بسم الله الرحمن الرحيم

***In the Name of Allah,
the Compassionate, the Merciful.
Praise be to Allah, Lord of the Universe,
and Peace and Prayers be upon
His Final Prophet and Messenger.***

This is indeed a Qur'an most honourable,
In a Book well-guarded
Which none shall touch
But those who are clean (56:77-79)

In the above passage "clean" means pure in body, mind, thought, intention, and soul; only those who have attained this level of purity can have real insight into its full meaning. There could be three ways of studying the Qur'an.

- **Daily reading** – Read every day at least one section of the Qur'an in Arabic (that is if you are able to do so), then read the translation, with the commentary. Do not worry about finishing the Book.

- **Brief reading** – Every morning before leaving home, just turn to any page of the Qur'an, and read the translation appearing on that page. You may consider this as Allah's Message to you for the day.

- **Subject reading** – Go through the detailed contents and the index to become acquainted with the themes and subjects in the Qur'an.

Read the Qur'an,
Study the Qur'an, and
Practice the
Message of the Qur'an.

THE MEANING OF
THE HOLY QUR'AN

Complete English Translation
with Selected Explanatory Notes

Translated by
'Abdullah Yusuf 'Ali

IPCI - Islamic Vision
Birmingham, U.K.

Published by
IPCI - Islamic Vision
426-434 Coventry Road
Birmingham B10 0UG
United Kingdom
Tel: 0121 773 0137 Fax: 0121 766 8577
Email: *info@ipci-iv.co.uk*
Website: *www.ipci-iv.co.uk*

ISBN No: 978-1-902480-07-7

Publisher's Note

The monumental work of 'Abdullah Yusuf 'Ali was first published in 1934. Since then there have been numerous reprintings and millions of copies distributed throughout the world. Regrettably this work was only available in the form of reprints of the original of over half a century ago, which was very old and faded to the point of illegibility.

IPCI, in 1997, published a new typeset edition with dramatic changes in style; the type for the English and Arabic text having been completely changed in order to make it more legible.

Since then there has been a growing demand for the translation of the Holy Quran by 'Abdullah Yusuf 'Ali in modern English. This edition will satisfy that need, insha Allah.

In this work essential explanatory notes have been included and edited wherever found necessary. The original numbering has been retained in a square bracket for cross referencing purposes.

The Holy Prophet Muhammad, peace be upon him, is reported to have said that the wonders of the Holy Qur'an will never cease to exist; it is a living miracle and it will unfold new meaning for every new age. It is hoped that this work will, insha Allah, help in furthering the aim of satisfying the ever changing needs and demands of the countless readers of today.

We would like to extend our gratitude to Haji Koya Kutty of Islamic Book Trust, Kuala Lumpur, Malaysia, without whose help and cooperation this publication would not have been possible.

Although we have made every effort to make this copy free from any error, we shall be grateful if our readers inform us of any typographical errors etc. they might come across, or any suggestions to improve future reprints of this edition, insha Allah.

IPCI - Islamic Vision
J.Awwal 1429 AH/April 2008
Birmingham, UK

Transliteration

For the pronunciation of Arabic names and terms, diacritical marks have been used throughout this book.

ā, *ī* and *ū* stand for the vowel sounds *aa* (as in *path*), *ee* (as in *feet*) and *oo* (as in *pool*) respectively.

Similarly, the signs (’) and (‘) have been used for the Arabic letters *hamzah* (as in *Qur’ān*) and *‘ayn* (as in *Sharī‘ah*).

Arabic Alphabet and its English Equivalent

ء	’	د	d	ض	ḍ	ك	k
ب	b	ذ	dh	ط	ṭ	ل	l
ت	t	ر	r	ظ	ẓ	م	m
ث	th	ز	z	ع	‘	ن	n
ج	j	س	s	غ	gh	هـ	h
ح	ḥ	ش	sh	ف	f	و	w
خ	kh	ص	ṣ	ق	q	ي	y

Contents

In the name of Allah,
Most Gracious, Most Merciful.

Translator's Introduction

Glory to Allah Most High, full of Grace and Mercy;
He created All, including Man.
To Man He gave a special place in His Creation.
He honoured man to be His Agent,
And to that end, endued him with understanding.
Purified his affections, and gave him spiritual insight;
So that man should understand Nature,
Understand himself,
And know Allah through His wondrous Signs,
And glorify Him in Truth, reverence, and unity.

For the fulfilment of this great trust
Man was further given a Will,
So that his acts should reflect
Allah's universal Will and Law,
And his mind, freely choosing,
Should experience the sublime joy
Of being in harmony with the Infinite,
And with the great drama of the world around him,
And with his own spiritual growth.

But, created though he was in the best of moulds,
Man fell from Unity when his Will was warped,
And he chose the crooked path of Discord.
And sorrow and pain, selfishness and degradation.
Ignorance and hatred, despair and unbelief
Poisoned his life, and he saw shapes of evil
In the physical, moral, and spiritual world,
And in himself

Then did his soul rise against himself,
And his self-discord made discord between kith and kin:

Men began to fear the strong and oppress the weak,
To boast in prosperity, and curse in adversity.
And to flee each other, pursuing phantoms,
For the truth and reality of Unity
Was gone from their minds.

When men spread themselves over the earth,
And became many nations,
Speaking diverse languages,
And observing diverse customs and laws;
The evils became multiplied,
As one race or nation
Became alienated from another.
The Brotherhood of Man was now doubly forgotten—
First, between individuals, and secondly,
between nations.
Arrogance, selfishness, and untruth
Were sown and reaped in larger fields;
And Peace, Faith, Love and Justice
Were obscured over masses of men,
As large tracts of land are starved
Of sunshine by clouds floating far on high.

But Allah, in His infinite mercy and love,
Who forgives and guides individuals and nations,
And turns to good even what seems to us evil,
Never forsakes the struggling soul that turns to Him,
Nor the groups of men and women
Who join together to obey His Will and Law
And strengthen each other in unity and truth,
Nor the Nations that dwell
In mountain or valley, heat or cold,
In regions fertile or arid,
In societies that roam over land or seas,
Or hunt, or tend flocks, or till the soil,
Or seek the seas for food or oil or fat or gems,
Or dig out from the bowels of the earth
Precious stones or metals or stored-up heat and energy,

Or practise arts and crafts, or produce abundant wealth
By machines of ingenious workmanship,
Or live a frugal life of contemplation:
For all are creatures of One God,
And share His loving care
And must be brought within the pale
Of His eternal unity and harmony.

And so this light of eternal Unity
Has shone in all ages and among all nations,
Through chosen Messengers of Allah, who came
As men to dwell among men,
To share their joys and sorrows,
To suffer for them and with them—
Aye, and to suffer more than falls
To ordinary mortal lot
That so their message and their life
Might fulfil the eternal
And unchanging purpose of the Most High
To lead man to his noblest destiny.

Ever this eternal light of Unity,
This mystic light of Allah's own Will,
Has shone and shines with undiminished splendour.
The names of many Messengers are inscribed
In the records of many nations and many tongues,
And many were the forms in which their
    message was delivered,
According to the needs of the times and the
    understanding of the people;
And manifold were the lives of the Messengers,
And manifold also was the response of their people;
But they all witnessed to the One Truth:
Of Allah's unity, might, grace and love.

As the records of man are imperfect,
And the memory of man unstable:
The names of many of these messengers

Are known in one place and not in another,
Or among one people and not among others;
And some of their names may have perished utterly;
But their message stands one and indivisible,
Even though it may have been forgotten,
Or twisted by ignorance, error, superstition or perversity;
Or misunderstood in the blinding light
Of time or tortuous Circumstances.

Many were the faiths in the composite world
Of Western Asia, Northern Africa, and Europe,
And many were the fragments of ancient wisdom,
Saved, transfomed, renewed, or mingled;
And many new streams of wisdom were poured
    through the crucibles
Of noble minds—prophets, poets, preachers,
Philosophers, and thinking men of action;
And many were the conflicts, and many
The noble attempts reaching out towards Unity,
And many were the subtle influences
Interchanged with the other worlds
Of further and Eastern Asia—
Aye, and perchance with the scattered Isles
Of the Pacific and the world between
The Atlantic and the Pacific.

At length came the time when the Voice of Unity
Should speak and declare to the People,
Without the need of Priests or Priest-craft,
Without miracles save those that happen
Now and always in the spiritual world,
Without mystery, save those mysteries
Which unfold themselves in the growing
Inner experience of man and his vision of Allah—
To declare with unfaltering voice
The Unity of Allah, the Brotherhood of Man,
And Grace and Mercy, Bounty and Love,
Poured out in unstinted measure forever and ever.

And this great healing light shone
Among a people steeped in ignorance,
Brave and free, but without cohesion or union,
Simple and rude, but with an easy familiarity with Nature,
Accustomed to Nature's hardships and her rugged
resistance to man,
But dreaming of the delights of gardens and fruitful fields,
Cruel, yet with a rough sense of equality,
And wielding a tongue, flexible, beautiful,
And able to respond, with brevity and eloquence,
To the sublimest thoughts which man could conceive.

Who were fit to be vehicles of this light?—
Not men intoxicated with words and mysteries,
Men whom politics had debauched or
tyranny had subdued,
Men whose refinement had ended in vices,
Who saw Nature only through books or artificial conceits,
Or in moods which bred softness, indolence, or luxury,
Who spoke of love and justice, but practised
Gross selfishness between class and class,
Sex and sex, condition and condition;
And had perverted their language, once beautiful,
Into jargons of empty elegance and unmeaning futility.

For the glory of Hellas, and her freedom and
wisdom had departed;
Rome's great systems of law, organisation,
and universal citizenship
Had sunk into the mire of ecclesiastical formalism,
And dogmatism, and exclusive arrogance;
The living fire of Persia's prophet scarce smouldered
In her votaries of luxury;
In India, countless castes and kingdoms
Cancelled the unity of Buddha's teaching;
The wounds of China had not yet been healed
by T'ang culture;

And Japan was still a disciple of China.

Then, in the sacred city of pagan Arabia,
Shone a light that spread in all directions.
It was centrally placed for the bounds of the world
Of men's habitations in Asia, Europe, and Africa.
It made the Arabs the leading nation of culture and science,
Of organised enterprise, law, and arts,
With a zeal for the conquest of Nature and her mysteries.

Behold! There was born into the world of sense
The unlettered Prophet, the comely child,
Noble of birth, but nobler still
In the grace and wisdom of human love
And human understanding; dowered with the key
Which opened to him the enchanted palace
Of nature; marked out to receive—
To receive and preach in burning words
The spiritual truth and message of the Most High.

Others before him had been born
In darkness, beyond the reach
Of history; others again it pleased Allah
To send as Messengers, preaching, working
In the dim twilight of history,
Wherein men fashion legends
After their own hearts and dimly seek
A light afar, remote from the lives
Mean and sordid, such as they knew.

But Muhammad came in the fullest blaze
Of history; with no learning he put to shame
The wisdom of the learned; with pasture folk
He lived and worked, and won their love; in hills
And valleys, caves and deserts, he wandered,
But never lost his way to truth and righteousness;
From his pure and spotless heart the Angels washed
Off the dust that flew around him; through the ways

Of crooked city folk, he walked upright and straight,
And won from them the ungrudging name
Of the Man of Faith[1] who never broke his word.

To the Praiseworthy[2] indeed be praise:
Born in the Sacred City[3] he destroyed
Its superstition; loyal to his people to the core,
He stood for all humanity; orphan-born
And poor, he envied not the rich,
And made his special care all those
Whom the world neglected or oppressed—
Orphans, women, slaves, and those in need
Of food or comforts, mental solace, spiritual strength,
Or virtues downtrodden in the haunts of men

His mother[4] and his foster-mother[5]
Loved and wondered at the child;
His grandfather, 'Abd al-Muṭṭalib,
Of all his twice-eight children and their offspring,
Loved him best and all his sweet and gentle ways;
His uncle Abū Ṭālib, loth though he was
To give up the cult of his fathers,
Knew well the purity of Muḥammad's
Mind and soul, and was his stoutest champion
When the other chiefs of Makkah sought to kill
The man who challenged in his person
Their narrow Pagan selfish lives.

To his cousin 'Alī, the well-beloved,[6]

---

1 Al-Amīn

2 Muḥammad

3 Makkah

4 Āminah

5 Ḥalīmah

6 *Murtaḍā*

Born when he was thirty, he appeared
As the very pattern of a perfect man,
As gentle as he was wise and true and strong,
The one in whose defence and aid
He spent his utmost strength and skill,
Holding life cheap in support of a cause so high,
And placing without reserve his chivalry,
His prowess, his wit and learning, and his sword
At the service of this mighty Messenger of Allah.

Not till the age of forty[7] did he receive
The Commission to stand forth and proclaim
The Bounty of Allah, and His gift, to lowly Man,
Of knowledge by Word and Pen; but all through
His years of preparation he did search
The Truth: he sought it in Nature's forms and laws,
Her beauty and her stern unflinching ways;
He sought it in the inner world
Of human lives, men's joys and sorrows;
Their kindly virtues and their sins
Of pride, injustice, cruel wrong,
And greed of gain; scarce checked by the inner voice
That spoke of duty, moral law, and higher still,
The Will Supreme of Allah, to which the will
Of man must tune itself to find its highest bliss.

But he grew steadfastly in virtue and purity;
Untaught by men, he learnt from them, and learned
To teach them; even as a boy of nine,
When he went in a trade caravan with Abū Ṭalib
To Syria,[8] his tender soul marked inwardly

---

7 The Arabian year preceding 10 A.H. was roughly luni-solar.

8 It was on such visits that he met and conversed with Nestorian Christian monks like Bahīrah who were quick to recognised his spiritual worth. Perhaps the meeting was in Busra in the Jabal Druze district of Syria, some 70 miles south of Damascus. There was another Busra in Edom, north of Petra in Transjordania. Busra was famous for trade in costly red dyes, and is referred to as Bozrah in Isaiah, xliii:i. Neither of these

How Allah did speak in the wide expanse
Of deserts, in the stern grandeur of rocks,
In the refreshing flow of streams, in the smiling
Bloom of gardens, in the art and skill with which
Men and birds and all life sought for light
From the Life of Lives, even as every plant
Seeks through devious ways the light of the Sun

Nor less was he grieved at Man's ingratitude
When he rebelled and held as naught the
Signs Of Allah, and turned His gifts to baser uses,
Driving rarer souls to hermit life,
Clouding the heavenly mirror of pure affections
With selfish passions, mad unseemly wrangles,
And hard unhallowed loathsome tortures of themselves.

He worked, and joyed in honest labour;
He traded with integrity to himself and to others;
He joined the throngs of cities and their busy life,
But saw its good and evil as types
Of an inner and more lasting life hereafter;
People gladly sought his help as umpire
And peacemaker because they knew his soul
Was just and righteous: he loved the society
Of old and young, but oft withdrew to solitude
For Prayer and inward spiritual strength;
He despised not wealth but used it for others;
He was happy in poverty and used it as his badge
And his pride[9] when wealth was within his reach
But not within his grasp, as a man among men.

At twenty-five he was united in the holy bonds

---

towns is to be confounded with the modern Basra. [The Prophet, peace be on him, went to Syria twice, and the incident of meeting Bahīrah took place in one of these visits. (Eds.)].

9 *Al faqru fakhrī* : "Poverty is my pride".

Of wedlock with Khadījah the Great, the noble lady
Who befriended him when he had no worldly resources,
Trusted him when his worth was little known,
Encouraged and understood him in his spiritual struggles,
Believed in him when with trembling steps
He took up the Call and withstood obloquy,
Persecution, insults, threats, and tortures,
And was a life-long helpmate till she was gathered
To the saints in his fifty-first year—
A perfect woman, the mother of those that believe

There is a cave in the side of Mount Hirā'
Some three miles north of the city of Makkah,
In a valley which turns left from the road to 'Arafāt.
To which Muhammad used to retire
for peaceful contemplation:
Often alone, but sometimes with Khadījah.[10]
Days and nights he spent there with his Lord.
Hard were the problems he revolved in his mind—
Harder and more cross-grained than the red granite
Of the rock around him—problems not his own,
But his people's, yea, and of human destiny,
Of the Mercy of Allah, and the age-long conflict
Of evil and righteousness, sin and abounding Grace.

Not till forty years of earthly life had passed
That the veil was lifted from the Preserved Tablet
And its contents began to be transferred to
    the tablet of his mind,
To be proclaimed to the world, and read and studied
For all time—a fountain of mercy and wisdom,
A warning to the heedless, a guide to the erring,
An assurance to those in doubt, a solace to the suffering,
A hope to those in despair—to complete the chain
Of Revelation through the mouths

---

10 This statement is not supported by any authentic evidence on record. [Ed.]

Of divinely inspired Prophets.

The Chosen One[11] was in the Cave of Ḥirā'.
For two years and more he had prayed there and adored
His Creator and wondered at the mystery
Of man with his corruptible flesh, just growing
Out of a clot,[12] and the soul in him
Reaching out to knowledge sublime, new
And ever new, taught by the bounty
Of Allah, and leading to that which man himself
Knoweth not. And now, behold! a dazzling
Vision of beauty and light overpowered his senses,
And he heard the word "*Iqra'!*"

"*Iqra*'!" which being interpreted may mean
"Read!" or "Proclaim!" or "Recite!"
The unlettered Prophet was puzzled;
He could not read. The Angel seemed
To press him to his breast in a close embrace,
And the cry rang clear *"Iqra'!"*
And so it happened three times; until
The first overpowering sensation yielded
To a collected grasp of the words which made clear
His Mission; its Author, Allah, the Creator,
Its subject, Man, Allah's wondrous handiwork,
Capable, by Grace, of rising to heights sublime;
And the instrument of that mission, the sanctified Pen,
And the sanctified Book, the Gift of Allah,
Which men might read, or write, or study, or
treasure in their souls.

The veil was lifted from the Chosen One's eyes,
And his soul for a moment was filled with divine Ecstasy. .
When this passed, And he returned to the world of Time

11 Al Muṣṭafā

12 See 96:2

And Circumstance and this world of Sense,
He felt like one whose eyes had seen
A light of dazzling beauty, and felt dazed
On his return to common sights.
The darkness now seemed tenfold dark;
The solitude seemed tenfold empty;
The mount of Ḥirā', henceforth known
As the Mountain of Light,[13] the mere shell
Of an intense memory. Was it a dream?
Terror seized his limbs and he straightway sought
Her who shared his inmost life,
And told her of his sense of exaltation,
And the awful void when the curtain closed.

She understood, rejoiced, and comforted him;
Gave strength to his shaken senses;
Wrapped up in warmth his shivering body,
Unused as yet to bear the strain and stress
Of an experience rare to mortal men.
She knew it was no dream or delusion.
She went and consulted her cousin Waraqah,
A devout worshipper of Allah in the Faith of Christ,
Learned in spiritual lore. He listened
And with her rejoiced that he, Muhammad,
Was Allah's Chosen One to renew the Faith.

She said: 'Blessed be thou, Chosen One!
Do we not see thy inner life—true and pure?
Do not all see thy outer life—kind and gentle?—
Loyal to kin, hospitable to strangers?
No thought of harm or mischief ever stained thy mind
Nor word ever passed thy lips that was not true
Or stilled not the passions of narrower men.
Ever ready in the service of Allah, thou art he
Of whom I bear witness: there's no god but He,

---

13 Jabal al-Nūr (The place where Prophet Muḥammad received the first revelation).

And thou art His Chosen Prophet.'

Khadījah believed, exalted in faith
Above all women; 'All, the well-beloved,
Then a child of ten, but lion-hearted,
Plighted his faith, and became from that moment
The right hand of Islam; Abu Bakr, the Sincere,[14]
The True-hearted, the man of wealth and influence,
Who used both without stint for the Cause,
The sober counsellor, the inseparable friend,
Never hesitated to declare his faith;
And Zayd, the freedman of Muḥammad,
Counted his freedom as naught compared
With the service of Muhammad and Islam.
These were the first fruits of the mission:
A woman, a child, a man of affairs, and a freedman,
All banded together in the equality of Islam.

The revelation had come, the mission
And the inspiration. But what was it leading to?
It was a miracle, but not in the sense
Of a reversing of Nature: Al Mustafa's vision
Was linked with Eternity, but he was no soothsayer
Foretelling passing events; the mysteries
Of knowledge were being opened out, but his message
Was no mere esoteric doctrine, to be grasped
By a few in contemplation, fleeing from action;
Nor was it the practice of single or social monasticism,
Undisturbed by the whims or passions of life.
He was asked to stand forth, to preach, to declare
The One Universal God, the Gracious, the Merciful,
And to lead men to the Right and forbid the Wrong.

The wrong?—The selfish pride of birth,
The massing of power and wealth in the hands

---

14 *Ṣadiq* or *Ṣiddīq*, the title of Abū Bakr.

Of a few, the slaughter of female infants,
The orgies of gambling and drunkenness,
The frauds of temples and idols and priests,
The feuds and arrogance of tribes and races,
The separation of Sacred and Profane,
As if the unity of All Life and All Truth
Did not flow from the unity of Allah, Most High.

He was loyal to his family, but could he support
Their monopoly of power?—To his tribe,
But were the Quraysh the only creatures
Of Allah? To the temple of Makkah, but
Could he wink at Lāt and 'Uzzā, and the other monsters,
Whose worship killed the spiritual growth of Man?
To the earlier Revelations, but could he hold
With the superstitions and falsehoods, the dogmas and creeds
Which went against reason and nature, and the inner light
Which was now fanned into flame by the Will of Allah?

And so his very virtues and loyalties pointed
To offence and conflict, mockery and misrepresentation,
Hatred and persecution, threats, tortures, and exile
For him and his, and martyrdoms, wars, revolutions,
And the shaking of the foundations of history
And the social order. But Islam meant
The willing submission of his will to Allah,
The active attainment of Peace through Conflict.

And he gave that submission, not without effort,
Even as Moses[15] did before him,
And Jesus[16] in the agony of the garden of Gethsemane.

For three and twenty years, in patience,
Conflict, hope, and final triumph,

---

15 Qur'an 20:25-32.

16 Matt.xxvi.

Did this Prophet of Allah receive
And teach the Message of the Most High.
It came, like the fruit of the soul's own yearning,
To teach profound spiritual truths,
Answer questions, appeal to men
In their doubts and fears, help and put heart
In them in moments of trial, and ordain
For them laws by which they could live
In society lives of purity, goodness and peace.

These messages came as inspiration
To Muhammad as the need arose,
On different occasions and in different places:
He recited them, and they were recorded
By the Pen: they were imprinted on his heart
And mind, and on the memory
Of his loving disciples: as the body
Of sacred Scripture grew, it was arranged
For purposes of public prayer and reading:
This is the Book, or the Reading, or the Qur'an.□

Chapter 1

Sūrah Al-Fātiḥah (The Opening)

Translator's Introduction

First comes that beautiful Sūrah,[1]
The Opening Chapter[2] of Seven Verses,[3]
Rightly called the Essence of the Book.
It teaches us the perfect Prayer.
For if we can pray aright, it means
That we have some knowledge of Allah
And His attributes, of His relations
To us and His creation, which includes
Ourselves; that we glimpse the source

---

1. Each chapter or portion of the Qur'an is called a Sūrah, which means a Degree or Step, by which we mount up. Sometimes whole Sūrahs were revealed, and sometimes portions, which were arranged under the Prophet's directions. Some Sūrahs are long, and some are short, but a logical thread runs through them all. Each verse of the Sūrah is called an *Āyah* (plural, *Āyāt),* which means also a sign. A verse of revelation is a Sign of Allah's wisdom and goodness just as much as Allah's beautiful handiwork in the material creation or His dealings in history are signs to us, if we would understand. Some *Āyāt* are long, and some are short. The *Āyah* is the true unit of the Qur'an. [15]
[Throughout this book 'Sūrah' will be used for Chapter in the text.—*Ed.*]

2. *Fātiḥah* = Opening Chapter: See note 1 at the end of this Sūrah. [16]
By universal consent it is rightly placed at the beginning of the Qur'an, as summing up, in marvellously terse and comprehensive words, man's relation to God in contemplation and prayer. In our spiritual contemplation the first words should be those of praise. If the praise is from our inmost being, it brings us into union with God's Will. Then our eyes see all good, peace, and harmony. Evil, rebellion, and conflict are purged out. They do not exist for us, for our eyes are lifted up above them in praise. Then we see God's attributes better (verses 2-4). This leads us to the attitude of worship and acknowledgement (verse 5). And finally comes prayer for guidance, and a contemplation of what guidance means (verses 6-7).
God needs no praise, for He is above all praise; He needs no petition, for He knows our needs better than we do ourselves; and His bounties are open without asking, to the righteous and the sinner alike. The prayer is for our own spiritual education, consolation, and. confirmation.
That is why the words in this Sūrah are given to us in the form in which we should utter them. When we reach enlightenment, they flow spontaneously from us. [18]

3. These seven verses form a complete unit by themselves, and are recited in every prayer and on many other occasions. *Cf.* 15:87. [17]

From which we come, and that final goal
Which is our spiritual destiny
Under Allah's true judgement: then
We offer ourselves to Allah and seek His light.

Prayer is the heart of Religion and Faith
But how shall we pray? What words shall convey
The yearnings of our miscrable ignorant hearts
To the Knower of all? Is it worthy of Him
Or of our spiritual nature to ask
For vanities, or even for such physical needs
As our daily bread? The Inspired One
Taught us a Prayer that sums up our faith,
Our hope, and our aspiration in things that matter.
We think in devotion of Allah's name and His Nature;
We praise Him for His creation and His Cherishing care;
We call to mind the Realities, seen and unseen;
We offer Him worship and ask for His guidance;
And we know the straight from the crooked path
By the light of His grace that illumines the righteous.

*** ***

1 In the name of Allah,
Most Gracious, Most Merciful.[4]

2 Praise be to Allah, the Cherisher and
Sustainer[5] of the Worlds;
3 Most Gracious, Most Merciful;
4 Master of the Day of Judgement.

5 You do we worship, and Your aid we seek.[6]

6 Show us the straight way,[7]
7 The way of those on whom You bestowed Your Grace,
those whose (portion) is not wrath,[8]
and who go not astray.[9] □

---

4. The Arabic words *Rahmān* and *Rahīm,* translated "Most Gracious" and "Most Merciful" are both intensive forms referring to different aspects of Allah's attribute of Mercy. The Arabic intensive is more suited to express Allah's attributes than the superlative degree in English. The latter implies a comparison with other beings, or with other times or places, while there is no being like unto Allah, and He is independent of Time and Place. Mercy may imply pity, long-suffering, patience, and forgiveness, all of which the sinner needs and Allah Most Merciful bestows in abundant measure. But there is a Mercy that goes before even the need arises, the Grace which is ever watchful, and flows from Allah Most Gracious to all His creatures, protecting them, preserving them, guiding them, and leading them to clearer light and higher life. For this reason the attribute *Rahmān* (Most Gracious) is not applied to any but Allah, but the attribute *Rahīm* (Merciful), is a general term, and may also be applied to Men. To make us contemplate these boundless gifts of Allah, the formula: "In the name of Allah Most Gracious, Most Merciful": is placed before every Sūrah of the Qur'an (except the ninth), and repeated at the beginning of every act by the Muslim who dedicates his life to Allah, and whose hope is in His Mercy

Opinion is divided whether the *Bismillāh* should be numbered as a separate verse or not. It is unanimously agreed that it is a part of the Qur'an. Therefore it is better to give it an independent number in the first Sūrah. For subsequent Sūrahs it is treated as an introduction or headline, and therefore not numbered. [19]

5. The Arabic word *Rabb,* usually translated Lord, has also the meaning of cherishing, sustaining, bringing to maturity. Allah cares for all the worlds He has created.

There are many worlds, astronomical and physical worlds, worlds of thought, spiritual world. and so on. In every one of them, Allah is all-in-all. We express only one aspect of it when we say: "In Him we live, and move, and have our being." The mystical division between (1) *Nāsūt,* the human world knowable by the senses, (2) *Malakūt,* the invisible world of angels, and (3) *Lāhūt,* the divine world of Reality, requires a whole volume to explain it. [20]

6. On realising in our souls Allah's love and care, His grace and mercy, and His power and justice (as Ruler of the Day of Judgement), the immediate result is that we bend in the act of worship, and see both our shortcomings and His all-sufficient power. The emphatic form means that not only do we reach the position of worshipping Allah and asking for His help, but we worship Him alone and ask for His aid only. For there is none other than He worthy of our devotion and able to help us. The plural "we" indicates that we associate ourselves with all who seek Allah, thus strengthening ourselves and strengthening them in a fellowship of faith. [21]

7. If we translate by the English word "guide", we shall have to say: "Guide us to and in the straight Way." For we may be wandering aimlessly, and the first step is to find the Way; and the second need is to keep in the Way: our own wisdom may fail in either case. The straight Way is often the narrow Way, or the steep Way, which many people shun (90:11). By the world's perversity the straight Way is sometimes stigmatized and the crooked Way praised. How are we to judge? We must ask for Allah's guidance. With a little spiritual insight we shall see which are the people who walk in the light of Allah's grace, and which are those that walk in the darkness of Wrath. This also would help our judgement. [22]

8. Note that words relating to Grace are connected actively with Allah; those relating to Wrath are impersonal. In the one case Allah's Mercy encompasses us beyond our deserts. In the other case our own actions are responsible for the Wrath—the negative of Grace, Peace, or Harmony. [23]

9. Are there two categories—those who are in the darkness of Wrath and those who stray? The first are those who deliberately break Allah's law; the second those who stray out of carelessness or negligence. Both are responsible for their own acts or omissions. In opposition to both are the people who are in the light of Allah's Grace: for His Grace not only protects them from active wrong (if they will only submit their will to Him) but also from straying into paths of temptation or carelessness. The negative *ghayr* should be construed as applying not to the way, but as describing men protected from two dangers by Allah's Grace. [24]

Chapter 2

Sūrah Al-Baqarah (The Heifer)

Translator's Introduction

As the Opening Sūrah (Chapter) sums up in seven beautiful verses the essence of the Qur'an, so this Sūrah sums up in 286 verses the whole teaching of the Qur'an. It is a closely reasoned argument.

Summary—It begins (verses 1-29) by classifying men into three broad categories, depending on how they receive Allah's message.

This leads to the story of the creation of man, the high destiny intended for him, his fall, and the hope held out to him (2:30-39).

Israel's story is then told according to their own records and traditions, what privileges they received and how they abused them (2:40-86), thus illustrating again as by a parable the general story of man.

In particular, reference is made to Moses and Jesus and their struggles with an unruly people: how the people of the Book played false their own lights and in their pride rejected Muḥammad, who came in the true line of Prophets (2:87-121).

They falsely laid claim to the virtues of Father Abraham: he was indeed a righteous Imām, but he was the progenitor of Ismā'īl's line (Arabs) as well as of Israel's line, and he with Ismā'īl built the Ka'bah (the House of Allah in Makkah) and purified it, thus establishing a common religion, of which Islam is the universal exponent (2:122-141). The Ka'bah was now to be the centre of universal worship and the symbol of Islamic unity (2:142-167).

The Islamic *Ummah* (brotherhood) having thus been established with its definite centre and symbol, ordinances are laid down for the social life of the community, with the proviso (2:177) that righteousness does not consist in formalities, but in faith, kindness, prayer, charity, probity, and patience under suffering. The ordinances relate to food and drink, bequests, fasts, *jihād*, wine and gambling, treatment of orphans and women, etc. (2:168-242).

Lest the subject of *jihād* should be misunderstood, it is taken up again in the story of Saul, Goliath and David, in contrast to the story of Jesus (2:243-253).

And so the lesson is enforced that true virtue lies in practical deeds of manliness, kindness, and good faith (2:254-283), and Allah's nature [Allah's Attributes—*Ed.*] is called to mind in the sublime Ā*yah al-Kursī,* the Verse of the

Throne (2:255).

The Sūrah ends with an exhortation to Faith, Obedience, a sense of Personal Responsibility, and Prayer (2:284-286).

This is the longest Sūrah of the Qur'an, and in it occurs the longest verse (2:282). The name of the Sūrah is from the Parable of the Heifer in 2:67-71, which illustrates the insufficiency of carping obedience. When faith is lost, people put off obedience with various excuses: even when at last they obey in the letter, they fail in the spirit, which means that they get fossilised, and their self-sufficiency prevents them from seeing that spiritually they are not alive but dead. For life is movement, activity, striving, fighting against baser things. And this is the burden of the Sūrah.

This is in the main an early Madīnan Sūrah.

*** *** ***

In the name of Allah,
Most Gracious, Most Merciful.

1 *Alif Lām Mīm.*[1]

2 This is the Book; in it is guidance sure, without doubt, to those who
fear[2] Allah; 3 Who believe in the Unseen, are steadfast in prayer, and

---

1. These are abbreviated letters, the *Muqatta'āt.* Certain Sūrahs have certain initials prefixed to them. A number of conjectures have been made as to their meaning. Opinions are divided as to the exact meaning of each particular letter or combination of letters, and it is agreed that only Allah knows their exact meaning.

The particular letters, *Alif, Lām, Mīm,* are found prefixed to this Sūrah, and Sūrahs 3, 29, 30, 31 and 32 (six in all). In 2 and 3 the argument is about the rise and fall of nations, their past, and their future in history, with ordinances for the new universal people of Islam. In 29 a similar argument about nations leads off to the mystery of Life and Death, Failure and Triumph, Past and Future, in the history of individual souls. The burden of 30 is that Allah is the source of all things and all things return to Him. In 31 and 32 the same lesson is enforced: Allah is the Creator and He will be the Judge on the Last Day. There is therefore a common thread, the mystery of Life and Death, Beginning and End.

Much has been written about the meaning of these letters, but most of it is pure conjecture. Some commentators are content to recognise them as some mystic symbols of which it is unprofitable to discuss the meaning by mere verbal logic. [25]

2. Arabic *Taqwā,* and the verbs and nouns connected with the root, signify: (1) the fear of Allah, which, according to the writer of Proverbs (i. 7) in the Old Testament, is the

spend out of what We have provided for them; 4 And who believe in the
Revelation sent to you, and sent before your time, and (in their hearts)
have the assurance of the Hereafter.

5 They are on (true) guidance, from their Lord, and it is these who will
prosper. 6 As to those who reject Faith,[3] it is the same to them whether
you warn them or do not warn them; they will not believe. 7 Allah has set
a seal on their hearts and on their hearing, and on their eyes is a veil;
great is the penalty they (incur).

SECTION 2

8 Of the people there are some who say: "We believe in Allah and the
Last Day;" but they do not (really) believe. 9 Fain would they deceive
Allah and those who believe, but they only deceive themselves, and
realise (it) not! 10 In their hearts is a disease; and Allah has increased their
disease: and grievous is the penalty they (incur), because they are false
(to themselves). 11 When it is said to them: "Make not mischief on the
earth," they say: "Why, we only want to make peace!" 12 Of a surety, they
are the ones who make mischief, but they realise (it) not. 13 When it is
said to them: "Believe as the others believe" they say: "Shall we believe
as the fools believe?"—Nay, of a surety they are the fools, but they do
not know. 14 When they meet those who believe, they say: "We believe;"
but when they are alone with their evil ones, they say: "We are really
with you: we (were) only jesting." 15 Allah will throw back their mockery
on them, and give them rope in their trespasses; so they will wander like
blind ones (to and fro). 16 These are they who have bartered Guidance for
error: but their traffic is profitless, and they have lost true direction.

17 Their similitude is that of a man who kindled a fire; when it lighted all

---

beginning of Wisdom; (2) restraint, or guarding one's tongue, hand, and heart from evil; (3) hence righteousness, piety, good conduct. All these ideas are implied: in the translation, only one or other of these ideas can be indicated, according to the context. See also 47:17 and 74:56. [26]

3. Arabic *Kafara, kufr, kāfir*, and derivative forms of the word, imply a deliberate rejection of Faith as opposed to a mistaken idea of Allah or faith, which is not inconsistent with an earnest desire to see the truth. Where there is such desire, the Grace and Mercy of Allah gives guidance. But that guidance is not efficacious when it is deliberately rejected, and the possibility of rejection follows from the grant of free will. The consequence of the rejection is that the spiritual faculties become dead or impervious to better influences. [30]

around him, Allah took away their light and left them in utter darkness.
So they could not see. 18 Deaf, dumb, and blind, they will not return (to
the path). 19 Or (another similitude) is that of a rain-laden cloud from the
sky: in it are zones of darkness, and thunder and lightning: they press
their fingers in their ears to keep out the stunning thunderclap, the while
they are in terror of death. But Allah is ever round the rejecters of Faith!
20 The lightning all but snatches away their sight; every time the light
(helps) them, they walk therein, and when the darkness grows on them,
they stand still. And if Allah willed, He could take away their faculty of
hearing and seeing; for Allah has power over all things.

SECTION 3

21 O you people! Adore your Guardian-Lord, Who created you and those
who came before you, that you may have the chance to learn
righteousness; 22 Who has made the earth your couch, and the heavens
your canopy; and sent down rain from the heavens; and brought forth
therewith fruits for your sustenance; then set not up rivals unto Allah
when you know (the truth). 23 And if you are in doubt as to what We have
revealed from time to time to Our servant, then produce a Sūrah like
thereunto; and call your witnesses or helpers (if there are any) besides
Allah, if your (doubts) are true. 24 But if you cannot—and of a surety you
cannot—then fear the Fire whose fuel is Men and Stones,—which is
prepared for those who reject Faith. 25 But give glad tidings to those who
believe and work righteousness, that their portion is Gardens, beneath
which rivers flow. Every time they are fed with fruits therefrom, they say:
"Why, this is what we were fed with before," for they are given things in
similitude; and they have therein companions pure (and holy); and they
abide therein (for ever).

26 Allah disdains not to use the similitude of things, lowest as well as
highest. Those who believe know that it is truth from their Lord; but those
who reject Faith say: "What means Allah by this similitude?" By it He
causes many to stray, and many He leads into the right path; but He
causes not to stray, except those who forsake (the path)—27 Those who
break Allah's Covenant[4] after it is ratified, and who sunder what Allah

---

4. Verses 26 and 27 form one sentence and should be read together. "Forsaking the path" is defined in 2:27; *viz.*, breaking solemn covenants which the sinner's own soul had ratified, causing division among mankind, who were meant to be one brotherhood, and

has ordered to be joined, and do mischief on earth: these cause loss (only)
to themselves. 28 How can you reject the faith in Allah? —seeing that you
were without life, and He gave you life; then will He cause you to die,
and will again bring you to life; and again to Him will you return. 29 It is
He Who has created for you all things that are on earth; moreover His
design comprehended the heavens, for He gave order and perfection to
the seven firmaments; and of all things He has perfect knowledge.

SECTION 4

30 Behold, your Lord said to the angels: "I will create a vicegerent on
earth." They said: "Will You place therein one who will make mischief
therein and shed blood?—whilst we do celebrate Your praises and glorify
Your holy (name)?" He said: "I know what you know not." 31 And He
taught Adam the nature of all things; then He placed them before the
angels, and said: "Tell Me the nature of these if you are right." 32 They
said: "Glory to You, of knowledge we have none, save what You have
taught us: in truth it is You Who are perfect in knowledge and wisdom."
33 He said: "O Adam! Tell them their natures." When he had told them,
Allah said: "Did I not tell you that I know the secrets of heaven and earth,
and I know what you reveal and what you conceal?" 34 And behold, We
said to the angels: "Bow down to Adam" and they bowed down. Not so
Iblīs:[5] he refused and was haughty; he was of those who reject Faith.

---

doing as much mischief as possible in the life on this earth, for the life beyond will be on another plane, where no rope will be given to evil.

The mention of the Covenant (2:27) has a particular and general signification. The particular one has reference to the Jewish tradition that a Covenant was entered into with "Father Abraham" that in return for Allah's favours the seed of Abraham would serve Allah faithfully. But as a matter of fact a great part of Abraham's progeny were in constant spiritual rebellion against Allah, as is testified by their own Prophets and Preachers and by Muḥammad Muṣṭafā. The general signification is that a similar Covenant is entered into by every creature of Allah: for Allah's loving care, we at least owe Him the fullest gratitude and willing obedience. The Sinner, before he darkens his own conscience, knows this, and yet he not only "forsakes the path" but resists the Grace of Allah which comes to save him. That is why his case becomes hopeless. But the loss is his own. He cannot spoil Allah's design. The good man is glad to retrace his steps from any lapses of which he may have been guilty and in his case Allah's Message reclaims him with complete understanding. [45]

5. The Arabic may also be translated: "They bowed down, except Iblīs." In that case Iblīs (Satan) would be one of the angels. But the theory of fallen angels is not accepted in Muslim theology. In 18:50, Iblīs is spoken of as a *Jinn*. We shall discuss later the meaning

35 We said: "O Adam! Dwell you and your wife in the Garden; and eat of
the bountiful things therein as (where and when) you will; but approach
not this tree, or you run into harm and transgression."[6] 36 Then did Satan
make them slip from the (Garden), and get them out of the state (of
felicity) in which they had been. We said: "Get you down, all (you
people), with enmity between yourselves. On earth will be your dwelling
place and your means of livelihood—for a time." 37 Then learnt Adam
from his Lord words of inspiration, and his Lord turned towards him; for
He is Oft-Returning, Most Merciful. 38 We said: "Get you down all from
here; and if, as is sure, there comes to you guidance from Me, whosoever
follows My guidance, on them shall be no fear, nor shall they grieve. 39
But those who reject Faith and belie Our Signs, they shall be Companions
of the Fire; they shall abide therein."

SECTION 5

40 O Children of Israel! Call to mind the (special) favour which I
bestowed upon you, and fulfil your Covenant with Me as I fulfil My
Covenant with you, and fear none but Me. 41 And believe in what I reveal,
confirming the revelation which is with you, and be not the first to reject
Faith therein, nor sell My Signs for a small price; and fear Me, and Me
alone. 42 And cover not Truth with falsehood, nor conceal the Truth when
you know (what it is). 43 And be steadfast in prayer; practise regular
charity; and bow down your heads with those who bow down (in
worship). 44 Do you enjoin right conduct on the people, and forget (to
practise it) yourselves, and yet you study the Scripture? Will you not
understand? 45 Nay, seek (Allah's) help with patient perseverance[7] and
prayer: it is indeed hard, except to those who bring a lowly spirit—46 Who

---

of this word. [49]

6. *Zulm* in Arabic (for transgression) implies harm, wrong, injustice, or transgression, and may have reference to oneself; when the wrong is done to others it implies tyranny and oppression; the idea of wrong naturally connects itself with darkness, which is another shade of meaning carried with the root word. [51]

7. The Arabic word *Sabr* (translated here "patient perseverance") implies many shades of meaning, which it is impossible to comprehend in one English word. It implies (1) patience in the sense of being thorough, not hasty; (2) patient perseverance, constancy, steadfastness, firmness of purpose; (3) systematic as opposed to spasmodic or chance action; (4) a cheerful attitude of resignation and understanding by the element of constancy or steadfastness. [61]

bear in mind the certainty that they are to meet their Lord, and that they are to return to Him.

SECTION 6

47 O Children of Israel! Call to mind the (special) favour which I
bestowed upon you, and that I preferred you to all others (for My
Message). 48 Then guard yourselves against a day when one soul shall not
avail another nor shall intercession be accepted for her, nor shall
compensation be taken from her, nor shall anyone be helped (from
outside).

49 And remember, We delivered you from the people of Pharaoh: they set you hard tasks and punishments, slaughtered your sons and let your womenfolk live; therein was a tremendous trial from your Lord.

50 And remember We divided the sea for you and saved you and drowned Pharaoh's people within your very sight.

51 And remember We appointed forty nights for Moses, and in his absence you took the calf (for worship), and you did grievous wrong.

52 Even then We did forgive you; there was a chance for you to be grateful.

53 And remember We gave Moses the Scripture and the Criterion (between right and wrong): there was a chance for you to be guided aright.

54 And remember Moses said to his people: "O my people! You have indeed wronged yourselves by your worship of the calf: so turn (in repentance) to your Maker, and slay yourselves (the wrong-doers); that will be better for you in the sight of your Maker." Then He turned towards you (in forgiveness): for He is Oft-Returning, Most Merciful.

55 And remember you said: "O Moses! We shall never believe in you until
we see Allah manifestly," but you were dazed with thunder and lightning
even as you looked on. 56 Then We raised you up after your death: you
had the chance to be grateful. 57 And We gave you the shade of clouds
and sent down to you Manna and quails, saying: "Eat of the good things
We have provided for you:" (but they rebelled); to Us they did no harm,
but they harmed their own souls.

58 And remember We said: "Enter this town, and eat of the plenty therein

as you wish; but enter the gate with humility, in posture and in words, and We shall forgive you your faults and increase (the portion of) those who do good." 59 But the transgressors changed the word from that which had been given them; so We sent on the transgressors a plague from heaven, for that they infringed(Our command) repeatedly.

SECTION 7

60 And remember Moses prayed for water for his people; We said: "Strike the rock with your staff." Then gushed forth therefrom twelve springs. Each group knew its own place for water. So eat and drink of the sustenance provided by Allah, and do no evil nor mischief on the (face of the) earth.

61 And remember you said: "O Moses! We cannot endure one kind of food (always); so beseech your Lord for us to produce for us of what the earth grows,—its pot-herbs, and cucumbers, its garlic, lentils, and onions." He said: "Will you exchange the better for the worse? Go you down to any town, and you shall find what you want!" They were covered with humiliation and misery; they drew on themselves the wrath of Allah. This because they went on rejecting the Signs of Allah and slaying His Messengers without just cause. This because they rebelled and went on transgressing.

SECTION 8

62 Those who believe (in the Qur'an), and those who follow the Jewish (scriptures), and the Christians and the Sabians,[8]—any who believe in

---

8. Latest researches have revealed a small remnant of a religious community numbering about 2,000 souls in Lower Iraq, near Basra. In Arabic they are called *Subbī* (plural, *Subbā*). They are also called Sabians and Nasoraeans, or Mandaeans, or Christians of St. John. They claim to be Gnostics, or Knowers of the Great Life. They dress in white, and believe in frequent immersions in water. Their Book Ginza is in a dialect of Aramaic. They have theories of Darkness and Light as in Zoroastrianism. They use the name *Yardan* (Jordan) for any river. They live in peace and harmony among their Muslim neighbours. They resemble the Ṣābi'ūn mentioned in the Qur'an, but are not probably identical with them.

The pseudo-Sabians of Ḥarrān, who attracted the attention of Khalīfah Ma'mūn al-Rashīd in A.C.830. by their long hair and peculiar dress probably adopted the name as it was mentioned in the Qur'an, in order to claim the privileges of the People of the Book. They were Syrian Star-worshippers with Hellenistic tendencies, like the Jews contemporary with Jesus.

Allah and the Last Day, and work righteousness, shall have their reward
with their Lord; on them shall be no fear, nor shall they grieve.

63 And remember We took your Covenant and We raised above you (the
towering height) of Mount (Sinai) (saying): "Hold firmly to what We have
given you and bring (ever) to remembrance what is therein: perchance you
may fear Allah." 64 But you turned back thereafter: had it not been for the
Grace and Mercy of Allah to you, you had surely been among the lost. 65
And well you knew those amongst you who transgressed in the matter of
the Sabbath. We said to them: "Be you apes, despised and rejected." 66 So
We made it an example to their own time and to their posterity, and a
lesson to those who fear Allah.

67 And remember Moses said to his people: "Allah commands that you
sacrifice a heifer." They said: "Make you a laughing-stock of us?" He
said: "Allah save me from being an ignorant (fool)!" 68 They said:
"Beseech on our behalf your Lord to make plain to us what (heifer) it is!"
He said: "He says: the heifer should be neither too old nor too young, but
of middling age. Now do what you are commanded!" 69 They said:
"Beseech on our behalf your Lord to make plain to us her colour." He
said: "He says: a fawn-coloured heifer, pure and rich in tone, the
admiration of beholders!" 70 They said: "Beseech on our behalf your Lord
to make plain to us what she is: to us are all heifers alike: we wish indeed
for guidance, if Allah wills." 71 He said: "He says: a heifer not trained to
till the soil or water the fields; sound and without blemish." They said:
"Now have you brought the truth." Then they offered her in sacrifice, but
not with goodwill.

SECTION 9

72 Remember you slew a man and fell into a dispute among yourselves as
to the crime: but Allah was to bring forth what you did hide. 73 So We

---

There was another people called the Sabaeans, who played an important part in the history of early Arabia, and are known through their inscriptions in an alphabet allied to the Phoenician and Babylonian. They had a flourishing kingdom in the Yemen tract in South Arabia about 800-700 B.C., though their origin may have been in North Arabia. They worshipped the planets and stars (Moon, Sun, Venus). Probably the Queen of Sheba is connected with them. They succumbed to Abyssinia about A.C.350. and to Persia about A.C.579. Their capital was near San'ā. They had beautiful stone buildings, in which the pointed arch is noticeable. *Cf.* 5:69. (See *Encyclopaedia Britannica* on Sabaeans.) [76]

said: "Strike the (body) with a piece of the (heifer)." Thus Allah brings
the dead to life and shows you His Signs: perchance you may understand.

74 Thenceforth were your hearts hardened: they became like a rock and
even worse in hardness. For among rocks there are some from which
rivers gush forth; others there are which when split asunder send forth
water; and others which sink for fear of Allah. And Allah is not
unmindful of what you do.

75 Can you (O you men of Faith) entertain the hope that they will believe
in you?—Seeing that a party of them heard the Word of Allah, and
perverted it knowingly after they understood it. 76 Behold! When they
meet the men of Faith, they say: "We believe" but when they meet each
other in private, they say: "Shall you tell them what Allah has revealed
to you, that they may engage you in argument about it before your
Lord?"—Do you not understand (their aim)? 77 Do they not know that
Allah knows what they conceal and what they reveal? 78 And there are
among them illiterates, who know not the Book, but (see therein their
own) desires, and they do nothing but conjecture. 79 Then woe to those
who write the Book with their own hands, and then say: "This is from
Allah," to traffic with it for a miserable price!—Woe to them for what
their hands do write, and for the gain they make thereby.

80 And they say: "The Fire shall not touch us but for a few numbered
days." Say: "Have you taken a promise from Allah, for He never breaks
His promise? Or is it that you say of Allah what you do not know?" 81
Nay, those who seek gain in evil, and are girt round by their sins,—they
are Companions of the Fire: therein shall they abide (for ever). 82 But
those who have faith and work righteousness, they are Companions of the
Garden: therein shall they abide (for ever).

SECTION 10

83 And remember We took a Covenant from the Children of Israel (to this
effect): worship none but Allah; treat with kindness your parents and
kindred, and orphans and those in need; speak fair to the people; be
steadfast in prayer; and practise regular charity. Then did you turn back,
except a few among you, and you backslide (even now). 84 And

remember We took[9] your Covenant (to this effect): shed no blood
amongst you, nor turn out your own people from your homes: and this
you solemnly ratified, and to this you can bear witness. 85 After this it is
you, the same people, who slay among yourselves, and banish a party of
you from their homes; assist (their enemies) against them, in guilt and
rancour; and if they come to you as captives, you ransom them, though
it was not lawful for you to banish them. Then is it only a part of the
Book that you believe in, and do you reject the rest? But what is the
reward for those among you who behave like this but disgrace in this
life?—and on the Day of Judgement they shall be consigned to the most
grievous penalty. For Allah is not unmindful of what you do. 86 These are
the people who buy the life of this world at the price of the Hereafter:
their penalty shall not be lightened nor shall they be helped.

SECTION 11

87 We gave Moses the Book and followed him up with a succession of
messengers; We gave Jesus the son of Mary clear (Signs) and
strengthened him with the Holy Spirit. Is it that whenever there comes to
you a messenger with what you yourselves desire not, you are puffed up
with pride?—some you called impostors, and others you slay! 88 They
say, "Our hearts are the wrappings (which preserve Allah's Word: we
need no more)." Nay, Allah's curse is on them for their blasphemy: little
is it they believe. 89 And when there comes to them a Book from Allah,
confirming what is with them,—although from of old they had prayed for
victory against those without Faith,—when there comes to them that
which they (should) have recognised, they refuse to believe in it but the
curse of Allah is on those without Faith. 90 Miserable is the price for
which they have sold their souls, in that they deny (the revelation) which
Allah has sent down, in insolent envy that Allah of His Grace should send
it to any of His servants He pleases: thus have they drawn on themselves
Wrath upon Wrath. And humiliating is the punishment of those who
reject Faith. 91 When it is said to them, "Believe in what Allah has sent

---

9. Verse 83 referred to the universal moral law. This verse 84 refers to its application under a special Covenant entered into with the Jews of Madīnah by the newborn Muslim Commonwealth under its Guide and teacher Muḥammad. This Covenant is given in Ibn Hishām's *Sīrat-ur-Rasūl*, and comments on it will be found in Ameer Ali's *Spirit of Islam* (London, 1922), pp.57-61. It was entered into in the second year of the Hijrah, and was treacherously broken by the Jews almost immediately afterwards. [88]

down," they say, "We believe in what was sent down to us," yet they
reject all besides, even if it be Truth confirming what is with them. Say:
"Why then have you slain the prophets of Allah in times gone by, if you
did indeed believe?" 92 There came to you Moses with clear (Signs); yet
you worshipped the Calf (even) after that, and you did behave
wrongfully. 93 And remember We took your Covenant and We raised
above you (the towering height) of Mount (Sinai): (saying): "Hold firmly
to what We have given you, and hearken (to the Law)": they said: "We
hear, and we disobey:" and they had to drink into their hearts (of the
taint) of the Calf because of their faithlessness. Say: "Vile indeed are the
behests of your Faith if you have any faith!" 94 Say: "If the last Home,
with Allah, be for you specially, and not for anyone else, then seek you
for death, if you are sincere." 95 But they will never seek for death, on
account of the (sins) which their hands have sent on before them, and
Allah is well-acquainted with the wrong-doers. 96 You will indeed find
them, of all people, most greedy of life,—even more than the idolaters:
each one of them wishes he could be given a life of a thousand years: but
the grant of such life will not save him from (due) punishment. For Allah
sees well all that they do.

SECTION 12

97 Say: Whoever is an enemy to Gabriel—for he brings down the
(revelation) to your heart by Allah's Will, a confirmation of what went
before, and guidance and glad tidings for those who believe,—98 Whoever
is an enemy to Allah and His angels and messengers, to Gabriel and
Michael,—lo! Allah is an enemy to those who reject Faith. 99 We have
sent down to you manifest Signs (*āyāt*); and none reject them but those
who are perverse. 100 Is it not (the case) that every time they make a
Covenant, some party among them throw it aside?—Nay, most of them
are faithless. 101 And when there came to them a messenger from Allah,
confirming what was with them, a party of the People of the Book threw
away the Book of Allah behind their backs, as if (it had been something)
they did not know! 102 They followed what the evil ones gave out (falsely)
against the power of Solomon: the blasphemers were, not Solomon, but
the evil ones, teaching men magic, and such things as came down at

Babylon to the angels Hārūt and Mārūt.[10] But neither of these taught anyone (such things) without saying: "We are only for trial; so do not blaspheme." They learned from them the means to sow discord between man and wife. But they could not thus harm anyone except by Allah's permission. And they learned what harmed them, not what profited them. And they knew that the buyers of (magic) would have no share in the happiness of the Hereafter. And vile was the price for which they did sell
their souls, if they but knew! 103 If they had kept their Faith and guarded
themselves from evil, far better had been the reward from their Lord, if they but knew!

SECTION 13

104 O you of Faith! Say not (to the Messenger) words of ambiguous import, but words of respect; and hearken (to him): to those without Faith
is a grievous punishment. 105 It is never the wish of those without Faith
among the People of the Book, nor of the Pagans, that anything good should come down to you from your Lord. But Allah will choose for His
special Mercy whom He will—for Allah is Lord of grace abounding. 106
None of Our revelations[11] do We abrogate or cause to be forgotten, but

---

10. Hārūt and Mārūt lived in Babylon, a very ancient seat of science, especially the science of astronomy. The period may be supposed to be anywhere about the time when the ancient Eastern Monarchies were strong and enlightened: probably even earlier, as Mā-rū-tu or Madruk was a deified hero afterwards worshipped as a god of magic in Babylon. Being good men, Hārūt and Mārūt of course dabbled in nothing evil, and their hands were certainly clean of fraud. But knowledge and the arts, if learned by evil men, can be applied to evil uses. The evil ones, besides their fraudulent magic, also learnt a little of this true science and applied it to evil uses. Hārūt and Mārūt did not withhold knowledge, yet never taught any one without plainly warning them of the trial and temptation of knowledge in the hands of evil men. Being men of insight, they also saw the blasphemy that might rise to the lips of the evil ones puffed up with science and warned them against it. Knowledge is indeed a trial or temptation: if we are warned, we know its dangers: if Allah has endowed us with free will, we must be free to choose between the benefit and the danger.

Among the Jewish traditions in the Midrash (Jewish *Tafsīrs*) was a story of two angels who asked Allah's permission to come down to earth but succumbed to temptation, and were hung up by their feet at Babylon for punishment. Such stories about sinning angels who were cast down to punishment were believed in by the early Christians also. (See the Second Epistle of Peter ii. 4, and the Epistle of Jude, verse 6.) [104]

11. The word which I have translated by the word "revelations" is *Āyāt*. It is not only used for verses of the Qur'an, but in a general sense for Allah's revelations, as in 2:39 and for other Signs of Allah in history or nature, or miracles, as in 2:61. It has even been used

We substitute something better or similar: Do you not know that Allah
has power over all things? 107 Do you not know that to Allah belongs the
dominion of the heavens and the earth? And besides Him you have
neither patron nor helper.

108 Would you question your Messenger as Moses was questioned of old?
But whoever changes from Faith to Unbelief, has strayed without doubt
from the even way. 109 Quite a number of the People of the Book wish
they could turn you (people) back to infidelity after you have believed,
from selfish envy, after the Truth has become manifest unto them: but
forgive and overlook, till Allah accomplishes His purpose; for Allah has
power over all things. 110 And be steadfast in prayer and regular in
charity: and whatever good you send forth for your souls before you, you
shall find it with Allah: for Allah sees well all that you do. 111 And they
say: "None shall enter Paradise unless he be a Jew or a Christian." Those
are their (vain) desires. Say: "Produce your proof if you are truthful." 112
Nay,—whoever submits his whole self to Allah and is a doer of
good,—he will get his reward with his Lord; on such shall be no fear, nor
shall they grieve.

SECTION 14

113 The Jews say: "The Christians have naught (to stand) upon" and the
Christians say: "The Jews have naught (to stand) upon." Yet they (profess
to) study the (same) Book. Like unto their word is what those say who

---

for human signs and tokens of wonder, as, for example, monuments or landmarks built by the ancient people of 'Ād (26:128). What is the meaning here? If we take it in a general sense, it means that Allah's Message from age to age is always the same, but that its form may differ according to the needs and exigencies of the time. That form was different as given to Moses and then to Jesus and then to Muhammad. Some commentators apply it also to the *Āyāt* of the Qur'an. There is nothing derogatory in this if we believe in progressive revelation. In 3:7 we are told distinctly about the Qur'an, that some of its verses are clear (and of established meaning), and others are not entirely clear, and it is mischievous to treat the verses that are not entirely clear and to follow them (literally). On the other hand, it is absurd to treat such a verse as 2:115 as if it were abrogated by 2:144 about the *Qiblah*.

There may be express abrogation, or there may be "causing or permitting to forget." How many good and wise institutions gradually become obsolete by afflux of time? Then there is the gradual process of disuse or forgetting in evolution. This does not mean that eternal principles change. It is only a sign of Allah's infinite Power that His creation should take so many forms and shapes not only in the material world but in the world of man's thought and expression. [107]

know not; but Allah will judge between them in their quarrel on the Day
of Judgement. 114 And who is more unjust than he who forbids that in
places for the worship of Allah, Allah's name should be
celebrated?—whose zeal is (in fact) to ruin them? It was not fitting that
such should themselves enter them except in fear. Fop them there is
nothing but disgrace in this world, and in the world to come, an
exceeding torment. 115 To Allah belong the East and the West: wherever
you turn, there is the presence of Allah. For Allah is All-pervading,
All-knowing. 116 They say: "Allah has begotten a son": glory be to
Him—nay, to Him belongs all that is in the heavens and on earth:
everything renders worship to Him.[12] 117 To Him is due the primal origin
of the heavens and the earth: when He decrees a matter, He says to it:
"Be," and it is. 118 Say those without knowledge: "Why does Allah not
speak unto us? Or why comes not unto us a Sign?" So said the people
before them words of similar import. Their hearts are alike. We have
indeed made clear the Signs unto any people who hold firmly to Faith (in
their hearts). 119 Verily, We have sent you in truth as a bearer of glad
tidings and a warner: but of you no question shall be asked of the
companions of the blazing Fire. 120 Never will the Jews or the Christians
be satisfied with you unless you follow their form of religion. Say: "The
Guidance of Allah,—that is the (only) Guidance." Were you to follow
their desires after the knowledge which has reached you, then would you
find neither protector nor helper against Allah. 121 Those to whom We
have sent the Book study it as it should be studied: they are the ones that
believe therein: those who reject faith therein,—the loss is their own.

SECTION 15

122 O Children of Israel! Call to mind the special favour which I bestowed
upon you, and that I preferred you to all others (for My Message). 123
Then guard yourselves against a Day when one soul shall not avail
another, nor shall compensation be accepted from her nor shall
intercession profit her nor shall anyone be helped (from outside).

---

12. It is a derogation from the glory of Allah—in fact it is blasphemy—to say that Allah begets sons, like a man or an animal. The Christian doctrine is here emphatically repudiated. If words have any meaning, it would mean an attribution to Allah of a material nature, and of the lower animal functions of sex. In a spiritual sense, we are all children of Allah. And all Creation celebrates His glory. Verse 117 should be read with this to complete the argument. [119]

124 And remember that Abraham was tried by his Lord with certain
Commands, which he fulfilled: He said: "I will make you an Imām to the
Nations." He pleaded: "And also (Imāms) from my offspring!" He
answered: "But My Promise is not within the reach of evil-doers." 125
Remember We made the House[13] a place of assembly for men and a
place of safety; and take you the station of Abraham as a place of prayer;
and We covenanted with Abraham and Ismā'īl, that they should sanctify
My House for those who compass it round, or use it as a retreat, or bow,
or prostrate themselves (therein in prayer). 126 And remember Abraham
said: "My Lord, Make this a City of Peace, and feed its people with
fruits,—such of them as believe in Allah and the Last Day." He said:
"(Yea), and such as reject Faith,—for a while will I grant them their
pleasure, but will soon drive them to the torment of Fire,—an evil
destination (indeed)!" 127 And remember Abraham and Ismā'īl raised the
foundations of the House (with this prayer): "Our Lord! Accept (this
service) from us: for You are the All-hearing, the All-knowing. 128 Our
Lord! Make of us Muslims, bowing to Your (Will), and of our progeny
a people Muslim, bowing to Your (Will); and show us our place for the
celebration of (due) rites; and turn unto us (in Mercy); for You are the
Oft-Returning, Most Merciful. 129 Our Lord! Send amongst them a
Messenger of their own, who shall rehearse Your Signs to them and
instruct them in scripture and wisdom, and sanctify them: for You are the
Exalted in Might, the Wise."

---

13. The Ka'bah, the House of Allah. Its foundation goes back by Arab tradition to Abraham. Its fourfold character is here referred to (1) It was the centre to which all the Arab tribes resorted for trade, for poetic contests, and for worship. (2) It was sacred territory, and was respected by friend and foe alike. At certain seasons, all fighting was and is forbidden within its limits, and even arms are not allowed to be carried, and no game or other thing is allowed to be killed. Like the Cities of Refuge under the Mosaic Dispensation, to which man-slayers could flee (Num. xxxv.6), or the Sanctuaries in Medieval Europe, to which criminals could not be pursued, Makkah was recognised by Arab custom as inviolable for the pursuit of revenge or violence. (3) It was a place of prayer: even today there is a Station of Abraham. (4) It must be held pure and sacred for all purposes.

Though the verse as a whole is expressed in the First Person Plural, the House is called "My House", to emphasise the personal relation of Allah, the One True God, to it, and repudiate the Polytheism which defiled it before it was *purified* again by Muḥammad. [125]

SECTION 16

130 And who turns away from the religion of Abraham but such as debase
their souls with folly? Him We chose and rendered pure in this world:
and he will be in the Hereafter in the ranks of the Righteous. 131 Behold!
His Lord said to him: "Bow (thy will to Me):" He said: "I bow (my will)
to the Lord and Cherisher of the Universe." 132 And this was the legacy
that Abraham left to his sons, and so did Jacob; "Oh my sons! Allah has
chosen the Faith for you; then die not except in the Faith of Islam." 133
Were you witnesses when death appeared before Jacob? Behold, he said
to his sons: "What will you worship after me?" They said: "We shall
worship your God and the God of your fathers,—of Abraham, Ismā'īl and
Isaac,—the one (True) God: to Him we bow (in Islam)." 134 That was a
people that has passed away. They shall reap the fruit of what they did,
and you of what you do! Of their merits there is no question in your case!

135 They say: "Become Jews or Christians if you would be guided (to
salvation)." Say you: "Nay! (I would rather) the Religion of Abraham the
True, and he joined not gods with Allah." 136 Say you: "We believe in
Allah, and the revelation given to us, and to Abraham, Ismā'īl , Isaac,
Jacob, and the Tribes, and that given to Moses and Jesus, and that given
to (all) prophets from their Lord: we make no difference between one and
another of them: and we bow to Allah (in Islam)." 137 So if they believe
as you believe, they are indeed on the right path; but if they turn back, it
is they who are in schism; but Allah will suffice you as against them, and
He is the All-hearing, the All-Knowing. 138 (Our religion is) the Baptism
of Allah: and who can baptize better than Allah? And it is He Whom we
worship.

139 Say: Will you dispute with us about Allah, seeing that He is our Lord
and your Lord; that we are responsible for our doings and you for yours;
and that we are sincere (in our faith) in Him? 140 Or do you say that
Abraham, Ismā'īl, Isaac, Jacob and the Tribes were Jews or Christians?
Say: Do you know better than Allah? Ah! Who is more unjust than those
who conceal the testimony they have from Allah? But Allah is not
unmindful of what you do! 141 That was a people that has passed away.
They shall reap the fruit of what they did, and you of what you do! Of
their merits there is no question in your case.

PART II

SECTION 17

142 The fools among the people will say: "What has turned them from the
Qiblah[14] to which they were used?" Say: To Allah belong both East and
West: He guides whom He will to a Way that is straight. 143 Thus, have
We made of you an *Ummah* justly balanced, that you might be witnesses
over the nations, and the Messenger a witness over yourselves; and We
appointed the *Qiblah* to which you were used, only to test those who
followed the Messenger from those who would turn on their heels (from
the Faith). Indeed it was (a change) momentous, except to those guided
by Allah. And never would Allah make your faith of no effect. For Allah
is to all people most surely full of kindness, Most Merciful. 144 We see the
turning of your face (for guidance) to the heavens: now shall We turn you
to a *Qiblah* that shall please you. Turn then your face in the direction of
the Sacred Mosque: wherever you are, turn your faces in that direction.
The People of the Book know well that that is the Truth from their Lord.
Nor is Allah unmindful of what they do. 145 Even if you were to bring to
the people of the Book all the Signs (together), they would not follow
your *Qiblah*; nor are you going to follow their *Qiblah*; nor indeed will
they follow each other's *Qiblah*. If you after the knowledge has reached
you, were to follow their (vain) desires,—then were you indeed (clearly)
in the wrong. 146 The People of the Book know this as they know their
own sons; but some of them conceal the truth which they themselves

---

14. *Qiblah*=the direction to which Muslims turn in prayer. Islam lays great stress on social prayer in order to emphasise our universal Brotherhood and mutual cooperation. For such prayer, order, punctuality, precision, symbolical postures, and a common direction are essential, so that the Imām (leader) and all his congregation may face one way and offer their supplications to Allah. In the early days, before they were organised as a people, they followed as a symbol for their *Qiblah* the sacred city of Jerusalem, sacred both to the Jews and the Christians, the people of the Book. This symbolised their allegiance to the continuity of Allah's revelation. When, despised and persecuted, they were turned out of Makkah and arrived in Madīnah, the Prophet under divine direction began to organise its people as an *Ummah,* an independent people, with laws and rituals of their own. At that stage the Ka'bah was established as *Qiblah,* thus going back to the earliest centre, with which the name of Abraham was connected, and traditionally also the name of Adam. Jerusalem still remained (and remains) sacred in the eyes of Islam on account of its past, but Islam is a progressive religion, and its new symbolism enabled it to shake off the tradition of a dead past and usher in the era of untrammelled freedom dear to the spirit of Arabia. The change took place about 16½ months after Hijrah. [141]

know. 147 The Truth is from your Lord; so be not at all in doubt.

SECTION 18

148 To each is a goal to which Allah turns him; then strive together (as in
a race) towards all that is good. Wheresoever you are, Allah will bring
you together. For Allah has power over all things. 149 From wherever you
start forth, turn your face in the direction of the Sacred Mosque; that is
indeed the truth from your Lord. And Allah is not unmindful of what you
do. 150 So from whencesoever you start forth, turn your face in the
direction of the Sacred Mosque; and wheresoever you are, turn your face
thither: that there be no ground of dispute against you among the people,
except those of them that are bent on wickedness; so fear them not, but
fear Me; and that I may complete My favours on you, and you may
(consent to) be guided; 151 A similar (favour have you already received)
in that We have sent among you a Messenger of your own, rehearsing to
you Our Signs, and sanctifying you, and instructing you in Scripture and
Wisdom, and in new knowledge. 152 Then do you remember[15] Me; I will
remember you. Be grateful to Me, and reject not Faith.

SECTION 19

153 O you who believe! Seek help with patient perseverance and prayer;
for Allah is with those who patiently persevere. 154 And say not of those
who are slain in the Way of Allah: "They are dead." Nay, they are living,
though you perceive (it) not. 155 Be sure We shall test you with something
of fear and hunger, some loss in goods or lives or the fruits (of your toil),
but give glad tidings to those who patiently persevere,—156 Who say,
when afflicted with calamity: "To Allah we belong, and to Him is our
return":—157 They are those on whom (descend) blessings from Allah,
and Mercy, and they are the ones that receive guidance.

158 Behold! Ṣafā and Marwah are among the Symbols of Allah. So if those
who visit the House in the Season or at other times, should compass them
round, it is no sin in them. And if any one obeys his own impulse to
good,—be sure that Allah is He Who recognises and knows. 159 Those

---

15. The word "remember" is too pale a word for *dhikr,* which has now acquired a large number of associations in our religious literature. In its verbal signification it implies: to remember; to praise by frequently mentioning; to rehearse; to celebrate or commemorate; to make much of; to cherish the memory of as a precious possession.[156]

who conceal the clear (Signs) We have sent down, and the Guidance,
after We have made it clear for the people in the Book,—on them shall
be Allah's curse, and the curse of those entitled to curse,— 160 Except
those who repent and make amends and openly declare (the Truth): to
them I turn; for I am Oft-Returning, Most Merciful. 161 Those who reject
Faith, and die rejecting,—on them is Allah's curse, and the curse of
angels, and of all mankind; 162 They will abide therein: their penalty will
not be lightened, nor will respite be their (lot). 163 And your Allah is One
Allah: there is no god but He, Most Gracious, Most Merciful.

SECTION 20

164 Behold! In the creation of the heavens and the earth; in the alternation of the night and the day; in the sailing of the ships through the ocean for the profit of mankind; in the rain which Allah sends down from the skies, and the life which He gives therewith to an earth that is dead; in the beasts of all kinds that He scatters through the earth; in the change of the winds, and the clouds which they trail like their slaves between the sky
and the earth;—(here) indeed are Signs for a people that are wise. 165 Yet
there are men who take (for worship) others besides Allah, as equal (with
Allah): they love them as they should love Allah. But those of Faith are
overflowing in their love for Allah. If only the unrighteous could see,
behold, they would see the Penalty: that to Allah belongs all power, and
Allah will strongly enforce the Penalty. 166 Then would those who are
followed clear themselves of those who follow (them): they would see the
Penalty, and all relations between them would be cut off. 167 And those
who followed would say: "If only we had one more chance, we would
clear ourselves of them, as they have cleared themselves of us." Thus will
Allah show them (the fruits of) their deeds as (nothing but) regrets. Nor
will there be a way for them out of the Fire.

SECTION 21

168 O you people! Eat of what is on earth, lawful and good; and do not
follow the footsteps of the Evil One, for he is to you an avowed enemy.
169. For he commands you what is evil and shameful, and that you should
say of Allah that of which you have no knowledge. 170 When it is said to
them: "Follow what Allah has revealed" they say: "Nay! We shall follow
the ways of our fathers." What! Even though their fathers were void of
wisdom and guidance? 171 The parable of those who reject Faith is as if

one were to shout like a goat-herd, to things that listen to nothing but
calls and cries: deaf, dumb, and blind, they are void of wisdom. 172 O you
who believe! Eat of the good things that We have provided for you, and
be grateful to Allah, if it is Him you worship. 173 He has only forbidden
you dead meat, and blood, and the flesh of swine, and that on which any
other name has been invoked besides that of Allah. But if one is forced
by necessity, without wilful disobedience, nor transgressing due
limits,—then is he guiltless. For Allah is Oft-Forgiving, Most Merciful.

174 Those who conceal Allah's revelations in the Book, and purchase for
them a miserable profit,—they swallow into themselves naught but Fire;
Allah will not address them on the Day of Resurrection. Nor purify them:
grievous will be their Penalty. 175 They are the ones who buy Error in
place of Guidance and Torment in place of Forgiveness. Ah! What
boldness (they show) for the Fire! 176 (Their doom is) because Allah sent
down the Book in truth but those who seek causes of dispute in the Book
are in a schism far (from the purpose).

SECTION 22

177 It is not righteousness that you turn your faces towards East or West;
but it is righteousness—to believe in Allah and the Last Day, and the
Angels, and the Book, and the Messengers; to spend of your substance,
out of love for Him, for your kin, for orphans, for the needy, for the
wayfarer, for those who ask, and for the ransom of slaves; to be steadfast
in prayer, and practise regular charity; to fulfil the contracts which you
have made; and to be firm and patient, in pain (or suffering) and
adversity, and throughout all periods of panic. Such are the people of
truth, the Allah-fearing.

178 O you who believe! The law of equality is prescribed to you in cases
of murder: the free for the free, the slave for the slave, the woman for the
woman. But if any remission is made by the brother of the slain, then
grant any reasonable demand, and compensate him with handsome
gratitude. This is a concession and a Mercy from your Lord. After this
whoever exceeds the limits shall be in grave penalty. 179 In the Law of
Equality there is (saving of) life to you, O you men of understanding; that
you may restrain yourselves.

180 It is prescribed, when death approaches any of you, if he leave any

goods that he make a bequest to parents and next of kin, according to
reasonable usage; this is due from the Allah-fearing. 181 If anyone changes
the bequest after hearing it, the guilt shall be on those who make the
change. For Allah hears and knows (all things). 182 But if anyone fears
partiality or wrongdoing on the part of the testator, and makes peace
between (the parties concerned), there is no wrong in him: for Allah is
Oft-Forgiving, Most Merciful.

SECTION 23

183 O you who believe! Fasting is prescribed to you as it was prescribed
to those before you, that you may (learn) self-restraint,— 184 (Fasting) for
a fixed number of days; but if any of you is ill, or on a journey, the
prescribed number (should be made up) from days later. For those who
can do it (with hardship), is a ransom, the feeding of one that is indigent.
But he that will give more, of his own free will,—it is better for him. And
it is better for you that you fast, if you only knew. 185 Ramaḍān is the
(month) in which was sent down the Qur'an, as a guide to mankind, also
clear (Signs) for guidance and judgement (between right and wrong). So
every one of you who is present (at his home) during that month should
spend it in fasting, but if any one is ill, or on a journey, the prescribed
period (should be made up) by days later. Allah intends every facility for
you; He does not want to put you to difficulties. (He wants you) to
complete the prescribed period, and to glorify Him in that He has guided
you; and perchance you shall be grateful. 186 When My servants ask you
concerning Me, I am indeed close (to them): I listen to the prayer of every
suppliant when he calls on Me: let them also, with a will, listen to My
call, and believe in Me: that they may walk in the right way. 187 Permitted
to you, on the night of the fasts, is the approach to your wives. They are
your garments and you are their garments. Allah knows what you used to
do secretly among yourselves; but He turned to you and forgave you; so
now associate with them, and seek what Allah has ordained for you, and
eat and drink, until the white thread of dawn appears to you distinct from
its black thread; then complete your fast till the night appears; but do not
associate with your wives while you are in retreat in the mosques. Those
are Limits (set by) Allah: approach not nigh thereto. Thus does Allah
make clear His Signs to men: that they may learn self-restraint. 188 And
do not eat up your property among yourselves for vanities, nor use it as
bait for the judges, with intent that you may eat up wrongfully and

knowingly a little of (other) people's property.

SECTION 24

189 They ask you concerning the New Moons. Say: They are but Signs to mark fixed periods of time in (the affairs of) men, and for Pilgrimage. It is no virtue if you enter your houses from the back:[16] it is virtue if you fear Allah. Enter houses through the proper doors: and fear Allah: that you may prosper.

190 Fight in the cause of Allah those who fight you, but do not transgress
limits; for Allah loves not transgressors. 191 And slay them wherever you
catch them, and turn them out from where they have turned you out; for
tumult and oppression are worse than slaughter; but fight them not at the
Sacred Mosque, unless they (first) fight you there; but if they fight you,
slay them. Such is the reward of those who suppress faith. 192 But if they
cease, Allah is Oft-Forgiving, Most Merciful. 193 And fight them on until
there is no more tumult or oppression, and there prevail justice and faith
in Allah; but if they cease,[17] let there be no hostility except to those who
practise oppression.[18]

---

16. There were many superstitions connected with the New Moon, as there are to the present day. We are told to disregard such superstitions. As a measure of time, where the lunar calendar is used, the New Moon is one great sign, for which people watch with eagerness. Muslim festivals, including the Pilgrimage are fixed by the appearance of the New Moon. The Arabs, among other superstitions, had one which made them enter their houses by the back door during or after the Pilgrimage. This is disapproved, for there is no virtue in any such artificial restrictions. All virtue proceeds from the love and fear of Allah. [202]

17. If the opposite party ceases to persecute you, your hostility ends with them as a party, but it does not mean that you become friends to oppression. Your fight is against wrong; there should not be any rancour against people as individuals or because they belong to a certain group, but rather, opposition to the wrong that any of them commit. [208] – Ed.

18. Verses 190-193 were revealed in connection with the ongoing attack and persecution by the Makkan idolaters that had started when the first small group of Muslims, who lived in Makkah, were persecuted for worshipping Allah as the One God at the same mosque (the Ka'bah in Makkah). So inveterate and merciless was the hostility that the Muslims were told to fight these hostile disbelievers wherever they encountered them, until worship at the sacred Ka'bah was for Allah alone. Worship at the Ka'bah has been for Allah alone since the peaceful conquest of Makkah in 630 CE (see also 9:5). – Ed.

194 The prohibited month[19] —for the prohibited month, and so for all things prohibited,—there is the law of equality. If then any one transgresses the prohibition against you, transgress you likewise against him. But fear Allah, and know that Allah is with those who restrain
themselves. 195 And spend of your substance in the cause of Allah, and
make not your own hands contribute to (your) destruction; but do good; for Allah loves those who do good.

196 And complete the *Ḥajj* or *'Umrah* in the service of Allah. But if you are prevented (from completing it), send an offering for sacrifice, such as you may find, and do not shave your heads until the offering reaches the place of sacrifice. And if any of you is ill, or has an ailment in his scalp, (necessitating shaving), (he should) in compensation either fast, or feed the poor, or offer sacrifice; and when you are in peaceful conditions (again), if any one wishes to continue the *'Umrah* on to the *Ḥajj*, he must make an offering, such as he can afford, but if he cannot afford it, he should fast three days during the *Ḥajj* and seven days on his return, making ten days in all. This is for those whose household is not in (the precincts of) the Sacred Mosque. And fear Allah, and know that Allah is strict in punishment.

SECTION 25

197 For *Ḥajj* are the months well known. If any one undertakes that duty therein, let there be no obscenity, nor wickedness, nor wrangling in the *Ḥajj*. And whatever good you do, (be sure) Allah knows it. And take a provision (with you) for the journey, but the best of provisions is right
conduct. So fear Me, O you that are wise. 198 It is no crime in you if you
seek of the bounty of your Lord (during pilgrimage). Then when you

---

19. *Harām* = prohibited, sacred. The month of Pilgrimage (*Dhū al-Ḥijjah*) was a sacred month, in which warfare was prohibited by Arab custom. The month preceding (*Dhū al-Qa'dah*) and the month following (*Muḥarram*) were included in the prohibition, and *Muharram* was specially called *al-Harām*. Possibly *Muharram* is meant in the first line, and the other months and other prohibited things in "all things prohibited". In *Rajab*, also, war was prohibited. If the pagan enemies of Islam broke the custom and made war in the prohibited months, the Muslims were free also to break the custom but only to the same extent as the others broke it. Similarly the territory of Makkah was sacred, in which war was prohibited. If the enemies of Islam broke that custom, the Muslims were free to do so to that extent. Any convention is useless if one party does not respect it. There must be a law of equality. Or perhaps the word reciprocity may express it better. [209]

pour down from (Mount) 'Arafāt, celebrate the praises of Allah at the
Sacred Monument, and celebrate His praises as He has directed you, even
though, before this, you went astray. 199 Then pass on at a quick pace
from the place whence it is usual for the multitude so to do, and ask for
Allah's forgiveness. For Allah is Oft-Forgiving, Most Merciful. 200 So
when you have accomplished your holy rites, celebrate the praises of
Allah, as you used to celebrate the praises of your fathers,—yea, with far
more heart and soul. There are men who say: "Our Lord! Give us (Thy
bounties) in this world!" but they will have no portion in the Hereafter.
201 And there are men who say: "Our Lord! Give us good in this world
and good in the Hereafter, and defend us from the torment of the Fire!"
202 To these will be allotted what they have earned; and Allah is quick in
account. 203 Celebrate the praises of Allah during the Appointed Days.[20]
But if any one hastens to leave in two days, there is no blame on him, and
if any one stays on, there is no blame on him, if his aim is to do right.
Then fear Allah, and know that you will surely be gathered unto Him.

204 There is the type of man whose speech about this world's life may
dazzle you, and he calls Allah to witness about what is in his heart; yet is
he the most contentious of enemies. 205 When he turns his back, his aim
everywhere is to spread mischief through the earth and destroy crops and
cattle. But Allah loves not mischief. 206 When it is said to him, "Fear
Allah", he is led by arrogance to (more) crime. Enough for him is
Hell;—an evil bed indeed (to lie on)! 207 And there is the type of man who
gives his life to earn the pleasure of Allah: and Allah is full of kindness
to (His) devotees.

208 O you who believe! Enter into Islam wholeheartedly; and follow not
the footsteps of the Evil One; for he is to you an avowed enemy. 209 If you
backslide after the clear (Signs) have come to you, then know that Allah
is Exalted in Power, Wise. 210 Will they wait until Allah comes to them in
canopies of clouds, with angels (in His train) and the question is (thus)
settled? But to Allah do all questions go back (for decision).

---

20. *The Appointed Days*: the three days after the tenth, when the Pilgrims stay on in the Valley of Minā for prayer and praise. They are the days of *Tashrīq* (see 2:200). It is optional for pilgrims to leave on the second or third day. [226]

SECTION 26

211 Ask the Children of Israel how many clear (Signs) We have sent them.
But if any one, after Allah's favour has come to him, substitutes
(something else), Allah is strict in punishment. 212 The life of this world
is alluring to those who reject faith, and they scoff at those who believe.
But the righteous will be above them on the Day of Resurrection; for
Allah bestows His abundance without measure on whom He will. 213
Mankind was one single nation, and Allah sent Messengers with glad
tidings and warnings; and with them He sent the Book in truth, to judge
between people in matters wherein they differed; but the People of the
Book, after the clear Signs came to them, did not differ among
themselves, except through selfish contumacy. Allah by His Grace guided
the Believers to the Truth, concerning that wherein they differed. For
Allah guides whom He will to a path that is straight. 214 Or do you think
that you shall enter the Garden (of Bliss) without such (trials) as came to
those who passed away before you? They encountered suffering and
adversity, and were so shaken in spirit that even the Messenger and those
of faith who were with him cried: "When (will come) the help of Allah?"
Ah! Verily, the help of Allah is (always) near!

215 They ask you what they should spend (in charity). Say: Whatever you
spend that is good, is for parents and kindred and orphans and those in
want and for wayfarers. And whatever you do that is good,— Allah
knows it well.

216 Fighting is prescribed for you, and you dislike it. But it is possible that
you dislike a thing which is good for you, and that you love a thing which
is bad for you. But Allah knows, and you know not.

SECTION 27

217 They ask you concerning fighting in the Prohibited Month.[21] Say:
"Fighting therein is a grave (offence); but graver is it in the sight of Allah
to prevent access to the path of Allah, to deny Him, to prevent access to
the Sacred Mosque, and drive out its members." Tumult and oppression
are worse than slaughter. Nor will they cease fighting you until they turn
you back from your faith if they can. And if any of you turn back from
their faith and die in unbelief, their works will bear no fruit in this life

---

21. *Prohibited Month*: See 2:194. [237]

and in the Hereafter; they will be Companions of the Fire and will abide
therein. 218 Those who believed and those who suffered exile and fought
(and strove and struggled) in the path of Allah,—they have the hope of
the Mercy of Allah: and Allah is Oft-Forgiving, Most Merciful.

219 They ask you concerning wine and gambling. Say: "In them is great
sin, and some profit, for men; but the sin is greater than the profit." They
ask you how much they are to spend. Say: "What is beyond your needs."
Thus does Allah make clear to you His Signs: in order that you may
consider—220 (Their bearings) on this life and the Hereafter. They ask you
concerning orphans. Say: "The best thing to do is what is for their good;
if you mix their affairs with yours, they are your brethren; but Allah
knows the man who means mischief from the man who means good. And
if Allah had wished, He could have put you into difficulties: He is indeed
Exalted in Power, Wise."

221 Do not marry unbelieving women (idolaters), until they believe: a
slave woman who believes is better than an unbelieving woman, even
though she allures you. Nor marry (your girls) to unbelievers until they
believe: a man slave who believes is better than an unbeliever, even
though he allures you. Unbelievers do (but) beckon you to the Fire. But
Allah beckons by His Grace to the Garden (of Bliss) and forgiveness, and
makes His Signs clear to mankind: that they may celebrate His praise.

SECTION 28

222 They ask you concerning women's courses. Say: They are a hurt and
a pollution: so keep away from women in their courses, and do not
approach them until they are clean. But when they have purified
themselves, you may approach them in any manner, time, or place
ordained for you by Allah. For Allah loves those who turn to Him
constantly and He loves those who keep themselves pure and clean. 223
Your wives are as a tilth unto you; so approach your tilth when or how
you will; but do some good act for your souls beforehand; and fear Allah.
And know that you are to meet Him (in the Hereafter), and give (these)
good tidings to those who believe.

224 And make not Allah's (name) an excuse in your oaths against doing
good, or acting rightly, or making peace between persons; for Allah is
One Who hears and knows all things. 225 Allah will not call you to account

for thoughtlessness in your oaths, but for the intention in your hearts; and
He is Oft-Forgiving, Most Forbearing. 226 For those who take an oath for
abstention from their wives, a waiting for four months is ordained; if then
they return, Allah is Oft-Forgiving, Most Merciful. 227 But if their
intention is firm for divorce, Allah hears and knows all things.

228 Divorced women shall wait concerning themselves for three monthly
periods. Nor is it lawful for them to hide what Allah has created in their
wombs, if they have faith in Allah and the Last Day. And their husbands
have the better right to take them back in that period, if they wish for
reconciliation. And women shall have rights similar to the rights against
them, according to what is equitable; but men have a degree (of
advantage) over them. And Allah is Exalted in Power, Wise.

SECTION 29

229 A divorce is only permissible twice: after that, the parties should either
hold together on equitable terms, or separate with kindness. It is not
lawful for you, (men), to take back any of your gifts (from your wives),
except when both parties fear that they would be unable to keep the limits
ordained by Allah. If you (judges) do indeed fear that they would be
unable to keep the limits ordained by Allah, there is no blame on either
of them if she give something for her freedom. These are the limits
ordained by Allah; so do not transgress them. If any do transgress the
limits ordained by Allah, such persons wrong (themselves as well as
others). 230 So if a husband divorces his wife (irrevocably), he cannot,
after that, re-marry her until after she has married another husband and
he has divorced her. In that case there is no blame on either of them if
they re-unite, provided they feel that they can keep the limits ordained by
Allah. Such are the limits ordained by Allah, which He makes plain to
those who understand. 231 When you divorce women, and they fulfil the
term of their *'Iddah*, either take them back on equitable terms or set them
free on equitable terms; but do not take them back to injure them, (or) to
take undue advantage; if any one does that; he wrongs his own soul. Do
not treat Allah's Signs as a jest, but solemnly rehearse Allah's favours on
you, and the fact that He sent down to you the Book and Wisdom, for
your instruction. And fear Allah, and know that Allah is well acquainted
with all things.

SECTION 30

232 When you divorce women, and they fulfil the term of their *'Iddah*, do
not prevent them from marrying their (former) husbands, if they mutually
agree on equitable terms. This instruction is for all amongst you, who
believe in Allah and the Last Day. That is (the course making for) most
virtue and purity amongst you and Allah knows, and you know not.

233 The mothers shall give suck to their offspring for two whole years, if
the father desires to complete the term. But he shall bear the cost of their
food and clothing on equitable terms. No soul shall have a burden laid on
it greater than it can bear. No mother shall be treated unfairly on account
of her child. Nor father on account of his child, an heir shall be
chargeable in the same way. If they both decide on weaning, by mutual
consent, and after due consultation, there is no blame on them. If you
decide on a foster-mother for your offspring, there is no blame on you,
provided you pay (the mother) what you offered, on equitable terms. But
fear Allah and know that Allah sees well what you do.

234 If any of you die and leave widows behind, they shall wait concerning
themselves four months and ten days: when they have fulfilled their term,
there is no blame on you if they dispose of themselves in a just and
reasonable manner. And Allah is well acquainted with what you do. 235
There is no blame on you if you make an offer of betrothal or hold it in
your hearts. Allah knows that you cherish them in your hearts: but do not
make a secret contract with them except in terms honourable, nor resolve
on the tie of marriage till the term prescribed is fulfilled. And know that
Allah knows what is in your hearts, and take heed of Him; and know that
Allah is Oft-Forgiving, Most Forbearing.

SECTION 31

236 There is no blame on you if you divorce women before consummation
or the fixation of their dower; but bestow on them (a suitable gift), the
wealthy according to his means, and the poor according to his means;—a
gift of a reasonable amount is due from those who wish to do the right
thing. 237 And if you divorce them before consummation, but after the
fixation of a dower for them, then the half of the dower (is due to them),
unless they remit it or (the man's half) is remitted by him in whose hands
is the marriage tie; and the remission (of the man's half) is the nearest to
righteousness. And do not forget liberality between yourselves. For Allah

sees well all that you do.

238 Guard strictly your (habit of) prayers, especially the Middle Prayer;[22]
and stand before Allah in a devout (frame of mind). 239 If you fear (an
enemy), pray on foot, or riding, (as may be most convenient), but when you are in security, celebrate Allah's praises in the manner He has taught you, which you knew not (before).

240 Those of you who die and leave widows should bequeath for their widows a year's maintenance and residence; but if they leave (the residence), there is no blame on you for what they do with themselves,
provided it is reasonable. And Allah is Exalted in Power, Wise. 241 For
divorced women maintenance (should be provided) on a reasonable
(scale). This is a duty on the righteous. 242 Thus does Allah make clear His
Signs to you: in order that you may understand.

SECTION 32

243 Did you not turn your vision to those who abandoned their homes, though they were thousands (in number), for fear of death? Allah said to them: "Die" then He restored them to life. For Allah is full of bounty to
mankind, but most of them are ungrateful. 244 Then fight in the cause of
Allah, and know that Allah hears and knows all things. 245 Who is he that
will loan to Allah a beautiful loan, which Allah will double unto his credit and multiply many times? It is Allah that gives (you) want or plenty, and to Him shall be your return.

246 Have you not turned your vision to the Chiefs of the Children of Israel after (the time of) Moses? They said to a prophet (that was) among them: "Appoint for us a king, that we may fight in the cause of Allah." He said: "Is it not possible, if you were commanded to fight, that you will not fight?" They said: "How could we refuse to fight in the cause of Allah, seeing that we were turned out of our homes and our families?" But when they were commanded to fight, they turned back, except a small band
among them. But Allah has full knowledge of those who do wrong. 247

---

22. The Middle Prayer: Arabic *Salāt al-wusṭā* may be translated "the best or most excellent prayer". Authorities differ as to the exact meaning of this phrase. The weight of authorities seems to be in favour of interpreting this as the *'Asr* prayer (in the middle of the afternoon). This is apt to be most neglected, and yet this is the most necessary to remind us of Allah in the midst of our worldly affairs. [271]

Their Prophet said to them: "Allah has appointed Ṭālūt as king over you." They said: "How can he exercise authority over us when we are better fitted than he to exercise authority, and he is not even gifted, with wealth in abundance?" He said: "Allah has chosen him above you, and has gifted him abundantly with knowledge and bodily prowess: Allah grants His authority to whom He pleases. Allah cares for all, and He knows all
things." 248 And (further) their Prophet said to them: "A Sign of His authority is that there shall come to you the Ark of the Covenant, with (an assurance) therein of security from your Lord, and the relics left by the family of Moses and the family of Aaron, carried by angels. In this is a Symbol for you if you indeed have faith."

SECTION 33

249 When Ṭālūt set forth with the armies, he said: "Allah will test you at the stream: if any drinks of its water, he goes not with my army; only those who taste not of it go with me; a mere sip out of the hand is excused." But they all drank of it, except a few. When they crossed the river,—he and the faithful ones with him,—they said: "This day we cannot cope with Goliath and his forces." But those who were convinced that they must meet Allah, said: "How oft, by Allah's will, has a small force vanquished a big one? Allah is with those who steadfastly
persevere." 250 When they advanced to meet Goliath and his forces, they prayed: "Our Lord! Pour out constancy on us and make our steps firm:
help us against those that reject faith." 251 By Allah's will they routed them; and David slew Goliath; and Allah gave him power and wisdom and taught him whatever (else) He willed. And did not Allah check one set of people by means of another, the earth would indeed be full of
mischief: but Allah is full of bounty to all the worlds. 252 These are the Signs of Allah: we rehearse them to you in truth: verily you are one of the messengers.

PART III

253 Those messengers We endowed with gifts, some above others: to one of them Allah spoke; others He raised to degrees (of honour); to Jesus the son of Mary We gave clear (Signs), and strengthened him with the holy spirit. If Allah had so willed, succeeding generations would not have fought among each other, after clear (Signs) had come to them, but they (chose) to wrangle, some believing and others rejecting. If Allah had so

willed, they would not have fought each other; but Allah fulfills His plan.

SECTION 34

254 O you who believe! Spend out of (the bounties) We have provided for
you, before the Day comes when no bargaining (will avail), nor
friendship nor intercession. Those who reject Faith—they are the
wrong-doers.

255 Allah! There is no god but He,—the Living, the Self-subsisting,
Eternal. No slumber can seize Him nor sleep. His are all things in the
heavens and on earth. Who is there can intercede in His presence except
as He permits? He knows what (appears to His creatures as) before or
after or behind them. Nor shall they compass aught of His knowledge
except as He wills. His Throne does extend over the heavens and the
earth, and He feels no fatigue in guarding and preserving them for He is
the Most High, the Supreme (in glory).

256 Let there be no compulsion in religion: Truth stands out clear from
Error: whoever rejects Evil and believes in Allah has grasped the most
trustworthy handhold, that never breaks. And Allah hears and knows all
things. 257 Allah is the Protector of those who have faith: from the depths
of darkness He will lead them forth into light. Of those who reject faith
the patrons are the evil ones: from light they will lead them forth into the
depths of darkness. They will be Companions of the Fire, to dwell therein
(for ever).

SECTION 35

258 Have you not turned your vision to one who disputed with Abraham
about his Lord, because Allah had granted him power? Abraham said:
"My Lord is He Who gives life and death." He said: "I give life and
death." Said Abraham: "But it is Allah that causes the sun to rise from the
East: do you then cause him to rise from the West?" Thus was he
confounded who (in arrogance) rejected faith. Nor does Allah give
guidance to a people unjust. 259 Or (take) the similitude of one who passed
by a hamlet, all in ruins to its roofs. He said: "Oh! How shall Allah bring
it (ever) to life, after (this) its death?" But Allah caused him to die for a
hundred years, then raised him up (again). He said: "How long did you
tarry (thus)?" He said: ("Perhaps) a day or part of a day." He said: "Nay,
you have tarried thus a hundred years; but look at your food and your

drink; they show no signs of age; and look at your donkey: and that We
may make of you a Sign unto the people, look further at the bones, how
We bring them together and clothe them with flesh." When this was
shown clearly to him, he said: "I know that Allah has power over all
things." 260 Behold! Abraham said: "My Lord! Show me how You give
life to the dead." He said: "Do you not then believe?" He said: "Indeed!
but to satisfy my own understanding." He said: "Take four birds; tame
them to turn to you; put a portion of them on every hill and call to them:
they will come to you (flying) with speed. Then know that Allah is
Exalted in Power, Wise."

SECTION 36

261 The parable of those who spend their substance in the way of Allah is
that of a grain of corn: it grows seven ears, and each ear has a hundred
grains. Allah gives manifold increase to whom He pleases: and Allah
cares for all and He knows all things. 262 Those who spend their substance
in the cause of Allah, and follow not up their gifts with reminders of their
generosity or with injury,—for them their reward is with their Lord: on
them shall be no fear, nor shall they grieve. 263 Kind words and the
covering of faults are better than charity followed by injury. Allah is free
of all wants, and He is Most Forbearing. 264 O you who believe! cancel
not your charity by reminders of your generosity or by injury,—like those
who spend their substance to be seen of men, but believe neither in Allah
nor in the Last Day. They are in Parable like a hard, barren rock, on
which is a little soil; on it falls heavy rain, which leaves it (just) a bare
stone. They will be able to do nothing with aught they have earned. And
Allah guides not those who reject faith. 265 And the likeness of those who
spend their substance, seeking to please Allah and to strengthen their
souls, is as a garden, high and fertile; heavy rain falls on it but makes it
yield a double increase of harvest, and if it receives not heavy rain, light
moisture suffices it. Allah sees well whatever you do. 266 Does any of you
wish that he should have a garden with date palms and vines and streams
flowing underneath, and all kinds of fruit, while he is stricken with old
age, and his children are not strong (enough to look after
themselves)—that it should be caught in a whirlwind, with fire therein,
and be burnt up? Thus does Allah make clear to you (His) Signs, that you
may consider.

SECTION 37

267 O you who believe! Give of the good things which you have
(honourably) earned, and of the fruits of the earth which We have
produced for you, and do not even aim at getting anything which is bad,
in order that out of it you may give away something, when you
yourselves would not receive it except with closed eyes. And know that
Allah is free of all wants, and worthy of all praise. 268 The Evil One
threatens you with poverty and bids you to conduct unseemly. Allah
promises you His forgiveness and bounties. And Allah cares for all and
He knows all things. 269 He grants wisdom to whom He pleases; and he
to whom wisdom is granted receives indeed a benefit overflowing; but
none will grasp the Message but men of understanding. 270 And whatever
you spend in charity or devotion, be sure Allah knows it all. But the
wrong-doers have no helpers. 271 If you disclose (acts of) charity, even so
it is well, but if you conceal them, and make them reach those (really) in
need, that is best for you: it will remove from you some of your (stains
of) evil. And Allah is well acquainted with what you do. 272 It is not
required of you (O Messenger), to set them on the right path, but Allah
sets on the right path whom He pleases. Whatever of good you give
benefits your own souls, and you shall only do so seeking the "Face" of
Allah. Whatever good you give, shall be rendered back to you, and you
shall not be dealt with unjustly. 273 (Charity is) for those in need, who, in
Allah's cause are restricted (from travel), and cannot move about in the
land, seeking (for trade or work): the ignorant man thinks, because of
their modesty, that they are free from want. You shall know them by their
(unfailing) mark: they beg not importunately from all and sundry. And
whatever of good you give, be assured Allah knows it well.

SECTION 38

274 Those who (in charity) spend of their goods by night and by day, in
secret and in public, have their reward with their Lord: on them shall be
no fear, nor shall they grieve. 275 Those who devour usury will not stand
except as stands one whom the Evil One by his touch has driven to
madness. That is because they say: "Trade is like usury," but Allah has
permitted trade and forbidden usury. Those who after receiving direction
from their Lord, desist, shall be pardoned for the past; their case is for
Allah (to judge); but those who repeat (the offence) are Companions of
the Fire: they will abide therein (for ever). 276 Allah will deprive usury of

all blessing, but will give increase for deeds of charity: for He loves not creatures ungrateful and wicked.
277 Those who believe, and do deeds of righteousness, and establish regular prayers and regular charity, will have their reward with their Lord: on them shall be no fear, nor shall they grieve.

SECTION 39

278 O you who believe! Fear Allah, and give up what remains of your demand for usury, if you are indeed believers.
279 If you do it not, take notice of war from Allah and His Messenger: but if you turn back, you shall have your capital sums; deal not unjustly, and you shall not be dealt with unjustly.
280 If the debtor is in a difficulty, grant him time till it is easy for him to repay. But if you remit it by way of charity, that is best for you if you only knew.
281 And fear the Day when you shall be brought back to Allah. Then shall every soul be paid what it earned, and none shall be dealt with unjustly.

282 O you who believe! When you deal with each other, in transactions involving future obligations in a fixed period of time, reduce them to writing, let a scribe write down faithfully as between the parties; let not the scribe refuse to write: as Allah has taught him, so let him write. Let him who incurs the liability dictate, but let him fear his Lord Allah, and not diminish aught of what he owes. If the party liable is mentally deficient, or weak, or unable himself to dictate, let his guardian dictate faithfully, and get two witnesses, out of your own men, and if there are not two men, then a man and two women,[23] such as you choose, for witnesses, so that if one of them errs, the other can remind her. The

---

23. This injunction refers to commercial or business transactions, which have traditionally been the realm of men. Women have usually been more involved in caring roles and those centred around the home.

In many societies, adult women have not been accustomed to being in close proximity with male strangers and so in the case of being a witness; this unfamiliar and potentially threatening situation can be very off putting.

Therefore, it is decreed that two women attend as witnesses, to support each other, obviously to protect their reputation, and generally to make them feel more comfortable. The less anxious and shy a witness is at the time, the more likely she is to remember the transaction and its details at a later date, if required. There are also in a woman's life occasions associated in one way or another with child bearing which can have physiological and psychological effects of varying degrees, (eg. monthly, pre-menopausal and post menopausal cycles, antenatal and post natal period etc.., that may give rise to temporary memory loss). During this time one woman might not be in a fit condition to remember what she witnessed some time ago, so the other woman, who is unlikely to be in a similar condition at the same time, can remind her. – Ed.

witnesses should not refuse when they are called on (for evidence).
Disdain not to reduce to writing (your contract) for a future period,
whether it be small or big: it is juster in the sight of Allah, more suitable
as evidence, and more convenient to prevent doubts among yourselves,
but if it be a transaction which you carry out on the spot among
yourselves, there is no blame on you if you reduce it not to writing. But
take witnesses whenever you make a commercial contract; and let neither
scribe nor witness suffer harm. If you do (such harm), it would be
wickedness in you. So fear Allah; for it is Allah that teaches you. And
Allah is well acquainted with all things. 283 If you are on a journey, and
cannot find a scribe, a pledge with possession (may serve the purpose).
And if one of you deposits a thing on trust with another, let the trustee
(faithfully) discharge his trust, and let him fear his Lord. Conceal not
evidence; for whoever conceals it,—his heart is tainted with sin. And
Allah knows all that you do.

SECTION 40

284 To Allah belongs all that is in the heavens and on earth. Whether you
show what is in your minds or conceal it, Allah calls you to account for
it. He forgives whom He pleases, and punishes whom He pleases, for
Allah has power over all things. 285 The Messenger believes in what has
been revealed to him from his Lord, as do the men of faith. Each one (of
them) believes in Allah, His angels, His books, and His messengers. "We
make no distinction (they say) between one and another of His
messengers." And they say: "We hear, and we obey: (we seek) Your
forgiveness, our Lord, and to You is the end of all journeys." 286 On no
soul does Allah place a burden greater than it can bear. It gets every good
that it earns, and it suffers every ill that it earns. (Pray:) "Our Lord!
Condemn us not if we forget or fall into error; Our Lord! Lay not on us
a burden like that which You did lay on those before us; Our Lord! Lay
not on us a burden greater than we have strength to bear. Blot out our
sins, and grant us forgiveness. Have mercy on us. You are our Protector;
help us against those who stand against Faith." □

Chapter 3

Sūrah Āl 'Imrān
(The Family of 'Imrān)

Translator's Introduction

This Sūrah is cognate to Sūrah 2, but the matter is here treated from a different point of view. The references to Badr (Ramaḍān, A.H. 2) and Uḥud (Shawwāl, A.H. 3) give a clue to the dates of those passages.

Like Sūrah 2, it takes a general view of the religious history of mankind, with special reference to the People of the Book, proceeds to explain the birth of the new people of Islam and their ordinances, insists on the need of struggle and fighting in the cause of Truth, and exhorts those who have been blessed with Islam to remain constant in Faith, pray for guidance, and maintain their spiritual hope for the future.

The new points of view developed are: (1) The emphasis is here laid on the duty of the Christians to accept the new light; the Christians are here specially appealed to, as the Jews were specially appealed to in the last Sūrah; (2) the lessons of the battles of Badr and Uḥud are set out for the Muslim community; and (3) the responsibilities of that community are insisted on both internally and in their relations to those outside.

Summary—Allah having revealed His Book, confirming previous revelations, we must accept it in all reverence, try to understand its meaning, and reject the base motives which make truth unacceptable to those who reject Faith (3:1-20).

The People of the Book had only a portion of the Book, and if they reject the complete Book, the People of Faith must part company with them, and their day is done (3:21-30).

The story of the family of 'Imrān (the father of Moses) leads us from the Mosaic Dispensation to the miracles connected with the birth of Jesus and his ministry (3:31-63).

Allah's revelation being continuous, all people are invited to accept its completion in Islam, and controversies are deprecated. The Muslims are asked to hold together in union and harmony, and are promised security from harm from their enemies, and enjoined to seek friendship among their own people (3:64-120).

The battle of Badr showed how Allah helps and upholds the virtuous, and how patience, perseverance, and discipline find their reward; on the other hand, the lessons of Uḥud must be learnt, not in despair, but in the exercise of the higher virtues and in contempt of pain and death (3:121-148).

The misfortunes at Uḥud are shown to be due to the indiscipline of some, the indecision and selfishness of others, and cowardice on the part of the hypocrites, but no enemy can hurt Allah's Cause (3:149-180).

The taunts of the enemy should be disregarded, and sincere prayer offered to Allah Who would grant His servants success and prosperity (3:181-200).

*** *** ***

In the name of Allah,
Most Gracious, Most Merciful.

1 *Alif Lām Mīm.*[1]

2 Allah! There is no god but He,—the Living, the Self-subsisting, Eternal.
3 It is He Who sent down to you (step by step), in truth, the Book,
confirming what went before it; and He sent down the Law (of Moses)
and the Gospel (of Jesus) before this, as a guide to mankind, and He sent
down the criterion (of judgement between right and wrong). 4 Then those
who reject Faith in the Signs of Allah will suffer the severest penalty, and
Allah is Exalted in Might, Lord of Retribution. 5 From Allah, verily
nothing is hidden on earth or in the heavens. 6 He it is Who shapes you
in the wombs as He pleases. There is no god but He, the Exalted in
Might, the Wise.

7 He it is Who has sent down to you the Book; in it are verses basic or fundamental (of established meaning); they are the foundation of the Book: others are allegorical. But those in whose hearts is perversity follow the part thereof that is allegorical, seeking discord, and searching for its hidden meanings, but no one knows its hidden meanings except Allah.[2] And those who are firmly grounded in knowledge say: "We

---

1. See note to 2:1.

2. This passage gives us an important clue to the interpretation of the Holy Qur'an. Broadly speaking it may be divided into two portions, not given separately, but intermingled: *viz.* (1) the nucleus or foundation of the Book, literally "the mother of the Book"; (2) the part which is not of well-established meaning. It is very fascinating to take up the latter, and exercise our ingenuity about its inner meaning, but it refers to such profound spiritual matters that human language is inadequate to it, and though people of wisdom may get some light from it, no one should be dogmatic, as the final meaning is known to Allah alone. The Commentators usually understand the verses "of established meaning" (*muḥkam*) to refer to the categorical orders of the *Sharī'ah* (or the Law), which

believe in the Book; the whole of it is from our Lord:" and none will grasp the Message except men of understanding.
8 "Our Lord!" (they say), "Let not our hearts deviate now after You have guided us, but grant us mercy from Your own Presence; for You are the Grantor of bounties without measure.
9 Our Lord! You are He that will gather mankind together against a day about which there is no doubt; for Allah never fails in His promise."

SECTION 2

10 Those who reject Faith,—neither their possessions nor their (numerous) progeny will avail them aught against Allah: they are themselves but fuel for the Fire.
11 (Their plight will be) no better than that of the people of Pharaoh, and their predecessors: they denied Our Signs, and Allah called them to account for their sins. For Allah is strict in punishment.
12 Say to those who reject Faith: "Soon will you be vanquished and gathered together to Hell,—an evil bed indeed (to lie on)!
13 There has already been for you a Sign in the two armies that met (in combat):[3] One was fighting in the cause of Allah, the other resisting Allah; these saw with their own eyes twice their number. But Allah does support with His aid whom He pleases. In this is a warning for such as have eyes to see."

14 Fair in the eyes of men is the love of things they covet: women and

---

are plain to everyone's understanding. But perhaps the meaning is wider: the "mother of the Book" must include the very foundation on which all law rests, the essence of God's Message, as distinguished from the various illustrative parables, allegories, and ordinances. [347]

3. This refers to the battle of Badr in Ramaḍān in the second year of the Hijrah. The little exiled community of Makkan Muslims, with their friends in Madīnah, had organised themselves into a God-fearing community, but were constantly in danger of being attacked by their Pagan enemies of Makkah, in alliance with some of the disaffected elements (Jews and Hypocrites) in or near Madīnah itself. The design of the Makkans was to gather all the resources they could, and with an overwhelming force, to crush and annihilate Muhammad and his party. To this end Abū Sufyān was leading a richly-laden caravan from Syria to Makkah. He called for armed aid from Makkah. The battle was fought in the plain of Badr, about 50 miles southwest of Madīnah. The Muslim force consisted of only about 313 men, mostly ill-armed, but they were led by Muḥammad, and they were fighting for their Faith. The Makkan army, well-armed and well-equipped, numbered over a thousand and had among its leaders some of the most experienced warriors of Arabia, including Abū Jahl, the inveterate foe and persecutor of Islam. Against all odds the Muslims won a brilliant victory, and many of the enemy leaders, including Abū Jahl, were killed. [352]

sons; heaped-up hoards of gold and silver; horses branded (for blood and
excellence); and (wealth of) cattle and well-tilled land. Such are the
possessions of this world's life; but in nearness to Allah is the best of the
goals (to return to). 15 Say: Shall I give you glad tidings of things far
better than those? For the righteous are Gardens in nearness to their Lord,
with rivers flowing beneath; therein is their eternal home; with
companions pure (and holy); and the good pleasure of Allah. For in
Allah's sight are (all) His servants,—16 (Namely), those who say: "Our
Lord! We have indeed believed: forgive us, then, our sins, and save us
from the agony of the Fire;"—17 Those who show patience, firmness and
self-control; who are true (in word and deed); who worship devoutly;
who spend (in the way of Allah); and who pray for forgiveness in the
early hours of the morning. 18 There is no god but He: that is the witness
of Allah, His angels, and those endued with knowledge, standing firm on
justice. There is no god but He, the Exalted in Power, the Wise. 19 The
Religion before Allah is Islam (submission to His Will): nor did the
People of the Book dissent therefrom except through envy of each other,
after knowledge had come to them. But if any deny the Signs of Allah,
Allah is swift in calling to account. 20 So if they dispute with you, say: "I
have submitted my whole self to Allah and so have those who follow
me." And say to the People of the Book and to those who are unlearned:
"Do you (also) submit yourselves?" If they do, they are in right guidance,
but if they turn back, your duty is to convey the Message; and in Allah's
sight are (all) His servants.

SECTION 3

21 As to those who deny the Signs of Allah and in defiance of right, slay
the prophets, and slay those who teach just dealing with mankind,[4]
announce to them a grievous penalty. 22 They are those whose works will
bear no fruit in this world and in the Hereafter nor will they have anyone
to help. 23 Have you not turned your vision to those who have been given
a portion of the Book? They are invited to the Book of Allah, to settle
their dispute, but a party of them turn back and decline (the arbitration).

---

4. Examples of the Prophets slain were: "the righteous blood shed upon the earth, from the blood of righteous Abel unto the blood of Zacharias, son of Barachias, whom ye slew between the temple and the altar": Matt.xxiii.35. *Cf.* 2.61. Again, John the Baptist (Yaḥyā, noble, chaste, and prophet, of the goodly company of the righteous, 3:39) was bound, imprisoned, and beheaded, and his head presented to a dancing harlot: Matt.xiv.1-11. [364]

24 This because they say: "The Fire shall not touch us but for a few
numbered days": for their forgeries deceive them as to their own religion.
25 But how (will they fare) when we gather them together against a day
about which there is no doubt, and each soul will be paid out just what it
has earned, without (favour or) injustice?

26 Say: "O Allah! Lord of Power (and Rule), You give power to whom
You please, and You strip off power from whom You please: You endue
with honour whom You please, and You bring low whom You please: in
Your hand is all good. Verily, over all things You have power. 27 You
cause the night to gain on the day, and You cause the day to gain on the
night; You bring the Living out of the Dead, and You bring the Dead out
of the Living;[5] and You give sustenance to whom You please, without
measure."[6]

28 Let not the believers take for friends or helpers Unbelievers rather than
believers: if any do that, in nothing will there be help from Allah: except
by way of precaution, that you may guard yourselves from them. But
Allah cautions you (to remember) Himself; for the final goal is to Allah.
29 Say: "Whether you hide what is in your hearts or reveal it, Allah knows
it all: He knows what is in the heavens, and what is on earth. And Allah
has power over all things. 30 On the Day when every soul will be
confronted with all the good it has done, and all the evil it has done, it
will wish there were a great distance between it and its evil. But Allah
cautions you (to remember) Himself. And Allah is full of kindness to
those that serve Him."

SECTION 4

31 Say: "If you do love Allah, follow me: Allah will love you and forgive
you your sins; for Allah is Oft-Forgiving, Most Merciful." 32 Say: "Obey
Allah and His Messenger": but if they turn back, Allah loves not those

---

5. We can interpret Dead and Living in even more senses than Day and Night: death physical, intellectual, emotional, spiritual. Life and Death may also apply to collective, group, or national life. And who has ever solved the mystery of Life? But Faith refers it to Allah's Will and Plan. [371]

6. Again true in all the senses suggested in the two previous notes. The only Eternal Reality is Allah. All else has its basis and sustenance in Him. Lest our little minds create fear out of "nicely calculated less or more", we are told at once that Allah's bounty is without measure or account. [372]

who reject Faith. 33 Allah did choose Adam and Noah, the family of
Abraham, and the family of 'Imrān above all people,—34 Offspring, one
of the other; and Allah hears and knows all things.

35 Behold! A woman of 'Imrān said: "O my Lord! I do dedicate unto You
what is in my womb for Your special service: so accept this of me: for
You hear and know all things." 36 When she was delivered, she said: "O
my Lord! Behold! I am delivered of a female child!"—and Allah knew
best what she brought forth—"and no wise is the male like the female. I
have named her Mary, and I commend her and her offspring to Your
protection from the Evil One, the Rejected." 37 Right graciously did her
Lord accept her: He made her grow in purity and beauty; to the care of
Zakarīyā was she assigned. Every time that he entered (her) chamber to
see her, he found her supplied with sustenance. He said: "O Mary!
Whence (comes) this to you?" She said: "From Allah: for Allah provides
sustenance to whom He pleases without measure."

38 There did Zakarīyā pray to his Lord, saying: "O my Lord! Grant unto
me from You a progeny that is pure: for You are He that hears prayer!"
39 While he was standing in prayer in the chamber, the angels called unto
him: "Allah does give you glad tidings of Yaḥyā, witnessing the truth of
a Word from Allah,[7] and (be besides) noble, chaste, and a prophet,—of
the (goodly) company of the righteous." 40 He said: "O my Lord! How
shall I have a son, seeing I am very old, and my wife is barren?" "Thus,"
was the answer, "does Allah accomplish what He wills." 41 He said: "O
my Lord! Give me a Sign!" "Thy Sign," was the answer, "shall be that
you shall speak to no man for three days but with signals. Then celebrate
the praises of your Lord again and again, and glorify Him in the evening
and in the morning."

SECTION 5

42 Behold! The angels said: "O Mary! Allah has chosen you and purified
you—chosen you above the women of all nations. 43 O Mary! Worship
your Lord devoutly: prostrate thyself, and bow down (in prayer) with
those who bow down." 44 This is part of the tidings of the things unseen,

---

7. Notice: "a Word from Allah", not "*the* Word of God", the epithet that mystical Christianity uses for Jesus. As stated in 3:59 below, Jesus was created by a miracle, by Allah's word "Be", and he was. [381]

which We reveal unto you (O Messenger!) by inspiration: you were not
with them when they cast lots with arrows, as to which of them should be
charged with the care of Mary: nor were you with them when they
disputed (the point). 45 Behold! The angels said: "O Mary! Allah gives
you glad tidings of a Word from Him: his name will be Christ Jesus, the
son of Mary, held in honour in this world and the Hereafter and of (the
company of) those nearest to Allah; 46 "He shall speak to the people in
childhood and in maturity. And he shall be (of the company) of the
righteous." 47 She said: "O my Lord! How shall I have a son when no
man has touched me?" He said: "Even so: Allah creates what He wills:
when He has decreed a plan, He but says to it, 'Be,' and it is! 48 And
Allah will teach him the Book and Wisdom, the Law and the Gospel, 49
And (appoint him) a messenger to the Children of Israel, (with this
message): 'I have come to you, with a Sign from your Lord, in that I
make for you out of clay, as it were, the figure of a bird, and breathe into
it, and it becomes a bird by Allah's leave: and I heal those born blind, and
the lepers, and I quicken the dead, by Allah's leave; and I declare to you
what you eat, and what you store in your houses. Surely therein is a Sign
for you if you did believe; 50 (I have come to you), to attest the Law
which was before me. And to make lawful to you part of what was
(before) forbidden to you; I have come to you with a Sign from your
Lord. So fear Allah, and obey me. 51 It is Allah Who is my Lord and your
Lord; then worship Him. This is a Way that is straight.'

52 When Jesus found Unbelief on their part, he said: "Who will be my
helpers to (the work of) Allah?" Said the disciples: "We are Allah's
helpers: we believe in Allah, and do you bear witness that we are
Muslims. 53 Our Lord! We believe in what You have revealed, and we
follow the Messenger; then write us down among those who bear
witness." 54 And (the unbelievers) plotted and planned, and Allah too
planned, and the best of planners is Allah.

SECTION 6

55 Behold! Allah said: "O Jesus! I will take you and raise you to Myself
and clear you (of the falsehoods) of those who blaspheme; I will make
those who follow you superior to those who reject faith, to the Day of
Resurrection: then shall you all return unto Me, and I will judge between
you of the matters wherein you dispute. 56 As to those who reject faith, I

will punish them with terrible agony in this world and in the Hereafter,
nor will they have anyone to help. 57 As to those who believe and work
righteousness, Allah will pay them (in full) their reward; but Allah loves
not those who do wrong." 58 This is what We rehearse unto you of the
Signs and the Message of Wisdom. 59 The similitude of Jesus before
Allah is as that of Adam; He created him from dust, then said to him:
"Be": and he was. 60 The Truth (comes) from Allah alone; so be not of
those who doubt. 61 If any one disputes in this matter with you, now after
(full) knowledge has come to you, say: "Come! Let us gather
together,—our sons and your sons, our women and your women,
ourselves and yourselves: then let us earnestly pray, and invoke the curse
of Allah on those who lie!" 62 This is the true account; there is no god
except Allah; and Allah—He is indeed the Exalted in Power, the Wise.
63 But if they turn back, Allah has full knowledge of those who do
mischief.

SECTION 7

64 Say: "O People of the Book! Come to common terms as between us
and you: that we worship none but Allah; that we associate no partners
with Him; that we erect not, from among ourselves, lords and patrons
other than Allah." If then they turn back, say you: "Bear witness that we
(at least) are Muslims (bowing to Allah's Will)." 65 You People of the
Book! Why dispute you about Abraham, when the Law and the Gospel
were not revealed till after him? Have you no understanding? 66 Ah! You
are those who fell to disputing (even) in matters of which you had some
knowledge! But why dispute you in matters of which you have no
knowledge? It is Allah Who knows, and you who know not! 67 Abraham
was not a Jew nor yet a Christian; but he was true in Faith, and bowed his
will to Allah's (which is Islam), and he joined not gods with Allah. 68
Without doubt, among men, the nearest of kin to Abraham, are those who
follow him, as are also this Messenger and those who believe: and Allah
is the Protector of those who have faith. 69 It is the wish of a section of the
People of the Book to lead you astray. But they shall lead astray (not
you), but themselves, and they do not perceive! 70 You People of the
Book! Why reject you the Signs of Allah, of which you are (yourselves)
witnesses? 71 You People of the Book! Why do you clothe Truth with
falsehood, and conceal the Truth, while you have knowledge?

SECTION 8

72 A section of the People of the Book say: "Believe in the morning what
is revealed to the believers, but reject it at the end of the day;[8] perchance
they may (themselves) turn back; 73 And believe no one unless he follows
your religion." Say: "True guidance is the Guidance of Allah: (fear you)
lest a revelation be sent to someone (else) like unto that which was sent
unto you? Or that those (receiving such revelation) should engage you in
argument before your Lord?" Say: "All bounties are in the hand of Allah:
He grants them to whom He pleases: and Allah cares for all, and He
knows all things." 74 For His Mercy He specially chooses whom He
pleases; for Allah is the Lord of bounties unbounded. 75 Among the
People of the Book are some who, if entrusted with a hoard of gold, will
(readily) pay it back; others, who, if entrusted with a single silver coin,
will not repay it unless you constantly stood demanding, because, they
say, "there is no call on us (to keep faith) with these ignorant (Pagans)."
But they tell a lie against Allah, and (well) they know it. 76 Nay—Those
that keep their plighted faith and act aright,—verily Allah loves those
who act aright. 77 As for those who sell the faith they owe to Allah and
their own plighted word for a small price, they shall have no portion in
the Hereafter: nor will Allah (deign to) speak to them or look at them on
the Day of Judgement, nor will He cleanse them (of sin): they shall have
a grievous penalty. 78 There is among them a section who distort the Book
with their tongues: (as they read) you would think it is a part of the Book,
but it is no part of the Book; and they say, "That is from Allah," but it is
not from Allah: it is they who tell a lie against Allah, and (well) they
know it! 79 It is not (possible) that a man, to whom is given the Book, and
Wisdom, and the prophetic office, should say to people: "Be you my
worshippers rather than Allah's": on the contrary (he would say): "Be you
worshippers of Him Who is truly the Cherisher of all: for you have taught
the Book and you have studied it earnestly." 80 Nor would he instruct you
to take angels and prophets for lords and patrons. What! Would he bid
you to unbelief after you have bowed your will (to Allah in Islam)?

SECTION 9

81 Behold! Allah took the covenant of the prophets, saying: "I give you

---

8. The cynics who plotted against Islam actually asked their accomplices to join the believers and then repudiate them. [406]

a Book and Wisdom; then comes to you a messenger, confirming what
is with you; do you believe in him and render him help." Allah said: "Do
you agree, and take this My Covenant as binding on you?" They said:
"We agree." He said: "Then bear witness, and I am with you among the
witnesses." 82 If any turn back after this, they are perverted transgressors.
83 Do they seek for other than the Religion of Allah?—while all creatures
in the heavens and on earth have, willing or unwilling, bowed to His Will
(accepted Islam), and to Him shall they all be brought back. 84 Say: "We
believe in Allah, and in what has been revealed to us and what was
revealed to Abraham, Ismā'īl, Isaac, Jacob, and the Tribes, and in (the
Books) given to Moses, Jesus, and the prophets, from their Lord: we
make no distinction between one and another among them, and to Allah
do we bow our will (in Islam)."

85 If anyone desires a religion other than Islam (submission to Allah),[9]
never will it be accepted of him; and in the Hereafter he will be in the
ranks of those who have lost (all spiritual good). 86 How shall Allah guide
those who reject Faith after they accepted it and bore witness that the
Messenger was true and that Clear Signs had come unto them? But Allah
guides not a people unjust. 87 Of such the reward is that on them (rests)
the curse of Allah, of His angels, and of all mankind;—88 In that will they
dwell; nor will their penalty be lightened, nor respite be (their lot);—89
Except for those that repent (even) after that, and make amends; for verily
Allah is Oft-Forgiving, Most Merciful. 90 But those who reject Faith after
they accepted it, and then go on adding to their defiance of Faith,—never
will their repentance be accepted; for they are those who have (of set
purpose) gone astray. 91 As to those who reject Faith, and die
rejecting,—never would be accepted from any such as much gold as the
earth contains, though they should offer it for ransom. For such is (in
store) a penalty grievous, and they will find no helpers.

---

9. The Muslim position is clear. The Muslim does not claim to have a religion peculiar to himself. Islam is not a sect or an ethnic religion. In its view all Religion is one, for the Truth is one. It was the religion preached by all the earlier prophets. It was the truth taught by all the inspired Books. In essence it amounts to a consciousness of the Will and Plan of Allah and a joyful submission to that Will and Plan. If any one wants a religion other than that, he is false to his own nature, as he is false to Allah's Will and Plan. Such a one cannot expect guidance, for he has deliberately renounced guidance. [418]

SECTION 10

92 By no means shall you attain righteousness unless you give (freely) of
that which you love; and whatever you give, of a truth Allah knows it
well.

PART IV

93 All food was lawful to the Children of Israel, except what Israel made
unlawful for itself, before the Law (of Moses) was revealed. Say: "Bring
you the Law and study it, if you be men of truth." 94 If any, after this,
invent a lie and attribute it to Allah, they are indeed unjust wrong-doers.
95 Say: "Allah speaks the Truth: follow the religion of Abraham, the sane
in faith; he was not of the Pagans."

96 The first House (of worship) appointed for men was that at Bakka:[10]
full of blessing and of guidance for all kinds of beings: 97 In it are Signs
Manifest; (for example), the Station of Abraham; whoever enters it attains
security; pilgrimage thereto is a duty men owe to Allah,—those who can
afford the journey; but if any deny faith, Allah stands not in need of any
of His creatures.

98 Say: "O People of the Book! Why reject you the Signs of Allah, when
Allah is Himself witness to all you do?" 99 Say: "O you People of the
Book! Why obstruct you those who believe, from the path of Allah,
seeking to make it crooked, while you were yourselves witnesses (to
Allah's Covenant)? But Allah is not unmindful of all that you do." 100 O
you who believe! If you listen to a faction among the People of the Book,
they would (indeed) render you apostates after you have believed! 101 And
how would you deny Faith while unto you are rehearsed the Signs of
Allah, and among you lives the Messenger? Whoever holds firmly to
Allah will be shown a way that is straight.

SECTION 11

102 O you who believe! Fear Allah as He should be feared, and die not
except in a state of Islam. 103 And hold fast, all together, by the rope which
Allah (stretches out for you), and be not divided among yourselves; and

---

10. Same as Makkah; perhaps an older name. The foundation of the Ka'bah goes back to Abraham, but there are place associations in the sacred territory with the names of Adam and Eve. [422]

remember with gratitude Allah's favour on you; for you were enemies and
He joined your hearts in love, so that by His Grace, you became brethren;
and you were on the brink of the pit of Fire, and He saved you from it.
Thus does Allah make His Signs clear to you: that you may be guided. 104
Let there arise out of you a band of people inviting to all that is good,
enjoining what is right, and forbidding what is wrong: they are the ones to
attain felicity. 105 Be not like those who are divided amongst themselves
and fall into disputations after receiving Clear Signs: for them is a dreadful
penalty,—106 On the Day when some faces will be (lit up with) white, and
some faces will be (in the gloom of) black: to those whose faces will be
black, (will be said): "Did you reject Faith after accepting it? Taste then the
penalty for rejecting Faith." 107 But those whose faces will be (lit with)
white,—they will be in (the light of) Allah's Mercy: therein to dwell (for
ever).

108 These are the Signs of Allah: We rehearse them to you in Truth: and
Allah means no injustice to any of His creatures. 109 To Allah belongs all
that is in the heavens and on earth; to Him do all questions go back (for
decision).

SECTION 12

110 You are the best of peoples, evolved for mankind, enjoining what is
right, forbidding what is wrong, and believing in Allah. If only the People
of the Book had faith, it were best for them: among them are some who
have faith, but most of them are perverted transgressors. 111 They will do
you no harm, barring a trifling annoyance; if they come out to fight you,
they will show you their backs, and no help shall they get. 112 Shame is
pitched over them (like a tent) wherever they are found, except when
under a covenant (of protection) from Allah and from men; they draw on
themselves wrath from Allah, and pitched over them is (the tent of)
destitution. This because they rejected the Signs of Allah, and slew the
prophets in defiance of right;[11] this because they rebelled and
transgressed beyond bounds. 113 Not all of them are alike: of the People
of the Book are a portion that stand (for the right): they rehearse the Signs
of Allah all night long, and they prostrate themselves[12] in adoration. 114

11. *Cf.* 3:21 and n. 49. [56]

12. In Islam we respect sincere faith and true righteousness in whatever form they appear. [437]

They believe in Allah and the Last Day; they enjoin what is right, and
forbid what is wrong; and they hasten (in emulation) in (all) good works:
they are in the ranks of the righteous. 115 Of the good that they do, nothing
will be rejected of them; for Allah knows well those that do right. 116
Those who reject Faith,—neither their possessions nor their (numerous)
progeny will avail them aught against Allah: they will be companions of
the Fire,—dwelling therein (for ever). 117 What they spend in the life of
this (material) world may be likened to a wind which brings a nipping
frost: it strikes and destroys the harvest of men who have wronged their
own souls: it is not Allah that has wronged them, but they wrong
themselves.

118 O you who believe! Take not into your intimacy those outside your
ranks: they will not fail to corrupt you. They only desire your ruin: rank
hatred has already appeared from their mouths: what their hearts conceal
is far worse. We have made plain to you the Signs, if you have wisdom.
119 Ah! You are those who love them, but they love you not,—though you
believe in the whole of the Book. When they meet you, they say, "We
believe": but when they are alone, they bite off the very tips of their
fingers at you in their rage. Say: "Perish in your rage; Allah knows well
all the secrets of the heart." 120 If aught that is good befalls you, it grieves
them; but if some misfortune overtakes you, they rejoice at it. But if you
are constant and do right, not the least harm will their cunning do to you;
for Allah compasses round about all that they do.

SECTION 13

121 Remember that morning you did leave your household (early) to post
the faithful at their stations for battle:[13] and Allah hears and knows all

---

13. The reference is to the Battle of Uḥud which was a great testing time for the young Muslim community. The Makkans were determined to wipe off their disgrace and to this end they collected a large force of some 3,000 men and marched to Madīnah. The Muslim leader, the Prophet himself, took his position at the foot of the Mount Uḥud and the Muslim warriors numbering 700 to 1,000 were up early. The passes in the hills at their back were filled with 50 archers to prevent an enemy attack from the rear. In the beginning the battle went well for the Muslims. The enemy wavered, and the Muslim archers, in disobedience of their orders, left their posts to join in the pursuit and share of the booty. The enemy took advantage of the opening left by the archers, and there was severe hand to hand fighting, in which numbers told in favour of the enemy. Many of the Companions were martyred, including the Prophet's uncle, the gallant Ḥamzah. The Messenger himself

things: 122 Remember two of your parties[14] meditated cowardice; but
Allah was their protector, and in Allah should the faithful (ever) put their
trust. 123 Allah had helped you at Badr, when you were a contemptible
little force; then fear Allah; thus may you show your gratitude. 124
Remember you said to the Faithful: "Is it not enough for you that Allah
should help you with three thousand angels (specially) sent down? 125
Yea,—if you remain firm, and act aright, even if the enemy should rush
here on you in hot haste, your Lord would help you with five thousand
angels making a terrific onslaught." 126 Allah made it but a message of
hope for you, and an assurance to your hearts: (in any case) there is no
help except from Allah, the Exalted, the Wise: 127 That He might cut off
a fringe of the Unbelievers or expose them to infamy, and they should
then be turned back, frustrated of their purpose. 128 Not for you, (but for
Allah), is the decision: whether He turn in mercy to them, or punish them;
for they are indeed wrong-doers. 129 To Allah belongs all that is in the
heavens and on earth. He forgives whom He pleases and punishes whom
He pleases; but Allah is Oft-Forgiving, Most Merciful.

SECTION 14

130 O you who believe! Devour not usury, doubled and multiplied; but
fear Allah; that you may (really) prosper. 131 Fear the Fire, which is
prepared for those who reject Faith: 132 And obey Allah and the
Messenger; that you may obtain mercy. 133 Be quick in the race for
forgiveness from your Lord, and for a Garden whose width is that (of the
whole) of the heavens and of the earth, prepared for the righteous,—134
Those who spend (freely), whether in prosperity, or in adversity; who
restrain anger, and pardon (all) men;—for Allah loves those who do
good;—135 And those who, having done something to be ashamed of, or
wronged their own souls, earnestly bring Allah to mind, and ask for
forgiveness for their sins,—and who can forgive sins except Allah?—and

---

was wounded in his head and face, and one of his front teeth was broken. Had it not been for his firmness, courage, and coolness, all would have been lost. As it was, the Prophet, inspite of his wound, and many of the wounded Muslims, inspired by his example, returned to the field the next day, and Abū Sufyān and his Makkah army withdrew. Madīnah was saved, but a lesson in faith, constancy, firmness, and steadfastness was learnt by the Muslims. [442]

14. The two parties wavering in their minds were probably the Banū Salamah Khazraj and the Banū Ḥarithah, but they rallied under the Prophet's inspiration. [443]

are never obstinate in persisting knowingly in (the wrong) they have
done. 136 For such the reward is forgiveness from their Lord, and Gardens
with rivers flowing underneath,—an eternal dwelling: how excellent a
recompense for those who work (and strive)!

137 Many were the Ways of Life that have passed away before you: travel
through the earth, and see what was the end of those who rejected Truth.
138 Here is a plain statement to men, a guidance and instruction to those
who fear Allah! 139 So lose not heart, nor fall into despair: for you must
gain mastery if you are true in Faith. 140 If a wound has touched you, be
sure a similar wound has touched the others. Such days (of varying
fortunes) We give to men and men by turns: that Allah may know those
that believe, and that He may take to Himself from your ranks
martyr-witnesses (to Truth). And Allah loves not those that do wrong. 141
Allah's object also is to purge those that are true in Faith and to deprive
of blessing those that resist Faith. 142 Did you think that you would enter
Heaven without Allah testing those of you who fought hard (in His
Cause) and remained steadfast? 143 You did indeed wish for death before
you met him: now you have seen him with your own eyes, (and you
flinch!)

SECTION 15

144 Muḥammad is no more than a messenger: many were the messengers
that passed away before him. If he died or were slain, will you then turn
back on your heels? If any did turn back on his heels, not the least harm
will he do to Allah; but Allah (on the other hand) will swiftly reward
those who (serve Him) with gratitude.[15] 145 Nor can a soul die except by
Allah's leave, the term being fixed as by writing. If any do desire a

---

15. This verse primarily applies to the Battle of Uḥud, in the course of which a cry was raised that the Messenger was slain. He had indeed been severely wounded, but Ṭalḥah, Abū Bakr, and 'Alī were at his side, and his own unexampled bravery saved the Muslim army from a rout. This verse was recalled again by Abū Bakr when the Messenger actually died a natural death eight years later, to remind people that Allah, Whose message he brought, lives for ever. And we have need to remember this now and often for two reasons: (1) when we feel inclined to pay more than human honour to one who was the truest, the purest, and the greatest of men, and thus in a sense to compound for our forgetting the spirit of his teaching, and (2) when we feel depressed at the chances and changes of time, and forget that the eternal Allah lives and watches over us and over all His creatures now as in all history in the past and in the future. [460]

reward in this life, We shall give it to him; and if any do desire a reward
in the Hereafter, We shall give it to him. And swiftly shall We reward
those that (serve Us with) gratitude. 146 How many of the prophets fought
(in Allah's way), and with them (fought) large bands of godly men? but
they never lost heart if they met with disaster in Allah's way, nor did they
weaken (in will) nor give in. And Allah loves those who are firm and
steadfast. 147 All that they said was: "Our Lord! Forgive us our sins and
anything we may have done that transgressed our duty: establish our feet
firmly, and help us against those that resist Faith." 148 And Allah gave
them a reward in this world, and the excellent reward of the Hereafter.
For Allah loves those who do good.

SECTION 16

149 O you who believe! If you obey the Unbelievers, they will drive you
back on your heels, and you will turn back (from Faith) to your own loss.
150 Nay, Allah is your protector, and He is the best of helpers. 151 Soon
shall We cast terror into the hearts of the Unbelievers, for that they joined
companions with Allah, for which He had sent no authority: their abode
will be the Fire: and evil is the home of the wrong-doers! 152 Allah did
indeed fulfil His promise to you when you with His permission were
about to annihilate your enemy,—until you flinched and fell to disputing
about the order,[16] and disobeyed it after He brought you in sight (of the
booty) which you covet. Among you are some that hanker after this world
and some that desire the Hereafter. Then did He divert you from your
foes in order to test you but He forgave you: for Allah is full of grace to
those who believe. 153 Behold! You were climbing up the high ground,
without even casting a side glance at any one, and the Messenger in your
rear was calling you back. There did Allah give you one distress after
another by way of requital, to teach you not to grieve for (the booty) that
had escaped you and for (the ill) that had befallen you. For Allah is well
aware of all that you do. 154 After (the excitement) of the distress, He sent
down calm on a band of you overcome with slumber, while another band
was stirred to anxiety by their own feelings, moved by wrong suspicions

---

16. The order was not to run after booty, but strictly to maintain discipline. Uḥud was in the beginning a victory for the Muslims. Many of the enemy were slain and they were retiring when a section of the Muslims against the orders of the Prophet, ran in pursuit, attracted by the prospect of booty. See note to 3:121. [462]

of Allah—suspicions due to ignorance. They said: "What affair is this of
ours?" Say you: "Indeed, this affair is wholly Allah's." They hide in their
minds what they dare not reveal to you. They say (to themselves): "If we
had had anything to do with this affair, we should not have been in the
slaughter here." Say: "Even if you had remained in your homes, those for
whom death was decreed would certainly have gone forth to the place of
their death"; but (all this was) that Allah might test what is in your breasts
and purge what is in your hearts. For Allah knows well the secrets of your
hearts. 155 Those of you who turned back on the day the two hosts
met,—it was Satan who caused them to fail, because of some (evil) they
had done. But Allah has blotted out (their fault): for Allah is Oft-
Forgiving, Most Forbearing.

SECTION 17

156 O you who believe! Be not like the Unbelievers, who say of their
brethren, when they are travelling through the Earth or engaged in
fighting: "If they had stayed with us, they would not have died, or been
slain." This that Allah may make it a cause of sighs and regrets in their
hearts. It is Allah that gives Life and Death, and Allah sees well all that
you do. 157 And if you are slain, or die, in the way of Allah, forgiveness
and mercy from Allah are far better than all they could amass. 158 And if
you die, or are slain, Lo! It is unto Allah that you are brought together.

159 It is part of the Mercy of Allah that you deal gently with them. Were
you severe or harsh-hearted, they would have broken away from about
you: so pass over (their faults), and ask for (Allah's) forgiveness for
them; and consult them in affairs (of moment). Then, when you have
taken a decision put your trust in Allah. For Allah loves those who put
their trust (in Him). 160 If Allah helps you, none can overcome you: if He
forsakes you, who is there, after that, that can help you? In Allah, then,
let believers put their trust.

161 No prophet could (ever) be false to his trust. If any person is so false,
he shall, on the Day of Judgement, restore what he misappropriated; then
shall every soul receive its due,—whatever it earned,—and none shall be
dealt with unjustly. 162 Is the man who follows the good pleasure of Allah
like the man who draws on himself the wrath of Allah, and whose abode
is in Hell?—A woeful refuge! 163 They are in varying grades in the sight
of Allah, and Allah sees well all that they do. 164 Allah did confer a great

favour on the believers when He sent among them a messenger from
among themselves, rehearsing unto them the Signs of Allah, sanctifying
them, and instructing them in Scripture and Wisdom, while, before that,
they had been in manifest error.

165 What! When a single disaster smites you, although you smote (your
enemies) with one twice as great, do you say?— "Whence is this?" Say
(to them): "It is from yourselves: for Allah has power over all things." 166
What you suffered on the day the two armies met, was with the leave of
Allah, in order that He might test the believers,—167 And the Hypocrites
also. These were told: "Come, fight in the way of Allah, or (at least) drive
(the foe from your city)." They said: "Had we known how to fight, we
should certainly have followed you." They were that day nearer to
Unbelief than to Faith, saying with their lips what was not in their hearts.
But Allah has full knowledge of all they conceal. 168 (They are) the ones
that say, (of their brethren slain), while they themselves sit (at ease): "If
only they had listened to us they would not have been slain." Say: "Avert
death from your own selves, if you speak the truth."

169 Think not of those who are slain in Allah's way as dead. Nay, they
live, finding their sustenance in the presence of their Lord; 170 They
rejoice in the bounty provided by Allah: and with regard to those left
behind, who have not yet joined them (in their bliss), the (Martyrs) glory
in the fact that on them is no fear, nor have they (cause to) grieve. 171
They glory in the Grace and the bounty from Allah, and in the fact that
Allah suffers not the reward of the Faithful to be lost (in the least).

SECTION 18

172 Of those who answered the call of Allah and the Messenger, even after
being wounded, those who do right and refrain from wrong have a great
reward;—173 Men said to them: "A great army is gathering against you,
and so fear them": but it (only) increased their Faith; they said: "For us
Allah suffices, and He is the best disposer of affairs." 174 And they
returned with Grace and Bounty from Allah; no harm ever touched them:
for they followed the good pleasure of Allah: and Allah is the Lord of
bounties unbounded.

175 It is only the Evil One that suggests to you the fear of his votaries: be
you not afraid of them, but fear Me, if you have Faith. 176 Let not those

grieve you who rush headlong into Unbelief: not the least harm will they
do to Allah: Allah's plan is that He will give them no portion in the
Hereafter, but a severe punishment. 177 Those who purchase Unbelief at
the price of faith,—not the least harm will they do to Allah, but they will
have a grievous punishment. 178 Let not the Unbelievers think that Our
respite to them is good for themselves: We grant them respite that they
may grow in their iniquity: but they will have a shameful punishment.

179 Allah will not leave the believers in the state in which you are now,
until He separates what is evil from what is good. Nor will He disclose to
you the secrets of the Unseen. But He chooses of His Messengers (for the
purpose) whom He pleases. So believe in Allah and His messengers; and
if you believe and do right, you have a reward without measure. 180 And
let not those who covetously withhold of the gifts which Allah has given
them of His Grace, think that it is good for them: nay, it will be the worse
for them: soon shall the things which they covetously withheld be tied to
their necks like a twisted collar, on the Day of Judgement. To Allah
belongs the heritage of the heavens and the earth; and Allah is
well-acquainted with all that you do.

SECTION 19

181 Allah has heard the taunt of those who say: "Truly, Allah is indigent
and we are rich!"—We shall certainly record their word and (their act) of
slaying the prophets in defiance of right, and We shall say: "Taste you the
penalty of the Scorching Fire! 182 This is because of the (unrighteous
deeds) which your hands sent on before you: for Allah never harms those
who serve Him." 183 They (also) said: "Allah took our promise not to
believe in a messenger unless he showed us a sacrifice consumed by fire
(from heaven)." Say: "There came to you messengers before me, with
Clear Signs and even with what you ask for: why then did you slay them,
if you speak the truth?" 184 Then if they reject you, so were rejected
messengers before you, who came with Clear Signs, Books of dark
prophecies, and the Book of Enlightenment.

185 Every soul shall have a taste of death: and only on the Day of
Judgement shall you be paid your full recompense. Only he who is saved
far from the Fire and admitted to the Garden will have attained the object
(of Life): for the life of this world is but goods and chattels of deception.
186 You shall certainly be tried and tested in your possessions and in your

personal selves; and you shall certainly hear much that will grieve you,
from those who received the Book before you and from those who
worship many gods. But if you persevere patiently, and guard against
evil,—then that will be a determining factor in all affairs. 187 And
remember Allah took a covenant from the People of the Book, to make
it known and clear to mankind, and not to hide it; but they threw it away
behind their backs, and purchased with it some miserable gain! And vile
was the bargain they made! 188 Think not that those who exult in what
they have brought about, and love to be praised for what they have not
done,—think not that they escape the penalty. For them is a penalty
grievous indeed. 189 To Allah belongs the dominion of the heavens and
the earth; and Allah has power over all things.

SECTION 20

190 Behold! In the creation of the heavens and the earth, and the
alternation of night and day,—there are indeed Signs for men of
understanding,—191 Men who celebrate the praises of Allah, standing,
sitting, and lying down on their sides, and contemplate the (wonders of)
creation in the heavens and the earth, (with the thought): "Our Lord! Not
for naught have You created (all) this! Glory to You! Give us salvation
from the penalty of the Fire. 192 Our Lord! Any whom You do admit to
the Fire, truly You cover with shame, and never will wrong-doers find
any helpers! 193 Our Lord! We have heard the call of one calling (us) to
Faith, 'Believe you in the Lord,' and we have believed, Our Lord!
Forgive us our sins, blot out from us our iniquities, and take to Thyself
our souls in the company of the righteous. 194 Our Lord! Grant us what
You did promise unto us through Your messengers, and save us from
shame on the Day of Judgement: for You never break Your promise." 195
And their Lord has accepted of them, and answered them: "Never will I
suffer to be lost the work of any of you, be he male or female: you are
members, one of another: those who have left their homes, or been driven
out therefrom, or suffered harm in My Cause, or fought or been
slain,—verily, I will blot out from them their iniquities, and admit them
into Gardens with rivers flowing beneath;—a reward from the presence
of Allah, and from His presence is the best of rewards."

196 Let not the strutting about of the Unbelievers through the land deceive
you: 197 Little is it for enjoyment: their ultimate abode is Hell: what an evil

bed (to lie on)! 198 On the other hand, for those who fear their Lord, are Gardens, with rivers flowing beneath; therein are they to dwell (for ever),—a gift from the presence of Allah; and that which is in the presence of Allah is the best (bliss) for the righteous. 199 And there are, certainly, among the People of the Book, those who believe in Allah, in the revelation to you, and in the revelation to them, bowing in humility to Allah: they will not sell the Signs of Allah for a miserable gain! For them is a reward with their Lord, and Allah is swift in account. 200 O you who believe! Persevere in patience and constancy; vie in such perseverance; strengthen each other; and fear Allah; that you may prosper.□

Chapter 4

Sūrah Al-Nisā'
(The Women)

Translator's Introduction

This Sūrah is closely connected chronologically with Sūrah 3. Its subject matter deals with the social problems which the Muslim community had to face immediately after Uḥud. While the particular occasion made the necessity urgent, the principles laid down have permanently governed Muslim Law and social practice.

Broadly speaking, the Sūrah consists of two parts: (1) that dealing with women, orphans, inheritance, marriage, and family rights generally, and (2) that dealing with the recalcitrants in the larger family, the community at Madīnah, *viz.*, the Hypocrites and their accomplices.

It should be kept in mind that these verses were revealed while the fledgling Muslim state of Madīnah, which included Muslims and non-Muslims, was under constant threat from secret treachery as well as open attack. Firm resolve for successful defence was needed. As ruler, the Prophet Muḥammad was responsible for defence.

Summary—It begins with an appeal to the solidarity of mankind, the rights of women and orphans, and the implications of family relationship, including an equitable distribution of property after death (4:1-14.)

While the decencies of family life should be enforced, women should be held in honour and their rights recognised, in marriage, property, and inheritance; and this principle of goodness should be extended to all beings, great and small (4:15-42).

The groups in Madīnah who had not yet become Muslims, but whose leaders had signed a covenant agreeing that the Prophet Muḥammad was their ruler, are advised not to go after false gods but to accept his rule under One God. They would then become part of a glorious fellowship. (The major external enemy, the Quraysh of Makkah, were the foremost polytheists of Arabia) (4:43-70).

The Believers should organise in self-defence against their enemies, and beware of the secret plots and mischiefs of the Hypocrites; how deserters should be treated (4:71-91).

Caution about the taking of life; recommendations for leaving places inimical to Islam; religious duties in the midst of war (4:92-104).

Treachery and the lure of evil (4:105-126).

Women and orphans be justly dealt with; Faith must go with justice, sincerity, and moderation in speech (4:127-152).

Where People of the Book went wrong, with honourable exceptions (4:153-176).

*** *** ***

In the name of Allah,
Most Gracious, Most Merciful.

1 O mankind! Reverence your Guardian-Lord, Who created you from a single person, created, of like nature, his mate, and from them twain scattered (like seeds) countless men and women;—reverence Allah, through Whom you demand your mutual (rights), and (reverence) the wombs (that bore you): for Allah ever watches over you.

2 To orphans restore their property (when they reach their age), nor substitute (your) worthless things for (their) good ones; and devour not their substance (by mixing it up) with your own. For this is indeed a great sin.

3 If you fear that you shall not be able to deal justly with the orphans,
marry women of your choice, two or three or four;[1] but if you fear that
you shall not be able to deal justly (with them), then only one, or (a
captive) that your right hands possess. That will be more suitable, to
prevent you from doing injustice. 4 And give the women (on marriage)
their dower as a free gift; but if they, of their own good pleasure, remit
any part of it to you, take it and enjoy it with right good cheer.

5 To those weak of understanding make not over your property, which Allah has made a means of support for you, but feed and clothe them therewith, and speak to them words of kindness and justice.

---

1. Before the advent of Islam, there was no limit to the number of women a man could marry. According to the Bible, Prophet Solomon had 700 wives and 300 concubines (1 Kings 11:3). Islam restricted the number of wives to four. However, it is normal to have one. "...but if you fear that you shall not be able to deal justly (with them), then only one..." (4:3)
In the times of war (for example the first and second world wars) when there are surplus women and orphans, sacrifices have to be made by men to undertake responsibility for more than one family, depending on their ability, capacity and resources. The wife also makes sacrifices by permitting her husband to fulfil additional responsibilities. There are other exceptional circumstances eg., if the first wife is infertile or chronically ill etc. that may be regarded as a valid reason for a man to take another wife, rather than abandoning the first wife, or "taking a mistress". – Ed.

6 Make trial of orphans until they reach the age of marriage; if then you
find sound judgement in them, release their property to them; but
consume it not wastefully, nor in haste against their growing up. If the
guardian is well-off, let him claim no remuneration, but if he is poor, let
him have for himself what is just and reasonable. When you release their
property to them, take witnesses in their presence: but all-sufficient is
Allah in taking account.

7 From what is left by parents and those nearest related there is a share for
men and a share for women, whether the property be small or large,—a
determinate share. 8 But if at the time of division other relatives, or
orphans or poor, are present, feed them out of the (property), and speak
to them words of kindness and justice. 9 Let those (disposing of an estate)
have the same fear in their minds as they would have for their own if they
had left a helpless family behind: let them fear Allah, and speak words of
appropriate (comfort). 10 Those who unjustly eat up the property of
orphans, eat up a Fire into their own bodies: they will soon be enduring
a Blazing Fire!

SECTION 2

11 Allah (thus) directs you as regards your children's[2] (inheritance): to
the male, a portion equal to that of two females: if only daughters, two or
more, their share is two-thirds of the inheritance; if only one, her share is
a half. For parents, a sixth share of the inheritance to each, if the deceased
left children; if no children, and the parents are the (only) heirs, the
mother has a third; if the deceased left brothers (or sisters) the mother has
a sixth. (The distribution in all cases is) after the payment of legacies and
debts. You know not whether your parents or your children are nearest to

---

2. The principle of inheritance law are laid down in broad outline in the Qur'an; the precise details have been worked out on the basis of the Prophet's practice and that of the Companions, and by interpretation and analogy. Muslim jurists have collected a vast amount of learning on this subject, and this body of law is enough by itself to form the subject of life-long study. Here we shall deal only with the broad principles to be gathered from the Text, as interpreted by the jurists.

(1) The power of testamentary disposition extends over only one-third of the property: the remaining two-thirds are distributed among heirs as laid down. (2) All distribution takes place after the legacies and debts (including funeral expenses) have first been paid. (3) Legacies cannot be left to any of the heirs included in the scheme of distribution; or it will amount to upsetting the shares and undue preference of one heir to another. (4) Generally, but not always, the male takes a share double that of a female in his own category. [516]

you in benefit. These are settled portions ordained by Allah; and Allah is All-Knowing, All-Wise.[3]

12 In what your wives leave, your share is a half, if they leave no child; but if they leave a child, you get a fourth; after payment of legacies and debts. In what you leave, their share is a fourth, if you leave no child; but if you leave a child, they get an eighth; after payment of legacies and debts.

If the man or woman whose inheritance is in question, has left neither ascendants nor descendants, but has left a brother or a sister, each one of the two gets a sixth; but if more than two, they share in a third; after payment of legacies and debts; so that no loss is caused (to any one). Thus is it ordained by Allah; and Allah is All-Knowing, Most Forbearing.

13 Those are limits set by Allah; those who obey Allah and His Messenger will be admitted to Gardens with rivers flowing beneath, to abide therein (for ever) and that will be the supreme achievement.
14 But those who disobey Allah and His Messenger and transgress His limits will be admitted to a Fire, to abide therein: and they shall have a humiliating punishment.

SECTION 3

15 If any of your women are guilty of lewdness, take the evidence of four

---

3. The principles of inheritance are laid down in broad outline in the Qur'an. The precise details have been worked out on the basis of the Prophet's practice and that of his Companions by Muslim jurists.
Distribution to heirs takes place after all debts and legacies (to non-heirs) have been paid. Two thirds of the wealth of the deceased is to be divided among his/her heirs. The heirs include parents, spouses, brothers, sisters and children, and can extend out to more distant relations, if no close ones are living.
No heir can also receive a legacy as this would unbalance the distribution to the heirs, because each heir receives a certain fraction of the wealth, dependent upon how many other heirs there are in each category and over all.
Generally, but not always, a male takes a share double to that of a female in his own category, for instance a son may receive a share double that of a daughter.
This takes into account the Qur'anic injunction that a man is expected to provide for his family out of his money/wealth, whereas a woman can do with hers as she chooses [516].-Ed.

(reliable) witnesses from amongst you against them; and if they testify,
confine them to houses until death do claim them, or Allah ordain for
them some (other) way. 16 If two men among you are guilty of lewdness,
punish them both. If they repent and amend, leave them alone; for Allah
is Oft-Returning, Most Merciful. 17 Allah accepts the repentance of those
who do evil in ignorance and repent soon afterwards; to them will Allah
turn in mercy: for Allah is full of knowledge and wisdom. 18 Of no effect
is the repentance of those who continue to do evil, until death faces one
of them, and he says, "Now have I repented indeed;" nor of those who die
rejecting Faith; for them have We prepared a punishment most grievous.

19 O you who believe! You are forbidden to inherit women against their
will.[4] Nor should you treat them with harshness, that you may take away
part of the dower[5] you have given them,—except where they have been
guilty of open lewdness; on the contrary live with them on a footing of
kindness and equity. If you take a dislike to them it may be that you
dislike a thing, and Allah brings about through it a great deal of good. 20
But if you decide to take one wife in place of another, even if you had
given the latter a whole treasure for dower, take not the least bit of it
back; would you take it by slander and manifest wrong? 21 And how
could you take it when you have gone in unto each other, and they have
taken from you a solemn covenant?

22 And marry not women whom your fathers married,—except what is
past: it was shameful and odious,—an abominable custom indeed.

SECTION 4

23 Prohibited to you (for marriage) are—your mothers, daughters, sisters;
father's sisters, mother's sisters; brother's daughters, sister's daughters;
foster-mothers (who gave you suck), foster-sisters; your wives' mothers;
your step-daughters under your guardianship, born of your wives to

---

4. Among many nations, including Arabs in the Days of Ignorance, a step-son or brother took possession of a dead man's widow or widows along with his goods and chattels. This shameful custom is forbidden. See also 4:22 below. [527]

5. Another trick, to detract from the freedom of married women was to treat them badly and force them to sue for a *Khul'* divorce (see 2:229) or its equivalent in pre-Islamic custom, when the dower could be claimed back. This is also forbidden. Or the harshness may be exercised in another way; a divorced woman may be prevented by those who have control of her, from re-marrying unless she remits her dower. All kinds of harshness are forbidden. [528]

whom you have gone in,—no prohibition if you have not gone in;—(those who have been) wives of your sons proceeding from your loins; and two sisters in wedlock at one and the same time, except for what is past; for Allah is Oft-Forgiving, Most Merciful;—

PART V

24 Also (prohibited are) women already married, except those whom your right hands possess:[6] thus has Allah ordained (prohibitions) against you: except for these, all others are lawful, provided you seek (them in marriage) with gifts from your property,—desiring chastity, not lust, seeing that you derive benefit from them, give them their dowers (at least) as prescribed; but if, after a dower is prescribed, you agree mutually (to vary it), there is no blame on you, and Allah is All-Knowing, All-
Wise. 25 If any of you have not the means wherewith to wed free
believing women, they may wed believing girls from among those whom your right hands possess: and Allah has full knowledge about your faith. You are one from another: wed them with the leave of their owners, and give them their dowers, according to what is reasonable: they should be chaste, not lustful, nor taking paramours: when they are taken in wedlock, if they fall into shame, their punishment is half that for free women. This (permission) is for those among you who fear sin; but it is better for you that you practise self-restraint. And Allah is Oft-Forgiving, Most Merciful.

SECTION 5

26 Allah does wish to make clear to you and to show you the ordinances
of those before you; and (He does wish to) turn to you (in Mercy): and
Allah is All-Knowing, All-Wise. 27 Allah does wish to turn to you, but the
wish of those who follow their lusts is that you should turn away (from
Him),—far, far away. 28 Allah does wish to lighten your (difficulties): for
man was created weak (in flesh). 29 O you who believe! Eat not up your
property among yourselves in vanities: but let there be amongst you
traffic and trade by mutual good-will: nor kill (or destroy) yourselves: for
verily Allah has been to you Most Merciful! 30 If any do that in rancour

6. *Whom your right hands possess i.e.*, captives in a *Jihād*, or war under the orders of the righteous Imām against those who persecute Faith. In such cases formal hostility dissolves civilities. [537]

and injustice,—soon shall We cast them into the Fire: and easy it is for
Allah. 31 If you (but) eschew the most heinous of the things which you are
forbidden to do, We shall expel out of you all the evil in you, and admit
you to a gate of great honour. 32 And in no wise covet those things in
which Allah has bestowed His gifts more freely on some of you than on
others: to men is allotted what they earn, and to women what they earn:
but ask Allah of His bounty. For Allah has full knowledge of all things.
33 To (benefit) every one, We have appointed sharers and heirs to
property left by parents and relatives. To those, also, to whom your right
hand was pledged, give their due portion. For truly Allah is witness to all
things.

SECTION 6

34 Men are the protectors and maintainers of women, because Allah has given the one more (strength) than the other, and because they support them from their means. Therefore the righteous women are devoutly obedient, and guard in (the husband's) absence what Allah would have them guard.[7] As to those women on whose part you fear disloyalty and ill-conduct, admonish them (first), (next), refuse to share their beds, (and last) chastise them[8] (lightly); but if they return to obedience, seek not

---

7. Or the sentence may be rendered: "and protect (the husband's interests) in his absence, as Allah has protected them." If we take the rendering as in the text, the meaning is: the good wife is obedient and harmonious in her husband's presence, and in his absence guards his reputation and property and her own virtue, as ordained by Allah. If we take the rendering as in the note, we reach the same result in a different way: the good wife, in her husband's absence, remembering how Allah has given her a sheltered position, does everything to justify that position by guarding her own virtue and his reputation and property. [546]

8. "*aḍribū*" to strike, to chastise, to part, to separate…
In this verse (4:34) the Arabic word, *aḍribū,* causes much debate. It is a verb in the imperative case (giving an instruction or advice) and is part of the verb *ḍaraba* which means to strike, to chastise, to part, to separate.
It is incorrect to interpret *aḍribū* as 'beat' or 'beat up', which both imply continual and heavy blows inflicting pain and injury. The verb meaning 'beat' and/or 'beat up' is *ḍarraba*. Please note the emphatic '*rr*' which changes the meaning to the intensive form of the verb.
The word *aḍribū* (from *ḍaraba*) found in this verse is NOT the intensive form.
Both traditional and modern commentators have taken the injunction to mean a symbolic single gesture, such as with a toothbrush or some such thing. It is reported that the Prophet Muḥammad detested the idea of a man beating his wife and there is no record whatsoever

against them means (of annoyance): for Allah is Most High, Great (above
you all). 35 If you fear a breach between them twain, appoint (two)
arbiters, one from his family, and the other from hers; if they wish for
peace, Allah will cause their reconciliation: for Allah has full knowledge,
and is acquainted with all things.

36 Serve Allah, and join not any partners with Him; and do good—to
parents, kinsfolk, orphans, those in need, neighbours who are near,
neighbours who are strangers, the companion by your side, the wayfarer
(you meet), and what your right hands possess: for Allah loves not the
arrogant, the vainglorious;—37 (Nor) those who are niggardly or enjoin
niggardliness on others, or hide the bounties which Allah has bestowed
on them; for We have prepared, for those who resist Faith, a punishment
that steeps them in contempt;—38 Nor those who spend of their substance,
to be seen of men, but have no faith in Allah and the Last Day: if any take
the Evil One for their intimate, what a dreadful intimate he is! 39 And
what burden were it on them if they had faith in Allah and in the Last
Day, and they spent out of what Allah has given them for sustenance? For
Allah has full knowledge of them. 40 Allah is never unjust in the least
degree: if there is any good (done), He doubles it, and gives from His
own presence a great reward. 41 How then if We brought from each
people a witness, and We brought you as a witness against these people!

---

of him ever having beaten anyone in his whole life. It is most reasonable to understand the instruction in this verse as follows:-

If you have good reason to fear disloyalty or misconduct on the part of your wife (4:34):-

(1) Speak to her firmly. If this fails then

(2) Make separate sleeping arrangements. If this fails

(3) Separate from her, with or without the symbolic gesture, (ie have nothing to do with her at anytime of the day). If she returns to obedience (some commentators take this to mean initially obedience to Allah), then make peace with her.

If it appears that husband and wife are unable to come to a reconciliation themselves (4:35), then

(4) A concerned party should appoint an arbiter from each side of the family to try and achieve reconciliation. If the married couple wish for peace, Allah will bring about their reconciliation.

(If all this fails completely then divorce is eventually permitted following considerate guidelines to be found elsewhere.) – Ed.

42 On that day those who reject Faith and disobey the Messenger will wish
that the earth were made one with them: but never will they hide a single
fact from Allah!

SECTION 7

43 O you who believe! Approach not prayers with a mind befogged, until
you can understand all that you say,—nor in a state of ceremonial
impurity (except when travelling on the road), until after washing your
whole body. If you are ill, or on a journey, or one of you comes from
offices of nature, or you have been in contact with women, and you find
no water, then take for yourselves clean sand or earth, and rub therewith
your faces and hands. For Allah does blot out sins and forgive again and
again.

44 Have you not turned your vision to those who were given a portion of
the Book? They traffic in error, and wish that you should lose the right
path. 45 But Allah has full knowledge of your enemies: Allah is enough
for a protector, and Allah is enough for a helper. 46 Of the Jews there are
those who displace words from their (right) places, and say: "We hear and
we disobey"; and "Hear what is not heard"; and "*Rā 'inā*";[9] with a twist
of their tongues and a slander to Faith. If only they had said: "We hear
and we obey"; and "Do hear"; and "Do look at us"; it would have been
better for them, and more proper; but Allah has cursed them for their
Unbelief; and but few of them will believe.

47 O you People of the Book! Believe in what We have (now) revealed,
confirming what was (already) with you, before We change the face and
fame of some (of you) beyond all recognition, and turn them hindwards,
or curse them as We cursed the Sabbath-breakers, for the decision of
Allah must be carried out. 48 Allah forgives not that partners should be set
up with Him; but He forgives anything else, to whom He pleases; to set
up partners with Allah is to devise a sin most heinous indeed.

49 Have you not turned your vision to those who claim sanctity for
themselves? Nay—but Allah does sanctify whom He pleases. But never

---

9. See 2:104. *Rā 'inā* if used respectfully in the Arabic way, would have meant "Please attend to us." With a twist of their tongue, they suggested an insulting meaning, such as "O thou that takes us to pasture!" or in Hebrew, "Our bad one!" [566]

will they fail to receive justice in the least little thing.[10] 50 Behold how
they invent a lie against Allah! But that by itself is a manifest sin!

SECTION 8

51 Have you not turned your vision to those who were given a portion of
the Book? They believe in Sorcery and Evil,[11] and say to the Unbelievers
that they are better guided in the (right) way than the Believers! 52 They
are (men) whom Allah has cursed: And those whom Allah has cursed,
you will find, have no one to help.[12] 53 Have they a share in dominion or
power? Behold, they give not a farthing to their fellow-men? 54 Or do
they envy mankind for what Allah has given them of His bounty? But We
had already given the people of Abraham the Book and Wisdom, and
conferred upon them a great kingdom. 55 Some of them believed, and
some of them averted their faces from him: and enough is Hell for a
burning fire. 56 Those who reject our Signs, We shall soon cast into the
Fire: as often as their skins are roasted through, We shall change them for
fresh skins, that they may taste the penalty: for Allah is Exalted in Power,
Wise. 57 But those who believe and do deeds of righteousness, We shall
soon admit to Gardens, with rivers flowing beneath,—their eternal home:
therein shall they have companions pure and holy: We shall admit them
to shades, cool and ever deepening. 58 Allah does command you to render
back your trusts to those to whom they are due; and when you judge
between man and man, that you judge with justice: verily how excellent
is the teaching which He gives you! For Allah is He Who hears and sees
all things. 59 O you who believe! Obey Allah, and obey the Messenger,

---

10. Literally, the small skin in the groove of a date stone, a thing of no value: *fatīlā*. [571]

11. The (Arabic) word I have translated *sorcery*, is *jibt* which may mean divination, sorcery, magic, or any false object of belief or worship, such as an idol. The word I have translated Evil (here and in 2:256) is *Ṭāghūt*, which means the evil one, the one who exceeds all bounds, Satan; or it may refer to some idol worshipped by the Pagan Arabs, with whom the Jews of Madīnah were intriguing against the Holy Prophet. The Jews had taken much to sorcery, magic, divination, and such superstitions. [573]

12. The Jews were then seeking the aid of the Makkan Pagans against Muḥammad, but far from getting any help from them, they and the Pagans were both overthrown. That was the immediate occasion, but the words have a perfectly general—a universal—meaning. [574]

and those charged with authority among you.[13] If you differ in anything among yourselves, refer it to Allah and His Messenger, if you do believe in Allah and the Last Day: that is best, and most suitable for final determination.

SECTION 9

60 Have you not turned your vision to those who declare that they believe
in the revelations that have come to you and to those before you? Their
(real) wish is to resort together for judgement (in their disputes) to the
Evil One, though they were ordered to reject him. But Satan's wish is to
lead them astray far away (from the right). 61 When it is said to them:
"Come to what Allah has revealed, and to the Messenger" you see the
Hypocrites avert their faces from you in disgust. 62 How then, when they
are seized by misfortune, because of the deeds which their hands have
sent forth? Then they come to you, swearing by Allah: "We meant no
more than good-will and conciliation!" 63 Those men,—Allah knows what
is in their hearts; so keep clear of them, but admonish them, and speak to
them a word to reach their very souls. 64 We sent not a Messenger, but to
be obeyed, in accordance with the Will of Allah. If they had only, when
they were unjust to themselves, come unto you and asked Allah's
forgiveness, and the Messenger had asked forgiveness for them, they
would have found Allah indeed Oft-Returning, Most Merciful. 65 But no,
by the Lord, they can have no (real) Faith, until they make you judge in
all disputes between them, and find in their souls no resistance against
your decisions, but accept them with the fullest conviction. 66 If We had
ordered them to sacrifice their lives or to leave their homes, very few of
them would have done it: but if they had done what they were (actually)
told, it would have been best for them, and would have gone farthest to
strengthen their (faith); 67 And We should then have given them from Our
presence a great reward; 68 And We should have shown them the Straight
Way.

69 All who obey Allah and the Messenger are in the company of those on

---

13. Arabic *Ulī al-amr* = those charged with authority or responsibility or decision, or the settlement of affairs. All ultimate authority rests in Allah. Prophets of Allah derive their authority from Him. As Islam makes no sharp division between sacred and secular affairs, it expects governments to be imbued with righteousness. Likewise Islam expects Muslims to respect the authority of such governments for otherwise there can be no order or discipline. [580]

whom is the Grace of Allah,—of the prophets (who teach), the sincere
(lovers of Truth), the witnesses (who testify), and the Righteous (who do
good): Ah! What a beautiful fellowship! 70 Such is the bounty from Allah:
and sufficient is it that Allah knows all.

SECTION 10

71 O you who believe! Take your precautions, and either go forth in parties
or go forth all together. 72 There are certainly among you men who would
tarry behind: if a misfortune befalls you, they say: "Allah did favour us in
that we were not present among them." 73 But if good fortune comes to
you from Allah, they would be sure to say—as if there had never been
ties of affection between you and them —"Oh! I wish I had been with
them; a fine thing should I then have made of it!"

74 Let those fight in the cause of Allah who sell the life of this world for
the Hereafter.[14] To him who fights in the cause of Allah,—whether he
is slain or gets victory—soon shall We give him a reward of great (value).
75 And why should you not fight in the cause of Allah and of those who,
being weak, are ill-treated (and oppressed)?—men, women, and children,
whose cry is: "Our Lord! Rescue us from this town, whose people are
oppressors; and raise for us from You one who will protect; and raise for
us from You one who will help!"[15] 76 Those who believe fight in the
cause of Allah, and those who reject Faith fight in the cause of Evil: So

---

14. It is not everyone – least of all a faint-hearted person – who is fit to fight in the cause of Allah. To do so is a privilege, and those who understand the privilege are prepared to sacrifice all their interests in this life, and this life itself; for they know that it is the sacrifice of something fleeting and of little value, for the sake of something everlasting, and of immense value. Whether (in appearance) they win or lose, in reality they win the prize for which they are fighting – viz., honour and glory in the sight of Allah. Note that the only alternatives here are Death or Victory! The true fighter knows no defeat. [591]–Ed.

15. Even from the human point of view the cause of Allah is the cause of justice, the cause of the oppressed. In the great persecution, before Makkah was won again, what sorrows, threats, tortures, and oppressions, were suffered by those whose faith was unshaken? Muḥammad's life and that of his adherents was threatened: they were mocked, assaulted, beaten and some tortured to death. Those within the power of the enemy were put into chains and cast into prison; others were boycotted; shut out of trade, business, and social intercourse; they could not even buy the food they needed, or perform their religious duties at the sacred mosque (the Ka'bah). The persecution was redoubled for the believing slaves, women, and children remaining in Makkah after the Hijrah. Their cry for a protector and helper from Allah was answered when Muḥammad the Chosen One, brought freedom and peace to Makkah again. [593] – Ed.

fight you against the friends of Satan: feeble indeed is the cunning of Satan.

SECTION 11

77 Have you not turned your vision to those who were told to hold back their hands (from fight) but establish regular prayers and spend in regular charity? When (at length) the order for fighting was issued to them, behold! A section of them feared men as—or even more than—they should have feared Allah. They said: "Our Lord! Why have You ordered us to fight? Would You not grant us respite to our (natural) term, near (enough)?" Say: "Short is the enjoyment of this world: the Hereafter is the best for those who do right: never will you be dealt with unjustly in
the very least! 78 Wherever you are, death will find you out, even if you
are in towers built up strong and high!"

If some good befalls them, they say, "This is from Allah"; but if evil, they say, "This is from you" (O Prophet). Say: "All things are from Allah."[16] But what has come to these people, that they fail to understand
a single fact? 79 Whatever good, (O man!) happens to you, is from Allah;
but whatever evil happens to you, is from your (own) soul. And We have sent you as a Messenger to (instruct) mankind. And enough is Allah for
a witness. 80 He who obeys the Messenger, obeys Allah: but if any turn
away, We have not sent you to watch over their (evil deeds). 81 They have
"Obedience" on their lips; but when they leave you, a section of them meditate all night on things very different from what you tell them. But Allah records their nightly (plots): so keep clear of them, and put your
trust in Allah, and enough is Allah as a disposer of affairs. 82 Do they not
consider the Qur'an (with care)? Had it been from other than Allah, they

16. The Hypocrites were inconsistent, and in this reflect unregenerate mankind. If a disaster happens, due to their own folly, they blame somebody else; but if they are fortunate, they claim reflected credit by pretending that Heaven has favoured them because of their own superior merits. The modern critic discards even this pretence, eliminates Heaven altogether, and claims all credit direct to himself, unless he brings in blind chance, but that he does mostly to "explain" misfortune. If we look to the Ultimate Cause of all things, all things come from Allah. But if we look to the proximate cause of things, our own merit is so small, that we can hardly claim credit for good ourselves with any fairness. In Allah's hand is all good: 3:26. On the other hand, the proximate cause of our evil is due to some wrong in our own inner selves; for never are we dealt with unjustly in the very least: 4:77. [597]

would surely have found therein much discrepancy.[17] 83 When there
comes to them some matter touching (public) safety or fear, they divulge
it. If they had only referred it to the Messenger, or to those charged with
authority among them, the proper investigators would have tested it from
them (direct). Were it not for the Grace and Mercy of Allah unto you, all
but a few of you would have fallen into the clutches of Satan.

84 Then fight in Allah's cause—you are held responsible only for
yourself—and rouse the believers. It may be that Allah will restrain the
fury of the Unbelievers; for Allah is the strongest in might and in
punishment.[18] 85 Whoever recommends and helps a good cause becomes
a partner therein: and whoever recommends and helps an evil cause,
shares in its burden: and Allah has power over all things.

86 When a (courteous) greeting is offered you, meet it with a greeting still
more courteous, or (at least) of equal courtesy. Allah takes careful
account of all things. 87 Allah! There is no god but He: of a surety He will
gather you together against the Day of Judgement, about which there is
no doubt. And whose word can be truer than Allah's?

SECTION 12

88 Why should you be divided into two parties about the Hypocrites?
Allah has upset them for their (evil) deeds. Would you guide those whom
Allah has thrown out of the Way? For those whom Allah has thrown out
of the Way, never shall you find the Way. 89 They but wish that you

---

17. The unity of the Qur'an is an admitted fact. How can we account for it except through the unity of Allah's purpose and design? From a mere human point of view, we should have expected much discrepancy, because (1) the Messenger who promulgated it was not a learned man or philosopher, (2) it was promulgated at various times and in various circumstances, and (3) it is addressed to all grades of mankind. Yet, when properly understood, its various pieces fit together better than a jig-saw puzzle even when arranged without any regard to chronological order. There was just the One Inspirer and the One Inspired. [601]

18. The courage of Muḥammad was as notable as his wisdom, his gentleness, and his trust in Allah. Facing fearful odds, he often stood alone, and took the whole responsibility on himself. But his example and visible trust in Allah inspired and roused the Muslims, and also – speaking purely from a human point of view – restrained the fury of his enemies. When we consider that he was Allah's inspired Messenger, to carry out His Plan, we can see that nothing can resist that Plan. If the enemy happens to have strength, power, or resources, Allah's strength, power, and resources are infinitely greater. If the enemy is meditating punishment of the righteous for their righteousness, Allah's punishment for such wickedness will be infinitely greater and more effective. [603]

should reject Faith, as they do, and thus be on the same footing (as they): but take not friends from their ranks until they flee[19] in the way of Allah (from what is forbidden). But if they turn renegades, seize them and slay them wherever you find them; and (in any case) take no friends or helpers from their ranks;—
90 Except those who join a group between whom and you there is a treaty (of peace), or those who approach you with hearts restraining them from fighting you as well as fighting their own people. If Allah had pleased, He could have given them power over you, and they would have fought you: therefore if they withdraw from you but fight you not, and (instead) send you (guarantees of) peace, then Allah has opened no way for you (to war against them).
91 Others you will find that wish to gain your confidence as well as that of their people: every time they are sent back to temptation, they succumb thereto: if they withdraw not from you nor give you (guarantees) of peace besides restraining their hands, seize them and slay them wherever you get them: in their case We have provided you with a clear argument against them.

SECTION 13

92 Never should a believer kill a believer; but (if it so happens) by mistake, (compensation is due): if one (so) kills a believer, it is ordained that he should free a believing slave, and pay compensation to the deceased's family, unless they remit it freely. If the deceased belonged to a people at war with you, and he was a believer, the freeing of a believing slave (is enough). If he belonged to a people with whom you have a treaty of mutual alliance, compensation should be paid to his family, and a believing slave be freed. For those who find this beyond their means, (is prescribed) a fast for two months running: by way of repentance to Allah: for Allah has all knowledge and all wisdom.
93 If a man kills a believer intentionally, his recompense is Hell, to abide therein (for ever):

---

19. Flee: the verbal form from which the noun *hijrah* is derived. Bukhārī, interprets this rightly as fleeing from all that is forbidden. This would include *hijrah* in the technical sense of leaving a place in which the practice of religion is not allowed. But it is more general. In time of war, if a man is willing to submit to discipline and refrain from infringing orders issued, he has proved his fidelity and may be treated as a member of the community at war. On the other hand if, by false pretences, he comes into the inner counsels merely to betray them, he may rightly be treated as a traitor or deserter and be punished for his treason or desertion; or if he escapes, he can be treated as an enemy and is entitled to no mercy. He is worse than an enemy; he has claimed to be of you in order to spy on you, and all the time been helping the enemy.[607] - Ed.

and the wrath and the curse of Allah are upon him, and a dreadful penalty
is prepared for him.

94 O you who believe! When you go abroad in the cause of Allah,
investigate carefully, and say not to any one who offers you a salutation:
"You are none of a believer!" coveting the perishable goods of this life:
with Allah are profits and spoils abundant. Even thus were you yourselves
before, till Allah conferred on you His favours: therefore carefully
investigate. For Allah is well aware of all that you do.

95 Not equal are those Believers who sit (at home) and receive no hurt,
and those who strive and fight in the cause of Allah with their goods and
their persons. Allah has granted a grade higher to those who strive and
fight with their goods and persons than to those who sit (at home). Unto
all (in Faith) has Allah promised good: but those who strive and fight has
He distinguished above those who sit (at home) by a special reward,—96
Ranks specially bestowed by Him, and Forgiveness and Mercy. For Allah
is Oft-Forgiving, Most Merciful.

SECTION 14

97 When angels take the souls of those who die in sin against their souls,
they say: "In what (plight) were you?" They reply: "Weak and oppressed
were we in the earth." They say: "Was not the earth of Allah spacious
enough for you to move yourselves away (from evil)?" Such men will
find their abode in Hell,—What an evil refuge!—98 Except those who are
(really) weak and oppressed—men, women, and children—who have no
means in their power, nor (a guide-post) to their way. 99 For these, there
is hope that Allah will forgive: for Allah does blot out (sins) and forgive
again and again. 100 He who forsakes his home in the cause of Allah, finds
in the earth many a refuge, wide and spacious: should he die as a refugee
from home for Allah and His Messenger, his reward becomes due and
sure with Allah: and Allah is Oft-Forgiving, Most Merciful.

SECTION 15

101 When you travel through the earth, there is no blame on you if you
shorten your prayers, for fear the Unbelievers may attack you: for the
Unbelievers are unto you open enemies. 102 When you (O Messenger) are
with them, and stand to lead them in prayer, let one party of them stand
up (in prayer) with you, taking their arms with them; when they finish

their prostrations, let them take their position in the rear. And let the other
party come up which has not yet prayed—and let them pray with you,
taking all precautions, and bearing arms: the Unbelievers wish, if you
were negligent of your arms and your baggage, to assault you in a single
rush. But there is no blame on you if you put away your arms because of
the inconvenience of rain or because you are ill; but take (every)
precaution for yourselves. For the Unbelievers Allah has prepared a
humiliating punishment. 103 When you pass (congregational) prayers,
celebrate Allah's praises, standing, sitting down, or lying down on your
sides; but when you are free from danger, set up Regular Prayers: for
such prayers are enjoined on believers at stated times. 104 And slacken not
in following up the enemy: if you are suffering hardships, they are
suffering similar hardships; but you have Hope from Allah, while they
have none. And Allah is full of knowledge and wisdom.

SECTION 16

105 We have sent down to you the Book in truth, that you might judge
between men, as guided by Allah: so be not (used) as an advocate by those
who betray their trust; 106 But seek the forgiveness of Allah; for Allah is
Oft-Forgiving, Most Merciful. 107 Contend not on behalf of such as betray
their own souls; for Allah loves not one given to perfidy and crime: 108
They may hide (their crimes) from men, but they cannot hide (them) from
Allah, seeing that He is in their midst when they plot by night, in words
that He cannot approve: and Allah does compass round all that they do. 109
Ah! These are the sort of men on whose behalf you may contend in this
world; but who will contend with Allah on their behalf on the Day of
Judgement, or who will carry their affairs through? 110 If any one does evil
or wrongs his own soul but afterwards seeks Allah's forgiveness, he will
find Allah Oft-Forgiving, Most Merciful. 111 And if any one earns sin, he
earns it against his own soul: for Allah is full of knowledge and wisdom.
112 But if any one earns a fault or a sin and throws it on to one that is
innocent, he carries (on himself) (both) a falsehood and a flagrant sin.

SECTION 17

113 But for the Grace of Allah to you and His Mercy, a party of them
would certainly have plotted to lead you astray. But (in fact) they will
only lead their own souls astray, and to you they can do no harm in the
least. For Allah has sent down to you the Book and wisdom and taught
you what you knew not (before): and great is the Grace of Allah unto

you. 114 In most of their secret talks there is no good; but if one exhorts
to a deed of charity or justice or conciliation between men, (secrecy is
permissible): to him who does this, seeking the good pleasure of Allah,
We shall soon give a reward of the highest (value). 115 If anyone contends
with the Messenger even after guidance has been plainly conveyed to
him, and follows a path other than that becoming to men of Faith, We
shall leave him in the path he has chosen, and land him in Hell,—what an
evil refuge!

SECTION 18

116 Allah forgives not (the sin of) joining other gods with Him; but He
forgives whom He pleases other sins than this: one who joins other gods
with Allah, has strayed far, far away (from the right). 117 (The Pagans),
leaving Him, call but upon female deities: they call but upon Satan the
persistent rebel! 118 Allah did curse him, but he said: "I will take of Your
servants a portion marked off; 119 I will mislead them, and I will create in
them false desires; I will order them to slit the ears of cattle, and to deface
the (fair) nature created by Allah." Whoever, forsaking Allah, takes Satan
for a friend, has of a surety suffered a loss that is manifest. 120 Satan
makes them promises, and creates in them false desires; but Satan's
promises are nothing but deception. 121 They (his dupes) will have their
dwelling in Hell, and from it they will find no way of escape. 122 But
those who believe and do deeds of righteousness,—we shall soon admit
them to Gardens, with rivers flowing beneath,—to dwell therein for ever.
Allah's promise is the truth, and whose word can be truer than Allah's?

123 Not your desires, nor those of the People of the Book (can prevail):
whoever works evil, will be requited accordingly. Nor will he find, besides
Allah, any protector or helper. 124 If any do deeds of righteousness,—be
they male or female—and have faith, they will enter Heaven, and not the
least injustice will be done to them. 125 Who can be better in religion than
one who submits his whole self to Allah, does good, and follows the way
of Abraham the true in Faith? For Allah did take Abraham for a friend. 126
But to Allah belong all things in the heavens and on earth: and He it is that
encompasses all things.

SECTION 19

127 They ask your instruction concerning the women. Say: Allah does
instruct you about them: and (remember) what has been rehearsed unto

you in the Book, concerning the orphans of women to whom you give not
the portions prescribed, and yet whom you desire to marry, as also
concerning the children who are weak and oppressed: that you stand firm
for justice to orphans. There is not a good deed which you do, but Allah
is well-acquainted therewith.

128 If a wife fears cruelty or desertion on her husband's part, there is no
blame on them if they arrange an amicable settlement between themselves;
and such settlement is best; even though men's souls are swayed by greed.
But if you do good and practise self-restraint, Allah is well-acquainted with
all that you do. 129 You are never able to be fair and just as between women,
even if it is your ardent desire: but turn not away (from a woman) altogether,
so as to leave her (as it were) hanging (in the air). If you come to a friendly
understanding, and practise self-restraint, Allah is Oft-Forgiving, Most
Merciful. 130 But if they disagree (and must part), Allah will provide
abundance for all from His all-reaching bounty: for Allah is He that cares for
all and is Wise.

131 To Allah belong all things in the heavens and on earth. Verily We have
directed the People of the Book before you, and you (O Muslims) to fear
Allah. But if you deny Him, lo! unto Allah belong all things in the
heavens and on earth, and Allah is free of all wants, worthy of all praise.
132 Yea, unto Allah belong all things in the heavens and on earth, and
enough is Allah to carry through all affairs. 133 If it were His will, He
could destroy you, O mankind, and create another race; for He has power
this to do. 134 If any one desires a reward in this life, in Allah's (gift) is
the reward (both) of this life and of the Hereafter: for Allah is He Who
hears and sees (all things).

SECTION 20

135 O you who believe! Stand out firmly for justice, as witnesses to Allah,
even as against yourselves, or your parents, or your kin, and whether it
be (against) rich or poor: for Allah can best protect both. Follow not the
lusts (of your hearts), lest you swerve, and if you distort (justice) or
decline to do justice, verily Allah is well-acquainted with all that you do.
136 O you who believe! Believe in Allah and His Messenger, and the
scripture which He has sent to His Messenger and the scripture which He
sent to those before (him). Any who denies Allah, His angels, His Books,
His Messengers, and the Day of Judgement, has gone far, far astray.

137 Those who believe, then reject faith, then believe (again) and (again)
reject faith, and go on increasing in unbelief,—Allah will not forgive them
nor guide them on the Way. 138 To the Hypocrites give the glad tidings that
there is for them (but) a grievous penalty;—139 Indeed, to those who take
for friends unbelievers rather than believers: is it honour they seek among
them? Nay,—all honour is with Allah. 140 Already has He sent you Word
in the Book, that when you hear the Signs of Allah held in defiance and
ridicule, you are not to sit with them unless they turn to a different theme:
if you did, you would be like them. For Allah will collect the hypocrites
and those who defy faith—all in Hell:—141 (These are) the ones who wait
and watch about you: if you do gain a victory from Allah, they say: "Were
we not with you?"—but if the unbelievers gain a success, they say (to
them): "Did we not gain an advantage over you, and did we not guard you
from the believers?" But Allah will judge betwixt you on the Day of
Judgment. And never will Allah grant to the unbelievers a way (to
triumph) over the believers.

SECTION 21

142 The Hypocrites—they think they are over-reaching Allah, but He will
over-reach them: when they stand up to prayer, they stand without
earnestness, to be seen of men, but little do they hold Allah in
remembrance; 143 (They are) distracted in mind even in the midst of
it,—being (sincerely) for neither one group nor for another. Whom Allah
leaves straying,—never will you find for him the Way. 144 O you who
believe! Take not for friends unbelievers rather than believers: do you
wish to offer Allah an open proof against yourselves? 145 The Hypocrites
will be in the lowest depths of the Fire: no helper will you find for
them;—146 Except for those who repent, mend (their lives), hold fast to
Allah, and purify their religion as in Allah's sight: if so they will be
(numbered) with the believers. And soon will Allah grant to the believers
a reward of immense value. 147 What can Allah gain by your punishment,
if you are grateful and you believe? Nay, it is Allah that recognises (all
good), and knows all things.

PART VI

148 Allah loves not that evil should be noised abroad in public speech, except

where injustice has been done;[20] for Allah is He Who hears and knows all
things. 149 Whether you publish a good deed or conceal it or cover evil with
pardon, verily Allah does blot out (sins) and has power (in the judgement of
values). 150 Those who deny Allah and His Messengers, and (those who)
wish to separate Allah from His Messengers, saying: "We believe in some
but reject others": and (those who) wish to take a course midway,—151 They
are in truth (equally) unbelievers; and we have prepared for unbelievers a
humiliating punishment. 152 To those who believe in Allah and His
Messengers and make no distinction between any of the Messengers, We
shall soon give their (due) rewards: for Allah is Oft-Forgiving, Most
Merciful.

SECTION 22

153 The People of the Book ask you to cause a book to descend to them
from heaven: indeed they asked Moses for an even greater (miracle), for
they said: "Show us Allah in public," but they were dazed for their
presumption, with thunder and lightning. Yet they worshipped the calf
even after clear Signs had come to them; even so We forgave them; and
gave Moses manifest proofs of authority. 154 And for their covenant We
raised over them (the towering height) of Mount (Sinai); and (on another
occasion) We said: "Enter the gate with humility"; and (once again) We
commanded them: "Transgress not in the matter of the Sabbath." And We
took from them a solemn covenant. 155 (They have incurred divine
displeasure): in that they broke their covenant; that they rejected the Signs
of Allah; that they slew the Messengers in defiance of right; that they said,
"Our hearts are the wrappings (which preserve Allah's Word; we need no

---

20. We can make a public scandal of evil in many ways. (1) It may be idle sensation-mongering: it often leads to more evil by imitation, as where criminal deeds are glorified in a cinema, or talked about shamelessly in a novel or drama. (2) It may be malicious gossip of a foolish, personal kind: it does no good, but it hurts people's feelings. (3) It may be malevolent slander or libel: it is intended deliberately to cause harm to people's reputation or injure them in other ways, and is rightly punishable under all laws. (4) It may be a public rebuke or correction or remonstrance, without malice. (1), (2) and (3) are absolutely forbidden. (4) may be by a person in authority; in which case the exception applies, for all wrong or injustice must be corrected openly, to prevent its recurrence. Or (4) may be by a person not vested with authority, but acting either from motives of public spirit, or in order to help some one who has been wronged: here again the exception will apply. But if the motive is different, the exception does not apply. (4) would also include a public complaint by a person who has suffered a wrong; he has every right to seek public redress. [654]

more)";—nay, Allah has set the seal on their hearts for their blasphemy,
and little is it they believe;— 156 That they rejected Faith; that they uttered
against Mary a grave false charge; 157 That they said (in boast), "We killed
Christ Jesus the son of Mary, the Messenger of Allah";—but they killed
him not, nor crucified him'[21] but so it was made to appear to them, and
those who differ therein are full of doubts, with no (certain) knowledge,
but only conjecture to follow, for of a surety they killed him not:— 158 Nay,
Allah raised him up[22] unto Himself; and Allah is Exalted in Power,
Wise;— 159 And there is none of the People of the Book but must believe
in him before his death; and on the Day of Judgement he will be a witness
against them;— 160 For the iniquity of the Jews We made unlawful for them
certain (foods) good and wholesome which had been lawful for them;—in
that they hindered many from Allah's Way;— 161 That they took usury,
though they were forbidden; and that they devoured men's substance
wrongfully;—We have prepared for those among them who reject Faith a
grievous punishment.

162 But those among them who are well-grounded in knowledge, and the believers, believe in what has been revealed to you and what was revealed

---

21. The end of the life of Jesus on earth is as much involved in mystery as his birth, and indeed the greater part of his private life, except the three main years of his ministry. It is not profitable to discuss the many doubts and conjectures among the early Christian sects and among Muslim theologians. The Orthodox Christian Churches make it a cardinal point of their doctrine that his life was taken on the Cross, that he died and was buried, that on the third day he rose in the body with his wounds intact, and walked about and conversed, and ate with his disciples, and was afterwards taken up bodily to heaven. This is necessary for the theological doctrine of blood sacrifice and vicarious atonement for sins, which is rejected by Islam. But some of the early Christian sects did not believe that Christ was killed on the Cross. The Basilidans believed that someone else was substituted for him. The Docetae held that Christ never had a real physical or natural body, but only an apparent or phantom body, and that his Crucifixion was only apparent, not real. The Marcionite Gospel (about A.C. 138) denied that Jesus was born, and merely said that he appeared in human form. The Gospel of St. Barnabas supported the theory of substitution on the Cross. The Qur'anic teaching is that Christ was not crucified nor killed by the Jews, notwithstanding certain apparent circumstances which produced that illusion in the minds of some of his enemies; that disputations, doubts, and conjectures on such matters are vain and that he was taken up to Allah (see next verse and note). [663]

22. There is difference of opinion as to the exact interpretation of this verse. The words are: The Jews did not kill Jesus, but Allah raised him up (*rafa'a*) to Himself. One school holds that Jesus did not die the usual human death, but still lives in the body in heaven, which is the generally accepted Muslim view. [664]

before you: and (especially) those who establish regular prayer and
practise regular charity and believe in Allah and in the Last Day: To them
shall We soon give a great reward.

SECTION 23

163 We have sent you inspiration, as We sent it to Noah and the
Messengers after him: We sent inspiration to Abraham, Ismā'īl, Isaac,
Jacob and the Tribes, to Jesus, Job, Jonah, Aaron, and Solomon, and to
David We gave the Psalms. 164 Of some Messengers We have already told
you the story; of others We have not;—and to Moses Allah spoke
direct;—165 Messengers who gave good news as well as warning, that
mankind, after (the coming) of the Messengers, should have no plea
against Allah: for Allah is Exalted in Power, Wise.

166 But Allah bears witness that what He has sent unto you He has sent
from His (own) knowledge, and the angels bear witness: but enough is
Allah for a witness. 167 Those who reject Faith and keep off (men) from
the way of Allah, have verily strayed far, far away from the Path. 168
Those who reject Faith and do wrong,—Allah will not forgive them nor
guide them to any way—169 Except the way of Hell, to dwell therein for
ever. And this to Allah is easy. 170 O Mankind! The Messenger has come
to you in truth from Allah: believe in him: it is best for you. But if you
reject Faith, to Allah belong all things in the heavens and on earth: and
Allah is All-Knowing, All-Wise. 171 O People of the Book! Commit no
excesses in your religion: nor say of Allah aught but the truth. Christ
Jesus the son of Mary was (no more than) a Messenger of Allah, and His
Word, which He bestowed on Mary, and a spirit proceeding from Him:
so believe in Allah and His Messengers. Say not "Trinity": desist: it will
be better for you: for Allah is one Allah: Glory be to Him: (far exalted is
He) above having a son. To Him belong all things in the heavens and on
earth. And enough is Allah as a Disposer of affairs.

SECTION 24

172 Christ disdains not to serve and worship Allah, nor do the angels, those
nearest (to Allah): those who disdain His worship and are arrogant,—He
will gather them all together unto Himself to (answer). 173 But to those
who believe and do deeds of righteousness, He will give their (due)
rewards,—and more, out of His bounty: but those who are disdainful and
arrogant, He will punish with a grievous penalty; nor will they find,

besides Allah, any to protect or help them. 174 O mankind! Verily there has come to you a convincing proof from your Lord: for We have sent unto you a light (that is) manifest.[23] 175 Then those who believe in Allah, and hold fast to Him,—soon will He admit them to mercy and grace from Himself, and guide them to Himself by a straight Way.

176 They ask you for a legal decision. Say: Allah directs (thus) about those who leave no descendants or ascendants as heirs. If it is a man that dies, leaving a sister but no child, she shall have half the inheritance: if (such a deceased was) a woman, who left no child, her brother takes her inheritance: if there are two sisters, they shall have two-thirds of the inheritance (between them): if there are brothers and sisters, (they share), the male having twice the share of the female. Thus does Allah make clear to you (His law), lest you err. And Allah has knowledge of all things.□

---

23. The Proof and the Light are the Qur'an and the Personality, Life and Teaching of Muḥammad Muṣtafā. [679]

Chapter 5

Sūrah Al-Mā'idah
(The Table Spread)

Translator's Introduction

This Sūrah deals, by way of recapitulation, with the backsliding of the Jews and Christians from their pure religions, to which the coping stone was placed by Islam. It refers particularly to the Christians, and to their solemn Sacrament of the Last Supper, to whose mystic meaning they are declared to have been false.

As a logical corollary to the corruption of the earlier religions of Allah, the practical precepts of Islam, about food, cleanliness, justice, and fidelity are recapitulated.

The third verse contains the memorable declaration: "This day have I perfected your religion for you": which was promulgated in A.H.10, during the Prophet's last Pilgrimage to Makkah. Chronologically it was the last verse to be revealed.

Summary—Beginning with an appeal to fulfil, as sacred, all obligations, human and divine, it points to certain regulations about food, as conducive to a sober and social life, without superstition and without bias or hatred (5:1-5).

Cleanliness of body, and justice and uprightness of dealing are nearest to Piety (5:6-11).

If the Jews and the Christians turned back from the Truth and violated their Covenants, they have had their warning (5:12-26).

The murder of Abel by Cain is the type of treatment which the just man suffers from the envious. There is punishment from Allah. The just man must not grieve (5:27-43).

Muslims must do impartial justice, but must protect their own Brotherhood and their Faith from insult and scorn; they must appreciate piety, humility, and other good points among the Christians (5:44-86).

They must enjoy with gratitude all that is good and lawful, but guard themselves against excess. Swearing, intoxication, gambling, violation of the Sanctuary, superstitions of all kinds, and false evidence are condemned (5:87-108).

The miracles of Jesus, and how they were misused by those who bore his name (5:109-120).

*** *** ***

In the name of Allah,
Most Gracious, Most Merciful.

1 O you who believe! Fulfil (all) obligations. Lawful unto you (for food)
are all four-footed animals, with the exceptions named: but animals of the
chase are forbidden while you are in the Sacred Precincts or in pilgrim
garb: for Allah does command according to His Will and Plan. 2 O you
who believe! Violate not the sanctity of the symbols of Allah, nor of the
sacred month, nor of the animals brought for sacrifice, nor the garlands
that mark out such animals, nor the people resorting to the Sacred House,
seeking of the bounty and good pleasure of their Lord. But when you are
clear of the Sacred Precincts and of pilgrim garb, you may hunt and let
not the hatred of some people in (once) shutting you out of the Sacred
Mosque lead you to transgression (and hostility on your part). Help you
one another in righteousness and piety, but help you not one another in
sin and rancour: fear Allah: for Allah is strict in punishment. 3 Forbidden
to you (for food) are: dead meat, blood, the flesh of swine, and that on
which has been invoked the name of other than Allah; that which has
been killed by strangling, or by a violent blow, or by a headlong fall, or
by being gored to death; that which has been (partly) eaten by a wild
animal; unless you are able to slaughter it (in due form); that which is
sacrificed on stone (altars); (forbidden) also is the division (of meat) by
raffling with arrows: that is impiety.

This day have those who reject Faith given up all hope of your religion:
yet fear them not but fear Me. This day have I perfected your religion for
you, completed My favour upon you, and have chosen for you Islam as
your religion. But if any is forced by hunger, with no inclination to
transgression, Allah is indeed Oft-Forgiving, Most Merciful. 4 They ask
you what is lawful to them (as food). Say: Lawful unto you are (all)
things good and pure: and what you have taught your trained hunting
animals (to catch) in the manner directed to you by Allah: eat what they
catch for you, but pronounce the name of Allah over it: and fear Allah;
for Allah is swift in taking account. 5 This day are (all) things good and
pure made lawful unto you. The food of the People of the Book is lawful
unto you and yours is lawful unto them. (Lawful unto you in marriage)
are (not only) chaste women who are believers, but chaste women among
the People of the Book, revealed before your time,—when you give them

their due dowers, and desire chastity, not lewdness, nor secret intrigues. If any one rejects faith, fruitless is his work, and in the Hereafter he will be in the ranks of those who have lost (all spiritual good).

SECTION 2

6 O you who believe! When you prepare for prayer, wash your faces, and
your hands (and arms) to the elbows; rub your heads (with water); and
(wash) your feet to the ankles. If you are in a state of ceremonial
impurity, bathe your whole body. But if you are ill, or on a journey, or
one of you comes from offices of nature, or you have been in contact
with women, and you find no water, then take for yourselves clean sand
or earth,[1] and rub therewith your faces and hands. Allah does not wish
to place you in a difficulty, but to make you clean, and to complete His
favour to you, that you may be grateful. 7 And call in remembrance the
favour of Allah unto you, and His covenant, which He ratified with you,
when you said: "We hear and we obey": and fear Allah, for Allah knows
well the secrets of your hearts. 8 O you who believe! Stand out firmly for
Allah, as witnesses to fair dealing, and let not the hatred of others to you
make you swerve to wrong and depart from justice. Be just: that is next
to piety: and fear Allah. For Allah is well-acquainted with all that you do.
9 To those who believe and do deeds of righteousness has Allah promised
forgiveness and a great reward. 10 Those who reject faith and deny Our
Signs will be companions of Hell-fire. 11 O you who believe! Call in
remembrance the favour of Allah unto you when certain men formed the
design to stretch out their hands against you, but (Allah) held back their
hands from you: so fear Allah. And on Allah let believers put (all) their
trust.

SECTION 3

12 Allah did aforetime take a covenant from the Children of Israel, and
We appointed twelve captains among them. [2] And Allah said: "I am with

1. This is *Tayammum,* or washing with clean sand or earth where water is not available. I take it that this substitute is permissible both for *Wuḍū* and for a full bath, in the circumstances mentioned. [704]

2. *Cf.* 2:63. "Moses... called for the elders of the people... and all the people answered together and said: 'All that the Lord hath spoken we will do'"(Exod.xix,7-8) This was under the towering height of Mount Sinai.

The captains or elders or leaders of the people were selected, one from each of the

you: if you (but) establish regular prayers, practise regular charity,
believe in My messengers, honour and assist them, and loan to Allah a
beautiful loan, verily I will wipe out from you your evils, and admit you
to Gardens with rivers flowing beneath; but if any of you, after this,
resists faith, he has truly wandered from the path of rectitude." 13 But
because of their breach of their covenant, We cursed them, and made
their hearts grow hard; they change the words from their (right) places
and forget a good part of the message that was sent them, nor will you
cease to find them—barring a few—ever bent on (new) deceits: but
forgive them, and overlook (their misdeeds): for Allah loves those who
are kind.

14 From those, too, who call themselves Christians, We did take a
Covenant,[3] but they forgot a good part of the message that was sent
them: so We estranged them, with enmity and hatred between the one and
the other, to the Day of Judgement. And soon will Allah show them what
it is they have done. 15 O People of the Book! There has come to you Our
Messenger, revealing to you much that you used to hide in the Book, and
passing over much (that is now unnecessary): there has come to you from
Allah a (new) light and a perspicuous Book,—16 Wherewith Allah guides
all who seek His good pleasure to ways of peace and safety, and leads
them out of darkness, by His Will, unto the light,—guides them to a path
that is straight.

17 In blasphemy indeed are those that say that Allah is Christ the son of
Mary. Say: "Who then has the least power against Allah, if His Will were
to destroy Christ the son of Mary, his mother, and all— every one that is
on the earth? For to Allah belongs the dominion of the heavens and the
earth, and all that is between. He creates what He pleases. For Allah has

---

twelve tribes (see 2:60). For census purposes the names of the elders of the tribes are given in Num.i. 4-16: they are called "every one the head of the house of his fathers". Later, twelve other "heads of the Children of Israel" were selected to spy out of the land of Canaan: their names are mentioned in Num. xiii. 1-16. See below 5:22-29 and notes. [709]

3. The Christian Covenant may be taken to be the charge which Jesus gave to his disciples, and which the disciples accepted, to welcome Aḥmad (61:6). Glimpses of this are to be found in the Gospel of St. John even as it exists now (John xv. 26, xvi. 7). It is those who call themselves "Christians" who reject this. True Christians have accepted it. The enmity between those who call themselves Christians and the Jews will continue till the Last Day. [715]

power over all things."

18 (Both) the Jews and the Christians say: "We are sons of Allah, and His
beloved." Say: "Why then does He punish you for your sins? Nay, you
are but men,—of the men He has created: He forgives whom He pleases,
and He punishes whom He pleases: and to Allah belongs the dominion of
the heavens and the earth, and all that is between: and unto Him is the
final goal (of all)." 19 O People of the Book! Now has come unto you,
making (things) clear unto you, Our Messenger, after the break in (the
series of) Our messengers, lest you should say: "There came unto us no
bringer of glad tidings and no warner (from evil)"; but now has come
unto you a bringer of glad tidings and a warner (from evil). And Allah
has power over all things.

SECTION 4

20 Remember Moses said to his people: "O my people! Call in
remembrance the favour of Allah unto you, when He produced prophets
among you, made you kings, and gave you what He had not given to any
other among the peoples. 21 O my people! Enter[4] the Holy Land which
Allah has assigned unto you, and turn not back ignominiously, for then
will you be overthrown, to your own ruin." 22 They said: "O Moses! In
this land are a people of exceeding strength: never shall we enter it until
they leave it: if (once) they leave, then shall we enter." 23 (But) among
(their) God-fearing men were two on whom Allah had bestowed His
grace:[5] they said: "Assault them at the (proper) Gate: when once you are
in, victory will be yours; but on Allah put your trust if you have faith."

---

4. We now come to the events detailed in the 13th and 14th chapters of the Book of Numbers in the Old Testament. Read these as Commentary, and examine a good map of the Sinai Peninsula, showing its connections with Egypt or the west, Northwest Arabia on the east, and Palestine on the northeast. We may suppose that Israel crossed from Egypt into the Peninsula somewhere near the northern extremity of the Gulf of Suez. Moses organised and numbered the people, and instituted the Priesthood. They went south about 200 miles to Mount Sinai where the Law was received. Then, perhaps a hundred and fifty miles north of their camp, about 20 miles south of the future Jerusalem. They saw a rich country, and brought from it pomegranates and figs and a bunch of grapes so heavy that it had to be carried by two men on a staff. They came back and reported that the land was rich, but the men there were too strong for them. The people of Israel had no courage and no faith, and Moses remonstrated with them. [724]

5. Among those who returned after spying out the land were two men who had faith and courage. They were Joshua and Caleb. [726]

24 They said: "O Moses! While they remain there, never shall we be able
to enter, to the end of time. Go you, and your Lord, and fight you two,
while we sit here (and watch)." 25 He said: "O my Lord! I have power
only over myself and my brother: so separate us from this rebellious
people!" 26 Allah said: "Therefore will the land be out of their reach for
forty years: in distraction will they wander through the land: but sorrow
you not over these rebellious people."

SECTION 5

27 Recite to them the truth of the story of the two sons of Adam. Behold!
they each presented a sacrifice (to Allah): it was accepted from one, but
not from the other. Said the latter: "Be sure I will slay you." "Surely,"
said the former, "Allah does accept of the sacrifice of those who are
righteous. 28 If you do stretch your hand against me, to slay me, it is not
for me to stretch my hand against you to slay you: for I do fear Allah, the
Cherisher of the worlds. 29 For me, I intend to let you draw on yourself
my sin as well as yours, for you will be among the companions of the
Fire, and that is the reward of those who do wrong." 30 The (selfish) soul
of the other led him to the murder of his brother: he murdered him, and
became (himself) one of the lost ones. 31 Then Allah sent a raven, who
scratched the ground, to show him how to hide the shame of his brother.
"Woe is me!" said he, "was I not even able to be as this raven, and to hide
the shame of my brother?" Then he became full of regrets—32 On that
account: We ordained for the Children of Israel that if any one slew a
person— unless it be for murder or for spreading mischief in the land—it
would be as if he slew the whole people: and if any one saved a life, it
would be as if he saved the life of the whole people. Then although there
came to them Our messengers with Clear Signs, yet, even after that, many
of them continued to commit excesses in the land.

33 The punishment of those who wage war against Allah and His
Messenger, and strive with might and main for mischief through the
land[6] is execution, or crucifixion, or the cutting off of hands and feet

---

6. For the double crime of treason against the State, combined with treason against Allah, as shown by overt crimes, four alternative punishments are mentioned, any one of which is to be applied according to circumstances. viz., execution (cutting off of the head), crucifixion, maiming, or exile. These were features of the Criminal Law then and for centuries afterwards, except that tortures such as "hanging, drawing, and quartering" in

from opposite sides, or exile from the land: that is their disgrace in this
world, and a heavy punishment is theirs in the Hereafter; 34 Except for
those who repent before they fall into your power: in that case, know that
Allah is Oft-Forgiving, Most Merciful.

SECTION 6

35 O you who believe! Do your duty to Allah, seek the means of approach
unto Him, and strive with might and main in His cause: that you may
prosper. 36 As to those who reject Faith,—if they had everything on earth,
and twice repeated, to give as ransom for the penalty of the Day of
Judgement, it would never be accepted of them; theirs would be a
grievous penalty. 37 Their wish will be to get out of the Fire, but never
will they get out therefrom: their penalty will be one that endures.

38 As to the thief,[7] male or female, cut off his or her hands: a punishment
by way of example, from Allah, for their crime: and Allah is Exalted in
power. 39 But if the thief repents after his crime, and amends his conduct,
Allah turns to him in forgiveness; for Allah is Oft-Forgiving, Most
Merciful. 40 Know you not that to Allah (alone) belongs the dominion of
the heavens and the earth? He punishes whom He pleases, and He
forgives whom He pleases: and Allah has power over all things.

41 O Messenger! Let not those grieve you, who race each other into
unbelief: (whether it be) among those who say "We believe" with their
lips but whose hearts have no faith; or it be among the Jews,—men who
will listen to any lie,—will listen even to others who have never so much
as come to you. They change the words from their (right) times and
places: they say, "If you are given this, take it, but if not, beware!" If any

---

English Law, and piercing of eyes and leaving the unfortunate victim exposed to a tropical sun, which was practised in Arabia, and all such tortures were abolished. In any case, sincere repentance before it was too late was recognised as a ground for mercy. [738]

7. Here we touch upon jurisprudence. The Canon Law jurists are not unanimous as to the value of the property stolen, which would involve the penalty of the cutting off of the hand. The majority hold that petty thefts (anything equal to, or less than the price of a shield), are exempt from this punishment. The general opinion is that only one hand should be cut off for the first theft, on the principle that "if thy hand or thy foot offend thee, cut them off, and cast them from thee" (Matt. xviii, 8). Apparently in the age of Jesus thieves were crucified (Matt. xxvii. 38). In the reign of the second Caliph, 'Umar, when there was famine for a short period of time, this punishment was suspended as the Muslim state could not guarantee to provide essentials to the citizens. – Ed.

one's trial is intended by Allah, you have no authority in the least for him
against Allah. For such—it is not Allah's will to purify their hearts. For
them there is disgrace in this world, and in the Hereafter a heavy
punishment. 42 (They are fond of) listening to falsehood, of devouring
anything forbidden. If they do come to you, either judge between them,
or decline to interfere. If you decline, they cannot hurt you in the least.
If you judge, judge in equity between them. For Allah loves those who
judge in equity. 43 But why do they come to you for decision, when they
have (their own) law before them?—therein is the (plain) command of
Allah; yet even after that, they would turn away. For they are not (really)
People of Faith.

SECTION 7

44 It was We Who revealed the Law (to Moses): therein was guidance and
light. By its standard have been judged the Jews, by the prophets who
bowed (as in Islam) to Allah's Will, by the rabbis and the doctors of law:
for to them was entrusted the protection of Allah's Book, and they were
witnesses thereto: therefore fear not men, but fear Me, and sell not My
Signs for a miserable price. If any do fail to judge by (the light of) what
Allah has revealed, they are (no better than) Unbelievers. 45 We ordained
therein for them: "Life for life, eye for eye, nose for nose, ear for ear,
tooth for tooth, and wounds equal for equal." But if any one remits the
retaliation by way of charity, it is an act of atonement for himself. And
if any fail to judge by (the light of) what Allah has revealed, they are (no
better than) wrong-doers.

46 And in their footsteps We sent Jesus the son of Mary, confirming the
Law that had come before him: We sent him the Gospel: therein was
guidance and light, and confirmation of the Law that had come before
him: a guidance and an admonition to those who fear Allah. 47 Let the
People of the Gospel judge by what Allah has revealed therein. If any do
fail to judge by (the light of) what Allah has revealed, they are (no better
than) those who rebel.

48 To you We sent the Scripture in truth, confirming the scripture that
came before it, and guarding it in safety: so judge between them by what
Allah has revealed, and follow not their vain desires, diverging from the
Truth that has come to you. To each among you have We prescribed a
Law and an open way. If Allah had so willed, He would have made you

a single people, but (His plan is) to test you in what He has given you: so
strive as in a race in all virtues. The goal of you all is to Allah; it is He
that will show you the truth of the matters in which you dispute; 49 And
this (He commands): Judge you between them by what Allah has
revealed, and follow not their vain desires, but beware of them lest they
beguile you from any of that (teaching) which Allah has sent down to
you. And if they turn away, be assured that for some of their crime it is
Allah's purpose to punish them. And truly most men are rebellious. 50 Do
they then seek after a judgement of (the days of) ignorance? But who, for
a people whose faith is assured, can give better judgement than Allah?

SECTION 8

51 O you who believe! Take not the Jews and the Christians for your
friends and protectors:[8] they are but friends and protectors to each other.
And he amongst you that turns to them (for friendship) is of them. Verily
Allah guides not a people unjust. 52 Those in whose hearts is a
disease—you see how eagerly they run about amongst them, saying: "We
do fear lest a change of fortune bring us disaster." Ah! Perhaps Allah will
give (thee) victory, or a decision according to His Will. Then will they
repent of the thoughts which they secretly harboured in their hearts. 53
And those who believe will say: "Are these the men who swore their
strongest oaths by Allah, that they were with you?" All that they do will
be in vain, and they will fall into (nothing but) ruin.

54 O you who believe! If any from among you turn back from his Faith,
soon will Allah produce a people whom He will love as they will love
Him,—lowly with the believers, mighty against the rejecters, fighting in
the Way of Allah, and never afraid of the reproaches of such as find fault.
That is the grace of Allah, which He will bestow on whom He pleases.
And Allah encompasses all, and He knows all things. 55 Your (real)
friends are (no less than) Allah, His Messenger, and the (fellowship of)
believers,—those who establish regular prayers and regular charity, and
they bow down humbly (in worship). 56 As to those who turn (for

---

8. That is, look not to them for help and comfort. They are more likely to combine against you than to help you. And this happened more than once in the lifetime of the Prophet, and in after-ages again and again. He who associates with them and shares their counsels must be counted as of them. The trimmer loses whichever way the wheel of fortune turns. [764]

friendship) to Allah, His Messenger, and the (fellowship of) believers,—it
is the fellowship of Allah that must certainly triumph.

SECTION 9

57 O you who believe! Take not for friends and protectors those who take
your religion for a mockery or sport,—whether among those who
received the Scripture before you, or among those who reject Faith; but
fear you Allah, if you have faith (indeed). 58 When you proclaim your call
to prayer, they take it (but) as mockery and sport; that is because they are
a people without understanding. 59 Say: "O People of the Book! Do you
disapprove of us for no other reason than that we believe in Allah, and the
Revelation that has come to us and that which came before (us), and
(perhaps) that most of you are rebellious and disobedient?" 60 Say: "Shall
I point out to you something much worse than this, (as judged) by the
treatment it received from Allah? Those who incurred the curse of Allah
and His wrath, those of whom some He transformed into apes and
swine,[9] those who worshipped evil;—these are (many times) worse in
rank, and far more astray from the even path!"

61 When they come to you, they say: "We believe": but in fact they enter
with a mind against Faith, and they go out with the same, but Allah
knows fully all that they hide. 62 Many of them do you see, racing each
other in sin and rancour, and their eating of things forbidden. Evil indeed
are the things that they do. 63 Why do not the rabbis and the doctors of
Law forbid them from their (habit of) uttering sinful words and eating
things forbidden? Evil indeed are their works.

64 The Jews say: "Allah's hand is tied up." Be their hands tied up and be
they accursed for the (blasphemy) they utter. Nay, both His hands are
widely outstretched: He gives and spends (of His bounty) as He pleases.
But the Revelation that comes to you from Allah increases in most of
them their obstinate rebellion and blasphemy. Amongst them We have
placed enmity and hatred till the Day of Judgement. Every time they
kindle the fire of war, Allah does extinguish it; but they (ever) strive to
do mischief on earth. And Allah loves not those who do mischief. 65 If
only the People of the Book had believed and been righteous, We should

---

9. For apes see 2:65. For men possessed by devils, and the devils being sent into swine, see Matt. viii. 28-32. [770]

indeed have blotted out their iniquities and admitted them to Gardens of
Bliss. 66 If only they had stood fast by the Law, the Gospel, and all the
Revelation that was sent to them from their Lord, they would have
enjoyed happiness from every side. There is from among them a party on
the right course: but many of them follow a course that is evil.

SECTION 10

67 O Messenger! Proclaim the (message) which has been sent to you from
your Lord. If you did not, you would not have fulfilled and proclaimed
His mission. And Allah will defend you from men (who mean mischief).
For Allah guides not those who reject Faith. 68 Say: "O People of the
Book! You have no ground to stand upon unless you stand fast by the
Law, the Gospel, and all the Revelation that has come to you from your
Lord." It is the Revelation that comes to you from your Lord, that
increases in most of them their obstinate rebellion and blasphemy. But
sorrow you not over (these) people without Faith. 69 Those who believe
(in the Qur'an), those who follow the Jewish (Scriptures), and the Sabians
and the Christians,—any who believe in Allah and the Last Day, and
work righteousness,—on them shall be no fear, nor shall they grieve. 70
We took the covenant of the Children of Israel and sent them messengers.
Every time, there came to them a messenger with what they themselves
desired not—some (of these) they called impostors, and some they (go so
far as to) slay. 71 They thought there would be no trial (or punishment);
so they became blind and deaf; yet Allah (in mercy) turned to them; yet
again many of them became blind and deaf. But Allah sees well all that
they do.

72 They do blaspheme who say: "Allah is Christ the son of Mary." But
said Christ: "O Children of Israel! Worship Allah, my Lord and your
Lord." Whoever joins other gods with Allah,—Allah will forbid him the
Garden, and the Fire will be his abode. There will for the wrong-doers be
no one to help! 73 They do blaspheme who say: "Allah is one of three in
a Trinity": for there is no god except One Allah. If they desist not from
their word (of blasphemy), verily a grievous penalty will befall the
blasphemers among them. 74 Why turn they not to Allah, and seek His
forgiveness? For Allah is Oft-Forgiving, Most Merciful. 75 Christ the son
of Mary was no more than a messenger; many were the messengers that

passed away before him. His mother was a woman of truth.[10] They had
both to eat their (daily) food. See how Allah does make His Signs clear
to them; yet see in what ways they are deluded away from the truth! 76
Say: "Will you worship, besides Allah, something which has no power
either to harm or benefit you? But Allah,—He it is that hears and knows
all things." 77 Say: "O People of the Book! Exceed not in your religion the
bounds (of what is proper), trespassing beyond the truth, nor follow the
vain desires of people who went wrong in times gone by,—who misled
many, and strayed (themselves) from the even Way."

SECTION 11

78 Curses were pronounced on those among the Children of Israel who
rejected Faith, by the tongue of David and of Jesus the son of Mary:
because they disobeyed and persisted in excesses. 79 Nor did they
(usually) forbid one another the iniquities which they committed: evil
indeed were the deeds which they did. 80 You see many of them turning
in friendship to the Unbelievers. Evil indeed are (the works) which their
souls have sent forward before them (with the result), that Allah's wrath
is on them, and in torment will they abide. 81 If only they had believed in
Allah, in the Messenger, and in what has been revealed to him, never
would they have taken them for friends and protectors, but most of them
are rebellious wrong-doers.

PART VII

82 Strongest among men in enmity to the believers will you find the Jews
and Pagans; and nearest among them in love to the believers will you find
those who say, "We are Christians": because amongst these are men
devoted to learning and men who have renounced the world, and they are
not arrogant. 83 And when they listen to the Revelation received by the
Messenger, you will see their eyes overflowing with tears, for they
recognise the truth: they pray: "Our Lord! We believe; write us down
among the witnesses. 84 What cause can we have not to believe in Allah
and the truth which has come to us, seeing that we long for our Lord to
admit us to the company of the righteous?" 85 And for this their prayer
has Allah rewarded them with Gardens, with rivers flowing underneath,

---

10. She never claimed that she was a mother of God, or that her son was God. She was a pious and virtuous woman. [783]

—their eternal home. Such is the recompense of those who do good. 86
But those who reject Faith and belie Our Signs,—they shall be
companions of Hell-fire.

SECTION 12

87 O you who believe! Make not unlawful the good things which Allah
has made lawful for you, but commit no excess: for Allah loves not those
given to excess. 88 Eat of the things which Allah has provided for you,
lawful and good; but fear Allah, in Whom you believe.

89 Allah will not call you to account for what is futile in your oaths, but He will call you to account for your deliberate oaths: for expiation, feed ten indigent persons, on a scale of the average for the food of your families; or clothe them; or give a slave his freedom. If that is beyond your means, fast for three days. That is the expiation for the oaths you have sworn. But keep to your oaths. Thus does Allah make clear to you His Signs, that you may be grateful.

90 O you who believe! Intoxicants and gambling, (dedication of) stones,[11]
and (divination by) arrows,[12] are an abomination,—of Satan's
handiwork: eschew such (abomination), that you may prosper. 91 Satan's
plan is (but) to excite enmity and hatred between you, with intoxicants
and gambling, and hinder you from the remembrance of Allah, and from
prayer: will you not then abstain? 92 Obey Allah, and obey the Messenger,
and beware (of evil): if you do turn back, know you that it is Our
Messenger's duty to proclaim (the message) in the clearest manner. 93 On
those who believe and do deeds of righteousness there is no blame for
what they ate (in the past), when they guard themselves from evil, and

11. *Cf.* 5:3. The stones there referred to were stone altars or stone columns on which oil was poured for consecration, or slabs on which meat was sacrificed to idols. Any idolatrous or superstitious practices are here condemned. The Arabic word *anṣāb* (translated here "stones") were objects of worship, and were common in Arabia before Islam. See Renan, *History of Israel*, Chapter iv, and *Corpus Inscriptionum Semiticarum,* Part I, p.154: Illustrations Nos. 123 and 123 *bis* are Phoenician columns of that kind, found in Malta. [794]

12. *Cf.* 5:3. The arrows there referred to were used for the division of meat by a sort of lottery or raffle. But arrows were also used for divination, *i.e.* for ascertaining lucky or unlucky moments, or learning the wishes of the heathen gods, as to whether men should undertake certain actions or not. All superstitions are condemned. [795]

believe, and do deeds of righteousness,—(or) again, guard themselves
from evil and believe,—(or) again, guard themselves from evil and do
good. For Allah loves those who do good.

SECTION 13

94 O you who believe! Allah does but make a trial of you in a little matter
of game well within reach of your hands and your lances, that He may
test who fears Him unseen: any who transgress thereafter, will have a
grievous penalty. 95 O you who believe! Kill not game while in the Sacred
Precincts or in pilgrim garb. If any of you does so intentionally, the
compensation is an offering, brought to the Ka'bah, of a domestic animal
equivalent to the one he killed, as adjudged by two just men among you;
or by way of atonement, the feeding of the indigent; or its equivalent in
fasts: that he may taste of the penalty of his deed. Allah forgives what is
past: for repetition Allah will exact from him the penalty. For Allah is
Exalted, and Lord of Retribution. 96 Lawful to you is the pursuit of
water-game and its use for food,—for the benefit of yourselves and those
who travel; but forbidden is the pursuit of land-game;—as long as you are
in the Sacred Precincts or in pilgrim garb. And fear Allah, to Whom you
shall be gathered back. 97 Allah made the Ka'bah, the Sacred House, an
asylum of security for men, as also the Sacred Months, the animals for
offerings, and the garlands that mark them: that you may know that Allah
has knowledge of what is in the heavens and on earth and that Allah is
well acquainted with all things. 98 Know you that Allah is strict in
punishment and that Allah is Oft-Forgiving, Most Merciful. 99 The
Messenger's duty is but to proclaim (the message). But Allah knows all
that you reveal and you conceal. 100 Say: "Not equal are things that are
bad and things that are good, even though the abundance of the bad may
dazzle you; so fear Allah, O you that understand; that (so) you may
prosper."

SECTION 14

101 O you who believe! Ask not questions about things which, if made
plain to you, may cause you trouble. But if you ask about things when the
Qur'an is being revealed, they will be made plain to you,[13] Allah will

---

13. Many secrets are wisely hidden from us. If the future were known to us, we need not necessarily be happy. In many cases we should be miserable. If the inner meaning of some

forgive those: for Allah is Oft-Forgiving, Most Forbearing. 102 Some
people before you did ask such questions,[14] and on that account lost their
faith. 103 It was not Allah who instituted (superstitions like those of) a
slit-ear she-camel, or a she-camel let loose for free pasture, or idol
sacrifices for twin-births in animals, or stallion-camels freed from work:
it is blasphemers who invent a lie against Allah; but most of them lack
wisdom. 104 When it is said to them: "Come to what Allah has revealed;
come to the Messenger": they say: "Enough for us are the ways we found
our fathers following." What! Even though their fathers were void of
knowledge and guidance? 105 O you who believe! Guard your own souls:
if you follow (right) guidance, no hurt can come to you from those who
stray. The goal of you all is to Allah: it is He that will show you the truth
of all that you do.

106 O you who believe! When death approaches any of you, (take)
witnesses among yourselves when making bequests,—two just men of
your own (brotherhood) or others from outside if you are journeying
through the earth, and the chance of death befalls you (thus). If you doubt
(their truth), detain them both after prayer, and let them both swear by
Allah: "We wish not in this for any worldly gain, even though the
(beneficiary) be our near relation: we shall hide not the evidence before
Allah: if we do, then behold! the sin be upon us!" 107 But if it gets known
that these two were guilty of the sin (of perjury), let two others stand
forth in their places,—nearest in kin from among those who claim a
lawful right: let them swear by Allah: "We affirm that our witness is truer
than that of those two, and that we have not trespassed (beyond the truth):
if we did, behold! the wrong be upon us!" 108 That is most suitable: that
they may give the evidence in its true nature and shape, or else they

---

of the things we see before our eyes were disclosed to us, it might cause a lot of mischief. Allah's Message, insofar as it is necessary for shaping our conduct, is plain and open to us. But there are many things too deep for us to understand, either individually or collectively. It would be foolish to pry into them, as some people tried to do in the time of the Prophet. Where a matter is mentioned in the Qur'an, we can reverently ask for its meaning. That is not forbidden. But we should never pass the bounds of (1) our own capacity to understand, (2) the time and occasion when we ask questions, and (3) the part of the Universal Plan which it is Allah's purpose to reveal to us. [807]

14. For example, the merely fractious questions asked of Moses by the Jews; 2:68-71. They showed that they had no faith. When foolish questions are asked, and there is no answer, it also shakes the faith of the foolish ones. [808]

would fear that other oaths would be taken after their oaths. But fear Allah, and listen (to His counsel): for Allah guides not a rebellious people.

SECTION 15

109 One day will Allah gather the messengers together, and ask: "What was the response you received (from men to your teaching)?" They will say: "We have no knowledge: it is You Who know in full all that is hidden."

110 Then will Allah say: "O Jesus the son of Mary! Recount My favour to you and to your mother. Behold! I strengthened you with the holy spirit, so that you did speak to the people in childhood and in maturity. Behold! I taught you the Book and Wisdom, the Law and the Gospel. And behold! you make out of clay, as it were, the figure of a bird, by My leave, and you breathes into it and it becomes a bird by My leave, and you heal those born blind, and the lepers, by My leave. And behold! you bring forth the dead by My leave. And behold! I did restrain the Children of Israel from (violence to) you when you did show them the clear Signs, and the unbelievers among them said: 'This is nothing but evident
magic.'[15]
111 And behold! I inspired the disciples to have faith in Me and My Messenger; they said, We have faith, and do you[16] bear witness that we bow to Allah as Muslims.'"

112 Behold! the disciples said: "O Jesus the son of Mary! Can your Lord send down to us a table set (with viands) from heaven?" Said Jesus: "Fear Allah,
if you have faith."
113 They said: "We only wish to eat thereof and satisfy our hearts, and to know that you have indeed told us the truth; and that we
ourselves may be witnesses to the miracle."
114 Said Jesus the son of Mary: "O Allah our Lord! Send us from heaven a table set (with viands), that there may be for us—for the first and the last of us—a solemn festival and a sign from You; and provide for our sustenance, for You are the best Sustainer (of
our needs)."
115 Allah said: "I will send it down unto you: but if any of you

---

15. According to Luke (xi. 15), when Christ performed the miracle of casting out devils, the Jews said he did it through the chief of the devils, *i.e.*, they accused him of black magic. No such miracle of casting out devils is mentioned in the Qur'an. But Moses, Jesus, and Muḥammad were all accused of magic and sorcery, by those who could find no other explanation of Allah's power. [822]

16. 'You' refers to Jesus, who is being addressed by his Disciples. *Cf.* 3:52. [823]

after that resists faith, I will punish him with a penalty such as I have not inflicted on any one among all the peoples."

SECTION 16

116 And behold! Allah will say: "O Jesus the son of Mary! Did you say
unto men, 'Worship me and my mother as gods in derogation of Allah'?"
He will say: "Glory to You! Never could I say what I had no right (to
say). Had I said such a thing, You would indeed have known it. You
know what is in my heart, though I know not what is in Yours. For You
know in full all that is hidden.[17] 117 Never said I to them aught except
what You did command me to say, to wit, 'Worship Allah, my Lord and
your Lord'; and I was a witness over them whilst I dwelt amongst them;
when You did take me up You were the Watcher over them, and You are
a witness to all things. 118 If You do punish them, they are Your servants:
if You do forgive them, You are the Exalted in power, the Wise." 119
Allah will say: "This is a day on which the truthful will profit from their
truth: theirs are Gardens, with rivers flowing beneath,—their eternal
Home: Allah well-pleased with them, and they with Allah: that is the
great salvation, (the fulfilment of all desires)." 120 To Allah does belong
the dominion of the heavens and the earth, and all that is therein, and it
is He Who has power over all things.□

17. Jesus disclaims here any knowledge of the sort of things that are attributed to him by those who take his name. The worship of Mary, though repudiated by the Protestants, was widely spread in the earlier Churches, both in the East and the West. [829]

Chapter 6

Sūrah Al-An'ām (The Cattle)

Translator's Introduction

This is a Sūrah of the late Makkan period. The greater part of it was revealed entire. Its place in the traditional order of arrangement is justified by logical considerations. We have already had the spiritual history of mankind, a discussion of the earlier revelations and how they were lost or corrupted, the regulations for the outer life of the new Community, and the points in which the Jews and Christians failed to maintain the central doctrine of Islam—the unity of Allah. The next step now taken is to expound this doctrine in relation to Pagan Arabia.

Summary—The nature of Allah and the method by which He reveals Himself are first expounded, and the weakness of Paganism is exposed (6:1-30.)

The emptiness of this world's life is contrasted with the evidence of Allah's wonderful handiwork in all Creation. It is He who holds the keys of the Unseen and the secrets of all that we see (6:31-60).

Allah's working in His world and His constant care and guidance should give a clue to His unity as it did to Abraham when he argued with those who worshipped false gods (6:61-82).

The succession of prophets after Abraham kept Allah's truth alive, and led up to the Qur'an. How can man fail to understand the majesty and goodness of Allah, when he contemplates Allah's creation and His Messages to mankind? (6:83-110).

The obstinate and the rebellious are deceived; they should be avoided. Though they turn for assistance to each other, they will receive due punishment (6:111-129).

Allah's decrees will come to pass, in spite of all the crimes and superstitions of the ungodly (6:130-150).

The better course is to follow the straight Way, the Way of Allah, as directed in the Qur'an, with unity and the full dedication of our lives (6:151-165).

*** *** ***

In the name of Allah,
Most Gracious, Most Merciful.

1 Praise be to Allah, Who created the heavens and the earth, and made the
Darkness and the Light. Yet those who reject Faith hold (others) as equal
with their Guardian-Lord. 2 He it is Who created you from clay, and then
decreed a stated term (for you). And there is in His presence another
determined term; yet you doubt within yourselves! 3 And He is Allah in
the heavens and on earth. He knows what you hide, and what you reveal,
and He knows the (recompense) which you earn (by your deeds).

4 But never did a single one of the Signs of their Lord reach them, but
they turned away therefrom. 5 And now they reject the truth when it
reaches them: but soon shall they learn the reality of what they used to
mock at. 6 See they not how many of those before them We did destroy?[1]
—generations We had established on the earth, in strength such as We
have not given to you—for whom We poured out rain from the skies in
abundance, and gave (fertile) streams flowing beneath their (feet): yet for
their sins We destroyed them, and raised in their wake fresh generations
(to succeed them).

7 If We had sent unto you a written (message) on parchment, so that they
could touch it with their hands, the Unbelievers would have been sure to
say: "This is nothing but obvious magic!" 8 They say: "Why is not an
angel sent down to him?" If We did send down an angel, the matter
would be settled at once, and no respite would be granted them. 9 If We
had made it an angel, We should have sent him as a man, and We should
certainly have caused them confusion in a matter which they have already
covered with confusion. 10 Mocked were (many) Messengers before you;
but their scoffers were hemmed in by the thing that they mocked.

SECTION 2

11 Say: "Travel through the earth and see what was the end of those who
rejected Truth." 12 Say: "To whom belongs all that is in the heavens and

---

1. Now comes the argument from history, looking backwards and forwards. If we are so short-sighted or arrogant as to suppose that we are firmly established on the earth, secure in our privileges, we are reminded of much greater nations in the past, who failed in their duty and were wiped out. In their fate we must read our own fate, if we fail likewise! But those without faith, instead of facing facts squarely, "turn away therefrom". [839]

on earth?" Say: "To Allah. He has inscribed for Himself (the rule of)
Mercy. That He will gather you together for the Day of Judgement, there
is no doubt whatever. It is they who have lost their own souls, that will
not believe. 13 To Him belongs all that dwells (or lurks) in the night and
the day. For He is the One Who hears and knows all things."[2] 14 Say:
"Shall I take for my protector any other than Allah, the Maker of the
heavens and the earth? And He it is that feeds but is not fed." Say: "Nay!
But I am commanded to be the first of those who bow to Allah (in Islam),
and be not you of the company of those who join gods with Allah." 15
Say: "I would, if I disobeyed my Lord, indeed have fear of the penalty of
a Mighty Day. 16 On that day, if the penalty is averted from any, it is due
to Allah's mercy; and that would be (salvation), the obvious fulfilment of
all desire.[3] 17 If Allah touch you with affliction, none can remove it but
He; if He touch you with happiness, He has power over all things. 18 He
is the irresistible, (watching) from above over His worshippers; and He
is the Wise, acquainted with all things." 19 Say: "What thing is most
weighty in evidence?" Say: "Allah is witness between me and you; this
Qur'an has been revealed to me by inspiration, that I may warn you and
all whom it reaches. Can you possibly bear witness that besides Allah
there is another god?" Say: "Nay! I cannot bear witness!" Say: "But in
truth He is the one Allah, and I truly am innocent of (your blasphemy of)
joining others with Him." 20 Those to whom We have given the Book

---

2. Throughout this section we have a sort of implied dialogue, of which one part is understood from the other part, which is expressed. In verse 11, we might have an imaginary objector saying: "Why go back to the past?" The answer is: "Well, travel through the world, and see whether it is not true that virtue and godliness exalt a nation, and the opposite are causes of ruin. Both the past and the present prove this." In verse 12, the objector may say: "But you speak of Allah's power?" The man of Allah replies: "Yes, but Mercy is Allah's own attribute, and knowledge and wisdom beyond what man can conceive." [846]

3. We continue the implied dialogue suggested in n. 94. In verse 14, the objector might say "But we have other interests in life than religion and Allah." "No," says the man of God. "My Creator is the one and only Power whose protection I seek; and I strive to be first in the race." In verse 15, the objector suggests: "Enjoy the good things of this life: it is short." The answer is: "The Hereafter is more real to me, and promises the true fulfilment of all desire; happiness or affliction comes not from the fleeting pettinesses or illusions of this life, but from the power and wisdom of Allah." In verse 19, the objector makes his final splash: "What evidence is there for all this?" The reply is: "I know it is true, for Allah's voice is within me, and my living Teacher awakens that voice; and there is the Book of Inspiration. Allah is one, and there is none other besides." [848]

know this as they know[4] their own sons. Those who have lost their own souls refuse therefore to believe.

SECTION 3

21 Who does more wrong than he who invents a lie against Allah or
rejects His signs? But verily the wrong-doers never shall prosper. 22 One
day shall We gather them all together: We shall say to those who ascribed
partners (to Us): "Where are the partners whom you (invented and) talked
about?" 23 There will then be (left) no subterfuge for them but to say: "By
Allah our Lord, we were not those who joined gods with Allah." 24
Behold! How they lie against their own souls! But the (lie) which they
invented will leave them[5] in the lurch. 25 Of them there are some who
(pretend to) listen to you; but We have thrown veils on their hearts, so
they understand it not,[6] and deafness in their ears; if they saw every one
of the Signs, not they will believe in them; in so much that when they
come to you, they (but) dispute with you; the Unbelievers say: "These are
nothing but tales of the ancients." 26 Others they keep away from it, and
themselves they keep away; but they only destroy their own souls, and
they perceive it not. 27 If you could but see when they are confronted with
the Fire! They will say: "Would that we were but sent back! Then would
we not reject the Signs of our Lord, but would be amongst those who
believe!" 28 Indeed, in their own (eyes) will become manifest what before
they concealed. But if they were returned, they would certainly relapse
to the things they were forbidden, for they are indeed liars. 29 And they
(sometimes) say: "There is nothing except our life on this earth, and
never shall we be raised up again." 30 If you could but see when they are
confronted with their Lord! He will say: "Is not this the truth?" They will
say: "Indeed, by our Lord!" He will say: "Taste you then the penalty,
because you rejected Faith."

---

4. *Cf.* 2:146. In both passages the pronoun translated 'this' may mean 'him' and refer to Muḥammad the Messenger of Allah, as some commentators think. [850]

5. The lies which they used to tell have now 'wandered' from the channels which they used to occupy, and left the liars in the lurch. In denying the indubitable fact that they took false gods, they admit the falsity of their notions and thus, are practically convicted out of their own mouths. [852]

6. *It* = The Qur'an. [852-A]

SECTION 4

31 Lost indeed are they who treat it as a falsehood that they must meet
Allah,— until on a sudden the hour is on them, and they say: "Ah! Woe
unto us that we took no thought of it"; for they bear their burdens on their
backs, and evil indeed are the burdens that they bear? 32 What is the life
of this world but play and amusement? But best is the home in the
Hereafter, for those who are righteous. Will you not then understand?

33 We know indeed the grief which their words do cause you: it is not you
they reject: it is the Signs of Allah, which the wicked condemn. 34
Rejected were the messengers before you: with patience and constancy
they bore their rejection and their wrongs, until Our aid did reach them:
there is none that can alter the Words (and decrees) of Allah. Already
have you received some account of those messengers. 35 If their spurning
is hard on your mind, yet if you were able to seek a tunnel in the ground
or a ladder to the skies and bring them a Sign,—(what good?). If it were
Allah's Will, He could gather them together unto true guidance: so be not
you amongst those who are swayed by ignorance (and impatience)! 36
Those who listen (in truth), be sure, will accept: as to the dead, Allah will
raise them up; then will they be turned unto Him.

37 They say: "Why is not a Sign sent down to him from his Lord?" Say:
"Allah has certainly power to send down a Sign: but most of them
understand not." 38 There is not an animal (that lives) on the earth, nor a
being that flies on its wings, but (forms part of) communities like you.
Nothing have we omitted from the Book, and they (all) shall be gathered
to their Lord in the end. 39 Those who reject Our Signs are deaf and
dumb,—in the midst of darkness profound: whom Allah wills, He leaves
to wander: whom He wills, He places on the Way that is straight. 40 Say:
"Think you to yourselves, if there come upon you the wrath of Allah, or
the Hour (that you dread), would you then call upon other than
Allah?—(reply) if you are truthful! 41 Nay,— on Him would you call, and
if it be His Will, He would remove (the distress) which occasioned your
call upon Him, and you would forget (the false gods) which you join with
Him!"

SECTION 5

42 Before you We sent (messengers) to many nations, and We afflicted the
nations with suffering and adversity, that they might learn humility. 43

When the suffering reached them from Us, why then did they not learn
humility? On the contrary their hearts became hardened, and Satan made
their (sinful) acts seem alluring to them. 44 But when they forgot the
warning they had received, We opened to them the gates of all (good)
things, until, in the midst of their enjoyment of Our gifts, suddenly, We
called them to account, when lo! they were plunged in despair! 45 Of the
wrong-doers the last remnant was cut off. Praise be to Allah, the
Cherisher of the Worlds.

46 Say: "Think you, if Allah took away your hearing and your sight, and
sealed up your hearts, who—a god other than Allah—could restore them
to you?" See how We explain the Signs by various (symbols); yet they
turn aside. 47 Say: "Think you, if the punishment of Allah comes to you,
whether suddenly or openly, will any be destroyed except those who do
wrong?" 48 We send the messengers only to give good news and to warn:
so those who believe and mend (their lives),—upon them shall be no fear,
nor shall they grieve. 49 But those who reject Our Signs,—them shall
punishment touch, for that they ceased not from transgressing." 50 Say: "I
tell you not that with me are the treasures of Allah,[7] nor do I know what
is hidden, nor do I tell you I am an angel. I but follow what is revealed to
me." Say: "Can the blind be held equal to the seeing?"[8] Will you then
consider not?

SECTION 6

51 Give this warning to those in whose (hearts) is the fear that they will be
brought (to judgement) before their Lord: except for Him they will have
no protector nor intercessor: that they may guard (against evil). 52 Send
not away those who call on their Lord morning and evening, seeking His

---

7. Literally, it might mean that the Prophets are not like vulgar soothsayers, who pretend to reveal hidden treasures, or peer into the future, or claim to be something of a different nature from men. But the meaning is wider: they deal out Allah's great treasures of truth, but the treasures are not theirs, but Allah's; they have greater insight into the higher things, but that insight is not due to their own wisdom, but to Allah's inspiration; they are of the same flesh and blood with us, and the sublimity of their words and teachings arises through Allah's grace—to them and to those who hear them. [867]

8. Therefore compare not the Prophets with ordinary men. The Prophets, although they be but men, have the higher light with them; therefore do not exact of them petty ephemeral services. Though they are men, they are not as other men, and are entitled to reverence. [868]

face. In naught are you accountable for them, and in naught are they accountable for you,[9] that you should turn them away, and thus be (one) of the unjust. 53 Thus did We try some of them by comparison[10] with others, that they should say: "Is it these then that Allah has favoured from amongst us?" Does not Allah know best those who are grateful? 54 When those come to you who believe in Our Signs, say: "Peace be on you: your Lord has inscribed for Himself (the rule[11] of) mercy: verily, if any of you did evil in ignorance, and thereafter repented, and amended (his conduct), lo! He is Oft-Forgiving, Most Merciful." 55 Thus do We explain the Signs in detail: that the way of the sinners may be shown up.

SECTION 7

56 Say: "I am forbidden to worship those—others than Allah—whom you call upon." Say: "I will not follow your vain desires: if I did, I would stray from the path, and be not of the company of those who receive guidance." 57 Say: "For me, I (work) on a Clear Sign from my Lord, but you reject Him. What you would see hastened, is not in my power. The command rests with none but Allah: He declares the truth, and He is the best of judges." 58 Say: "If what you would see hastened were in my power, the matter would be settled at once between you and me. But Allah knows best those who do wrong." 59 With Him are the keys of the

---

9. Some of the rich and influential Quraysh thought it beneath their dignity to listen to Muḥammad's teaching in company with the lowly disciples, who were gathered round him. But he refused to send away these lowly disciples, who were sincere seekers after Allah. From a worldly point of view they had nothing to gain from Muḥammad as he was himself poor, and he had nothing to gain from them as they had no influence. But that was no reason for turning them away; indeed their true sincerity entitled them to precedence over worldly men in the kingdom of Allah, Whose justice was vindicated in Muḥammad's daily life in this as in other things. If their sincerity was in any way doubtful, it involved no responsibility for the Preacher. [871]

10. Pursue the argument of the last note. The influential people who were not given precedence over the poor and humble but sincere disciples, were on their trial as to their spiritual insight. Their temptation was to say (and they said it in scorn): "We are much greater than they: has Allah then selected these lowly people for His teaching?" But that was so. And Allah knew best those who were grateful to Him for His guidance. [872]

11. The humble who had sincere faith, were not only not sent away to humour the wealthy: they were honoured and were given a special salutation, which has become the characteristic salutation in Islam: "Peace be on you",—the word peace, 'salām' having special affinity with the word '*Islām*'. In words they are given the salutation; in life they are promised Mercy by the special grace of Allah.[873]

unseen, the treasures that none knows but He. He knows whatever there
is on the land and in the sea. Not a leaf does fall but with His knowledge:
there is not a grain in the darkness (or depths) of the earth, nor anything
fresh or dry (green or withered), but is (inscribed) in a record clear (to
those who can read). 60 It is He Who does take your souls by night, and
has knowledge of all that you have done by day: by day does He raise
you up again; that a term appointed be fulfilled; in the end unto Him will
be your return; then will He show you the truth of all that you did.

SECTION 8

61 He is the Irresistible, (watching) from above over His worshippers, and
He sets guardians over you. At length, when death approaches one of
you, Our angels take his soul, and they never fail in their duty. 62 Then are
men returned unto Allah, their Protector, the (only) reality: is not His the
command? And He is the swiftest in taking account.

63 Say: "Who is it that delivers you from the dark recesses of land and sea,
when you call upon Him in humility and silent terror: 'If He only delivers
us from these (dangers), (we vow) we shall truly show our gratitude'?"
64 Say "It is Allah that delivers you from these and all (other) distresses:
and yet you worship false gods!" 65 Say: "He has power to send
calamities[12] on you, from above and below, or to cover you with
confusion in party strife, giving you a taste of mutual vengeance—each
from the other." See how We explain the Signs by various (symbols); that
they may understand. 66 But your people reject this, though it is the truth.
Say: "Not mine is the responsibility for arranging your affairs; 67 For
every message is a limit of time, and soon shall you know it."

68 When you see men engaged in vain discourse about Our Signs, turn
away from them unless they turn to a different theme. If Satan ever makes
you forget, then after recollection, sit not you in the company of those
who do wrong. 69 On their account no responsibility falls on the righteous,
but (their duty) is to remind them, that they may (learn to) fear Allah. 70
Leave alone those who take their religion to be mere play and
amusement, and are deceived by the life of this world. But proclaim (to
them) this (truth): that every soul delivers itself to ruin by its own acts: it

---

12. *Calamities from above and below*: such as storms and blizzards, torrential rain, etc., or earthquakes, floods, landslides, etc. [888]

will find for itself no protector or intercessor except Allah: if it offered
every ransom, (or reparation), none will be accepted: such is (the end of)
those who deliver themselves to ruin by their own acts: they will have for
drink (only) boiling water, and for punishment, one most grievous: for
they persisted in rejecting Allah.

SECTION 9

71 Say: "Shall we indeed call on others besides Allah,—things that can do
us neither good nor harm,—and turn on our heels after receiving
guidance from Allah?— like one whom the evil ones have made into a
fool, wandering bewildered through the earth, his friends calling, 'Come
to us', (vainly) guiding him to the path."

Say: "Allah's guidance is the (only) guidance, and we have been directed
to submit ourselves to the Lord of the Worlds;—72 To establish regular
prayers and to fear Allah: for it is to Him that we shall be gathered
together." 73 It is He Who created the heavens and the earth in true
(proportions): the day He said, "Be," behold! it is. His Word is the truth.
His will be the dominion the day the trumpet will be blown. He knows
the unseen as well as that which is open. For He is the Wise, well
acquainted (with all things).

74 Lo! Abraham said to his father Āzar: "Take you idols for gods? For I
see you and your people in manifest error." 75 So also did We show
Abraham the power and the laws of the heavens and the earth, that he
might (with understanding) have certitude. 76 When the night covered him
over, he saw a star: he said: "This is my Lord." But when it set, he said:
"I love not those that set." 77 When he saw the moon rising in splendour,
he said: "This is my Lord." But when the moon set, he said: "Unless my
Lord guide me, I shall surely be among those who go astray." 78 When he
saw the sun rising in splendour, he said: "This is my Lord; this is the
greatest (of all)." But when the sun set, he said: "O my people! I am
indeed free from your (guilt) of giving partners to Allah. 79 For me, I have
set my face, firmly and truly, towards Him Who created the heavens and
the earth, and never shall I give partners to Allah." 80 His people disputed
with him. He said: "(Come) you to dispute with me, about Allah, when
He (Himself) has guided me? I fear not (the beings) you associate with
Allah: unless my Lord wills, (nothing can happen). My Lord
comprehends in His knowledge all things. Will you not (yourselves) be

admonished? 81 How should I fear (the beings) you associate with Allah, when you fear not to give partners to Allah without any warrant having been given to you? Which of (us) two parties has more right to security? (Tell me) if you know. 82 It is those who believe and confuse not their beliefs with wrong—that are (truly) in security, for they are on (right) guidance."

SECTION 10

83 That was the reasoning about Us, which We gave to Abraham (to use) against his people: We raise whom We will, degree after degree: for your Lord is full of wisdom and knowledge. 84 We gave him Isaac and Jacob: all (three) we guided:[13] and before him, We guided Noah,[14] and among his progeny, David, Solomon, Job, Joseph, Moses, and Aaron: thus do We reward those who do good: 85 And Zakarīyā and John,[15] and Jesus and Elias: all in the ranks of the righteous: 86 And Ismā'īl and Elisha,[16]

13. We have now a list of eighteen Prophets in four groups, covering the great Teachers accepted among the three great religions based on Moses, Jesus, and Muḥammad. The first group to be mentioned is that of Abraham, his son Isaac, and Isaac's son, Jacob. Abraham was the first to have a Book. His Book is mentioned in 87:19, though it is now lost. They were therefore the first to receive Guidance in the sense of a Book. [903]

14. In the second group, we have the great founders of families, apart from Abraham, *viz.*, Noah, of the time of the Flood, David and Solomon, the real establishers of the Jewish monarchy; Job, who lived for 140 years, saw four generations of descendants, and was blessed at the end of his life with large pastoral wealth (Job xlii.16, 12); Joseph, who as Minister of State did great things in Egypt and was the progenitor of two Tribes; and Moses and Aaron, the leaders of the Exodus from Egypt. They led active lives and are called "doers of good". [904]

15. The third group consists not of men of action, but Preachers of Truth, who led solitary lives. Their epithet is: "the Righteous." They were mystic prophets and form a connected group round Jesus. Zakarīyā was the father of John the Baptist, the precursor of Jesus (3:37-41); and Jesus referred to John the Baptist as Elias: "this is Elias, which was for to come" (Matt. xi.14); and Elias is said to have been present and talked to Jesus at the Transfiguration on the Mount (Matt. xvii.3). Elias is the same as Elijah (*Cf.* 37:123). [905]

16. This is the last group, described as those "favoured above the nations." It consists of four men who all had great misfortunes to contend with, and were concerned in the clash of nations, but they kept in the path of Allah, and came through above the clash of nations. Ismā'īl was the eldest son of Abraham; when he was a baby, he and his mother had nearly died of thirst in the desert round Makkah; but they were saved by the well of Zamzam, and he became the founder of the new Arab nation. Elisha (Al-Yasa') succeeded to the mantle of the Prophet Elijah (same as Elias, see last note); he lived in troublesome times for both the Jewish kingdoms (of Judah and Israel); there were wicked kings, and other nations were

and Jonas, and Lot: and to all We gave favour above the nations: 87 (To
them) and to their fathers,[17] and progeny and brethren: We chose them,
and We guided them to a straight Way. 88 This is the guidance of Allah:
He gives that guidance to whom He pleases, of His worshippers. If they
were to join other gods with Him, all that they did would be vain for
them. 89 These were the men to whom We gave the Book, and authority,
and prophethood: if these (their descendants) reject them, behold! We
shall entrust their charge to a new people who reject them not. 90 Those
were the (prophets) who received Allah's guidance: copy the guidance
they received; say: "No reward for this do I ask of you: this is no less
than a message for the nations."

SECTION 11

91 No just estimate of Allah do they make when they say: "Nothing does
Allah send down to man (by way of revelation)". Say: "Who then sent
down the Book which Moses brought?—a light and guidance to man: but
you make it into (separate) sheets for show, while you conceal much (of
its contents): therein were you taught that which you knew not—neither
you nor your fathers." Say: "Allah (sent it down)"; then leave them to
plunge in vain discourse and trifling. 92 And this is a Book which We
have sent down, bringing blessings, and confirming (the revelations)
which came before it: that you may warn the Mother of Cities and all
around her. Those who believe in the Hereafter believe in this (Book),
and they are constant in guarding their prayers.[18]

93 Who can be more wicked than one who invents a lie against Allah, or
says, "I have received inspiration," when he has received none, or (again)

---

pressing in on them; but he performed many miracles, and some check was given to the enemies under his advice. The story of Jonah (Yūnus) is well known: he was swallowed by a fish or whale, but was saved by Allah's mercy: through his preaching, his city (Nineveh) was saved (10: 98). Lot was a contemporary and nephew of Abraham: when the city of Sodom was destroyed for its wickedness, he was saved as a just man (7:80-84). [906]

17. I take verse 87 to refer back to all the four groups just mentioned. [907]

18. Mother of Cities: Makkah, now the *Qiblah* and Centre of Islam. If this verse was (like the greater part of the Chapter) revealed in Makkah before the Hijrah, and before Makkah was made the *Qiblah* of Islam, Makkah was nonetheless the Mother of Cities, being traditionally associated with Abraham and with Adam and Eve (see 2:125 and 2:197).

'All around Makkah' would mean, the whole world if we look upon Makkah as the Centre. [913]

who says, "I can reveal the like of what Allah has revealed"? If you could
but see how the wicked (do fare) in the flood of confusion at death!—the
angels stretch forth their hands, (saying),"Yield up your souls: this day
shall you receive your reward,—a penalty of shame, for that you used to
tell lies against Allah, and scornfully to reject of His Signs!" 94 "And
behold! You come to Us bare and alone as We created you for the first
time: you have left behind you all (the favours) which We bestowed on
you: We see not with you your intercessors whom you thought to be
partners in your affairs: so now all relations between you have been cut
off, and your (pet) fancies have left you in the lurch!"

SECTION 12

95 It is Allah Who causes the seed-grain and the date-stone to split and
sprout. He causes the living to issue from the dead, and He is the One to
cause the dead to issue from the living. That is Allah: then how are you
deluded away from the truth? 96 He it is that cleaves the day-break (from
the dark): He makes the night for rest and tranquillity, and the sun and
moon for the reckoning (of time): such is the judgement and ordering of
(Him), the Exalted in Power, the Omniscient. 97 It is He Who makes the
stars (as beacons) for you, that you may guide yourselves, with their help,
through the dark spaces of land and sea: We detail Our Signs for people
who know. 98 It is He Who has produced you from a single person: here
is a place of sojourn and a place of departure: We detail Our Signs for
people who understand. 99 It is He Who sends down rain from the skies:
with it We produce vegetation of all kinds: from some We produce green
(crops), out of which We produce grain, heaped up (at harvest); out of the
date-palm and its sheaths (or spathes) (come) clusters of dates hanging
low and near: and (then there are) gardens of grapes, and olives, and
pomegranates, each similar (in kind) yet different (in variety): when they
begin to bear fruit, feast your eyes with the fruit and the ripeness thereof.
Behold! in these things there are Signs for people who believe.

100 Yet they make the *Jinns* equals[19] with Allah, though Allah did create

---

19. *Jinns*: who are they? In 18:50 we are told that Iblīs was one of the *Jinns*, and it is suggested that that was why he disobeyed the Command of Allah. But in that passage and other similar passages, we are told that Allah commanded the angels to bow down to Adam, and they obeyed except Iblīs. That implies that Iblīs had been of the company of angels. In many passages *Jinns* and men are spoken of together. In 55:14-15, man is stated to have

the *Jinns*; and they falsely, having no knowledge, attribute to Him sons and daughters. Praise and glory be to Him! (for He is) above what they attribute to Him!

SECTION 13

101 To Him is due the primal origin of the heavens and the earth: how can
He have a son when He has no consort? He created all things, and He has
full knowledge of all things. 102 That is Allah, your Lord! There is no god
but He, the Creator of all things: then worship you Him: and He has
power to dispose of all affairs. 103 No vision can grasp Him, but His grasp
is over all vision: He is above all comprehension, yet is acquainted with
all things.

104 "Now have come to you, from your Lord, proofs (to open your eyes):
if any will see, it will be for (the good of) his own soul; if any will be
blind, it will be to his own (harm): I am not (here) to watch over your
doings." 105 Thus do We explain the Signs by various (symbols): that they
may say, "You have taught (us) diligently," and that We may make the
matter clear to those who know. 106 Follow what you are taught by
inspiration from your Lord: there is no god but He: and turn aside from
those who join gods with Allah. 107 If it had been Allah's plan, they would
not have taken false gods: but We made you not one to watch over their
doings, nor are you set over them to dispose of their affairs.

108 Revile not you those whom they call upon besides Allah, lest they out
of spite revile Allah in their ignorance. Thus have We made alluring to
each people its own doings. In the end will they return to their Lord, and
We shall then tell them the truth of all that they did.

109 They swear their strongest oaths by Allah, that if a (special) Sign came
to them, by it they would believe. Say: "Certainly (all) Signs are in the
power of Allah: but what will make you (Muslims) realise that (even) if

---

been created from clay, while *Jinns* from a flame of fire. The root meaning of *janna, yajinnu,* is "to be covered or hidden," and *janna, yajunnu*, in the active voice, "to cover or hide," as in 6:76. (Both the Qur'an and *Hadīth* describe the Jinn as a definite species of living beings. They are created out of fire and like man, may believe or disbelieve, accept or reject guidance. The authoritative Islamic texts show that they are not merely a hidden force, or a spirit. They are personalised beings who enjoy a certain amount of free will and thus will be called to account. [929]

for your Lord is not unmindful of anything that they do. 133 Your Lord is
Self-sufficient, full of Mercy: if it were His Will, He could destroy you,
and in your place appoint whom He will as your successors, even as He
raised you up from the posterity of other people. 134 All that has been
promised unto you will come to pass: nor can you frustrate it (in the least
bit). 135 Say: "O my people! Do whatever you can: I will do (my part):
soon will you know who it is whose end will be (best) in the Hereafter:
certain it is that the wrong-doers will not prosper." 136 Out of what Allah
has produced in abundance in tilth and in cattle, they assigned Him a
share: they say, according to their fancies: "This is for Allah, and
this"—for our "partners"! But the share of their "partners" reaches not
Allah, whilst the share of Allah reaches their "partners"! Evil (and unjust)
is their assignment! 137 Even so, in the eyes of most of the Pagans, their
"partners" made alluring the slaughter of their children, in order to lead
them to their own destruction, and cause confusion in their religion. If
Allah had willed, they would not have done so: but leave alone them and
their inventions. 138 And they say that such and such cattle and crops are
taboo, and none should eat of them except those whom—so they
say—We wish; further, there are cattle forbidden to yoke or burden, and
cattle on which, (at slaughter), the name of Allah is not
pronounced;—inventions against Allah's name: soon will He requite
them for their inventions. 139 They say: "What is in the wombs of such
and such cattle is specially reserved (for food) for our men, and forbidden
to our women; but if it is still-born, then all have shares therein." For their
(false) attribution (of superstitions to Allah), He will soon punish them:
for He is full of wisdom and knowledge. 140 Lost are those who slay their
children, from folly, without knowledge, and forbid food which Allah has
provided for them, inventing (lies) against Allah. They have indeed gone
astray and heeded no guidance.

SECTION 17

141 It is He Who produces Gardens, with trellises and without, and dates,
and tilth with produce of all kinds, and olives and pomegranates, similar
(in kind) and different (in variety): eat of their fruit in their season, but
render the dues that are proper on the day that the harvest is gathered. But
waste not by excess: for Allah loves not the wasters. 142 Of the cattle are
some for burden and some for meat: eat what Allah has provided for you,
and follow not the footsteps of Satan: for he is to you an avowed enemy.

143 (Take) eight (head of cattle)[20] in (four) pairs: of sheep a pair, and of
goats a pair; say, has He forbidden the two males, or the two females, or
(the young) which the wombs of the two females enclose? Tell me with
knowledge if you are truthful: 144 Of camels a pair, and oxen a pair; say,
has He forbidden the two males, or the two females, or (the young) which
the wombs of the two females enclose?—were you present when Allah
ordered you such a thing? But who does more wrong than one who
invents a lie against Allah, to lead astray men without knowledge? For
Allah guides not people who do wrong.

SECTION 18

145 Say: "I find not in the message received by me by inspiration any
(meat) forbidden to be eaten by one who wishes to eat it, unless it be dead
meat, or blood poured forth,[21] or the flesh of swine,—for it is an
abomination—or, what is impious, (meat) on which a name has been
invoked, other than Allah's." But (even so), if a person is forced by
necessity, without wilful disobedience, nor transgressing due limits,
—your Lord is Oft-Forgiving, Most Merciful. 146 For those who followed
the Jewish Law, We forbade every (animal) with undivided hoof, and We
forbade them the fat of the ox and the sheep, except what adheres to their
backs or their entrails, or is mixed up with a bone: this in recompense for
their wilful disobedience: for We are true (in Our ordinances). 147 If they
accuse you of falsehood, say: "Your Lord is full of mercy all-embracing;"
but from people in guilt never will His wrath be turned back.

148 Those who give partners (to Allah) will say: "If Allah had wished, we
should not have given partners to Him, nor would our fathers; nor should we
have had any taboos." So did their ancestors argue falsely, until they tasted
of Our wrath. Say: "Have you any (certain) knowledge? If so, produce it
before us. You follow nothing but conjecture: you do nothing but lie." 149
Say: "With Allah is the argument that reaches home: if it had been His Will,
He could indeed have guided you all." 150 Say: "Bring forward your
witnesses to prove that Allah did forbid so and so." If they bring such
witnesses, be not you amongst them: nor follow you the vain desires of such

---

20. The superstitions referred to in 6:139 and 5:103 are further ridiculed in this verse and the next. [968]

21. *Blood poured forth*: as distinguished from blood adhering to flesh, or the liver, or such other internal organs purifying the blood. [969]

as treat Our Signs as falsehoods, and such as believe not in the Hereafter: for they hold others as equal with their Guardian-Lord.

SECTION 19

151 Say: "Come, I will rehearse what Allah has (really) prohibited you from":
Join not anything as equal with Him; be good to your parents; kill not your
children on a plea of want;—We provide sustenance for you and for
them;—come not nigh to shameful deeds, whether open or secret; take not
life, which Allah has made sacred, except by way of justice and law: thus
does He command you, that you may learn wisdom. 152 And come not nigh
to the orphan's property, except to improve it, until he attain the age of full
strength; give measure and weight with (full) justice;—no burden do We
place on any soul, but that which it can bear;—whenever you speak, speak
justly, even if a near relative is concerned; and fulfil the covenant of Allah:
thus does He command you, that you may remember. 153 Verily, this is My
Way, leading straight: follow it: follow not (other) paths: they will scatter
you about from His (great) path: thus does He command you, that you may
be righteous. 154 Moreover, We gave Moses the Book, completing (Our
favour) to those who would do right, and explaining all things in
detail,—and a guide and a mercy, that they might believe in the meeting with
their Lord.

SECTION 20

155 And this is a Book which We have revealed as a blessing: so follow it
and be righteous, that you may receive mercy: 156 Lest you should say:
"The Book was sent down to two Peoples[22] before us, and for our part,
we remained unacquainted with all that they learned by assiduous study;"
157 Or lest you should say: "If the Book had only been sent down to us,
we should have followed its guidance better than they." Now then has
come unto you a clear (Sign)[23] from your Lord,—and a guide and a
mercy: then who could do more wrong than one who rejects Allah's
Signs, and turns away therefrom? In good time shall We requite those
who turn away from Our Signs, with a dreadful penalty, for their turning
away. 158 Are they waiting to see if the angels come to them, or your Lord

22. That is, to the Jews and the Christians, who were the only two communities known to the Arabs as possessing revealed scriptures. [Muhammad Asad.—*Ed.*]

23. The Qur'an and the life and the teaching of Muḥammad, the Messenger of Allah. [982]

(Himself), or certain of the Signs of your Lord! The day that certain of
the Signs of your Lord do come, no good will it do to a soul to believe in
them then, if it believed not before nor earned righteousness through its
faith. Say: "Wait you: we too are waiting." 159 As for those who divide[24]
their religion and break up into sects, you have no part in them in the
least: their affair is with Allah: He will in the end tell them the truth of all
that they did. 160 He that does good shall have ten times as much to his
credit: he that does evil shall only be recompensed according to his evil:
no wrong shall be done unto (any of) them.

161 Say: "Verily, my Lord has guided me to a Way that is straight,—a
religion of right,—the path (trod) by Abraham the true in Faith, and he
(certainly) joined not gods with Allah." 162 Say: "Truly, my prayer and
my service of sacrifice, my life and my death, are (all) for Allah, the
Cherisher of the Worlds: 163 No partner has He: this am I commanded,
and I am the first of those who bow to His will."

164 Say: "Shall I seek for (my) Cherisher other than Allah, when He is the
Cherisher of all things (that exist)? Every soul draws the meed of its acts
on none but itself: no bearer of burdens can bear the burden of another.
Your goal in the end is towards Allah: He will tell you the truth of the
things wherein you disputed." 165 It is He Who has made you (His) agents,
inheritors of the earth: He has raised you in ranks, some above others:
that He may try you in the gifts He has given you: for your Lord is quick
in punishment: yet He is indeed Oft-Forgiving, Most Merciful.□

---

24. Divide their religion (*farraqū*) *i.e.*, (1) make a distinction between one part of it and another, take the part which suits them and reject the rest; or (2) have religion one day of the week and the world the rest of the six days; or (3) keep "religion in its right place," as if it did not claim to govern the whole life; make a sharp distinction between the secular and the religious, or (4) show a sectarian bias, seek differences in views, so as to break up the unity of Islam. [985]

Chapter 7

***Sūrah Al-A'rāf* (The Heights)**

Translator's Introduction

This Sūrah is closely connected, both chronologically and in respect of the argument, with the previous Sūrah. But it expounds the doctrine of revelation and man's spiritual history by illustrations from Adam onwards, through various Prophets, and the details of Moses' struggles, to the time of the Prophet Muḥammad, in whom Allah's revelation is completed.

Summary—The note, "learn from the past" is struck from the very beginning. The opposition of Evil to Good is illustrated by the story of Adam and Iblīs. Arrogance leads to rebellion; the rebel is jealous and tempts the natural man, who is warned against deceit and all excess (7:1-31).

If the warning is not heeded, the future penalties are indicated, while the privileges and the bliss and peace of the righteous are shown in a picture of the Hereafter, as well as in the power and goodness of Allah in the world that we see around us (7:32-58).

The story of Noah and the Flood, and the stories of Hūd, Ṣāliḥ, Lot, and Shu'ayb, all point to the lesson that the Prophets were resisted and rejected, but truth triumphed in the end, and evil was humbled, for Allah's Plan never fails (7:59-99).

The story of Moses is told in greater detail, not only in his struggles with Pharaoh, but in his preparation for his mission, and his struggles with his own rebellious people. Even from the time of Moses, the coming of the unlettered Prophet was foreshadowed (7:100-157).

But the people of Moses frequently lapsed from Allah's Law as promulgated to them, and transgressed Allah's Covenant, and they were scattered through the earth in sections (7:158-171).

The children of Adam have multiplied, but many of them have rejected truth and go by degrees to destruction in ways that they do not realise. The righteous listen to the Message of Allah, and serve Him in humility (7:172-206).

*** *** ***

In the name of Allah,
Most Gracious, Most Merciful.

1 *Alif Lām Mīm Ṣād.*[1] 2 A Book revealed unto you,—so let your heart be
oppressed no more by any difficulty on that account,—that with it you
might warn (the erring) and teach the Believers. 3 Follow (O men!) the
revelation given unto you from your Lord, and follow not, as friends or
protectors, other than Him. Little it is you remember of admonition.

4 How many towns have We destroyed (for their sins)? Our punishment
took them suddenly by night or while they slept for their afternoon rest.
5 When (thus) Our punishment took them, no cry did they utter but this:
"Indeed we did wrong."

6 Then shall We question those to whom Our Message was sent and those
by whom We sent it. 7 And verily, We shall recount their whole story
with knowledge, for We were never absent (at any time or place). 8 The
balance that day will be true (to a nicety): those whose scale (of good)
will be heavy, will prosper: 9 Those whose scale will be light, will find
their souls in perdition, for that they wrongfully treated Our Signs. 10 It
is We Who have placed you with authority on earth, and provided you
therein with means for the fulfilment of your life: small are the thanks
that you give!

SECTION 2

11 It is We Who created you and gave you shape; then We bade the angels
bow down to Adam, and they bowed down; not so Iblīs; he refused to be
of those who bow down. 12 (Allah) said: "What prevented you from
bowing down when I commanded you?" He said: "I am better than he:

---

1. This is a combination of four Abbreviated Letters. For Abbreviated Letters generally, see note to 2:1. The combination here includes the three letters *Alif, Lām, Mīm,* which occurred at the beginning of Sūrah 2, and are discussed in note 26 to 2:1.

The additional letter *Ṣād* occurs in combination here and in Sūrah 19, and by itself at the beginning of Sūrah 38, and nowhere else. The factor common to Sūrahs 7, 19, and 38 is that in each case the core of the Sūrah consists in the stories (*qaṣaṣ*) of the Prophets. In this Sūrah we have the stories of Noah, Hūd, Ṣāliḥ, Lot, Shu'ayb, and Moses, leading up to Muḥammad, and in Sūrah 38, the stories of David, Solomon, and Job similarly lead up to Muḥammad, occupying three out of the five sections. Sūrah 19 consists almost entirely of such stories. Can we understand *Ṣād* to stand for *qaṣas,* of which it is the most characteristic letter? In this Sūrah 7, we have the religious history of mankind traced—the Beginning, the Middle, and the End. [989]

You did create me from fire, and him from clay." 13 (Allah) said: "Get
you down from this: it is not for you to be arrogant here: get out, for you
are of the meanest (of creatures)." 14 He said: "Give me respite till the day
they are raised up." 15 (Allah) said: "Be you among those who have
respite." 16 He said: "Because You have thrown me out of the Way, lo! I
will lie in wait for them on Your straight Way: 17 Then will I assault them
from before them and behind them, from their right and their left: nor will
You find, in most of them, gratitude (for Your mercies)." 18 (Allah) said:
"Get out from this, disgraced and expelled. If any of them follow
you,—Hell will I fill with you all.

19 "O Adam! Dwell you and your wife in the Garden, and enjoy (its good
things) as you wish: but approach not this tree, or you run into harm and
transgression." 20 Then began Satan to whisper suggestions to them,
bringing openly before their minds all their shame that was hidden from
them (before): he said: "Your Lord only forbade you this tree, lest you
should become angels or such beings as live for ever." 21 And he swore
to them both, that he was their sincere adviser. 22 So by deceit he brought
about their fall: when they tasted of the tree, their shame became manifest
to them, and they began to sew together the leaves of the Garden over
their bodies. And their Lord called unto them: "Did I not forbid you that
tree, and tell you that Satan was an avowed enemy unto you?" 23 They
said: "Our Lord! We have wronged our own souls: if You forgive us not
and bestow not upon us Your Mercy, we shall certainly be lost." 24
(Allah) said: "Get you down, with enmity between yourselves. On earth
will be your dwelling-place and your means of livelihood,—for a time."
25 He said: "Therein shall you live, and therein shall you die; but from it
shall you be taken out (at last)."

SECTION 3

26 O you Children of Adam! We have bestowed raiment upon you to
cover your shame, as well as to be an adornment to you. But the raiment
of righteousness,—that is the best. Such are among the Signs of Allah,
that they may receive admonition! 27 O you Children of Adam! Let not
Satan seduce you, in the same manner as he got your parents out of the
Garden, stripping them of their raiment, to expose their shame: for he and
his tribe watch you from a position where you cannot see them: We made
the Evil Ones friends (only) to those without Faith.

28 When they do aught that is shameful, they say: "We found our fathers
doing so"; and "Allah commanded us thus": Say: "Nay, Allah never
commands what is shameful: do you say of Allah what you know not?"
29 Say: "My Lord has commanded justice; and that you set your whole
selves (to Him) at every time and place of prayer, and call upon Him,
making your devotion sincere as in His sight: such as He created you in
the beginning, so shall you return." 30 Some He has guided: others have
(by their choice) deserved the loss of their way; in that they took the Evil
Ones, in preference to Allah, for their friends and protectors, and think
that they receive guidance. 31 O Children of Adam! Wear your beautiful
apparel at every time and place of prayer: eat and drink: but waste not by
excess, for Allah loves not the wasters.

SECTION 4

32 Say: Who has forbidden the beautiful (gifts) of Allah, which He has
produced for His servants, and the things, clean and pure, (which He has
provided) for sustenance? Say: They are, in the life of this world, for
those who believe, (and) purely for them on the Day of Judgement. Thus
do We explain the Signs in detail for those who understand. 33 Say: The
things that my Lord has indeed forbidden are: shameful deeds, whether
open or secret; sins and trespasses against truth or reason; assigning of
partners to Allah, for which He has given no authority; and saying things
about Allah of which you have no knowledge.

34 To every people is a term appointed: when their term is reached, not an
hour can they cause delay, nor (an hour) can they advance (it in
anticipation). 35 O you Children of Adam! Whenever there come to you
messengers from amongst you, rehearsing My Signs unto you,—those
who are righteous and mend (their lives),—on them shall be no fear nor
shall they grieve. 36 But those who reject Our Signs and treat them with
arrogance,—they are companions of the Fire, to dwell therein (for ever).
37 Who is more unjust than one who invents a lie against Allah or rejects
His Signs? For such, their portion appointed must reach them from the
Book (of decrees): until, when our messengers (of death) arrive and take
their souls, they say: "Where are the things that you used to invoke
besides Allah?" They will reply, "They have left us in the lurch," and
they will bear witness against themselves, that they had rejected Allah. 38
He will say: "Enter you in the company of the peoples who passed away

before you—men and *Jinns,*—into the Fire." Every time a new people
enters, it curses its sister-people (that went before), until they follow each
other, all into the Fire. Says the last about the first: "Our Lord! It is these
that misled us: so give them a double penalty in the Fire." He will say:
"Doubled for all": but this you do not understand. 39 Then the first will
say to the last: "See then! No advantage have you over us; so taste you of
the Penalty for all that you did!"

SECTION 5

40 To those who reject Our Signs and treat them with arrogance, no
opening will there be of the gates of heaven, nor will they enter the
Garden, until the camel can pass through the eye of the needle: such is
Our reward for those in sin. 41 For them there is Hell, as a couch (below)
and folds and folds of covering above: such is Our requital of those who
do wrong.

42 But those who believe and work righteousness,—no burden do We
place on any soul, but that which it can bear,—they will be companions
of the Garden, therein to dwell (for ever). 43 And We shall remove from
their hearts any lurking sense of injury;—beneath them will be rivers
flowing;—and they shall say: "Praise be to Allah, Who has guided us to
this (felicity): never could we have found guidance, had it not been for
the Guidance of Allah: indeed it was the truth, that the messengers of our
Lord brought unto us." And they shall hear the cry: "Behold! the Garden
before you! You have been made[2] its inheritors, for your deeds (of
righteousness)." 44 The companions of the Garden will call out to the
companions of the Fire: "We have indeed found the promises of our Lord
to us true: Have you also found your Lord's promises true?" They shall
say, "Yes"; but a crier shall proclaim between them: "The curse of Allah
is on the wrong-doers;—45 Those who would hinder (men) from the path
of Allah and would seek in it something crooked: they were those who
denied the Hereafter." 46 Between them shall be a veil, and on the heights

2. Jesus said: "Blessed are the meek, for they shall inherit the earth": Matt. v. 5. Here we are told: blessed are the righteous, for they shall inherit the kingdom of Heaven. The stress here is on actual practical deeds of righteousness: whether they find their rewards on earth or not is immaterial: their attention is directed to an infinitely greater reward, the kingdom of Heaven. In the Sermon on the Mount this is promised to the "poor in spirit": Matt. v. 3. [1022]

will be men who would know every one by his marks: they will call out
to the companions of the Garden, "Peace on you": they will not have
entered, but they will have an assurance (thereof). 47 When their eyes
shall be turned towards the companions of the Fire, they will say: "Our
Lord! Send us not to the company of the wrong-doers."

SECTION 6

48 The men on the heights will call to certain men whom they will know
from their marks, saying: "Of what profit to you were your hoards and
your arrogant ways? 49 Behold! Are these not the men whom you swore
that Allah with His Mercy would never bless? Enter you the Garden: no
fear shall be on you, nor shall you grieve." 50 The companions of the Fire
will call to the companions of the Garden: "Pour down to us water or
anything that Allah does provide for your sustenance." They will say:
"Both these things has Allah forbidden to those who rejected Him;—51
Such as took their religion to be mere amusement and play, and were
deceived by the life of the world." That day shall We forget them as they
forgot the meeting of this day of theirs, and as they were wont to reject
Our Signs. 52 For We had certainly sent unto them a Book, based on
knowledge, which We explained in detail,—a guide and a mercy to all
who believe. 53 Do they just wait for the final fulfilment of the event? On
the day the event is finally fulfilled, those who disregarded it before will
say: "The messengers of our Lord did indeed bring true (tidings). Have
we no intercessors now to intercede on our behalf? Or could we be sent
back? Then should we behave differently from our behaviour in the past."
In fact they will have lost their souls, and the things they invented will
leave them in the lurch.

SECTION 7

54 Your Guardian-Lord is Allah, Who created the heavens and the earth
in six days, and is firmly established on the throne (of authority): He
draws the night as a veil over the day, each seeking the other in rapid
succession: He created the sun, the moon, and the stars, (all) governed by
laws under His command. Is it not His to create and to govern? Blessed
be Allah, the Cherisher and Sustainer of the Worlds! 55 Call on your Lord
with humility and in private: for Allah loves not those who trespass
beyond bounds. 56 Do no mischief on the earth, after it has been set in
order, but call on Him with fear and longing (in your hearts): for the

Mercy of Allah is (always) near to those who do good. 57 It is He Who
sends the winds like heralds of glad tidings, going before His Mercy:
when they have carried the heavy-laden clouds, We drive them to a land
that is dead, make rain to descend thereon, and produce every kind of
harvest therewith: thus shall We raise up the dead: perchance you may
remember. 58 From the land that is clean and good, by the Will of its
Cherisher, springs up produce, (rich) after its kind: but from the land that
is bad, springs up nothing but that which is niggardly: thus do We explain
the Signs by various (symbols) to those who are grateful.

SECTION 8

59 We sent Noah to his people. He said: "O my people! Worship Allah!
You have no other god but Him. I fear for you the punishment of a
dreadful day!" 60 The leaders of his people said: "Ah! We see you
evidently wandering (in mind)." 61 He said: "O my people! No wandering
is there in my (mind): on the contrary I am a messenger from the Lord
and Cherisher of the Worlds! 62 I but fulfil towards you the duties of my
Lord's mission: sincere is my advice to you, and I know from Allah
something that you know not. 63 Do you wonder that there has come to
you a message from your Lord, through a man of your own people, to
warn you,—so that you may fear Allah and haply receive His Mercy?"
64 But they rejected him, and We delivered him, and those with him, in
the Ark: but We overwhelmed in the Flood those who rejected Our Signs.
They were indeed a blind people!

SECTION 9

65 To the 'Ād people,[3] (We sent) Hūd, one of their (own) brethren: he

---

3. The 'Ād people, with their prophet Hūd, are mentioned in many places. See especially 26:123-140, and 46:21-26. Their story belongs to Arabian tradition. Their eponymous ancestor 'Ād was fourth in generation from Noah, having been a son of 'Aus, the son of Aram, the son of Sām, the son of Noah. They occupied a large tract of country in Southern Arabia, extending from 'Umān at the mouth of the Persian Gulf to Ḥadramawt and Yemen at the southern end of the Red Sea. The people were tall in stature and were great builders. Probably the long, winding tracts of sands (*aḥqāf*) in their dominions (46:21) were irrigated with canals. They forsook the true God, and oppressed their people. A three-year famine visited them, but yet they took no warning. At length a terrible blast of wind destroyed them and their land, but a remnant, known as the second 'Ād or the Thamūd (see below) were saved, and afterwards suffered a similar fate for their sins.

The tomb of the Prophet Hūd (*qabr Nabī Hūd*) is still traditionally shown in Hadramawt, latitude 15°N and longitude 49½°E, about 90 miles north of Mukalla. There are ruins and

said: "O my people! Worship Allah! You have no other god but Him.
Will you not fear (Allah)?" 66 The leaders of the Unbelievers among his
people said: "Ah! We see you are an imbecile!" and "We think you are
a liar!" 67 He said: "O my people! I am no imbecile, but (I am) a
messenger from the Lord and Cherisher of the Worlds! 68 I but fulfil
towards you the duties of my Lord's mission: I am to you a sincere and
trustworthy adviser. 69 Do you wonder that there has come to you a
Message from your Lord through a man of your own people, to warn
you? Call in remembrance that He made you inheritors after the people
of Noah, and gave you a stature tall among the nations. Call in
remembrance the benefits (you have received) from Allah: that so you
may prosper." 70 They said: "Come you to us, that we may worship Allah
alone, and give up the cult of our fathers? Bring us what you threaten us
with, if so be that you tell the truth!" 71 He said: "Punishment and wrath
have already come upon you from your Lord: dispute you with me over
names which you have devised—you and your fathers,—without
authority from Allah? Then wait: I am amongst you, also waiting." 72 We
saved him and those who adhered to him. By Our Mercy, and We cut off
the roots of those who rejected Our Signs and did not believe.

SECTION 10

73 To the Thamūd people[4] (We sent) Ṣāliḥ, one of their own brethren: he

---

inscriptions in the neighbourhood. There is an annual pilgrimage to it in the month of Rajab. See *Hadramawt, Some of its Mysteries Unveiled*, by D. van der Meulen and H.von Wissmann, Leiden, 1932. [1040]

4. The Thamūd people were the successors to the culture and civilisation of the 'Ād people, for whom see n.119 and 7:65 above. They were cousins to the `Ād, apparently a younger branch of the same race. Their story also belongs to Arabian tradition, according to which their eponymous ancestor Thamūd was a son of 'Ābir (a brother of Aram), the son of Sām, the son of Noah. Their seat was in the northwest corner of Arabia (Arabia Petraea), between Madīnah and Syria. It included both rocky country (15:80), and the spacious fertile valley (*Wādī*) and plains country of Qurā, which begins just north of the City of Madīnah and was traversed by the Hijāz Railway. When the Holy Prophet in the 9th year of the Hijrah led his expedition to Tabūk (about 400 miles north of Madīnah) against the Roman forces, on a reported Roman invasion from Syria, he and his men came across the archaeological remains of the Thamūd. The recently excavated rock city of Petra, near Ma'ān, may go back to the Thamūd, though its architecture has many features connecting it with Egyptian and Graeco-Roman culture overlaying what is called by European writers Nabataean culture. Who were the Nabataeans? They were an old Arab tribe which played a considerable part in history after they came into conflict with Antigonus I in 312 B.C. Their capital was Petra, but they extended their territory right up to the Euphrates. In 85 B.C. they were lords of Damascus under their king Ḥāritha (Aretas of Roman

said: "O my people! Worship Allah; you have no other god but Him.
Now has come unto you a clear (Sign) from your Lord! This she-camel
of Allah is a Sign unto you: so leave her to graze in Allah's earth, and let
her come to no harm, or you shall be seized with a grievous
punishment.[5] 74 And remember how He made you inheritors after the
'Ād people and gave you habitations in the land: you build for yourselves
palaces and castles in (open) plains, and carve out homes in the
mountains; so bring to remembrance the benefits (you have received)
from Allah, and refrain from evil and mischief on the earth." 75 The
leaders of the arrogant party among his people said to those who were
reckoned powerless—those among them who believed: "Know you
indeed that Ṣāliḥ is a messenger from his Lord?" They said: "We do
indeed believe in the revelation which has been sent through him." 76 The
arrogant party said: "For our part, we reject what you believe in." 77 Then
they hamstrung the she-camel, and insolently defied the order of their
Lord, saying: "O Ṣāliḥ! Bring about your threats, if you are a messenger
(of Allah)!" 78 So the earthquake took them unawares, and they lay
prostrate in their homes in the morning! 79 So Ṣāliḥ left them, saying: "O
my people! I did indeed convey to you the message for which I was sent
by my Lord: I gave you good counsel, but you love not good

---

history). For some time they were allies of the Roman Empire and held the Red Sea littoral. The Emperor Trajan reduced them and annexed their territory in A.C. 105. The Nabataeans succeeded the Thamūd of Arabian tradition. The Thamūd are mentioned by name in an inscription of the Assyrian King Sargon, dated 715 B.C., as a people of Eastern and Central Arabia (*Encyclopaedia of Islam*).

With the advance of material civilisation, the Thamūd people became godless and arrogant, and were destroyed by an earthquake. Their prophet and warner was Ṣāliḥ, and the crisis in their history is connected with the story of a wonderful she-camel: see next note. [1043]

5. The story of this wonderful she-camel, that was a sign to the Thamūd, is variously told in tradition. We need not follow the various versions in the traditional story. What we are told in the Qur'an is: that (1) she was a Sign or Symbol, which the Prophet Ṣāliḥ, used for a warning to the haughty oppressors of the poor; (2) there was scarcity of water, and the arrogant or privileged classes tried to prevent the access of the poor or their cattle to the springs, while Ṣāliḥ intervened on their behalf (26:155, 54:28); (3) like water, pasture was considered a free gift of nature, in this spacious earth of Allah (7:73), but the arrogant ones tried to monopolise the pasture also; (4) this particular she-camel was made a test case (54:27) to see if the arrogant ones would come to reason; (5) the arrogant ones, instead of yielding to the reasonable rights of the people, hamstrung the poor she-camel and slew her, probably secretly (91:14, 54:29); the cup of their iniquities was full, and the Thamūd people were destroyed by a dreadful earthquake, which threw them prone on the ground and buried them with their houses and their fine buildings. [1044]

counsellors!"

80 We also (sent) Lūṭ:[6] he said to his people: "Do you commit lewdness
such as no people in creation (ever) committed before you? 81 For you
practise your lusts on men in preference to women: you are indeed a
people transgressing beyond bounds." 82 And his people gave no answer
but this: they said, "Drive them out of your city: these are indeed men
who want to be clean and pure!" 83 But We saved him and his family,
except his wife: she was of those who lagged behind. 84 And We rained
down on them a shower (of brimstone): then see what was the end of
those who indulged in sin and crime!

SECTION 11

85 To the Madyan people[7] We sent Shu'ayb,[8] one of their own

---

6. Lūṭ is the Lot of the English Bible. His story is biblical, but freed from some shameful features which are a blot on the biblical narrative (*e.g.*, see Gen. xix. 30-36). He was a nephew of Abraham, and was sent as a Prophet and warner to the people of Sodom and Gomorrah, cities utterly destroyed for their unspeakable sins. They cannot be exactly located, but it may be supposed that they were somewhere in the plain east of the Dead Sea. The story of their destruction is told in the 19th chapter of Genesis. Two angels in the shape of handsome young men came to Lot in the evening and became his guests by night. The inhabitants of Sodom in their lust for unnatural crime invaded Lot's house but were repulsed. In the morning, the angels warned Lot to escape with his family. "Then the Lord rained upon Sodom and upon Gomorrah brimstone and fire from the Lord out of heaven: and He overthrew those cities, and all the plain, and all the inhabitants of the cities, and that which grew upon the ground. But his wife looked back from behind him, and she became a pillar of salt." (Gen. xix. 24-26).

Note that Lūṭ's people are the people to whom he is sent on a mission. He was not one of their own brethren, as was Ṣāliḥ or Shu'ayb. But he looked upon his people as his brethren (50:13), as a man of God always does. [1049]

7. 'Madyan' may be identified with 'Midian.' Midian and the Midianites are frequently mentioned in the Old Testament, though the particular incident here mentioned belongs to Arab rather than to Jewish tradition. The Midianites were of Arab race, though, as neighbours of the Canaanites, they probably intermixed with them. They were a wandering tribe; it was Midianite merchants to whom Joseph was sold into slavery, and who took him to Egypt. Their principal territory in the time of Moses was in the northeast of the Sinai Peninsula, and east of the Amalekites. Under Moses the Israelites waged a war of extermination against them: they slew the kings of Midian, slaughtered all the males, burnt their cities and castles, and captured their cattle (Num. xxxi. 7-11). This sounds like total extermination. Yet a few generations afterwards, they were so powerful that the Israelites for their sins were delivered into the captivity of the Midianites for seven years: both the Midianites and their camels were without number: and the Israelites hid from them in "dens... caves, and strongholds" (Judges vii. 1-6). Gideon destroyed them again, (Judges

brethren: he said: "O my people! Worship Allah; you have no other god but Him. Now has come unto you a clear (Sign) from your Lord! Give just measure and weight, nor withhold from the people the things that are their due; and do no mischief on the earth after it has been set in order: that will be best for you, if you have Faith. 86 And squat not on every road, breathing threats, hindering from the path of Allah those who believe in Him, and seeking in it something crooked; but remember how you were little, and He gave you increase. And hold in your mind's eye what was the end of those who did mischief.[9] 87 And if there is a party

---

vii. 1-25), say about two centuries after Moses. As the decisive battle was near the hill of Moreh, not far south of Mount Tabor, we may localise the Midianites on this occasion in the northern parts of the Jordan valley, at least 200 miles north of the Sinai Peninsula.

This and the previous destruction under Moses were local, and mention no *town* of Midian. In later times there was a town of Madyan on the east side of the Gulf of `Aqaba. It is mentioned in Josephus, Eusebius, and Ptolemy: (*Encyclopaedia of Islam.*) Then it disappears from geography. In Muslim times it was a revived town with quite a different kind of population, but it never flourished. The Midianites disappeared from history. [1053]

8. Shu'ayb belongs to Arab rather than to Jewish tradition, to which he is unknown. His identification with Jethro, the father-in-law of Moses, has no warrant, and I reject it. There is no similarity either in names or incidents, and there are chronological difficulties. If, as the commentators tell us, Shu`ayb was in the fourth generation from Abraham, being a great-grandson of Madyan (a son of Abraham), he would be only about a century from the time of Abraham, whereas the Hebrew Bible would give us a period of four to six centuries between Abraham and Moses. The mere fact that Jethro was a Midianite and that another name, Hobab, is mentioned for a father-in-law of Moses in Num. x. 29, is slender ground for identification. As the Midianites were mainly a nomad tribe, we need not be surprised that their destruction in one or two settlements did not affect their life in wandering sections of the tribe in other geographical regions. Shu'ayb's mission was apparently in one of the settled towns of the Midianites, which was completely destroyed by an earthquake (7:91). If this happened in the century after Abraham, there is no difficulty in supposing that they were again a numerous tribe three or five centuries later, in the time of Moses (see last note). As they were a mixed wandering tribe, both their resilience and their eventual absorption can be easily understood. But the destruction of the settlement or settlements (if the Wood or Ayka was a separate settlement, see 15:78) to which Shu'ayb was sent to preach was complete, and no traces of it now remain. [1054]

9. The Midianites were in the path of a commercial highway of Asia, *viz.*, that between two such opulent and highly organised nations as Egypt and the Mesopotamian group comprising Assyria and Babylonia. Their besetting sins are thus characterised here: (1) giving short measure or weight, whereas the strictest commercial probity is necessary for success, (2) a more general form of such fraud, depriving people of rightful dues, (3) producing mischief and disorder, whereas peace and order had been established (again in a literal as well as a metaphorical sense); (4) not content with upsetting settled life, taking

among you who believes in the Message with which I have been sent, and
a party which does not believe, hold yourselves in patience until Allah
does decide between us: for He is the best to decide."

PART IX

88 The leaders, the arrogant party among his people, said: "O Shu'ayb!
We shall certainly drive you out of our city—(you) and those who believe
with you; or else you (you and they) shall have to return to our ways and
religion." He said: "What! Even though we do detest (them)? 89 We
should indeed invent a lie against Allah, if we returned to your ways after
Allah has rescued us therefrom; nor could we by any manner of means
return thereto unless it be as in the Will and plan of Allah, Our Lord. Our
Lord can reach out to the utmost recesses of things by His knowledge. In
Allah is our trust. Our Lord! Decide You between us and our people in
truth, for You are the best to decide." 90 The leaders, the Unbelievers
among his people, said: "If you follow Shu'ayb, be sure then you are
ruined!" 91 But the earthquake took them unawares, and they lay prostrate
in their homes before the morning! 92 The men who rejected Shu'ayb
became as if they had never been in the homes where they had flourished:
the men who rejected Shu'ayb—it was they who were ruined! 93 So
Shu'ayb left them, saying: "O my people! I did indeed convey to you the
Messages for which I was sent by my Lord: I gave you good counsel, but
how shall I lament over a people who refuse to believe!"[10]

---

to highway robbery, literally as well as (5) metaphorically, in two ways, *viz.*, cutting off people from access to the worship of Allah, and abusing religion and piety for crooked purposes, *i.e.*, exploiting religion itself for their crooked ends, as when a man builds houses of prayer out of unlawful gains or ostentatiously gives charity out of money which he has obtained by force or fraud, etc. After setting out this catalogue of besetting sins, Shu'ayb makes two appeals to the past: (1) You began as an insignificant tribe, and by Allah's favour you increased and multiplied in numbers and resources; do you not then owe a duty to Allah to fulfil His Law? (2) What was the result in the case of those who fell into sin? Will you not take warning by their example?

So Shu'ayb began his argument with faith in Allah as the source of all virtue, and ended it with destruction as the result of all sin. In the next verse he pleads with them to end their controversies and come to Allah. [1055]

10. Can we get any idea of the chronological place of the destruction of the Midianites? In 7:85 we have discussed the geographical aspects. The following considerations will help us in getting some idea of their period: (1) The stories of Noah, Hūd, Ṣāliḥ, Lūṭ, and Shu'ayb seem to be in chronological order. Therefore Shu'ayb came after Abraham, whose

SECTION 12

94 Whenever We sent a prophet to a town, We took up its people in
suffering and adversity, in order that they might learn humility. 95 Then
We changed their suffering into prosperity, until they grew and
multiplied, and began to say: "Our fathers (too) were touched by
suffering and affluence" ... Behold! We called them to account of a
sudden, while they realised not (their peril). 96 If the people of the towns
had but believed and feared Allah, We should indeed have opened out to
them (all kinds of) blessings from heaven and earth; but they rejected (the
truth), and We brought them to book for their misdeeds. 97 Did the people
of the towns feel secure against the coming of Our wrath by night while
they were asleep? 98 Or else did they feel secure against its coming in
broad daylight while they played about (care-free)? 99 Did they then feel
secure against the plan of Allah?—but no one can feel secure from the
Plan of Allah, except those (doomed) to ruin!

SECTION 13

100 To those who inherit the earth in succession to its (previous)
possessors, is it not a guiding, (lesson) that, if We so willed, We could
punish them (too) for their sins, and seal up their hearts so that they could
not hear? 101 Such were the towns whose story We (thus) relate unto you:
there came indeed to them their messengers with clear (Signs): but they
would not believe what they had rejected before. Thus does Allah seal up
the hearts of those who reject Faith. 102 Most of them We found not men
(true) to their covenant: but most of them We found rebellious and
disobedient.

---

nephew Lūṭ was; (2) If Shu'ayb was in the fourth generation from Abraham, (see 11:89), it would be impossible for him to have been a contemporary of Moses, who came many centuries later—this difficulty is recognised by Ibn Kathīr and other classical commentators; (3) The identification of Shu'ayb with Jethro the father-in-law of Moses is without warrant; see 7:85; (4) Shu'ayb must have been before Moses; see 7:103; (5) The Midianites who were destroyed by Moses and by Gideon after him were local remnants, as we may speak of the Jews at the present day but their existence as a nation in their original homelands seems to have ended before Moses: "they became as if they had never been in the homes where they had flourished" (7:92); (6) Josephus, Eusebius, and Ptolemy mention a town of Madyan, but it was not of any importance; (7) After the first centuries of the Christian era, Madyan as a town appears as an unimportant place resting on its past. [1064]

103 Then after them We sent Moses with Our Signs to Pharaoh and his
chiefs, but they wrongfully rejected them: so see what was the end of
those who made mischief. 104 Moses said: "O Pharaoh! I am a messenger
from the Lord of the Worlds,—105 One for whom it is right to say nothing
but truth about Allah. Now have I come unto you (people), from your
Lord, with a clear (Sign): so let the Children of Israel depart along with
me." 106 (Pharaoh) said: "If indeed you have come with a Sign, show it
forth,—if you tell the truth." 107 Then (Moses) threw his rod, and behold!
it was a serpent, plain (for all to see)! 108 And he drew out his hand, and
behold! it was white to all beholders!

SECTION 14

109 Said the chiefs of the people of Pharaoh: "This is indeed a sorcerer
well-versed. 110 His plan is to get you out of your land: then what is it you
counsel?" 111 They said: "Keep him and his brother in suspense (for a
while); and send to the cities men to collect—112 And bring up to you all
(our) sorcerers well-versed."

113 So there came the sorcerers to Pharaoh: they said, "Of course we shall
have a (suitable) reward if we win!" 114 He said: "Indeed, (and
more),—for you shall in that case be (raised to posts) nearest (to my
person)." 115 They said: "O Moses! Will you throw (first), or shall we
have the (first) throw?" 116 Said Moses: "Throw you (first)." So when
they threw, they bewitched the eyes of the people, and struck terror into
them: for they showed a great (feat of) magic. 117 We put it into Moses'
mind by inspiration: "Throw (now) your rod": and behold! it swallows up
straightaway all the falsehoods which they fake! 118 Thus truth was
confirmed, and all that they did was made of no effect. 119 So the (great
ones) were vanquished there and then, and were made to look small.

120 But the sorcerers fell down prostrate in adoration. 121 Saying: "We
believe in the Lord of the Worlds,—122 The Lord of Moses and Aaron."
123 Said Pharaoh: "Believe you in Him before I give you permission?
Surely this is a trick which you have planned in the city to drive out its
people: but soon shall you know (the consequences). 124 Be sure I will cut
off your hands and your feet on opposite sides, and I will cause you all
to die on the cross." 125 They said: "For us, we are but sent back unto our
Lord: 126 But you do wreak your vengeance on us simply because we
believed in the Signs of our Lord when they reached us! Our Lord! Pour

out on us patience and constancy, and take our souls unto You as
Muslims (who bow to Your Will)!

SECTION 15

127 Said the chiefs of Pharaoh's people: "Will you leave Moses and his
people, to spread mischief in the land, and to abandon you and your gods?"
He said: "Their male children will we slay; (only) their females will we save
alive; and we have over them (power) irresistible." 128 Said Moses to his
people: "Pray for help from Allah, and (wait) in patience and constancy: for
the earth is Allah's, to give as a heritage to such of His servants as He
pleases; and the end is (best) for the righteous." 129 They said: "We have had
(nothing but) trouble, both before and after you came to us." He said: "It
may be that your Lord will destroy your enemy and make you inheritors in
the earth; that so He may try you by your deeds."

SECTION 16

130 We punished the people of Pharaoh with years (of droughts) and
shortness of crops; that they might receive admonition. 131 But when good
(times) came, they said, "This is due to us;" when gripped by calamity,
they ascribed it to evil omens connected with Moses and those with him!
Behold! In truth the omens of evil are theirs in Allah's sight, but most of
them do not understand! 132 They said (to Moses): "Whatever be the Signs
you bring, to work therewith your sorcery on us, we shall never believe
in you." 133 So We sent (plagues) on them: Wholesale Death, Locusts,
Lice, Frogs, and Blood: Signs openly self-explained: but they were
steeped in arrogance,—a people given to sin. 134 Every time the Penalty
fell on them, they said: "O Moses! On our behalf call on your Lord in
virtue of His promise to you: if you will remove the Penalty from us, we
shall truly believe in you, and we shall send away the Children of Israel
with you." 135 But every time We removed the Penalty from them
according to a fixed term which they had to fulfil,—behold! they broke
their word! 136 So We exacted retribution from them: We drowned them
in the sea, because they rejected Our Signs and failed to take warning
from them. 137 And We made a people, considered weak (and of no
account), inheritors of lands in both east and west,—lands whereon We
sent down Our blessings. The fair promise of your Lord was fulfilled for
the Children of Israel, because they had patience and constancy, and We
levelled to the ground the great works and fine buildings which Pharaoh
and his people erected (with such pride).

138 We took the Children of Israel (with safety) across the sea. They came
upon a people devoted entirely to some idols they had. They said: "O
Moses! Fashion for us a god like unto the gods they have." He said:
"Surely you are a people without knowledge. 139 As to these folk,—the
cult they are in is (but) a fragment of a ruin, and vain is the (worship)
which they practise." 140 He said: "Shall I seek for you a god other than
the (true) Allah, when it is Allah Who has endowed you with gifts above
the nations?" 141 And remember We rescued you from Pharaoh's people,
who afflicted you with the worst of penalties, who slew your male
children and saved alive your females: in that was a momentous trial from
your Lord.

SECTION 17

142 We appointed for Moses thirty nights, and completed (the period) with
ten (more): thus was completed the term (of communion) with his Lord,
forty nights. And Moses had charged his brother Aaron (before he went
up): "Act for me amongst my people: do right, and follow not the way of
those who do mischief." 143 When Moses came to the place appointed by
Us, and his Lord addressed him, he said: "O my Lord! Show (Yourself)
to me, that I may look upon you." Allah said: "By no means can you see
Me (direct); but look upon the mount; if it abide in its place, then shall
you see Me." When his Lord manifested His glory on the Mount, He
made it as dust. And Moses fell down in a swoon. When he recovered his
senses he said: "Glory be to You! To You I turn in repentance, and I am
the first to believe." 144 (Allah) said: "O Moses! I have chosen you above
(other) men, by the mission I (have given you) and the words I (have
spoken to you): take then the (revelation) which I give you, and be of
those who give thanks." 145 And We ordained laws for him in the Tablets
in all matters, both commanding and explaining all things, (and said):
"Take and hold these with firmness, and enjoin your people to hold fast
by the best in the precepts: soon shall I show you the homes of the
wicked,—(how they lie desolate)." 146 Those who behave arrogantly on
the earth in defiance of right—them will I turn away from My Signs:
even if they see all the Signs, they will not believe in them; and if they
see the way of right conduct, they will not adopt it as the Way; but if they
see the way of error, that is the Way they will adopt. For they have
rejected Our Signs, and failed to take warning from them. 147 Those who
reject Our Signs and the meeting in the Hereafter,—vain are their deeds:

can they expect to be rewarded except as they have wrought?

SECTION 18

148 The people of Moses made, in his absence, out of their ornaments, the
image of a calf, (for worship): it seemed to low: did they not see that it
could neither speak to them, nor show them the Way? They took it for
worship and they did wrong. 149 When they repented, and saw that they
had erred, they said: "If our Lord have not mercy upon us and forgive us,
we shall indeed be of those who perish." 150 When Moses came back to
his people, angry and grieved, he said: "Evil it is that you have done in
my place in my absence: did you make haste to bring on the judgement
of your Lord?" He put down the Tablets, seized his brother by (the hair
of) his head, and dragged him to him. Aaron said: "Son of my mother!
The people did indeed reckon me as naught, and went near to slaying me!
Make not the enemies rejoice over my misfortune, nor count you me
amongst the people of sin." 151 Moses prayed: "O my Lord! Forgive me
and my brother! Admit us to Your Mercy! For You are the Most Merciful
of those who show mercy!"

SECTION 19

152 Those who took the calf (for worship) will indeed be overwhelmed
with wrath from their Lord, and with shame in this life: thus do We
recompense those who invent (falsehoods). 153 But those who do wrong
but repent thereafter and (truly) believe,—verily your Lord is thereafter
Oft-Forgiving, Most Merciful. 154 When the anger of Moses was
appeased, he took up the Tablets: in the writing thereon was Guidance
and Mercy for such as fear their Lord.

155 And Moses chose seventy of his people for Our place of meeting:
when they were seized with violent quaking, he prayed: "O my Lord! If
it had been Your Will You could have destroyed, long before, both them
and me: would You destroy us for the deeds of the foolish ones among
us? This is no more than Your trial: by it You cause whom You will to
stray, and You lead whom You will into the right path. You are our
Protector: so forgive us and give us Your Mercy; for You are the best of
those who forgive. 156 And ordain for us that which is good, in this life
and in the Hereafter: for we have turned unto You." He said: "With My
punishment I visit whom I will; but My Mercy extends to all things. That
(Mercy) I shall ordain for those who do right, and practise regular charity,

and those who believe in Our Signs;—157 Those who follow the
Messenger, the unlettered Prophet, whom they find mentioned in their
own (Scriptures)[11],—in the Law and the Gospel;—for he commands
them what is just and forbids them what is evil; he allows them as lawful
what is good (and pure) and prohibits them from what is bad (and
impure); he releases them from their heavy burdens and from the yokes
that are upon them. So it is those who believe in him, honour him, help
him, and follow the light which is sent down with him,—it is they who
will prosper."

SECTION 20

158 Say: "O men! I am sent unto you all, as the Messenger of Allah, to
Whom belongs the dominion of the heavens and the earth: there is no god
but He: it is He that gives both life and death. So believe in Allah and His
Messenger, the unlettered Prophet, who believes in Allah and His Words:
follow him that (so) you may be guided." 159 Of the people of Moses there
is a section who guide and do justice in the light of truth. 160 We divided
them into twelve tribes or nations. We directed Moses by inspiration,
when his (thirsty) people asked him for water: "Strike the rock with your
staff": out of it there gushed forth twelve springs: each group knew its
own place for water. We gave them the shade of clouds, and sent down
to them manna and quails, (saying): "Eat of the good things We have
provided for you": (but they rebelled); to Us they did no harm, but they
harmed their own souls. 161 And remember it was said to them: "Dwell in
this town and eat therein as you wish, but say the word of humility and
enter the gate in a posture of humility: We shall forgive you your faults;
We shall increase (the portion of) those who do good." 162 But the
transgressors among them changed the word from that which had been
given them so We sent on them a plague from heaven. For that they

---

11. In this verse is a prefiguring, to Moses, of the Arabian Messenger, the last and greatest of the Messengers of Allah. Prophecies about him will be found in the *Torah* and the *Injīl*. In the reflex of the *Torah* as now accepted by the Jews, Moses says, "The Lord thy God will raise up unto thee, of thy brethren, like unto me" (Deut.xviii.15): the only Prophet who brought a *Sharī'ah* like that of Moses was Muḥammad Muṣṭafā and he came of the house of Ismā'īl, the brother of Isaac, the father of Israel. In this reflex of the Gospel as now accepted by the Christians, Christ promised another Comforter (John xiv.16): the Greek word *Paraclete* which the Christians interpret as referring to the Holy Spirit is by our Doctors taken to be *Periclyte*, which would be the Greek form of Aḥmad. See 61:6. [1127]

repeatedly transgressed.

SECTION 21

163 Ask them concerning the town standing close by the sea. Behold! They
transgressed in the matter of the Sabbath. For on the day of their Sabbath
their fish did come to them, openly holding up their heads, but on the day
they had no Sabbath, they came not: thus did We make a trial of them, for
they were given to transgression. 164 When some of them said: "Why do
you preach to a people whom Allah will destroy or visit with a terrible
punishment?"—said the preachers: "To discharge our duty to your Lord,
and perchance they may fear Him." 165 When they disregarded the
warnings that had been given them, We rescued those who forbade Evil;
but We visited the wrong-doers with a grievous punishment because they
were given to transgression. 166 When in their insolence they transgressed
(all) prohibitions, We said to them: "Be you apes, despised and rejected."

167 Behold! Your Lord did declare that He would send against them, to the
Day of Judgement, those who would afflict them with grievous penalty.
Your Lord is quick in retribution, but He is also Oft-Forgiving, Most
Merciful. 168 We broke them up into sections on this earth. There are
among them some that are the righteous, and some that are the opposite.
We have tried them with both prosperity and adversity: in order that they
might turn (to Us). 169 After them succeeded an (evil) generation: they
inherited the Book, but they chose (for themselves) the vanities of this
world, saying (for excuse): "(Everything) will be forgiven us." (Even so),
if similar vanities came their way, they would (again) seize them. Was not
the Covenant of the Book taken from them, that they would not ascribe
to Allah anything but the truth? And they study what is in the Book. But
best for the righteous is the home in the Hereafter. Will you not
understand? 170 As to those who hold fast by the Book and establish
regular prayer,—never shall We suffer the reward of the righteous to
perish. 171 When We shook the Mount over them, as if it had been a
canopy, and they thought it was going to fall on them (We said): "Hold
firmly to what We have given you, and bring (ever) to remembrance what
is therein; perchance you may fear Allah."

SECTION 22

172 When your Lord drew forth[12] from the Children of Adam—from their
loins—their descendants, and made them testify concerning themselves,
(saying): "Am I not your Lord (Who cherishes and sustains
you)?"—They said: "Indeed! We do testify!"[13] (This), lest you should
say on the Day of Judgement: "Of this we were never mindful": 173 Or lest
you should say: "Our fathers before us may have taken false gods, but we
are (their) descendants after them: will You then destroy us because of
the deeds of men who were futile?" 174 Thus do We explain the Signs in
detail; and perchance they may turn (unto Us).

175 Relate to them the story[14] of the man to whom We sent Our Signs, but
he passed them by: so Satan followed him up, and he went astray. 176 If
it had been Our Will, We should have elevated him with Our Signs; but
he inclined to the earth, and followed his own vain desires. His similitude
is that of a dog: if you attack him, he lolls out his tongue, or if you leave
him alone, he (still) lolls out his tongue. That is the similitude of those

12. This passage has led to differences of opinion in interpretation. Does it mean that each individual in the posterity of Adam had a separate existence from the time of Adam, and that a Covenant was taken from all of them, which is binding accordingly on each individual? That question really does not arise. The words in the text refer to the descendants of the Children of Adam, *i.e.*, to all humanity, born or unborn, without any limit of time. Adam's seed carries on the existence of Adam and succeeds to his spiritual heritage. Humanity as such has a corporate aspect. Humanity has been given by Allah certain powers and faculties, whose possession creates on our side special spiritual obligations which we must faithfully discharge: see 5:1. These obligations may from a legal point of view be considered as arising from implied Covenants. In the preceding verse (7:171) a reference was made to the implied Covenant of the Jewish nation. Now we consider the implied Covenant of the whole of humanity, for the Holy Prophet's mission was worldwide. [1146]

13. The Covenant is completed in this way. We acknowledge that Allah is our Creator, Cherisher, and Sustainer: therefore we acknowledge our duty to Him: when we so testify concerning ourselves, the obligation is, as it were, assumed by us; for it follows from our very nature when it is pure and uncorrupted. [1147]

14. Commentators differ as to whether this story or parable refers to a particular individual, and if so, to whom. The story of Balaam, the seer, who was called out by Israel's enemies to curse Israel, but who blessed Israel instead (Num. xxii., xxiii., xxiv) is quite different. It is better to take the parable in a general sense. These are men, of talents and position, to whom great opportunities of spiritual insight come, but they perversely pass them by. Satan sees his opportunity and catches them up. Instead of rising higher in the spiritual world, their selfish and worldly desires and ambitions pull them down, and they are lost. [1149]

who reject Our Signs; so relate the story; perchance they may reflect. 177
Evil as an example are people who reject Our Signs and wrong their own
souls. 178 Whom Allah does guide,—he is on the right path: whom He
rejects from His Guidance,—such are the persons who perish. 179 Many
are the *Jinns* and men We have made for Hell: they have hearts
wherewith they understand not, eyes wherewith they see not, and ears
wherewith they hear not. They are like cattle,—nay more misguided: for
they are heedless (of warning).

180 The most beautiful names[15] belong to Allah: so call on Him by them; but shun such men as use profanity in His names: for what they do, they will soon be requited.

181 Of those We have created are people who direct (others) with truth. And dispense justice therewith.

SECTION 23

182 Those who reject Our Signs, We shall gradually visit with punishment,
in ways they perceive not; 183 Respite will I grant unto them: for My
scheme is strong (and unfailing). 184 Do they not reflect? Their companion
is not seized with madness: he is but a perspicuous warner. 185 Do they
see nothing in the government of the heavens and the earth and all that
Allah has created? (Do they not see) that it may well be that their term is
nigh drawing to an end? In what Message after this will they then
believe? 186 To such as Allah rejects from His Guidance, there can be no
guide: He will leave them in their trespasses, wandering in distraction.

187 They ask you about the (final) Hour—when will be its appointed time? Say: "The knowledge thereof is with my Lord (alone): none but He can reveal as to when it will occur. Heavy were its burden through the heavens and the earth. Only, suddenly will it come to you." They ask you as if you were eager in search thereof: say: "The knowledge thereof is

---

15. As we contemplate Allah's nature, we can use the most beautiful names we can think of, to express His attributes. There are ninety-nine such attributes. In the opening chapter, we have these indicated in a few comprehensive words, such as *al-Raḥmān* (most Gracious), *al-Raḥīm* (most Merciful), *Rabb al-'ālamīn* (Cherisher and Sustainer of the worlds). Our bringing such names to remembrance is part of our Prayer and Praise. But we must not associate with people who use Allah's names profanely, or so as to suggest anything derogatory to His dignity or His unity. *Cf.* 17:110. [1154]

with Allah (alone), but most men know not." 188 Say: "I have no power
over any good or harm to myself except as Allah wills. If I had
knowledge of the unseen, I should have multiplied all good, and no evil
should have touched me: I am but a warner, and a bringer of glad tidings
to those who have faith."

SECTION 24

189 It is He Who created you from a single person, and made his mate of
like nature, in order that he might dwell with her (in love). When they are
united, she bears a light burden and carries it about (unnoticed). When
she grows heavy, they both pray to Allah their Lord, (saying): "If You
give us a goodly child, we vow we shall (ever) be grateful." 190 But when
He gives them a goodly child, they ascribe to others a share in the gift
they have received: but Allah is exalted high above the partners they
ascribe to Him. 191 Do they indeed ascribe to Him as partners things that
can create nothing, but are themselves created? 192 No aid can they give
them, nor can they aid themselves! 193 If you call them to guidance, they
will not obey: for you it is the same whether you call them or you hold
your peace!

194 Verily those whom you call upon besides Allah are servants like unto
you: call upon them, and let them listen to your prayer, if you are
(indeed) truthful! 195 Have they feet to walk with? Or hands to lay hold
with? Or eyes to see with? Or ears to hear with? Say: "Call your
'god-partners', scheme (your worst) against me, and give me no respite!
196 For my Protector is Allah, Who revealed the Book (from time to time),
and He will choose and befriend the righteous. 197 But those you call upon
besides Him, are unable to help you, and indeed to help themselves." 198
If you call them to guidance, they hear not. You will see them looking at
you, but they see not.

199 Hold to forgiveness; command what is right; but turn away from the
ignorant. 200 If a suggestion from Satan assail your (mind), seek refuge
with Allah; for He hears and knows (all things). 201 Those who fear Allah,
when a thought of evil from Satan assaults them, bring Allah to
remembrance, when lo! they see (aright)!

202 But their brethren (the Evil Ones) plunge them deeper into error, and
never relax (their efforts). 203 If you bring them not a revelation, they say:

"Why have you not got it together?" Say: "I but follow what is revealed to me from my Lord: this is (nothing but) lights from your Lord, and Guidance, and Mercy, for any who have Faith."

204 When the Qur'an is read, listen to it with attention, and hold your
peace: that you may receive Mercy. 205 And do you (O reader!) bring your
Lord to remembrance in your (very) soul, with humility and in reverence,
without loudness in words, in the mornings and evenings; and be not you
of those who are unheedful. 206 Those who are near to your Lord, disdain
not to do Him worship: they celebrate His praises, and bow down before
Him.□

Chapter 8

Sūrah Al-Anfāl
(The Spoils of War)

Translator's Introduction

In the previous Introductions to the Sūrahs we have shown how each Sūrah is a step or gradation in the teaching of the Qur'an. The first seven Sūrahs, comprising a little less than one-third of the Qur'an, form a gradation, sketching the early spiritual history of man and leading up to the formation of the new *Ummah* or Community of the Holy Messenger. Now we begin another gradation, consolidating that *Ummah* and directing us as to various phases in our new collective life.

In this chapter we have the lessons of the Battle of Badr enforced in their larger aspects: (1) the question of war booty; (2) the true virtues necessary for fighting the good fight; (3) victory against odds; (4) clemency and consideration for one's own and for others in the hour of victory.

As regards booty taken in battle, the first point to note is that that should never be our aim in war. It is only an adventitious circumstance, a sort of windfall. Secondly, no soldier or troop has any inherent right to it. A righteous war is a community affair, and any accessions resulting from it belong to Allah, or the community or Cause. Thirdly, certain equitable principles of division should be laid down to check human greed and selfishness. A fifth share goes to the Commander, and he can use it at his discretion; for his own expenses, and for the relief of the poor and suffering, and the orphans and widows (8:41). The remainder was divided, according to the Prophet's practice, not only among those who were actually in the fight physically, but all who were in the enterprise, young and old, provided they loyally did some duty assigned to them. Fourthly, there should be no disputes, as they interfere with internal discipline and harmony.

These principles are followed in the best modern practice of civilised nations. All acquisitions of war belong absolutely to the Sovereign as representing the commonwealth. In the distribution of booty not only the actual captors but also the "joint captors" and the "constructive captors" share. See Sir R. Phillimore's *International Law* (1885), vol. 3, pp. 209-10, 221-24. As regards the military virtues, which are the types of virtues throughout life, we are shown by an analysis of the incidents of Badr how against the greatest odds, Allah's help will give victory if men are fighting not for themselves but for the sacred Cause of Allah. And directions are given for the treatment of prisoners and for maintaining the solidarity of the Muslim community.

The date of this Sūrah is shortly after the battle of Badr, which was fought on Friday, the 17th of Ramaḍān in the second year of the Hijrah. A short account of the battle is given in note to 3:13.

Summary—All booty is really at the disposal of Allah's Messenger under directions from Allah. Men of faith accept and obey these directions with cheerfulness. Victory and the prize of victory come from Allah, as was proved at Badr (8:1-19).

Obedience and intelligent discipline, zeal, faith, and gratitude to Allah, are the true passports to success and protection from the assaults of evil. Evil will be piled up with evil and destroyed (8:20-37).

The battle of Badr was a testing time, and showed how virtue and valour can conquer against odds. Steadfastness and obedience; faith, courage, and fearlessness; due preparation and free expenditure of resources and energy—these are expected from you by Allah, and His help is all-sufficient (8:38-64).

Even ten-fold odds against you do not count if you are fighting for truth and faith against enemies of truth and faith; but remember clemency and consideration in the hour of victory (8:65-75).

*** *** ***

In the name of Allah,
Most Gracious, Most Merciful.

1 They ask you[1] concerning (things taken as) spoils of war. Say: "(Such)
spoils are at the disposal of Allah and the Messenger: so fear Allah, and
keep straight the relations between yourselves: obey Allah and His
Messenger, if you do believe." 2 For, Believers are those who, when Allah
is mentioned, feel a tremor in their hearts, and when they hear His Signs
rehearsed, find their faith strengthened, and put (all) their trust in their
Lord; 3 Who establish regular prayers and spend (freely) out of the gifts
We have given them for sustenance: 4 Such in truth are the Believers:
they have grades of dignity with their Lord, and forgiveness, and
generous sustenance: 5 Just as your Lord ordered you out of your house
in truth, even though a party among the Believers disliked it, 6 Disputing
with you concerning the truth after it was made manifest, as if they were
being driven to death and they (actually) saw it. 7 Behold! Allah promised

---

1. The occasion was the question of the division of the booty after the battle of Badr. See Introduction to this Sūrah. [1178].

you one of the two (enemy) parties,[2] that it should be yours: you wished
that the one unarmed should be yours, but Allah willed to justify the
Truth according to His words and to cut off the roots of the
Unbelievers;—8 That He might justify Truth and prove Falsehood false,
distasteful though it be to those in guilt. 9 Remember you implored the
assistance of your Lord, and He answered you: "I will assist you with a
thousand of the angels, ranks on ranks." 10 Allah made it but a message
of hope, and an assurance to your hearts: (in any case) there is no help
except from Allah: and Allah is Exalted in Power, Wise.

SECTION 2

11 Remember He covered you with a sort of drowsiness, to give you calm
as from Himself, and He caused rain to descend on you from heaven, to
clean you therewith, to remove from you the stain of Satan, to strengthen
your hearts, and to plant your feet firmly therewith. 12 Remember your
Lord inspired the angels (with the message): "I am with you: give
firmness to the Believers: I will instil terror into the hearts of the
Unbelievers: smite you above their necks and smite all their finger-tips
off them." 13 This because they contended against Allah and His
Messenger: if any contend against Allah and His Messenger, Allah is
strict in punishment. 14 Thus (will it be said): "Taste you then of the
(punishment): for those who resist Allah, is the penalty of the Fire."

15 O you who believe! When you meet the Unbelievers in hostile array,
never turn your backs to them. 16 If any do turn his back to them on such
a day—unless it be in a stratagem of war, or to retreat to a troop (of his
own)—he draws on himself the wrath of Allah, and his abode is

2. Just before Badr there were two alternatives before the Muslims in Madīnah, to save themselves from being overwhelmed by the Makkan Quraysh with all their resources from the rich Syrian trade. One, which had least danger for the time being, and also promised much booty, was to fall upon the Quraysh caravan returning from Syria to Makkah richly laden, and led by Abū Sufyān with only 40 unarmed men. From a worldly point of view this was the safest and most lucrative course. The other alternative, which was actually adopted on the recommendation of the Prophet by the guidance of Allah, was to leave the booty alone and march out boldly against the well-armed and well-equipped Quraysh army of 1,000 men coming from Makkah. The Muslims had no more than 300 men, ill-armed, to oppose the force. But if they could defeat it, it would shake the selfish autocracy which was in possession of Makkah. By Allah's help they won a splendid victory, and the standard of Truth was established, never to be lowered again.[1183]

Hell,—an evil refuge (indeed)! 17 It is not you who slew them; it was
Allah: when you threw (a handful of dust), it was not your act, but
Allah's: in order that He might test the Believers by a gracious trial from
Himself: for Allah is He Who hears and knows (all things). 18 That, and
also because Allah is He Who makes feeble the plans and stratagem of
the Unbelievers. 19 (O Unbelievers!) If you prayed for victory and
judgement, now has the judgement come to you: if you desist (from
wrong), it will be best for you: if you return (to the attack), so shall We.
Not the least good will your forces be to you even if they were
multiplied: for verily Allah is with those who believe!

SECTION 3

20 O you who believe! Obey Allah and His Messenger, and turn not away
from him when you hear (him speak). 21 Nor be like those who say, "We
hear," but listen not: 22 For the worst of beasts in the sight of Allah are the
deaf and the dumb,—those who understand not. 23 If Allah had found in
them any good, He would indeed have made them listen: (as it is), if He
had made them listen, they would but have turned back and declined
(faith). 24 O you who believe! Give your response to Allah and His
Messenger, when He calls you to that which will give you life; and know
that Allah comes in between a man and his heart, and that it is He to
Whom you shall (all) be gathered. 25 And fear tumult or oppression,
which affects not in particular (only) those of you who do wrong: and
know that Allah is strict in punishment. 26 Call to mind when you were a
small (band), despised through the land, and afraid that men might
despoil and kidnap you; but He provided a safe asylum for you,
strengthened you with His aid, and gave you good things for sustenance:
that you might be grateful.

27 O you that believe! Betray not the trust of Allah and the Messenger, nor
misappropriate knowingly things entrusted to you. 28 And know you that
your possessions and your progeny are but a trial; and that it is Allah with
Whom lies your highest reward.

SECTION 4

29 O you who believe! If you fear Allah, He will grant you a criterion (to
judge between right and wrong), remove from you (all) evil (that may
afflict) you, and forgive you: for Allah is the Lord of grace unbounded.

30 Remember how the Unbelievers plotted against you, to keep you in
bonds, or slay you, or get you out (of your home). They plot and plan,
and Allah too plans; but the best of planners is Allah.

31 When Our Signs are rehearsed to them, they say: "We have heard this
(before): if we wished, we could say (words) like these: these are nothing
but tales of the ancients." 32 Remember how they said: "O Allah! If this
is indeed the Truth from You, rain down on us a shower of stones from
the sky, or send us a grievous penalty." 33 But Allah was not going to
send them a Penalty whilst you were amongst them; nor was He going to
send it whilst they could ask for pardon. 34 But what plea have they that
Allah should not punish them, when they keep out (men) from the Sacred
Mosque—and they are not its guardians? No men can be its guardians
except the righteous; but most of them do not understand. 35 Their prayer
at the House (of Allah) is nothing but whistling and clapping of hands:
(its only answer can be), "Taste you the Penalty because you
blasphemed."

36 The Unbelievers spend their wealth to hinder (men) from the path of
Allah, and so will they continue to spend; but in the end they will have
(only) regrets and sighs; at length they will be overcome: and the
Unbelievers will be gathered together to Hell;—37 In order that Allah may
separate the impure from the pure, put the impure, one on another, heap
them together, and cast them into Hell. They will be the ones to have lost.

SECTION 5

38 Say to the Unbelievers, if (now) they desist (from Unbelief), their past
would be forgiven them; but if they persist, the punishment of those
before them is already (a matter of warning for them). 39 And fight them
on until there is no more tumult or oppression, and there prevail justice
and faith in Allah; but if they cease, verily Allah does see all that they
do.[3] 40 If they refuse, be sure that Allah is your Protector—the best to
protect and the best to help.

---

3. If they desist from fighting and from the persecution of truth, Allah judges them by their actions and their motives, and would not wish that they should be harassed with further hostility. But if they refuse all terms, the righteous have nothing to fear: Allah will help and protect them. See also Note 17 to 2:193. [1208] – Ed.

PART X

41 And know that out of all the booty that you may acquire (in war), a
fifth share is assigned to Allah,—and to the Messenger, and to near
relatives, orphans, the needy, and the wayfarer,—if you do believe in
Allah and in the revelation We sent down to Our servant on the Day of
Testing,—the Day of the meeting of the two forces. For Allah has power
over all things. 42 Remember you were on the hither side of the valley,
and they on the farther side, and the caravan on lower ground than you.
Even if you had made a mutual appointment to meet, you would certainly
have failed in the appointment: but (thus you met), that Allah might
accomplish a matter already enacted; that those who died might die after
a clear Sign (had been given), and those who lived might live after a clear
Sign (had been given). And verily Allah is He Who hears and knows (all
things). 43 Remember in your dream Allah showed them to you as few: if
He had shown them to you as many, you would surely have been
discouraged, and you would surely have disputed in (your) decision; but
Allah saved (you): for He knows well the (secrets) of (all) hearts. 44 And
remember when you met, He showed them to you as few in your eyes,
and He made you appear as contemptible in their eyes: that Allah might
accomplish a matter already enacted. For to Allah do all questions go
back (for decision).

SECTION 6

45 O you who believe! When you meet a force, be firm, and call Allah in
remembrance much (and often); that you may prosper: 46 And obey Allah
and His Messenger; and fall into no disputes, lest you lose heart and your
power depart; and be patient and persevering: for Allah is with those who
patiently persevere: 47 And be not like those who started from their homes
insolently and to be seen of men, and to hinder (men) from the path of
Allah: for Allah compasses round about all that they do. 48 Remember
Satan made their (sinful) acts seem alluring to them, and said: "No one
among men can overcome you this day, while I am near to you": but
when the two forces came in sight of each other, he turned on his heels,
and said: "Lo! I am clear of you; lo! I see what you see not; lo! I fear
Allah: for Allah is strict in punishment."

SECTION 7

49 Lo! the Hypocrites say, and those in whose hearts is a disease: "These

people,—their religion has misled them." But if any trust in Allah,
behold! Allah is Exalted in might, Wise. 50 If you could see, when the
angels take the souls of the Unbelievers (at death), (how) they smite their
faces and their backs, (saying): "Taste the Penalty of the blazing Fire— 51
Because of (the deeds) which your (own) hands sent forth; for Allah is
never unjust to His servants: 52 (Deeds) after the manner of the people of
Pharaoh and of those before them: they rejected the Signs of Allah, and
Allah punished them for their crimes: for Allah is strong, and strict in
punishment: 53 Because Allah will never change the grace which He has
bestowed on a people until they change what is in their (own) souls: and
verily Allah is He Who hears and knows (all things)." 54 "(Deeds) after
the manner of the people of Pharaoh and those before them": they treated
as false the Signs of their Lord: so We destroyed them for their crimes,
and We drowned the people of Pharaoh: for they were all oppressors and
wrong-doers.

55 For the worst of beasts in the sight of Allah are those who reject Him:
they will not believe. 56 They are those with whom you did make a
covenant, but they break their covenant every time, and they have not the
fear (of Allah). 57 If you gain the mastery over them in war, disperse, with
them, those who follow them, that they may remember. 58 If you fear
treachery from any group, throw back (their covenant) to them, (so as to
be) on equal terms: for Allah loves not the treacherous.

SECTION 8

59 Let not the Unbelievers think that they can get the better (of the godly):
they will never frustrate (them). 60 Against them make ready your strength
to the utmost of your power, including steeds of war, to strike terror into
(the hearts of) the enemies, of Allah and your enemies, and others
besides, whom you may not know, but whom Allah does know. Whatever
you shall spend in the cause of Allah, shall be repaid unto you, and you
shall not be treated unjustly.

61 But if the enemy incline towards peace, do you (also) incline towards
peace, and trust in Allah: for He is the One that hears and knows (all
things). 62 Should they intend to deceive you,—verily Allah suffices you:
He it is that has strengthened you with His aid and with (the company of)
the Believers; 63 And (moreover) He has put affection between their
hearts: not if you had spent all that is in the earth, could you have

produced that affection, but Allah has done it: for He is Exalted in might,
Wise. 64 O Prophet! Sufficient unto you is Allah,—(unto you) and unto
those who follow you among the Believers.

SECTION 9

65 O Prophet! Rouse the Believers to the fight. If there are twenty amongst
you, patient and persevering, they will vanquish two hundred: if a
hundred, they will vanquish a thousand of the Unbelievers: for these are
a people without understanding. 66 For the present, Allah has lightened
your (task), for He knows that there is a weak spot in you: but (even so),
if there are a hundred of you, patient and persevering, they will vanquish
two hundred, and if a thousand, they will vanquish two thousand, with the
leave of Allah: for Allah is with those who patiently persevere.

67 It is not fitting for a Prophet that he should have prisoners of war until
he has thoroughly subdued the land. You look for the temporal goods of
this world; but Allah looks to the Hereafter: and Allah is Exalted in
might, Wise. 68 Had it not been for a previous ordainment from Allah, a
severe penalty would have reached you for the (ransom) that you took.
69 But (now) enjoy what you took in war, lawful and good: but fear Allah:
for Allah is Oft-Forgiving, Most Merciful.

SECTION 10

70 O Prophet! Say to those who are captives in your hands: "If Allah finds
any good in your hearts, He will give you something better than what has
been taken from you, and He will forgive you: for Allah is Oft-Forgiving,
Most Merciful." 71 But if they have treacherous designs against you, (O
Messenger!), they have already been in treason against Allah, and so has
He given (you) power over them. And Allah is He Who has (full)
knowledge and wisdom.

72 Those who believed, and adopted exile, and fought for the Faith, with
their property and their persons, in the cause of Allah, as well as those who
gave (them) asylum[4] and aid,—these are (all) friends and protectors, one

---

4. The reference is to the *Muhājirīn* and *Anṣār*, the Emigrants and the Helpers, the people who forsook their homes and adopted voluntary exile from Makkan company with their beloved Leader, and their good friends in Madīnah, who gave them asylum and every kind of assistance, moral and material. Under the magnetic personality of the Holy Prophet these two groups became like blood-brothers, and they were so treated in matters of

of another. As to those who believed but came not into exile, you owe no
duty of protection to them until they come into exile; but if they seek your
aid in religion, it is your duty to help them, except against a people with
whom you have a treaty of mutual alliance. And (remember) Allah sees all
that you do. 73 The Unbelievers are protectors, one of another: unless you
do this, (protect each other), there would be tumult and oppression on earth,
and great mischief. 74 Those who believe, and adopt exile, and fight for the
Faith, in the cause of Allah, as well as those who give (them) asylum and
aid,—these are (all) in very truth the Believers: for them is the forgiveness
of sins and a provision most generous. 75 And those who accept Faith
subsequently, and adopt exile, and fight for the Faith in your
company,—they are of you. But kindred by blood have prior rights against
each other in the Book of Allah. Verily Allah is well-acquainted with all
things.□

---

inheritance during the period when they were cut off from their kith and kin. [1239]

Chapter 9

Sūrah Al-Tawbah or *Barā'ah* (The Repentance *or* Immunity)

Translator's Introduction

Logically this Sūrah follows up the argument of the last Sūrah (8), and indeed may be considered a part of it, although chronologically the two are separated by an interval of seven years.

We saw that Sūrah 8 dealt with the large questions arising at the outset of the life of a new *Ummah* or organised nation: questions of defence under attack, distribution of war acquisitions after victory, the virtues needed for concerted action, and clemency and consideration for one's own and for enemies in the hour of victory. We pass on in this Sūrah to deal with the question: what is to be done if the enemy breaks faith and is guilty of treachery? No nation can go on with a treaty if the other party violates it at will; but it is laid down that a period of four months should be allowed by way of notice after denunciation of the treaty; that due protection should be accorded in the intervening period; that there should always be open the door to repentance and reunion with the people of Allah; and that if all these fail, and war must be undertaken, it must be pushed with the utmost vigour.

These are the general principles deducible from the Sūrah. The immediate occasion for their promulgation may be considered in connection with the chronological place of the Sūrah.

Chronologically, verses 1-29 were a notable declaration of state policy promulgated about the month of Shawwāl, A.H. 9, and read out by 'Alī at the Pilgrimage two months later in order to give the policy the widest publicity possible. The remainder of the Sūrah, verses 30-129, was revealed a little earlier, say about the month of Ramaḍān, A.H. 9, and sums up the lessons of the Prophet's Tabūk expedition in the late summer of A.H. 9 (say October 630).

Tabūk is a place near the frontier of Arabia, quite close to what was then Byzantine territory in the Province of Syria (which includes Palestine). It is on the Ḥijaz Railway, about 350 miles northwest of Madīnah, and 150 miles south of Ma'ān. It had a fort and a spring of sweet water. In consequence of strong and persistent rumours that the Byzantines (Romans) were preparing to invade Arabia and that the Byzantine Emperor himself had arrived near the frontier for the purpose, the Prophet collected as large a force as he could, and marched to Tabūk. The Byzantine invasion did not take place. But the Prophet took the opportunity of consolidating the Muslim position in that direction and making treaties of alliance with certain Christian and Jewish tribes near the Gulf of

'Aqabah. On his return to Madīnah he considered the situation. During his absence the Hypocrites had played, as always, a double game; and the policy hitherto followed, of free access to the sacred centre of Islam to Muslims and Pagans alike—was now altered, as it had been abused by the enemies of Islam.

This is the only Sūrah to which the usual formula of *Bismillāh* is not prefixed. It was among the last of the Sūrahs revealed, and though the Prophet had directed that it should follow Sūrah 8, it was not clear whether it was to form a separate Sūrah or only a part of Sūrah 8. It is now treated as a separate Sūrah, but the *Bismillāh* is not prefixed to it, as there is no warrant for supposing that the Prophet used the *Bismillāh* before it in his recitation of the Qur'an. The Sūrah is known under many names: the most commonly used are (1) *Al-Tawbah* (Repentance), with reference to 9:104 and (2) *Barā'ah* (The Disavowal), the opening word of the Sūrah.

Summary—Treaties with those Pagans who have treacherously broken their terms are denounced, but four months' time is given for adjustments or repentance. Pagans to be excluded from the sacred Mosques. Infidelity to be fought (9:1-29).

The People of the Book have obscured the light of Allah, but the Truth of Allah must prevail over all. We must be ready to fight for the Faith that is in us; otherwise we shall be unworthy to uphold Allah's banner, and He will raise other people in our place (9:30-42).

The Hypocrites and their double dealing: their evil ways pointed out. Their punishment will be as sure as the blessings of the righteous (9:43-72).

All evil should be resisted, unless there is repentance: falsehood is not content with breach of faith but mocks all good: it should not be envied but shunned (9:73-99).

The good pleasure of Allah is with those who are sincere and make sacrifices in His cause; He will forgive those who do wrong and repent, but not those who intend mischief and foment unbelief and disunion among believers. The Believers by their self-surrender obtain eternal Felicity. Allah will turn in mercy even to those who, though they waver or fail in duty, turn at last to Him (9:100-118).

Those who believe should associate with the righteous and the truthful, actively doing their duty. But if the Community marches out, a part of them should remain behind for the purpose of diligently studying religion and teaching their brethren when they return. Every Sūrah increases the faith of those who believe, though those diseased in heart may add doubt to doubt. Trust in Allah, Lord of the Throne of Glory (9:119-129).

*** *** ***

1 A (declaration) of immunity from Allah and His Messenger, to those of
the Pagans with whom you have contracted mutual alliances:—2 Go you,
then, for four months, backwards and forwards, (as you will), throughout
the land, but know you that you cannot frustrate Allah (by your
falsehood) but that Allah will cover with shame those who reject Him. 3
And an announcement from Allah and His Messenger, to the people
(assembled) on the day of the Great Pilgrimage,—that Allah and His
Messenger dissolve (treaty) obligations with the Pagans. If then, you
repent, it were best for you; but if you turn away, know you that you
cannot frustrate Allah. And proclaim a grievous penalty to those who
reject Faith. 4 (But the treaties are) not dissolved with those Pagans with
whom you have entered into alliance and who have not subsequently
failed you in aught, nor aided any one against you. So fulfil your
engagements with them to the end of their term: for Allah loves the
righteous.

5 But when the forbidden months are past, then fight and kill the
polytheists (idolaters) wherever you encounter them, and seize them,
besiege them (in the battlefield), and lie in wait for them in every
stratagem (of war); but if they repent, and establish regular prayers and
practise regular charity, then open the way for them: for Allah is Oft-
Forgiving, Most Merciful.[1] 6 If one amongst the Polytheists (idolaters)
asks you for asylum, grant it to him, so that he may hear the Word of
Allah; and then escort him to where he can be secure.[2] That is because

---

1. When war becomes inevitable, it must be prosecuted with vigour. According to the English phrase, you cannot fight with kid gloves on. The fighting may take the form of killing, or capture, or siege, or ambush and other stratagems. But, even then there is room for repentance and the making of amends on the part of the guilty party, and if that takes place, our duty is forgiveness and the establishment of peace. [1251]
The repentance must be sincere, and that is shown by conduct – a religious spirit of true prayer and charity. In that case, we are not to bar the gate against the repentant. On the contrary, we must do all we can to make their way easy, remembering that Allah is Oft-forgiving, Most Merciful. [1252]

2. Even among the enemies of Islam, actively fighting against Islam, there may be individuals who may be in a position to require protection. Full asylum is to be given to them, and opportunities provided for hearing the Word of Allah. If they accept the Word, they become Muslims and brethren, and no further question arises. If they do not see their way to accept Islam, they will require double protection: (1) from the Muslim forces openly fighting against their people, and (2) from their own people, as they have detached themselves from them. Both kinds of protection should be ensured for them, and they

they are men without knowledge.

SECTION 2

7 How can there be a league, before Allah and His Messenger, with the
Pagans, except those with whom you made a treaty near the Sacred
Mosque? As long as these stand true to you, stand you true to them: for
Allah does love the righteous. 8 How (can there be such a league), seeing
that if they get an advantage over you, they respect not in you the ties
either of kinship or of covenant? With (fair words from) their mouths
they entice you, but their hearts are averse from you; and most of them
are rebellious and wicked. 9 The Signs of Allah have they sold for a
miserable price, and (many) have they hindered from His Way: evil
indeed are the deeds they have done. 10 In a Believer they respect not the
ties either of kinship or of covenant! It is they who have transgressed all
bounds.

11 But (even so), if they repent, establish regular prayers, and practise
regular charity,—they are your brethren in Faith: (thus) do We explain
the Signs in detail, for those who understand. 12 But if they violate their
oaths after their covenant, and taunt you for your Faith,—fight you the
chiefs of Unfaith: for their oaths are nothing to them: that thus they may
be restrained.

13 Will you not fight people who violated their oaths, plotted to expel the
Messenger,[3] and took the aggressive by being the first (to assault) you?
Do you fear them? Nay, it is Allah Whom you should more justly fear,
if you believe! 14 Fight them, and Allah will punish them by your hands,
cover them with shame, help you (to victory) over them, heal the breasts

---

should be safely escorted to a place where they can be safe. Such persons only err through ignorance, and there may be much good in them. [1253]

3. The argument now takes a new turn. An appeal is made to the Muslims on various grounds: (1) the shameless disregard of treaties by the enemy, (2) the underhand plots to discredit the Prophet, and turn him out of Madīnah as he had been turned out of Makkah, (3) the aggressive stance taken by the Quraysh of Makkah and their confederates in Madīnah after the treaty of Ḥudaybiyah (A.H. 6, Dhū al Qa‘dah, February 628), (4) the courageous attitude that fears Allah rather than human beings, and (5) the need to prove our sincere faith by test and trial and struggle and sacrifice (9:16). [1261] -Ed.

of Believers,[4] 15 And still the indignation of their hearts. For Allah will
turn (in mercy) to whom He will; and Allah is All-Knowing, All-Wise.
16 Or think you that you shall be abandoned, as though Allah did not
know those among you who strive with might and main, and take none
for friends and protectors except Allah, His Messenger, and the
(community of) Believers? But Allah is well-acquainted with (all) that
you do.

SECTION 3

17 It is not for such as join gods with Allah, to visit or maintain the
mosques of Allah while they witness against their own souls to infidelity.
The works of such bear no fruit: in Fire shall they dwell. 18 The mosques
of Allah shall be visited and maintained by such as believe in Allah and
the Last Day, establish regular prayers, and practise regular charity, and
fear none (at all) except Allah. It is they who are expected to be on true
guidance. 19 Do you make the giving of drink to pilgrims, or the
maintenance of the Sacred Mosque, equal to (the pious service of) those
who believe in Allah and the Last Day, and strive with might and main
in the Cause of Allah? They are not comparable in the sight of Allah: and
Allah guides not those who do wrong. 20 Those who believe, and suffer
exile and strive with might and main, in Allah's Cause, with their goods
and their persons, have the highest rank in the sight of Allah: they are the
people who will achieve (salvation). 21 Their Lord does give them glad
tidings of a Mercy from Himself, of His good pleasure, and of Gardens
for them, wherein are delights that endure: 22 They will dwell therein for
ever. Verily in Allah's presence is a reward, the greatest (of all).

23 O you who believe! Take not for protectors your fathers and your
brothers if they love infidelity above Faith: if any of you do so, they do
wrong. 24 Say: If it be that your fathers, your sons, your brothers, your
mates, or your kindred; the wealth that you have gained; the commerce
in which you fear a decline: or the dwellings in which you delight—are
dearer to you than Allah, or His Messenger, or the striving in His
Cause;—then wait until Allah brings about His decision: and Allah guides
not the rebellious.

---

4. *Heal the breasts of believers*, this means encourage, enhearten, grant satisfaction and tranquillity to the believers after the stress and injury, both psychological and physical, and the losses that they have suffered during the cruel onslaughts of the enemy. [1262] – Ed.

SECTION 4

25 Assuredly Allah did help you in many battlefields and on the day of
Ḥunayn:[5] Behold! Your great numbers elated you, but they availed you
naught: the land, for all that it is wide, did constrain you, and you turned
back in retreat.[6] 26 But Allah did pour His calm[7] on the Messenger and
on the Believers, and sent down forces which you saw not: He punished
the Unbelievers; thus does He reward those without Faith. 27 Again will
Allah, after this,[8] turn (in mercy) to whom He will: for Allah is Oft-
Forgiving, Most Merciful.

28 O you who believe! Truly the Pagans are unclean; so let them not, after
this year of theirs, approach the Sacred Mosque. And if you fear poverty,

---

5. Ḥunayn is on the road to Ṭā'if from Makkah, about fourteen miles to the east of Makkah. It is a valley in the mountainous country between Makkah and Ṭā'if. Immediately after the conquest of Makkah, (A.H. 8), the Pagan idolaters, who were surprised and chagrined at the wonderful reception which Islam was receiving, organised a great gathering near Ṭā'if to concert plans for attacking the Prophet. The Hawāzin and the Thaqīf tribes took the lead and prepared a great expedition for Makkah, boasting of their strength and military skill. There was on the other hand a wave of confident enthusiasm among the Muslims at Makkah, in which the new Muslims joined. The enemy forces numbered about 4,000 but the Muslim force reached a total of ten or twelve thousand, as everyone wished to join. The battle was joined at Ḥunayn, as described in the next note. [1274]

6. For the first time the Muslims had at Ḥunayn tremendous odds in their favour. But this itself constituted a danger. Many in their ranks had more enthusiasm than wisdom, more a spirit of elation than of faith and confidence in the righteousness of their cause. The enemy had the advantage of knowing the ground thoroughly. They laid an ambush in which the advance guard of the Muslim forces was caught. The country is hilly, in which the enemy concealed himself. As soon as the Muslim vanguard entered the Ḥunayn valley, the enemy fell upon them with fury and caused havoc with their arrows from their places of concealment. In such ground the numbers of the Muslims were themselves a disadvantage. Many were slain, and many turned back in confusion and retreat. But the Prophet, as ever, was calm in his wisdom and faith. He rallied his forces and inflicted the most crushing defeat on the enemy. [1275]

7. *Sakīn* calm, peace, security, tranquillity. *Cf.* 2:248. The Prophet never approved of over-weening confidence, or reliance merely upon human strength, or human resources or numbers. In the hour of danger and seeming disaster, he was perfectly calm, and with cool courage relied upon the help of Allah, Whose standard he carried. His calmness inspired all around him, and stopped the rout of those who had turned their backs. It was with Allah's help that they won, and their victory was complete. They followed it up with an energetic pursuit of the enemies, capturing their camps, their flocks and herds, and their families, whom they had boastfully brought with them in expectation of an easy victory. [1276]

8. Examples of Allah's mercy and grace in difficult circumstances in one case illustrate His grace and mercy at all times to those who have faith. [1277]

soon will Allah enrich you, if He wills, out of His bounty, for Allah is
All-Knowing, All-Wise. 29 Fight those who believe not in Allah nor the
Last Day, nor hold that forbidden which has been forbidden by Allah and
His Messenger, nor acknowledge the religion of Truth, (even if they are)
of the People of the Book,[9] until they pay the *Jizyah*[10] with willing
submission,[11] and feel themselves subdued.

SECTION 5

30 The Jews call 'Uzayr a son of Allah, and the Christians call Christ the
son of Allah. That is a saying from their mouth; (in this) they but imitate
what the Unbelievers of old used to say. Allah's curse be on them: how
they are deluded away from the Truth! 31 They take their priests and their
anchorites to be their lords in derogation of Allah, and (they take as their
Lord) Christ the son of Mary; yet they were commanded to worship but
One Allah: there is no god but He. Praise and glory to Him: (far is He)
from having the partners they associate (with Him).

---

9. This was revealed when the area of Arabia ruled by Prophet Muḥammad was gradually expanding as a result of various tribal chiefs, most notably the Quraysh of Makkah, taking oaths of allegiance to the Prophet. Tribal representatives were visiting the Prophet to give their allegiance and learn about Islam. Once under this rule, tribal members were not obliged to "become Muslims", but were expected to be loyal. Non-Muslim citizens were exempt from taking up arms against an external foe hostile to the new rule, but were expected to pay annually a nominal tax (*jizyah*) as a token of their loyalty and acknowledgment of the protection they were now receiving. Any of these people who refused to pay the *jizyah*, or attacked from within, were to be subdued by force, as they had reneged on their oaths of allegiance. – Ed.

10. *Jizyah* the root meaning is compensation. The derived meaning, which became the technical meaning, was a poll tax levied from those who did not accept Islam, but were willing to live under the protection of Islam, and were thus tacitly willing to submit to its ideals being enforced in the Muslim State. There was no amount permanently fixed for it, and in any case it was merely symbolic—an acknowledgement that those whose religion was tolerated would in their turn not interfere with the preaching and progress of Islam. Imām Shāfi'ī' suggests one dinār per year, which would be the Arabian gold dinār of the Muslim States, equivalent in value to about half a sovereign, or about 5 or 7 rupees. See 3:75. The tax varied in amount, and there were exemptions for the poor, for females and children (according to Abū Ḥanīfah), for slaves, and for monks and hermits. Being a tax on able-bodied males of military age, it was in a sense a commutation for military service. But see the next note. [1281]

11. *'An Yadin* (literally, from the hand) has been variously interpreted. The hand being the symbol of power and authority, I accept the interpretation "in token of willing submission." The *Jizyah* was thus partly symbolic and partly a commutation for military service, but as the amount was insignificant and the exemptions numerous, its symbolic character predominated. See the last note. [1282]

32 Fain would they extinguish Allah's Light with their mouths, but Allah
will not allow but that His Light should be perfected, even though the
Unbelievers may detest (it). 33 It is He Who has sent His Messenger with
Guidance and the Religion of Truth, to proclaim it over all religion, even
though the Pagans may detest (it). 34 O you who believe! There are indeed
many among the priests and anchorites, who in falsehood devour the
substance of men and hinder (them) from the Way of Allah. And there
are those who bury gold and silver and spend it not in the Way of Allah:
announce unto them a most grievous penalty—35 On the Day when heat
will be produced out of that (wealth) in the fire of Hell, and with it will
be branded their foreheads, their flanks, and their backs.—"This is the
(treasure) which you buried for yourselves: taste you, then, the (treasures)
you buried!"

36 The number of months in the sight of Allah is twelve (in a year)—so
ordained by Him the day He created the heavens and the earth; of them
four are sacred: that is the straight usage. So wrong not yourselves
therein, and fight the Pagans all together as they fight you all together.
But know that Allah is with those who restrain themselves. 37 Verily the
transposing (of a prohibited month) is an addition to Unbelief: the
Unbelievers are led to wrong thereby: for they make it lawful one year,
and forbidden another year, in order to adjust the number of months
forbidden by Allah and make such forbidden ones lawful. The evil of
their course seems pleasing to them. But Allah guides not those who
reject Faith.

SECTION 6

38 O you who believe! What is the matter with you, that, when you are
asked to go forth in the Cause of Allah, you cling heavily to the earth? Do
you prefer the life of this world to the Hereafter? But little is the comfort
of this life, as compared with the Hereafter. 39 Unless you go forth, He
will punish you with a grievous penalty, and put others in your place; but
Him you would not harm in the least. For Allah has power over all things.
40 If you help not (your leader), (it is no matter): for Allah did indeed help
him, when the Unbelievers drove him out: he had no more than one
companion; they two were in the cave, and he said to his companion,
"Have no fear, for Allah is with us": then Allah sent down His peace
upon him, and strengthened him with forces which you saw not, and

humbled to the depths the word of the Unbelievers. But the word of Allah
is exalted to the heights: for Allah is Exalted in might, Wise. 41 Go you
forth, (whether equipped) lightly or heavily, and strive and struggle, with
your goods and your persons, in the Cause of Allah. That is best for you,
if you (but) knew. 42 If there had been immediate gain (in sight), and the
journey easy, they would (all) without doubt have followed you, but the
distance was long, (and weighed) on them. They would indeed swear by
Allah, "If we only could, we should certainly have come out with you": they
would destroy their own souls; for Allah does know that they are certainly
lying.

SECTION 7

43 Allah give you grace! why did you grant them exemption until those
who told the truth were seen by you in a clear light, and you had proved
the liars? 44 Those who believe in Allah and the Last Day ask you for no
exemption from fighting with their goods and persons. And Allah knows
well those who do their duty. 45 Only those ask you for exemption who
believe not in Allah and the Last Day, and whose hearts are in doubt, so
that they are tossed in their doubts to and fro. 46 If they had intended to
come out, they would certainly have made some preparation therefor; but
Allah was averse to their being sent forth; so He made them lag behind,
and they were told, "Sit you among those who sit (inactive)." 47 If they had
come out with you, they would not have added to your (strength) but only
(made for) disorder, hurrying to and fro in your midst and sowing sedition
among you, and there would have been some among you who would have
listened to them. But Allah knows well those who do wrong. 48 Indeed they
had plotted sedition before, and upset matters for you,—until the Truth
arrived, and the Decree of Allah became manifest, much to their disgust.

49 Among them is (many) a man who says: "Grant me exemption and
draw me not into trial." Have they not fallen into trial already? And
indeed Hell surrounds the Unbelievers (on all sides). 50 If good befalls
you, it grieves them; but if a misfortune befalls you, they say, "We took
indeed our precautions beforehand," and they turn away rejoicing. 51 Say:
"Nothing will happen to us except what Allah has decreed for us: He is
our Protector": and on Allah let the Believers put their trust. 52 Say: "Can
you expect for us (any fate) other than one of two glorious
things—(martyrdom or victory)? But we can expect for you either that
Allah will send His punishment from Himself, or by our hands. So wait

(expectant); we too will wait with you." 53 Say: "Spend (for the Cause)
willingly or unwillingly: not from you will it be accepted: for you are
indeed a people rebellious and wicked." 54 The only reasons why their
contributions are not accepted are: that they reject Allah and His
Messenger; that they come to prayer without earnestness; and that they
offer contributions unwillingly. 55 Let not their wealth nor their (following
in) sons dazzle you: in reality Allah's plan is to punish them with these
things in this life, and that their souls may perish in their (very) denial of
Allah. 56 They swear by Allah that they are indeed of you; but they are
not of you: yet they are afraid (to appear in their true colours). 57 If they
could find a place to flee to, or caves, or a place of concealment, they
would turn straightaway thereto, with an obstinate rush. 58 And among
them are men who slander you in the matter of (the distribution of) the
alms: if they are given part thereof, they are pleased, but if not, behold!
they are indignant! 59 If only they had been content with what Allah and
His Messenger gave them, and had said, "Sufficient unto us is Allah!
Allah and His Messenger will soon give us of His bounty: to Allah do we
turn our hopes!" (that would have been the right course).

SECTION 8

60 Alms are for the poor and the needy, and those employed to administer
the (funds); for those whose hearts have been (recently) reconciled (to
Truth); for those in bondage and in debt; in the Cause of Allah; and for
the wayfarer: (thus is it) ordained by Allah, and Allah is full of
knowledge and wisdom. 61 Among them are men who molest the Prophet
and say, "He is (all) ear." Say, "He listens to what is best for you: he
believes in Allah, has faith in the Believers, and is a Mercy to those of
you who believe." But those who molest the Messenger will have a
grievous penalty. 62 To you they swear by Allah. In order to please you:
but it is more fitting that they should please Allah and His Messenger, if
they are Believers. 63 Know they not that for those who oppose Allah and
His Messenger, is the Fire of Hell?—wherein they shall dwell. That is the
supreme disgrace.

64 The Hypocrites are afraid lest a Sūrah should be sent down about them,
showing them what is (really passing) in their hearts. Say: "Mock you!
But verily Allah will bring to light all that you fear (should be revealed)."
65 If you do question them, they declare (with emphasis): "We were only

talking idly and in play." Say: "Was it at Allah, and His Signs, and His
Messenger, that you were mocking?" 66 Make you no excuses: you have
rejected Faith after you had accepted it. If We pardon some of you, We
will punish others amongst you, for that they are in sin.

SECTION 9

67 The Hypocrites, men and women, (have an understanding) with each
other: they enjoin evil, and forbid what is just, and are close with their
hands. They have forgotten Allah; so He has forgotten them. Verily the
Hypocrites are rebellious and perverse. 68 Allah has promised the
Hypocrites men and women, and the rejecters, of Faith, the fire of Hell:
therein shall they dwell: sufficient is it for them: for them is the curse of
Allah, and an enduring punishment,—69 As in the case of those before
you: they were mightier than you in power, and more flourishing in
wealth and children. They had their enjoyment of their portion: and you
have of yours, as did those before you; and you indulge in idle talk as
they did. They!—their works are fruitless in this world and in the
Hereafter, and they will lose (all spiritual good). 70 Has not the story
reached them of those before them?—the people of Noah, and 'Ād, and
Thamūd; the people of Abraham, the men of Midian, and the Cities
overthrown. To them came their messengers with clear Signs. It is not
Allah Who wrongs them, but they wrong their own souls.

71 The Believers, men and women, are protectors one of another: they
enjoin what is just, and forbid what is evil: they observe regular prayers,
practise regular charity, and obey Allah and His Messenger. On them will
Allah pour His mercy: for Allah is Exalted in power, Wise. 72 Allah has
promised to Believers, men and women, Gardens under which rivers
flow, to dwell therein, and beautiful mansions in Gardens of everlasting
bliss. But the greatest bliss is the good pleasure of Allah: that is the
supreme felicity.

SECTION 10

73 O Prophet! strive hard against the Unbelievers and the Hypocrites, and
be firm against them. Their abode is Hell,—an evil refuge indeed. 74 They
swear by Allah that they said nothing (evil), but indeed they uttered
blasphemy, and they did it after accepting Islam; and they meditated a
plot which they were unable to carry out: this revenge of theirs was
(their) only return for the bounty with which Allah and His Messenger

had enriched them! If they repent, it will be best for them; but if they turn
back (to their evil ways), Allah will punish them with a grievous penalty
in this life and in the Hereafter: they shall have none on earth to protect
or help them. 75 Amongst them are men who made a covenant with Allah,
that if He bestowed on them of His bounty, they would give (largely) in
charity, and be truly amongst those who are righteous. 76 But when He did
bestow of His bounty, they became covetous, and turned back (from their
covenant), averse (from its fulfilment). 77 So He has put as a consequence
hypocrisy into their hearts, (to last) till the Day whereon they shall meet
Him: because they broke their covenant with Allah, and because they lied
(again and again). 78 Know they not that Allah does know their secret
(thoughts) and their secret counsels, and that Allah knows well all things
unseen?

79 Those who slander such of the believers as give themselves freely to
(deeds of) charity, as well as such as can find nothing to give except the
fruits of their labour,—and throw ridicule on them,—Allah will throw
back their ridicule on them: and they shall have a grievous penalty. 80
Whether you ask for their forgiveness, or not, (their sin is unforgivable):
if you ask seventy times for their forgiveness, Allah will not forgive
them: because they have rejected Allah and His Messenger: and Allah
guides not those who are perversely rebellious.

SECTION 11

81 Those who were left behind (in the Tabūk expedition) rejoiced in their
inaction behind the back of the Messenger of Allah: they hated to strive
and fight, with their goods and their persons, in the Cause of Allah: they
said, "Go not forth in the heat." Say, "The fire of Hell is fiercer in heat."
If only they could understand! 82 Let them laugh a little: much will they
weep: a recompense for the (evil) that they do. 83 If, then, Allah bring you
back to any of them, and they ask your permission to come out (with
you), say: "Never shall you come out with me, nor fight an enemy with
me: for you preferred to sit inactive on the first occasion: then sit you
(now) with those who lag behind." 84 Nor do you ever pray for any of
them that dies, nor stand at his grave; for they rejected Allah and His
Messenger, and died in a state of perverse rebellion. 85 Nor let their
wealth nor their (following in) sons dazzle you: Allah's plan is to punish
them with these things in this world, and that their souls may perish in

their (very) denial of Allah.

86 When a Sūrah comes down, enjoining them to believe in Allah and to
strive and fight along with His Messenger, those with wealth and
influence among them ask you for exemption, and say: "Leave us
(behind): we would be with those who sit (at home)." 87 They prefer to be
with (the women), who remain behind (at home): their hearts are sealed
and so they understand not. 88 But the Messenger, and those who believe
with him, strive and fight with their wealth and their persons: for them are
(all) good things: and it is they who will prosper. 89 Allah has prepared for
them Gardens under which rivers flow, to dwell therein: that is the
supreme felicity.

SECTION 12

90 And there were, among the desert Arabs (also), men who made excuses
and came to claim exemption; and those who were false to Allah and His
Messenger (merely) sat inactive.[12] Soon will a grievous penalty seize the
Unbelievers among them. 91 There is no blame on those who are infirm,
or ill, or who find no resources to spend (on the Cause), if they are
sincere (in duty) to Allah and His Messenger: no ground (of complaint)
can there be against such as do right: and Allah is Oft-Forgiving, Most
Merciful. 92 Nor (is there blame) on those who came to you to be
provided with mounts, and when you said, "I can find no mounts for
you," they turned back, their eyes streaming with tears of grief that they
had no resources wherewith to provide the expenses.

PART XI

93 The ground (of complaint) is against such as claim exemption while
they are rich. They prefer to stay with the (women) who remain behind:
Allah has sealed their hearts; so they know not (What they miss). 94 They
will present their excuses to you when you return to them. Say you:

---

12. Not only had the Hypocrites a nest in Madīnah, but their tactics affected some of the village or desert Bedouins, who loved war and would have followed a standard of war even if no question of Faith or a sacred Cause was involved. But some of them, though professing Islam, were frightened by the hardships of the Tabūk expedition and the prospect of meeting the trained armies of the great Roman (Byzantine) Empire. They made all sorts of lying excuses, but really their want of faith made them ineligible for being enlisted in a sacred Cause, in the terms of 9:46-47 and 9:53-54. Some came to make excuses; others did not even come but sat at home, ignoring the summons. [1342]

"Present no excuses: we shall not believe you: Allah has already informed
us of the true state of matters concerning you: it is your actions that Allah
and His Messenger will observe: in the end will you be brought back to
Him Who knows what is hidden and what is open: then will He show you
the truth of all that you did." 95 They will swear to you by Allah, when you
return to them, that you may leave them alone. So leave them alone: for
they are an abomination, and Hell is their dwelling-place,—a fitting
recompense for the (evil) that they did. 96 They will swear unto you, that
you may be pleased with them. But if you are pleased with them, Allah is
not pleased with those who disobey.

97 The Arabs of the desert are the worst in Unbelief and hypocrisy, and
most fitted to be in ignorance of the command which Allah has sent down
to His Messenger: but Allah is All-Knowing, All-Wise. 98 Some of the
desert Arabs look upon their payments as a fine, and watch for disasters
for you: on them be the disaster of evil: for Allah is He Who hears and
knows (all things). 99 But some of the desert Arabs believe in Allah and
the Last Day, and look on their payments as pious gifts bringing them
nearer to Allah and obtaining the prayers of the Messenger. Aye, indeed
they bring them nearer (to Him): soon will Allah admit them to His
Mercy: for Allah is Oft-Forgiving, Most Merciful.

SECTION 13

100 The vanguard (of Islam)—the first of those who forsook (their homes)
and of those who gave them aid, and (also) those who follow them in (all)
good deeds,—well-pleased is Allah with them, as are they with Him: for
them has He prepared Gardens under which rivers flow, to dwell therein
for ever: that is the supreme felicity.

101 Certain of the desert Arabs round about you are Hypocrites, as well as
(desert Arabs) among the Madīnah folk: they are obstinate in hypocrisy:
you know them not: We know them: twice shall We punish them: and in
addition shall they be sent to a grievous Penalty. 102 Others (there are
who) have acknowledged their wrong-doings: they have mixed an act that
was good with another that was evil. Perhaps Allah will turn unto them
(in mercy): for Allah is Oft-Forgiving, Most Merciful. 103 Of their goods,
take alms, that so you might purify and sanctify them; and pray on their
behalf. Verily your prayers are a source of security for them: and Allah
is One Who hears and knows.

104 Know they not that Allah does accept repentance from His votaries
and receives their gifts of charity, and that Allah is verily He, the Oft-
Returning, Most Merciful? 105 And say: "Work (righteousness): soon will
Allah observe your work, and His Messenger, and the Believers: soon
will you be brought back to the Knower of what is hidden and what is
open: then will He show you the truth of all that you did." 106 There are
(yet) others, held in suspense for the command of Allah, whether He will
punish them, or turn in mercy to them: and Allah is All-Knowing, Wise.

107 And there are those who put up a mosque by way of mischief and
infidelity—to disunite the Believers—and in preparation for one who
warred against Allah and His Messenger aforetime. They will indeed
swear that their intention is nothing but good; but Allah does declare that
they are certainly liars. 108 Never stand you forth therein. There is a
mosque whose foundation was laid from the first day on piety; it is more
worthy of the standing forth (for prayer) therein. In it are men who love
to be purified; and Allah loves those who make themselves pure. 109
Which then is best—he that lays his foundation on piety to Allah and His
good pleasure—or he that lays his foundation on an undermined
sand-cliff ready to crumble to pieces? And it does crumble to pieces with
him, into the fire of Hell. And Allah guides not people that do wrong.[13]
110 The foundation of those who so build is never free from suspicion and
shakiness in their hearts, until their hearts are cut to pieces. And Allah is
All-Knowing, Wise.

SECTION 14

111 Allah has purchased of the believers their persons and their goods; for
theirs (in return) is the Garden (of Paradise): they fight in His Cause, and

---

13. Three categories of Hypocrites having already been mentioned (9:101-106), a fourth class of insidious evil doers is now mentioned, whose type is illustrated in the story of the Qubā "Mosque of mischief (*ḍirār*)". Qubā is a suburb of Madīnah, about three miles to the southeast. When the Holy Prophet arrived at Madīnah for Hijrah, he rested four days in Qubā before entering the town of Madīnah. Here was built the first mosque, the "Mosque of Piety" *(Taqwā)*, or the mosque of the power of Islam (*Qūwah al-Islam*), to which he frequently came during his subsequent stay in Madīnah. Taking advantage of these sacred associations, some Hypocrites of the tribe of Banī Ghanam built an opposition mosque in Qubā, pretending to advance Islam. In reality they were in league with a notorious enemy of Islam, one Abū 'Āmir, who had fought against Islam at Uḥud and who was now, after the battle of Ḥunayn (A.H. 9), in Syria: his confederates wanted a mosque for him to come to, but it would only be a source of mischief and division, and the scheme was disapproved. [1355]

slay and are slain: a promise binding on Him in truth, through the Law,
the Gospel, and the Qur'an: and who is more faithful to his covenant than
Allah? Then rejoice in the bargain which you have concluded: that is the
achievement supreme. 112 Those that turn (to Allah) in repentance; that
serve Him, and praise Him; that wander in devotion to the Cause of
Allah; that bow down and prostrate themselves in prayer; that enjoin good
and forbid evil; and observe the limits set by Allah;—(these do rejoice).
So proclaim the glad tidings to the Believers.

113 It is not fitting, for the Prophet and those who believe, that they should
pray for forgiveness for Pagans, even though they be of kin, after it is
clear to them that they are companions of the Fire. 114 And Abraham
prayed for his father's forgiveness only because of a promise he had
made to him. But when it became clear to him that he was an enemy to
Allah, he dissociated himself from him: for Abraham was most
tender-hearted, forbearing. 115 And Allah will not mislead a people after
He has guided them, in order that He may make clear to them what to
fear (and avoid)—for Allah has knowledge of all things.

116 Unto Allah belongs the dominion of the heavens and the earth. He
gives life and He takes it. Except for Him you have no protector nor
helper. 117 Allah turned with favour to the Prophet, the *Muhājirs*,[14] and
the *Anṣār*,—who followed him in a time of distress, after that the hearts
of a part of them had nearly swerved (from duty); but He turned to them
(also): for He is unto them Most Kind, Most Merciful. 118 (He turned in
mercy also) to the three who were left behind; (they felt guilty) to such
a degree that the earth seemed constrained to them, for all its
spaciousness, and their (very) souls seemed straitened to them,—and they
perceived that there is no fleeing from Allah (and no refuge) but to
Himself. Then He turned to them, that they might repent: for Allah is Oft-
Returning, Most Merciful.

---

14. *Cf.* 9:100. The *Muhājirs* were the people who originally forsook their homes in Makkah and followed Muṣṭafā in exile to Madīnah. The *Anṣār* were the Madīnah people who received them with honour and hospitality into their city. Both these groups were staunch supporters of Islam, and proved their Faith by great sacrifices. But in the difficult days of the Tabūk expedition some of them, not perversely, but out of lethargy and human weakness, had failed to follow the standard. They were forgiven, and they afterwards acquitted themselves with zeal. [1368]

SECTION 15

119 O you who believe! Fear Allah and be with those who are true (in
word and deed). 120 It was not fitting for the people of Madīnah and the
Bedouin Arabs of the neighbourhood, to refuse to follow Allah's
Messenger, nor to prefer their own lives to his: because nothing could
they suffer or do, but was reckoned to their credit as a deed of
righteousness,—whether they suffered thirst, or fatigue, or hunger, in the
Cause of Allah, or trod paths to raise the ire of the Unbelievers, or
received any injury whatever from an enemy: for Allah suffers not the
reward to be lost of those who do good;—121 Nor could they spend
anything (for the Cause)—small or great—nor cut across a valley, but the
deed is inscribed to their credit: that Allah may requite their deed with the
best (possible reward).

122 Nor should the Believers all go forth together: if a contingent from
every expedition remained behind, they could devote themselves to
studies in religion, and admonish the people when they return to
them,—that thus they (may learn) to guard themselves (against evil).[15]

SECTION 16

123 O you who believe! Fight the Unbelievers who gird you about, and let
them find firmness in you: and know that Allah is with those who fear
Him. 124 Whenever there comes down a Sūrah, some of them say: "Which
of you has had his faith increased by it?" Yea, those who believe,—their
faith is increased and they do rejoice. 125 But those in whose hearts is a
disease,—it will add doubt to their doubt, and they will die in a state of
Unbelief. 126 See they not that they are tried every year once or twice? Yet
they turn not in repentance, and they take no heed. 127 Whenever there
comes down a Sūrah, they look at each other, (saying), "Does anyone see
you?" Then they turn aside: Allah has turned their hearts (from the light);
for they are a people that understand not.

128 Now has come unto you a Messenger from amongst yourselves: it

---

15. Fighting may be inevitable, and where a call is made by the righteous Imām, it should be obeyed. But fighting is not to be glorified to the exclusion of all else. Even among those who are able to go forth, a party should remain behind—one in each township or circle—for purposes of study; so that when the fighters return home, their minds may be attuned again to the more normal interests of religious life, under properly instructed teachers. The students and teachers are soldiers of the *Jihād* in their spirit of obedience and discipline. [1373]

grieves him that you should perish: ardently anxious is he over you: to the
Believers is he most kind and merciful. 129 But if they turn away, Say:
"Allah suffices me: there is no god but He: on Him is my trust,—He the
Lord of the Throne (of Glory) Supreme!"□

Chapter 10

Sūrah Yūnus (Jonah)

Translator's Introduction

Chronologically this Sūrah and the five that follow (Sūrahs 11-15) are closely connected, and were revealed in the late Makkan period, as the great event of the Hijrah was gradually approaching down the stream of Time. But their chronology has no particular significance.

On the other hand their arrangement in the gradation of Qur'anic teaching fits in with the subject matter. Sūrahs 8 and 9 were mainly concerned with the first questions that arose on the formation of the new and organised Community of Islam in its conflict with those who wished to suppress or destroy it or use force to prevent its growth and the consolidation of its ideals. See Introductions to those Sūrahs. The present group leads us to the questions that face us when external hostility has been met, and our relations to Allah have to be considered from a higher standpoint than that of self-preservation. How does revelation work? What is the meaning of divine grace and its withdrawal? How do the Messengers of Allah deliver their Message? How should we receive it?

All these questions revolve around the revelation of the Qur'an and each Sūrah of this group except the 13th has the Abbreviated Letters *Alif, Lām, Rā'* attached to it. Sūrah 13 has the letters *Alif, Lām, Mīm, Rā'* and we shall discuss this variation when we come to Sūrah 13.

The Abbreviated Letters are mystic symbols, about whose meaning there is no authoritative explanation. If the theory advanced in the note to 2:1 has any validity, and the present group, *Alif, Lām, Rā'*, is cognate to the group *Alif, Lām, Mīm*, we have to consider and form some idea in our minds as to the probable meaning of the variation. We took *Alif, Lām, Mīm* to be a symbol of those Sūrahs that deal with the beginning, the middle, and the end of man's spiritual history—the origin, the present position, and the things to come in the Last Days (eschatology, to use a theological term). We took *Alif, Lām*, to stand as symbols of the first two, and *Mīm*, of the last. In the present group of Sūrahs we find hardly any eschatological matter, and therefore we can understand the absence of *Mīm*, the symbol standing for such matter. In its place comes *Rā'*, which is phonetically allied to *Lām*. *Lām* is produced by the impact of the tongue to the front of the palate, and *Rā'* to the middle of the palate. In many languages the letters *Lām* and *Rā'* are interchangeable; *e.g.*, in Arabic, *Al-Raḥmān* becomes ar-Raḥmān, and *Rā'* in imperfect enunciation *Lām*, in Chinese lallations. If *Lām* is a symbol of present-day things looking to the future, we may take *Rā'* as a symbol of present-day things looking within, *i.e.*, into the interior of the organisation of the *Ummah*. And this symbolism fits in with the subject matter of the Sūrahs in question. But no one should be dogmatic in speculation about mystic Symbols.

Let us now consider Sūrah 10 alone. The central theme is that Allah's wonderful Creation must not be viewed by us as a creation of material things only, once made and finished with. Most wonderful of all is how He reveals Himself to men through Prophets and Scriptures; how prophets are rejected by men, and the Message disbelieved until it is too late for repentance; and how, as in the case of Yūnus (Jonah) and his people, even the rejection (when repentance supervenes) does not prevent Allah's grace and mercy from working, and how far that working is beyond man's comprehension.

Summary—The wonderful working of the Spirit through man by revelation seems like magic to men; yet they could find Signs and Messages from Him in the sun and the moon and the constantly varying yet regular phenomena of nature, from which men should take a lesson of constancy and Faith (10:1-20).

All the goodness or beauty that man meets in the life around him proceeds from Allah. Yet man is blind and will not understand (10:21-40).

As all things and beings proceed from Allah, so will they return to Him, and He is ever true. Why then does ungrateful man make untrue phantoms for himself instead of rejoicing in the good news which He sends? (10:41-70).

Allah revealed Himself through Noah, but Noah's people rejected him and perished. He spoke through Moses to Pharaoh, but Pharaoh was stiff-necked and arrogant, and when he repented at all, it was too late (10:71-92).

Everywhere want of faith causes people to perish. But the people of Yūnus repented, and Allah saved them by His wonderful grace. So Allah will deliver the Believers. When the Truth comes from Allah, follow it and be patient, for Allah is the most righteous of Judges (10:93-109).

*** *** ***

In the name of Allah,
Most Gracious, Most Merciful.

1 *Alif Lām Rā'*.[1] These are the *Āyāt*[2] of the Book of Wisdom. 2 Is it a
matter of wonderment to men that We have sent Our inspiration to a man
from among themselves?—that he should warn mankind (of their
danger), and give the good news to the Believers that they have before
their Lord the lofty rank of Truth. (But) say the Unbelievers: "This is
indeed an evident sorcerer!" 3 Verily your Lord is Allah, Who created the
heavens and the earth in six days, and is firmly established on the Throne
(of authority), regulating and governing all things. No intercessor (can
plead with Him) except after His leave (has been obtained). This is Allah
your Lord; Him therefore serve you: will you not receive admonition? 4
To Him will be your return—of all of you. The promise of Allah is true
and sure. It is He Who begins the process of creation, and repeats it, that
He may reward with justice those who believe and work righteousness;
but those who reject Him will have draughts of boiling fluids, and a
Penalty grievous, because they did reject Him. 5 It is He Who made the
sun to be a shining glory and the moon to be a light (of beauty), and
measured out stages for her; that you might know the number of years
and the count (of time). Nowise did Allah create this but in truth and
righteousness. (Thus) does He explain His Signs in detail, for those who
understand. 6 Verily, in the alternation of the night and the day, and in all
that Allah has created, in the heavens and the earth, are Signs for those
who fear Him.

7 Those who rest not their hope on their meeting with Us, but are pleased
and satisfied with the life of the present, and those who heed not Our
Signs,—8 Their abode is the Fire, because of the (evil) they earned. 9
Those who believe, and work righteousness,—their Lord will guide them

---

1. For the Abbreviated Letters generally, see note to 2:1. For this particular combination see the Introduction to this Sūrah. [1381]

2. *Āyāt* = Signs, or Verses of the Qur'an. Here both meanings are to be understood. Each verse is a nugget of wisdom. And in the verses immediately following, *e.g.*, 10:3-6, examples are given of the wonders of Allah's material Creation. If the starry heavens impress us with their sublimity as signs of Allah's wisdom and power, how much more wonderful is it that He should speak to lowly man through His Messengers, in man's language, so that he can understand? [1382]

because of their Faith: beneath them will flow rivers in Gardens of bliss.
10 (This will be) their cry therein: "Glory to You, O Allah!" And "Peace" will be their greeting therein! And the close of their cry will be: "Praise be to Allah, the Cherisher and Sustainer of the Worlds!"

SECTION 2

11 If Allah were to hasten for men the ill (they have earned) as they would fain hasten on the good,—then would their respite be settled at once. But We leave those who rest not their hope on their meeting with Us, in their
trespasses, wandering in distraction to and fro.
12 When trouble touches a man, he cries unto Us (in all postures)—lying down on his side, or sitting, or standing. But when We have solved his trouble, he passes on his way as if he had never cried to Us for a trouble that touched him! Thus do the deeds of transgressors seem fair in their eyes!

13 Generations before you We destroyed when they did wrong: their messengers came to them with clear Signs, but they would not believe! Thus do We requite those who sin!
14 Then We made you heirs in the land
after them, to see how you would behave![3]
15 But when Our clear Signs are rehearsed unto them, those who rest not their hope on their meeting with Us, say: "Bring us a Reading[4] other than this, or change this," say: "It is not for me, of my own accord, to change it: I follow naught but what is revealed unto me: if I were to disobey my Lord, I should myself
fear the Penalty of a Great Day (to come)."
16 Say: "If Allah had so willed, I should not have rehearsed it to you, nor would He have made it known to you. A whole lifetime before this have I tarried amongst you: will you not then understand?"

---

3. This is addressed to the Quraysh in the first instance, for they have succeeded to the 'Ād and the Thamūd heritage. But the application is universal, and was true to the 'Abbāsī Empire in the time of Hārūn al-Rashīd, or the Muslim Empire in Spain or the Turkish Empire in its palmiest days, and indeed, apart from political power, to the Muslims and non-Muslims of our own days. [1401]

4. *Reading*: in the Arabic, the word is *Qur'ān*: which may mean Reading or in the special sense, the Qur'an. The duty of Allah's Messenger is to deliver Allah's Message as it is revealed to him, whether it please or displease those who hear it. Selfish men want to read their own desires or fancies into religious precepts, and thus they are often willing to use Religion for their own ends. Most of the corruptions of Religion are due to this cause. But Religion is not to be so prostituted. [1402]

17 Who does more wrong than such as forge a lie against Allah, or deny
His Signs? But never will prosper those who sin. 18 They serve, besides
Allah, things that hurt them not nor profit them, and they say: "These are
our intercessors with Allah." Say: "Do you indeed inform Allah of
something He knows not, in the heavens or on earth?—Glory to Him!
And far is He above the partners they ascribe (to Him)!" 19 Mankind was
but one nation, but differed (later). Had it not been for a Word that went
forth before from your Lord, their differences would have been settled
between them. 20 They say: "Why is not a Sign sent down to him from his
Lord?" Say: "The Unseen is only for Allah (to know), then wait you: I
too will wait with you."

SECTION 3

21 When We make mankind taste of some mercy after adversity has
touched them, behold! they take to plotting against Our Signs! Say:
"Swifter to plan is Allah!" Verily, Our messengers record all the plots
that you make! 22 He it is Who enables you to traverse through land and
sea; so that you even board ships;—they sail with them with a favourable
wind, and they rejoice thereat; then comes a stormy wind and the waves
come to them from all sides, and they think they are being overwhelmed:
they cry unto Allah, sincerely offering (their) duty unto Him, saying, "If
You do deliver us from this, we shall truly show our gratitude!" 23 But
when He delivers them, behold! they transgress insolently through the
earth in defiance of right! O mankind! Your insolence is against your own
souls,—an enjoyment of the life of the present: in the end, to Us is your
return, and We shall show you the truth of all that you did.

24 The likeness of the life of the present is as the rain which We send
down from the skies: by its mingling arises the produce of the
earth—which provides food for men and animals: (it grows) till the earth
is clad with its golden ornaments and is decked out (in beauty): the
people to whom it belongs think they have all powers of disposal over it:
there reaches it Our command by night or by day, and We make it like a
harvest clean-mown, as if it had not flourished only the day before! Thus
do We explain the Signs in detail for those who reflect. 25 But Allah does
call to the Home of Peace: He does guide whom He pleases to a way that
is straight. 26 To those who do right is a goodly (reward)—Indeed, more
(than in measure)! No darkness nor shame shall cover their faces! They

are companions of the Garden; they will abide therein (for ever)! 27 But
those who have earned evil will have a reward of like evil: ignominy will
cover their (faces): no defender will they have from (the wrath of) Allah:
their faces will be covered, as it were, with pieces from the depth of the
darkness of night: they are companions of the Fire: they will abide therein
(for aye)! 28 One day shall We gather them all together. Then shall We
say to those who joined gods (with Us): "To your place! you and those
you joined as 'partners'. We shall separate them, and their 'partners' shall
say: 'It was not us that you worshipped! 29 Enough is Allah for a witness
between us and you: we certainly knew nothing of your worship of us!'"
30 There will every soul prove (the fruits of) the deeds it sent before: they
will be brought back to Allah their rightful Lord, and their invented
falsehoods will leave them in the lurch.

SECTION 4

31 Say: "Who is it that sustains you (in life) from the sky and from the
earth? Or who is it that has power over hearing and sight? And who is it
that brings out the living from the dead and the dead from the living? And
who is it that rules and regulates all affairs?" They will soon say, "Allah".
Say, "Will you not then show piety (to Him)?" 32 Such is Allah, your real
Cherisher and Sustainer: apart from Truth, what (remains) but error? How
then are you turned away? 33 Thus is the Word of your Lord proved true
against those who rebel: verily they will not believe.

34 Say: "Of your 'partners', can any originate creation and repeat it?" Say:
"It is Allah Who originates creation and repeats it: then how are you
deluded away (from the truth)?" 35 Say: "Of your 'partners' is there any
that can give any guidance towards Truth?" Say: "It is Allah Who gives
guidance towards Truth. Is then He Who gives guidance to Truth more
worthy to be followed, or he who finds not guidance (himself) unless he
is guided? What then is the matter with you? How judge you?" 36 But
most of them follow nothing but fancy: truly fancy can be of no avail
against Truth. Verily Allah is well aware of all that they do.

37 This Qur'an is not such as can be produced by other than Allah; on the
contrary it is a confirmation of (revelations) that went before it, and a

fuller explanation of the Book[5]—wherein there is no doubt—from the
Lord of the Worlds. 38 Or do they say, "He forged it"? Say: "Bring then
a Sūrah like unto it, and call (to your aid) anyone you can besides Allah,
if it be you speak the truth!" 39 Nay, they charge with falsehood that
whose knowledge they cannot compass, even before the elucidation
thereof has reached them: thus did those before them make charges of
falsehood: but see what was the end of those who did wrong! 40 Of them
there are some who believe therein, and some who do not: and your Lord
knows best those who are out for mischief.

SECTION 5

41 If they charge you with falsehood, say: "My work to me, and yours to
you! You are free from responsibility for what I do, and I for what you
do!" 42 Among them are some who (pretend to) listen to you: but can you
make the deaf to hear,—even though they are without understanding? 43
And among them are some who look at you: but can you guide the
blind,—even though they will not see? 44 Verily Allah will not deal
unjustly with man in aught: it is man that wrongs his own soul. 45 One day
He will gather them together: (it will be) as if they had tarried but an hour
of a day: they will recognise each other: assuredly those will be lost who
denied the meeting with Allah and refused to receive true guidance. 46
Whether We show you (realised in your lifetime) some part of what We
promise them,—or We take your soul (to Our Mercy) (before that),—in
any case, to Us is their return: ultimately Allah is witness to all that they
do.

47 To every people (was sent) a messenger:[6] when their messenger comes

---

5. *The Book*: *Cf.*3:23. God's revelation throughout the ages is one. The Qur'an confirms, fulfils, completes, and further explains the one true revelation, which has been sent by the One True God in all ages. [1429]

6. Every people or generation or nation had its Message or Messenger: Allah revealed Himself to it in some way or another. If that Messenger was ignored or rejected, or his Message was twisted or misused, the Day of Reckoning will come, when perfect justice will be done and the whole Truth revealed. The Unbelievers mockingly say: "If that is true, pray tell us when that Day will come!" The answer of the Messenger is: "It will come in good time: no one can either hasten or retard it. If you want me then to save you or if you fear that I shall harm you for your treatment of me, know that this matter is in the hands of Allah alone, Who will do perfect justice. Even in regard to myself, any harm or good that befalls me is by the command and in the power of Allah." [1439]

(before them), the matter will be judged between them with justice, and
they will not be wronged. 48 They say: "When will this promise come to
pass,—if you speak the truth?" 49 Say: "I have no power over any harm
or profit to myself except as Allah wills. To every people is a term
appointed: when their term is reached, not an hour can they cause delay,
nor (an hour) can they advance (it in anticipation)." 50 Say: "Do you
see,—if His punishment should come to you by night or by day,—what
portion of it would the sinners wish to hasten? 51 Would you then believe
in it at last, when it actually comes to pass? (It will then be said): 'Ah!
Now? and you wanted (aforetime) to hasten it on!' 52 At length will be
said to the wrong-doers: 'Taste you the enduring punishment! You get
but the recompense of what you earned!'" 53 They seek to be informed by
you: "Is that true?" Say: "Aye! By my Lord! It is the very truth! and you
cannot frustrate it!"

SECTION 6

54 Every soul that has sinned, if it possessed all that is on earth, would
fain give it in ransom: they would declare (their) repentance when they
see the Penalty: but the judgement between them will be with justice, and
no wrong will be done unto them. 55 Is it not (the case) that to Allah
belongs whatever is in the heavens and on earth? Is it not (the case) that
Allah's promise is assuredly true? Yet most of them understand not. 56 It
is He Who gives life and Who takes it, and to Him shall you all be
brought back.

57 O mankind! There has come to you a direction from your Lord and a
healing for the (diseases) in your hearts,—and for those who believe, a
guidance and a Mercy. 58 Say: "In the bounty of Allah. And in His
Mercy,—in that let them rejoice": that is better than the (wealth) they
hoard. 59 Say: "See you what things Allah has sent down to you for
sustenance? Yet you hold forbidden some things thereof and (some
things) lawful." Say: "Has Allah indeed permitted you, or do you invent
(things) to attribute to Allah?" 60 And what think those who invent lies
against Allah, of the Day of Judgement? Verily Allah is full of bounty to
mankind, but most of them are ungrateful.

SECTION 7

61 In whatever business you may be, and whatever portion you may be
reciting from the Qur'an,—and whatever deed you (mankind) may be

doing,—We are witnesses thereof when you are deeply engrossed therein.
Nor is hidden from your Lord (so much as) the weight of an atom on the
earth or in heaven. And not the least and not the greatest of these things
but are recorded in a clear record. 62 Behold! Verily on the friends of
Allah there is no fear, nor shall they grieve; 63 Those who believe and
(constantly) guard against evil;— 64 For them are glad tidings, in the life
of the present and in the Hereafter; no change can there be in the Words
of Allah. This is indeed the supreme felicity. 65 Let not their speech grieve
you: for all power and honour belong to Allah: it is He Who hears and
knows (all things). 66 Behold! Verily to Allah belong all creatures, in the
heavens and on earth. What do they follow who worship as His "partners"
other than Allah? They follow nothing but fancy, and they do nothing but
lie. 67 He it is Who has made you the night that you may rest therein, and
the day to make things visible (to you). Verily in this are Signs for those
who listen (to His Message).

68 They say: "Allah has begotten a son!"—Glory be to Him! He is
self-sufficient! His are all things in the heavens and on earth! No warrant
have you for this! Say you about Allah what you know not? 69 Say:
"Those who invent a lie against Allah will never prosper." 70 A little
enjoyment in this world!—and then, to Us will be their return, then shall
We make them taste the severest Penalty for their blasphemies.

SECTION 8

71 Relate to them the story of Noah. Behold! he said to his people: "O my
people, if it be hard on your (mind) that I should stay (with you) and
commemorate the Signs of Allah,—yet I put my trust in Allah. Get you
then an agreement about your plan and among your partners, so your plan
be not to you dark and dubious. Then pass your sentence on me, and give
me no respite. 72 But if you turn back, (consider): no reward have I asked
of you: my reward is only due from Allah, and I have been commanded
to be of those who submit to Allah's will (in Islam)." 73 They rejected
him, but We delivered him, and those with him, in the Ark, and We made
them inherit (the earth), while We overwhelmed in the flood those who
rejected Our Signs. Then see what was the end of those who were warned
(but heeded not)!

74 Then after him We sent (many) messengers to their peoples: they
brought them clear Signs, but they would not believe what they had

already rejected beforehand. Thus do We seal the hearts of the transgressors.

75 Then after them sent We Moses and Aaron to Pharaoh and his Chiefs
with Our Signs. But they were arrogant: they were a people in sin. 76
When the Truth did come to them from Us, they said: "This is indeed
evident sorcery!" 77 Said Moses: "Say you (this) about the Truth when it
has (actually) reached you? Is sorcery (like) this? But sorcerers will not
prosper." 78 They said: "Have you come to us to turn us away from the
ways we found our fathers following,—in order that you and your brother
may have greatness in the land? But not we shall believe in you!" 79 Said
Pharaoh: "Bring me every sorcerer well versed." 80 When the sorcerers
came, Moses said to them: "Throw you what you (wish) to throw!" 81
When they had had their throw, Moses said: "What you have brought is
sorcery: Allah will surely make it of no effect: for Allah prospers not the
work of those who make mischief. 82 And Allah by His Words does prove
and establish His Truth, however much the sinners may hate it!"

SECTION 9

83 But none believed in Moses except some children of his people,
because of the fear of Pharaoh and his Chiefs, lest they should persecute
them; and certainly Pharaoh was mighty on the earth and one who
transgressed all bounds. 84 Moses said: "O my people! If you do (really)
believe in Allah, then in Him put your trust if you submit (your will to
His)." 85 They said: "In Allah do we put our trust. Our Lord! Make us not
a trial for those who practise oppression; 86 And deliver us by Your
Mercy from those who reject (You)."

87 We inspired Moses and his brother with this Message: "Provide
dwellings for your people in Egypt, make your dwellings into places of
worship, and establish regular prayers: and give glad tidings to those who
believe!" 88 Moses prayed: "Our Lord! You have indeed bestowed on
Pharaoh and his Chiefs splendour and wealth in the life of the present,
and so, our Lord, they mislead (men) from Your Path. Deface, our Lord,
the features of their wealth, and send hardness to their hearts, so they will
not believe until they see the grievous Penalty." 89 Allah said: "Accepted
is your prayer (O Moses and Aaron)! So stand you straight, and follow
not the path of those who know not."

90 We took the Children of Israel across the sea: Pharaoh and his hosts
followed them in insolence and spite. At length, when overwhelmed with
the flood, he said: "I believe that there is no god except Him Whom the
Children of Israel believe in: I am of those who submit (to Allah in
Islam)." 91 (It was said to him): "Ah now!—But a little while before, were
you in rebellion!—and you did mischief (and violence)! 92 This day shall
We save you in your body, that you may be a Sign to those who come
after you! But verily, many among mankind are heedless of Our Signs!"

SECTION 10

93 We settled the Children of Israel in a beautiful dwelling-place, and
provided for them sustenance of the best: it was after knowledge had been
granted to them, that they fell into schisms. Verily Allah will judge
between them as to the schisms amongst them, on the Day of Judgement.
94 If you were in doubt as to what We have revealed unto you, then ask
those who have been reading the Book from before you: the Truth has
indeed come to you from your Lord: so be in no way of those in doubt.
95 Nor be of those who reject the Signs of Allah, or you shall be of those
who perish.

96 Those against whom the Word of your Lord has been verified would
not believe—97 Even if every Sign was brought unto them,—until they
see (for themselves) the grievous Penalty. 98 Why was there not a single
township (among those We warned), which believed,—so its Faith should
have profited it,—except the people of Jonah? When they believed, We
removed from them the Penalty of Ignominy in the life of the present, and
permitted them to enjoy (their life) for a while.

99 If it had been your Lord's Will, they would all have believed,—all who
are on earth! Will you then compel mankind, against their will, to
believe! 100 No soul can believe, except by the Will of Allah, and He will
place doubt (or obscurity) on those who will not understand. 101 Say:
"Behold all that is in the heavens and on earth"; but neither Signs nor
Warners profit those who believe not. 102 Do they then expect (anything)
but (what happened in) the days of the men who passed away before
them? Say: "Wait you then: for I, too, will wait with you." 103 In the end
We deliver Our messengers and those who believe: thus is it fitting on
Our part that We should deliver those who believe!

SECTION 11

104 Say: "O you men! If you are in doubt as to my religion, (behold!) I
worship not what you worship, other than Allah! But I worship
Allah—Who will take your souls (at death): I am commanded to be (in
the ranks) of the Believers, 105 And further (thus): 'set your face towards
religion with true piety, and never in anyway be of the Unbelievers; 106
Nor call on any, other than Allah;—such will neither profit you nor hurt
you: if you do, behold! you shall certainly be of those who do wrong.'"
107 If Allah does touch you with hurt, there is none can remove it but He:
if He does design some benefit for you, there is none can keep back His
favour: He causes it to reach whomsoever of His servants He pleases.
And He is the Oft-Forgiving, Most Merciful. 108 Say: "O you men! Now
Truth has reached you from your Lord! Those who receive guidance, do
so for the good of their own souls; those who stray, do so to their own
loss: and I am not (set) over you to arrange your affairs." 109 Follow you
the inspiration sent unto you, and be patient and constant, till Allah does
decide: for He is the best to decide.□

Chapter 11

Sūrah Hūd
(The Prophet Hūd)

Translator's Introduction

For the chronological place of this Sūrah and the general argument of Sūrahs 10 to 15, see Introduction to Sūrah 10.

In subject matter this Sūrah supplements the preceding one. In the last Sūrah stress was laid on that side of Allah's dealings with man which leans to Mercy: here stress is laid on the side which deals with justice and the punishment of Sin when all Grace is resisted.

Summary—Allah's revelation of mercy, His dealing with man, and His long-suffering patience are contrasted with man's ingratitude, his love of falsehood and vanity, and his crookedness (11:1-24).

Noah's unselfishness and humility in teaching his people the Truth of Allah were traduced by the ungodly, and his Message ridiculed and rejected. But he built his Ark under directions from Allah, and was saved, with peace and blessings, while his rejecters perished (11:25-49).

The Prophet Hūd preached to his people, the 'Ād, against false gods, and the Prophet Ṣāliḥ to his people, the Thamūd, against dishonouring the symbol of Allah's bounty. In both cases Allah's Signs were rejected, and the rejecters were blotted out (11:50-68).

Lot's people were given to abominations: Abraham pleaded for them, and Lot was sent out to them, but they went deeper and deeper into sin and suffered the Penalty. Shu'ayb's people, the Midianites, were warned against fraud and mischief, but they reproached him with helplessness and were themselves destroyed (11:69-95).

It is arrogant leaders like Pharaoh who mislead men, and men bring ruin on themselves. But Allah is Just. The penalty for sin is real and abiding; therefore shun all wrongdoing, and serve Allah wholeheartedly (11:96-123).

*** *** ***

In the name of Allah,
Most Gracious, Most Merciful

1 *Alif Lām Rā'*.[1] (This is) a Book, with verses basic or fundamental (of
established meaning), further explained in detail,—from One Who is
Wise and Well-acquainted (with all things): 2 (It teaches) that you should
worship none but Allah. (Say): "Verily I am (sent) unto you from Him to
warn and to bring glad tidings: 3 (And to preach thus), 'Seek you the
forgiveness of your Lord, and turn to Him in repentance; that He may
grant you enjoyment, good (and true), for a term appointed, and bestow
His abounding grace on all who abound in merit! But if you turn away,
then I fear for you the Penalty of a Great Day: 4 'To Allah is your return,
and He has power over all things.'" 5 Behold! They fold up their hearts,
that they may lie hid from Him! Ah! Even when they cover themselves
with their garments, He knows what they conceal, and what they reveal:
for He knows well the (inmost secrets) of the hearts.

PART XII

6 There is no moving creature on earth but its sustenance depends on
Allah: He knows the time and place of its definite abode and its
temporary deposit: all is in a clear record.[2] 7 He it is Who created the
heavens and the earth in six Days—and His Throne was over the
Waters[3]—that He might try you, which of you is best in conduct. But if
you were to say to them, "You shall indeed be raised up after death", the
Unbelievers would be sure to say, "This is nothing but obvious sorcery!"
8 If We delay the Penalty for them for a definite term, they are sure to say,
"What keeps it back?" Ah! On the day it (actually) reaches them, nothing
will turn it away from them, and they will be completely encircled by that
which they used to mock at!

---

1. For the meaning of these Letters, see Introduction to Sūrah 10. [1492]

2. *Cf.* 6:59 and 10:61. [1500]

3. It is scientifically correct to say that all life was evolved out of the waters, and this statement also occurs in the Qur'an, 21:30. The throne of Allah's authority is metaphorically expressed as over the waters, *i.e.*, as regulating all life. Some such mystic meaning, I think, also attaches to the Gen. i. 2. The past tense "was" refers to the time before life developed in solid forms, on land and in air. [1502]

SECTION 2

9 If We give man a taste of mercy from Ourselves, and then withdraw it
from him, behold! he is in despair and (falls into) blasphemy. 10 But if We
give him a taste of (Our) favours after adversity has touched him, he is
sure to say, "All evil has departed from me:" behold! he falls into
exultation and pride. 11 Not so do those who show patience and
constancy, and work righteousness; for them is forgiveness (of sins) and
a great reward.

12 Perchance you may (feel the inclination) to give up a part of what is
revealed[4] unto you, and your heart feels straitened lest they say, "Why
is not a treasure sent down unto him, or why does not an angel come
down with him?" But you are there only to warn! It is Allah that arranges
all affairs! 13 Or they may say, "He forged it." Say, "Bring you then ten
Sūrahs forged, like unto it, and call (to your aid) whomsoever you can,
other than Allah!—if you speak the truth![5] 14 If then they (your false
gods) answer not your (call), know you that this Revelation is sent down
(replete) with the knowledge of Allah, and that there is no god but He!
Will you even then submit (to Islam)?"

15 Those who desire the life of the present and its glitter,—to them We
shall pay (the price of) their deeds therein,—without diminution. 16 They
are those for whom there is nothing in the Hereafter but the Fire: vain are
the designs they frame therein, and of no effect and the deeds that they
do! 17 Can they be (like) those who accept a clear (Sign) from their Lord,
and whom a witness from Himself does teach, as did the Book of Moses
before it,—a guide and a mercy? They believe therein; but those of the
Sects that reject it,—the Fire will be their promised meeting-place. Be not
then in doubt thereon: for it is the Truth from your Lord: yet many among

---

4. Every Prophet of Allah, when he not only encounters opposition, but is actually accused of falsehood and those very evils which he is protesting against, may feel inclined, in his human weakness, to ask himself the question, "Supposing I omit this little point, will Allah's Truth then be accepted more readily?" Or he may think to himself, "If I had only more money to organise my campaign, or something which will draw people's attention, like the company of an angel, how much better can I push my Message?" He is told that truth must be delivered as it is revealed, even though portions of it may be unpalatable, and that resources and other means to draw people to him are beside the point. He must use just such resources and opportunities as he has, and leave the rest to Allah. [1509]

5. *Cf.* 2:23 and 10.38.

men do not believe!

18 Who does more wrong than those who invent a lie against Allah? They
will be turned back to the presence of their Lord, and the witnesses will
say, "These are the ones who lied against their Lord! Behold! the Curse
of Allah is on those who do wrong!— 19 Those who would hinder (men)
from the path of Allah and would seek in it something crooked: these
were they who denied the Hereafter!" 20 They will in no way frustrate
(His design) on earth, nor have they protectors besides Allah! Their
penalty will be doubled! They lost the power to hear, and they did not
see! 21 They are the ones who have lost their own souls: and the (fancies)
they invented have left them in the lurch! 22 Without a doubt, these are the
very ones who will lose most in the Hereafter! 23 But those who believe
and work righteousness, and humble themselves before their Lord,—they
will be companions of the Gardens, to dwell therein for ever! 24 These
two kinds (of men) may be compared to the blind and deaf, and those
who can see and hear well. Are they equal when compared? Will you not
then take heed?

SECTION 3

25 We sent Noah to his people (with a mission): "I have come to you with
a clear Warning: 26 That you serve none but Allah: verily I do fear for you
the Penalty of a grievous Day."

27 But the Chiefs of the Unbelievers among his people said: "We see (in)
you nothing but a man like ourselves: nor do we see that any follow you
but the meanest among us, in judgement immature: nor do we see in you
(all) any merit above us: in fact we think you are liars!" 28 He said: "O my
people! See you if (it be that) I have a clear Sign from my Lord, and that
He has sent Mercy unto me from His own presence, but that the Mercy
has been obscured from your sight? Shall we compel you to accept it
when you are averse to it? 29 And O my people! I ask you for no wealth
in return: my reward is from none but Allah: but I will not drive away (in
contempt) those who believe: for verily they are to meet their Lord, and
you I see are the ignorant ones! 30 And O my people! Who would help me
against Allah if I drove them away? Will you not then take heed? 31 I tell
you not that with me are the treasures of Allah, nor do I know what is
hidden, nor claim I to be an angel. Nor yet do I say, of those whom your

eyes do despise that Allah will not grant them (all) that is good: Allah
knows best what is in their souls: I should, if I did, indeed be a wrong-
doer." 32 They said: "O Noah! You have disputed with us, and (much)
have you prolonged the dispute with us: now bring upon us what you
threaten us with, if you speak the truth!?" 33 He said: "Truly, Allah will
bring it on you if He wills,—and then, you will not be able to frustrate it!
34 Of no profit will be my counsel to you, much as I desire to give you
(good) counsel, if it be that Allah wills to leave you astray: He is your
Lord! and to Him will you return!"

35 Or do they say, "He has forged it"? Say: "If I had forged it, on me were
my sin! and I am free of the sins of which you are guilty!"

SECTION 4

36 It was revealed to Noah: "None of your people will believe except
those who have believed already! So grieve no longer over their (evil)
deeds. 37 But construct an Ark under Our eyes and Our inspiration, and
address Me no (further) on behalf of those who are in sin: for they are
about to be overwhelmed (in the Flood)." 38 Forthwith he (starts)
constructing the Ark: every time that the Chiefs of his people passed by
him, they threw ridicule on him. He said: "If you ridicule us now, we (in
our turn) can look down on you with ridicule likewise! 39 But soon will
you know who it is on whom will descend a Penalty that will cover them
with shame,—on whom will be unloosed a Penalty lasting:"

40 At length, behold! there came Our command, and the fountains of the
earth gushed forth! We said: "Embark therein, of each kind two, male and
female, and your family—except those against whom the Word has
already gone forth,—and the Believers." But only a few believed with
him. 41 So he said: "Embark you on the Ark, in the name of Allah,
whether it move or be at rest! For my Lord is, be sure, Oft-forgiving,
Most Merciful!" 42 So the Ark floated with them on the waves (towering)
like mountains, and Noah called out to his son, who had separated
himself (from the rest): "O my son! Embark with us, and be not with the
Unbelievers!" 43 The son replied: "I will betake myself to some mountain:
it will save me from the water." Noah said: "This day nothing can save,

from the command of Allah, any but those on whom He has mercy!" And the waves came between them, and the son was among those overwhelmed in the Flood.

44 Then the word went forth: "O earth! swallow up your water, and O sky! Withhold (your rain)!" and the water abated, and the matter was ended. The Ark rested on Mount Jūdī,[6] and the word went forth: "Away with those who do wrong!"

45 And Noah called upon his Lord, and said: "O my Lord! Surely my son
is of my family! and Your promise is true, and You are the justest of
Judges!" 46 He said: "O Noah! He is not of your family: for his conduct
is unrighteous. So ask not of Me that of which you have no knowledge!
I give you counsel, lest you act like the ignorant!" 47 Noah said: "O my
Lord! I do seek refuge with You, lest I ask You for that of which I have
no knowledge. And unless you forgive me and have Mercy on me, I
should indeed be lost!" 48 The word came: "O Noah! Come down (from
the Ark) with peace from Us, and blessing on you and on some of the
peoples (who will spring) from those with you: but (there will be other)
peoples to whom We shall grant their pleasures (for a time), but in the

6. Let us get a little idea of the geography of the place. The letters *Jīm, Bā* and *Kāf* are philologically interchangeable, and Jūdī, Gūdī, Kūdī are sounds that can pass into each other. There is no doubt that the name is connected with the name "Kurd", in which the letter *r* is a later interpolation, for the oldest Sumerian records name a people called Kūtī or Gūtū as holding the middle Tigris region not later than 2000 B.C. (see *E.B.*, Kurdistan). That region comprises the modern Turkish district of Bohtan, in which Jabal Jūdī is situated (near the frontiers of modern Turkey, modern Iraq, and modern Syria), and the town of Jazirah ibn 'Umar, (on the present Turco-Syrian frontier), and it extends into Iraq and Iran. The great mountain mass of the Ararat plateau dominates this district. This mountain system "is unique in the Old World in containing great sheets of water that are bitter lakes without outlets, Lake Van and Lake Urumiya being the chief" (*E.B.*, Asia). Such would be the very region for a stupendous Deluge if the usual scanty rainfall were to be changed into a very heavy downpour. A glacier damming of Lake Van in the Ice Age would have produced the same result. The region has many local traditions connected with Noah and the Flood. The Biblical legend of Mount Ararat being the resting place of Noah's Ark is hardly plausible, seeing that the highest peak of Ararat is over 16,000 feet high. If it means one of the lower peaks of the Ararat system, it agrees with the Muslim tradition about Mount Jūdī (or Gūdī), and this is in accordance with the oldest and best local traditions. These traditions are accepted by Josephus, by the Nestorian Christians, and indeed by all the Eastern Christians and Jews, and they are the best in touch with local traditions. See (Viscount) J. Bryce, *Transcaucasia and Ararat*, 4th ed., 1896, p. 216. [1539]

end will a grievous Penalty reach them from Us."

49 Such are some of the stories of the Unseen, which We have revealed unto you: before this, neither you nor your people knew them. So persevere patiently: for the End is for those who are righteous.

SECTION 5

50 To the 'Ād people (We sent) Hūd, one of their own brethren. He said:
"O my people! Worship Allah! You have no other god but Him. (Your
other gods) you do nothing but invent! 51 O my people! I ask of you no
reward for this (Message). My reward is from none but Him who created
me: will you not then understand? 52 And O my people! Ask forgiveness
of your Lord, and turn to Him (in repentance): He will send you the skies
pouring abundant rain, and add strength to your strength: so turn you not
back in sin!" 53 They said: "O Hūd! No clear (Sign) have you brought us,
and we are not the ones to desert our gods on your word! Nor shall we
believe in you! 54 We say nothing but that (perhaps) some of our gods
may have seized you with imbecility." He said: "I call Allah to witness,
and do you bear witness, that I am free from the sin of ascribing, to Him,
55 Other gods as partners! so scheme (your worst) against me, all of you,
and give me no respite. 56 I put my trust in Allah, my Lord and your
Lord! There is not a moving creature, but He has grasp of its forelock.
Verily, it is my Lord that is on a straight Path. 57 If you turn away,—I (at
least) have conveyed the Message with which I was sent to you. My Lord
will make another people to succeed you, and you will not harm Him in
the least. For my Lord has care and watch over all things."

58 So when Our decree issued, We saved Hūd and those who believed
with him, by (special) Grace from Ourselves: We saved them from a
severe Penalty. 59 Such were the 'Ād People: they rejected the Signs of
their Lord and Cherisher; disobeyed His messengers; and followed the
command of every powerful, obstinate transgressor. 60 And they were
pursued by a Curse in this life,—and on the Day of Judgement. Ah!
Behold! for the 'Ād rejected their Lord and Cherisher! Ah! Behold!
removed (from sight) were 'Ād the people of Hūd!

SECTION 6

61 To the Thamūd people (We sent) Ṣāliḥ, one of their own brethren. He
said: "O my people! Worship Allah: you have no other god but Him. It

is He Who has produced you from the earth and settled you therein: then
ask forgiveness of Him, and turn to Him (in repentance): for my Lord is
(always) near, ready to answer." 62 They said: "O Ṣāliḥ! You have been
of us! a centre of our hopes hitherto! Do you (now) forbid us the worship
of what our fathers worshipped? But we are really in suspicious
(disquieting) doubt as to that to which you invite us." 63 He said: "O my
people! Do you see? if I have a clear (Sign) from my Lord and He has
sent Mercy unto me from Himself,—who then can help me against Allah
if I were to disobey Him? What then would you add to my (portion) but
perdition? 64 And O my people! This she-camel of Allah is a symbol to
you: leave her to feed on Allah's (free) earth, and inflict no harm on her,
or a swift Penalty will seize you!" 65 But they did hamstring her. So he
said: "Enjoy yourselves in your homes for three days: (then will be your
ruin): (behold) there a promise not to be belied!" 66 When Our decree
issued, We saved Ṣāliḥ and those who believed with him, by (special)
Grace from Ourselves—and from the Ignominy of that Day. For your
Lord—He is the Strong One, and able to enforce His Will. 67 The
(mighty) Blast overtook the wrong-doers, and they lay prostrate in their
homes before the morning,—68 As if they had never dwelt and flourished
there. Ah! Behold! for the Thamūd rejected their Lord and Cherisher! Ah!
Behold! removed (from sight) were the Thamūd!

SECTION 7

69 There came Our messengers to Abraham with glad tidings. They said,
"Peace!" He answered, "Peace!" and hastened to entertain them with a
roasted calf. 70 But when he saw their hands went not towards the (meal),
he felt some mistrust of them, and conceived a fear of them. They said:
"Fear not: we have been sent against the people of Lūt." 71 And his wife
was standing (there), and she laughed: but we gave her glad tidings of
Isaac, and after him, of Jacob. 72 She said: "Alas for me! Shall I bear a
child, seeing I am an old woman, and my husband here is an old man?
That would indeed be a wonderful thing!" 73 They said: "Do you wonder
at Allah's decree? The grace of Allah and His blessings on you, O you
people of the house! For He is indeed worthy of all praise, full of all
glory!"

74 When fear had passed from (the mind of) Abraham and the glad tidings
had reached him, he began to plead with Us for Lūṭ's people. 75 For

Abraham was, without doubt, forbearing (of faults), compassionate, and given to look to Allah. 76 O Abraham! Seek not this. The decree of your Lord has gone forth: for them there comes a Penalty that cannot be turned back!

77 When Our messengers came to Lūṭ, he was grieved on their account and felt himself powerless (to protect) them. He said: "This is a distressful day."[7] 78 And his people came rushing towards him, and they had been long in the habit of practising abominations. He said: "O my people! Here are my daughters: they are purer for you (if you marry)![8] Now fear Allah, and cover me not with shame about my guests! Is there not among you a single right-minded man?" 79 They said: "Well do you know we have no need of your daughters: indeed you know quite well what we want!" 80 He said: "Would that I had power to suppress you or that I could betake myself to some powerful support."[9] 81 (The Messengers) said: "O Lūṭ! We are Messengers from your Lord! By no means shall they reach you! Now travel with your family while yet a part

---

7. The story of Lot, as referred to in 7:80-84, laid emphasis on the rejection of Lot's mission by men who practised unnatural abominations. Here the emphasis is laid on Allah's dealings with men—in mercy for true spiritual service and in righteous wrath and punishment for those who defy the laws of nature established by Him; also, on men's dealings with each other and the contrast between the righteous and the wicked who respect no laws human or divine. [1574]

8. The Biblical narrative suggests that the daughters were married and their husbands were close by (Gen. xix. 14) and that these same daughters afterwards committed incest with their father and had children by him (Gen. xix. 31). The Holy Qur'an nowhere suggests such abominations. Some Commentators suggest that "my daughters" in the mouth of a venerable man like Lūṭ, the father of his people, may mean any young girls of those Towns. "My son" (*waladī*) is still a common mode of address in Arabic-speaking countries when an elderly man addresses a young man. [1575]

9. Lūṭ seemed helpless in the situation in which he found himself—alone against a rabble of people inflamed with evil passions. He wished he had had the strength to suppress them himself or had had some powerful support to lean on! But the powerful support was there, though he had not realised it till then. It was the support of Allah. His guests were not ordinary men, but Angels who had come to test the people before they inflicted the punishment. They now declared themselves, and gave him directions to get away before the morning, when the punishment would descend on the doomed Cities of the Plain. [1576]

of the night remains, and let not any of you look back: but your wife[10]
(will remain behind): to her will happen what happens to the people.
Morning is their time appointed: is not the morning nigh?"
82 When Our
decree issued, We turned (the cities) upside down, and rained down on
them brimstones hard as baked clay, spread, layer on layer,—
83 Marked
as from your Lord: nor are they[11] ever far from those who do wrong!

SECTION 8

84 To the Madyan people (We sent) Shu'ayb, one of their own brethren:
he said: "O my people! Worship Allah: you have no other god but Him.
And give not short measure or weight: I see you in prosperity, but I fear
for you the Penalty of a Day that will compass (you) all round.
85 And O
my people! Give just measure and weight, nor withhold from the people
the things that are their due:[12] commit not evil in the land with intent to
do mischief.
86 That which is left you by Allah is best for you, if you (but)
believed! But I am not set over you to keep watch!"
87 They said: "O
Shu'ayb! Does your (religion of) prayer command you that we leave off
the worship which our fathers practised, or that we leave off doing what
we like with our property? Truly, you are the one that forbears with faults
and is right-minded!"
88 He said: "O my people! See you whether I have
a clear (Sign) from my Lord, and He has given me sustenance (pure and)
good as from Himself? I wish not, in opposition to you, to do that which
I forbid you to do. I only desire (your) betterment to the best of my
power; and my success (in my task) can only come from Allah. In Him
I trust, and unto Him I look.
89 And O my people! Let not my dissent

10. Even in Lot's household was one who detracted from the harmony of the family. She was disobedient to her husband, and he was here obeying Allah's Command. She looked back and shared the fate of the wicked inhabitants of the Cities of the Plain: see also 66:10. The Biblical narrative suggests that she was turned into a pillar of salt (Gen. xix. 26). [1577]

11. *They*: Arabic *hiya*: some Commentators take the pronoun to refer to the wicked cities so destroyed: the meaning then would be: those wicked cities were not so different from other cities that do wrong, for they would all suffer similar punishment! Perhaps it would be better to refer "they" to the stones of punishment by a metonymy for "punishment": 'punishment would not be far from any people that did wrong.' [1581]

12. Both Plato and Aristotle define justice as the virtue which gives everyone his due. From this point of view Justice becomes the master virtue, and includes most other virtues. It was the lack of this that ruined the Midianites. Their selfishness was "intent on mischief:" *i.e.*, spoiling other people's business by not giving them their just dues. [1584]

(from you) cause you to sin, lest you suffer a fate similar to that of the
people of Noah or of Hūd or of Ṣāliḥ, nor are the people of Lūṭ far off
from you! 90 But ask forgiveness of your Lord, and turn unto Him (in
repentance): for my Lord is indeed full of mercy and loving-kindness."
91 They said: "O Shu'ayb! Much of what you say we do not understand!
In fact among us we see that you have no strength! Were it not for your
family, we should certainly have stoned you! For you have among us no
great position!" 92 He said: "O my people! Is then my family of more
consideration with you than Allah? For you cast Him away behind your
backs (with contempt). But verily my Lord encompasses on all sides all
that you do! 93 And O my people! Do whatever you can: I will do (my
part): soon will you know who it is on whom descends the Penalty of
Ignominy; and who is a liar! And watch you! For I too am watching with
you!" 94 When Our decree issued, We saved Shu'ayb and those who
believed with him, by (special) mercy from Ourselves: but the (mighty)
Blast did seize the wrong-doers, and they lay prostrate in their homes by
the morning,—95 As if they had never dwelt and flourished there! Ah!
Behold! how the Madyan were removed (from sight) as were removed
the Thamūd!

SECTION 9

96 And We sent Moses, with Our clear (Signs) and an authority manifest,
97 Unto Pharaoh and his Chiefs: but they followed the command of
Pharaoh and the command of Pharaoh was no right (guide). 98 He will go
before his people on the Day of Judgement, and lead them into the Fire
(as cattle are led to water): but woeful indeed will be the place to which
they are led! 99 And they are followed by a curse in this (life) and on the
Day of Judgement: and woeful is the gift which shall be given (unto
them)!

100 These are some of the stories of communities which We relate unto
you: of them some are standing, and some have been mown down (by the
sickle of time). 101 It was not We that wronged them: they wronged their
own souls: the deities, other than Allah, whom they invoked, profited
them not at all when there issued the decree of your Lord: nor did they
add aught (to their lot) but perdition! 102 Such is the chastisement of your
Lord when He chastises communities in the midst of their wrong:
grievous, indeed, and severe is His chastisement. 103 In that is a Sign for

those who fear the Penalty of the Hereafter: that is a Day for which
mankind will be gathered together: that will be a Day of Testimony. 104
Nor shall We delay it but for a term appointed.

105 The day it arrives, no soul shall speak except by His leave: of those
(gathered) some will be wretched and some will be blessed. 106 Those who
are wretched shall be in the Fire: there will be for them therein (nothing
but) the heaving of sighs and sobs: 107 They will dwell therein for all the
time that the heavens and the earth endure, except as your Lord wills: for
your Lord is the (sure) accomplisher of what He plans. 108 And those who
are blessed shall be in the Garden: they will dwell therein for all the time
that the heavens and the earth endure, except as your Lord wills: a gift
without break. 109 Be not then in doubt as to what these men worship.
They worship nothing but what their fathers worshipped before (them):
but verily We shall pay them back (in full) their portion without (the
least) abatement.

SECTION 10

110 We certainly gave the Book to Moses, but differences arose therein:
had it not been that a Word had gone forth before from your Lord, the
matter would have been decided between them, but they are in suspicious
doubt concerning it. 111 And, of a surety, to all will your Lord pay back
(in full the recompense) of their deeds: for He knows well all that they
do. 112 Therefore stand firm (in the straight Path) as you are
commanded,—you and those who with you turn (unto Allah); and
transgress not (from the Path): for He sees well all that you do. 113 And
incline not to those who do wrong, or the Fire will seize you; and you
have no protectors other than Allah, nor shall you be helped. 114 And
establish regular prayers at the two ends of the day[13] and at the
approaches of the night:[14] for those things that are good remove those

---

13. *The two ends of the day*: Morning and afternoon. The morning prayer is the *Fajr*, after the light is up but before sunrise: we thus get up betimes and begin the day with the remembrance of Allah and of our duty to Him. The early afternoon prayer, *Ẓuhr*, is immediately after noon: we are in the midst of our daily life, and again we remember Allah. [1616]

14. *Approaches of the night*: Arabic *Zulafun*, plural of *Zulfatun*, an approach, something near at hand. As Arabic has, like Greek, a dual number distinct from the plural, and the plural number is used here, and not the dual, it is reasonable to argue that at least three "approaches of the night" are meant. The later afternoon prayer, *'Aṣr*, can be one of these

that are evil: be that the word of remembrance to those who remember
(their Lord): 115 And be steadfast in patience; for verily Allah will not
suffer the reward of the righteous to perish.

116 Why were there not, among the generations before you, persons
possessed of balanced good sense, prohibiting (men) from mischief in the
earth—except a few among them whom We saved (from harm)? But the
wrong-doers pursued the enjoyment of the good things of life which were
given them, and persisted in sin. 117 Nor would your Lord be the One to
destroy communities for a single wrong-doing, if its members were likely
to mend. 118 If your Lord had so willed, He could have made mankind one
people: but they will not cease to dispute, 119 Except those on whom your
Lord has bestowed His Mercy: and for this did He create them: and the
Word of your Lord shall be fulfilled: "I will fill Hell with *jinns* and men
all together."

120 All that We relate to you of the stories of the messengers,—with it We
make firm your heart: in them there comes to you the Truth, as well as an
exhortation and a message of remembrance to those who believe. 121 Say to
those who do not believe: "Do whatever you can: we shall do our part; 122
And wait you! we too shall wait." 123 To Allah belong the unseen (secrets)
of the heavens and the earth, and to Him goes back every affair (for
decision): then worship Him, and put your trust in Him: and your Lord is
not unmindful of aught that you do.□

---

three, and the evening prayer, *Maghrib*, just after sunset, can be the second. The early night prayer, *'Ishā'*, at supper time when the glow of sunset is disappearing, would be the third of the "approaches of the night", when we commit ourselves to Allah before sleep. These are the five canonical prayers of Islam. [1617]

Chapter 12

Sūrah Yūsuf
(Joseph)

Translator's Introduction

For the chronological place of this Sūrah and the general argument of Sūrahs 10 to 15, see Introduction to Sūrah 10.

In subject matter this Sūrah is entirely taken up with the story (recapitulated rather than told) of Joseph, the youngest (but one) of the twelve sons of the patriarch Jacob. The story is called the most beautiful of stories (12:3) for many reasons: (1) it is the most detailed of any in the Qur'an; (2) it is full of human vicissitudes, and has therefore deservedly appealed to men and women of all classes; (3) it paints in vivid colours, with their spiritual implications, the most varied aspects of life—the patriarch's old age and the confidence between him and his little best-beloved son, the elder brothers' jealousy of this little son, their plot and their father's grief, the sale of the father's darling into slavery for a miserable little price, carnal love contrasted with purity and chastity, false charges, prison, the interpretation of dreams, low life and high life, Innocence raised to honour, the sweet "revenge" of Forgiveness and Benevolence, high matters of state and administration, humility in exaltation, filial love, and the beauty of Piety and Truth.

The story is similar to but not identical with the Biblical story; but the atmosphere is wholly different. The Biblical story is like a folktale in which morality has no place. Its tendency is to exalt the clever and financially-minded Jew against the Egyptian, and to explain certain ethnic and tribal peculiarities in later Jewish history. Joseph is shown as buying up all the cattle and the land of the poor Egyptians for the State under the stress of famine conditions, and making the Israelites "rulers" over Pharaoh's cattle. The Qur'anic story, on the other hand, is less a narrative than a highly spiritual sermon or allegory explaining the seeming contradictions in life, the enduring nature of virtue in a world full of flux and change, and the marvellous working of Allah's eternal purpose in His Plan as unfolded to us on the wide canvas of history. This aspect of the matter has been a favourite with Muslim poets and Sufi exegetists.

Summary—Life is a dream and a vision, to be explained by stories and parables, as in the perspicuous Arabic Qur'an. The truth, which Joseph the Prophet of Allah saw in his vision, was unpalatable to his ten half-brothers, who plotted against him and sold him into slavery to a merchant for a few pieces of silver (12:1-20).

Joseph was taken by the merchant into Egypt, was bought by a great

Egyptian court dignitary ('Azīz), who adopted him. The dignitary's wife sought, but in vain, to attract Joseph to the delights of earthly love. His resistance brought him disgrace and imprisonment, but he taught the truth even in prison and was known for his kindness. One of his fellow prisoners, to whom he had interpreted a dream, was released and received into favour as the King's cupbearer (12:21-42).

The King had a vision, which Joseph (through the cupbearer) got an opportunity to explain. Joseph insisted that all the scandal that had been raised about him should be publicly cleared. He was received into favour, and was appointed *wazīr* by the King. His half-brothers (driven by famine) came to Egypt and were treated kindly by Joseph without their knowing his identity. He asks them to bring his full brother, the youngest son, Benjamin. (12:43-68).

Joseph detains Benjamin and by a stratagem convicts his half-brothers of their hatred and crime against himself, forgives them, and sends them to bring Jacob and the whole family from Canaan to Egypt (12:69-93).

Israel (Jacob) comes, is comforted, and settles in Egypt. The name of Allah is glorified. The truth of Allah endures forever, and Allah's purpose is fully revealed in the Hereafter (12:94-111).

*** *** ***

In the name of Allah,
Most Gracious, Most Merciful.

1 *Alif Lām Rā'*.[1] These are the Symbols (or Verses) of the perspicuous
Book. 2 We have sent it down as an Arabic Qur'an, in order that you may
learn wisdom. 3 We do relate unto you the most beautiful of stories, in
that We reveal to you this (portion of the) Qur'an: before this, you too
were among those who knew it not.

4 Behold! Joseph said to his father: "O my father! I did see eleven stars
and the sun and the moon: I saw them prostrate themselves to me!" 5 Said
(the father): "My (dear) little son! Relate not your vision to your brothers,
lest they concoct a plot against you: for Satan is to man an avowed
enemy! 6 Thus will your Lord choose you and teach you the interpretation
of stories (and events) and perfect His favour to you and to the posterity
of Jacob—even as He perfected it to your fathers Abraham and Isaac
aforetime! For Allah is full of knowledge and wisdom."

---

1. For the meaning of these mystic letters, see Introduction to Sūrah 10. [1627]

SECTION 2

7 Verily in Joseph and his brethren are Signs (or Symbols) for seekers
(after Truth).

8 They said: "Truly Joseph and his brother are loved more by our father
than we: but we are a goodly body! Really our father is obviously
wandering (in his mind)! 9 Slay you Joseph or cast him out to some
(unknown) land, that so the favour of your father may be given to you
alone: (there will be time enough) for you to be righteous after that!" 10
Said one of them: "Slay not Joseph, but if you must do something, throw
him down to the bottom of the well: he will be picked up by some
caravan of travellers."

11 They said: "O our father! Why do you not trust us with Joseph,—seeing
we are indeed his sincere well-wishers? 12 Send him with us tomorrow to
enjoy himself and play, and we shall take every care of him." 13 (Jacob)
said: "Really it saddens me that you should take him away: I fear lest the
wolf should devour him while you attend not to him." 14 They said: "If
the wolf were to devour him while we are (so large) a party, then should
we indeed (first) have perished ourselves!"

15 So they did take him away, and they all agreed to throw him down to
the bottom of the well: and We put into his heart (this Message): "Of a
surety you shall (one day) tell them the truth of this their affair while they
know (you) not."

16 Then they came to their father in the early part of the night, weeping.
17 They said: "O our father! We went racing with one another, and left
Joseph with our things; and the wolf devoured him, but you will never
believe us even though we tell the truth." 18 They stained his shirt with
false blood. He said: "Nay, but your minds have made up a tale (that may
pass) with you. (For me) patience is most fitting: against that which you
assert, it is Allah (alone) Whose help can be sought."

19 Then there came a caravan of travellers: they sent their water-carrier
(for water), and he let down his bucket (into the well)... He said: "Ah
there! Good news! Here is a (fine) young man!" So they concealed him
as a treasure! But Allah knows well all that they do! 20 The (brethren) sold
him for a miserable price, for a few dirhams counted out: in such low
estimation did they hold him!

SECTION 3

21 The man in Egypt who bought him, said to his wife: "Make his stay (among us) honourable: maybe he will bring us much good, or we shall adopt him as a son." Thus did We establish Joseph in the land, that We might teach him the interpretation of stories (and events). And Allah has full power and control over His affairs; but most among mankind know
it not. 22 When Joseph attained his full manhood, We gave him power and knowledge: thus do We reward those who do right.

23 But she in whose house he was, sought to seduce him from his (true) self: she fastened the doors, and said: "Now come, you (dear one)!" He said: "Allah forbid! Truly (your husband) is my lord! He made my sojourn agreeable! Truly to no good come those who do wrong!" 24 And
(with passion) did she desire him, and he would have desired her, but that he saw the evidence of his Lord: thus (did We order) that We might turn away from him (all) evil and shameful deeds: for he was one of Our servants, sincere and purified.

25 So they both raced each other to the door, and she tore his shirt from the back: they both found her lord near the door. She said: "What is the (fitting) punishment for one who formed an evil design against your wife,
but prison or a grievous chastisement?" 26 He said: "It was she that sought
to seduce me—from my (true) self." And one of her household saw (this) and bore witness, (thus):—"If it be that his shirt is rent from the front,
then is her tale true, and he is a liar! 27 But if it be that his shirt is torn
from the back, then is she the liar, and he is telling the truth!" 28 So when
he saw his shirt,—that it was torn at the back,—(her husband) said: "Behold! It is a snare of you women! Truly, mighty is your snare! 29 O
Joseph, pass this over! (O wife), ask forgiveness for your sin, for truly you have been at fault!"

SECTION 4

30 Ladies said in the City: "The wife of the (great) 'Azīz[2] is seeking to seduce her slave from his (true) self: truly has he inspired her with violent

---

2. *'Azīz*: title of a nobleman or officer of Court, of high rank. Considering all the circumstances, the office of Grand Chamberlain or minister may be indicated. But "*'Azīz*" I think is a title, not an office. I have not translated the title but left it as it is. "Excellency" or "Highness" would have specialised modern associations which I want to avoid. [1677]

love: we see she is evidently going astray." 31 When she heard of their
malicious talk, she sent for them and prepared a banquet for them: she
gave each of them a knife: and she said (to Joseph), "Come out before
them." When they saw him, they did extol him, and (in their amazement)
cut their hands: they said, "Allah preserve us! No mortal is this! This is
none other than a noble angel!" 32 She said: "There before you is the man
about whom you did blame me! I did seek to seduce him from his (true)
self but he did firmly save himself guiltless!... and now, if he does not my
bidding, he shall certainly be cast into prison, and (what is more) be of
the company of the vilest!" 33 He said: "O my Lord! The prison is more
to my liking than that to which they invite me: unless You turn away their
snare from me, I should (in my youthful folly) feel inclined towards them
and join the ranks of the ignorant."

34 So his Lord hearkened to him (in his prayer), and turned away from
him their snare: verily He hears and knows (all things).

35 Then it occurred to the men, after they had seen the Signs, (that it was
best) to imprison him for a time.

SECTION 5

36 Now with him there came into the prison two young men. Said one of
them: "I see myself (in a dream) pressing wine." Said the other: "I see
myself (in a dream) carrying bread on my head, and birds are eating
thereof." "Tell us" (they said) "the truth and meaning thereof: for we see
you are one that does good (to all)." 37 He said: "Before any food comes
(in due course) to feed either of you, I will surely reveal to you the truth
and meaning of this before it befall you: that is part of the (duty) which
my Lord has taught me. I have (I assure you) abandoned the ways of a
people that believe not in Allah and that (even) deny the Hereafter. 38 And
I follow the ways of my fathers,—Abraham, Isaac, and Jacob; and never
could we attribute any partners whatever to Allah: that (comes) of the
grace of Allah to us and to mankind: yet most men are not grateful. 39 O
my two companions of the prison! (I ask you): Are many lords differing
among themselves better, or the One Allah, Supreme and Irresistible? 40
If not Him, you worship nothing but names which you have named,—you
and your fathers,—for which Allah has sent down no authority: the
command is for none but Allah: He has commanded that you worship
none but Him: that is the right religion, but most men understand not... 41

O my two companions of the prison! As to one of you, he will pour out the wine for his lord to drink: as for the other, he will hang from the cross, and the birds will eat from off his head. (So) has been decreed that matter whereof you both do enquire"...

42 And of the two, to that one whom he considered about to be saved, he said: "Mention me to your lord." But Satan made him forget to mention him to his lord: and (Joseph) lingered in prison a few (more) years.

SECTION 6

43 The king (of Egypt) said: "I do see (in a vision) seven fat cows, whom
seven lean ones devour, and seven green ears of corn, and seven (others)
withered. O you chiefs! Expound to me my vision if it be that you can
interpret visions." 44 They said: "A confused medley of dreams: and we
are not skilled in the interpretation of dreams."

45 But the man who had been released, one of the two (who had been in
prison) and who now remembered him after (so long) a space of time,
said: "I will tell you the truth of its interpretation: send you me
(therefore)." 46 "O Joseph!" (he said) "O man of truth! Expound to us (the
dream) of seven fat cows whom seven lean ones devour, and of seven
green ears of corn and (seven) others withered: that I may return to the
people, and that they may understand." 47 (Joseph) said: "For seven years
shall you diligently sow as is your wont: and the harvests that you reap,
you shall leave them in the ear,—except a little, of which you shall eat.
48 Then will come after that (period) seven dreadful (years), which will
devour what you shall have laid by in advance for them,—(all) except a
little which you shall have (specially) guarded. 49 Then will come after
that (period) a year in which the people will have abundant water, and in
which they will press (wine and oil)."

SECTION 7

50 So the king said: "Bring you him unto me." But when the messenger
came to him, (Joseph) said: "Go you back to your lord, and ask him,
'What is the state of mind of the ladies who cut their hands'? For my
Lord is certainly well aware of their snare." 51 (The king) said (to the
ladies): "What was your affair when you did seek to seduce Joseph from
his (true) self?" The ladies said: "Allah preserve us! No evil know we
against him!" Said the 'Azīz's wife: "Now is the truth manifest (to all):

it was I who sought to seduce him from his (true) self: he is indeed of
those who are (ever) true (and virtuous). 52 This (say I), in order that he
may know that I have never been false to him in his absence, and that
Allah will never guide the snare of the false ones.

PART XIII

53 "Nor do I absolve my own self (of blame): the (human) soul is certainly
prone to evil, unless my Lord do bestow His Mercy: but surely my Lord
is Oft-forgiving, Most Merciful."

54 So the king said: "Bring him unto me; I will take him specially to serve
about my own person." Therefore when he had spoken to him, he said:
"Be assured this day, you are, before our own presence, with rank firmly
established, and fidelity fully proved!" 55 (Joseph) said: "Set me over the
store-houses of the land: I will indeed guard them, as one that knows
(their importance)."

56 Thus did We give established power to Joseph in the land, to take
possession therein as, when, or where he pleased. We bestow of Our
Mercy on whom We please, and We suffer not, to be lost, the reward of
those who do good. 57 But verily the reward of the Hereafter is the best,
for those who believe, and are constant in righteousness.

SECTION 8

58 Then came Joseph's brethren: they entered his presence, and he knew
them, but they knew him not. 59 And when he had furnished them forth
with provisions (suitable) for them, he said: "Bring unto me a brother you
have, of the same father as yourselves, (but a different mother): see you
not that I pay out full measure, and that I do provide the best hospitality?
60 Now if you bring him not to me, you shall have no measure (of corn)
from me, nor shall you (even) come near me." 61 They said: "We shall
certainly seek to get our wish about him from his father: indeed we shall
do it."

62 And (Joseph) told his servants to put their stock in trade (with which
they had bartered) into their saddlebags, so they should know it only
when they returned to their people, in order that they might come back.

63 Now when they returned to their father, they said: "O our father! No
more measure of grain shall we get (unless we take our brother): So send

our brother with us, that we may get our measure; and we will indeed
take every care of him." 64 He said: "Shall I trust you with him with any
result other than when I trusted you with his brother aforetime? But Allah
is the best to take care (of him), and He is the Most Merciful of those who
show mercy!"

65 Then when they opened their baggage, they found their stock in trade
had been returned to them. They said: "O our father! What (more) can we
desire? This our stock in trade has been returned to us: so we shall get
(more) food for our family; we shall take care of our brother; and add (at
the same time) a full camel's load (of grain to our provisions). This is but
a small quantity." 66 (Jacob) said: "Never will I send him with you until
you swear a solemn oath to me, in Allah's name, that you will be sure to
bring him back to me unless you are yourselves hemmed in (and made
powerless)." And when they had sworn their solemn oath, he said: "Over
all that we say, be Allah the witness and guardian!" 67 Further he said: "O
my sons! Enter not all by one gate: enter you by different gates. Not that
I can profit you aught against Allah (with my advice): None can
command except Allah: on Him do I put my trust: and let all that trust put
their trust on Him." 68 And when they entered in the manner their father
had enjoined, it did not profit them in the least against (the plan of) Allah:
It was but a necessity of Jacob's soul, which he discharged. For he was,
by Our instruction, full of knowledge (and experience): but most men
know not.

SECTION 9

69 Now when they came into Joseph's presence, he received his (full)
brother to stay with him. He said (to him): "Behold! I am your (own)
brother; so grieve not at aught of their doings." 70 At length when he had
furnished them forth with provisions (suitable) for them, he put the
drinking cup into his brother's saddlebag. Then shouted out a crier: "O
you (in) the caravan! Behold, you are thieves, without doubt!" 71 They
said, turning towards them: "What is it that you miss?" 72 They said: "We
miss the great beaker of the king; for him who produces it, is (the reward
of) a camel load; I will be bound by it." 73 (The brothers) said: "By Allah!
Well you know that we came not to make mischief in the land, and we
are no thieves!" 74 (The Egyptians) said: "What then shall be the penalty
of this, if you are (proved) to have lied?" 75 They said: "The penalty

should be that he in whose saddlebag it is found, should be held (as bondman) to atone for the (crime). Thus it is we punish the wrong-doers!"

76 So he began (the search) with their baggage, before (he came to) the baggage of his brother: at length he brought it out of his brother's baggage. Thus did We plan for Joseph.[3] He could not take his brother by the law of the king except that Allah willed it (so). We raise to degrees (of wisdom) whom We please: but over all endued with knowledge is One, the All-knowing. 77 They said: "If he steals, there was a brother of his who did steal before (him)." But these things did Joseph keep locked in his heart, revealing not the secrets to them. He (simply) said (to himself): "You are the worse situated; and Allah knows best the truth of what you assert!"

78 They said: "O exalted one! Behold! he has a father, aged and venerable, (who will grieve for him); so take one of us in his place; for we see that you are (gracious) in doing good." 79 He said: "Allah forbid that we take other than him with whom we found our property: indeed (if we did so), we should be acting wrongfully."

---

3. When the packs of Benjamin, Joseph's younger brother, were being readied, Joseph put his drinking cup in his younger brother's saddle bag. This was not malicious subterfuge on the part of Joseph, but was done out of great love and affection for his younger brother. This was neither known to Benjamin nor to the courtiers. [Previously Joseph had done something similar when he put all the money in his brothers' packs, which they had brought to buy grain. The brothers had only realized it when they opened their packs upon arrival at their home.] In the meantime, the measuring beaker of the king had been misplaced (Allah's planning), and the courtiers suspected Joseph's brothers of stealing it.

After searching the bags, a *siqāyah* (drinking cup) was found in Benjamin's bag. The issue here is with the translation of the word "it" in this verse. The word for the king's measuring beaker is *sūwa'* (12:72), and the pronoun which refers to this is *hee* ("be<u>hee</u>", 12:72), and not *ha* (*istakhrajahā*; 12:76), which is the pronoun actually used in this verse. Therefore, it was not the king's measuring beaker that was found in Benjamin's baggage but Joseph's drinking cup.

The case was referred to Joseph to decide what should happen. Joseph was able to realise immediately that this was Allah's planning, because he was a Prophet, and therefore acted accordingly. It was clearly not a trick on the part of Joseph (as mentioned in the Bible, Genesis 44:1-15), to prevent his brother from leaving, as the Qur'an tells us: *'Thus We planned (kidnā) for Joseph'* (12:76). (See *The Encyclopaedia of the Qur'an*, The Islamic Centre, New Delhi). [1737] – Ed.

SECTION 10

80 Now when they saw no hope of his (yielding), they held a conference
in private. The leader among them said: "Know you not that your father
did take an oath from you in Allah's name, and how, before this, you did
fail in your duty with Joseph? Therefore will I not leave this land until
my father permits me, or Allah commands me; and He is the best to
command. 81 Turn you back to your father, and say, 'O our father!
Behold! your son committed theft! We bear witness only to what we
know, and we could not well guard against the unseen! 82 Ask at the town
where we have been and the caravan in which we returned, and (you will
find) we are indeed telling the truth'."

83 Jacob said: "Nay, but you have yourselves contrived a story (good
enough) for you. So patience is most fitting (for me). Maybe Allah will
bring them (back) all to me (in the end). For He is indeed full of
knowledge and wisdom." 84 And he turned away from them, and said:
"How great is my grief for Joseph!" And his eyes became white with
sorrow, and he fell into silent melancholy. 85 They said: "By Allah!
(Never) will you cease to remember Joseph until you reach the last
extremity of illness, or until you die!" 86 He said: "I only complain of my
distraction and anguish to Allah, and I know from Allah that which you
know not... 87 O my sons! Go you and enquire about Joseph and his
brother, and never give up hope of Allah's Soothing Mercy: truly no one
despairs of Allah's Soothing Mercy, except those who have no faith."

88 Then, when they came (back) into (Joseph's) presence they said: "O
exalted one! Distress has seized us and our family: we have (now)
brought but scanty capital: so pay us full measure, (we pray you), and
treat it as charity to us: for Allah does reward the charitable." 89 He said:
"Know you how you dealt with Joseph and his brother, not knowing
(what you were doing)?" 90 They said: "Are you indeed Joseph?" He said,
"I am Joseph, and this is my brother: Allah has indeed been gracious to
us (all): behold, he that is righteous and patient,—never will Allah suffer
the reward to be lost, of those who do right." 91 They said: "By Allah!
Indeed has Allah preferred you above us, and we certainly have been
guilty of sin!" 92 He said: "This day let no reproach be (cast) on you:
Allah will forgive you, and He is the Most Merciful of those who show
mercy! 93 Go with this my shirt, and cast it over the face of my father: he

will come to see (clearly). Then come you (here) to me together with all
your family."

SECTION 11

94 When the caravan left (Egypt), their father said: "I do indeed scent the
presence of Joseph: nay, think me not a dotard." 95 They said: "By Allah!
Truly you are in your old wandering mind." 96 Then when the bearer of
the good news came, he cast (the shirt) over his face, and he forthwith
regained clear sight. He said: "Did I not say to you, 'I know from Allah
that which you know not?'" 97 They said: "O our father! Ask for us
forgiveness for our sins, for we were truly at fault." 98 He said: "Soon will
I ask my Lord for forgiveness for you: for he is indeed Oft-forgiving,
Most Merciful."

99 Then when they entered the presence of Joseph, he provided a home for
his parents with himself, and said: "Enter you Egypt (all) in safety if it
please Allah." 100 And he raised his parents high on the throne (of
dignity), and they fell down in prostration, (all) before him. He said: "O
my father! This is the fulfilment of my vision of old! Allah has made it
come true! He was indeed good to me when He took me out of prison and
brought you (all here) out of the desert, (even) after Satan had sown
enmity between me and my brothers. Verily my Lord understands best
the mysteries of all that He plans to do, for verily He is full of knowledge
and wisdom. 101 O my Lord! You have indeed bestowed on me some
power, and taught me something of the interpretation of dreams and
events,—O You Creator of the heavens and the earth! You are my
Protector in this world and in the Hereafter. Take You my soul (at death)
as one submitting to Your will (as a Muslim), and unite me with the
righteous."

102 Such is one of the stories of what happened unseen, which We reveal
by inspiration unto you; nor were you (present) with them then when they
concerted their plans together in the process of weaving their plots. 103
Yet no faith will the greater part of mankind have, however ardently you
do desire it. 104 And no reward do you ask of them for this: it is no less
than a Message for all creatures.

SECTION 12

105 And how many Signs in the heavens and the earth do they pass by?

Yet they turn (their faces) away from them! 106 And most of them believe
not in Allah without associating (others as partners) with Him! 107 Do they
then feel secure from the coming against them of the covering veil of the
wrath of Allah,—or of the coming against them of the (final) Hour
suddenly while they perceive not?

108 Say you: "This is my way: I do invite unto Allah,—on evidence clear
as the seeing with one's eyes,—I and whoever follows me. Glory to
Allah! And never will I join gods with Allah!" 109 Nor did We send before
you (as messengers) any but men, whom We did inspire,—(men) living
in human habitations. Do they not travel through the earth, and see what
was the end of those before them? But the home of the Hereafter is best,
for those who do right. Will you not then understand? 110 (Respite will be
granted) until, when the messengers give up hope (of their people) and
(come to) think that they were treated as liars, there reaches them Our
help, and those whom We will are delivered into safety. But never will
be warded off Our punishment from those who are in sin. 111 There is, in
their stories, instruction for men endued with understanding. It is not a
tale invented, but a confirmation of what went before it,—a detailed
exposition of all things, and a Guide and a Mercy to any such as
believe.□

Chapter 13

Sūrah Al-Ra'd
(The Thunder)

Translator's Introduction

The chronological place of this Sūrah and the general argument of Sūrahs 10 to 15 has been described in the Introduction to Sūrah 10.

The special argument of this Sūrah deals with that aspect of Allah's revelation of Himself to man and His dealings with him, which is concerned with certain contrasts which are here pointed out. There is the revelation of the Prophets, which comes in spoken words adapted to the language of the various men and groups of men to whom it comes; and there is the parallel revelation or Signs in the constant laws of external nature, on this earth and in the visible heavens. There is the contrast between recurring life and death already in the external world: why should men disbelieve in the life after death? They mock at the idea of punishment because it is deferred: but can they not see Allah's power and glory in thunder and the forces of nature? All creation praises Him: it is the good that endures and the evil that is swept away like froth or scum. Not only in miracles but in the normal working of the world, are shown Allah's power and mercy. What is Punishment in this world, compared to that in the life to come? Even here there are Signs of the working of His law: plot or plan as men will, it is Allah's Will that must prevail. This is illustrated in Joseph's story in the preceding Sūrah.

Summary—The Book of Revelation is true, and is confirmed by the Signs to be seen in visible nature. Allah Who created such mighty forces in outer nature can raise up man again after death. Allah's knowledge is all-encompassing: so are His power and goodness (13:1-18).

The righteous seek the pleasure of Allah and find Peace; the evil ones break His Law, cavil and dispute, and reject faith; the wrath of Allah will take them unawares, but in His Own good time (13:19-31).

So was it with Prophets before: they were mocked, but the mockers were destroyed, while the righteous rejoiced and were established (13:32-43).

*** *** ***

In the name of Allah,
Most Gracious, Most Merciful.

1 *Alif Lām Mīm Rā'.*[1] These are the Signs (or Verses) of the Book: that
which has been revealed unto you from your Lord is the Truth; but most
men believe not. 2 Allah is He Who raised the heavens without any pillars
that you can see; is firmly established on the Throne (of Authority); He
has subjected the sun and the moon (to His Law)! Each one runs (its
course) for a term appointed. He does regulate all affairs, explaining the
Signs in detail, that you may believe with certainty in the meeting with
your Lord. 3 And it is He Who spread out the earth, and set thereon
mountains standing firm and (flowing) rivers: and fruit of every kind He
made in pairs, two and two: He draws the night as a veil over the Day.
Behold, verily in these things there are Signs for those who consider! 4
And in the earth are tracts (diverse though) neighbouring, and Gardens
of vines and fields sown with corn, and palm trees—growing out of
single roots or otherwise: watered with the same water, yet some of them
We make more excellent than others to eat. Behold, verily in these things
there are Signs for those who understand!

5 If you do marvel (at their want of faith), strange is their saying: "When
we are (actually) dust, shall we indeed then be in a creation renewed?"
They are those who deny their Lord! They are those round whose necks
will be yokes (of servitude): they will be companions of the Fire, to dwell
therein (for ever)! 6 They ask you to hasten on the evil in preference to the
good: yet have come to pass, before them, (many) exemplary
punishments! But verily your Lord is full of forgiveness for mankind for
their wrong-doing, and verily your Lord is (also) strict in punishment.

7 And the Unbelievers say: "Why is not a Sign sent down to him from his
Lord?" But you are truly a warner, and to every people a guide.

---

1. For *Alif, Lām, Mīm*, see 2:1 and note. For *Alif, Lām, Rā'*, see Introduction to Sūrah 10. Here there seems to be a combination of the groups *Alif, Lām, Mīm* and *Alif, Lām, Rā'*. We consider here not only the beginning (*Alif*), the middle (*Lām*), and the end (*Mīm*), of man's spiritual history, but also the immediate future of the interior of our organisation, such as it appeared to our *Ummah* towards the close of the Makkan period. But in trying to understand mystic symbolism, we must not be dogmatic. The befitting attitude is to say: Allah knows best. [1798]

SECTION 2

8 Allah does know what every female (womb) does bear, by how much
the wombs fall short (of their time or number) or do exceed. Every single
thing is before His sight, in (due) proportion. 9 He knows the Unseen and
that which is open: He is the Great, the Most High. 10 It is the same (to
Him) whether any of you conceal his speech or declare it openly; whether
he lie hid by night or walk forth freely by day. 11 For each (such person)
there are (angels) in succession, before and behind him: they guard him
by command of Allah. Verily never will Allah change the condition of a
people until they change it themselves (with their own souls). But when
(once) Allah wills a people's punishment, there can be no turning it back,
nor will they find, besides Him, any to protect. 12 It is He Who does show
you the lightning, by way both of fear and of hope: it is He Who does
raise up the clouds, heavy with (fertilising) rain! 13 Nay, thunder repeats
His praises, and so do the angels, with awe: He flings the loud-voiced
thunderbolts, and therewith He strikes whomsoever He will. Yet these
(are the men) who (dare to) dispute about Allah, with the strength of His
power (supreme)!

14 For Him (alone) is prayer in Truth: any others that they call upon
besides Him hear them no more than if they were to stretch forth their
hands for water to reach their mouths but it reaches them not: for the
prayer of those without Faith is nothing but (futile) wandering (in the
mind). 15 Whatever beings there are in the heavens and the earth do
prostrate themselves to Allah (acknowledging subjection),—with good-will or in spite of themselves: so do their shadows in the mornings and
evenings.

16 Say: "Who is the Lord and Sustainer of the heavens and the earth?"
Say: "(It is) Allah." Say: "Do you then take (for worship) protectors other
than Him, such as have no power either for good or for harm to
themselves?" Say: "Are the blind equal with those who see? Or the depths
of darkness equal with light?" Or do they assign to Allah partners who
have created (anything) as He has created, so that the creation seemed to
them similar? Say: "Allah is the Creator of all things: He is the One, the
Supreme and Irresistible." 17 He sends down water from the skies, and the
channels flow, each according to its measure: but the torrent bears away
the foam that mounts up to the surface. Even so, from that (ore) which

they heat in the fire, to make ornaments or utensils therewith, there is a
scum likewise. Thus does Allah (by parables) show forth Truth and
Vanity. For the scum disappears like froth cast out; while that which is
for the good of mankind remains on the earth. Thus does Allah set forth
parables. 18 For those who respond to their Lord, are (all) good things. But
those who respond not to Him,—even if they had all that is in the heavens
and on earth, and as much more, (in vain) would they offer it for ransom.
For them will the reckoning be terrible: their abode will be Hell,—what
a bed of misery!

SECTION 3

19 Is then one who does know that that which has been revealed unto you
from your Lord is the Truth, like one who is blind? It is those who are
endued with understanding that receive admonition;—20 Those who fulfil
the Covenant of Allah and fail not in their plighted word; 21 Those who
join together those things which Allah has commanded to be joined, hold
their Lord in awe, and fear the terrible reckoning; 22 Those who patiently
persevere, seeking the countenance of their Lord; establish regular
prayers; spend, out of (the gifts) We have bestowed for their sustenance,
secretly and openly; and turn off Evil with good: for such there is the
final attainment of the (eternal) Home,—23 Gardens of perpetual bliss:
they shall enter there, as well as the righteous among their fathers, their
spouses, and their offspring: and angels shall enter unto them from every
gate (with the salutation): 24 "Peace unto you for that you persevered in
patience! Now how excellent is the final Home!"

25 But those who break the Covenant of Allah, after having plighted their
word thereto, and cut asunder those things which Allah has commanded
to be joined, and work mischief in the land;—on them is the Curse; for
them is the terrible Home!

26 Allah does enlarge, or grant by (strict) measure, the sustenance (which
He gives) to whom so He pleases. (The worldly) rejoice in the life of this
world: but the life of this world is but little comfort in the Hereafter.

SECTION 4

27 The Unbelievers say: "Why is not a Sign sent down to him from his
Lord?" Say: "Truly Allah leaves to stray, whom He will; but He guides
to Himself those who turn to Him in penitence,—28 Those who believe,

and whose hearts find satisfaction in the remembrance of Allah: for
without doubt in the remembrance of Allah do hearts find satisfaction. 29
For those who believe and work righteousness, is (every) blessedness, and
a beautiful place of (final) return."

30 Thus have We sent you amongst a people before whom (long since)
have (other) peoples (gone and) passed away; in order that you might
rehearse unto them what We send down unto you by inspiration; yet do
they reject (Him), the Most Gracious! Say: "He is my Lord! There is no
god but He! On Him is my trust, and to Him do I turn!" 31 If there were
a Qur'an with which mountains were moved, or the earth were cloven
asunder, or the dead were made to speak, (this would be the one!) But,
truly, the command is with Allah in all things! Do not the Believers
know, that, had Allah (so) willed, He could have guided all mankind (to
the Right)? But the Unbelievers,—never will disaster cease to seize them
for their (ill) deeds, or to settle close to their homes, until the promise of
Allah come to pass, for, verily, Allah will not fail in His promise.

SECTION 5

32 Mocked were (many) messengers before you: but I granted respite to
the Unbelievers, and finally I punished them: then how (terrible) was My
requital! 33 Is then He Who stands over every soul (and knows) all that it
does, (like any others)? And yet they ascribe partners to Allah. Say: "But
name them! Is it that you will inform Him of something He knows not on
earth, or is it (just) a show of words?" Nay! To those who believe not,
their pretence seems pleasing, but they are kept back (thereby) from the
Path. And those whom Allah leaves to stray, no one can guide. 34 For
them is a Penalty in the life of this world, but harder, truly, is the Penalty
of the Hereafter: and defender have they none against Allah. 35 The
parable of the Garden which the righteous are promised!—beneath it flow
rivers: perpetual is the enjoyment thereof and the shade therein: such is
the end of the Righteous; and the end of Unbelievers is the Fire.

36 Those to whom We have given the Book rejoice at what has been
revealed unto you: but there are among the clans those who reject a part
thereof. Say: "I am commanded to worship Allah, and not to join partners
with Him. Unto Him do I call, and unto Him is my return." 37 Thus have
We revealed it to be a judgement of authority in Arabic. Were you to
follow their (vain) desires after the knowledge which has reached you,

then would you find neither protector nor defender against Allah.

SECTION 6

38 We did send messengers before you, and appointed for them wives and
children: and it was never the part of a messenger to bring a Sign except
as Allah permitted (or commanded).[2] For each period is a Book
(revealed).[3] 39 Allah does blot out or confirm what He pleases: with Him
is the Mother of the Book.[4]

40 Whether We shall show you (within your lifetime) part of what We
promised them or take to ourselves your soul (before it is all
accomplished),—your duty is to make (the Message) reach them: it is Our
part to call them to account. 41 See they not that We gradually reduce the
land (in their control) from its outlying borders? (Where) Allah
commands, there is none to put back His command: and He is swift in
calling to account. 42 Those before them did (also) devise plots; but in all
things the master-planning is Allah's. He knows the doings of every soul:
and soon will the Unbelievers know who gets home in the end. 43 The
Unbelievers say: "No messenger are you." Say: "Enough for a witness
between me and you is Allah, and such as have knowledge of the
Book."□

---

2. No Prophet performed any miracle or showed forth any "Signs", except as Allah willed. Allah's will (Arabic *Mashī'ah*) is an All-Wise, universal Plan, which is not formed for the benefit of one tribe or *millah* or of one age or country (see also next verse). The greatest Miracle in history was and is the Qur'an. We can apprehend its beauty and grandeur today as much as did the people of Al-Muṣṭafā's day—even more, as our collective knowledge of nature and of Allah's creation has increased. [1862]

3. For Arabic *Kitāb*, I have translated "a Book (revealed)"; it can also mean "a Law decreed" or "a Decree established." Ultimately the meaning is the same; for each age, according to Allah's wisdom, His Message is renewed. [1863]

4. Mother of the Book: (*Umm al-Kitāb*) the original foundation of all revelation; the essence of Allah's Will and Law. *Cf.* 3:7. [1864]

Chapter 14

Sūrah Ibrāhīm (Abraham)

Translator's Introduction

For the chronology and the general argument of this Sūrah in the series Sūrahs 10 to 15, see Introduction to Sūrah 10.

The special subject matter of this Sūrah is a continuation of the concluding portion of the last Sūrah, which explained how Allah's revelation gains ground in spite of selfish men's opposition. Here illustrations are given from the story of Moses and Abraham, and Abraham's Prayer for Makkah forms the core of the Sūrah.

Summary—Revelation leads man from darkness to light. It comes to each nation in its own language and for its own special circumstances. So was it with Moses and other Prophets. There was a conflict of evil with good, but evil was destroyed. Parable of the Goodly Tree (14:1-27).

Why will men not receive Allah's grace? Why will they choose to go astray? Abraham prayed to be saved from infidelity, himself and his posterity, and he prayed for Makkah, the city of the new revelation through Arabia. Good and Evil will find their proper retribution, and Allah's Plan of Unity will prevail (14:28-52).

*** *** ***

In the name of Allah,
Most Gracious, Most Merciful.

1 *Alif Lām Rā'*.[1] A Book which We have revealed unto you, in order that
you might lead mankind out of the depths of darkness into light —by the
leave of their Lord—to the Way of (Him) the Exalted in Power, Worthy
of all praise!—2 Of Allah, to Whom do belong all things in the heavens
and on earth! But alas for the Unbelievers for a terrible Penalty (their
Unfaith will bring them)!—3 Those who love the life of this world more
than the Hereafter, who hinder (men) from the Path of Allah and seek
therein something crooked: they are astray by a long distance.

1. For those mystic Letters see Introduction to Sūrah 10. [1869]

4 We sent not a messenger except (to teach) in the language of his (own)
people, in order to make (things) clear to them. Now Allah leaves
straying those whom He pleases and guides whom He pleases: and He is
Exalted in Power, full of Wisdom.

5 We sent Moses with Our Signs (and the command): "Bring out your
people from the depths of darkness into light, and teach them to
remember the Days of Allah." Verily in this there are Signs for such as
are firmly patient and constant,—grateful and appreciative. 6 Remember!
Moses said to his people: "Call to mind the favour of Allah to you when
He delivered you from the people of Pharaoh: they set you hard tasks and
punishments, slaughtered your sons, and let your women-folk live:
therein was a tremendous trial from your Lord."

SECTION 2

7 And remember your Lord caused to be declared (publicly): "If you are
grateful, I will add more (favours) unto you; but if you show ingratitude,
truly My punishment is terrible indeed." 8 And Moses said: "If you show
ingratitude, you and all on earth together, yet is Allah free of all wants,
worthy of all praise."

9 Has not the story reached you, (O people!), of those who (went) before
you?—of the people of Noah, and 'Ād, and Thamūd?—and of those who
(came) after them? None knows them but Allah. To them came
messengers with clear (Signs); but they put their hands up to their
mouths, and said: "We do deny (the mission) on which you have been
sent, and we are really in suspicious (disquieting) doubt as to that to
which you invite us." 10 Their messengers said: "Is there a doubt about
Allah, the Creator of the heavens and the earth? It is He Who invites you,
in order that He may forgive you your sins and give you respite for a term
appointed!" They said: "Ah! You are no more than human, like
ourselves! You wish to turn us away from the (gods) our fathers used to
worship: then bring us some clear authority." 11 Their messengers said to
them: "True, we are human like yourselves, but Allah does grant His
grace to such of His servants as He pleases. It is not for us to bring you
an authority except as Allah permits. And on Allah let all men of faith put
their trust. 12 No reason have we why we should not put our trust on
Allah. Indeed He has guided us to the Ways we (follow). We shall
certainly bear with patience all the hurt you may cause us. For those who

put their trust should put their trust on Allah."

SECTION 3

13 And the Unbelievers said to their messengers: "Be sure we shall drive
you out of our land, or you shall return to our religion." But their Lord
inspired (this Message) to them: "Verily We shall cause the wrong-doers
to perish! 14 And verily We shall cause you to abide in the land, and
succeed them. This for such as fear the Time when they shall stand before
My tribunal,—such as fear the punishment denounced." 15 But they
sought victory and decision (there and then), and frustration was the lot
of every powerful obstinate transgressor. 16 In front of such a one is Hell,
and he is given, for drink, boiling fetid water. 17 In gulps will he sip it, but
never will he be near swallowing it down his throat: death will come to
him from every quarter, yet will he not die: and in front of him will be a
chastisement unrelenting.

18 The parable of those who reject their Lord is that their works are as
ashes, on which the wind blows furiously on a tempestuous day: no
power have they over aught that they have earned: that is the straying far,
far (from the goal). 19 See you not that Allah created the heavens and the
earth in Truth? If He so wills, He can remove you and put (in your place)
a new creation? 20 Nor is that for Allah any great matter. 21 They will all
be marshalled before Allah together: then will the weak say to those who
were arrogant, "For us, we but followed you; can you then avail us at all
against the wrath of Allah?" They will reply, "If we had received the
Guidance of Allah, we should have given it to you: to us it makes no
difference (now) whether we rage, or bear (these torments) with patience:
for ourselves there is no way of escape."

SECTION 4

22 And Satan will say when the matter is decided: "It was Allah Who gave
you a promise of Truth: I too promised, but I failed in my promise to you.
I had no authority over you except to call you, but you listened to me:
then reproach not me, but reproach your own souls. I cannot listen to
your cries, nor can you listen to mine. I reject your former act in
associating me with Allah. For wrong-doers there must be a grievous
Penalty."

23 But those who believe and work righteousness will be admitted to

Gardens beneath which rivers flow,—to dwell therein for ever with the
leave of their Lord. Their greeting therein will be: "Peace!"

24 See you not how Allah sets forth a parable?—a goodly Word like a
goodly tree, whose root is firmly fixed, and its branches (reach) to the
heavens,—25 It brings forth its fruit at all times, by the leave of its Lord.
So Allah sets forth parables for men, in order that they may receive
admonition. 26 And the parable of an evil Word is that of an evil tree: it
is torn up by the root from the surface of the earth: it has no stability. 27
Allah will establish in strength those who believe, with the Word that
stands firm, in this world and in the Hereafter; but Allah will leave, to
stray, those who do wrong: Allah does what He wills.

SECTION 5

28 Have you not turned your vision to those who have changed the favour
of Allah into blasphemy and caused their people to descend to the House
of Perdition?—29 Into Hell? They will burn therein,—an evil place to stay
in! 30 And they set up (idols) as equal to Allah, to mislead (men) from the
Path! Say: "Enjoy (your brief power)! But verily you are making
straightway for Hell!"

31 Speak to My servants who have believed, that they may establish
regular prayers, and spend (in charity) out of the sustenance We have
given them, secretly and openly, before the coming of a Day in which
there will be neither mutual bargaining nor befriending.

32 It is Allah Who has created the heavens and the earth and sends down
rain from the skies, and with it brings out fruits wherewith to feed you;
it is He Who has made the ships subject to you, that they may sail through
the sea by His command; and the rivers (also) has He made subject to
you. 33 And He has made subject to you the sun and the moon, both
diligently pursuing their courses; and the night and the day has He (also)
made subject to you. 34 And He gives you of all that you ask for. But if
you count the favours of Allah, never will you be able to number them.
Verily, man is given up to injustice and ingratitude.

SECTION 6

35 Remember Abraham said: "O my Lord! Make this city one of peace
and security: and preserve me and my sons from worshipping idols. 36 O
my Lord! They have indeed led astray many among mankind; he then

who follows my (ways) is of me, and he that disobeys me,—but You are
indeed Oft-forgiving, Most Merciful. 37 O our Lord! I have made some
of my offspring to dwell in a valley without cultivation, by Your Sacred
House; in order, O our Lord, that they may establish regular prayer: so fill
the hearts of some among men with love towards them, and feed them
with fruits: so that they may give thanks. 38 O our Lord! Truly You do
know what we conceal and what we reveal: for nothing whatever is
hidden from Allah, whether on earth or in heaven. 39 Praise be to Allah,
Who has granted unto me in old age Ismā'īl and Isaac: for truly my Lord
is He, the Hearer of prayer![2] 40 O my Lord! Make me one who
establishes regular prayer, and also (raise such) among my offspring O
our Lord! and accept You my prayer. 41 O our Lord! Cover (us) with
Your Forgiveness—me, my parents, and (all) Believers, on the Day that
the Reckoning will be established!"

SECTION 7

42 Think not that Allah does not heed the deeds of those who do wrong.
He but gives them respite against a Day when the eyes will fixedly stare
in horror,—43 They running forward with necks outstretched, their heads
uplifted, their gaze returning not towards them, and their hearts a (gaping)
void!

44 So warn mankind of the Day when the Wrath will reach them: then will
the wrong-doers say: "Our Lord! Respite us (if only) for a short term: we
will answer Your call, and follow the messengers!" "What! Were you not
wont to swear aforetime that you should suffer no decline? 45 And you
dwelt in the dwellings of men who wronged their own souls; you were
clearly shown how We dealt with them; and We put forth (many)
Parables on your behalf!" 46 Mighty indeed were the plots which they
made, but their plots were (well) within the sight of Allah, even though
they were such as to shake the hills! 47 Never think that Allah would fail
His messengers in His promise: for Allah is Exalted in Power,—the Lord
of Retribution.

---

2. Abraham was 100 years old when Isaac was born (Gen. xxi. 5); and as Ismā'īl was 13 years old when Abraham was 99, (Gen. xvii. 24-25), Ismā'īl was also a son of his father's old age, having been born when Abraham was 86 years old. The younger son's progeny developed the Faith of Israel and that of Christ; the elder son's progeny perfected the more universal Faith of Islam, the Faith of Abraham the True. [1917]

48 One day the earth will be changed to a different earth, and so will be
the heavens, and (men) will be marshalled forth, before Allah, the One,
the Irresistible; 49 And you will see the sinners that day bound together in
fetters;—50 Their garments of liquid pitch, and their faces covered with
Fire; 51 That Allah may requite each soul according to its deserts; and
verily Allah is swift in calling to account.

52 Here is a Message for mankind: let them take warning therefrom, and let them know that He is (no other than) One Allah: let men of understanding take heed.□

Chapter 15

Sūrah Al-Ḥijr
(The Rocky Tract)

Translator's Introduction

This is the last of the six Sūrahs of the *Alif, Lām, Mīm* series (10 to 15). Its place in chronology is the late Makkan period, probably somewhere near the middle of that period. See Introduction to Sūrah 10, where will be found also an indication of the general subject matter of the whole series in the gradation of Qur'anic teaching.

The special subject matter of this Sūrah is the protection of Allah's Revelation and Allah's Truth. Evil arose from Pride and the warping of man's will, but Allah's Mercy is the antidote, as was proved in the case of Abraham and Lot, and might have been proved by the people of the Aykah and the Ḥijr if they had only attended to Allah's "Signs". The Qur'an, beginning with the Seven Oft-Repeated Verses, is the precious vehicle for the praises of Allah.

Summary—Allah will guard His Revelation, in spite of the cavils of the Unbelievers: Allah is the source of all things; He knows His own people, whom He will gather to Himself (15:1-25).

How Evil arose through the pride of Iblīs, to whom a respite was granted for a period: but neither fear nor evil affect those who receive Allah's Message (15:26-50).

The Mercy of Allah to Abraham was conveyed by the same messengers that were sent to destroy the people of Lot for their unspeakable crimes; Evil brought its retribution also on the Companions of the Wood (*Al-Aykah*) and of the Rocky Tract *(Al-Ḥijr)* (15:51-84).

The Qur'an and its Sūrahs teach you to celebrate Allah's praises, learn humility in worship, and serve Allah all your life (15:85-99).

*** *** ***

PART XIV

In the name of Allah,
Most Gracious, Most Merciful.

1 *Alif Lām Rā'*.[1] These are the Āyāt of Revelation,—of a Qur'an that
makes things clear.

2 Again and again will those who disbelieve, wish that they had bowed (to
Allah's Will) in Islam. 3 Leave them alone, to enjoy (the good things of
this life) and to please themselves: let (false) hope amuse them: soon will
knowledge (undeceive them).

4 Never did We destroy a population that had not a term decreed and
assigned beforehand. 5 Neither can a people anticipate its term, nor delay
it. 6 They say: "O you to whom the Message is being revealed! Truly you
are mad (or possessed)! 7 Why bring you not angels to us if it be that you
have the Truth?" 8 We send not the angels down except for just cause: if
they came (to the ungodly), behold! no respite would they have!

9 We have, without doubt, sent down the Message; and We will assuredly
guard it (from corruption).

10 We did send messengers before you amongst the religious sects of old:
11 But never came a messenger to them but they mocked him. 12 Even so
do We let it creep into the hearts of the sinners—13 That they should not
believe in the (Message); but the ways of the ancients have passed away.

14 Even if We opened out to them a gate from heaven, and they were to
continue (all day) ascending therein, 15 They would only say: "Our eyes
have been intoxicated: nay, we have been bewitched by sorcery."

SECTION 2

16 It is We Who have set out the zodiacal signs in the heavens, and made
them fair-seeming to (all) beholders; 17 And (moreover) We have guarded
them from every evil spirit accursed:[2] 18 But any that gains a hearing by
stealth, is pursued by a flaming fire, bright (to see). 19 And the earth We

---

1. For these mystic Letters, see Introduction to Sūrah 10.[1932]

2. Arabic *Rajīm* literally means: driven away with stones, rejected, accursed. *Cf.* 3:36.[1952]

have spread out (like a carpet); set thereon mountains firm and
immovable; and produced therein all kinds of things in due balance. 20
And We have provided therein means of subsistence,—for you and for
those for whose sustenance you are not responsible.

21 And there is not a thing but its (sources and) treasures (inexhaustible)
are with Us; but We only send down thereof in due and ascertainable
measures. 22 And We send the fecundating winds, then cause the rain to
descend from the sky, therewith providing you with water (in abundance),
though you are not the guardians of its stores.

23 And verily, it is We Who give life, and Who give death: it is We Who
remain inheritors (after all else passes away).

24 To Us are known those of you who hasten forward, and those who lag
behind. 25 Assuredly it is your Lord Who will gather them together: for
He is perfect in Wisdom and Knowledge.

SECTION 3

26 We created man from sounding clay, from mud moulded into shape; 27
And the *Jinn* race, We had created before, from the fire of a scorching
wind.

28 Behold! Your Lord said to the angels: "I am about to create man, from
sounding clay from mud moulded into shape; 29 When I have fashioned
him (in due proportion) and breathed into him of My spirit, fall you down
in obeisance unto him." 30 So the angels prostrated themselves, all of
them together: 31 Not so Iblīs: he refused to be among those who
prostrated themselves. 32 (Allah) said: "O Iblīs! What is your reason for
not being among those who prostrated themselves?" 33 (Iblīs) said: "I am
not one to prostrate myself to man, whom You did create from sounding
clay, from mud moulded into shape." 34 (Allah) said: "Then get you out
from here; for you are rejected, accursed. 35 And the Curse shall be on
you till the Day of Judgement." 36 (Iblīs) said: "O my Lord! Give me then
respite till the Day the (dead) are raised." 37 (Allah) said: "Respite is
granted you— 38 Till the Day of the Time appointed." 39 (Iblīs) said: "O
my Lord! Because You have put me in the wrong, I will make (wrong)
fair-seeming to them on the earth, and I will put them all in the
wrong,—40 Except Your servants among them, sincere and purified (by
Your Grace)." 41 (Allah) said: "This (Way of My sincere servants) is

indeed a Way that leads straight to Me. 42 For over My servants no
authority shall you have, except such as put themselves in the wrong and
follow you."

43 And verily, Hell is the promised abode for them all! 44 To it are seven
gates: for each of those gates is a (special) class (of sinners) assigned.

SECTION 4

45 The righteous (will be) amid Gardens and fountains (of clear-flowing
water). 46 (Their greeting will be): "Enter you here in peace and security."
47 And We shall remove from their hearts any lurking sense of injury:
(they will be) brothers (joyfully) facing each other on thrones (of
dignity). 48 There no sense of fatigue shall touch them, nor shall they
(ever) be asked to leave.

49 Tell My servants that I am indeed the Oft-forgiving, Most Merciful; 50
And that My Penalty will be indeed the most grievous Penalty.

51 Tell them about the guests of Abraham.[3] 52 When they entered his
presence and said, "Peace!" he said, "We feel afraid of you!"[4] 53 They
said: "Fear not! We give you glad tidings of a son endowed with
wisdom." 54 He said: "Do you give me glad tidings that old age has seized
me? Of what, then, is your good news?" 55 They said: "We give you glad
tidings in truth: be not then in despair!" 56 He said: "And who despairs of
the mercy of his Lord, but such as go astray?"

57 Abraham said: "What then is the business on which you (have come),
O you messengers (of Allah)?" 58 They said: "We have been sent to a

---

3. In illustration of the contrasts between Good and Evil, and the consequences that flow from them, we now have a reference to four incidents from the past, *viz*.: (1) an incident from the story of Abraham; (2) from that of Lot, nephew of Abraham and the end of the Cities of the Plain, which he was sent to warn; (3) the People of the Wood; and (4) the People of the Rocky Tract (*Al-Ḥijr*), after whom this Sūrah is called. As usual, the recital of Allah's abounding Grace comes first. [1980]

4. For a full understanding of this reference to the angels who were Abraham's guests and came to announce the birth of a son to him in his old age, read 11:69-73. The appearance of two strangers of uncommon appearance, who refused to partake of the host's sumptuous hospitality, made Abraham at first suspicious and afraid. [1981]

people (deep) in sin,[5] 59 Excepting the adherents of Lūṭ: them we are
certainly (charged) to save (from harm),—all—60 Except his wife, who,
we have ascertained, will be among those who will lag behind."[6]

SECTION 5

61 At length when the messengers arrived among the adherents of Lūṭ, 62
He said: "You appear to be uncommon folk." 63 They said: "Indeed, we
have come to you to accomplish that of which they doubt. 64 We have
brought to you that which is inevitably due, and assuredly we tell the
truth. 65 Then travel by night with your household, when a portion of the
night (yet remains), and do you bring up the rear: let no one amongst you
look back, but pass on whither you are ordered." 66 And We made known
this decree to him, that the last remnants of those (sinners) should be cut
off by the morning.

67 The inhabitants of the City came in (mad) joy (at news of the young
men). 68 Lūṭ said: "These are my guests: disgrace me not: 69 But fear
Allah, and shame me not." 70 They said: "Did we not forbid you (to
speak) for all and sundry?" 71 He said: "There are my daughters (to
marry), if you must act (so)."[7] 72 Verily, by your life (O Prophet), in their
wild intoxication, they wander in distraction, to and fro. 73 But the
(mighty) Blast overtook them before morning, 74 And We turned (the
Cities) upside down, and rained down on them brimstones hard as baked
clay. 75 Behold! In this are Signs for those who by tokens do understand.
76 And the (Cities were) right on the high-road. 77 Behold! In this is a Sign
for those who believe!

78 And the Companions of the Wood[8] were also wrong-doers; 79 So We

---

5. The Cities of the Plain round the Dead Sea, which to this day is called Bahr Lūṭ. They were given to unspeakable abominations. Read in this connection 11:77-83. [1985]

6. See 11:81, and note.

7. *Cf.* 11:78. "My daughters" in the mouth of a venerable man may mean young girls of the city, which would be appropriate considering the large number of men who came to besiege Lot's house. [1994]

8. "Companions of the Wood": *Aṣḥāb al-Aykah.* Perhaps *Aykah* is after all a proper noun, the name of a town or tract. Who were the Companions of the Aykah? They are mentioned four times in the Qur'an, *viz*., here, and in 26:176-191; 38:13; and 50:14. The only passage in which any details are given is 26:176-191. There we are told that their Prophet was Shu'ayb, and other details given correspond to those of the Madyan, to whom

exacted retribution from them. They were both on an open highway, plain to see.

SECTION 6

80 The Companions of the Rocky Tract[9] also rejected the messengers: 81
We sent them Our Signs, but they persisted in turning away from them.
82 Out of the mountains did they hew (their) edifices, (feeling themselves)
secure. 83 But the (mighty) Blast seized them of a morning, 84 And of no
avail to them was all that they did (with such art and care)!

85 We created not the heavens, the earth, and all between them, but for just
ends. And the Hour is surely coming (when this will be manifest). So
overlook (any human faults) with gracious forgiveness. 86 For verily it is
your Lord Who is the Master-Creator, knowing all things. 87 And We
have bestowed upon you the Seven Oft-repeated (verses)[10] and the
Grand Qur'an. 88 Strain not your eyes, (wistfully) at what We have
bestowed on certain classes of them, nor grieve over them: but lower your
wing (in gentleness) to the Believers.

89 And say: "I am indeed he that warns openly and without
ambiguity,"—90 (Of just such wrath) as We sent down on those who
divided (Scripture into arbitrary parts),—91 (So also on such) as have
made the Qur'an into shreds (as they please). 92 Therefore, by your Lord,
We will, of a surety, call them to account, 93 For all their deeds. 94
Therefore expound openly what you are commanded, and turn away from
those who join false gods with Allah. 95 For sufficient are We unto you
against those who scoff,—96 Those who adopt, with Allah, another god:

Shu'ayb was sent as Prophet: see 7:85-93. In my notes to that passage I have discussed the question of Shu'ayb and the Madyan people. It is reasonable to suppose that the Companions of the Wood were either the same as the Madyan, or a group among them or in their neighbourhood. [2000]

9. "The Rocky Tract" is undoubtedly a geographical name. On the maps of Arabia will be found a tract called the *Ḥijr,* north of Madīnah. Jabal Ḥijr is about 150 miles north of Madīnah. The tract would fall on the highway to Syria. This was the country of the Thamūd. For them and the country see 7:73, n. 120. [2002]

10. The Seven Oft-repeated Verses are usually understood to be the Opening Sūrah, the *Fātiḥah.* They sum up the whole teaching of the Qur'an. What can be a more precious gift to a Muslim than the glorious Qur'an or any Sūrah of it? Worldly wealth, honour, possessions, or anything else, sinks into insignificance in comparison with it (*Cf.* n.17). [2008]

but soon will they come to know. 97 We do indeed know how your heart
is distressed at what they say. 98 But celebrate the praises of your Lord,
and be of those who prostrate themselves in adoration. 99 And serve your
Lord until there come unto you the Hour that is certain.□

Chapter 16

Sūrah Al-Naḥl
(The Bee)

Translator's Introduction

Chronologically this Sūrah, like the six which preceded it, belongs to the late Makkan period, except perhaps verse 110 and some of the verses that follow. But the chronology has no significance. In subject matter it sums up, from a new point of view, the arguments on the great questions of Allah's dealings with man, His Self-revelation to man, and how the Messengers and the Message are writ large in every phase of Allah's Creation and the life of Man. The new point of view is that Nature points to Nature's Allah.

Summary—Everything in Creation proclaims the glory of Allah. To man is given dominion over Nature, that man may recognise Allah's Unity and Allah's Truth (16:1-25).

Man should never lose sight of his goal, which is the good, or dispute with the great Teachers, who are sent to all Peoples, to bring about Unity: all creatures serve Allah (16:26-50).

Allah's favours and man's ingratitude recounted, His Signs in the rain-bearing clouds, the cattle that give milk, the bee that produces honey, the wonderful relations of family and social life, and the refinements and comforts of civilisation (16:51-83).

The Messengers of Truth will bear witness against those who reject the Truth. Allah will judge us according to our faith and deeds (16:84-100).

The Qur'an is true: it guides and gives glad tidings. Believe, and make the most of life in all things good and lawful. Follow the example of Abraham: be true in Faith and righteousness, and do good (16:101-128).

*** *** ***

In the name of Allah,
Most Gracious, Most Merciful.

1 (Inevitably) comes (to pass) the Command of Allah: seek you not then
to hasten it:[1] Glory to Him, and far is He above having the partners they

---

1. This is an answer to the taunt of the Pagans, who said: "If there is a god, the One True God as you say, with unified control, why does He not punish the wrong-doers at

ascribe unto Him! 2 He does send down His angels with inspiration of His
Command, to such of His servants as He pleases, (saying): "Warn (Man)
that there is no god but I: so do your duty unto Me." 3 He has created the
heavens and the earth for just ends: far is He above having the partners
they ascribe to Him!

4 He has created man from a sperm-drop; and behold this same (man)
becomes an open disputer!

5 And cattle He has created for you (men): from them you derive warmth,
and numerous benefits, and of their (meat) you eat. 6 And you have a
sense of pride and beauty in them as you drive them home in the evening,
and as you lead them forth to pasture in the morning. 7 And they carry
your heavy loads to lands that you could not (otherwise) reach except
with souls distressed: for your Lord is indeed Most Kind, Most Merciful.
8 And (He has created) horses, mules, and donkeys, for you to ride and
use for show; and He has created (other) things of which you have no
knowledge.

9 And unto Allah leads straight the Way, but there are ways that turn
aside: if Allah had willed, He could have guided all of you.

SECTION 2

10 It is He Who sends down rain from the sky: from it you drink, and out
of it (grows) the vegetation on which you feed your cattle. 11 With it He
produces for you corn, olives, date-palms, grapes and every kind of fruit:
verily in this is a Sign for those who give thought.

12 He has made subject to you the night and the day; the sun and the
moon; and the stars are in subjection by His Command: verily in this are
Signs for men who are wise. 13 And the things on this earth which He has
multiplied in varying colours (and qualities): verily in this is a Sign for
men who celebrate the praises of Allah (in gratitude).

14 It is He Who has made the sea subject, that you may eat thereof flesh
that is fresh and tender, and that you may extract therefrom ornaments to
wear; and you see the ships therein that plough the waves, that you may

---

once?" The answer is: "The decree of Allah will inevitably come to pass; it will come soon enough; when it comes, you will wish it were delayed; how foolish of you to wish even to cut off your last hope of forgiveness?" [2019]

seek (thus) of the bounty of Allah and that you may be grateful.

15 And He has set up on the earth mountains[2] standing firm, lest it should
shake with you; and rivers and roads; that you may guide yourselves; 16
And marks and sign-posts; and by the stars (men) guide themselves.

17 Is then He Who creates like one that creates not? Will you not receive
admonition? 18 If you would count up the favours of Allah, never would
you be able to number them: for Allah is Oft-forgiving, Most Merciful.
19 And Allah does know what you conceal, and what you reveal. 20 Those
whom they invoke besides Allah create nothing and are themselves
created. 21 (They are things) dead, lifeless: nor do they know when they
will be raised up.

SECTION 3

22 Your Allah is one Allah: as to those who believe not in the Hereafter,
their hearts refuse to know, and they are arrogant. 23 Undoubtedly Allah
does know what they conceal, and what they reveal: verily He loves not
the arrogant. 24 When it is said to them, "What is it that your Lord has
revealed?" they say, "Tales of the ancients!" 25 Let them bear, on the Day
of Judgement, their own burdens in full, and also (something) of the
burdens of those without knowledge, whom they misled.[3] Alas, how
grievous the burdens they will bear!

SECTION 4

26 Those before them did also plot (against Allah's Way): but Allah took
their structures from their foundations, and the roof fell down on them
from above; and the Wrath seized them from directions they did not
perceive. 27 Then, on the Day of Judgement, He will cover them with
shame, and say: "Where are My 'partners' concerning whom you used to

---

2. *Cf.* 13:3 and 15:19. Here and elsewhere the earth is spoken of as a spacious carpet beneath our feet and the hills as a steadying agent to keep the carpet from rolling or shaking about. In 78:7 they are spoken of as pegs or stakes. [2038]

3. Their responsibility or crime is twofold: (1) that they rejected Allah's Message, and (2) that they misled others. Their Penalty will also be double. In 6:164, we are told that "no bearer of burdens can bear the burden of another". This is against the doctrine of vicarious atonement. Every man is responsible for his own sins; but the sin of misleading others is a sin of the misleader himself, and he must suffer the penalty for that also, without relieving those misled, of their responsibility. [2048]

dispute (with the godly)?" Those endued with knowledge will say: "This
Day, indeed, are the Unbelievers covered with shame and misery,—28
(Namely) those whose lives the angels take in a state of wrong-doing to
their own souls." Then would they offer submission (with the pretence),
"We did no evil (knowingly)." (The angels will reply), "Nay, but verily
Allah knows all that you did; 29 So enter the gates of Hell, to dwell
therein." Thus evil indeed is the abode of the arrogant.

30 To the righteous (when) it is said, "What is it that your Lord has
revealed?" they say, "All that is good." To those who do good, there is
good in this world, and the Home of the Hereafter is even better and
excellent indeed is the Home of the righteous,—31 Gardens of Eternity
which they will enter: beneath them flow (pleasant) rivers: they will have
therein all that they wish: thus does Allah reward the righteous,—32
(Namely) those whose lives the angels take in a state of purity, saying (to
them), "Peace be on you; enter you the Garden, because of (the good)
which you did (in the world)."

33 Do the (ungodly) wait until the angels come to them, or there comes the
Command of your Lord (for their doom)? So did those who went before
them. But Allah wronged them not: nay, they wronged their own souls.
34 But the evil results of their deeds overtook them, and that very (Wrath)
at which they had scoffed hemmed them in.

SECTION 5

35 The worshippers of false gods say: "If Allah had so willed, we should
not have worshipped aught but Him—neither we[4] nor our fathers,—nor
should we have prescribed prohibitions other than His." So did those who
went before them. But what is the mission of messengers but to preach
the clear Message? 36 For We assuredly sent amongst every people a
messenger, (with the Command), "Serve Allah, and eschew Evil": of the
people were some whom Allah guided, and some on whom error became
inevitably (established). So travel through the earth, and see what was the
end of those who denied (the Truth). 37 If you are anxious for their

---

4. The age-old argument: if Allah is All-Powerful, why did He not force all persons to His Will? This ignores the limited free-will granted to man, which is the whole basis of Ethics. Allah gives man every opportunity of knowing and understanding things, but He does not force him, for that would be against the whole Plan on which our present Life is constituted. [2057]

guidance, yet Allah guides not such as He leaves to stray, and there is none to help them.

38 They swear their strongest oaths[5] by Allah, that Allah will not raise up
those who die: nay, but it is a promise (binding) on Him in truth: but most
among mankind realise it not. 39 (They must be raised up), in order that
He may manifest to them the truth of that wherein they differ, and that the
rejecters of Truth may realise that they had indeed (surrendered to)
Falsehood. 40 For to anything which We have willed, We but say the
word, "Be", and it is.

SECTION 6

41 To those who leave their homes in the cause of Allah, after suffering
oppression,—We will assuredly give a goodly home in this world; but
truly the reward of the Hereafter will be greater. If they only realised
(this)! 42 (They are) those who persevere in patience, and put their trust
in their Lord.

43 And before you also the messengers We sent were but men, to whom
We granted inspiration: if you realise this not, ask of those who possess
the Message. 44 (We sent them) with clear Signs and Books of dark
prophecies; and We have sent down unto you (also) the Message; that
you may explain clearly to men what is sent for them, and that they may
give thought.

45 Do then those who devise evil (plots) feel secure that Allah will not
cause the earth to swallow them up, or that the Wrath will not seize them
from directions they little perceive?—46 Or that He may not call them to
account in the midst of their goings to and fro, without a chance of their
frustrating Him?—47 Or that He may not call them to account by a
process of slow wastage—for your Lord is indeed full of kindness and
mercy.

48 Do they not look at Allah's creation, (even) among (inanimate)
things,—how their (very) shadows turn round, from the right and the left,

5. The usual Pagan creed is (as is the creed of the present materialistic civilisation): "If there is a God, it does not follow that He will raise us up; why should He?" The answer is twofold: (1) Allah has promised it, and Allah's promise is true, (2) He must finally manifest the Truth to them, convict them of their falsehood, and enforce their personal responsibility (16:39). [2064]

prostrating themselves to Allah, and that in the humblest manner? 49 And
to Allah does obeisance all that is in the heavens and on earth, whether
moving (living) creatures or the angels: for none are arrogant (before
their Lord). 50 They all revere their Lord, high above them, and they do
all that they are commanded.

SECTION 7

51 Allah has said: "Take not (for worship) two gods:[6] for He is just One
Allah: then fear Me (and Me alone)." 52 To Him belongs whatever is in
the heavens and on earth, and to Him is duty due always: then will you
fear other[7] than Allah? 53 And you have no good thing but is from Allah:
and moreover, when you are touched by distress, unto Him you cry with
groans;[8] 54 Yet, when He removes the distress from you, behold! some
of you turn to other gods to join with their Lord—55 (As if) to show their
ingratitude for the favours We have bestowed on them! Then enjoy (your
brief day); but soon will you know (your folly)! 56 And they (even)
assign, to things they do not know, a portion out of that which We have
bestowed for their sustenance! By Allah, you shall certainly be called to
account for your false inventions.

57 And they assign daughters[9] for Allah!—Glory be to Him!—and for
themselves (sons—the issue) they desire! 58 When news is brought to one
of them, of (the birth of) a female (child), his face darkens, and he is
filled with inward grief! 59 With shame does he hide himself from his

---

6. The ancient Persians believed in two powers in the Universe, one good and the other evil. The pagan Arabs also had pairs of deities: *e.g., Jibt* (Sorcery) and *Ṭāghūt* (Evil), referred to in 4:51, or the idols on Ṣafā and Marwah referred to in note to 2:158: their names were Isāf and Nā'ilah. [2077]

7. The Pagans might have a glimmering of the One True God, but they had also a haunting fear of malevolent Powers of Evil. They are told that such fears are groundless. Evil has no power over those who trust in Allah: 15:42. The only fear they should have is that of the Wrath of Allah. To the righteous all good things come from Allah, and they have no fear in their hearts. [2078]

8. Which shows that the natural tendency of man is to seek Allah, the only Power which can truly relieve distress. [2079]

9. Some of the Pagan Arabs called angels `the daughters of Allah'. In their own life they hated to have daughters, as explained in the next two verses. They practised female infanticide. In their state of perpetual war, sons were a source of strength to them; daughters only made them subject to humiliating raids! [2082]

people, because of the bad news he has had! Shall he retain it on
(sufferance and) contempt, or bury it in the dust? Ah! What an evil
(choice) they decide on? 60 To those who believe not in the Hereafter,
applies the similitude of evil: to Allah applies the highest similitude: for
He is the Exalted in Power, full of Wisdom.

SECTION 8

61 If Allah were to punish men for their wrong-doing, He would not leave,
on the (earth), a single living creature: but He gives them respite for a
stated Term: when their Term expires, they would not be able to delay
(the punishment) for a single hour, just as they would not be able to
anticipate it (for a single hour). 62 They attribute to Allah what they hate
(for themselves), and their tongues assert the falsehood that all good
things are for themselves: without doubt for them is the Fire, and they
will be the first to be hastened on into it!

63 By Allah, We (also) sent (Our messengers) to peoples before you; but
Satan made, (to the wicked), their own acts seem alluring: he is also their
patron today, but they shall have a most grievous penalty. 64 And We sent
down the Book to you for the express purpose, that you should make
clear to them those things in which they differ, and that it should be a
guide and a mercy to those who believe. 65 And Allah sends down rain
from the skies, and gives therewith life to the earth after its death: verily
in this is a Sign for those who listen.

SECTION 9

66 And verily in cattle (too) will you find an instructive Sign. From what
is within their bodies, between excretions and blood, We produce, for
your drink, milk, pure and agreeable to those who drink it. 67 And from
the fruit of the date palm and the vine, you get out wholesome drink and
food: behold, in this also is a Sign for those who are wise. 68 And your
Lord taught the Bee to build its cells in hills, on trees, and in (men's)
habitations; 69 Then to eat of all the produce (of the earth), and find with
skill the spacious paths of its Lord: there issues from within their bodies
a drink of varying colours, wherein is healing for men: verily in this is a
Sign for those who give thought. 70 It is Allah Who creates you and takes
your souls at death; and of you there are some who are sent back to a
feeble age, so that they know nothing after having known (much): for
Allah is All-knowing, All-powerful.

SECTION 10

71 Allah has bestowed His gifts of sustenance more freely on some of you
than on others: those more favoured are not going to throw back their
gifts to those whom their right hands possess, so as to be equal in that
respect. Will they then deny the favours of Allah? 72 And Allah has made
for you mates (and companions) of your own nature, and made for you,
out of them, sons and daughters and grandchildren, and provided for you
sustenance of the best: will they then believe in vain things, and be
ungrateful for Allah's favours?—73 And worship others than Allah,—such
as have no power of providing them, for sustenance, with anything in the
heavens or earth, and cannot possibly have such power?

74 Invent not similitudes for Allah: for Allah knows, and you know not.
75 Allah sets forth the Parable (of two men: one) a slave under the
dominion of another; he has no power of any sort; and (the other) a man
on whom We have bestowed goodly favours from Ourselves, and he
spends thereof (freely), privately and publicly: are the two equal? (By no
means;) praise be to Allah. But most of them understand not. 76 Allah sets
forth (another) Parable of two men: one of them dumb, with no power of
any sort; a wearisome burden is he to his master; whichever way be
directs him, he brings no good: is such a man equal with one who
commands justice, and is on a straight Way?

SECTION 11

77 To Allah belongs the Mystery of the heavens and the earth. And the
Decision of the Hour (of Judgement) is as the twinkling of an eye, or
even quicker: for Allah has power over all things. 78 It is He Who brought
you forth from the wombs of your mothers when you knew nothing; and
He gave you hearing and sight and intelligence and affection: that you
may give thanks (to Allah). 79 Do they not look at the birds, held poised
in the midst of (the air and) the sky? Nothing holds them up but (the
power of) Allah. Verily in this are Signs for those who believe. 80 It is
Allah Who made your habitations homes of rest and quiet for you; and
made for you, out of the skins of animals, (tents for) dwellings, which
you find so light (and handy) when you travel and when you stop (in your
travels); and out of their wool, and their soft fibres (between wool and
hair), and their hair, rich stuff and articles of convenience (to serve you)
for a time. 81 It is Allah Who made out of the things He created, some

things to give you shade; of the hills He made some for your shelter; He
made you garments to protect you from heat, and coats of mail to protect
you from your (mutual) violence. Thus does He complete His favours on
you, that you may bow to His Will (in Islam). 82 But if they turn away,
your duty is only to preach the clear Message. 83 They recognise the
favours of Allah; then they deny them; and most of them are (creatures)
ungrateful.

SECTION 12

84 One day We shall raise from all peoples a Witness: then will no excuse
be accepted from Unbelievers, nor will they receive any favours. 85 When
the wrong-doers (actually) see the Penalty, then will it in no way be
mitigated, nor will they then receive respite. 86 When those who gave
partners to Allah will see their "partners", they will say: "Our Lord!
These are our `partners', those whom we used to invoke besides You."
But they will throw back their word at them (and say): "Indeed you are
liars!" 87 That day shall they (openly) show (their) submission to Allah;
and all their inventions shall leave them in the lurch. 88 Those who reject
Allah and hinder (men) from the Path of Allah—for them will We add
Penalty to Penalty; for that they used to spread mischief.

89 One day We shall raise from all peoples a witness against them, from
amongst themselves: and We shall bring you as a witness against these
(your people): and We have sent down to you the Book explaining all
things, a Guide, a Mercy, and Glad Tidings to Muslims.

SECTION 13

90 Allah commands justice, the doing of good, and liberality to kith and
kin, and He forbids all shameful deeds, and injustice and rebellion: He
instructs you, that you may receive admonition. 91 Fulfil the Covenant of
Allah when you have entered into it, and break not your oaths after you
have confirmed them; indeed you have made Allah your surety; for Allah
knows all that you do. 92 And be not like a woman who breaks into
untwisted strands the yarn which she has spun, after it has become strong.
Nor take your oaths to practise deception between yourselves, lest one
party should be more numerous than another: for Allah will test you by
this; and on the Day of Judgement He will certainly make clear to you
(the truth of) that wherein you disagree. 93 If Allah so willed, He could
make you all one people: but He leaves straying whom He pleases, and

He guides whom He pleases: but you shall certainly be called to account
for all your actions. 94 And take not your oaths, to practise deception
between yourselves, with the result that someone's foot may slip after it
was firmly planted, and you may have to taste the evil (consequences) of
having hindered (men) from the Path of Allah, and a mighty Wrath
descend on you.

95 Nor sell the Covenant of Allah for a miserable price: for with Allah is
(a prize) far better for you, if you only knew. 96 What is with you must
vanish: what is with Allah will endure. And We will certainly bestow, on
those who patiently persevere, their reward according to the best of their
actions. 97 Whoever works righteousness, man or woman, and has Faith,
verily, to him will We give a new Life, a life that is good and pure and
We will bestow on such their reward according to the best of their
actions.

98 When you do read the Qur'an, seek Allah's protection from Satan the
rejected one. 99 No authority has he over those who believe and put their
trust in their Lord. 100 His authority is over those only, who take him as
patron and who join partners with Allah.

SECTION 14

101 When We substitute one revelation for another,—and Allah knows
best what He reveals (in stages),—they say, "You are but a forger": but
most of them understand not. 102 Say, the Holy Spirit[10] has brought the
revelation from your Lord in Truth, in order to strengthen those who
believe, and as a Guide and Glad Tidings to Muslims. 103 We know
indeed that they say, "It is a man that teaches him." The tongue of him
they wickedly point to is notably foreign, while this is Arabic, pure and
clear. 104 Those who believe not in the Signs of Allah,—Allah will not
guide them, and theirs will be a grievous Penalty. 105 It is those who
believe not in the Signs of Allah, that forge falsehood: it is they who lie!

106 Anyone who, after accepting faith in Allah, utters Unbelief,[11]

---

10. The title of the Angel Gabriel, through whom the revelation came down. [2141]

11. The exception refers to a case like that of 'Ammār, whose father Yāsir and mother Sumayyah, were subjected to unspeakable tortures for their belief in Islam, but never recanted. 'Ammār, himself was of less mature age and faith, and in a weak moment, suffering under tortures himself and his mind acted on by the sufferings of his parents,

—except under compulsion, his heart remaining firm in Faith—but such
as open their breast to Unbelief,— on them is Wrath from Allah, and
theirs will be a dreadful Penalty. 107 This because they love the life of this
world better than the Hereafter: and Allah will not guide those who reject
Faith. 108 Those are they whose hearts, ears, and eyes Allah has sealed up,
and they take no heed. 109 Without doubt, in the Hereafter they will perish.
110 But verily your Lord,—to those who leave their homes after trials and
persecutions,—and who thereafter strive and fight for the Faith and
patiently persevere,—your Lord, after all this is Oft-forgiving, Most
Merciful.

SECTION 15

111 One Day every soul will come up struggling for itself, and every soul
will be recompensed (fully) for all its actions, and none will be unjustly
dealt with. 112 Allah sets forth a Parable: a city enjoying security[12] and
quiet, abundantly supplied with sustenance from every place: yet was it
ungrateful for the favours of Allah: so Allah made it taste of hunger and
terror (in extremes) (closing in on it) like a garment[13] (from every side),
because of the (evil) which (its people) wrought. 113 And there came to
them a Messenger from among themselves, but they falsely rejected him;
so the Wrath seized them even in the midst of their iniquities.

114 So eat of the sustenance which Allah has provided for you, lawful and
good; and be grateful for the favours of Allah, if it is He Whom you

---

uttered a word construed as recantation, though his heart never wavered and he came back at once to the Prophet, who consoled him for his pain and confirmed his faith. There is no permission in this for weakness or dissembling under torture or persecution. [2145]

12. The reference may be to any of the cities or populations in ancient or modern times, which were favoured with security and other blessings from Allah, but which rebelled from Allah's Law and tasted the inevitable penalty, even in the midst of their iniquities. Some commentators see here a reference to the city of Makkah under Pagan control. See next note. [2149]

13. There is a double metaphor: (1) the *tasting* of hunger and terror after the abundant supplies and the full security which it had enjoyed; and (2) the complete *enfolding* of the city as with a *garment*, by these two scourges, hunger and a state of subjective alarm. If the reference is to Makkah shortly before its fall to the Muslims, the "hunger" was the seven years' severe famine which afflicted it, and the alarm was the constant fear in the minds of the Pagans that their day was done. Peace and prosperity were restored after the re-entry of the Prophet. [2150]

serve. 115 He has only forbidden you dead meat, and blood, and the flesh
of swine, and any (food) over which the name of other than Allah has
been invoked. But if one is forced by necessity, without wilful
disobedience, nor transgressing due limits,—then Allah is Oft-forgiving,
Most Merciful. 116 But say not—for any false thing[14] that your tongues
may put forth,—"This is lawful, and this is forbidden," so as to ascribe
false things to Allah. For those who ascribe false things to Allah, will
never prosper. 117 (In such falsehood) is but a paltry profit; but they will
have a most grievous Penalty.

118 To the Jews We prohibited such things as We have mentioned to you
before: We did them no wrong, but they were used to doing wrong to
themselves. 119 But verily your Lord,—to those who do wrong in
ignorance, but who thereafter repent and make amends,—your Lord, after
all this, is Oft-forgiving, Most Merciful.

SECTION 16

120 Abraham was indeed a model, devoutly obedient to Allah, (and) true
in Faith, and he joined not gods with Allah: 121 He showed his gratitude
for the favours of Allah, Who chose him, and guided him to a straight
Way. 122 And We gave him Good in this world, and he will be, in the
Hereafter, in the ranks of the Righteous. 123 So We have taught you the
inspired (Message), "Follow the ways of Abraham the True in Faith, and
he joined not gods with Allah." 124 The Sabbath was only made (strict) for
those who disagreed (as to its observance); but Allah will judge between
them on the Day of Judgement, as to their differences.

125 Invite (all) to the Way of your Lord with wisdom and beautiful
preaching; and argue with them in ways that are best and most gracious:
for your Lord knows best, who have strayed from His Path, and who
receive guidance. 126 And if you do catch them out, catch them out no
worse than they catch you out: but if you show patience, that is indeed the
best (course) for those who are patient. 127 And do you be patient, for your
patience is but from Allah; nor grieve over them: and distress not yourself
because of their plots. 128 For Allah is with those who restrain themselves,
and those who do good.□

---

14. Men are apt to create taboos for themselves, out of superstition, and often for selfish ends, and enforce them in the name of religion. Nothing can be more reprehensible. [2153]

Chapter 17

Al-Isra' or *Banī Isrā'īl*
(The Night Journey *or* The Children of Israel)

Translator's Introduction

In the gradation of spiritual teaching (see Introduction to Sūrah 8), we saw that the first seven Sūrahs sketched the early spiritual history of man, and led up to the formation of the new *Ummah* of Islam. Sūrahs 8 to 16 formed another series dealing with the formation of the new *Ummah* and its consolidation, and Allah's dealing with man taken as an *Ummah* and considered in his social relations in organised communities (see Introduction to Sūrahs 8, 10, and 16). We now come to a fresh series, (Sūrahs 17-29), which may be considered in three parts. Sūrahs 17-21 begin with a allusion to the *Mi'rāj* (of which more later), and proceed to spiritual history as touching individuals rather than nations. The old prophets and stories of the past are now referred to from this point of view. Sūrahs 22-25 refer to *Hajj* (pilgrimage), worship and prayer, chastity, privacy, etc., as related to a man's individual spiritual growth. Sūrahs 26-29 go back to the old prophets and stories of the past, as illustrating the growth of the individual soul in its reactions against the lives of the communities and the reactions of the communities to the lives of its great individual souls.

Let us now consider Sūrah 17 by itself. It opens with the mystic Vision of the Ascension of the Holy Prophet: he was transported from the Sacred Mosque (of Makkah) to the Farthest Mosque (of Jerusalem) in a night and shown some of the Signs of Allah. The majority of Commentators take this Night Journey literally, but allow that there were other occasions on which a spiritual Journey or Vision occurred. Even on the supposition of a miraculous bodily Journey, it is conceded that the body was almost transformed into spiritual fineness. The *Hadīth* literature gives details of this Journey and its study helps to elucidate its meaning. The Holy Prophet was first transported to the seat of the earlier revelations in Jerusalem, and then taken through the seven heavens even to the Sublime Throne, and initiated into the spiritual mysteries of the human soul struggling in Space and Time. The Spaniard, Miguiel Asin, Arabic Professor in the University of Madrid, has shown that this *Mi'rāj* literature had a great influence on the Medieval literature of Europe, and especially on the great Italian poem, the *Divine Comedy* (or Drama) of Dante, which towers like a landmark in Medieval European literature.

The reference to this great mystic story of the *Mi'rāj* is a fitting prelude to the journey of the human soul in its spiritual growth in life. The first steps in such growth must be through moral conduct—the reciprocal rights of parents and children, kindness to our fellow-men, courage and firmness in the hour of danger, and sense of personal responsibility, and a sense of Allah's Presence through prayer and praise.

The *Mi'rāj* is usually dated to the 27th night of the month of Rajab (though other dates, *e.g.*, 17th of Rabī' al-Awwal, are also given) in the year before the Hijrah. This fixes the date of the opening verse of the Sūrah, though portions of the Sūrah may have been a little earlier.

Summary—The spiritual experiences of the men of Allah are given in order that Allah's Signs may be made clear to men: man is misled into evil, and must be guided to a sense of personal responsibility (17:1-22).

Our service to Allah is shown also in our human relations, goodness to parents and kinsmen and strangers in want, as well as kindness to children, purity in sex relations, justice and respect for human life, protection of orphans, probity in all dealings, and avoidance of arrogance (17:23-40).

Allah's glory is above all comparison, and the reception of His revelation marks off the man of faith from those who do not believe. But the Believers should speak fair and avoid dissensions, for Allah encompasses all men (17:41-60).

Pride caused the fall of Iblīs, but the children of Adam have been raised in excellence above other Creation. They will be judged by their deeds. Prayer is good at stated times and at night, and the Qur'an is offered as healing and mercy (17:61-84).

Inspiration (the Qur'an) is a Sign of Allah's grace, and men should accept it without making carping excuses. Be humble in prayer and praise (17:85-111).

*** *** ***

PART XV

In the name of Allah,
Most Gracious, Most Merciful.

1 Glory to (Allah) Who did take His servant for a Journey by night[1] from the Sacred Mosque[2] to the Farthest Mosque,[3] whose precincts We did

---

1. The reference is to the *Mi'rāj* for which see the Introduction to this Sūrah. [2166]

2. *Masjid* is a place of prayer: here it refers to the Ka'bah at Makkah. It had not yet been cleared of its idols and rededicated exclusively to the One True God. It was symbolical of the new Message which was being given to mankind. [2167]

3. *The Farthest Mosque* must refer to the site of the Temple of Solomon in Jerusalem on the hill of Moriah, at or near which stands the Dome of the Rock. This and the Mosque known as the Farthest Mosque (*Masjid al-Aqṣā*) were completed by the Amīr 'Abd al-

bless,—in order that We might show him some of Our Signs: for He is the One Who hears and sees (all things). 2 We gave Moses the Book, and made it a Guide to the Children of Israel, (commanding): "Take not other than Me as Disposer of (your) affairs." 3 O you that are sprung from those whom We carried (in the Ark) with Noah! Verily he was a devotee most grateful. 4 And We gave (clear) Warning to the Children of Israel[4] in the Book, that twice[5] would they do mischief on the earth and be elated with mighty arrogance (and twice would they be punished)! 5 When the first of the warnings came to pass, We sent against you Our servants given to terrible warfare: they entered the very inmost parts of your homes; and it was a warning (completely) fulfilled. 6 Then did We grant you the Return as against them:[6] We gave you increase in resources and sons,

---

Malik in A.H 68. *Farthest,* because it was the place of worship farthest west which was known to the Arabs in the time of the Holy Prophet: it was a sacred place to both Jews and Christians, but the Christians then had the upper hand, as it was included in the Byzantine (Roman) Empire, which maintained a Patriarch at Jerusalem. The chief dates in connection with the Temple are: it was finished by Solomon about 1004 B.C.; destroyed by the Babylonians under Nebuchadnezzar about 586 B.C.; rebuilt under Ezra and Nehemiah about 515 B.C.; turned into a heathen idol-temple by one of Alexander's successors, Antiochus Epiphanes, 167 B.C.; restored by Herod, 17 B.C. to A.C. 29; and completely razed to the ground by the Emperor Titus in A.C. 70. These ups and downs are among the greater Signs in religious history. [2168]

4. The Book is the revelation given to the Children of Israel. Here it seems to refer to the burning words of Prophets like Isaiah. For example, see Isaiah, chap. xxiv, or Isaiah v. 20-30, or Isaiah iii.16-26. [2173]

5. What are the two occasions referred to? It may be that "twice" is a figure of speech for "more than once", "often". Or it may be that the two occasions refer to (1) the destruction of the Temple by the Babylonian Nebuchadnezzar in 586 B.C., when the Jews were carried off into captivity, and (2) the destruction of Jerusalem by Titus in A.C. 70, after which the Temple was never rebuilt. See n. 199 above. On both occasions it was a judgement of Allah for the sins of the Jews, their backslidings, and their arrogance. [2174]

6. The return of the Jews from the Captivity was about 520 B.C. They started life afresh. They rebuilt the Temple. They carried out various reforms and built up a new Judaism in connection with Ezra. For a time they prospered. Meanwhile their old oppressors the Babylonians had been absorbed by Persia. Subsequently Persia was absorbed in Alexander's Empire. The whole of western Asia was Hellenized, and the new school of Jews was Hellenized also, and had a strong centre in Alexandria. But their footing in Palestine continued, and under the Asmonaean Dynasty (167-63 B.C.), they had a national revival, and the names of the Maccabees are remembered as those of heroes. Another dynasty, that of the Idumaeans, (63 B.C. to 4 B.C.), to which Herod belonged, also enjoyed some semi-independent power. The sceptre of Syria (including Palestine) passed to the Romans in

and made you the more numerous in manpower. 7 If you did well, you did
well for yourselves; if you did evil, (you did it) against yourselves. So
when the second of the warnings came to pass, (We permitted your
enemies) to disfigure your faces,[7] and to enter your Temple[8] as they had
entered it before, and to visit with destruction all that fell into their
power. 8 It may be that your Lord may (yet) show Mercy unto you; but if
you revert (to your sins), We shall revert (to Our punishments): and We
have made Hell a prison for those who reject (all Faith). 9 Verily this
Qur'an does guide to that which is most right (or stable), and gives the
Glad Tidings to the Believers who work deeds of righteousness, that they
shall have a magnificent reward; 10 And to those who believe not in the
Hereafter, (it announces) that We have prepared for them a Penalty
grievous (indeed).

SECTION 2

11 The prayer that man should make for good, he makes for evil; for man
is given to hasty (deeds). 12 We have made the Night and the Day as two
(of Our) Signs: the Sign of the Night have We obscured, while the Sign
of the Day We have made to enlighten you; that you may seek bounty
from your Lord, and that you may know the number and count of the
years: all things have We explained in detail. 13 Every man's fate We
have fastened on his own neck: on the Day of Judgement We shall bring
out for him a scroll, which he will see spread open. 14 (It will be said to
him:) "Read your (own) record: sufficient is your soul this day to make
out an account against you."

15 Who receives guidance, receives it for his own benefit: who goes astray
does so to his own loss: no bearer of burdens can bear the burden of
another: nor would We visit with Our Wrath until We had sent a

---

65 B.C., and Jewish feudatory Kings held power under them. But the Jews again showed a stiff-necked resistance to Allah's Messenger in the time of Jesus, and the inevitable doom followed in the complete and final destruction of the Temple under Titus in A.C. 70. [2176]

7. The second doom was due to the rejection of the Message of Jesus. "To disfigure your faces" means to destroy any credit or power you may have got: the face shows the personality of the man. [2178]

8. Titus's destruction of Jerusalem in A.C. 70 was complete. He was a son of the Roman Emperor Vespasian, and at the date of the destruction of Jerusalem, had the title of Caesar as heir to the throne. He ruled as Roman Emperor from A.C. 79 to 81. [2179]

messenger (to give warning). 16 When We decide to destroy a population,
We (first) send a definite order to those among them who are given the
good things of this life and yet transgress; so that the word is proved true
against them: then (it is) We destroy them utterly. 17 How many
generations have We destroyed after Noah? And enough is your Lord to
note and see the sins of His servants.

18 If any do wish for the transitory things (of this life), We readily grant
them—such things as We will, to such person as We will: in the end have
We provided Hell for them: they will burn therein, disgraced and rejected.
19 Those who do wish for the (things of) the Hereafter, and strive for them
with all due striving, and have Faith,—they are the ones whose striving
is acceptable (to Allah). 20 Of the bounties of your Lord We bestow freely
on all—these as well as those: the bounties of your Lord are not closed
(to anyone). 21 See how We have bestowed more on some than on others;
but verily the Hereafter is more in rank and gradation and more in
excellence. 22 Take not with Allah another object of worship; or you (O
man!) will sit in disgrace and destitution.

SECTION 3

23 Your Lord has decreed that you worship none but Him, and that you be
kind to parents. Whether one or both of them attain old age in your life,
say not to them a word of contempt, nor repel them, but address them in
terms of honour. 24 And, out of kindness, lower to them the wing of
humility, and say: "My Lord! Bestow on them Your Mercy even as they
cherished me in childhood." 25 Your Lord knows best what is in your
hearts: if you do deeds of righteousness, verily He is Most Forgiving to
those who turn to Him again and again (in true penitence).

26 And render to the kindred their due rights, as (also) to those in want,
and to the wayfarer: but squander not (your wealth) in the manner of a
spendthrift. 27 Verily spendthrifts are brothers of the Evil Ones; and the
Evil One is to his Lord (Himself) ungrateful. 28 And even if you have to
turn away from them in pursuit of the Mercy from your Lord which you
do expect, yet speak to them a word of easy kindness. 29 Make not your
hand tied (like a niggard's) to your neck, nor stretch it forth to its utmost
reach, so that you become blameworthy and destitute. 30 Verily your Lord
does provide sustenance in abundance for whom He pleases, and He
provides in a just measure. For He does know and regard all His servants.

SECTION 4

31 Kill not your children[9] for fear of want: We shall provide sustenance
for them as well as for you. Verily the killing of them is a great sin. 32 Nor
come near to adultery: for it is a shameful (deed) and an evil, opening the
road (to other evils). 33 Nor take life—which Allah has made
sacred—except for just cause. And if anyone is slain wrongfully, We
have given his heir authority (to demand *Qiṣāṣ*[10] or to forgive): but let
him not exceed bounds in the matter of taking life; for he is helped (by
the Law).

34 Come not near to the orphan's property except to improve it, until he
attains the age of full strength; and fulfil (every) engagement, for (every)
engagement will be enquired into (on the Day of Reckoning). 35 Give full
measure when you measure, and weigh with a balance that is straight: that
is the most fitting and the most advantageous in the final determination.
36 And pursue not that of which you have no knowledge;[11] for every act
of hearing, or of seeing or of (feeling in) the heart will be enquired into
(on the Day of Reckoning). 37 Nor walk on the earth with insolence: for
you cannot rend the earth asunder, nor reach the mountains in height. 38
Of all such things the evil is hateful in the sight of your Lord. 39 These are

---

9. The Arabs were addicted to female infanticide. In a society perpetually at war a son was a source of strength whereas a daughter was a source of weakness. Even now infanticide is not unknown in other countries for economic reasons. This crime against children's lives is here characterised as one of the greatest of sins. [2214]

10. On the subject of *Qiṣāṣ* see 2:178 and the notes thereto. Under the strict limitations there laid down, a life may be taken for a life. The heir is given the right to demand the life; but he must not exceed due bounds, because he is helped by the Law. Some commentators understand "he" in "he is helped (by the Law)" to refer to the heir of the person against whom *Qiṣāṣ* is sought. He too will be helped by the Law, if the heir of the first slain exceeds the bounds of Law. [2216]

11. Idle curiosity may lead us to nose into evil, through our ignorance that it is evil. We must guard against every such danger. We must only hear the things that are known to us to be of good report, and see things that are good and instructive, and entertain in our hearts feelings or in our minds ideas that we have reason to expect will be spiritually profitable to us. We shall be called to account for the exercise of every faculty that has been given to us. This goes a little farther than a famous sculpture on a Japanese temple in which three monkeys are shown as putting their hands to their ears, eyes and mouths, respectively, to show that they were not prepared to hear any evil, see any evil, or speak any evil. Here idle curiosity is condemned. Futility is to be avoided even if it does not reach the degree of positive evil. [2222]

among the (precepts of) wisdom, which your Lord has revealed to you.
Take not, with Allah, another object of worship, lest you should be
thrown into Hell, blameworthy and rejected.

40 Has then your Lord (O Pagans!) preferred for you sons, and taken for
Himself daughters among the angels? Truly you utter a most dreadful
saying!

SECTION 5

41 We have explained (things) in various (ways) in this Qur'an, in order
that they may receive admonition, but it only increases their flight (from
the Truth)! 42 Say: If there had been (other) gods with Him, as they
say,—behold, they would certainly have sought out a way to the Lord of
the Throne! 43 Glory to Him! He is high above all that they say!—Exalted
and Great (beyond measure)! 44 The seven heavens and the earth, and all
beings therein, declare His glory: there is not a thing but celebrates His
praise; and yet you understand not how they declare His glory! Verily He
is Oft-forbearing, Most Forgiving!

45 When you do recite the Qur'an, We put, between you and those who
believe not in the Hereafter, a veil invisible: 46 And We put coverings
over their hearts (and minds) lest they should understand the Qur'an, and
deafness into their ears: when you do commemorate your Lord—and Him
alone—in the Qur'an, they turn on their backs, fleeing (from the Truth).
47 We know best why it is they listen, when they listen to you; and when
they meet in private conference, behold, the wicked say, "You follow
none other than a man bewitched!" 48 See what similes they strike for
you: but they have gone astray, and never can they find a way.

49 They say: "What! When we are reduced to bones and dust, should we
really be raised up (to be) a new creation?"50 Say: "(Nay!) Be you stones
or iron, 51 Or created matter which, in your minds, is hardest (to be raised
up),—(yet shall you be raised up)!" Then will they say: "Who will cause
us to return?" Say: "He Who created you first!" Then will they wag their
heads towards you, and say, "When will that be?" Say, "Maybe it will be
quite soon! 52 It will be on a Day when He will call you, and you will
answer (His call) with (words of) His praise, and you will think that you
tarried but a little while!"

SECTION 6

53 Say to My servants that they should (only) say those things that are
best: for Satan does sow dissensions among them: for Satan is to man an
avowed enemy. 54 It is your Lord that knows you best: if He please, He
grants you mercy, or if He please, punishment: We have not sent you to
be a disposer of their affairs for them. 55 And it is your Lord that knows
best all beings that are in the heavens and on earth: We did bestow on
some prophets more (and other) gifts than on others: and We gave to
David (the gift of) the Psalms.

56 Say: "Call on those—besides Him—whom you fancy: they have neither
the power to remove your troubles from you nor to change them." 57
Those whom they call upon do desire (for themselves) means of access
to their Lord,—even those who are nearest: they hope for His Mercy and
fear His Wrath: for the Wrath of your Lord is something to take heed of.

58 There is not a population but We shall destroy it before the Day of
Judgement or punish it with a dreadful Penalty: that is written in the
(eternal) record. 59 And We refrain from sending the Signs, only because
the men of former generations treated them as false: We sent the
she-camel to the Thamūd to open their eyes, but they treated her
wrongfully: We only send the Signs by way of terror (and warning from
evil). 60 Behold! We told you that your Lord does encompass mankind
round about: We granted the vision which We showed you, but as a trial
for men,—as also the Cursed Tree (mentioned) in the Qur'an: We put
terror (and warning) into them, but it only increases their inordinate
transgression!

SECTION 7

61 Behold! We said to the angels: "Bow down unto Adam": they bowed
down except Iblīs: he said, "Shall I bow down to one whom You did
create from clay?" 62 He said: "See You? This is the one whom You have
honoured above me! If You will but respite me to the Day of Judgement,
I will surely bring his descendants under my sway—all but a few!" 63
(Allah) said: "Go your way; if any of them follow you, verily Hell will
be the recompense of you (all)—an ample recompense. 64 Lead to
destruction those whom you can among them, with your (seductive)
voice; make assaults on them with your cavalry and your infantry;
mutually share with them wealth and children; and make promises to

them. But Satan promises them nothing but deceit. 65 As for My servants,
no authority shall you have over them." Enough is your Lord for a
Disposer of affairs.

66 Your Lord is He that makes the ship go smoothly for you through the
sea, in order that you may seek of His Bounty. For He is unto you Most
Merciful. 67 When distress seizes you at sea, those that you call
upon—besides Himself—leave you in the lurch! But when He brings you
back safe to land, you turn away (from Him). Most ungrateful is man! 68
Do you then feel secure that He will not cause you to be swallowed up
beneath the earth when you are on land, or that He will not send against
you a violent tornado (with showers of stones) so that you shall find no
one to carry out your affairs for you? 69 Or do you feel secure that He will
not send you back a second time to sea and send against you a heavy gale
to drown you because of your ingratitude, so that you find no helper
therein against Us? 70 We have honoured the sons of Adam; provided
them with transport on land and sea; given them for sustenance things
good and pure; and conferred on them special favours, above a great part
of Our creation.

SECTION 8

71 One day We shall call together all human beings with their (respective)
Imāms: those who are given their record in their right hand will read it
(with pleasure), and they will not be dealt with unjustly in the least. 72 But
those who were blind in this world, will be blind in the Hereafter, and
most astray from the Path.

73 And their purpose was to tempt you away from that which We had
revealed unto you, to substitute in Our name something quite different;
(in that case), behold! they would certainly have made you (their) friend!
74 And had We not given you strength, you would nearly have inclined to
them a little. 75 In that case We should have made you taste an equal
portion (of punishment) in this life, and an equal portion in death: and
moreover you would have found none to help you against Us! 76 Their
purpose was to scare you off the land, in order to expel you; but in that
case they would not have stayed (therein) after you, except for a little
while. 77 (This was Our) way with the messengers We sent before you:
you will find no change in Our ways.

SECTION 9

78 Establish regular prayers[12]—at the sun's decline till the darkness of the
night, and the morning prayer and reading: for the prayer and reading in
the morning carry their testimony.[13] 79 And pray in the small watches of
the morning: (it would be) an additional prayer (or spiritual profit) for
you: soon will your Lord raise you to a Station of Praise and Glory! 80
Say: "O my Lord! Let my entry be[14] by the Gate of Truth and Honour,
and likewise my exit by the Gate of Truth and Honour; and grant me
from Your Presence an authority to aid (me)." 81 And say: "Truth has
(now) arrived, and Falsehood perished: for Falsehood is (by its nature)
bound to perish." 82 We send down (stage by stage) in the Qur'an that
which is a healing and a mercy to those who believe: to the unjust it
causes nothing but loss after loss.

83 Yet when We bestow Our favours on man, he turns away and becomes
remote on his side (instead of coming to Us), and when evil seizes him

---

12. The Commentators understand here the command for the five daily canonical prayers, *viz.*: the four from the declination of the sun from the zenith to the fullest darkness of the night, and the early morning prayer, *Fajr*, which is usually accompanied by a reading of the Holy Qur'an. The four afternoon prayers are: *Zuhr*, immediately after the sun begins to decline in the afternoon; *'Asr*, the late afternoon; *Maghrib*, immediately after sunset; and *'Ishā'*, after the glow of sunset has disappeared and the full darkness of the night has set in. There is difference of opinion as to the meaning of particular words and phrases but none as to the general effect of this passage. [2275]

13. The morning prayer is specially singled out for separate mention, because the morning is a "Holy hour" and special spiritual influences act on the soul awaking from the night's rest. Special testimony is borne to the prayers of this hour by the angelic host. [2276]

14. The entry and exit here referred to may be interpreted in four senses: (1) entry into death and exit at the resurrection; for the righteous, who have purified their souls by prayer (last verse) and spiritual teaching from the Qur'an (next verse), there is on each occasion a fuller and fuller realisation and enjoyment of truth and honour; for those who are estranged from Allah, the effect is the opposite: the truth becomes bitter and there is ignominy and exposure instead of honour; (2) entry for the holy Prophet into the new life at Madīnah, which was still in the womb of futurity, and exit from the life of persecution and the milieu of falsehood, which surrounded him in his native city of Makkah still given up to idolatry; (3) referring to the impending Hijrah again, the prayer may mean, "Let it be from pure motives of truth and spiritual honour, and not from motives of anger against the city of Makkah or its persecutors, or of ambition or worldly power from the city of Madīnah, which was ready to lay everything at the Prophet's feet"; (4) generally, entry and exit at every stage of life. [2279]

he gives himself up to despair! 84 Say: "Everyone acts according to his
own disposition: but your Lord knows best who it is that is best guided
on the Way."

SECTION 10

85 They ask you concerning the Spirit (of inspiration). Say: "The Spirit
(comes) by command of my Lord: of knowledge it is only a little that is
communicated to you, (O men!)" 86 If it were Our Will, We could take
away that which We have sent you by inspiration: then would you find
none to plead your affair in that matter as against Us,—87 Except for
Mercy from your Lord: for His Bounty is to you (indeed) great.

88 Say: "If the whole of mankind and *Jinns*[15] were to gather together to
produce the like of this Qur'an, they could not produce the like thereof,
even if they backed up each other with help and support." 89 And We
have explained to man, in this Qur'an, every kind of similitude: yet the
greater part of men refuse (to receive it) except with ingratitude! 90 They
say: "We shall not believe in you, until you cause a spring to gush forth
for us from the earth, 91 Or (until) you have a garden of date trees and
vines, and cause rivers to gush forth in their midst, carrying abundant
water; 92 Or you cause the sky to fall in pieces, as you say (will happen),
against us; or you bring Allah and the angels before (us) face to face; 93
Or you have a house adorned with gold, or you mount a ladder right into the
skies. No, we shall not even believe in your mounting until you send down
to us a book that we could read." Say: "Glory to my Lord! Am I aught but a
man,—a messenger?"

SECTION 11

94 What kept men back from belief when Guidance came to them, was
nothing but this: they said, "Has Allah sent a man (like us) to be (His)
Messenger?" 95 Say, "If there were settled, on earth, angels walking about
in peace and quiet, We should certainly have sent them down from the
heavens an angel for a messenger." 96 Say: "Enough is Allah for a witness
between me and you: for He is well acquainted with His servants, and He
sees (all things)."

97 It is he whom Allah guides, that is on true Guidance; but he whom He

15. For the meaning of "*Jinns*", see note to 6:100. [2288]

leaves astray—for such will you find no protector besides Him. On the
Day of Judgement We shall gather, them together, prone on their faces,
blind, dumb, and deaf: their abode will be Hell: every time it shows
abatement, We shall increase for them the fierceness of the Fire. 98 That
is their recompense, because they rejected Our Signs, and said, "When we
are reduced to bones and broken dust, should we really be raised up (to
be) a new creation?" 99 See they not that Allah, Who created the heavens
and the earth, has power to create the like of them (anew)? Only He has
decreed a term appointed, of which there is no doubt. But the unjust
refuse (to receive it) except with ingratitude. 100 Say: "If you had control
of the Treasures of the Mercy of my Lord, behold, you would keep them
back, for fear of spending them: for man is (ever) niggardly!"

SECTION 12

101 To Moses We did give Nine clear Signs: ask the Children of Israel:
when he came to them, Pharaoh said to him: "O Moses! I consider you,
indeed, to have been worked upon by sorcery!" 102 Moses said, "You
know well that these things have been sent down by none but the Lord of
the heavens and the earth as eye-opening evidence: and I consider you
indeed, O Pharaoh, to be one doomed to destruction!" 103 So he resolved
to remove them from the face of the earth: but We did drown him and all
who were with him. 104 And We said thereafter to the Children of Israel,
"Dwell securely in the land (of promise)": but when the second of the
warnings came to pass, We gathered you together in a mingled crowd.

105 We sent down the (Qur'an) in Truth, and in Truth has it descended:
and We sent you but to give Glad Tidings and to warn (sinners). 106 (It is)
a Qur'an which We have divided (into parts from time to time), in order
that you might recite it to men at intervals: We have revealed it by stages.
107 Say: "Whether you believe in it or not, it is true that those who were
given knowledge beforehand, when it is recited to them, fall down on
their faces in humble prostration, 108 And they say: `Glory to our Lord!
Truly has the promise of our Lord been fulfilled!'" 109 They fall down on
their faces in tears, and it increases their (earnest) humility.[16] 110 Say:

---

16. A feeling of earnest humility comes to the man who realises how, in spite of his own unworthiness, he is brought, by Allah's Mercy, into touch with the most sublime Truths. Such a man is touched with the deepest emotion, which finds its outlet in tears. [2320]

"Call upon Allah, or call upon *Raḥmān*:[17] by whatever name you call upon Him, (it is well): for to Him belong the Most Beautiful Names.[18] Neither speak your prayer aloud, nor speak it in a low tone, but seek a middle course between."
111 Say: "Praise be to Allah, Who begets no son, and has no partner in (His) dominion: nor (needs) He any to protect Him from humiliation: indeed, magnify Him for His greatness and glory!"□

---

17. *Cf.*7:180. *Raḥmān* describes one of the attributes of Allah—His Grace and Mercy which come to the sinner even before he feels conscious of the need of it—the preventive Grace which saves Allah's servants from sin. See note to Sūrah *Fātiḥah*:1. Allah can be invoked, either by His simple name, which includes all attributes, or by one of the names implying the attributes by which we try to explain His nature to our limited understanding. The attribute of Mercy in *Raḥmān* was particularly repugnant to the Pagan Arabs (see 25:60 and 21:36): that is why special stress is laid on it in the Qur'an. [2321]

18. These Beautiful Names of Allah are many. For *tasbīḥ* purposes a list of 99 is made out in *Ḥadīth* literature: that in Tirmidhī is considered authoritative. Qāḍī Muḥammad Sulaimān has published an Urdu monograph on the subject, published by the Daftar Raḥmatun-lil Ālamīn, Patiala, India, 1930. Those who wish to see a poetic Commentary on the names in the form of stories in English may consult Sir Edwin Arnold's *Pearls of the Faith.* Sir Edwin's stories are of unequal merit, but a fine example is furnished by No. 4, *al-Mālik,* "The King". [2322]

Chapter 18

Sūrah Al-Kahf
(The Cave)

Translator's Introduction

It has been explained in the Introduction to Sūrah 17 how the five Sūrahs 17 to 21 develop the theme of the individual soul's spiritual history, and how they fit into the general scheme of exposition.

This particular Makkan Sūrah may be called a lesson in the brevity and mystery of Life. First there is the story of the Companions of the Cave who slept therein for a long period, and yet thought they had been there only a day or less. Then there is the story of the mysterious Teacher who shows Moses how Life itself is a parable. And further there is the story of Dhū al-Qarnayn, the two-horned one, the powerful ruler of west and east, who made an iron wall to protect the weak against the strong. The parables refer to the brevity, uncertainty, and vanity of this life; to the many paradoxes in it, which can only be understood by patience and the fullness of knowledge; and to the need of guarding our spiritual gains against the incursions of evil.

Summary—The Qur'an is a direction and a warning. This life is brief and subject to vicissitudes. Our ideas of Time are defective, as shown in the story of the Companions of the Cave, who had faith, truth, patience, and other virtues. But their life was a mystery that can be fathomed but by few (18:1-22).

Knowledge is for Allah: be on your guard against idle conjectures and cocksure hopes. Learn from the Qur'an the Parable of the man who is puffed up with this world's goods and is brought to nought (18:23-44).

This life is uncertain and variable: goodness and virtue are better and more durable. For the Day of Reckoning will come, with its Mercy and its Wrath (18:45-59).

Moses in his thirst for knowledge forgot his limitations. Patience and faith were enjoined on him, and he understood when the paradoxes of Life were explained (18:60-82).

Dhū al-Qarnayn had a wide dominion: he punished the guilty and rewarded the good; he protected the weak from the lawless; but he had faith, and valued the guidance of Allah. Allah is One, and His service is righteousness (18:83-110).

*** *** ***

In the name of Allah,
Most Gracious, Most Merciful.

1 Praise be to Allah, Who has sent to His Servant the Book, and has
allowed therein no crookedness: 2 (He has made it) straight (and clear) in
order that He may warn (the godless) of a terrible Punishment from Him,
and that He may give Glad Tidings to the Believers who work righteous
deeds, that they shall have a goodly Reward, 3 Wherein they shall remain
for ever: 4 Further, that He may warn those (also) who say, "Allah has
begotten a son": 5 No knowledge have they of such a thing, nor had their
fathers. It is a grievous thing that issues from their mouths as a saying.
What they say is nothing but falsehood!

6 You would only, perchance, fret yourself to death, following after them,
in grief, if they believe not in this Message. 7 That which is on earth We
have made but as a glittering show for the earth, in order that We may
test them—as to which of them are best in conduct. 8 Verily what is on
earth We shall make but as dust and dry soil (without growth or herbage).

9 Or do you reflect that the Companions of the Cave and of the Inscription
were wonders among Our Signs? 10 Behold, the youths betook
themselves[1] to the Cave: they said, "Our Lord! Bestow on us Mercy

1. The bare Christian story (without the spiritual lessons taught in the Qur'an) is told in Gibbon's *Decline and Fall of the Roman Empire* (end of chapter 33). In the reign of a Roman Emperor who persecuted the Christians, seven Christian youths of Ephesus left the town and hid themselves in a cave in a mountain nearby. They fell asleep, and remained asleep for some generations or centuries. When the wall which sealed up the cave was being demolished, the youths awoke. They still thought of the world in which they had previously lived. They had no idea of the duration of time. But when one of them went to the town to purchase provisions, he found that the whole world had changed. The Christian religion, instead of being persecuted was fashionable: in fact it was now the State religion. His dress and speech, and the money which he brought, seemed to belong to another world. This attracted attention. The great ones of the land visited the Cave, and verified the tale by questioning the man's Companions.

When the story became very popular and circulated throughout the Roman Empire, we may well suppose that an Inscription was put up at the mouth of the Cave. See verse 9. This inscription was probably to be seen for many years afterwards, as Ephesus was a famous city on the west coast of Asia Minor, about forty to fifty miles south of Smyrna. Later on, the Khalīfah Wāthiq (A.C. 842-846) sent an expedition to examine and identify the locality, as he did about the Dhū al-Qarnayn barrier in Central Asia.

A popular story circulating from mouth to mouth would necessarily be vague as to dates and vary very much in details. Somewhere about the 6th century A.C. a Syriac writer reduced

from Yourself, and dispose of our affair for us in the right way!" 11 Then
We drew (a veil) over their ears, for a number of years, in the Cave, (so
that they heard not): 12 Then We roused them, in order to test which of the
two parties was best at calculating the term of years they had tarried!

SECTION 2

13 We relate to you their story in truth: they were youths who believed in
their Lord, and We advanced them in guidance: 14 We gave strength to
their hearts: behold, they stood up and said: "Our Lord is the Lord of the
heavens and of the earth: never shall we call upon any god other than
Him: if we did, we should indeed have uttered an enormity! 15 These our
people have taken for worship gods other than Him: why do they not
bring forward an authority clear (and convincing) for what they do? Who
does more wrong than such as invent a falsehood against Allah? 16 When
you turn away from them and the things they worship other than Allah,
go yourselves to the Cave: your Lord will shower His mercies on you and
dispose of your affair towards comfort and ease."

17 You would have seen the sun, when it rose, declining to the right from their Cave, and when it set, turning away from them to the left, while they lay in the open space in the midst of the Cave. Such are among the Signs of Allah: he whom Allah guides is rightly guided; but he whom Allah leaves to stray,—for him will you find no protector to lead him to the right Way.

SECTION 3

18 You would have deemed them awake, whilst they were asleep, and We
turned them on their right and on their left sides: their dog stretching forth
his two fore-legs on the threshold: if you had come up on to them, you
would have certainly turned back from them in flight, and would certainly
have been filled with terror of them. 19 Such (being their state), We raised
them up (from sleep), that they might question each other. Said one of

---

it to writing. He suggested that the youths were seven in number; that they went to sleep in the reign of the Emperor Decius (who reigned from A.C. 249 to 251, and who was a violent persecutor of Christians) and that they awoke in the reign of Theodosius II, who reigned from A.C. 408 to 450. In our literature Decius is known as Daqyānūs (from the adjectival Latin from Decianus), and the name stands as a symbol of injustice and oppression, and also of things old fashioned and out-of-date, as *res decianae* must have been two to three centuries after Decius. [2337]

them, "How long have you stayed (here)?" They said, "We have stayed
(perhaps) a day, or part of a day." (At length) they (all) said, "Allah
(alone) knows best how long you have stayed here.... Now send you then
one of you with this money of yours to the town: let him find out which
is the best food (to be had) and bring some to you, that (you may) satisfy
your hunger therewith: and let him behave with care and courtesy, and let
him not inform anyone about you. 20 For if they should come upon you,
they would stone you or force you to return to their cult, and in that case
you would never attain prosperity."

21 Thus did We make their case known to the people, that they might
know that the promise of Allah is true, and that there can be no doubt
about the Hour of Judgement. Behold, they dispute among themselves as
to their affair. (Some) said, "Construct a building over them": their Lord
knows best about them: those who prevailed over their affair said, "Let
us surely build a place of worship over them." 22 (Some) say they were
three, the dog being the fourth among them; (others) say they were five,
the dog being the sixth,—doubtfully guessing at the unknown; (yet
others) say they were seven, the dog being the eighth. Say you: "My Lord
knows best their number; it is but few that know their (real case)." Enter
not, therefore, into controversies concerning them, except on a matter that
is clear, nor consult any of them about (the affair of) the Sleepers.

SECTION 4

23 Nor say of anything, "I shall be sure to do so and so tomorrow" —24
Without adding, "So please Allah!". And call your Lord to mind when
you forget, and say, "I hope that my Lord will guide me ever closer
(even) than this to the right road."

25 So they stayed in their Cave three hundred years, and (some) add nine
(more) 26 Say: "Allah knows best how long they stayed: with Him is (the
knowledge of) the secrets of the heavens and the earth: how clearly He
sees, how finely He hears (everything)! They have no protector other than
Him; nor does He share His Command with any person whatsoever." 27
And recite (and teach) what has been revealed to you of the Book of your
Lord: none can change His Words, and none will you find as a refuge
other than Him. 28 And keep your soul content with those who call on
their Lord morning and evening, seeking His Face; and let not your eyes
pass beyond them, seeking the pomp and glitter of this life; nor obey any

whose heart We have permitted to neglect the remembrance of Us, one
who follows his own desires, whose case has gone beyond all bounds.

29 Say, "The Truth is from your Lord": let him who will, believe, and let
him who will, reject (it): for the wrong-doers We have prepared a Fire
whose (smoke and flames), like the walls and roof of a tent, will hem
them in: if they implore relief they will be granted water like melted
brass, that will scald their faces. How dreadful the drink! How
uncomfortable a couch to recline on! 30 As to those who believe and work
righteousness, verily We shall not suffer to perish the reward of any who
do a (single) righteous deed. 31 For them will be Gardens of Eternity;
beneath them rivers will flow; they will be adorned therein with bracelets
of gold, and they will wear green garments of fine silk and heavy
brocade: they will recline therein on raised thrones. How good the
recompense! How beautiful a couch to recline on!

SECTION 5

32 Set forth to them the parable of two men: for one of them We provided
two gardens of grape-vines and surrounded them with date palms; in
between the two We placed corn-fields. 33 Each of those gardens brought
forth its produce, and failed not in the least therein: in the midst of them
We caused a river to flow. 34 (Abundant) was the produce this man had:
he said to his companion, in the course of a mutual argument: "More
wealth have I than you, and more honour and power in (my following of)
men." 35 He went into his garden in a state (of mind) unjust to his soul: he
said, "I deem not that this will ever perish. 36 Nor do I deem that the Hour
(of Judgement) will (ever) come: even if I am brought back to my Lord,
I shall surely find (there) something better in exchange." 37 His
companion said to him, in the course of the argument with him: "Do you
deny Him Who created you out of dust, then out of a sperm-drop, then
fashioned you into a man? 38 But (I think) for my part that He is Allah,
my Lord, and none shall I associate with my Lord. 39 Why did you not,
as you went into your garden, say: 'Allah's Will (be done)! There is no
power but with Allah!' If you do see me less than you in wealth and sons,
40 It may be that my Lord will give me something better than your garden,
and that He will send on your garden thunderbolts (by way of reckoning)
from heaven, making it (but) slippery sand!—41 Or the water of the
garden will run off underground so that you will never be able to find it."
42 So his fruits (and enjoyment) were encompassed (with ruin), and he

remained twisting and turning his hands over what he had spent on his
property, which had (now) tumbled to pieces to its very foundations, and
he could only say, "Woe is me! Would I had never ascribed partners to
my Lord and Cherisher!" 43 Nor had he numbers to help him against
Allah, nor was he able to deliver himself. 44 There, the (only) protection
comes from Allah, the True One. He is the best to reward, and the best to
give success.

SECTION 6

45 Set forth to them the similitude of the life of this world: it is like the
rain which We send down from the skies: the earth's vegetation absorbs
it, but soon it becomes dry stubble, which the winds do scatter: it is (only)
Allah Who prevails over all things. 46 Wealth and sons are allurements of
the life of this world: but the things that endure, good deeds, are best in
the sight of your Lord, as rewards, and best as (the foundation for) hopes.
47 One Day We shall remove the mountains, and you will see the earth as
a level stretch, and We shall gather them, all together, nor shall We leave
out any one of them. 48 And they will be marshalled before your Lord in
ranks, (with the announcement), "Now have you come to Us (bare) as We
created you first: indeed, you thought We shall not fulfil the appointment
made to you to meet (Us)!": 49 And the book (of deeds) will be placed
(before you); and you will see the sinful in great terror because of what
is (recorded) therein; they will say, "Ah! Woe to us! What a book is this!
It leaves out nothing small or great, but takes account thereof!" They will
find all that they did, placed before them: and not one will your Lord treat
with injustice.

SECTION 7

50 Behold! We said to the angels, "Bow down to Adam": they bowed
down except Iblīs. He was one of the *Jinns*, and he broke the Command
of his Lord. Will you then take him and his progeny as protectors rather
than Me? And they are enemies to you! Evil would be the exchange for
the wrong-doers! 51 I called them not to witness the creation of the
heavens and the earth, nor (even) their own creation: nor is it for Me to
take as helpers such as lead (men) astray! 52 One Day He will say, "Call
on those whom you thought to be My partners," and they will call on
them, but they will not listen to them; and We shall make for them a place
of common perdition. 53 And the Sinful shall see the Fire and apprehend

that they have to fall therein: no means will they find to turn away
therefrom.

SECTION 8

54 We have explained in detail in this Qur'an, for the benefit of mankind,
every kind of similitude: but man is, in most things, contentious. 55 And
what is there to keep back men from believing, now that guidance has
come to them, nor from praying for forgiveness from their Lord, but that
(they ask that) the ways of the ancients be repeated with them, or the
Wrath be brought to them face to face? 56 We only send the messengers
to give Glad Tidings and to give warnings: but the Unbelievers dispute
with vain argument, in order therewith to weaken the truth, and they treat
My Signs as a jest, as also the fact that they are warned! 57 And who does
more wrong than one who is reminded of the Signs of his Lord, but turns
away from them, forgetting the (deeds) which his hands have sent forth?
Verily We have set veils over their hearts lest they should understand this,
and over their ears, deafness. If you call them to guidance, even then will
they never accept guidance. 58 But your Lord is Most Forgiving, full of
Mercy. If He were to call them (at once) to account for what they have
earned, then surely He would have hastened their punishment: but they
have their appointed time, beyond which they will find no refuge. 59 Such
were the populations We destroyed when they committed iniquities; but
we fixed an appointed time for their destruction.

SECTION 9

60 Behold, Moses said to his attendant, "I will not give up until I reach the
junction of the two seas[2] or (until) I spend years and years in travel." 61
But when they reached the Junction, they forgot (about) their Fish, which
took its course through the sea (straight) as in a tunnel. 62 When they had
passed on (some distance), Moses said to his attendant: "Bring us our
early meal; truly we have suffered much fatigue at this (stage of) our
journey." 63 He replied: "Saw you (what happened) when we betook
ourselves to the rock? I did indeed forget (about) the Fish: none but Satan
made me forget to tell (you) about it: it took its course through the sea in

---

2. The most probable geographical location (if any is required in a story that is a parable) is where the two arms of the Red Sea join together, *viz.*, the Gulf of 'Aqabah and the Gulf of Suez. They enclose the Sinai Peninsula, in which Moses and the Israelites spent many years in their wanderings. [2405]

a marvellous way!" 64 Moses said: "That was what we were seeking
after": so they went back on their footsteps, following (the path they had
come).

65 So they found one[3] of Our servants, on whom We had bestowed
Mercy from Ourselves and whom We had taught knowledge from Our
own Presence. 66 Moses said to him: "May I follow you, on the footing
that you teach me something of the (higher) Truth which you have been
taught?" 67 (The other) said: "Verily you will not be able to have patience
with me! 68 And how can you have patience about things about which
your understanding is not complete?" 69 Moses said: "You will find me,
if Allah so wills, (truly) patient: nor shall I disobey you in aught." 70 The
other said: "If then you would follow me, ask me no questions about
anything until I myself speak to you concerning it."

SECTION 10

71 So they both proceeded: until, when they were in the boat, he scuttled
it. Said Moses: "Have you scuttled it in order to drown those in it? Truly
a strange thing have you done!" 72 He answered: "Did I not tell you that
you can have no patience with me?" 73 Moses said: "Rebuke me not for
forgetting, nor grieve me by raising difficulties in my case."

74 Then they proceeded: until, when they met a young man, he slew him.
Moses said: "Have you slain an innocent person who had slain none?
Truly a foul (unheard of) thing have you done!"

PART XVI

75 He answered: "Did I not tell you that you can have no patience with
me?" 76 (Moses) said: "If ever I ask you about anything after this, keep
me not in your company: then would you have received (full) excuse
from my side."

---

3. *One of Our servants*: his name is not mentioned in the Qur'an, but Tradition gives it as Khidr. Round him have gathered a number of picturesque folk tales, with which we are not here concerned. *Khidr* means "Green": his knowledge is fresh and green, and drawn out of the living sources of life for it is drawn from Allah's own Presence. He is a mysterious being, who had to be sought out. He has the secrets of the paradoxes of Life, which ordinary people do not understand, or understand in a wrong sense, as we shall see further on. The nearest equivalent figure in the literature of the People of the Book is Melchizedek or Melchisedek (the Greek form in the New Testament). In Gen. xiv. 18-20, he appears as king of Salem, priest of the Most High God: he blesses Abraham, and Abraham gives him tithes. [2411]

77 Then they proceeded: until, when they came to the inhabitants of a
town, they asked them for food, but they refused them hospitality. They
found there a wall on the point of falling down, but he set it up straight.
(Moses) said: "If you had wished, surely you could have exacted some
recompense for it!" 78 He answered: "This is the parting between me and
you: now will I tell you the interpretation of (those things) over which
you were unable to hold patience.

79 "As for the boat, it belonged to certain men in dire want: they plied on
the water: I but wished to render it unserviceable, for there was after them
a certain king who seized on every boat by force. 80 As for the youth, his
parents were people of Faith, and we feared that he would grieve them by
obstinate rebellion and ingratitude (to Allah and man). 81 So we desired
that their Lord would give them in exchange (a son) better in purity (of
conduct) and closer in affection. 82 As for the wall, it belonged to two
youths, orphans, in the Town; there was, beneath it, a buried treasure, to
which they were entitled: their father had been a righteous man: so your
Lord desired that they should attain their age of full strength and get out
their treasure—a mercy (and favour) from your Lord. I did it not of my
own accord. Such is the interpretation of (those things) over which you
were unable to hold patience."

SECTION 11

83 They ask you concerning Dhū al-Qarnayn.[4] Say, "I will rehearse to
you something of his story." 84 Verily We established his power on earth,
and We gave him the ways and the means to all ends.

85 One (such) way he followed, 86 Until, when he reached the setting of the
sun, he found it set in a spring of murky water: near it he found a people:

---

4. Literally, "the Two-horned One" the King with the Two Horns, or the Lord of the Two Epochs. Who was he? In what age, and where did he live? The Qur'an gives us no material on which we can base a positive answer. Nor is it necessary to find an answer, as the story is treated as a Parable. Popular opinion identifies Dhū al-Qarnayn with Alexander the Great. An alternative suggestion is an ancient Persian King, or a prehistoric Ḥimyarite King.

Dhū al-Qarnayn was a most powerful king, but it was Allah, Who, in His universal Plan, gave him power and provided him with the ways and means for his great work. His sway extended over East and West, and over people of diverse civilisations. He was just and righteous, not selfish or grasping. He protected the weak and punished the unlawful and the turbulent. Three of his expeditions are described in the text, each embodying a great ethical idea involved in the possession of kingship or power. [2428]

We said: "O Dhū al-Qarnayn! (You have authority,) either to punish
them, or to treat them with kindness." 87 He said: "Whoever does wrong,
him shall we punish; then shall he be sent back to his Lord; and He will
punish him with a punishment unheard of (before). 88 But whoever
believes, and works righteousness,—he shall have a goodly reward, and
easy will be his task as we order it by our command."

89 Then followed he (another) way, 90 Until, when he came to the rising
of the sun, he found it rising on a people for whom We had provided no
covering protection against the sun. 91 (He left them) as they were: We
completely understood what was before him.

92 Then followed he (another) way, 93 Until, when he reached (a tract)
between two mountains, he found, beneath them, a people who scarcely
understood a word. 94 They said: "O Dhū al-Qarnayn! The Gog and
Magog (people)[5] do great mischief on earth: shall we then render you
tribute in order that you might erect a barrier between us and them?

95 He said: "(The power) in which my Lord has established me is better
(than tribute): help me therefore with strength (and labour): I will erect
a strong barrier between you and them: 96 Bring me blocks of iron." At
length, when he had filled up the space between the two steep
mountain-sides, he said, "Blow (with your bellows)." Then, when he had
made it (red) as fire, he said: "Bring me, that I may pour over it, molten
lead." 97 Thus were they made powerless to scale it or to dig through it.
98 He said: "This is a mercy from my Lord: but when the promise of my
Lord comes to pass, He will make it into dust; and the promise of my
Lord is true."

99 On that Day We shall leave them to surge like waves on one another:
the trumpet will be blown, and We shall collect them all together. 100 And

---

5. Who were the Gog and Magog people? This question is connected with the question, who was Dhū al-Qarnayn? What we are mainly concerned with is the spiritual interpretation. The Conqueror had now arrived among a people who were different in speech and race from him, but not quite primitive, for they were skilled in the working of metals, and could furnish blocks (or bricks) of iron, melt metals with bellows or blowpipes, and prepare molten lead (18:96). Apparently they were a peaceable and industrious race, much subject to incursions from wild tribes who are called Gog and Magog. Against these tribes they were willing to purchase immunity by paying the Conqueror tribute in return for protection. The permanent protection they wanted was the closing of a mountain gap through which the incursions were made. [2439]

We shall present Hell that day for Unbelievers to see, all spread out,—101
(Unbelievers) whose eyes had been under a veil from remembrance of
Me, and who had been unable even to hear.

SECTION 12

102 Do the Unbelievers think that they can take My servants as protectors
besides Me? Verily We have prepared Hell for the Unbelievers for (their)
entertainment. 103 Say: "Shall we tell you of those who lose most in
respect of their deeds?—104 Those whose efforts have been wasted in this
life, while they thought that they were acquiring good by their works?"
105 They are those who deny the Signs of their Lord and the fact of their
having to meet Him (in the Hereafter): vain will be their works, nor shall
We, on the Day of Judgement, give them any weight. 106 That is their
reward, Hell, because they rejected Faith, and took My Signs and My
messengers by way of jest.

107 As to those who believe and work righteous deeds, they have, for their
entertainment, the Gardens of Paradise, 108 Wherein they shall dwell (for
ever): no change will they wish for from them. 109 Say: "If the ocean were
ink (wherewith to write out) the words of my Lord,[6] sooner would the
ocean be exhausted than would the words of my Lord, even if we added
another ocean like it, for its aid." 110 Say: "I am but a man like yourselves,
(but) the inspiration has come to me, that your Allah is one Allah:
whoever expects to meet his Lord, let him work righteousness, and, in the
worship of his Lord, admit no one as partner."□

6. The Words and Signs and Mercies of Allah are in all Creation, and can never be fully set out in human language, however extended our means may be imagined to be. [2453]

Chapter 19

Sūrah Maryam
(Mary)

Translator's Introduction

The spiritual growth of man as an individual soul having been explained in Sūrah 17 as beginning with the first principles of moral conduct and in Sūrah 18. as being dependent upon our realisation of the brevity and mystery of this life and the true use of power as in the story of Dhū al-Qarnayn, we now pass on to the story of individual Messengers of Allah in their personal relations with their environment—Yaḥyā with his father Zakarīyā, Jesus with his mother Mary, Abraham with his unbelieving father, Moses with his brother Aaron, Ismā'īl with his family, and Idrīs in the high station to which he was called. Seeing how these great ones fitted into the scheme of life, man is condemned for his want of faith, or for degrading his faith to superstition, and warned of the Hereafter.

In chronology, it was revealed before the first resort of the batch of Muslims to Abyssinia, say seven years before Hijrah.

Summary—Zakarīyā was anxious to have an heir to carry on Allah's work in a world of unrighteousness, and Yaḥyā was given to him (19:1-15).

Mary, the mother of Jesus was maligned by her people, but Jesus comforted her and was good to her (19:16-40).

Abraham was persecuted for his Faith by his people, including his unbelieving father, but he withdrew from them, and was blessed; Moses was helped by his brother Aaron; Ismā'īl brought up his family in piety; and Idrīs was truthful and pious in a high station: they showed the way; yet men will not learn the good of life (19:41-65).

Man should not disbelieve in the Hereafter, nor sully his faith by false notions about Allah (19:66-98).

*** *** ***

In the name of Allah,
Most Gracious, Most Merciful.

1 *Kāf Hā Yā 'Ayn Ṣād.*[1] 2 (This is) a recital of the Mercy of your Lord to

1. This is the only Sūrah which begins with these five Abbreviated Letters, *Kāf, Hā, Yā, 'Ayn, Ṣād*. For Abbreviated Letters generally, see note to 2:1.

His servant Zakarīyā. 3 Behold! he cried to his Lord in secret, 4 Praying:
"O my Lord! Infirm indeed are my bones, and the hair of my head does
glisten with grey: but never am I unblest, O my Lord, in my prayer to
You! 5 Now I fear (what) my relatives (and colleagues) (will do) after me:
but my wife is barren: so give me an heir as from Yourself,—6 (One that)
will (truly) represent me, and represent the posterity of Jacob; and make
him, O my Lord! one with whom You are well-pleased!" 7 (His prayer
was answered): "O Zakarīyā! We give you good news of a son: his name
shall be Yaḥyā: on none by that name have We conferred distinction
before."[2] 8 He said: "O my Lord! How shall I have a son, when my wife
is barren and I have grown quite decrepit from old age?" 9 He said:[3] "So
(it will be): your Lord says, 'that is easy for Me: I did indeed create you
before, when you had been nothing!'" 10 (Zakarīyā) said: "O my Lord!
Give me a Sign." "Your Sign," was the answer, "shall be that you shall
speak to no man for three nights, although you are not dumb." 11 So
Zakarīyā came out to his people from his chamber: he told them by signs
to celebrate Allah's praises in the morning and in the evening.

12 (To his son came the command): "O Yaḥyā! Take hold of the Book
with might": and We gave him Wisdom even as a youth, 13 And piety (for

---

As stated in my note above, such Letters are Symbols, of which the true meaning is known to Allah alone. We should not be dogmatic about any conjectures that we make.
I offer this suggestion with some diffidence. The suggestion of the *Tafsīr Kabīr* is that the letters stand for attributes of Allah: K for *Kāfī* (the one sufficient in Himself): H for *Hādī* (He Who guides); Y for *Yad* (Hand as a symbol of Power and Authority; *Cf.* 48:10, "The Hand of Allah is above their hands"); 'A' for *'Alīm* (the All-Knowing); and 'Ṣ' for *Ṣādiq* (The True One). [2455]

2. This was John the Baptist, the forerunner of Jesus. In accordance with his father's prayer he, and Jesus for whom he prepared the way, renewed the Message of Allah, which had been corrupted and lost among the Israelites. The Arabic form Yaḥyā suggests "Life". The Hebrew form is Johanan, which means "Jehovah has been Gracious". *Cf. Ḥanāna* in verse 13 below. It does not mean that the name was given for the first time, for we read of a Johanan the son of Careah in II Kings, xxv. 23, an otherwise obscure man. It means that Allah had, for the first time, called one of His elect by that name. [2461]

3. Who is the "He" in this clause? As I have construed it, following the majority of Commentators, it means the angel who brought the message from Allah. *Cf.* 19:21 below. But some Commentators construe it to refer to Zakarīyā. In that case the meaning will be: Zakarīyā after a little reflection said (in his wonder) "So!" *i.e.*"Can it really be so? Can I really have a son in my old age?" The speech following, "Thy Lord said," etc., will then be that of the angel-messenger. [2462]

all creatures) as from Us, and purity:[4] he was devout, 14 And kind to his
parents, and he was not overbearing or rebellious. 15 So Peace on him the
day he was born, the day that he dies, and the day that he will be raised
up to life (again)!

SECTION 2

16 Relate in the Book (the story of) Mary, when she withdrew from her
family to a place in the East. 17 She placed a screen (to screen herself)
from them; then We sent to her Our angel, and he appeared before her as
a man in all respects. 18 She said: "I seek refuge from you to (Allah) Most
Gracious: (come not near) if you do fear Allah." 19 He said: "Nay, I am
only a messenger from your Lord, (to announce) to you the gift of a holy
son." 20 She said: "How shall I have a son, seeing that no man has
touched me, and I am not unchaste?" 21 He said: "So (it will be): your
Lord says, `that is easy for Me: and (We wish) to appoint him as a Sign
unto men and a Mercy from Us': it is a matter (so) decreed."

22 So she conceived him, and she retired with him to a remote place. 23
And the pains of childbirth drove her to the trunk of a palm tree: she cried
(in her anguish): "Ah! Would that I had died before this! Would that I
had been a thing forgotten and out of sight!" 24 But (a voice) cried to her
from beneath the (palm tree): "Grieve not! for your Lord has provided a
rivulet beneath you; 25 And shake towards yourself the trunk of the palm
tree: it will let fall fresh ripe dates upon you. 26 So eat and drink and cool
(thine) eye. And if you do see any man, say, 'I have vowed a fast to
(Allah) Most Gracious, and this day will I enter into no talk with any
human being'"

27 At length she brought the (baby) to her people, carrying him (in her
arms). They said: "O Mary! Truly an amazing thing have you brought!

4. John the Baptist did not live long. He was imprisoned by Herod, the tetrarch (provincial ruler under the Roman Empire), whom he had reproved for his sins, and eventually beheaded at the instigation of a woman with whom Herod was infatuated. But even in his young life, he was granted (1) wisdom by Allah, for he boldly denounced sin; (2) gentle pity and love for all Allah's creatures, for he moved among the humble and lowly, and despised "soft raiment"; and (3) purity of life, for he renounced the world and lived in the wilderness. All his work he did in his youth. These things showed themselves in his conduct, for he was devout, showing love to Allah and to Allah's creatures, and more particularly to his parents (for we are considering that aspect of his life); this was also shown by the fact that he never used violence, from an attitude of arrogance, nor entertained a spirit of rebellion against divine Law. [2468]

28 O sister of Aaron! Your father was not a man of evil, nor your mother
a woman unchaste!" 29 But she pointed to the baby. They said: "How can
we talk to one who is a child in the cradle?" 30 He said: "I am indeed a
servant of Allah: He has given me revelation and made me a prophet; 31
And He has made me blessed wheresoever I be, and has enjoined on me
prayer and charity as long as I live; 32 (He) has made me kind to my
mother, and not overbearing or miserable; 33 So peace is on me the day
I was born, the day that I die, and the day that I shall be raised up to life
(again)"!

34 Such (was) Jesus the son of Mary: (it is) a statement of truth, about
which they (vainly) dispute. 35 It is not befitting to (the majesty of) Allah
that He should beget a son. Glory be to Him! When He determines a
matter, He only says to it, "Be", and it is.[5] 36 Verily Allah is my Lord and
your Lord: Him therefore serve you: this is a Way that is straight. 37 But
the sects differ among themselves: and woe to the unbelievers because of
the (coming) Judgement of a momentous Day! 38 How plainly will they
see and hear, the Day that they will appear before Us! But the unjust
today are in error manifest! 39 But warn them of the Day of Distress,
when the matter will be determined: for (behold,) they are negligent and
they do not believe! 40 It is We Who will inherit the earth, and all beings
thereon: to Us will they all be returned.

SECTION 3

41 (Also) mention in the Book (the story of) Abraham: he was a man of
Truth, a prophet. 42 Behold, he said to his father: "O my father! Why
worship that which hears not and sees not, and can profit you nothing? 43
O my father! To me has come knowledge which has not reached you: so
follow me: I will guide you to a Way that is even and straight. 44 O my
father! Serve not Satan: for Satan is a rebel against (Allah) Most
Gracious. 45 O my father! I fear lest a Penalty afflict you from (Allah)
Most Gracious, so that you become to Satan a friend." 46 (The father)
replied: "Do you hate my gods, O Abraham? If you forbear not, I will

5. Begetting a son is a physical act depending on the needs of men's animal nature. Allah Most High is independent of all needs, and it is derogatory to Him to attribute such an act to Him. It is merely a relic of pagan and anthropomorphic materialist superstitions. [2487]

indeed stone you: now get away from me for a good long while!" 47
Abraham said: "Peace be on you: I will pray to my Lord for your
forgiveness: for He is to me Most Gracious. 48 And I will turn away from
you (all) and from those whom you invoke besides Allah: I will call on
my Lord: perhaps, by my prayer to my Lord, I shall be not unblest." 49
When he had turned away from them and from those whom they
worshipped besides Allah, We bestowed on him Isaac and Jacob, and
each one of them We made a prophet. 50 And We bestowed of Our Mercy
on them, and We granted them lofty honour on the tongue of truth.

SECTION 4

51 Also mention in the Book (the story of) Moses: for he was specially
chosen, and he was a messenger (and) a prophet. 52 And We called him
from the right side of Mount (Sinai), and made him draw near to Us, for
mystic (converse). 53 And, out of Our Mercy, We gave him his brother
Aaron, (also) a prophet.

54 Also mention in the Book (the story of) Ismā'īl: he was (strictly) true
to what he promised, and he was a messenger (and) a prophet. 55 He used
to enjoin on his people prayer and charity, and he was most acceptable in
the sight of his Lord.

56 Also mention in the Book the case of Idrīs: he was a man of truth (and
sincerity), (and) a prophet: 57 And We raised him to a lofty station.

58 Those were some of the prophets on whom Allah did bestow His
Grace,—of the posterity of Adam, and of those who We carried (in the
Ark) with Noah, and of the posterity of Abraham and Israel—of those
whom We guided and chose. Whenever the Signs of (Allah) Most
Gracious were rehearsed to them, they would fall down in prostrate
adoration and in tears. 59 But after them there followed a posterity who
missed prayers and followed after lusts; soon, then, will they face
Destruction,—60 Except those who repent and believe, and work
righteousness: for these will enter the Garden and will not be wronged in
the least,—61 Gardens of Eternity, those which (Allah) Most Gracious has
promised to His servants in the Unseen: for His promise must
(necessarily) come to pass. 62 They will not there hear any vain discourse,
but only salutations of Peace: and they will have therein their sustenance,
morning and evening. 63 Such is the Garden which We give as an

inheritance to those of Our servants who guard against evil.

64 (The angels say:) "We descend not but by command of your Lord: to
Him belongs what is before us and what is behind us, and what is
between: and your Lord never does forget,—65 Lord of the heavens and
of the earth, and of all that is between them; so worship Him, and be
constant and patient in His worship: know you of any who is worthy of
the same name as He?"

SECTION 5

66 Man says: "What! When I am dead, shall I then be raised up alive?" 67
But does not man call to mind that We created him before out of nothing?
68 So, by your Lord, without doubt, We shall gather them together, and
(also) the Evil Ones (with them); then shall We bring them forth on their
knees round about Hell; 69 Then shall We certainly drag out from every
sect all those who were worst in obstinate rebellion against (Allah) Most
Gracious. 70 And certainly We know best those who are most worthy of
being burned therein. 71 Not one of you but will pass over it: this is, with
your Lord, a Decree which must be accomplished. 72 But We shall save
those who guarded against evil, and We shall leave the wrong-doers
therein, (humbled) to their knees.

73 When Our clear Signs are rehearsed to them, the Unbelievers say to
those who believe, "Which of the two sides is best in point of position?
Which makes the best show in council?" 74 But how many (countless)
generations before them have We destroyed, who were even better in
equipment and in glitter to the eye? 75 Say: "If any men go astray, (Allah)
Most Gracious extends (the rope) to them, until, when they see the
warning of Allah (being fulfilled)—either in punishment or in (the
approach of) the Hour,—they will at length realise who is worst in
position, and (who) weakest in forces! 76 And Allah does advance in
guidance those who seek guidance: and the things that endure, good
deeds, are best in the sight of your Lord, as rewards, and best in respect
of (their) eventual returns."

77 Have you then seen the (sort of) man who rejects Our Signs, yet says:
"I shall certainly be given wealth and children?" 78 Has he penetrated to
the Unseen, or has he taken a contract with (Allah) Most Gracious? 79
Nay! We shall record what he says, and We shall add and add to his

punishment. 80 To Us shall return all that he talks of and he shall appear
before Us bare and alone. 81 And they have taken (for worship) gods other
than Allah, to give them power and glory! 82 Instead, they shall reject
their worship, and become adversaries against them.

SECTION 6

83 See you not that We have set the Evil Ones on against the Unbelievers,
to incite them with fury? 84 So make no haste against them, for We but
count out to them a (limited) number (of days). 85 The day We shall gather
the righteous to (Allah) Most Gracious, like a band presented before a
king for honours, 86 And We shall drive the sinners to Hell, like thirsty
cattle driven down to water,—87 None shall have the power of
intercession, but such a one as has received permission (or promise) from
(Allah) Most Gracious.

88 They say: "(Allah) Most Gracious has begotten a son!" 89 Indeed you
have put forth a thing most monstrous![6] 90 At it the skies are ready to
burst, the earth to split asunder, and the mountains to fall down in utter
ruin, 91 That they should invoke a son for (Allah) Most Gracious. 92 For
it is not consonant with the majesty of (Allah) Most Gracious that He
should beget a son.

93 Not one of the beings in the heavens and the earth but must come to
(Allah) Most Gracious as a servant. 94 He does take an account of them
(all), and has numbered them (all) exactly. 95 And everyone of them will
come to Him singly on the Day of Judgement. 96 On those who believe
and work deeds of righteousness, will (Allah) Most Gracious bestow love.

97 So have We made the (Qur'an) easy in your own tongue, that with it
you may give Glad Tidings to the righteous, and warnings to people
given to contention. 98 But how many (countless) generations before them
have We destroyed? Can you find a single one of them (now) or hear (so
much as) a whisper of them?□

---

6. The belief in Allah begetting a son is not a question of words or of speculative thought. It is a stupendous blasphemy against Allah. It lowers Allah to the level of an animal. If combined with the doctrine of vicarious atonement, it amounts to a negation of Allah's justice and man's personal responsibility. It is destructive of all moral and spiritual order, and is condemned in the strongest possible terms. [2529]

Chapter 20

Sūrah Ṭā Hā

Translator's Introduction

The chronology of the Sūrah has some significance: it has some relation to the spiritual lessons which it teaches.

It was used with great effect in that remarkable scene which resulted in 'Umar's conversion, and which took place about the seventh year before the Hijrah.

The scene is described with dramatic details by Ibn Hishām. 'Umar had previously been one of the greatest enemies and persecutors of Islam. Like his bloodthirsty kinsmen the Quraysh, he meditated slaying the Prophet, when it was suggested to him that there were near relations of his that had embraced Islam. His sister Fāṭimah and her husband Sa'īd were Muslims, but in those days of persecution they had kept their faith secret. When 'Umar went to their house, he heard them reciting this Sūrah from a written copy they had. For a while they concealed the copy. 'Umar attacked his sister and her husband, but they bore the attack with exemplary patience, and declared their faith. 'Umar was so struck with their sincerity and fortitude that he asked to see the leaf from which they had been reading. It was given to him: his soul was touched, and he not only came into the Faith but became one of its strongest supporters and champions.

The leaf contained some portion of the Sūrah, perhaps the introductory portion. The mystic letters *Tā Hā* are prefixed to this Sūrah. What do they mean? The earliest tradition is that they denote a dialectical interjection meaning "O man!" If so, the title is particularly appropriate in two ways. (1) It was a direct and personal address to a man in a high state of excitement, tempted by his temper to do grievous wrong, but called by Allah's Grace, as by a personal appeal, to face the realities, for Allah knew his inmost secret thoughts (20:7): the revelation was sent by Allah, Most Gracious, out of His Grace and Mercy (20:5). (2) It takes up the story from the last Sūrah, of man as a spiritual being and illustrates it in further details. It tells the story of Moses in the crisis of his life when he received Allah's Commission and in his personal relations with his mother, and how he came to be brought up in the Pharaoh's house, to learn all the wisdom of the Egyptians, for use in Allah's service, and in his personal relations with Pharaoh, whom we take to be his adoptive father (28:9). It further tells the story of a fallen soul who misled the Israelites into idolatry, and recalls how man's Arch-enemy Satan caused his fall. Prayer and praise are necessary to man to cure his spiritual blindness and enable him to appreciate Allah's revelation.

Summary—The revelation of Allah (the Qur'an) is not an occasion of distress, but is a gift of mercy from Allah Most Gracious (20:1-8).

How Moses was first chosen, and led to his mission to Pharaoh with his brother Aaron (20:9-36).

How the mother of Moses was directed to cast the infant Moses into the river, to be brought up in Pharaoh's house under Allah's own supervision, in order to preach to Pharaoh and declare Allah's glory (20:37-76).

How Moses was directed to lead his people and quell their rebellious spirit, and how that spirit was stirred up by Sāmirī (20:77-104).

On the Day of Judgement personal responsibility will be enforced, and Allah's Truth acknowledged: man should guard against Adam's enemy, Satan, and should renounce vanities, purify himself with prayer and praise, and await the call to Allah (20:105-135).

*** *** ***

In the name of Allah,
Most Gracious, Most Merciful.

1 *Ṭā Hā*.[1] 2 We have not sent down the Qur'an to you to be (an occasion)
for your distress, 3 But only as an admonition to those who fear
(Allah),—4 A revelation from Him Who created the earth and the heavens
on high. 5 (Allah) Most Gracious is firmly established on the throne (of
authority). 6 To Him belongs what is in the heavens and on earth, and all
between them, and all beneath the soil. 7 If you pronounce the word
aloud, (it is no matter): for verily He knows what is secret and what is yet
more hidden. 8 Allah! there is no god but He! To Him belong the Most
Beautiful Names.

9 Has the story of Moses reached you? 10 Behold, he saw a fire: so he said
to his family, "Tarry you; I perceive a fire; perhaps I can bring you some
burning brand therefrom, or find some guidance at the fire." 11 But when
he came to the fire, a voice was heard: "O Moses! 12 Verily I am your
Lord! Therefore (in My presence) put off your shoes: you are in the
sacred valley Ṭuwā.[2] 13 I have chosen you: listen, then, to the inspiration
(sent to you). 14 Verily, I am Allah: there is no god but I: so serve you Me

1. For an explanation see the Introduction to this Sūrah. [2534]

2. This was the valley just below Mount Sinai, where subsequently he was to receive the Torah. [2544]

(only), and establish regular prayer for celebrating My praise. 15 Verily
the Hour is coming—My design is to keep it hidden—for every soul to
receive its reward by the measure of its Endeavour. 16 Therefore let not
such as believe not therein but follow their own lusts, divert you
therefrom, lest you perish!"

17 "And what is that in your right hand, O Moses?" 18 He said, "It is my
rod: on it I lean; with it I beat down fodder for my flocks; and in it I find
other uses." 19 (Allah) said, "Throw it, O Moses!" 20 He threw it, and
behold! it was a snake, active in motion. 21 (Allah) said, "Seize it, and fear
not: We shall return it at once to its former condition."

22 "Now draw your hand[3] close to your side: it shall come forth white
(and shining), without harm (or stain),—as another Sign,—23 In order that
We may show you (two) of Our greater Signs. 24 Go you to Pharaoh, for
he has indeed transgressed all bounds."

SECTION 2

25 (Moses) said: "O my Lord! Expand me my breast; 26 Ease my task for
me; 27 And remove the impediment from my speech,[4] 28 So they may
understand what I say: 29 And give me a Minister from my family, 30
Aaron, my brother; 31 Add to my strength through him, 32 And make him
share my task: 33 That we may celebrate Your praise without stint, 34 And
remember You without stint: 35 For You are He that (ever) regards us."
36 (Allah) said: "Granted is your prayer, O Moses!"

37 "And indeed We conferred a favour on you another time (before). 38
Behold! We sent to your mother, by inspiration, the message: 39 'Throw
(the child) into the chest, and throw (the chest) into the river: the river
will cast him up on the bank, and he will be taken up by one who is an
enemy to Me and an enemy to him': but I cast (the garment of) love over
you from Me: and (this) in order that you may be reared under Mine
eye." 40 "Behold! your sister goes forth and says, 'Shall I show you one

---

3. The second of the greater Miracles shown to Moses was the "White (shining) Hand". Ordinarily, when the skin becomes white, it is a sign of disease, leprosy or something loathsome. Here there was no question of disease: on the contrary, the hand was glorified and it shone as with a divine light. Such a miracle was beyond Egyptian or human magic. [2550]

4. Literally, (in Arabic) "Loosen a knot from my tongue". [2553]

who will nurse and rear the (child)?' So We brought you back to your
mother, that her eye might be cooled and she should not grieve. Then you
did slay a man, but We saved you from trouble, and We tried you in
various ways. Then did you tarry a number of years with the people of
Midian. Then did you come hither as ordained, O Moses! 41 And I have
prepared you for Myself (for service)"...

42 "Go, you and your brother, with My Signs, and slacken not, either of
you, in keeping Me in remembrance. 43 Go, both of you, to Pharaoh, for
he has indeed transgressed all bounds; 44 But speak to him mildly;
perchance he may take warning or fear (Allah)." 45 They (Moses and
Aaron) said: "Our Lord! We fear lest he hasten with insolence against us,
or lest he transgress all bounds." 46 He said: "Fear not: for I am with you:
I hear and see (everything). 47 So go you both to him, and say, 'Verily we
are messengers sent by your Lord: send forth, therefore, the Children of
Israel with us, and afflict them not: with a Sign, indeed, have we come
from your Lord! And peace to all who follow guidance! 48 'Verily it has
been revealed to us that the Penalty (awaits) those who reject and turn
away.'"

49 (When this message was delivered), (Pharaoh) said: "Who, then, O
Moses, is the Lord of you two?" 50 He said: "Our Lord is He Who gave
to each (created) thing its form and nature, and further, gave (it)
guidance." 51 (Pharaoh) said: "What then is the condition of previous
generations?" 52 He replied: "The knowledge of that is with my Lord,
duly recorded: my Lord never errs, nor forgets,—53 He Who has made for
you the earth like a carpet spread out; has enabled you to go about therein
by roads (and channels); and has sent down water from the sky." With it
have We produced diverse pairs of plants each separate from the others.
54 Eat (for yourselves) and pasture your cattle: verily, in this are Signs for
men endued with understanding.

SECTION 3

55 From the (earth) did We create you, and into it shall We return you, and
from it shall We bring you out once again.

56 And We showed Pharaoh all Our Signs, but he did reject and refuse. 57
He said: "Have you come to drive us out of our land with your magic, O
Moses? 58 But we can surely produce magic to match yours! So make a

tryst between us and you, which we shall not fail to keep—neither we nor
you—in a place where both shall have even chances." 59 Moses said:
"Your tryst is the Day of the Festival, and let the people be assembled
when the sun is well up." 60 So Pharaoh withdrew: he concerted his plan,
and then came (back). 61 Moses said to him: "Woe to you! Forge not you
a lie against Allah, lest He destroy you (at once) utterly by chastisement:
the forger must suffer frustration!" 62 So they disputed, one with another,
over their affair, but they kept their talk secret. 63 They said: "These two
are certainly (expert) magicians: their object is to drive you out from your
land with their magic, and to do away with your most cherished
institutions. 64 Therefore concert your plan, and then assemble in (serried)
ranks: he wins (all along) today who gains the upper hand."

65 They said: "O Moses! Whether will you that you throw (first) or that
we be the first to throw?" 66 He said, "Nay, throw you first!" Then behold
their ropes and their rods—so it seemed to him on account of their
magic—began to be in lively motion! 67 So Moses conceived in his mind
a (sort of) fear. 68 We said: "Fear not! for you have indeed the upper
hand: 69 Throw that which is in your right hand: quickly will it swallow
up that which they have faked; what they have faked is but a magician's
trick: and the magician thrives not, (no matter) where he goes."

70 So the magicians were thrown down to prostration: they said, "We
believe in the Lord of Aaron and Moses". 71 (Pharaoh) said: "Believe you
in Him before I give you permission? Surely this must be your leader,
who has taught you magic! Be sure I will cut off your hands and feet on
opposite sides, and I will have you crucified on trunks of palm-trees: so
shall you know for certain, which of us can give the more severe and the
more lasting punishment!" 72 They said: "Never shall we regard you as
more than the clear Signs that have come to us, or than Him Who created
us! So decree whatever you desire to decree: for you can only decree
(touching) the life of this world. 73 For us, we have believed in our Lord:
may He forgive us our faults, and the magic to which you did compel us:
for Allah is Best and Most Abiding." 74 Verily he who comes to his Lord
as a sinner (at Judgement),—for him is Hell: therein shall he neither die
nor live. 75 But such as come to Him as Believers who have worked
righteous deeds,—for them are ranks exalted,—76 Gardens of Eternity,
beneath which flow rivers: they will dwell therein for ever: such is the
reward of those who purify themselves (from evil).

SECTION 4

77 We sent an inspiration to Moses: "Travel by night with My servants,
and strike a dry path for them through the sea, without fear of being
overtaken (by Pharaoh) and without (any other) fear." 78 Then Pharaoh
pursued them with his forces, but the waters completely overwhelmed
them and covered them up. 79 Pharaoh led his people astray instead of
leading them aright.

80 O you Children of Israel! We delivered you from your enemy, and We
made a Covenant with you on the right side of Mount (Sinai), and We
sent down to you Manna and quails: 81 (Saying): "Eat of the good things
We have provided for your sustenance, but commit no excess therein, lest
My Wrath should justly descend on you: and those on whom descends
My Wrath do perish indeed! 82 But, without doubt, I am (also) He that
forgives again and again, to those who repent, believe, and do right,
who,—in fine, are ready to receive true guidance."

83 (When Moses was up on the Mount, Allah said:) "What made you
hasten in advance of your people, O Moses?" 84 He replied: "Behold, they
are close on my footsteps: I hastened to You, O my Lord, to please You."
85 (Allah) said: "We have tested your people in your absence: the Sāmirī
has led them astray." 86 So Moses returned to his people in a state of
indignation and sorrow. He said: "O my people! Did not your Lord make
a handsome promise to you? Did then the promise seem to you long (in
coming)? Or did you desire that Wrath should descend from your Lord
on you, and so you broke your promise to me?" 87 They said: "We broke
not the promise to you, as far as lay in our power: but we were made to
carry the weight of the ornaments of the (whole) people, and we threw
them (into the fire), and that was what the Sāmirī suggested. 88 Then he
brought out (of the fire) before the (people) the image of a calf: it seemed
to low: so they said: 'This is your god, and the god of Moses, but (Moses)
has forgotten!'" 89 Could they not see that it could not return them a word
(for answer), and that it had no power either to harm them or to do them
good?

SECTION 5

90 Aaron had already, before this said to them: "O my people! You are
being tested in this: for verily your Lord is (Allah) Most Gracious; so
follow me and obey my command." 91 They had said: "We will not

abandon this cult, but we will devote ourselves to it until Moses returns
to us." 92 (Moses) said: "O Aaron! What kept you back, when you saw
them going wrong, 93 From following me? Did you then disobey my
order?" 94 (Aaron) replied: "O son of my mother! Seize (me) not by my
beard nor by (the hair of) my head! Truly I feared lest you should say,
'You have caused a division among the Children of Israel, and you did
not respect my word!'" 95 (Moses) said: "What then is your case, O
Sāmirī?" 96 He replied: "I saw what they saw not: so I took a handful (of
dust) from the footprint of the Messenger, and threw it (into the calf):
thus did my soul suggest to me."[5] 97 (Moses) said: "Get you gone! But
your (punishment) in this life will be that you will say, 'Touch me not';[6]
and moreover (for a future penalty) you have a promise that will not fail:
now look at your god, of whom you have become a devoted worshipper:
we will certainly (melt) it in a blazing fire and scatter it broadcast in the
sea!" 98 But the god of you all is the One Allah: there is no god but He:
all things He comprehends in His knowledge.

99 Thus do We relate to you some stories of what happened before: for
We have sent you a Message from Our own Presence. 100 If any do turn
away therefrom, verily they will bear a burden on the Day of Judgement;
101 They will abide in this (state): and grievous will the burden be to them
on that Day,— 102 The Day when the Trumpet will be sounded: that Day,
We shall gather the sinful, blear-eyed (with terror). 103 In whispers will
they consult each other: "You tarried not longer than ten (Days);" 104 We
know best what they will say, when their leader most eminent in conduct

---

5. This answer of the Sāmirī is a fine example of unblushing effrontery, careful evasion of issues, and invented falsehoods. He takes upon himself to pretend that he had far more insight than anybody else: he saw what the vulgar crowd did not see. He saw something supernatural. "The Messenger" is construed by many Commentators to mean the angel Gabriel. "*Rasūl*" (plural *rusul*) is used in several places for "angels", *e.g.*, in 11:69,77; 19:19; and 35:1. But if we take it to mean the Messenger Moses, it means that the Sāmirī saw something sacred or supernatural in his footprints: perhaps he thinks a little flattery would make Moses forgive him. The dust became sacred, and his throwing it into the calf's image made the calf utter a lowing sound! As if that was the point at issue! He does not answer the charge of making an image for worship. But finally, with arrogant effrontery, he says, "Well, that is what my soul suggested to me, and that should be enough!" [2621]

6. He and his kind were to become social lepers, untouchables; perhaps also sufficiently arrogant to hold others at arm's length, and say "*Noli me tangere*" (touch me not). [2622]

will say: "You tarried not longer than a day!"

SECTION 6

105 They ask you concerning the Mountains: say, "My Lord will uproot
them and scatter them as dust;" 106 "He will leave them as plains smooth
and level;" 107 "Nothing crooked or curved will you see in their place."

108 On that Day will they follow the Caller (straight): no crookedness (can
they show) him: all sounds shall humble themselves in the Presence of
(Allah) Most Gracious: nothing shall you hear but the tramp of their feet
(as they march). 109 On that Day shall no intercession avail except for
those for whom permission has been granted by (Allah) Most Gracious
and whose word is acceptable to Him. 110 He knows what (appears to His
creatures as) before or after or behind them: but they shall not compass
it with their knowledge. 111 (All) faces shall be humbled before
(Him)—the Living, the Self-subsisting, Eternal: hopeless indeed will be
the man that carries iniquity (on his back). 112 But he who works deeds of
righteousness, and has faith, will have no fear of harm nor of any
curtailment (of what is his due).

113 Thus have We sent this down—an Arabic Qur'an—and explained
therein in detail some of the warnings, in order that they may fear Allah,
or that it may cause their remembrance (of Him). 114 High above all is
Allah, the King, the Truth! Be not in haste with the Qur'an before its
revelation to you is completed, but say, "O my Lord! Advance me in
knowledge." 115 We had already, beforehand, taken the covenant of
Adam, but he forgot: and We found on his part no firm resolve.

SECTION 7

116 When We said to the angels, "Prostrate yourselves to Adam", they
prostrated themselves, but not Iblīs: he refused. 117 Then We said: "O
Adam! Verily, this is an enemy to you and your wife: so let him not get
you both out of the Garden, so that you are landed in misery.

118 There is therein (enough provision) for you not to go hungry nor to go
naked, 119 Nor to suffer from thirst, nor from the sun's heat."

120 But Satan whispered evil to him: he said, "O Adam! Shall I lead you
to the Tree of Eternity and to a kingdom that never decays?" 121 In the
result, they both ate of the tree, and so their nakedness appeared to them:

they began to sew together, for their covering, leaves from the Garden:
thus did Adam disobey his Lord, and allow himself to be seduced. 122 But
his Lord chose him (for His Grace): He turned to him, and gave him
guidance. 123 He said: "Get you down, both of you,—all together, from
the Garden, with enmity one to another: but if, as is sure, there comes to
you guidance from Me, whosoever follows My guidance, will not lose his
way, nor fall into misery. 124 But whosoever turns away from My
Message, verily for him is a life narrowed down, and We shall raise him
up blind on the Day of Judgement." 125 He will say: "O my Lord! Why
have You raised me up blind, while I had sight (before)?" 126 (Allah) will
say: "Thus did you, when Our Signs came unto you, disregard them: so
will you, this day, be disregarded." 127 And thus do We recompense him
who transgresses beyond bounds and believes not in the Signs of his
Lord: and the Penalty of the Hereafter is far more grievous and more
enduring. 128 Is it not a warning to such men (to call to mind) how many
generations before them We destroyed, in whose haunts they (now)
move? Verily, in this are Signs for men endued with understanding.

SECTION 8

129 Had it not been for a Word that went forth before from your Lord,
(their punishment) must necessarily have come; but there is a term
appointed (for respite). 130 Therefore be patient with what they say, and
celebrate (constantly) the praises of your Lord, before the rising of the
sun, and before its setting; indeed, celebrate them for part of the hours of
the night, and at the sides[7] of the day: that you may have (spiritual) joy.
131 Nor strain your eyes in longing for the things We have given for
enjoyment to parties of them, the splendour of the life of this world,
through which We test them: but the provision of your Lord is better and

---

7. The Arabic *Taraf, (*plural *atrāf*) translated here as "sides" as may also mean ends, extremities. If the day be compared to a tubular figure standing erect, the top and bottom are clearly marked, but the sides are not so clearly marked: they would be *atrāf* (plural), not *tarafayn* (dual). Now the prayer before sunrise is clearly *Fajr*; that before sunset is *'Asr*: "part of the hours of the night" would indicate *Maghrib* (early night, just after sunset), and *'Ishā'*, before going to bed. There is left *Zuhr,* which is the indefinite side or middle of the day; it may be soon after the sun's decline from noon, but there is considerable latitude about the precise hour. The majority of Commentators interpret in favour of the five Canonical prayers, and some include optional prayers. But I think the words are even more comprehensive. A good man's life is all one sweet Song of Praise to Allah. [2655]

more enduring. 132 Enjoin prayer on your people, and be constant therein.
We ask you not to provide sustenance: We provide it for you. But the
(fruit of) the Hereafter is for righteousness.

133 They say: "Why does he not bring us a Sign from his Lord?" Has not
a clear Sign come to them of all that was in the former Books of
revelation? 134 And if We had inflicted on them a penalty before this, they
would have said: "Our Lord! If only You had sent us a messenger, we
should certainly have followed Your Signs before we were humbled and
put to shame." 135 Say: "Each one (of us) is waiting: wait you, therefore,
and soon shall you know who it is that is on the straight and even Way,
and who it is that has received Guidance."□

Chapter 21

Sūrah Al-Anbiyā' (The Prophets)

Translator's Introduction

The last Sūrah dealt with the individual story (spiritual) of Moses and Aaron, and contrasted it with the growth of evil in individuals like the Pharaoh and the Sāmirī, and ended with a warning against Evil, and an exhortation to the purification of the soul with prayer and praise. This Sūrah begins with the external obstacles placed by Evil against such purification, and gives the assurance of Allah's power to defend men, illustrating this with reference to Abraham's fight against idolatry, Lot's fight against unnatural wickedness, Noah's against unbelief, that of David and Solomon against injustice and failure to proclaim God's glory by making full use of man's God-given faculties and powers, that of Job against impatience and want of self-confidence, that of Ismā'īl, Idrīs, and Dhū al-Kifl against want of steady perseverance, that of Dhū al-Nūn against hasty anger, that of Zakarīyā against spiritual isolation, and that of Mary against the lusts of this world. In each allusion there is a special point about the soul's purification. The common point is that the Prophets were not, as the vulgar suppose, just irresistible men. They had to win their ground inch by inch against all kinds of resistance from evil.

The chronology of this Sūrah has no significance. It probably dates from the middle of the Makkan period of inspiration.

Summary—Man treats, as he has always treated, the serious things of life with jest or contempt; but the Judgement must come, and Truth must triumph (21:1-29).

Unity of Design, and certainty of Allah's Promise: Allah's protection and mercy, and His justice (21:30-50).

How Abraham triumphed over idols, as did others among Allah's chosen ones over various forms of evil (21:51-93).

Work righteousness while there is yet time, for the Judgement will come, and only the righteous will inherit (21:94-112).

*** *** ***

PART XVII

In the name of Allah,
Most Gracious, Most Merciful.

1 Closer and closer to mankind comes their Reckoning: yet they heed not
and they turn away. 2 Never comes (aught) to them of a renewed Message
from their Lord, but they listen to it as in jest,—3 Their hearts toying as
with trifles. The wrong-doers conceal their private counsels, (saying), "Is
this (one) more than a man like yourselves? Will you go to witchcraft
with your eyes open?" 4 Say: "My Lord knows (every) word (spoken) in
the heavens and on earth: He is the One That hears and knows (all
things)." 5 "Nay," they say, "(These are) medleys of dreams!—Nay, he
forged it!—Nay, he is (but) a poet! Let him then bring us a Sign like the
ones that were sent to (prophets) of old!" 6 (As to those) before them, not
one of the populations which We destroyed believed: will these believe?
7 Before you, also, the messengers We sent were but men, to whom We
granted inspiration: if you realise this not, ask of those who possess the
Message. 8 Nor did We give them bodies that ate no food, nor were they
exempt from death. 9 In the end We fulfilled to them Our promise, and
We saved them and those whom We pleased, but We destroyed those
who transgressed beyond bounds. 10 We have revealed for you (O men!)
a Book in which is a Message for you: will you not then understand?

SECTION 2

11 How many were the populations We utterly destroyed because of their
iniquities, setting up in their places other peoples? 12 Yet, when they felt
Our Punishment (coming), behold, they (tried to) flee from it. 13 Flee not,
but return to the good things of this life which were given you, and to
your homes, in order that you may be called to account. 14 They said:
"Ah! Woe to us! We were indeed wrong-doers!" 15 And that cry of theirs
ceased not, till We made them as a field that is mown, as ashes silent and
quenched.

16 Not for (idle) sport did We create the heavens and the earth and all that
is between! 17 If it had been Our wish to take (just) a pastime, We should
surely have taken it from the things nearest to Us, if We would do (such
a thing)! 18 Nay, We hurl the Truth against falsehood, and it knocks out
its brain, and behold, falsehood does perish! Ah! Woe be to you for the

(false) things you ascribe (to Us). 19 To Him belong all (creatures) in the
heavens and on earth: even those who are in His (very) Presence are not
too proud to serve Him, nor are they (ever) weary (of His service): 20
They celebrate His praises night and day, nor do they ever flag or
intermit.

21 Or have they taken (for worship) gods from the earth who can raise (the
dead)? 22 If there were, in the heavens and the earth, other gods besides
Allah, there would have been confusion in both! But glory to Allah, the
Lord of the Throne: (High is He) above what they attribute to Him! 23 He
cannot be questioned for His acts, but they will be questioned (for theirs).

24 Or have they taken for worship (other) gods besides Him? Say, "Bring
your convincing proof: this is the Message of those with me and the
Message of those before me." But most of them know not the Truth, and
so turn away. 25 Not a messenger did We send before you without this
inspiration sent by Us to him: that there is no god but I; therefore worship
and serve Me.

26 And they say: "(Allah) Most Gracious has begotten offspring." Glory
to Him! they are (but) servants raised to honour. 27 They speak not before
He speaks, and they act (in all things) by His Command. 28 He knows
what is before them, and what is behind them, and they offer no
intercession except for those who are acceptable, and they stand in awe
and reverence of His (Glory). 29 If any of them should say, "I am a god
besides Him", such a one We should reward with Hell: thus do We
reward those who do wrong.

SECTION 3

30 Do not the Unbelievers see that the heavens and the earth were joined
together (as one unit of creation), before We clove them asunder? We
made from water every living thing. Will they not then believe? 31 And
We have set on the earth mountains standing firm, lest it should shake
with them, and We have made therein broad highways (between
mountains) for them to pass through: that they may receive Guidance. 32
And We have made the heavens as a canopy well guarded: yet do they
turn away from the Signs which these things (point to)! 33 It is He Who
created the Night and the Day, and the sun and the moon: all (the celestial
bodies) swim along, each in its rounded course.

34 We granted not to any man before you permanent life (here): if then
you should die, would they live permanently? 35 Every soul shall have a
taste of death: and We test you by evil and by good by way of trial. To
Us must you return. 36 When the Unbelievers see you, they treat you not
except with ridicule. "Is this," (they say), "the one who talks of your
gods?" And they blaspheme at the mention of (Allah) Most Gracious! 37
Man is a creature of haste: soon (enough) will I show you My Signs; then
you will not ask Me to hasten them! 38 They say: "When will this promise
come to pass, if you are telling the truth?" 39 If only the Unbelievers knew
(the time) when they will not be able to ward off the Fire from their faces,
nor yet from their backs, and (when) no help can reach them! 40 Nay, it
may come to them suddenly and confound them: no power will they have
then to avert it, nor will they (then) get respite. 41 Mocked were (many)
messengers before you; but their scoffers were hemmed in by the thing
that they mocked.

SECTION 4

42 Say: "Who can keep you safe by night and by day from (the Wrath of)
(Allah) Most Gracious?" Yet they turn away from the mention of their
Lord. 43 Or have they gods that can guard them from Us? They have no
power to aid themselves, nor can they be defended from Us. 44 Nay, We
gave the good things of this life to these men and their fathers until the
period grew long for them; see they not that We gradually reduce the land
(in their control) from its outlying borders? Is it then they who will win?
45 Say, "I do but warn you according to revelation": but the deaf will not
hear the call, (even) when they are warned! 46 If but a breath of the Wrath
of your Lord do touch them, they will then say, "Woe to us! We did
wrong indeed!"

47 We shall set up scales of justice for the Day of Judgement, so that not
a soul will be dealt with unjustly in the least. And if there be (no more
than) the weight of a mustard seed, We will bring it (to account): and
enough are We to take account.

48 In the past We granted to Moses and Aaron the Criterion (for
judgement), and a Light and a Message for those who would do right,—49
Those who fear their Lord in their most secret thoughts, and who hold the
Hour (of Judgement) in awe. 50 And this is a blessed Message which We
have sent down: will you then reject it?

SECTION 5

51 We bestowed aforetime on Abraham his rectitude of conduct, and well
were We acquainted with him. 52 Behold! he said to his father and his
people, "What are these images, to which you are (so assiduously)
devoted?" 53 They said, "We found our fathers worshipping them." 54 He
said, "Indeed you have been in manifest error—you and your fathers." 55
They said, "Have you brought us the Truth, or are you one of those who
jest?" 56 He said, "Nay, your Lord is the Lord of the heavens and the
earth, He Who created them (from nothing): and I am a witness to this
(Truth). 57 And by Allah, I have a plan for your idols—after you go away
and turn your backs."

58 So he broke them to pieces, (all) but the biggest of them, that they
might turn (and address themselves) to it. 59 They said, "Who has done
this to our gods? He must indeed be some man of impiety!" 60 They said,
"We heard a youth talk of them: he is called Abraham." 61 They said,
"Then bring him before the eyes of the people, that they may bear
witness." 62 They said, "Are you the one that did this with our gods, O
Abraham?" 63 He said: "Nay, this was done by—this is their biggest one!
Ask them, if they can speak intelligently!" 64 So they turned to themselves
and said, "Surely you are the ones in the wrong!" 65 Then were they
confounded with shame: (they said), "You know full well that these
(idols) do not speak!" 66 (Abraham) said, "Do you then worship, besides
Allah, things that can neither be of any good to you nor do you harm? 67
Fie upon you, and upon the things that you worship besides Allah! Have
you no sense?"

68 They said, "Burn him and protect your gods, if you do (anything at
all)!" 69 We said, "O Fire! Be you cool, and (a means of) safety for
Abraham!" 70 Then they sought a stratagem against him: but We made
them the ones that lost most! 71 But We delivered him and (his nephew)
Lūṭ (and directed them) to the land which We have blessed for the
nations.

72 And We bestowed on him Isaac and, as an additional gift, (a grandson),
Jacob, and We made righteous men of every one (of them). 73 And We
made them leaders, guiding (men) by Our Command, and We sent them
inspiration to do good deeds, to establish regular prayers, and to practise
regular charity; and they constantly served Us (and Us only).

74 And to Lūṭ, too, We gave Judgement and Knowledge, and We saved him from the town which practised abominations: truly they were a people given to Evil, a rebellious people.
75 And We admitted him to Our Mercy: for he was one of the Righteous.

SECTION 6

76 (Remember) Noah, when he cried (to Us) aforetime: We listened to his (prayer) and delivered him and his family from great distress.

77 We helped him against people who rejected Our Signs: truly they were a people given to Evil: so We drowned them (in the Flood) all together.

78 And remember David and Solomon, when they gave judgement in the matter of the field into which the sheep of certain people had strayed by night: We did witness their judgement.
79 To Solomon We inspired the (right) understanding of the matter: to each (of them) We gave Judgement and Knowledge; it was Our power that made the hills and the birds celebrate Our praises, with David: it was We Who did (all these things).
80 It was We Who taught him the making of coats of mail for your benefit, to guard you from each other's violence: will you then be grateful?

81 (It was Our power that made) the violent (unruly) wind flow (tamely) for Solomon, to his order, to the land which We had blessed: for We do know all things.
82 And of the evil ones, were some who dived for him, and did other work besides; and it was We Who guarded them.

83 And (remember) Job, when he cried to his Lord, "Truly distress has seized me, but You are the Most Merciful of those that are merciful."
84
So We listened to him: We removed the distress that was on him, and We restored his people to him, and doubled their number,—as a Grace from Ourselves, and a thing for commemoration, for all who serve Us.
85 And (remember) Ismā'īl, Idrīs, and Dhū al-Kifl, all (men) of constancy and patience;
86 We admitted them to Our Mercy: for they were of the Righteous ones.

87 And remember Dhū al-Nūn,[1] when he departed in wrath: he imagined

---

1. *Dhū al-Nūn,* "the man of the Fish or the Whale", is the title of Jonah (Yūnus), because he was swallowed by a large Fish or Whale. He was the prophet raised to warn the Assyrian capital Nineveh. His story is told in 37:139-149. When his first warning was unheeded by the

that We had no power over him! But he cried through the depths of
darkness, "There is no god but You: glory to You: I was indeed wrong!"
88 So We listened to him: and delivered him from distress: and thus do We
deliver those who have faith.

89 And (remember) Zakarīyā, when he cried to his Lord: "O my Lord!
Leave me not without offspring, though You are the best of inheritors."
90 So We listened to him: and We granted him Yaḥyā: We cured his wife's
(barrenness) for him. These (three) were ever quick in emulation in good
works; they used to call on Us with love and reverence, and humble
themselves before Us. 91 And (remember) her who guarded her chastity:
We breathed into her of Our Spirit, and We made her and her son a Sign
for all peoples.

92 Verily, this brotherhood of yours is a single brotherhood, and I am your
Lord and Cherisher: therefore serve Me (and no other). 93 But (later
generations) cut off their affair (of unity), one from another: (yet) will
they all return to Us.

SECTION 7

94 Whoever works any act of righteousness and has Faith,—his endeavour
will not be rejected: We shall record it in his favour. 95 But there is a ban
on any population which We have destroyed: that they shall not return,
96 Until the Gog and Magog (people)[2] are let through (their barrier), and
they swiftly swarm from every hill. 97 Then will the True Promise draw

---

people, he denounced Allah's wrath on them. But they repented and Allah forgave them for the time being. Jonah, meanwhile, departed in wrath, discouraged at the apparent failure of his mission. He should have remained in the most discouraging circumstances, and relied on the power of Allah; for Allah had power both over Nineveh and over the Messenger He had sent to Nineveh. He went away to the sea and took a ship, but apparently the sailors threw him out as a man of bad omen in a storm. He was swallowed by a big Fish (or Whale), but in the depth of the darkness, he cried out to Allah and confessed his weakness. The "darkness" may be interpreted both physically and spiritually: physically, as the darkness of the night and the storm and the Fish's body; spiritually, as the darkness in his soul, his extreme distress in the situation which he had brought on himself. Allah Most Gracious forgave him. He was cast out ashore; he was given the shelter of a plant in his state of physical and mental lassitude. He was refreshed and strengthened, and the work of his mission prospered. Thus he overcame all his disappointment by repentance and Faith, and Allah accepted him. [2744]

2. For Gog and Magog see note to 18:94. The name stands for wild and lawless tribes who will break their barriers and swarm through the earth. This will be one of the prognostications of the approaching Judgement. [2753]

nigh (of fulfilment): then behold! the eyes of the Unbelievers will fixedly
stare in horror: "Ah! Woe to us! We were indeed heedless of this; nay, we
truly did wrong!" 98 Verily you, (Unbelievers), and the (false) gods that
you worship besides Allah, are (but) fuel for Hell! To it will you (surely)
come! 99 If these had been gods, they would not have got there! But each
one will abide therein. 100 There, sobbing will be their lot, nor will they
there hear (aught else).

101 Those for whom the good (record) from Us has gone before, will be
removed far therefrom. 102 Not the slightest sound will they hear of Hell:
what their souls desired, in that will they dwell. 103 The Great Terror will
bring them no grief: but the angels will meet them (with mutual
greetings): "This is your Day,—(the Day) that you were promised." 104
The Day that We roll up the heavens like a scroll rolled up for books
(completed),—even as We produced the first creation, so shall We produce a new
one: a promise We have undertaken: truly shall We fulfil it.

105 Before this We wrote in the Psalms, after the Message (given to
Moses): "My servants, the righteous, shall inherit the earth." 106 Verily in
this (Qur'an) is a Message for people who would (truly) worship Allah.
107 We sent you not, but as a mercy for all creatures. 108 Say: "What has
come to me by inspiration is that your Allah is One Allah: will you
therefore bow to His Will (in Islam)?" 109 But if they turn back, say: "I
have proclaimed the Message to you all alike and in truth; but I know not
whether that which you are promised is near or far. 110 It is He Who
knows what is open in speech and what you hide (in your hearts). 111 I
know not but that it may be a trial for you, and a grant of (worldly)
livelihood (to you) for a time." 112 Say: "O my Lord! Judge You in
truth!"[3] "Our Lord Most Gracious is the One Whose assistance should
be sought against the blasphemies you utter!"[4]□

---

3. That is, Allah's judgement as between the Teacher and those who refuse the Message, or between the righteous and those who taunt them for their poverty, will be the true one, and both the Teacher and the *Ummah* must leave the judgement to Allah. [2768]

4. Blasphemy is a dreadful sin. We must guard ourselves from it. But as regards others, if we cannot prevent it, we must pray to Allah for assistance and not rely upon carnal weapons. [2769]

Chapter 22

Sūrah Al-Ḥajj
(The Pilgrimage)

Translator's Introduction

We now come to a new series of four Sūrahs, dealing with the environments and methods contributing to our spiritual progress, as the last five Sūrahs dealt with the Messengers who came in various ways to proclaim the Truth and conquer evil. See Introduction to Sūrah 17.

The subject matter of this particular Sūrah is concerned mainly with the spiritual implications of the Sacred House, the Pilgrimage, the Sacrifice, Striving and Fighting in defence of Truth when attacked, and other acts that make for Unselfishness and uproot Falsehood.

On the chronology of this Sūrah, opinion is divided. Some parts were probably revealed in the later Makkan period, and some in Madīnah. But the chronological question has no significance here.

Summary—Importance of the spiritual Future, and need of firmness in Faith: help for Truth and punishment for Evil (22:1-25).

Purity, Prayer, Humility, and Faith are implied in the Pilgrimage; in solemn Sacrifice we express our gratitude and reverence to Allah, and our desire to share food with our poorer brethren; Striving and Fighting in defence of Truth when attacked are necessary as tests of self-sacrifice (22:26-48).

The promptings of Evil may hinder the work of Allah's Prophet, but that work must triumph, and the Mercy and Truth of Allah must be established; therefore serve Allah humbly, and He will protect and help you (22:49-78).

*** *** ***

In the name of Allah,
Most Gracious, Most Merciful.

1 O mankind! Fear your Lord! For the convulsion of the Hour (of
Judgement) will be a thing terrible! 2 The Day you shall see it, every
mother giving suck shall forget her suckling baby, and every pregnant
female shall drop her load (unformed): you shall see mankind as in a
drunken riot, yet not drunk: but dreadful will be the Wrath of Allah. 3
And yet among men there are such as dispute about Allah, without
knowledge, and follow every evil one obstinate in rebellion! 4 About the

(Evil One) it is decreed that whoever turns to him for friendship, him will
he lead astray, and he will guide him to the Penalty of the Fire.

5 O mankind! If you have a doubt about the Resurrection, (consider) that
We created you out of dust, then out of sperm, then out of a leech-like
clot, then out of a morsel of flesh, partly formed and partly unformed, in
order that We may manifest (Our Power) to you; and We cause whom We
will to rest in the wombs for an appointed term, then do We bring you out
as babies, then (foster you) that you may reach your age of full strength;
and some of you are called to die, and some are sent back to the feeblest
old age, so that they know nothing after having known (much), and
(further), you see the earth barren and lifeless, but when We pour down
rain on it, it is stirred (to life), it swells, and it puts forth every kind of
beautiful growth (in pairs). 6 This is so, because Allah is the Reality: it is
He Who gives life to the dead, and it is He Who has power over all
things. 7 And verily the Hour will come: there can be no doubt about it,
or about (the fact) that Allah will raise up all who are in the graves. 8 Yet
there is among men such a one as disputes about Allah, without
knowledge, without guidance, and without a Book of Enlightenment,—9
(Disdainfully) bending his side, in order to lead (men) astray from the
Path of Allah: for him there is disgrace in this life, and on the Day of
Judgement We shall make him taste the Penalty of burning (Fire). 10 (It
will be said): "This is because of the deeds which your hands sent forth,
for verily Allah is not unjust to His servants."

SECTION 2

11 There are among men some who serve Allah, as it were, on the verge:[1]
if good befalls them, they are, therewith, well content; but if a trial comes
to them, they turn on their faces: they lose both this world and the
Hereafter: that is loss for all to see! 12 They call on such deities, besides
Allah, as can neither hurt nor profit them: that is straying far indeed (from

---

1. They are men whose minds are not firm: they will have faith, if all goes well with them, but as soon as they are tried, they are found wanting. They differ from hypocrites. It is not fraud or double dealing that is their sin: it is a weak mind, petty standards of judging right by success, a selfishness that gives nothing but asks for all, a narrow-mindedness that does not go beyond petty mundane calculations—a "nicely calculated less or more" of the good things of this world. They fail in both worlds and their failure in this world is patent for every onlooker. [2782]

the Way)! 13 (Perhaps) they call on one whose hurt is nearer than his
profit: evil, indeed, is the patron, and evil the companion (for help)!

14 Verily Allah will admit those who believe and work righteous deeds,
to Gardens, beneath which rivers flow: for Allah carries out all that He
plans. 15 If any think that Allah will not help him (His Messenger) in this
world and the Hereafter, let him stretch out a rope to the ceiling and cut
(himself) off: then let him see whether his plan will remove that which
enrages (him)! 16 Thus have We sent down clear Signs; and verily Allah
does guide whom He will! 17 Those who believe (in the Qur'an), those
who follow the Jewish (scriptures), and the Sabians, Christians, Magians,
and Polytheists,—Allah will judge between them on the Day of
Judgement: for Allah is witness of all things.

18 See you not that to Allah bow down in worship all things that are in the
heavens and on earth,—the sun, the moon, the stars; the hills, the trees,
the animals; and a great number among mankind? But a great number are
(also) such as are fit for Punishment: and such as Allah shall
disgrace,—none can raise to honour: for Allah carries out all that He
wills. 19 These two antagonists dispute with each other about their Lord:
but those who deny (their Lord),—for them will be cut out a garment of
Fire: over their heads will be poured out boiling water. 20 With it will be
scalded what is within their bodies, as well as (their) skins. 21 In addition
there will be maces of iron (to punish) them. 22 Every time they wish to
get away therefrom, from anguish, they will be forced back therein, and
(it will be said), "Taste you the Penalty of Burning!"

SECTION 3

23 Allah will admit those who believe and work righteous deeds, to
Gardens beneath which rivers flow: they shall be adorned therein with
bracelets of gold and pearls; and their garments there will be of silk. 24
For they have been guided (in this life) to the purest of speeches; they
have been guided to the Path of Him Who is Worthy of (all) Praise. 25 As
to those who have rejected (Allah), and would keep back (men) from the
Way of Allah, and from the Sacred Mosque, which We have made (open)
to (all) men—equal is the dweller there and the visitor from the
country—and any whose purpose therein is profanity or wrong-
doing—them will We cause to taste of a most grievous Penalty.

SECTION 4

26 Behold! We gave the site, to Abraham, of the (Sacred) House, (saying):
"Associate not anything (in worship) with Me; and sanctify My House for
those who compass it round, or stand up, or bow, or prostrate themselves
(therein in prayer). 27 And proclaim the Pilgrimage among men: they will
come to you on foot and (mounted) on every kind of camel, lean on
account of journeys through deep and distant mountain highways; 28 That
they may witness the benefits (provided) for them, and celebrate the name
of Allah, through the Days appointed, over the cattle which He has
provided for them (for sacrifice): then eat you thereof and feed the
distressed ones in want. 29 Then let them complete the rites prescribed for
them, perform their vows, and (again) circumambulate the Ancient
House."

30 Such (is the Pilgrimage): whoever honours the sacred rites of Allah, for
him it is good in the sight of his Lord. Lawful to you (for food in
Pilgrimage) are cattle, except those mentioned to you (as exceptions): but
shun the abomination of idols, and shun the word that is false,— 31 Being
true in faith to Allah, and never assigning partners to Him: if anyone
assigns partners to Allah, he is as if he had fallen from heaven and been
snatched up by birds, or the wind had swooped (like a bird on its prey)
and thrown him into a far-distant place. 32 Such (is his state): and whoever
holds in honour the symbols of Allah, (in the sacrifice of animals), such
(honour) should come truly from piety of heart. 33 In them you have
benefits for a term appointed: in the end their place of sacrifice is near the
Ancient House.

SECTION 5

34 To every people did We appoint rites (of sacrifice), that they might
celebrate the name of Allah over the sustenance He gave them from
animals (fit for food). But your Allah is One Allah: submit then your
wills to Him (in Islam): and give you the good news to those who humble
themselves,—35 To those whose hearts, when Allah is mentioned, are
filled with fear, who show patient perseverance over their afflictions,
keep up regular prayer, and spend (in charity) out of what We have
bestowed upon them.

36 The sacrificial camels We have made for you as among the symbols
from Allah: in them is (much) good for you: then pronounce the name of

Allah over them as they line up (for sacrifice): when they are down on
their sides (after slaughter), eat you thereof, and feed such as (beg not
but) live in contentment, and such as beg with due humility: thus have
We made animals subject to you, that you may be grateful. 37 It is not
their meat nor their blood, that reaches Allah: it is your piety that reaches
Him: He has thus made them subject to you, that you may glorify Allah
for His Guidance to you: and proclaim the good news to all who do right.
38 Verily Allah will defend (from ill) those who believe: verily, Allah
loves not any that is a traitor to faith, or shows ingratitude.

SECTION 6

39 To those against whom war is made, permission is given (to fight),
because they are wronged;—and verily, Allah is Most Powerful for their
aid;—40 (They are) those who have been expelled from their homes in
defiance of right,—(for no cause) except that they say, "Our Lord is
Allah." Did not Allah check one set of people by means of another, there
would surely have been pulled down monasteries, churches, synagogues,
and mosques, in which the name of Allah is commemorated in abundant
measure. Allah will certainly aid those who aid His (cause);—for verily
Allah is full of Strength, Exalted in Might, (able to enforce His Will). 41
(They are) those who, if We establish them in the land, establish regular
prayer and give regular charity, enjoin the right and forbid wrong: with
Allah rests the end (and decision) of (all) affairs.

42 If they treat your (mission) as false, so did the peoples before them
(with their prophets),—the people of Noah, and 'Ād and Thamūd; 43
Those of Abraham and Lūṭ; 44 And the Companions of the Madyan
people; and Moses was rejected (in the same way). But I granted respite
to the Unbelievers, and (only) after that did I punish them: but how
(terrible) was My rejection (of them)! 45 How many populations have We
destroyed, which were given to wrong-doing? They tumbled down on
their roofs. And how many wells are lying idle and neglected, and castles
lofty and well-built? 46 Do they not travel through the land, so that their
hearts (and minds) may thus learn wisdom and their ears may thus learn
to hear? Truly it is not their eyes that are blind, but their hearts which are
in their breasts. 47 Yet they ask you to hasten on the Punishment! But
Allah will not fail in His Promise. Verily a Day in the sight of your Lord
is like a thousand years of your reckoning. 48 And to how many

populations did I give respite, which were given to wrong-doing? In the
end I punished them. To Me is the destination (of all).

SECTION 7

49 Say: "O men! I am (sent) to you only to give a clear warning: 50 Those
who believe and work righteousness, for them is forgiveness and a
sustenance most generous. 51 But those who strive against Our Signs, to
frustrate them,—they will be companions of the Fire."

52 Never did We send a messenger or a prophet before you, but, when he
framed a desire, Satan threw some (vanity) into his desire: but Allah will
cancel anything (vain) that Satan throws in, and Allah will confirm (and
establish) His Signs: for Allah is full of knowledge and wisdom: 53 That
He may make the suggestions thrown in by Satan, but a trial for those in
whose hearts is a disease and who are hardened of heart: verily the
wrong-doers are in a schism far (from the Truth): 54 And that those on
whom knowledge has been bestowed may learn that the (Qur'an) is the
Truth from your Lord, and that they may believe therein, and their hearts
may be made humbly (open) to it: for verily Allah is the Guide of those
who believe, to the straight Way. 55 Those who reject Faith will not cease
to be in doubt concerning (Revelation) until the Hour (of Judgement)
comes suddenly upon them, or there comes to them the Penalty of a Day
of Disaster. 56 On that Day the Dominion will be that of Allah: He will
judge between them: so those who believe and work righteous deeds will
be in Gardens of Delight. 57 And for those who reject Faith and deny Our
Signs, there will be a humiliating Punishment.

SECTION 8

58 Those who leave their homes in the cause of Allah, and are then slain
or die,—on them will Allah bestow verily a goodly Provision: truly Allah
is He Who bestows the best Provision. 59 Verily He will admit them to a
place with which they shall be well pleased: for Allah is All-knowing,
Most Forbearing. 60 That (is so). And if one has retaliated to no greater
extent than the injury he received, and is again set upon inordinately,
Allah will help him: for Allah is One that blots out (sins) and forgives
(again and again).

61 That is because Allah merges night into day, and He merges day into
night, and verily it is Allah Who hears and sees (all things). 62 That is

because Allah—He is the Reality; and those besides Him whom they
invoke,—they are but vain Falsehood: verily Allah is He, Most High,
Most Great. 63 See you not that Allah sends down rain from the sky, and
forthwith the earth becomes clothed with green? For Allah is He Who
understands the finest mysteries, and is well-acquainted (with them). 64 To
Him belongs all that is in the heavens and on earth: for verily Allah,—He
is free of all wants, worthy of all Praise.

SECTION 9

65 See you not that Allah has made subject to you (men) all that is on the
earth, and the ships that sail through the sea by His Command? He
withholds the sky (rain) from falling on the earth except by His leave: for
Allah is Most Kind and Most Merciful to man. 66 It is He Who gave you
life, will cause you to die, and will again give you life: truly man is a
most ungrateful creature!

67 To every people have We appointed rites and ceremonies which they
must follow: let them not then dispute with you on the matter, but do you
invite (them) to your Lord: for you are assuredly on the right Way. 68 If
they do wrangle with you, say, "Allah knows best what it is you are
doing." 69 "Allah will judge between you on the Day of Judgement
concerning the matters in which you differ." 70 Know you not that Allah
knows all that is in heaven and on earth? Indeed it is all in a record, and
that is easy for Allah. 71 Yet they worship, besides Allah, things for which
no authority has been sent down to them, and of which they have (really)
no knowledge: for those that do wrong there is no helper. 72 When Our
clear Signs are rehearsed to them, you will notice a denial on the faces of
the Unbelievers! They nearly attack with violence those who rehearse Our
Signs to them. Say, "Shall I tell you of something (far) worse than these
Signs? It is the Fire (of Hell)! Allah has promised it to the Unbelievers!
And evil is that destination!"

SECTION 10

73 O men! Here is a parable set forth! Listen to it! Those on whom,
besides Allah, you call, cannot create (even) a fly, if they all met together
for the purpose! And if the fly should snatch away anything from them,
they would have no power to release it from the fly. Feeble are those who
petition and those whom they petition! 74 No just estimate have they made
of Allah: for Allah is He Who is strong and able to carry out His Will. 75

Allah chooses messengers from angels and from men for Allah is He Who hears and sees (all things). 76 He knows what is before them and what is behind them: and to Allah go back all questions (for decision).

77 O you who believe! Bow down, prostrate yourselves, and adore your Lord; and do good; that you may prosper. 78 And strive in His cause as you ought to strive, (with sincerity and under discipline). He has chosen you, and has imposed no difficulties on you in religion; it is the cult of your father Abraham. It is He Who has named you Muslims, both before and in this (Revelation); that the Messenger may be a witness for you, and you be witnesses for mankind! So establish regular prayer, give regular charity, and hold fast to Allah! He is your Protector—the Best to protect and the Best to help!□

Chapter 23

Sūrah Al-Mu'minūn
(The Believers)

Translator's Introduction

This Sūrah deals with the virtues which are the seed-bed of Faith, especially in an environment in which Truth is denied and its votaries insulted and persecuted. But Truth is One and must prevail. Those who do wrong will be filled with vain regrets when it is too late for repentance.

It belongs to the late Makkan period.

Summary—Faith, coupled with humility in prayer, charity, abstinence from vanity and from indulgence in appetites, and strict probity, must lead to final success, even though people mock and accuse the righteous of false motives, as did the contemporaries of Noah, of Moses, and of Jesus (23:1-50).

The prophets of Allah and the righteous form one Brotherhood, but those who make schisms and refuse to believe have ample evidence pointing to Truth and the goodness and greatness of Allah (23:51-92).

Evil must be repelled by goodness and faith in Allah; for the future life is sure, and those who disbelieve will wish for another chance when it is too late (23:93-118).

*** *** ***

PART XVIII

In the name of Allah,
Most Gracious, Most Merciful.

1 The Believers must (eventually) win through,—2 Those who humble
themselves in their prayers;[1] 3 Who avoid vain talk; 4 Who are active in
deeds of charity; 5 Who abstain from sex, 6 Except with those joined to
them in the marriage bond, or (the captives) whom their right hands
possess,—for (in their case) they are free from blame, 7 But those whose

---

1. Humility in prayer as regards (1) their estimate of their own worth in Allah's presence, (2) as regards their estimate of their own powers or strength unless they are helped by Allah, and (3) as regards the petitions they offer to Allah. [2866]

desires exceed those limits are transgressors;—8 Those who faithfully
observe their trusts and their covenants; 9 And who (strictly) guard their
prayers;—10 These will be the heirs, 11 Who will inherit Paradise: they
will dwell therein (for ever).

12 Man We did create from a quintessence (of clay); 13 Then We placed
him as (a drop of) sperm in a place of rest, firmly fixed; 14 Then We made
the sperm into a clot of congealed blood; then of that clot We made a
(foetus) lump; then We made out of that lump bones and clothed the
bones with flesh; then We developed out of it another creature. So blessed
be Allah, the Best to create! 15 After that, at length you will die, 16 Again,
on the Day of Judgement, will you be raised up. 17 And We have made,
above you, seven tracts; and We are never unmindful of (Our) Creation.

18 And We send down water from the sky according to (due) measure, and
We cause it to soak in the soil; and We certainly are able to drain it off
(with ease). 19 With it We grow for you gardens of date palms and vines:
in them have you abundant fruits: and of them you eat (and have
enjoyment),—20 Also a tree springing out of Mount Sinai, which produces
oil, and relish for those who use it for food. 21 And in cattle (too) you
have an instructive example: from within their bodies We produce (milk)
for you to drink; there are, in them, (besides), numerous (other) benefits
for you; and of their (meat) you eat; 22 And on them, as well as in ships,
you ride.

SECTION 2

23 (Further, We sent a long line of prophets for your instruction). We sent
Noah to his people: he said, "O my people! Worship Allah! You have no
other god but Him. Will you not fear (Him)?" 24 The chiefs of the
Unbelievers among his people said: "He is no more than a man like
yourselves: his wish is to assert his superiority over you: if Allah had
wished (to send messengers), He could have sent down angels; never did
we hear such a thing (as he says), among our ancestors of old." 25 (And
some said): "He is only a man possessed: wait (and have patience) with
him for a time." 26 (Noah) said: "O my Lord! Help me: for that they
accuse me of falsehood!" 27 So We inspired him (with this message):
"Construct the Ark within Our sight and under Our guidance: then when
comes Our Command, and the fountains of the earth gush forth, take you
on board pairs of every species, male and female, and your

family—except those of them against whom the Word has already gone
forth: and address Me not in favour of the wrong-doers; for they shall be
drowned (in the Flood). 28 And when you have embarked on the
Ark—you and those with you,—say: 'Praise be to Allah, Who has saved
us from the people who do wrong.' 29 And say: 'O my Lord! Enable me
to disembark with Your blessing: for You are the Best to enable (us) to
disembark.'" 30 Verily in this there are Signs (for men to understand);
(thus) do We try (men).

31 Then We raised after them another generation. 32 And We sent to them
a messenger from among themselves, (saying), "Worship Allah! You
have no other god but Him. Will you not fear (Him)?"

SECTION 3

33 And the chiefs of his people, who disbelieved and denied the Meeting
in the Hereafter, and on whom We had bestowed the good things of this
life, said: "He is no more than a man like yourselves: he eats of that of
which you eat, and drinks of what you drink. 34 If you obey a man like
yourselves, behold, it is certain you will be lost.[2] 35 Does he promise that
when you die and become dust and bones, you shall be brought forth
(again)? 36 Far, very far is that which you are promised! 37 There is
nothing but our life in this world! We shall die and we live! But we shall
never be raised up again! 38 He is only a man who invents a lie against
Allah, but we are not the ones to believe in him!" 39 (The prophet) said:
"O my Lord! Help me: for that they accuse me of falsehood." 40 (Allah)
said: "In but a little while, they are sure to be sorry!" 41 Then the Blast
overtook them with justice, and We made them as rubbish of dead leaves
(floating on the stream of Time)! So away with the people who do wrong!

42 Then We raised after them other generations. 43 No people can hasten
their term, nor can they delay (it). 44 Then sent We Our messengers in
succession: every time there came to a people their messenger, they
accused him of falsehood: so We made them follow each other (in

---

2. The type of the narrow Sybarite, who enjoys the good things of this life, denies a future life, and is jealous of anyone who presumes to widen his horizon, is here described in a few masterly strokes. He is bored by any mention of the serious things beyond his ken. What good is it, he says, to talk about the future? Enjoy the present. The gain is all in the present: the loss is all in the future. [2895]

punishment): We made them as a tale (that is told): so away with a people
that will not believe!

45 Then We sent Moses and his brother Aaron, with Our Signs and
authority manifest, 46 To Pharaoh and his Chiefs: but these behaved
insolently: they were an arrogant people. 47 They said: "Shall we believe
in two men like ourselves? And their people are subject to us!" 48 So they
accused them of falsehood, and they became of those who were
destroyed. 49 And We gave Moses the Book, in order that they might
receive guidance.

50 And We made the son of Mary and his mother as a Sign: We gave them
both shelter on high ground, affording rest and security and furnished
with springs.

SECTION 4

51 O you messengers! Enjoy (all) things good and pure, and work
righteousness: for I am well-acquainted with (all) that you do. 52 And verily
this Brotherhood of yours is a single Brotherhood, and I am your Lord and
Cherisher: therefore fear Me (and no other). 53 But people have cut off their
affair (of unity), between them, into sects: each party rejoices in that which
is with itself. 54 But leave them in their confused ignorance for a time.

55 Do they think that because We have granted them abundance of wealth
and sons, 56 We would hasten them on in every good? Nay, they do not
understand.

57 Verily those who live in awe for fear of their Lord; 58 Those who
believe in the Signs of their Lord; 59 Those who join not (in worship)
partners with their Lord; 60 And those who dispense their charity with
their hearts full of fear, because they will return to their Lord;—61 It is
these who hasten in every good work, and these who are foremost in
them.

62 On no soul do We place a burden greater than it can bear: before Us is
a record which clearly shows the truth: they will never be wronged. 63 But
their hearts are in confused ignorance of this; and there are, besides that,
deeds of theirs, which they will (continue) to do,—64 Until, when We
seize in Punishment those of them who received the good things of this
world, behold, they will groan in supplication! 65 (It will be said): "Groan

not in supplication this day; for you shall certainly not be helped by Us.
66 My Signs used to be rehearsed to you, but you used to turn back on
your heels— 67 In arrogance: talking nonsense about the (Qur'an), like
one telling fables by night."

68 Do they not ponder over the Word (of Allah), or has anything (new)
come to them that did not come to their fathers of old? 69 Or do they not
recognise their Messenger, that they deny him? 70 Or do they say, "He is
possessed"? Nay, he has brought them the Truth, but most of them hate
the Truth. 71 If the Truth had been in accord with their desires, truly the
heavens and the earth, and all beings therein would have been in
confusion and corruption! Nay, We have sent them their admonition, but
they turn away from their admonition. 72 Or is it that you ask them for
some recompense? But the recompense of your Lord is best: He is the
Best of those who give sustenance. 73 But verily you call them to the
straight Way; 74 And verily those who believe not in the Hereafter are
deviating from that Way.

75 If We had mercy on them and removed the distress which is on them,
they would obstinately persist in their transgression, wandering in
distraction to and fro. 76 We inflicted Punishment on them, but they
humbled not themselves to their Lord, nor do they submissively entreat
(Him)!—77 Until We open on them a gate leading to a severe Punishment:
then lo! they will be plunged in despair therein!

SECTION 5

78 It is He Who has created for you (the faculties of) hearing, sight,
feeling and understanding: little thanks it is you give! 79 And He has
multiplied you through the earth, and to Him shall you be gathered back.
80 It is He Who gives life and death, and to Him (is due) the alternation of
Night and Day: will you not then understand? 81 On the contrary they say
things similar to what the ancients said. 82 They say: "What! When we die
and become dust and bones, could we really be raised up again? 83 Such
things have been promised to us and to our fathers before! They are
nothing but tales of the ancients!" 84 Say: "To whom belong the earth and
all beings therein? (Say) if you know!" 85 They will say, "To Allah!" Say:
"Yet will you not receive admonition?" 86 Say: "Who is the Lord of the
seven heavens, and the Lord of the Throne (of Glory) Supreme?" 87 They
will say, "(They belong) to Allah." Say: "Will you not then be filled with

awe?" 88 Say: "Who is it in whose hands is the governance of all
things,—Who protects (all), but is not protected (of any)? (Say) if you
know." 89 They will say, "(It belongs) to Allah." Say: "Then how are you
deluded?"

90 We have sent them the Truth: but they indeed practise falsehood! 91 No
son did Allah beget, nor is there any god along with Him: (if there were
many gods), behold, each god would have taken away what he had
created, and some would have lorded it over others! Glory to Allah! (He
is free) from the (sort of) things they attribute to Him! 92 He knows what
is hidden and what is open: too high is He for the partners they attribute
to Him!

SECTION 6

93 Say: "O my Lord! If You will show me (in my lifetime) that which they
are warned against,—94 Then, O my Lord! put me not amongst the people
who do wrong!" 95 And We are certainly able to show you (in fulfilment)
that against which they are warned. 96 Repel evil with that which is best:
We are well acquainted with the things they say. 97 And say "O my Lord!
I seek refuge with You from the suggestions of the Evil Ones. 98 And I
seek refuge with You O my Lord! Lest they should come near me."

99 (In Falsehood will they be) until, when death comes to one of them, he
says: "O my Lord! send me back (to life),—100 In order that I may work
righteousness in the things I neglected."—"By no means! It is but a word
he says."—Before them is a Partition[3] till the Day they are raised up.

101 Then when the Trumpet is blown, there will be no more relationships
between them that Day, nor will one ask after another! 102 Then those
whose balance (of good deeds) is heavy,—they will attain salvation: 103
But those whose balance is light, will be those who have lost their souls;
in Hell will they abide. 104 The Fire will burn their faces, and they will
therein grin, with their lips displaced. 105 "Were not My Signs rehearsed
to you, and you did but treat them as falsehoods?" 106 They will say: "Our
Lord! Our misfortune overwhelmed us, and we became a people astray!

---

3. Partition (Arabic *Barzakh*): a bar or barrier; the place or state in which people will be after death and before Judgement. *Cf.* 25:53 and 55:20. Behind them is the barrier of death, and in front of them is the *Barzakh*, partition, a quiescent state until the judgement comes. [2940]

107 Our Lord! Bring us out of this: if ever we return (to evil), then shall we
be wrong-doers indeed!" 108 He will say: "Be you driven into it (with
ignominy)! And speak you not to Me! 109 A part of My servants there
was, who used to pray 'Our Lord! We believe; then do You forgive us,
and have mercy upon us: for You are the Best of those who show mercy!'
110 But you treated them with ridicule, so much so that (ridicule of) them
made you forget My Message while you were laughing at them! 111 I have
rewarded them this Day for their patience and constancy: they are indeed
the ones that have achieved Bliss. . ." 112 He will say: "What number of
years did you stay on earth?" 113 They will say: "We stayed a day or part
of a day: but ask those who keep account." 114 He will say: "You stayed
not but a little,—if you had only known! 115 Did you then think that We
had created you in jest, and that you would not be brought back to Us (for
account)?"

116 Therefore exalted be Allah, the King, the Reality: there is no god but
He, the Lord of the Throne of Honour! 117 If anyone invokes, besides
Allah, any other god, he has no authority therefor; and his reckoning will
be only with his Lord! And verily the Unbelievers will fail to win
through! 118 So say: "O my Lord! Grant You forgiveness and mercy for
You are the Best of those who show mercy!"□

Chapter 24

Sūrah Al-Nūr
(The Light)

Translator's Introduction

The environmental and social influences which most frequently wreck our spiritual ideals have to do with sex and especially with its misuse, whether in the form of unregulated behaviour, or false charges or scandals, or breach of the refined conventions of personal or domestic privacy. Our complete conquest of all pitfalls in such matters enables us to rise to the higher regions of Light and of God-created Nature, about which a mystic doctrine is suggested. This subject is continued in the next Sūrah.

As the reprobation of false slanders about women (24:11-20) is connected with an incident that happened to 'Ā'ishah in A.H. 5-6, that fixes the chronological place of this Madīnan Sūrah.

Summary—Sex offences should be severely punished, but the strictest evidence should be required, and false slanderers are also worthy of punishment. Light talk about women is reprobated (24:1-26).

Privacy should be respected, and the utmost decorum should be observed in dress and manners (24:27-34).

Parable of Light and Darkness: order and obedience in Nature point to the spiritual duty of man (24:35-57).

Domestic manners and manners in public or collective life all contribute to the highest virtues, and are part of our spiritual duties leading up to Allah (24:58-64).

*** *** ***

In the name of Allah,
Most Gracious, Most Merciful.

1 A Sūrah which We have sent down and which We have ordained: in it have We sent down clear Signs, in order that you may receive admonition.[1]

---

1. It must not be thought that the checking of sex offences or of minor improprieties, that relate to sex or privacy, are matters that do not affect spiritual life in the highest degree. These matters are intimately connected with spiritual teaching such as Allah has

2 The woman and the man guilty of adultery or fornication,[2]—flog each
of them with a hundred stripes: let not compassion move you in their
case, in a matter prescribed by Allah, if you believe in Allah and the Last
Day: and let a party of the Believers witness their punishment. 3 Let no
man guilty of adultery or fornication marry any but a woman similarly
guilty, or an Unbeliever: nor let any but such a man or an Unbeliever
marry such a woman: to the Believers such a thing is forbidden.

4 And those who launch a charge against chaste women, and produce not
four witnesses (to support their allegations),—flog them with eighty
stripes; and reject their evidence ever after: for such men are wicked
transgressors;—5 Unless they repent thereafter and mend (their conduct);
for Allah is Oft-Forgiving, Most Merciful.

6 And for those who launch a charge against their spouses, and have (in
support) no evidence but their own,—their solitary evidence (can be
received) if they bear witness four times (with an oath) by Allah that they
are solemnly telling the truth; 7 And the fifth (oath) (should be) that they
solemnly invoke the curse of Allah on themselves if they tell a lie. 8 But
it would avert the punishment from the wife, if she bears witness four
times (with an oath) by Allah, that (her husband) is telling a lie; 9 And the
fifth (oath) should be that she solemnly invokes the wrath of Allah on
herself if (her accuser) is telling the truth. 10 If it were not for Allah's
grace and mercy on you, and that Allah is Oft-Returning, full of
Wisdom,—(you would be ruined indeed).

---

sent down in this Sūrah. The emphasis is on "We": these things are not mere matters of convenience, but Allah has ordained them for our observance in life. [2953]

2. *Zinā* includes sexual intercourse between a man and a woman not married to each other. It therefore applies both to adultery (which implies that one or both of the parties are married to a person or persons other than the ones concerned) and to fornication, which, in its strict signification, implies that both parties are unmarried. The law of marriage and divorce is made easy in Islam, so that there may be less temptation for intercourse outside the well-defined institution of marriage. This makes for greater self-respect for both man and woman. Other sex offences are also punishable, but this section applies strictly to *Zinā* as above defined. The punishment for adultery according to be Bible is death by stoning (Deuteronomy 22:22-24. [2954] -Ed.

SECTION 2

11 Those who brought forward[3] the lie are a body among yourselves:
think it not to be an evil to you; on the contrary it is good for you: to
every man among them (will come the punishment) of the sin that he
earned, and to him who took on himself the lead among them, will be a
Penalty grievous. 12 Why did not the Believers—men and women—when
you heard of the affair,—put the best construction on it in their own
minds and say, "This (charge) is an obvious lie"? 13 Why did they not
bring four witnesses to prove it? When they have not brought the
witnesses, such men, in the sight of Allah, (stand forth) themselves as
liars! 14 Were it not for the grace and mercy of Allah on you, in this world
and the Hereafter, a grievous penalty would have seized you in that you
rushed glibly into this affair. 15 Behold, you received it on your tongues,
and said out of your mouths things of which you had no knowledge; and
you thought it to be a light matter, while it was most serious in the sight
of Allah. 16 And why did you not, when you heard it, say?—"It is not
right of us to speak of this: Glory to Allah! This is a most serious
slander!"

17 Allah does admonish you, that you may never repeat such (conduct),
if you are (true) Believers. 18 And Allah makes the Signs plain to you: for
Allah is full of knowledge and wisdom. 19 Those who love (to see)
scandal published broadcast among the Believers, will have a grievous
Penalty in this life and in the Hereafter: Allah knows, and you know not.
20 Were it not for the grace and mercy of Allah on you, and that Allah is
full of kindness and mercy, (you would be ruined indeed).

---

3. The particular incident here referred to occurred on the return from the expedition to the Banū Musṭaliq, A.H. 5-6. When the march was ordered, 'Ā'ishah was not in her tent, having gone to search for a valuable necklace she had dropped. As her litter was veiled, it was not noticed that she was not in it, until the army reached the next halt. Meanwhile, finding the camp had gone, she sat down to rest, hoping that someone would come back to fetch her when her absence was noticed. It was night, and she fell asleep. Next morning she was found by Ṣafwān, a *Muhājir*, who had been left behind in the camp expressly to pick up anything inadvertently left behind. He put her on his camel and brought her, leading the camel on foot. This gave occasion for enemies to raise a malicious scandal. The ringleader among them was the chief of the Madīnan Hypocrites, 'Abdullāh ibn Ubayy who is referred to in the last clause of the verse. He had other sins and enormities to his debit, and was left to the spiritual punishment of an unrepentant sinner, for he died in that state. The minor tools were given the legal punishment of the law, after penitence mended their lives. They made good. [2962]

SECTION 3

21 O you who believe! Follow not Satan's footsteps: if any will follow the
footsteps of Satan, he will (but) command what is shameful and wrong:
and were it not for the grace and mercy of Allah on you, not one of you
would ever have been pure: but Allah does purify whom He pleases: and
Allah is One Who hears and knows (all things). 22 Let not those among
you who are endued with grace and amplitude of means resolve by oath
against helping their kinsmen, those in want, and those who have left
their homes in Allah's cause: let them forgive and overlook, do you not
wish that Allah should forgive you? For Allah is Oft-Forgiving, Most
Merciful. 23 Those who slander chaste women, indiscreet but believing,
are cursed in this life and in the Hereafter: for them is a grievous
Penalty,—24 On the Day when their tongues, their hands, and their feet
will bear witness against them as to their actions. 25 On that Day Allah
will pay them back (all) their just dues, and they will realise that Allah is
the (very) Truth, that makes all things manifest. 26 Women impure are for
men impure, and men impure for women impure and women of purity are
for men of purity, and men of purity are for women of purity: these are
not affected by what people say: for them there is forgiveness, and a
provision honourable.

SECTION 4

27 O you who believe! Enter not houses other than your own, until you
have asked permission and saluted those in them: that is best for you, in
order that you may heed (what is seemly). 28 If you find no one in the
house, enter not until permission is given to you: if you are asked to go
back, go back: that makes for greater purity for yourselves: and Allah
knows well all that you do. 29 It is no fault on your part to enter houses
not used for living in, which serve some (other) use for you: and Allah
has knowledge of what you reveal and what you conceal.

30 Say to the believing men that they should lower their gaze and guard
their modesty: that will make for greater purity for them: and Allah is
well acquainted with all that they do. 31 And say to the believing women
that they should lower their gaze and guard their modesty; that they
should not display their beauty and ornaments except what (must
ordinarily) appear thereof; that they should draw their veils over their
bosoms and not display their beauty except to their husbands, their

fathers, their husbands' fathers, their sons, their husbands' sons, their
brothers or their brothers' sons, or their sisters' sons, or their women, or
the slaves whom their right hands possess, or male servants free of
physical needs, or small children who have no sense of the shame of sex;
and that they should not strike their feet in order to draw attention to their
hidden ornaments. And O you Believers! Turn you all together towards
Allah, that you may attain Bliss.

32 Marry those among you who are single, or the virtuous ones among
your slaves, male or female: if they are in poverty, Allah will give them
means out of His grace: for Allah encompasses all, and He knows all
things. 33 Let those who find not the wherewithal for marriage keep
themselves chaste, until Allah gives them means out of His grace. And if
any of your slaves ask for a deed in writing (to enable them to earn their
freedom for a certain sum), give them such a deed if you know any good
in them: indeed, give them something yourselves out of the means which
Allah has given to you. But force not your maids to prostitution when
they desire chastity, in order that you may make a gain in the goods of
this life. But if anyone compels them, yet, after such compulsion, is
Allah, Oft-Forgiving, Most Merciful (to them).

34 We have already sent down to you verses making things clear, an
illustration from (the story of) people who passed away before you, and
an admonition for those who fear (Allah).

SECTION 5

35 Allah is the Light of the heavens and the earth. The Parable of His
Light is as if there were a Niche and within it a Lamp: the Lamp enclosed
in Glass: the glass as it were a brilliant star: lit from a blessed Tree, an
Olive, neither of the East nor of the West, whose oil is well-nigh
luminous, though fire scarce touched it: Light upon Light! Allah does
guide whom He will to His light: Allah does set forth Parables for men:
and Allah does know all things. 36 (Lit is such a light) in houses, which
Allah has permitted to be raised to honour; for the celebration, in them,
of His name: in them is He glorified in the mornings and in the evenings,
(again and again),—37 By men whom neither traffic nor merchandise can
divert from the remembrance of Allah, nor from regular Prayer, nor from
the practice of regular Charity: their (only) fear is for the Day when
hearts and eyes will be transformed (in a world wholly new),—38 That

Allah may reward them according to the best of their deeds, and add even more for them out of His Grace: for Allah does provide for those whom He will, without measure.

39 But the Unbelievers,—their deeds are like a mirage in sandy deserts,
which the man parched with thirst mistakes for water; until when he
comes up to it, he finds it to be nothing: but he finds Allah (ever) with
him, and Allah will pay him his account: and Allah is swift in taking
account. 40 Or (the Unbelievers' state) is like the depths of darkness in a
vast deep ocean, overwhelmed with billow topped by billow, topped by
(dark) clouds: depths of darkness, one above another: if a man stretches
out his hand, he can hardly see it! For any to whom Allah gives not light,
there is no light!

SECTION 6

41 See you not that it is Allah Whose praises all beings in the heavens and
on earth do celebrate, and the birds (of the air) with wings outspread?
Each one knows its own (mode of) prayer and praise. And Allah knows
well all that they do. 42 Indeed, to Allah belongs the dominion of the
heavens and the earth; and to Allah is the final goal (of all). 43 See you not
that Allah makes the clouds move gently, then joins them together, then
makes them into a heap?—then will you see rain issue forth from their
midst. And He sends down from the sky mountain masses (of clouds)
wherein is hail: He strikes therewith whom He pleases and He turns it
away from whom He pleases. The vivid flash of His lightning well-nigh
blinds the sight. 44 It is Allah Who alternates the Night and the Day: verily
in these things is an instructive example for those who have vision! 45
And Allah has created every animal from water:[4] of them there are some
that creep on their bellies; some that walk on two legs; and some that
walk on four. Allah creates what He wills for verily Allah has power over
all things. 46 We have indeed sent down Signs that make things manifest:
and Allah guides whom He wills to a Way that is straight.

---

4. *Cf.* 21:30. Protoplasm is the basis of all living matter, and "the vital power of protoplasm seems to depend on the constant presence of water" (Lowson's *Textbook of Botany*, Indian Edition, London, 1922, p. 23). Textbooks of Zoology are also clear on the point. For example, see T. J. Parker and W. A. Haswell, *Textbook of Zoology*, London, 1910, vol.I, p.15: "Living protoplasm always contains a large amount of water." [3021]

47 They[5] say, "We believe in Allah and in the Messenger, and we obey":
but even after that, some of them turn away: they are not (really)
Believers. 48 When they are summoned to Allah and His Messenger, in
order that he may judge between them, behold, some of them decline (to
come). 49 But if the right is on their side, they come to him with all
submission. 50 Is it that there is a disease in their hearts? Or do they doubt,
or are they in fear, that Allah and His Messenger will deal unjustly with
them? Nay, it is they themselves who do wrong.

SECTION 7

51 The answer of the Believers, when summoned to Allah and His
Messenger, in order that he may judge between them, is no other than
this: they say, "We hear and we obey": it is such as these that will attain
felicity. 52 It is such as obey Allah and His Messenger, and fear Allah and
do right, that will win (in the end), 53 They swear their strongest oaths by
Allah that, if only you would command them, they would leave (their
homes). Say: "Swear you not; obedience is (more) reasonable; verily,
Allah is well acquainted with all that you do." 54 Say: "Obey Allah, and
obey the Messenger." But if you turn away, he is only responsible for the
duty placed on him and you for that placed on you. If you obey him, you
shall be on right guidance. The Messenger's duty is only to preach the
clear (Message).

55 Allah has promised, to those among you who believe and work
righteous deeds, that He will, of a surety, grant them in the land,
inheritance (of power), as He granted it to those before them; that He will
establish in authority their religion—the one which He has chosen for
them; and that He will change (their state), after the fear in which they
(lived), to one of security and peace: 'They will worship Me (alone) and
not associate aught with Me.' If any do reject Faith after this, they are
rebellious and wicked. 56 So establish regular prayer and give regular
charity; and obey the Messenger; that you may receive mercy. 57 Never
think you that the Unbelievers are going to frustrate (Allah's Plan) on
earth: their abode is the Fire,—and it is indeed an evil refuge!

---

5. The Hypocrites, far from profiting from Allah's Light and Revelation, or declaring their open hostility, play fast and loose according to their selfish worldly aims. [3024]

SECTION 8

58 O you who believe![6] Let those whom your right hands possess, and the
(children) among you who have not come of age ask your permission
(before they come to your presence), on three occasions: before morning
prayer; the while you take off your clothes for the noonday heat; and after
the late-night prayer: these are your three times of undress: outside those
times it is not wrong for you or for them to move about attending to each
other: thus does Allah make clear the Signs to you: for Allah is full of
knowledge and wisdom. 59 But when the children among you come of
age, let them (also) ask for permission, as do those senior to them (in
age): thus does Allah make clear His Signs to you: for Allah is full of
knowledge and wisdom. 60 Such elderly women as are past the prospect
of marriage,—there is no blame on them if they lay aside their (outer)
garments, provided they make not a wanton display of their beauty: but
it is best for them to be modest: and Allah is One Who sees and knows
all things.

61 It is no fault in the blind nor in one born lame, nor in one afflicted with illness, nor in yourselves, that you should eat in your own houses, or those of your fathers, or your mothers, or your brothers, or your sisters, or your father's brothers or your father's sisters, or your mother's brothers, or your mother's sisters, or in houses of which the keys are in your possession, or in the house of a sincere friend of yours: there is no blame on you, whether you eat in company or separately. But if you enter houses, salute each other—a greeting of blessing and purity as from Allah. Thus does Allah make clear the Signs to you: that you may understand.

SECTION 9

62 Only those are Believers, who believe in Allah and His Messenger:

---

6. We now come to rules of decorum within the family circle in refined society. Servants and children have rather more freedom of access, as they come and go at all hours, and there is less ceremony with them. But even in their case there are limitations. During the night, before morning prayer, *i.e.,* before dawn, they must discreetly ask for permission before they enter, partly because they must not unnecessarily disturb people asleep, and partly because the people are then undressed. The same applies to the time for the midday siesta, and again to the time after night prayers, when people usually undress and turn in to sleep. For grown-ups the rule is stricter: they must ask permission to come in at all times (24:59). [3033]

when they are with him on a matter requiring collective action, they do not depart until they have asked for his leave; those who ask for your leave are those who believe in Allah and His Messenger; so when they ask for your leave, for some business of theirs, give leave to those of them whom you will, and ask Allah for their forgiveness: for Allah is Oft-Forgiving, Most Merciful. 63 Deem not the summons of the Messenger among yourselves like the summons of one of you to another: Allah does know those of you who slip away under shelter of some excuse: then let those beware who withstand the Messenger's order, lest some trial befall them, or a grievous Penalty be inflicted on them. 64 Be quite sure that to Allah does belong whatever is in the heavens and on earth. Well does He know what you are intent upon: and one day they will be brought back to Him, and He will tell them the truth of what they did: for Allah does know all things.□

Chapter 25

Sūrah Al-Furqān
(The Criterion)

Translator's Introduction

This Sūrah further develops the contrast between Light and Darkness, as symbolical of knowledge and ignorance, righteousness and sin, spiritual progress and degradation. It closes with a definition of the deeds by which the righteous are known in the environment of this world.

It is mainly an early Makkan Sūrah, but its date has no significance.

Summary—Allah's highest gift to man is that He has furnished a Criterion for judgement between right and wrong—in His revelation, which teaches us the true significance of our eternal Future (25:1-20).

Those who do not use that Criterion will be full of woe when the Judgement comes, for Allah gave full warning at all times (25:21-44).

In the contrasts of shade and sun, night and day, death and life, and the whole ordering of Allah's Creation, men may learn of Allah Most Gracious; and the virtues of the righteous respond to Allah's care for them (25:45-77).

*** *** ***

In the name of Allah,
Most Gracious, Most Merciful.

1 Blessed is He Who sent down the Criterion to His servant, that it may
be an admonition to all creatures;—2 He to Whom belongs the dominion
of the heavens and the earth: no son has He begotten, nor has He a
partner in His dominion: it is He Who created all things, and ordered
them in due proportions. 3 Yet have they taken, besides Him, gods that
can create nothing but are themselves created; that have no control of hurt
or good to themselves; nor can they control Death nor Life nor
Resurrection.

4 But the Misbelievers say: "Naught is this but a lie which he has forged,
and others have helped him at it." In truth it is they who have put forward
an iniquity and a falsehood. 5 And they say: "Tales of the ancients, which
he has caused to be written: and they are dictated before him morning and

evening." 6 Say: "The (Qur'an) was sent down by Him Who knows the
Mystery (that is) in the heavens and the earth: verily He is Oft-Forgiving,
Most Merciful."

7 And they say: "What sort of a messenger is this, who eats food, and
walks through the streets? Why has not an angel been sent down to him
to give admonition with him? 8 Or (why) has not a treasure been
bestowed on him, or why has he (not) a garden for enjoyment?" The
wicked say: "You follow none other than a man bewitched." 9 See what
kinds of comparisons they make for you! But they have gone astray, and
never a way will they be able to find!

SECTION 2

10 Blessed is He Who, if that were His Will, could give you better (things)
than those,—Gardens beneath which rivers flow; and He could give you
Palaces (secure to dwell in). 11 Nay, they deny the Hour (of the
Judgement to come): but We have prepared a blazing Fire for such as
deny the Hour: 12 When it sees them from a place far off, they will hear
its fury and its raging sigh. 13 And when they are cast, bound together,
into a constricted place therein, they will plead for destruction there and
then! 14 "This day plead not for a single destruction: plead for destruction
oft-repeated!" 15 Say: "Is that best, or the eternal Garden, promised to the
righteous? For them, that is a reward as well as a goal (of attainment). 16
For them there will be therein all that they wish for: they will dwell
(there) for ever: a promise to be prayed for from your Lord."

17 The Day He will gather them together as well as those whom they
worship besides Allah, He will ask: "Was it you who led these My
servants astray, or did they stray from the Path themselves?" 18 They will
say: "Glory to You! Not meet was it for us that we should take for
protectors others besides You: but You did bestow, on them and their
fathers, good things (in life), until they forgot the Message: for they were
a people (worthless and) lost." 19 (Allah will say): "Now have they proved
you liars in what you say: so you cannot avert (your penalty) nor (get)
help." And whoever among you does wrong, him shall We cause to taste
of a grievous Penalty. 20 And the messengers whom We sent before you
were all (men) who ate food and walked through the streets: We have
made some of you as a trial for others: will you have patience? For Allah
is One Who sees (all things).

PART XIX

SECTION 3

21 Such as fear not the meeting with Us (for Judgement) say: "Why are
not the angels sent down to us, or (why) do we not see our Lord?" Indeed
they have an arrogant conceit of themselves, and mighty is the insolence
of their impiety! 22 The Day they see the angels,—no joy will there be to
the sinners that Day: the (angels) will say: "There is a barrier forbidden
(to you) altogether!" 23 And We shall turn to whatever deeds they did (in
this life), and We shall make such deeds as floating dust scattered about.
24 The Companions of the Garden will be well, that Day, in their abode,
and have the fairest of places for repose. 25 The Day the heaven shall be
rent asunder with clouds, and angels shall be sent down, descending (in
ranks),—26 That Day, the dominion as of right and truth, shall be (wholly)
for (Allah) Most Merciful: it will be a Day of dire difficulty for the
Misbelievers.

27 The Day that the wrong-doer will bite at his hands, he will say, "Oh!
Would that I had taken a (straight) path with the Messenger! 28 Ah! Woe
is me! Would that I had never taken such a one for a friend! 29 He did
lead me astray from the Message (of Allah) after it had come to me! Ah!
The Evil One is but a traitor to man!" Then the Messenger will say: 30 "O
my Lord! Truly my people took this Qur'an for just foolish nonsense." 31
Thus have We made for every prophet an enemy among the sinners: but
enough is your Lord to guide and to help.

32 Those who reject Faith say: "Why is not the Qur'an revealed to him all
at once?" Thus (is it revealed), that We may strengthen your heart
thereby, and We have rehearsed it to you in slow, well-arranged stages,
gradually. 33 And no question do they bring to you but We reveal to you
the truth and the best explanation (thereof). 34 Those who will be gathered
to Hell (prone) on their faces,—they will be in an evil plight, and, as to
Path, most astray.

SECTION 4

35 (Before this,) We sent Moses the Book, and appointed his brother
Aaron with him as minister; 36 And We commanded: "Go you both, to the
people who have rejected Our Signs."—and those (people) We destroyed
with utter destruction. 37 And the people of Noah,—when they rejected

the messengers, We drowned them, and We made them as a Sign for mankind; and We have prepared for (all) wrong-doers a grievous Penalty;—
38 As also 'Ād and Thamūd, and the Companions of the *Rass*,[1] and many a generation between them.
39 To each one We set forth parables and examples; and each one We broke to utter annihilation (for their sins).
40 And the (Unbelievers) must indeed have passed by the town on which was rained a shower of evil: did they not then see it (with their own eyes)? But they fear not the Resurrection.

41 When they see you, they treat you no otherwise than in mockery: "Is this the one whom Allah has sent as a messenger?
42 He indeed would well-nigh have misled us from our gods, had it not been that we were constant to them!"—Soon will they know, when they see the Penalty, who it is that is most misled in Path!
43 See you such a one as takes for his god his own passion (or impulse)? Could you be a disposer of affairs for him?
44 Or think you that most of them listen or understand? They are only like cattle;—Nay, they are worse astray in Path.

SECTION 5

45 Have you not turned your vision to your Lord?—How He does prolong the Shadow! If He willed, He could make it stationary! Then do We make the sun its guide;
46 Then We draw it in towards Ourselves,—a contraction by easy stages.

47 And He it is Who makes the Night as a Robe for you, and Sleep as Repose, and makes the Day (as it were) a Resurrection.

48 And He it is Who sends the winds as heralds of glad tidings, going before His Mercy, and We send down pure water from the sky,—
49 That

---

1. Commentators are not clear as to who the "Companions of the *Rass*" were. The root meaning of *Rass* is an old well or shallow water-pit. Another root connects it with the burial of the dead. But it is probably the name of a town or place. The "Companions of the *Rass*" may well have been the people of Shu'ayb, as they are here mentioned with the 'Ād, the Thamūd, and Lot's people, and the people of Shu'ayb are mentioned in a similar connection in 26:176-190 and in 11:84-95. Shu'ayb was the prophet of the Madyan people in the northwest of Arabia, where many old wells are found. There is however, an oasis town *al-Rass* in the district of Qasim in Middle Najd, about thirty-five miles southwest of the town of 'Unayzah, reputed to be the central point of the Arabian Peninsula, and situated midway between Makkah and Baṣrah. See Doughty's *Arabia Deserta*, thin paper one-volume edition, London, 1926, II, 435 and Map, Lat.26°N. and Long.43°E. [3094]

with it We may give life to a dead land, and slake the thirst of things We
have created,—cattle and men in great numbers. 50 And We have
distributed the (water) amongst them, in order that they may celebrate
(Our) praises, but most men are averse (to aught) but (rank) ingratitude.

51 Had it been Our Will, We could have sent a warner to every centre of
population. 52 Therefore listen not to the Unbelievers, but strive against
them with the utmost strenuousness, with the (Qur'an).

53 It is He Who has let free the two bodies of flowing water: one palatable
and sweet, and the other salt and bitter; yet has He made a barrier
between them, a partition that is forbidden to be passed.[2]

54 It is He Who has created man from water: then has He established
relationships of lineage and marriage: for your Lord has power (over all
things).

55 Yet do they worship, besides Allah, things that can neither profit them
nor harm them: and the Misbeliever is a helper (of Evil), against his own
Lord! 56 But you We only sent to give glad tidings and admonition. 57 Say:
"No reward do I ask of you for it but this: that each one who will may
take a (straight) Path to his Lord."

58 And put your trust in Him Who lives and dies not; and celebrate His
praise; and enough is He to be acquainted with the faults of His
servants;—59 He Who created the heavens and the earth and all that is
between, in six days, and is firmly established on the Throne (of
Authority): Allah Most Gracious: ask you, then, about Him of any
acquainted (with such things). 60 When it is said to them, "Adore you
(Allah) Most Gracious!", they say, "And what is (Allah) Most Gracious?
Shall we adore that which you command us?" And it increases their flight
(from the Truth).

---

2. In Allah's overall scheme of things, bodies of salt and sweet water, which are adjoining and yet separate, have significant functions. Weaving a harmonious fabric out of these different fibres shows both Allah's power and wisdom. Incidentally, this verse points to a fact which has only recently been discovered by science. This fact relates to the oceans of the world: they meet and yet each remains separate for Allah has placed "a barrier, a partition" between them. [3112]

SECTION 6

61 Blessed is He Who made constellations in the skies, and placed therein
a Lamp and a Moon giving light; 62 And it is He Who made the night and
the day to follow each other: for such as have the will to celebrate His
praises or to show their gratitude.

63 And the servants of (Allah) Most Gracious are those who walk on the
earth in humility, and when the ignorant address them, they say,
"Peace!"; 64 Those who spend the night in adoration of their Lord
prostrate and standing; 65 Those who say, "Our Lord! Avert from us the
Wrath of Hell, for its Wrath is indeed an affliction grievous,—66 Evil
indeed is it as an abode, and as a place to rest in"; 67 Those who, when
they spend, are not extravagant and not niggardly, but hold a just
(balance) between those (extremes); 68 Those who invoke not, with Allah,
any other god, nor slay such life as Allah has made sacred, except for just
cause, nor commit[3] fornication;—and any that does this (not only) meets
punishment. 69 (But) the Penalty on the Day of Judgement will be doubled
to him, and he will dwell therein in ignominy,—70 Unless he repents,
believes, and works righteous deeds, for Allah will change the evil of
such persons into good, and Allah is Oft-Forgiving, Most Merciful, 71 And
whoever repents and does good has truly turned to Allah with an
(acceptable) conversion;—72 Those who witness no falsehood, and, if
they pass by futility, they pass by it with honourable (avoidance); 73 Those
who, when they are admonished with the Signs of their Lord, droop not
down at them as if they were deaf or blind; 74 And those who pray, "Our
Lord! Grant unto us wives and offspring who will be the comfort of our
eyes, and give us (the grace) to lead the righteous." 75 Those are the ones
who will be rewarded with the highest place in heaven, because of their
patient constancy: therein shall they be met with salutations and peace,

---

3. Here three things are expressly condemned: (1) false worship, which is a crime against Allah; (2) the taking of life, which is a crime against our fellow creatures; and (3) fornication, which is a crime against our self-respect, against ourselves. Every crime is against Allah, His creatures, and ourselves, but some may be viewed more in relation to one than to another. The prohibition against taking life is qualified: "except for just cause": *e.g.*, in judicial punishment for murder, or in self-preservation, which may include not only self-defence in the legal sense, but also the clearing out of pests, and the provision of meat under conditions of *Ḥalāl*: see 5:5. After this comes a long parenthesis, which ends with verse 71, below. [3128]

76 Dwelling therein;—how beautiful an abode and place of rest!

77 Say (to the Rejecters): "My Lord is not uneasy because of you if you call not on Him: but you have indeed rejected (Him), and soon will come the inevitable (punishment)!"□

Chapter 26

Sūrah Al-Shu'arā'
(The Poets)

Translator's Introduction

This Sūrah begins a new series of four Sūrahs (26-29), which illustrate the contrast between the spirit of Prophecy and spiritual Light and the reactions to it in the communities among whom it appeared, by going back to old Prophets and the stories of the Past, as explained in the Introduction to Sūrah 17.

In this particular Sūrah we have the story of Moses in his fight with Pharaoh and of Pharaoh's discomfiture. Other Prophets mentioned are Abraham, Noah, Hūd, Ṣāliḥ, Lūṭ, and Shu'ayb. The lesson is drawn that the Qur'an is a continuation and fulfilment of previous Revelations, and is pure Truth, unlike poetry of vain poets.

Chronologically the Sūrah belongs to the middle Makkan period, when the contact of the Light of Prophecy with the milieu of Pagan Makkah was testing the Makkans in their most arrogant mood.

Summary—The conflict of Unbelief with Truth is vain: so was the conflict of Pharaoh with Moses: Pharaoh's magicians bowed to the Truth, and Pharaoh and his hosts were drowned (26:1-69).

Nor did Abraham's people gain anything by their resisting of the Truth he preached, and Noah's people perished by their Unbelief (26:70-122).

Hūd warned his people against reliance on their material strength and Ṣāliḥ against sacrilege, but in both cases the evil ones were brought low (26:123-159).

Lūṭ had to deal with unspeakable crimes, and Shu'ayb against dishonest dealings and mischief: their teaching was rejected, but the rejecters were wiped out (26:160-191).

So, when the spirit of Prophecy came to Makkah, it was resisted by the votaries of evil: but Truth is not like vain poetry, and must triumph at last (26:192-277).

*** *** ***

In the name of Allah,
Most Gracious, Most Merciful.

1 *Ṭā Sīn Mīm.*[1] 2 These are Verses of the Book that makes (things) clear.

3 It may be you fret your soul with grief, that they do not become
Believers. 4 If (such) were Our Will, We could send down to them from
the sky a Sign, to which they would bend their necks in humility. 5 But
there comes not to them a newly-revealed Message from (Allah) Most
Gracious, but they turn away therefrom. 6 They have indeed rejected (the
Message): so they will know soon (enough) the truth of what they
mocked at! 7 Do they not look at the earth,—how many noble things of
all kinds We have produced therein? 8 Verily, in this is a Sign: but most
of them do not believe. 9 And verily, your Lord is He, the Exalted in
Might, Most Merciful.

SECTION 2

10 Behold, your Lord called Moses: "Go to the people of iniquity,—11 The
people of Pharaoh: will they not fear Allah?" 12 He said: "O my Lord! I
do fear that they will charge me with falsehood: 13 My breast will be
straitened. And my speech may not go (smoothly): so send unto Aaron.
14 And (further), they have a charge of crime against me; and I fear they
may slay me." 15 Allah said: "By no means! proceed then, both of you,
with Our Signs; We are with you, and will listen (to your call). 16 So go
forth, both of you, to Pharaoh, and say: 'We have been sent by the Lord
and Cherisher of the Worlds; 17 Send you with us the Children of Israel.'"
18 (Pharaoh) said: "Did we not cherish you as a child among us, and did
you not stay in our midst many years of your life? 19 And you did a deed
of yours which (you know) you did, and you are an ungrateful (wretch)!"
20 Moses said: "I did it then, when I was in error. 21 So I fled from you
(all) when I feared you; but my Lord has (since) invested me with
judgement (and wisdom) and appointed me as one of the messengers. 22
And this is the favour with which you do reproach me,—that you have
enslaved the Children of Israel!"

23 Pharaoh said: "And what is the 'Lord and Cherisher of the Worlds'?"

1. This is a combination of three Abbreviated Letters, as to which, generally, see note to Sūrah 2:1. [3137]

24 (Moses) said: "The Lord and Cherisher of the heavens and the earth,
and all between,—if you want to be quite sure." 25 (Pharaoh) said to those
around: "Did you not listen (to what he says)?" 26 (Moses) said: "Your
Lord and the Lord of your fathers from the beginning!" 27 (Pharaoh) said:
"Truly your messenger who has been sent to you is a veritable madman!"
28 (Moses) said: "Lord of the East and the West, and all between! If you
only had sense!" 29 (Pharaoh) said: "If you do put forward any god other
than me, I will certainly put you in prison!" 30 (Moses) said: "Even if I
showed you something clear (and) convincing?" 31 (Pharaoh) said: "Show
it then, if you tell the truth!" 32 So (Moses) threw his rod, and behold, it
was a serpent, plain (for all to see)! 33 And he drew out his hand, and
behold, it was white to all beholders!

SECTION 3

34 (Pharaoh) said to the Chiefs around him: "This is indeed a sorcerer
well-versed: 35 His plan is to get you out of your land by his sorcery; then
what is it you counsel?" 36 They said: "Keep him and his brother in
suspense (for a while), and dispatch to the Cities heralds to collect—37
And bring up to you all (our) sorcerers well-versed."

38 So the sorcerers were got together for the appointment of a day
well-known, 39 And the people were told: "Are you (now) assembled?
—40 That we may follow the sorcerers (in religion) if they win?" 41 So
when the sorcerers arrived, they said to Pharaoh: "Of course—shall we
have a (suitable) reward if we win?" 42 He said: "Indeed, (and
more),—for you shall in that case be (raised to posts) nearest (to my
person)." 43 Moses said to them: "Throw you—that which you are about
to throw!" 44 So they threw their ropes and their rods, and said: "By the
might of Pharaoh, it is we who will certainly win!" 45 Then Moses threw
his rod, when, behold, it straightway swallows up all the falsehoods
which they fake!

46 Then did the sorcerers fall down, prostrate in adoration, 47 Saying: "We
believe in the Lord of the Worlds, 48 The Lord of Moses and Aaron." 49
Said (Pharaoh): "Believe you in Him before I give you permission?
Surely he is your leader, who has taught you sorcery! But soon shall you
know! Be sure I will cut off your hands and your feet on opposite sides,
and I will cause you all to die on the cross!" 50 They said: "No matter! For
us, we shall but return to our Lord! 51 Only, our desire is that our Lord

will forgive us our faults, that we may become foremost among the
believers!"

SECTION 4

52 By inspiration We told Moses: "Travel by night with My servants; for
surely you shall be pursued." 53 Then Pharaoh sent heralds to (all) the
Cities, 55 (Saying): "These (Israelites) are but a small band, 55 And they
are raging furiously against us; 56 But we are a multitude amply
forewarned."

57 So We expelled them from gardens, springs, 58 Treasures, and every
kind of honourable position; 59 Thus it was, but We made the Children of
Israel inheritors of such things.

60 So they pursued them at sunrise. 61 And when the two bodies saw each
other, the people of Moses said: "We are sure to be overtaken." 62(Moses)
said: "By no means! My Lord is with me! Soon will He guide me!" 63
Then We told Moses by inspiration: "Strike the sea with your rod." So it
divided, and each separate part became like the huge, firm mass of a
mountain. 64 And We made the other party approach thither. 65 We
delivered Moses and all who were with him; 66 But We drowned the
others. 67 Verily in this is a Sign: but most of them do not believe. 68 And
verily your Lord is He, the Exalted in Might, Most Merciful.

SECTION 5

69 And rehearse to them (something of) Abraham's story. 70 Behold, he
said to his father and his people: "What worship you?" 71 They said: "We
worship idols, and we remain constantly in attendance on them." 72 He
said: "Do they listen to you when you call (on them), 73 or do you good
or harm?" 74 They said: "Nay, but we found our fathers doing thus (what
we do)." 75 He said: "Do you then see whom you have been
worshipping,—76 You and your fathers before you?—77 For they are
enemies to me; not so the Lord and Cherisher of the Worlds; 78 Who
created me, and it is He Who guides me; 79 Who gives me food and drink,
80 And when I am ill, it is He Who cures me; 81 Who will cause me to die,
and then to live (again); 82 And who, I hope, will forgive me my faults on
the Day of Judgement...

83 "O my Lord! Bestow wisdom on me, and join me with the righteous;
84 Grant me honourable mention on the tongue of truth among the latest

(generations); 85 Make me one of the inheritors of the Garden of Bliss; 86
Forgive my father, for that he is among those astray; 87 And let me not be
in disgrace on the Day when (men) will be raised up—

88 "The Day whereon neither wealth nor sons will avail, 89 But only he
(will prosper) that brings to Allah a sound heart; 90 To the righteous, the
Garden will be brought near, 91 And to those straying in Evil, the Fire will
be placed in full view; 92 And it shall be said to them: 'Where are the
(gods) you worshipped—93 Besides Allah? Can they help you or help
themselves?' 94 Then they will be thrown headlong into the (Fire),—they
and those straying in Evil, 95 And the whole hosts of Iblīs together. 96
They will say there in their mutual bickerings: 97 'By Allah, we were truly
in an error manifest, 98 When we held you as equals with the Lord of the
Worlds; 99 And our seducers were only those who were steeped in guilt.
100 Now, then, we have none to intercede (for us), 101 Nor a single friend
to feel (for us). 102 Now if we only had a chance of return, we shall truly
be of those who believe!'"

103 Verily in this is a Sign but most of them do not believe. 104 And verily
your Lord is He, the Exalted in Might, Most Merciful.

SECTION 6

105 The people of Noah rejected the messengers. 106 Behold, their brother
Noah said to them: "Will you not fear (Allah)? 107 I am to you a
messenger worthy of all trust: 108 So fear Allah, and obey me. 109 No
reward do I ask of you for it: my reward is only from the Lord of the
Worlds: 110 So fear Allah, and obey me." 111 They said: "Shall we believe
in you when it is the meanest that follow you?" 112 He said: "And what do
I know as to what they do? 113 Their account is only with my Lord, if you
could (but) understand. 114 I am not one to drive away those who believe.
115 I am sent only to warn plainly in public." 116 They said: "If you desist
not, O Noah! you shall be stoned (to death)." 117 He said: "O my Lord!
Truly my people have rejected me. 118 Judge You, then, between me and
them openly, and deliver me and those of the Believers who are with
me." 119 So We delivered him and those with him, in the Ark filled (with
all creatures). 120 Thereafter We drowned those who remained behind. 121
Verily in this is a Sign: but most of them do not believe. 122 And verily
your Lord is He, the Exalted in Might, Most Merciful.

SECTION 7

123 The 'Ād (people) rejected the messengers. 124 Behold, their brother
Hūd said to them: "Will you not fear (Allah)? 125 I am to you a messenger
worthy of all trust: 126 So fear Allah and obey me. 127 No reward do I ask
of you for it: my reward is only from the Lord of the Worlds. 128 Do you
build a landmark on every high place to amuse yourselves? 129 And do
you get for yourselves fine buildings in the hope of living therein (for
ever)? 130 And when you exert your strong hand, do you do it like men of
absolute power? 131 Now fear Allah, and obey me. 132 Indeed, fear Him
Who has bestowed on you freely all that you know. 133 Freely has He
bestowed on you cattle and sons,—134 And Gardens and Springs. 135 Truly
I fear for you the Penalty of a great Day."

136 They said: "It is the same to us whether you admonish us or be not
among (our) admonishers! 137 This is no other than a customary device of
the ancients, 138 And we are not the ones to receive Pains and Penalties!"
139 So they rejected him, and We destroyed them. Verily in this is a Sign:
but most of them do not believe. 140 And verily your Lord is He, the
Exalted in Might, Most Merciful.

SECTION 8

141 The Thamūd (people) rejected the messengers. 142 Behold, their brother
Ṣāliḥ said to them: "Will you not fear (Allah)? 143 I am to you a
messenger worthy of all trust. 144 So fear Allah, and obey me. 145 No
reward do I ask of you for it: my reward is only from the Lord of the
Worlds. 146 Will you be left secure, in (the enjoyment of) all that you have
here?—147 Gardens and Springs, 148 And cornfields and date palms with
spathes near breaking (with the weight of fruit)? 149 And you carve houses
out of (rocky) mountains with great skill. 150 But fear Allah and obey me;
151 And follow not the bidding of those who are extravagant,—152 Who
make mischief in the land, and mend not (their ways)."

153 They said: "You are only one of those bewitched! 154 You are no more
than a mortal like us: then bring us a Sign, if you tell the truth!" 155 He
said: "Here is a she-camel: she has a right of watering, and you have a
right of watering, (severally) on a day appointed. 156 Touch her not with
harm, lest the Penalty of a great Day seize you." 157 But they hamstrung
her: then did they become full of regrets. 158 But the Penalty seized them.
Verily in this is a Sign: but most of them do not believe. 159 And verily

your Lord is He, the Exalted in Might, Most Merciful.

SECTION 9

160 The people of Lūṭ rejected the messengers. 161 Behold, their brother
Lūṭ said to them: "Will you not fear (Allah)? 162 I am to you a messenger
worthy of all trust. 163 So fear Allah and obey me. 164 No reward do I ask
of you for it: my reward is only from the Lord of the Worlds. 165 Of all
the creatures in the world, will you approach males, 166 And leave those
whom Allah has created for you to be your mates? Nay, you are a people
transgressing (all limits)!"

167 They said: "If you desist not, O Lūṭ! you will assuredly be cast out!"
168 He said: "I do detest your doings. 169 O my Lord! Deliver me and my
family from such things as they do!" 170 So We delivered him and his
family,—all, 171 Except an old woman[2] who lingered behind. 172 But the
rest We destroyed utterly. 173 We rained down on them a shower (of
brimstone): and evil was the shower on those who were admonished (but
heeded not)! 174 Verily in this is a Sign: but most of them do not believe.
175 And verily your Lord is He, the Exalted in Might, Most Merciful.

SECTION 10

176 The Companions of the Wood[3] rejected the messengers. 177 Behold,
Shu'ayb said to them: "Will you not fear (Allah)? 178 I am to you a
messenger worthy of all trust. 179 So fear Allah and obey me. 180 No
reward do I ask of you for it: my reward is only from the Lord of the
Worlds. 181 Give just measure, and cause no loss (to others by fraud). 182
And weigh with scales true and upright. 183 And withhold not things justly
due to men, nor do evil in the land, working mischief. 184 And fear Him
Who created you and (Who created) the generations before (you)."

185 They said: "You are only one of those bewitched! 186 You are no more
than a mortal like us, and indeed we think you are a liar! 187 Now cause
a piece of the sky to fall on us, if you are truthful!" 188 He said: "My Lord
knows best what you do." 189 But they rejected him. Then the punishment
of a day of overshadowing gloom seized them, and that was the Penalty

---

2. This was Lūṭ's wife, who lingered behind and was among those who perished. See 7:83. [3212]

3. See note to 15:78. [3214]

of a great Day. 190 Verily in that is a Sign: but most of them do not
believe. 191 And verily your Lord is He, the Exalted in Might, Most
Merciful.

SECTION 11

192 Verily this is a Revelation from the Lord of the Worlds: 193 With it
came down the spirit of Faith and Truth—194 To your heart and mind, that
you may admonish, 195 In the perspicuous Arabic tongue. 196 Without
doubt it is (announced) in the mystic Books of former peoples. 197 Is it not
a Sign to them that the Learned of the Children of Israel knew it (as true)?
198 Had We revealed it to any of the non-Arabs, 199 And had he recited it
to them, they would not have believed in it.

200 Thus have We caused it to enter the hearts of the sinners. 201 They will
not believe in it until they see the grievous Penalty; 202 But the (Penalty)
will come to them suddenly, while they perceive it not; 203 Then they will
say: "Shall we be respited?"

204 Do they then ask for Our Penalty to be hastened on? 205 See you? If We
do let them enjoy (this life) for a few years, 206 Yet there comes to them
at length the (Punishment) which they were promised! 207 It will profit
them not that they enjoyed (this life)! 208 Never did We destroy a
population, but had its warners—209 By way of reminder; and We never
are unjust.

210 No evil ones have brought down this (Revelation): 211 It would neither
suit them nor would they be able (to produce it). 212 Indeed they have been
removed far from even (a chance of) hearing it. 213 So call not on any
other god with Allah, or you will be among those under the Penalty. 214
And admonish your nearest kinsmen, 215 And lower your wing to the
Believers who follow you. 216 Then if they disobey you, say: "I am free
(of responsibility) for what you do!" 217 And put your trust on the Exalted
in Might, the Merciful,—218 Who see you standing forth (in prayer), 219
And your movements among those who prostrate themselves, 220 For it is
He Who hears and knows all things.

221 Shall I inform you, (O people!), on whom it is that the evil ones
descend? 222 They descend on every lying, wicked person, 223 (Into whose
ears) they pour hearsay vanities, and most of them are liars. 224 And the
Poets,—it is those straying in Evil, who follow them: 225 See you not that

they wander distracted in every valley?—226 And that they say what they practise not?—227 Except those who believe, work righteousness, engage much in the remembrance of Allah, and defend themselves only after they are unjustly attacked. And soon will the unjust assailants know what vicissitudes their affairs will take!□

Chapter 27

Sūrah Al-Naml
(The Ants)

Translator's Introduction

This Sūrah is cognate in subject to the one preceding it and the two following it. Its chronological place is also in the same group of four, in the middle Makkan period.

Here there is much mystic symbolism. Wonders in the physical world are types of greater wonders in the spiritual world. The Fire, the White Hand, and the Rod, in the story of Moses; the speech of birds, the crowds of *Jinns* and men pitted against a humble ant, and the Hoopoe and the Queen of Sheba, in Solomon's story; the defeat of the plot of the nine wicked men in the story of Ṣāliḥ; and the crime of sin with open eyes in the story of Lūṭ—lead up to the lessons of true and false worship and the miracles of Allah's grace and revelation.

Summary—Wonderful in Revelation, like the Fire which Moses saw, which was a glimpse of Allah's Glory, and His Miracles, which searched out those who refused Faith in spite of the light they had received (27:1-14).

Solomon knew the speech of Birds and had hosts of *Jinns* and men; yet the wise ant had ample defence against them: the Hoopoe who was absent at his muster, was yet serving him: the Queen of Sheba had a kingdom, but it submitted with conviction to the Wisdom of Solomon and the Kingdom of Allah (27:15-44).

Fools ascribe ill-luck to godliness as in Ṣālih's story, or fall into the lusts with their eyes open, as in Lūṭ's story; but their plots and their rage will be foiled by Allah (27:45-58).

Allah's glory and goodness are supreme over all Creation: Unfaith will yield to Faith in the final adjustment of values: so follow Revelation, serve Allah, and trust in Him (27:59-93).

*** *** ***

In the name of Allah,
Most Gracious, Most Merciful.

1 *Ṭā Sīn.*[1] These are verses of the Qur'an,—a Book that makes (things)
clear; 2 A Guide; and Glad Tidings for the Believers,—3 Those who
establish regular prayers and give in regular charity, and also have (full)
assurance of the Hereafter. 4 As to those who believe not in the Hereafter,
We have made their deeds pleasing in their eyes; and so they wander
about in distraction. 5 Such are they for whom a grievous Penalty is
(waiting); and in the Hereafter theirs will be the greatest loss. 6 As to you,
the Qur'an is bestowed upon you from the presence of One Who is Wise
and All-Knowing.

7 Behold! Moses said to his family: "I perceive a fire; soon will I bring
you from there some information, or I will bring you a burning brand to
light our fuel, that you may warm yourselves." 8 But when he came to the
(Fire), a voice was heard: "Blessed are those in the Fire and those around:
and Glory to Allah, the Lord of the Worlds. 9 O Moses! Verily, I am
Allah, the Exalted in Might, the Wise! 10 Now do you throw your rod!"
But when he saw it moving (of its own accord) as if it had been a snake,
he turned back in retreat, and retraced not his steps: "O Moses!" (it was
said), "Fear not: truly, in My presence, those called as messengers have
no fear,—11 But if any have done wrong and have thereafter substituted
good to take the place of evil, truly, I am Oft-Forgiving, Most Merciful.
12 Now put your hand into your bosom, and it will come forth white
without stain (or harm): (these are) among the nine Signs (you will
take)[2] to Pharaoh and his people: for they are a people rebellious in
transgression." 13 But when Our Signs came to them, that should have
opened their eyes, they said: "This is sorcery manifest!" 14 And they
rejected those Signs in iniquity and arrogance, though their souls were
convinced thereof: so see what was the end of those who acted corruptly!

---

1. See note to 26:1.

2. *Cf.* 7:133; 17:101. These are (1) the Rod (7:107), (2) the Radiant Hand (7:108), (3) the years of drought or shortage of water (7:130), (4) short crops (7:130), (5) epidemics among men and beasts (7:133), (6) locusts, (7) lice, (8) frogs, and (9) water turning to blood.(7:133) [1091]

SECTION 2

15 We gave (in the past) knowledge to David and Solomon: and they both
said: "Praise be to Allah, Who has favoured us above many of His
servants who believe!" 16 And Solomon was David's heir. He said: "O
you people! We have been taught the speech of birds, and on us has been
bestowed (a little) of all things: this is indeed Grace manifest (from
Allah)." 17 And before Solomon were marshalled his hosts,—of *Jinns* and
men and birds, and they were all kept in order and ranks. 18 At length,
when they came to a (lowly) valley of ants, one of the ants said: "O you
ants, get into your habitations, lest Solomon and his hosts crush you
(under foot) without knowing it." 19 So he smiled, amused at her speech;
and he said: "O my Lord! So order me that I may be grateful for Your
favours, which You have bestowed on me and on my parents, and that I
may work the righteousness that will please You: and admit me, by Your
Grace, to the ranks of Your righteous Servants."

20 And he took a muster of the Birds; and he said: "Why is it I see not the
Hoopoe? Or is he among the absentees? 21 I will certainly punish him
with a severe penalty, or execute him, unless he bring me a clear reason
(for absence)."

22 But the Hoopoe tarried not far: he (came up and) said: "I have
compassed (territory) which you have not compassed, and I have come
to you from Sabā'[3] with tidings true. 23 I found (there) a woman ruling[4]

---

3. Sabā' may reasonably be identified as the Biblical Sheba (1 Kings x. 1-10). It is further referred to in the Sūrah called after its name: 34:15-20. It was a city in Yemen, said to have been three days' journey (say 50 miles) from the city of Ṣan'ā'. A recent German explorer, Dr. Hans Helfritz, claims to have located it in what is now Ḥadhramawt territory. The famous dam of Ma'rīb made the country very prosperous and enabled it to attain a high degree of civilisation ("provided with every requisite" in the next verse). The Queen of Sheba therefore rightly held her head high until she saw the glories of Solomon. [3263]

4. The Queen of Sheba (by name Bilqīs in Arabian tradition) came apparently from Yemen, but she had affinities with Abyssinia and possibly ruled over Abyssinia also. The Ḥabasha tribe (after whom Abyssinia was named) came from Yemen. Between the southern coast of Yemen and the northeastern coast of Abyssinia there are only the Straits of Bāb al-Mandab, barely twenty miles across. In the 10th or 11th century B.C. there were frequent invasions of Abyssinia from Arabia, and Solomon's reign of 40 years is usually synchronised with 992 to 952 B.C. The Sabaean and Ḥimyarite alphabets, in which we find the south Arabian pre-Islamic inscriptions, passed into Ethiopic, the language of Abyssinia. The Abyssinians possess a traditional history called "The Book of the Glory of Kings"

over them and provided with every requisite; and she has a magnificent throne. 24 I found her and her people worshipping the sun besides Allah:[5] Satan has made their deeds seem pleasing in their eyes, and has kept them away from the Path,—so they receive no guidance,—25 (Kept them away from the Path), that they should not worship Allah, Who brings to light what is hidden in the heavens and the earth, and knows what you hide and what you reveal. 26 Allah!—there is no god but He!—Lord of the Throne Supreme!"

27 (Solomon) said: "Soon shall we see whether you have told the truth or lied! 28 Go you, with this letter of mine, and deliver it to them: then draw back from them, and (wait to) see what answer they return" 29 (The Queen) said: "You chiefs! Here is—delivered to me—a letter worthy of respect. 30 It is from Solomon, and is (as follows): 'In the name of Allah, Most Gracious, Most Merciful: 31 Be you not arrogant against me, but come to me in submission (to the true Religion).'"

SECTION 3

32 She said: "You chiefs! Advise me in (this) my affair: no affair have I decided except in your presence." 33 They said: "We are endued with strength, and given to vehement war: but the command is with you; so consider what you will command." 34 She said: "Kings, when they enter a country, despoil it, and make the noblest of its people its meanest; thus do they behave. 35 But I am going to send him a present, and (wait) to see with what (answer) return (my) ambassadors."

(*Kebra Negast*), which has been translated from Ethiopic into English by Sir E.A. Wallis Budge (Oxford, 1932). It gives an account of the Queen of Sheba and her only son Menyelek I, as founders of the Abyssinian dynasty. [3264]

5. The ancient religion of the people of Sabā' (the Ḥimyar or Sabaeans) consisted in the worship of the heavenly bodies, the sun, the planets, and the stars. Possibly the cult was connected with that of Chaldea, the homeland of Abraham: see 6:75-79 and notes thereon. Yemen had easy access to Mesopotamia and the Persian Gulf by way of the sea, as well as with Abyssinia. That accounts for the Christians of Najrān and the Jewish dynasty of kings (*e.g.*, Dhū Nuwās, d. A.C. 525) who persecuted them in the century before Islam—also for the Christian Abyssinian Governor Abrahah and his discomfiture in the year of the Prophet's birth (Sūrah 105), say A.C. 570. Jewish-Christian influences were powerful in Arabia in the sixth century of the Christian era.

The religion of these Sabaeans (written in Arabic with a *Sīn*) should not be confused with that of the Sabians (with a *Ṣād*), as to whom see 2:62. [3266]

36 Now when (the embassy) came to Solomon, he said: "Will you give me
abundance in wealth? But that which Allah has given me is better than
that which He has given you! Nay it is you who rejoice in your gift! 37 Go
back to them, and be sure we shall come to them with such hosts as they
will never be able to meet: we shall expel them from there in disgrace,
and they will feel humbled (indeed)." 38 He said (to his own men): "You
Chiefs! Which of you can bring me her throne before they come to me in
submission?" 39 Said an `Ifrīt,[6] of the *Jinns*: "I will bring it to you before
you rise from your council: indeed I have full strength for the purpose,
and may be trusted." 40 Said one who had knowledge of the Book: "I will
bring it to you within the twinkling of an eye!" Then when (Solomon)
saw it placed firmly before him, he said: "This is by the Grace of my
Lord!—to test me whether I am grateful or ungrateful! And if any is
grateful, truly his gratitude is (a gain) for his own soul; but if any is
ungrateful, truly my Lord is Free of all needs, Supreme in Honour!" 41 He
said: "Transform her throne out of all recognition by her: let us see
whether she is guided (to the truth) or is one of those who receive no
guidance."

42 So when she arrived, she was asked, "Is this your throne?" She said, "It
was just like this; and knowledge was bestowed on us in advance of this,
and we have submitted to Allah (in Islam)." 43 And he diverted her from
the worship of others besides Allah: for she was (sprung) of a people that
had no faith. 44 She was asked to enter the lofty Palace: but when she saw
it, she thought it was a lake of water, and she (tucked up her skirts),
uncovering her legs. He said: "This is but a palace paved smooth with
slabs of glass." She said: "O my Lord! I have indeed wronged my soul:
I do (now) submit (in Islam), with Solomon, to the Lord of the Worlds."

SECTION 4

45 We sent (aforetime), to the Thamūd, their brother Ṣāliḥ, saying, "Serve
Allah": but behold, they became two factions quarrelling with each other.
46 He said: "O my people! Why ask you to hasten on the evil in
preference to the good? If only you ask Allah for forgiveness, you may
hope to receive mercy." 47 They said: "Ill omen do we augur from you

---

6. *'Ifrīt*: a large, powerful *jinn*, reputed to be wicked and crafty: hence he is anxious to be recognised as one that "could be trusted". [3274]

and those that are with you." He said: "Your ill omen is with Allah;
indeed, you are a people under trial." 48 There were in the city nine men
of a family, who made mischief in the land, and would not reform. 49
They said: "Swear a mutual oath by Allah that we shall make a secret
night attack on him and his people, and that we shall then say to his heir
(when he seeks vengeance): 'We were not present at the slaughter of his
people, and we are positively telling the truth.'" 50 They plotted and
planned, but We too planned, even while they perceived it not. 51 Then
see what was the end of their plot!—this, that We destroyed them and
their people, all (of them). 52 Now such were their houses,—in utter
ruin,—because they practised wrong-doing. Verily in this is a Sign for
people of knowledge. 53 And We saved those who believed and practised
righteousness.

54 (We also sent) Lūṭ (as a messenger): behold, he said to his people, "Do
you do what is shameful though you see (its iniquity)? 55 Would you
really approach men in your lusts rather than women? Nay, you are a
people (grossly) ignorant!" 56 But his people gave no other answer but
this: they said, "Drive out the followers of Lūṭ from your city: these are
indeed men who want to be clean and pure!" 57 But We saved him and his
family, except his wife; her We destined to be of those who lagged
behind. 58 And We rained down on them a shower (of brimstone): and evil
was the shower on those who were admonished (but heeded not)!

SECTION 5

59 Say: Praise be to Allah, and Peace on His servants whom He has
chosen (for His Message). (Who) is better?—Allah or the false gods they
associate (with Him)?

PART XX

60 Or, who has created the heavens and the earth, and Who sends you
down rain from the sky? Indeed, with it We cause to grow well-planted
orchards full of beauty and delight: it is not in your power to cause the
growth of the trees in them. (Can there be another) god besides Allah?
Nay, they are a people who swerve from justice. 61 Or, who has made the
earth firm to live in; made rivers in its midst; set thereon mountains
immovable; and made a separating bar between the two bodies of flowing
water? (Can there be another) god besides Allah? Nay, most of them

know not. 62 Or, who listens to the (soul) distressed when it calls on Him,
and who relieves its suffering, and makes you (mankind) inheritors of the
earth? (Can there be another) god besides Allah? Little it is that you heed!
63 Or, who guides you through the depths of darkness on land and sea,
and who sends the winds as heralds of glad tidings, going before His
mercy? (Can there be another) god besides Allah?—High is Allah above
what they associate with Him! 64 Or, who originates Creation, then repeats
it, and who gives you sustenance from heaven and earth? (Can there be
another) god besides Allah? Say, "Bring forth your argument, if you are
telling the truth!" 65 Say: None in the heavens or on earth, except Allah,
knows what is hidden: nor can they perceive when they shall be raised up
(for Judgement). 66 Still less can their knowledge comprehend the
Hereafter: nay, they are in doubt and uncertainty thereof; nay, they are
blind thereunto!

SECTION 6

67 The Unbelievers say: "What! When we become dust,—we and our
fathers,—shall we really be raised (from the dead)? 68 It is true we were
promised this,—we and our fathers before (us): these are nothing but tales
of the ancients." 69 Say: "Go you through the earth and see what has been
the end of those guilty (of sin)." 70 But grieve not over them, nor distress
yourself because of their plots.

71 They also say: "When will this promise (come to pass)? (Say) if you
are truthful." 72 Say: "It may be that some of the events which you wish
to hasten on may be (close) in your pursuit!" 73 But verily your Lord is
full of grace to mankind: yet most of them are ungrateful. 74 And verily
your Lord knows all that their hearts do hide. As well as all that they
reveal. 75 Nor is there aught of the Unseen, in heaven or earth, but is
(recorded) in a clear record.

76 Verily this Qur'an does explain to the Children of Israel most of the
matters in which they disagree. 77 And it certainly is a Guide and a Mercy
to those who believe. 78 Verily your Lord will decide between them by
His Decree: and He is Exalted in Might, All-Knowing. 79 So put your trust
in Allah: for you are on (the path of) manifest Truth. 80 Truly you cannot
cause the Dead to listen, nor can you cause the Deaf to hear the call,
(especially) when they turn back in retreat. 81 Nor can you be a guide to
the Blind, (to prevent them) from straying: only those will you get to

listen who believe in Our Signs, and they will bow in Islam. 82 And when
the Word is fulfilled against them (the unjust), We shall produce from the
earth a Beast to (face) them:[7] he will speak to them, for that mankind did
not believe with assurance in Our Signs.

SECTION 7

83 One day We shall gather together from every people a troop of those
who reject Our Signs, and they shall be kept in ranks,—84 Until, when
they come (before the Judgement Seat), (Allah) will say: "Did you reject
My Signs, though you comprehended them not in knowledge, or what
was it you did?" 85 And the Word will be fulfilled against them, because
of their wrong-doing, and they will be unable to speak (in plea). 86 See
they not that We have made the night for them to rest in and the day to
give them light? Verily in this are Signs for any people that believe! 87
And the Day that the Trumpet will be sounded—then will be smitten with
terror those who are in the heavens, and those who are on earth, except
such as Allah will please (to exempt): and all shall come to His
(Presence) as beings conscious of their lowliness. 88 You see the
mountains and think them firmly fixed: but they shall pass away as the
clouds pass away: (such is) the artistry of Allah, Who disposes of all
things in perfect order: for He is well acquainted with all that you do. 89
If any do good, good will (accrue) to them therefrom; and they will be
secure from terror that Day. 90 And if any do evil, their faces will be
thrown headlong into the Fire: "Do you receive a reward other than that
which you have earned by your deeds?"

91 For me, I have been commanded to serve the Lord of this City, Him
Who has sanctified it and to Whom (belong) all things: and I am
commanded to be of those who bow in Islam to Allah's Will,—92 And to
rehearse the Qur'an: and if any accept guidance, they do it for the good
of their own souls, and if any stray, say: "I am only a Warner." 93 And
say: "Praise be to Allah, Who will soon show you His Signs, so that you
shall know them"; and your Lord is not unmindful of all that you do.□

---

7. The Beast will be one of the Signs of the Last Day to come, before the present World passes away and the new World is brought into being. If *taklimuhum* is read instead of *tukallimuhum,* it would mean that the Beast would wound them. [3313].

Chapter 28

Sūrah Al-Qaṣaṣ
(The Narration)

Translator's Introduction

This Sūrah continues the subject of Revelation and its reception by those to whom it is sent. But it emphasises new points: how the recipient of inspiration is prepared for his high destiny, even in the growth of his ordinary life, and how the rejection of Allah's Message by groups of men or by individuals is caused by overweening arrogance or avarice. The plight of those who reject the Truth is contrasted with the reward of the righteous.

With the possible exception of a few verses, it belongs to the late Makkan period, just preceding the Hijrah.

Summary—Pharaoh was arrogant and unjust, but Allah's Plan was to strengthen the weak: in infancy Moses was prepared for his mission; in youth he trusted in the Lord and was guided; in his exile he found help and love; and when he was called, he was supported by Allah (28:1-42).

So was the Holy Prophet Muḥammad fed spiritually by Allah's Grace, and his Revelation was recognised by those who knew the earlier Revelations: it came to an old and sacred Centre, to warn those seduced by this world's life (28:43-60).

The Future is with those who repent, have faith, and do good: for all Mercy and Truth are with Allah (28:61-75).

But men puffed up with wealth, like Qārūn, will come to an evil end, while the lowly and the righteous will attain Allah's Mercy (28:76-88).

*** *** ***

In the name of Allah,
Most Gracious, Most Merciful.

1 *Ṭā Sīn Mīm*.[1] 2 These are Verses of the Book that makes (things) clear.
3 We rehearse to you some of the story of Moses and Pharaoh in Truth,
for people who believe.

4 Truly Pharaoh elated himself in the land and broke up its people into
sections, depressing a small group among them: their sons he slew, but

1. See 26:1. [3326]

he kept alive their females: for he was indeed a maker of mischief. 5 And
We wished to be gracious to those who were being depressed in the land,
to make them leaders (in faith) and make them heirs, 6 To establish a firm
place for them in the land, and to show Pharaoh, Hāmān,[2] and their
hosts, at their hands, the very things against which they were taking
precautions.

7 So We sent this inspiration to the mother of Moses: "Suckle (your
child), but when you have fears about him, cast him into the river, but
fear not nor grieve: for We shall restore him to you, and We shall make
him one of Our messengers." 8 Then the people of Pharaoh picked him up
(from the river): (it was intended) that (Moses) should be to them an
adversary and a cause of sorrow: for Pharaoh and Hāmān and (all) their
hosts were men of sin. 9 The wife of Pharaoh said: "(Here is) a joy of the
eye, for me and for you: slay him not. It may be that he will be of use to
us, or we may adopt him as a son." And they perceived not (what they
were doing)! 10 But there came to be a void in the heart of the mother of
Moses: she was going almost to disclose his (case), had We not
strengthened her heart (with faith), so that she might remain a (firm)
believer. 11 And she said to the sister of (Moses), "Follow him" so she (the
sister) watched him in the character of a stranger. And they knew not. 12
And We ordained that he refused suck at first, until (his sister came up
and) said: "Shall I point out to you the people of a house that will nourish
and bring him up for you and be sincerely attached to him?"... 13 Thus did
We restore him to his mother, that her eye might be comforted, that she
might not grieve, and that she might know that the promise of Allah is
true: but most of them do not understand.

SECTION 2

14 When he reached full age, and was firmly established (in life), We
bestowed on him wisdom and knowledge: for thus do We reward those
who do good. 15 And he entered the City at a time when its people were
not watching: and he found there two men fighting,—one of his own
religion, and the other, of his foes. Now the man of his own religion
appealed to him against his foe, and Moses struck him with his fist and

2. Hāmān was evidently Pharaoh's minister, not to be confused with a Hāmān who is mentioned in the Old Testament (Esther iii. 1), as a minister of Ahasuerus (Xerxes) King of Persia, the same who invaded Greece, and ruled from 485 to 464 B.C. [3331]

made an end of him. He said: "This is a work of Evil (Satan): for he is an
enemy that manifestly misleads!" 16 He prayed: "O my Lord! I have
indeed wronged my soul! Do You then forgive me!" So (Allah) forgave
him: for He is Oft-forgiving, Most Merciful. 17 He said: "O my Lord! For
that You have bestowed Your Grace on me, never shall I be a help to
those who sin!" 18 So he saw the morning in the City, looking about, in a
state of fear, when behold, the man who had, the day before, sought his
help called aloud for his help (again). Moses said to him: "You are truly,
it is clear, a quarrelsome fellow!" 19 Then, when he decided to lay hold
of the man who was an enemy to both of them, that man said: "O Moses!
Is it your intention to slay me as you slew a man yesterday? Your
intention is none other than to become a powerful violent man in the land,
and not to be one who sets things right!" 20 And there came a man,
running, from the furthest end of the City. He said: "O Moses! The Chiefs
are taking counsel together about you, to slay you: so get you away, for
I do give you sincere advice." 21 He therefore got away therefrom,
looking about, in a state of fear. He prayed: "O my Lord! Save me from
people given to wrong-doing."

SECTION 3

22 Then, when he turned his face towards (the land of) Madyan, he said:
"I do hope that my Lord will show me the smooth and straight Path." 23
And when he arrived at the watering (place) in Madyan, he found there
a group of men watering (their flocks), and besides them he found two
women who were keeping back (their flocks). He said: "What is the
matter with you?" They said: "We cannot water (our flocks) until the
shepherds take back (their flocks): and our father is a very old man." 24
So he watered (their flocks) for them; then he turned back to the shade,
and said: "O my Lord! Truly am I in (desperate) need of any good that
You do send me!" . . .

25 Afterwards one of the (damsels) came (back) to him, walking bashfully.
She said: "My father invites you that he may reward you for having
watered (our flocks) for us." So when he came to him and narrated the
story, he said: "Fear you not: (well) have you escaped from unjust
people." 26 Said one of the (damsels): "O my (dear) father! Engage him
on wages: truly the best of men for you to employ is the (man) who is
strong and trusty". . . 27 He said: "I intend to wed one of these my

daughters to you, on condition that you serve me for eight years; but if
you complete ten years, it will be (grace) from you. But I intend not to
place you under a difficulty: you will find me, indeed, if Allah wills, one
of the righteous." 28 He said: "Be that (the agreement) between me and
you: whichever of the two terms I fulfil, let there be no ill-will to me. Be
Allah a witness to what we say."

SECTION 4

29 Now when Moses had fulfilled the term, and was travelling with his
family, he perceived a fire in the direction of Mount Ṭūr. He said to his
family: "Tarry you; I perceive a fire; I hope to bring you from there some
information, or a burning firebrand, that you may warm yourselves." 30
But when he came to the (Fire), a voice was heard from the right bank of
the valley, from a tree in hallowed ground: "O Moses! Verily I am Allah,
the Lord of the Worlds. 31 Now do you throw your rod!" But when he saw
it moving (of its own accord) as if it had been a snake, he turned back in
retreat, and retraced not his steps: "O Moses!" (it was said), "Draw near,
and fear not: for you are of those who are secure. 32 Move your hand into
your bosom, and it will come forth white without stain (or harm), and
draw your hand close to your side (to guard) against fear. Those are the
two credentials from your Lord to Pharaoh and his Chiefs: for truly they
are a people rebellious and wicked." 33 He said: "O my Lord! I have slain
a man among them, and I fear lest they slay me. 34 And my brother
Aaron—he is more eloquent in speech than I: so send him with me as a
helper, to confirm (and strengthen) me: for I fear that they may accuse me
of falsehood." 35 He said: "We will certainly strengthen your arm through
your brother, and invest you both with authority, so they shall not be able
to touch you: with Our Signs shall you triumph,—you two as well as
those who follow you."

36 When Moses came to them with Our clear Signs, they said: "This is
nothing but sorcery faked up: never did we hear the like among our
fathers of old!" 37 Moses said: "My Lord knows best who it is that comes
with guidance from Him and whose End will be best in the Hereafter:
certain it is that the wrong-doers will not prosper." 38 Pharaoh said: "O
Chiefs! No god do I know for you but myself: therefore, O Hāmān! light
me a (kiln to bake bricks) out of clay, and build me a lofty palace, that I
may mount up to the god of Moses: but as far as I am concerned, I think

(Moses) is a liar!" 39 And he was arrogant and insolent in the land, beyond
reason,—he and his hosts: they thought that they would not have to return
to Us! 40 So We seized him and his hosts, and We flung them into the sea:
now behold what was the end of those who did wrong! 41 And We made
them (but) leaders inviting to the Fire; and on the Day of Judgement no
help shall they find. 42 In this world We made a curse to follow them: and
on the Day of Judgement they will be among the loathed (and despised).

SECTION 5

43 We did reveal to Moses the Book after We had destroyed the earlier
generations, (to give) Insight to men, and Guidance and Mercy, that they
might receive admonition. 44 You were not on the Western side when We
decreed the commission to Moses, nor were you a witness (of those
events).[3] 45 But We raised up (new) generations, and long were the ages
that passed over them; but you were not a dweller among the people of
Madyan, rehearsing Our Signs to them; but it is We Who send
messengers (with inspiration). 46 Nor were you at the side of (the
Mountain of) Ṭūr when We called (to Moses). Yet (are you sent) as a
Mercy from your Lord, to give warning to a people to whom no warner
had come before you: in order that they may receive admonition. 47 If
(We had) not (sent you to the Quraysh),—in case a calamity should seize
them for (the deeds) that their hands have sent forth, they might say: "Our
Lord! Why did You not send us a messenger? We should then have
followed Your Signs and been amongst those who believe!"

48 But (now), when the Truth has come to them from Ourselves, they say,
"Why are not (Signs) sent to him, like those which were sent to Moses?"
Do they not then reject (the Signs) which were formerly sent to Moses?
They say: "Two kinds of sorcery, each assisting the other!" And they say:
"For us, we reject all (such things)!" 49 Say: "Then bring you a Book from
Allah, which is a better guide than either of them, that I may follow it!
(Do), if you are truthful!" 50 But if they listen not to you, know that they
only follow their own lusts: and who is more astray than one who follows
his own lusts, devoid of guidance from Allah? For Allah guides not
people given to wrong-doing.

---

3. The Sinai peninsula is in the northwest corner of Arabia. But the reference here is, I think, to the western side of the valley of Ṭuwā. Mount Ṭūr where Moses received the prophetic commission, is on the western side of the valley. [3376]

SECTION 6

51 Now have We caused the Word to reach them themselves, in order that
they may receive admonition. 52 Those to whom We sent the Book before
this,—they do believe in this (Revelation); 53 And when it is recited to
them, they say: "We believe therein, for it is the Truth from our Lord:
indeed we have been Muslims (bowing to Allah's Will) from before this.
54 Twice will they be given their reward, for that they have persevered,
that they avert Evil with Good, and that they spend (in charity) out of
what We have given them. 55 And when they hear vain talk, they turn
away therefrom and say: "To us our deeds, and to you yours; peace be to
you: we seek not the ignorant." 56 It is true you will not be able to guide
everyone,[4] whom you love; but Allah guides those whom He will and He
knows best those who receive guidance.

57 They say: "If we were to follow the guidance with you, we should be
snatched away from our land." Have We not established for them a secure
sanctuary, to which are brought as tribute fruits of all kinds,—a provision
from Ourselves? But most of them understand not. 58 And how many
populations We destroyed, which exulted in their life (of ease and
plenty)! Now those habitations of theirs, after them, are deserted,—all but
a (miserable) few! And We are their heirs! 59 Nor was your Lord the one
to destroy a population until He had sent to its Centre a messenger,
rehearsing to them Our Signs; nor are We going to destroy a population
except when its members practise iniquity. 60 The (material) things which
you are given are but the conveniences of this life and the glitter thereof;
but that which is with Allah is better and more enduring: will you not
then be wise?

SECTION 7

61 Are (these two) alike?—one to whom We have made a goodly promise,

---

4. The immediate occasion for this was the death of Abū Ṭālib, an uncle whom the Holy Prophet loved dearly and who had befriended and protected him. The Prophet was naturally anxious that he should die in the profession of the true Faith, but the pagan Quraysh leaders persuaded him to remain true to the faith of his fathers. This was an occasion of disappointment and grief to the Prophet. We are told that in such circumstances we should not grieve. All whom we love do not necessarily share our views or beliefs. We must not judge. Allah will guide whom He pleases and as He pleases. He alone knows the true inwardness of things. [3388]

and who is going to reach its (fulfilment), and one to whom We have
given the good things of this life, but who, on the Day of Judgement, is
to be among those brought up (for punishment)? 62 That Day (Allah) will
call to them, and say "Where are My `partners'?—whom you imagined
(to be such)?" 63 Those against whom the charge will be proved, will say:
"our Lord! These are the ones whom we led astray: we led them astray,
as we were astray ourselves: we free ourselves (from them) in Your
presence: it was not us they worshipped." 64 It will be said (to them):
"Call upon your `partners' (for help)": they will call upon them, but they
will not listen to them; and they will see the Penalty (before them); (how
they will wish) `if only they had been open to guidance!'

65 That Day (Allah) will call to them, and say: "What was the answer you
gave to the messengers?" 66 Then the (whole) story that Day will seem
obscure to them (like light to the blind) and they will not be able (even)
to question each other.

67 But any that (in this life) had repented, believed, and worked
righteousness, will have hopes to be among those who achieve salvation.

68 Your Lord does create and choose as He pleases: no choice have they
(in the matter): Glory to Allah! And far is He above the partners they
ascribe (to Him)! 69 And your Lord knows all that their hearts conceal and
all that they reveal. 70 And He is Allah: there is no god but He. To Him be
praise, at the first and at the last: for Him is the Command, and to Him
shall you (all) be brought back.

71 Say: See you? If Allah were to make the night perpetual over you to the
Day of Judgement, what god is there other than Allah, who can give you
enlightenment? Will you not then listen? 72 Say: See you? If Allah were
to make the day perpetual over you to the Day of Judgement, what god
is there other than Allah, who can give you a night in which you can rest?
Will you not then see? 73 It is out of His Mercy that He has made for you
night and day,—that you may rest therein, and that you may seek of His
Grace;—and in order that you may be grateful.

74 The Day that He will call on them, He will say: "Where are My
`partners'?—whom you imagined (to be such)?" 75 And from each people

shall We draw a witness, and We shall say: "Produce your Proof": then shall they know that the Truth is in Allah (alone), and the (lies) which they invented will leave them in the lurch.

SECTION 8

76 Qārūn was doubtless,[5] of the people of Moses; but he acted insolently
towards them: such were the treasures We had bestowed on him that their
very keys would have been a burden to a body of strong men. Behold, his
people said to him: "Exult not, for Allah loves not those who exult (in
riches). 77 But seek, with the (wealth) which Allah has bestowed on you,
the Home of the Hereafter, nor forget your portion in this world: but do
you good, as Allah has been good to you, and seek not (occasions for)
mischief in the land: for Allah loves not those who do mischief." 78 He
said: "This has been given to me because of a certain knowledge which
I have." Did he not know that Allah had destroyed, before him, (whole)
generations,—which were superior to him in strength and greater in the
amount (of riches) they had collected? But the wicked are not called
(immediately) to account for their sins. 79 So he went forth among his
people in the (pride of his worldly) glitter. Said those whose aim is the
Life of this World: "Oh! That we had the like of what Qārūn has got! For
he is truly a lord of mighty good fortune!" 80 But those who had been
granted (true) knowledge said: "Alas for you! The reward of Allah (in the
Hereafter) is best for those who believe and work righteousness: but this
none shall attain, save those who steadfastly persevere (in good)." 81 Then
We caused the earth to swallow up him and his house; and he had not (the
least little) party to help him against Allah, nor could he defend himself.
82 And those who had envied his position the day before began to say on
the morrow: "Ah! It is indeed Allah Who enlarges the provision or
restricts it, to any of His servants He pleases! Had it not been that Allah

---

5. Qārūn is identified with the Korah of the English Bible. His story is told in Num. xvi. 1-35. He and his followers, numbering 250 men, rose in rebellion against Moses and Aaron, on the ground that their position and fame in the congregation entitled them to equality in spiritual matters with the Priests—that they were as holy as any, and they claimed to burn incense at the sacred Altar reserved for the Priests. They had an exemplary punishment: "the earth opened her mouth, and swallowed them up, and their houses, and all the men that appertained unto Korah, and all their goods: they, and all that appertained to them, went down alive into the pit, and the earth closed upon them: and they perished from among the congregation." [3404]

was gracious to us, He could have caused the earth to swallow us up! Ah! Those who reject Allah will assuredly never prosper."

SECTION 9

83 That Home of the Hereafter We shall give to those who intend not
high-handedness or mischief on earth: and the End is (best) for the
righteous. 84 If any does good, the reward to him is better than his deed;
but if any does evil, the doers of evil are only punished (to the extent) of
their deeds. 85 Verily He Who ordained the Qur'an for you, will bring you
back to the Place[6] of Return. Say: "My Lord knows best who it is that
brings true guidance, and who is in manifest error." 86 And you had not
expected that the Book would be sent to you except as a Mercy from your
Lord: therefore lend not you support in any way to those who reject
(Allah's Message). 87 And let nothing keep you back from the Signs of
Allah after they have been revealed to you: and invite (men) to your
Lord, and be not of the company of those who join gods with Allah. 88
And call not, besides Allah, on another god. There is no god but He.
Everything (that exists) will perish except His own Face. To Him belongs
the Command, and to Him will you (all) be brought back.□

---

6. *Place of Return*: (1) a title of Makkah; (2) the occasion when we shall be restored to the Presence of our Lord. It is said that this verse was revealed at *Juhfa*, on the road from Makkah to Madīnah, a short distance from Makkah, on the Hijrah journey. The Prophet was sad at heart, and this was given as consolation to him. If this was the particular occasion, the general meaning would refer the Place of Return to the occasion of the Resurrection, when all true values will be restored, however they may be disturbed by the temporary interference of Evil in this life. [3416]

Chapter 29

Sūrah Al-'Ankabūt (The Spider)

Translator's Introduction

This Sūrah is the last of the series begun with Sūrah 17, in which the growth of the spiritual man as an individual is considered, especially illustrated by the way in which the great Prophets were prepared for their work and received their mission, and the nature of Revelation in relation to the environments in which it was promulgated. (See Introduction to Sūrah 17.) It also closes the sub-series beginning with Sūrah 26, which is concerned with the spiritual Light, and the reactions to it at certain periods of spiritual history. (See Introduction to Sūrah 26.)

The last Sūrah closed with a reference to the doctrine of the *Ma'ād,* or final Return of Man to Allah. This theme is further developed here, and as it is continued in the subsequent three Sūrahs all bearing the Abbreviated Letters, *Alif Lām Mīm,* it forms a connecting link between the present series and those three Sūrahs.

In particular, emphasis is laid here on the necessity of linking actual conduct with the reception of Allah's revelation, and reference is again made to the stories of Noah, Abraham, and Lot among the Prophets, and the stories of Madyan, 'Ād, Thamūd, and Pharaoh among the rejecters of Allah's Message. This world's life is contrasted with the real Life of the Hereafter.

Chronologically the main Sūrah belongs to the late Middle Makkan period, but the chronology has no significance except as showing how clearly the vision of the Future was revealed long before the Hijrah, to the struggling Brotherhood of Islam.

Summary—Belief is tested by trial in life and practical conduct: though Noah lived 950 years, his people refused Faith, and Abraham's generation threatened to burn Abraham (29:1-27).

Lot's people not only rejected Allah's Message but publicly defied him in sin: the 'Ād and the Thamūd had intelligence but misused it, and Qārūn, Pharaoh, and Hāmān perished for their overweening arrogance: they found their worldly power as frail as a spider's web (29:28-44).

The Qur'an as a revelation stands on its own merits and is a Sign: it teaches the distinction between Right and Wrong, and shows the importance and excellence of the Hereafter (29:45-69).

*** *** ***

In the name of Allah,
Most Gracious, Most Merciful.

1 *Alif Lām Mīm.*[1]

2 Do men think that they will be left alone on saying, "We believe", and
that they will not be tested? 3 We did test those before them, and Allah
will certainly know those who are true from those who are false. 4 Do
those who practise evil think that they will get the better of Us? Evil is
their judgement! 5 For those whose hopes are in the meeting with Allah
(in the Hereafter, let them strive); for the Term (appointed) by Allah is
surely coming and He hears and knows (all things). 6 And if any strive
(with might and main), they do so for their own souls: for Allah is Free
of all needs from all creation.

7 Those who believe and work righteous deeds,—from them shall We blot
out all evil (that may be) in them, and We shall reward them according
to the best of their deeds. 8 We have enjoined on man kindness to parents:
but if they (either of them) strive (to force) you to join with Me (in
worship) anything of which you have no knowledge, obey them not. You
have (all) to return to Me, and I will tell you (the truth) of all that you did.
9 And those who believe and work righteous deeds,—them shall We
admit to the company of the Righteous.

10 Then there are among men such as say, "We believe in Allah"; but
when they suffer affliction in (the cause of) Allah, they treat men's
oppression as if it were the Wrath of Allah! And if help comes (to you)
from your Lord, they are sure to say, "We have (always) been with you!"
Does not Allah know best all that is in the hearts of all Creation? 11 And
Allah most certainly knows those who believe, and as certainly those who
are Hypocrites. 12 And the Unbelievers say to those who believe: "Follow
our path, and we will bear (the consequences) of your faults." Never in
the least will they bear their faults: in fact they are liars! 13 They will bear
their own burdens, and (other) burdens along with their own, and on the
Day of Judgement they will be called to account for their falsehoods.

---

1. For these Abbreviated Letters see note to 2:1 and see Introduction to this Sūrah. [3422]

SECTION 2

14 We (once) sent Noah to his people, and he tarried among them a
thousand years less fifty: but the Deluge overwhelmed them while they
(persisted in) sin. 15 But We saved him and the Companions of the Ark,
and We made the (Ark) a Sign for all peoples!

16 And (We also saved) Abraham: behold, he said to his people, "Serve
Allah and fear Him: that will be best for you—if you understand! 17 For
you do worship idols besides Allah, and you invent falsehood. The things
that you worship besides Allah have no power to give you sustenance:
then seek you sustenance from Allah, serve Him, and be grateful to Him:
to Him will be your return. 18 And if you reject (the Message), so did
generations before you: and the duty of the apostle is only to preach
publicly (and clearly)."

19 See they not how Allah originates creation, then repeats it: truly that is
easy for Allah. 20 Say: "Travel through the earth and see how Allah did
originate creation; so will Allah produce a later creation: for Allah has
power over all things. 21 He punishes whom He pleases, and He grants
mercy to whom He pleases, and towards Him are you turned. 22 Not on
earth nor in heaven will you be able (fleeing) to frustrate (His Plan), nor
have you, besides Allah, any protector or helper."

SECTION 3

23 Those who reject the Signs of Allah and the Meeting with Him (in the
Hereafter),—it is they who shall despair of My mercy: it is they who will
(suffer) a most grievous Penalty.

24 So naught was the answer of (Abraham's) people except that they said:
"Slay him or burn him." But Allah did save him from the Fire. Verily in
this are Signs for people who believe. 25 And he said: "For you, you have
taken (for worship) idols besides Allah, out of mutual love and regard
between yourselves in this life; but on the Day of Judgement you shall
disown each other and curse each other: and your abode will be the Fire,
and you shall have none to help." 26 But Lūṭ had faith in Him: He said: "I
will leave home for the sake of my Lord: for He is Exalted in Might, and
Wise." 27 And We gave (Abraham) Isaac and Jacob, and ordained among
his progeny Prophethood and Revelation, and We granted him his reward
in this life; and he was in the Hereafter (of the company) of the

Righteous.

28 And (remember) Lūṭ: behold, he said to his people: "You do commit
lewdness, such as no people in Creation (ever) committed before you. 29
Do you indeed approach men, and cut off the highway?—and practise
wickedness (even) in your councils?" But his people gave no answer but
this: they said: "Bring us the Wrath of Allah if you tell the truth." 30 He
said: "O my Lord! Help You me against people who do mischief!"

SECTION 4

31 When Our Messengers came to Abraham with the good news, they
said: "We are indeed going to destroy the people of this township: for
truly they are (addicted to) crime." 32 He said: "But there is Lūṭ there."
They said: "Well do we know who is there: we will certainly save him
and his following,—except his wife: she is of those who lag behind!" 33
And when Our Messengers came to Lūṭ, he was grieved on their account,
and felt himself powerless (to protect) them: but they said: "Fear you not,
nor grieve: we are (here) to save you and your following, except your
wife: she is of those who lag behind. 34 For we are going to bring down
on the people of this township a Punishment from heaven, because they
have been wickedly rebellious." 35 And We have left thereof an evident
Sign, for any people who (care to) understand.

36 To the Madyan (people) (We sent) their brother Shu'ayb. Then he said:
"O my people! Serve Allah, and fear the Last Day: nor commit evil on
the earth, with intent to do mischief." 37 But they rejected him: then the
mighty Blast seized them, and they lay prostrate in their homes by the
morning.

38 (Remember also) the 'Ād and the Thamūd (people): clearly will appear
to you from (the traces) of their buildings (their fate): the Evil One made
their deeds alluring to them, and kept them back from the Path, though
they were gifted with intelligence and skill. 39 (Remember also) Qārūn,
Pharaoh, and Hāmān: there came to them Moses with clear Signs, but
they behaved with insolence on the earth; yet they could not overreach
(Us). 40 Each one of them We seized for his crime: of them, against some
We sent a violent tornado (with showers of stones); some were caught by
a (mighty) Blast; some We caused the earth to swallow up; and some We
drowned (in the waters): it was not Allah Who injured (or oppressed)

them: they injured (and oppressed) their own souls.

41 The parable of those who take protectors other than Allah is that of the
Spider, who builds (to itself) a house; but truly the flimsiest of houses is
the Spider's house;—if they but knew. 42 Verily Allah does know of
(every thing) whatever that they call upon besides Him: and He is Exalted
(in power), Wise. 43 And such are the Parables We set forth for mankind,
but only those understand them who have Knowledge. 44 Allah created
the heavens and the earth in true (proportions): verily in that is a Sign for
those who believe.

PART XXI

SECTION 5

45 Recite what is sent of the Book by inspiration to you, and establish
regular Prayer: for Prayer restrains from shameful and unjust deeds; and
remembrance of Allah is the greatest (thing in life) without doubt. And
Allah knows the (deeds) that you do. 46 And dispute you not with the
People of the Book, except with means better (than mere disputation),
unless it be with those of them who inflict wrong (and injury): but say,
"We believe in the Revelation which has come down to us and in that
which came down to you; our Allah and your Allah is One; and it is to
Him we bow (in Islam)." 47 And thus (it is) that We have sent down the
Book to you. So the People of the Book believe therein, as also do some
of these (pagan Arabs): and none but Unbelievers reject Our Signs. 48 And
you were not (able) to recite a Book before this (Book came), nor are you
(able) to transcribe it with your right hand: in that case, indeed, would the
talkers of vanities have doubted. 49 Nay, here are Signs self-evident in the
hearts of those endowed with knowledge: and none but the unjust reject
Our Signs. 50 Yet they say: "Why are not Signs sent down to him from his
Lord?" Say: "The Signs are indeed with Allah: and I am indeed a clear
Warner." 51 And is it not enough for them that We have sent down to you
the Book which is rehearsed to them? Verily, in it is Mercy and a
Reminder to those who believe.

SECTION 6

52 Say: "Enough is Allah for a Witness between me and you: He knows
what is in the heavens and on earth. And it is those who believe in
vanities and reject Allah, that will perish (in the end)."

53 They ask you to hasten on the Punishment (for them): had it not been
for a term (of respite) appointed, the Punishment would certainly have
come to them: and it will certainly reach them,—suddenly, while they
perceive not! 54 They ask you to hasten on the Punishment: but, of a
surety, Hell will encompass the rejecters of Faith!—55 On the Day that the
Punishment shall cover them from above them and from below them, and
(a Voice) shall say: "Taste you (the fruits) of your deeds!"

56 O My servants who believe! Truly, spacious is My Earth: therefore
serve you Me—(and Me alone)! 57 Every soul shall have a taste of death:
in the end to Us shall you be brought back. 58 But those who believe and
work deeds of righteousness—to them shall We give a Home in
Heaven,—lofty mansions beneath which flow rivers,—to dwell therein
for ever;—an excellent reward for those who do (good)!—59 Those who
persevere in patience, and put their trust in their Lord and Cherisher.

60 How many are the creatures that carry not their own sustenance? It is
Allah Who feeds (both) them and you: for He hears and knows (all
things). 61 If indeed you ask them who has created the heavens and the
earth and subjected the sun and the moon (to His Law), they will certainly
reply, "Allah". How are they then deluded away (from the truth)? 62 Allah
enlarges the sustenance (which He gives) to whichever of His servants He
pleases; and He (similarly) grants by (strict) measure, (as He pleases): for
Allah has full knowledge of all things. 63 And if indeed you ask them who
it is that sends down rain from the sky, and gives life therewith to the
earth after its death, they will certainly reply, "Allah!" Say, "Praise be to
Allah!" But most of them understand not.

SECTION 7

64 What is the life of this world but amusement and play? But verily the
Home in the Hereafter,—that is life indeed, if they but knew. 65 Now, if
they embark on a boat, they call on Allah, making their devotion
sincerely (and exclusively) to Him; but when He has delivered them
safely to (dry) land, behold, they give a share (of their worship to
others)!—66 Disdaining ungratefully Our gifts, and giving themselves up
to (worldly) enjoyment! But soon will they know. 67 Do they not then see
that We have made a sanctuary secure, and that men are being snatched
away from all around them? Then, do they believe in that which is vain,
and reject the Grace of Allah? 68 And who does more wrong than he who

invents a lie against Allah or rejects the Truth when it reaches him? Is
there not a home in Hell for those who reject Faith? 69 And those who
strive in Our (Cause),—We will certainly guide them to Our Paths: for
verily Allah is with those who do right.□

Chapter 30

Sūrah Al-Rūm
(The Roman Empire)

Translator's Introduction

This Sūrah, as remarked in the Introduction to the last Sūrah, deals with the question of *Ma'ād* or the Final End of Things, from various points of view. In the last Sūrah, we saw that Revelation was linked up with Life and Conduct, and Time (looking backwards and forwards) figured forth the frailty of this Life. In this Sūrah the Time theme and its mystery are brought into relation with human history in the foreground and the evolution of the world in all its aspects in the background. The corruption introduced by man is cleared away by Allah, Whose Universal Plan points to the Hereafter. We shall see that the next two Sūrahs (31 and 32) present the theme in other aspects. All four are introduced with the Abbreviated Letters *Alif, Lām, Mīm*, which (without being dogmatic) I have suggested as symbolical of the Past, Present and Future.

The chronology of this Sūrah is significant. It was revealed about the 7th or 6th year *before* the Hijrah, corresponding to 615-616 of the Christian era, when the tide of Persian conquest over the Roman Empire was running strong. The Christian Empire of Rome had lost Jerusalem to the Persians, and Christianity had been humbled in the dust. At that time it seemed outside the bounds of human possibility, even to one intimately acquainted with the inner resources and conditions of the Persian and Roman armies and empires, that the tables would be turned and the position reversed within the space of eight or nine years. The pro-Persian Pagan Quraysh rejoiced exceedingly, and redoubled their taunts and persecution against the Holy Prophet, whose Message was a renewal of the Message of Christ preached in Jerusalem. Then was this passage 30:1-6 revealed, clearly foreshadowing the final defeat of Persia as a prelude to the destruction of the Persian Empire. There is no doubt about the prophecy and its fulfilment. For the exulting Pagans of Makkah laid a heavy wager against the fulfilment of the prophecy with Abū Bakr, and they lost it on its fulfilment.

But the rise and fall even of such mighty empires as the Persian and Roman Empires, were but small events on the chequerboard of Time, compared to a mightier movement that was taking birth in the promulgation of Islam. In the seventh or sixth year *before* the Hijrah, and for a year or two after the Hijrah, Islam was struggling in the world like the still small voice in the conscience of humanity. It was scarcely heeded, and when it sought to insist upon its divine claim, it was insulted, assaulted, persecuted, boycotted, and (as it seemed) suppressed. The agony of Ṭā'if (two years before the Hijrah) and the murder-plot on the eve of the Hijrah were yet to come. But the purpose of Allah is not to be thwarted. Badr (A.H. 2 = A.C. 624), rightly called the critical Day of Decision, began to redress the balance of outward events in early Islam, in the same year in which Issus began to redress the balance of outward events in Perso-Roman relations. Mightier events were yet to come. A new inner World was being created through Islam. The spiritual Revolution was an infinitely greater moment in world history. The toppling down of priestcraft and false worship, the restoration of simplicity in faith and life, the rehabilitation of this life as the first step to the understanding of the Hereafter, the displacement of superstition and hair-splitting theology by a spirit of rational enquiry and knowledge, and the recognition of the divine as covering not merely an isolated thing called "Religion" but the whole way of Life, Thought, and Feeling—this was and is the true Message of Islam and its mission. Its struggle—its fight—continues, but it is not without effect, as may be seen in the march of centuries in world history.

Summary—The ebb and flow of worldly power—as symbolised in the conflict of the Persian and Roman Empires—are but outward events: the deeper meaning is in the working of Allah's Universe—how Good and Evil reach their final End (30:1-19).

The changes and changing variety in Allah's Creation, physical, moral, and spiritual, yet point to Unity in Nature and Religion: man should not break away from that Unity, but glorify Him, the One, for there is none like unto Him (30:20-40).

The hands of men have wrought corruption and mischief: but Allah purifies the moral world as He does the world of physical nature, strengthening the weak and pulling down the mighty in due season: wait therefore in patience and constancy, and be not depressed (30:41-60).

*** *** ***

In the name of Allah,
Most Gracious, Most Merciful.

1 *Alif Lām Mīm.*[1] 2 The Roman Empire[2] has been defeated,—3 In a land close by; but they, (even) after (this) defeat of theirs, will soon be

---

1. See 2:1 and Introduction to this Sūrah. [3504]

2. The remarkable defeats of the Roman Empire under Heraclius and the straits to which it was reduced were not merely isolated defeats; the Roman Empire lost most of its Asiatic territory and was hemmed in on all sides at its capital, Constantinople. The defeat, "in a land close by" must refer to Syria and Palestine. Jerusalem was lost in A.C. 614-15, shortly before this Sūrah was revealed. [3505]

victorious,[3]—4 Within a few years.[4] With Allah is the Decision, in the Past and in the Future: on that Day shall the Believers rejoice,—5 With the help of Allah. He helps whom He will, and He is Exalted in Might, Most Merciful. 6 (It is) the promise of Allah. Never does Allah depart from His promise: but most men understand not. 7 They know but the outer (things) in the life of this world: but of the End of things they are heedless.

8 Do they not reflect in their own minds? Not but for just ends and for a term appointed, did Allah create the heavens and the earth, and all between them: yet are there truly many among men who deny the meeting with their Lord (at the Resurrection)! 9 Do they not travel through the earth, and see what was the End of those before them? They were superior to them in strength: they tilled the soil and populated it in greater numbers than these have done: there came to them their messengers with clear (Signs). (Which they rejected, to their own destruction): it was not Allah Who wronged them, but they wronged their own souls. 10 In the long run evil in the extreme will be the End of those who do evil; for that they rejected the Signs of Allah, and held them up to ridicule.

SECTION 2

11 It is Allah Who begins (the process of) creation; then repeats it; then shall you be brought back to Him. 12 On the Day that the Hour will be established, the guilty will be struck dumb with despair. 13 No intercessor will they have among their "Partners" and they will (themselves) reject their "Partners". 14 On the Day that the Hour will be established,—that Day shall (all men) be sorted out. 15 Then those who have believed and

---

3. The Pagan Quraysh of Makkah rejoiced at the overthrow of Rome by Persia. They were pro-Persian, and in their heart of hearts they hoped that the nascent movement of Islam, which at that time was, from a worldly point of view, very weak and helpless, would also collapse under their persecution. But they misread the true Signs of the times. They are told here that they would soon be disillusioned in both their calculations, and it actually so happened at the battle of Issus in 622 (the year of Hijrah) and in 624, when Heraclius carried his campaign into the heart of Persia and the Makkan Quraysh were beaten off at Badr. [3506]

4. *Biḍ'* in the text means a short period—a period of from three to nine years. The period between the loss of Jerusalem (614-15) by the Romans and their victory at Issus (622) was seven years, and that to the penetration of Persia by Heraclius was nine years. See last note. [3507]

worked righteous deeds, shall be made happy in a Mead of Delight. 16
And those who have rejected Faith and falsely denied Our Signs and the
meeting of the Hereafter,—such shall be brought forth to Punishment.

17 So (give) glory to Allah, when you reach eventide and when you rise
in the morning; 18 Indeed, to Him be praise, in the heavens and on earth;
and in the late afternoon and when the day begins to decline. 19 It is He
Who brings out the living from the dead, and brings out the dead from the
living, and Who gives life to the earth after it is dead: and thus shall you
be brought out (from the dead).

SECTION 3

20 Among His Signs is this, that He created you from dust; and
then,—behold, you are men scattered (far and wide)! 21 And among His
Signs is this, that He created for you mates from among yourselves, that
you may dwell in tranquillity with them, and He has put love and mercy
between your (hearts): verily in that are Signs for those who reflect. 22
And among His Signs is the creation of the heavens and the earth, and the
variations in your languages and your colours: verily in that are Signs for
those who know. 23 And among His Signs is the sleep that you take by
night and by day, and the quest that you (make for livelihood) out of His
Bounty: verily in that are Signs for those who listen. 24 And among His
Signs, He shows you the lightning, by way both of fear and of hope, and
He sends down rain from the sky and with it gives life to the earth after
it is dead: verily in that are Signs for those who are wise. 25 And among
His Signs is this, that heaven and earth stand by His Command: then
when He calls you, by a single call, from the earth, behold, you
(straightway) come forth. 26 To Him belongs every being that is in the
heavens and on earth: all are devoutly obedient to Him. 27 It is He Who
begins (the process of) creation; then repeats it; and for Him it is most
easy. To Him belongs the loftiest similitude (we can think of) in the
heavens and the earth: for He is Exalted in Might, full of wisdom.

SECTION 4

28 He does propound to you a similitude from your own (experience): do
you have partners among those whom your right hands possess, to share

as equals in the wealth We have[5] bestowed on you? Do you fear them as
you fear each other? Thus do We explain the Signs in detail to a people
that understand. 29 Nay, the wrong-doers (merely) follow their own lusts,
being devoid of knowledge. But who will guide those whom Allah leaves
astray? To them there will be no helpers.

30 So set you your face steadily and truly to the Faith: (establish) Allah's
handiwork according to the pattern on which He has made mankind: no
change (let there be) in the work (wrought) by Allah: that is the standard
Religion: but most among mankind understand not. 31 Turn you back in
repentance to Him, and fear Him: establish regular prayers, and be not
you among those who join gods with Allah,—32 Those who split up their
Religion, and become (mere) Sects,—each party rejoicing in that which
is with itself!

33 When trouble touches men, they cry to their Lord, turning back to Him
in repentance: but when He gives them a taste of Mercy as from Himself,
behold, some of them pay part-worship to other gods besides their
Lord,—34 (As if) to show their ingratitude for the (favours) We have
bestowed on them! Then enjoy (your brief day); but soon will you know
(your folly). 35 Or have We sent down authority to them, which points out
to them the things to which they pay part-worship? 36 When We give men
a taste of Mercy, they exult thereat: and when some evil afflicts them
because of what their (own) hands have sent forth, behold, they are in
despair! 37 See they not that Allah enlarges the provision and restricts it,
to whomsoever He pleases? Verily in that are Signs for those who
believe.

38 So give what is due to kindred, the needy, and the wayfarer. That is
best for those who seek the Countenance, of Allah, and it is they who will
prosper. 39 That which you lay out for increase through the property of
(other) people, will have no increase with Allah: but that which you lay
out for charity, seeking the Countenance of Allah, (will increase): it is

---

5. Allah is far higher above His Creation than any, the highest, of His creatures can be above any, the lowest, of His creatures. And yet would a man share his wealth on equal terms with his dependants? Even what he calls his wealth is not really his own, but given by Allah. It is "his" in common speech by reason merely of certain accidental circumstances. How then can men raise Allah's creatures to equality with Allah in worship? [3536]

these who will get a recompense multiplied. 40 It is Allah Who has created
you: further, He has provided for your sustenance; then He will cause you
to die; and again He will give you life. Are there any of your (false)
"Partners" who can do any single one of these things? Glory to Him! And
High is He above the partners they attribute (to Him)!

SECTION 5

41 Mischief has appeared on land and sea because of (the meed) that the
hands of men have earned, that (Allah) may give them a taste of some of
their deeds: in order that they may turn back (from Evil). 42 Say: "Travel
through the earth and see what was the End of those before (you): most
of them worshipped others besides Allah." 43 But set you your face to the
right Religion, before there come from Allah the Day which there is no
chance of averting: on that Day shall men be divided (in two). 44 Those
who reject Faith will suffer from that rejection: and those who work
righteousness will spread their couch (of repose) for themselves (in
heaven): 45 That He may reward those who believe and work righteous
deeds, out of His Bounty. For He loves not those who reject Faith.

46 Among His Signs is this, that He sends the Winds, as heralds of Glad
Tidings, giving you a taste of His (Grace and) Mercy,—that the ships
may sail (majestically) by His Command and that you may seek of His
Bounty: in order that you may be grateful. 47 We did indeed send, before
you, messengers to their (respective) peoples, and they came to them with
clear Signs: then, to those who transgressed, We meted out Retribution:
and it was due from Us to aid those who believed.

48 It is Allah Who sends the Winds, and they raise the Clouds: then does
He spread them in the sky as He wills, and break them into fragments,
until you see raindrops issue from the midst thereof: then when He has
made them reach such of His servants as He wills, behold, they do
rejoice!—49 Even though, before they received (the rain)—just before
this—they were dumb with despair! 50 Then contemplate (O man!) the
memorials of Allah's Mercy!—how He gives life to the earth after its
death: verily the Same will give life to the men who are dead: for He has
power over all things. 51 And if We (but) send a Wind from which they
see (their tilth) turn yellow,—behold, they become, thereafter, ungrateful
(Unbelievers)! 52 So verily you cannot make the dead to hear, nor can you
make the deaf to hear the call, when they show their backs and turn away.

53 Nor can you lead back the blind from their straying: only those will you
make to hear, who believe in Our Signs and submit (their wills in Islam).

SECTION 6

54 It is Allah Who created you in a state of (helpless) weakness, then gave
(you) strength after weakness, then, after strength, gave (you) weakness
and a hoary head: He creates as He wills, and it is He Who has all
knowledge and power. 55 On the Day that the Hour (of reckoning) will be
established, the transgressors will swear that they tarried not but an hour:
thus were they used to being deluded! 56 But those endued with
knowledge and faith will say: "Indeed you did tarry, within Allah's
Decree, to the Day of Resurrection, and this is the Day of Resurrection:
but you—you were not aware!" 57 So on that Day no excuse of theirs will
avail the transgressors, nor will they be invited (then) to seek grace (by
repentance).

58 Verily We have propounded for men, in this Qur'an, every kind of
Parable: but if you bring to them any Sign, the Unbelievers are sure to
say, "You do nothing but talk vanities." 59 Thus does Allah seal up the
hearts of those who understand not. 60 So patiently persevere: for verily
the promise of Allah is true: nor let those shake your firmness, who have
(themselves) no certainty of faith.□

Chapter 31

Sūrah Luqmān

Translator's Introduction

The argument of the Final End of Things is here continued from another point of view. What is Wisdom? Where shall it be found? Will it solve the mysteries of Time and Nature, and that world higher than physical Nature, which brings us nearer to Allah? "Yes," is the answer: "if, as in the advice of Luqmān the Wise, human wisdom looks to Allah in true worship, ennobles every act of life with true kindness, but avoids the false indulgence that infringes the divine law—and in short follows the golden mean of virtue." And this is indicated by every Sign in nature.

The chronology of this Sūrah has no significance. In the main, it belongs to the late Makkan period.

Summary—The earnest seekers after righteousness receive guidance, unlike the seekers after vanity, who perish: all Creation bears witness to this: Wisdom, as expounded by Luqmān the Wise, is true service to Allah, and consists in moderation (31:1-19).

True Wisdom is firm and enduring, and discerns Allah's Law in the working of His Creation: it looks to the Final End of Things, whose mystery is only known to Allah (31:20-34).

*** *** ***

In the name of Allah,
Most Gracious, Most Merciful.

1 *Alif Lām Mīm*.[1] 2 These are Verses of the Wise Book,[2]—3 A Guide and

1. See n. 25 to 2:1 and Introduction to Sūrah 30. [3579]

2. This Sūrah relates to Wisdom and the Qur'an is appropriately called the Wise Book, or the Book of Wisdom. In verse 12 below there is a reference to Luqmān the Wise. "Wise" in this sense (*Ḥakīm*) means not only a man versed in knowledge human and divine, but one carrying out in practical conduct (*'amal*) the right course in life to the utmost of his power. His knowledge is correct and practical, but not necessarily complete: for no man is perfect. Such an ideal involves the conception of a man of heroic action as well as of deep and workman-like knowledge of nature and human nature—not merely dreams or speculation. That ideal was fulfilled in a most remarkable degree in the Holy Prophet, and in the sacred Book which was revealed through him. "The Wise Book" *(al-*

a Mercy to the Doers of Good,—4 Those who establish regular prayer,
and give regular charity, and have (in their hearts) the assurance of the
Hereafter. 5 These are on (true) guidance from their Lord; and these are
the ones who will prosper.

6 But there are, among men, those who purchase idle tales, without
knowledge (or meaning), to mislead (men) from the Path of Allah and
throw ridicule (on the Path): for such there will be a humiliating Penalty.
7 When Our Signs are rehearsed to such a one, he turns[3] away in
arrogance, as if he heard them not, as if there were deafness in both his
ears: announce to him a grievous Penalty. 8 For those who believe and
work righteous deeds, there will be Gardens of Bliss,—9 To dwell therein.
The promise of Allah is true: and He is Exalted in power, Wise.

10 He created the heavens without any pillars that you can see; He set on
the earth mountains standing firm, lest it should shake with you; and He
scattered through it beasts of all kinds. We send down rain from the sky,
and produce on the earth every kind of noble creature, in pairs. 11 Such is
the Creation of Allah: now show Me what is there that others besides Him
have created: nay, but the Transgressors are in manifest error.

SECTION 2

12 We bestowed (in the past) wisdom on Luqmān:[4] "Show (your)
gratitude to Allah." Any who is (so) grateful does so to the profit of his
own soul: but if any is ungrateful, verily Allah is free of all wants,
Worthy of all praise. 13 Behold, Luqmān said to his son by way of

---

kitāb al-ḥakīm) is one of the titles of the Qur'an. [3580]

3. Such men behave as if they had heard nothing of serious import, or laugh at serious teaching. The loss will be their own. They will miss the higher things of life and be left out of Allah's blessings. Ignorance and arrogance are in most cases the causes of their fall. [3585]

4. The sage Luqmān, after whom this Sūrah is called, belongs to Arab tradition. Very little is known of his life. He is usually associated with a long life, and his title is *Mu'ammar* (the long-lived). He is referred by some to the age of the 'Ād people, for whom see note to 7:65. He is the type of perfect wisdom. It is said that he belonged to a humble station in life, being a slave or a carpenter, and that he refused worldly power and a kingdom. Many instructive apologues are credited to him, similar to Aesop's Fables in Greek tradition. The identification of Luqmān and Aesop has no historical foundation, though it is true that the traditions about them influenced each other. [3593]

instruction: "O my son! Join not in worship (others) with Allah: for false
worship is indeed the highest wrong-doing." 14 And We have enjoined on
man (to be good) to his parents: in travail upon travail did his mother bear
him, and in years twain was his weaning: (hear the command), "Show
gratitude to Me and to your parents: to Me is (your final) Goal. 15 But if
they strive to make you join in worship with Me things of which you
have no knowledge, obey them not; yet bear them company in this life
with justice (and consideration), and follow the way of those who turn to
Me (in love): in the End the return of you all is to Me, and I will tell you
the truth (and meaning) of all that you did." 16 "O my son!" (said
Luqmān), "If there be (but) the weight of a mustard seed and it were
(hidden) in a rock, or (anywhere) in the heavens or on earth, Allah will
bring it forth: for Allah understands the finest mysteries, (and) is
well-acquainted (with them). 17 O my son! Establish regular prayer, enjoin
what is just, and forbid what is wrong: and bear with patient constancy
whatever betide you; for this is firmness (of purpose) in (the conduct of)
affairs. 18 And swell not your cheek (for pride) at men, nor walk in
insolence through the earth; for Allah loves not any arrogant boaster. 19
And be moderate in your pace, and lower your voice; for the harshest of
sounds without doubt is the braying of the ass."

SECTION 3

20 Do you not see that Allah has subjected to your (use) all things in the
heavens and on earth, and has made His bounties flow to you in
exceeding measure, (both) seen and unseen? Yet there are among men
those who dispute about Allah, without knowledge and without guidance,
and without a Book to enlighten them! 21 When they are told to follow the
(Revelation) that Allah has sent down, they say: "Nay, we shall follow the
ways that we found our fathers (following)." What! Even if it is Satan
beckoning them to the Penalty of the (blazing) Fire?

22 Whoever submits his whole self to Allah, and is a doer of good, has
grasped indeed the most trustworthy handhold: and with Allah rests the
End and Decision of (all) affairs. 23 But if any reject Faith, let not his
rejection grieve you: to Us is their return, and We shall tell them the truth
of their deeds: for Allah knows well all that is in (men's) hearts. 24 We
grant them their pleasure for a little while: in the end shall We drive them
to a chastisement unrelenting.

25 If you ask them, who it is that created the heavens and the earth, they
will certainly say, "Allah". Say: "Praise be to Allah!" But most of them
understand not. 26 To Allah belong all things in heaven and earth: verily
Allah is He (that is) Free of all wants, Worthy of all praise. 27 And if all
the trees on earth were pens and the Ocean (were ink), with seven Oceans
behind it to add to its (supply), yet would not the Words of Allah be
exhausted (in the writing): for Allah is Exalted in power, full of Wisdom.
28 And your creation or your resurrection is in no wise but as an
individual soul: for Allah is He Who hears and sees (all things). 29 See
you not that Allah merges Night into Day and He merges Day into Night;
that He has subjected the sun, and the moon (to His Law), each running
its course for a term appointed; and that Allah is well-acquainted with all
that you do? 30 That is because Allah is the (only) Reality, and because
whatever else they invoke besides Him is Falsehood; and because
Allah,—He is the Most High, Most Great.

SECTION 4

31 See you not that the ships sail through the Ocean by the grace of
Allah?—that He may show you of His Signs? Verily in this are Signs for
all who constantly persevere and give thanks. 32 When a wave covers
them like the canopy (of clouds), they call to Allah, offering Him sincere
devotion. But when He has delivered them safely to land, there are among
them those that halt between (right and wrong). But none reject Our Signs
except only a perfidious ungrateful (wretch)! 33 O mankind! Do your duty
to your Lord, and fear (the coming of) a Day when no father can avail
aught for his son, nor a son avail aught for his father. Verily, the promise
of Allah is true: let not then this present life deceive you, nor let the Chief
Deceiver deceive you about Allah. 34 Verily the knowledge of the Hour
is with Allah (alone). It is He Who sends down rain, and He Who knows
what is in the wombs. Nor does anyone know what it is that he will earn
on the morrow; nor does anyone know in what land he is to die. Verily
with Allah is full knowledge and He is acquainted (with all things).□

Chapter 32

Sūrah Al-Sajdah
(The Prostration)

Translator's Introduction

This short Sūrah closes the series of four *Alif, Lām, Mīm* Sūrahs, which began with the 29th. Its theme is the mystery of Creation, the mystery of Time and the mystery of the *Ma'ād* (the Final End) as viewed through the light of Allah's revelation. The contemplation of these mysteries should lead to Faith and the adoration of Allah. In chronology it belongs to the middle Makkan period and is therefore a little earlier than the last, but its chronology has no significance.

Summary—The mystery of Creation, the mystery of Time, and the mystery of the End of Things are but known by external symbols to man; Revelation brings faith and humble adoration, and is a blessing like Rain, which brings life to dead soil (32:1-30).

*** *** ***

In the name of Allah,
Most Gracious, Most Merciful.

1 *Alif Lām Mīm.*[1]

2 (This is) the revelation of the Book in which there is no doubt,—from
the Lord of the Worlds. 3 Or do they say, "He has forged it"? Nay, it is
the Truth from your Lord, that you may admonish a people to whom no
warner has come before you: in order that they may receive guidance.

4 It is Allah Who has created the heavens and the earth, and all between
them, in six Days, and is firmly established on the Throne (of authority):
you have none, besides Him, to protect or intercede (for you): will you
not then receive admonition? 5 He rules (all) affairs from the heavens to
the earth: in the end will (all affairs) go up to Him, on a Day, the space
whereof will be (as) a thousand years of your reckoning. 6 Such is He, the
Knower of all things, hidden and open, the Exalted (in power), the

1. See note to 2:1 and Introduction to Sūrah 30. [3628]

Merciful;—7 He Who has made everything which He has created most
good: He began the creation of man with (nothing more than) clay, 8 And
made his progeny from a quintessence of the nature of a fluid despised:
9 But He fashioned him in due proportion, and breathed into him
something of His spirit. And He gave you (the faculties of) hearing and
sight and feeling (and understanding): little thanks do you give! 10 And
they say: "What! When we lie, hidden and lost, in the earth, shall we
indeed be in a Creation renewed?" Nay, they deny the Meeting with their
Lord! 11 Say: "The Angel of Death, put in charge of you, will (duly) take
your souls: then shall you be brought back to your Lord."

SECTION 2

12 If only you could see when the guilty ones will bend low their heads
before their Lord, (saying:) "Our Lord! We have seen and we have heard:
now then send us back (to the world): we will work righteousness: for we
do indeed (now) believe." 13 If We had so willed, We could certainly have
brought every soul its true guidance: but the Word from Me will come
true, "I will fill Hell with *Jinns* and men all together." 14 "Taste you
then—for you forgot the Meeting of this Day of yours, and We too will
forget you—taste you the Penalty of Eternity for your (evil) deeds!" 15
Only those believe in Our Signs, who, when they are recited to them, fall
down in adoration, and celebrate the praises of their Lord, nor are they
(ever) puffed up with pride. 16 Their limbs do forsake their beds of sleep,
the while they call on their Lord, in Fear and Hope: and they spend (in
charity) out of the sustenance which We have bestowed on them. 17 Now
no person knows what delights of the eye are kept hidden (in reserve) for
them—as a reward for their (good) deeds.

18 Is then the man who believes no better than the man who is rebellious
and wicked? Not equal are they. 19 For those who believe and do
righteous deeds, are Gardens as hospitable homes, for their (good) deeds.
20 As to those who are rebellious and wicked, their abode will be the Fire:
every time they wish to get away therefrom, they will be forced thereinto,
and it will be said to them: "Taste you the Penalty of the Fire, the which
you were wont to reject as false." 21 And indeed We will make them taste
of the Penalty of this (life) prior to the supreme Penalty, in order that they
may (repent and) return. 22 And who does more wrong than one to whom
are recited the Signs of his Lord, and who then turns away therefrom?

Verily from those who transgress We shall exact (due) Retribution.

SECTION 3

23 We did indeed aforetime give the Book to Moses: be not then in doubt
of its reaching (you): and We made it a guide to the Children of Israel. 24
And We appointed, from among them, leaders, giving guidance under
Our command, so long as they persevered with patience and continued to
have faith in Our Signs. 25 Verily your Lord will judge between them on
the Day of Judgement, in the matters wherein they differ (among
themselves), 26 Does it not teach them a lesson, how many generations
We destroyed before them, in whose dwellings they (now) go to and fro?
Verily in that are Signs: do they not then listen? 27 And do they not see
that We do drive rain to parched soil (bare of herbage), and produce
therewith crops, providing food for their cattle and themselves? Have
they not the vision?

28 They say: "When will this decision be, if you are telling the truth?" 29
Say: "On the Day of Decision, no profit will it be to Unbelievers if they
(then) believe! Nor will they be granted a respite." 30 So turn away from
them, and wait: they too are waiting.□

Chapter 33

Sūrah Al-Aḥzāb (The Confederates)

Translator's Introduction

The series of mystic Sūrahs beginning with Sūrah 26 having been closed with the last Sūrah, we now come back to the hard facts of this life. Two questions are mainly considered here, *viz*., (1) the attempt by violence and brute force to crush the truth, and (2) the attempt by slander or unseemly conduct, to poison the relations of women with men.

As regards the first, the story of *Al-Aḥzāb* or the Confederates, who tried to surround and annihilate the Muslim community in Madīnah, is full of underhand intrigues on the part of such diverse enemies as the Pagan Quraysh, the Jews (Banū Naḍīr) who had already been expelled from Madīnah for their treachery, the Ghaṭfān tribe of Bedouin Arabs from the interior, and the Jewish tribe of Banū Qurayẓah in Madīnah. This was the unholy Confederacy against Islam. But though they caused a great deal of anxiety and suffering to the beleaguered Muslims, Islam came triumphantly out of the trial and became more firmly established than ever.

The Quraysh in Makkah had tried all sorts of persecution, boycott, insult, and bodily injuries to the Muslims, leading to their partial *Hijrah* to Abyssinia and their Hijrah as a body to Madīnah. The first armed conflict between them and the Muslims took place at Badr in Ramaḍān A.H. 2, when the Quraysh were signally defeated. (See note 3:13.) Next year (Shawwāl A.H. 3) they came to take revenge on Madīnah. The battle was fought at Uḥud, and though the Muslims suffered severely, Madīnah was saved and the Makkans had to return to Makkah with their object frustrated. Then they began to make a network of intrigues and alliances, and besieged Madīnah with a force of 10,000 men in Shawwāl and Dhū al-Qa'dah A.H. 5. This is the siege of the Confederates referred to in 33:9-27, which lasted over two weeks: some accounts give 27 days. It caused much suffering, from hunger, cold, an unceasing shower of arrows, and constant general or concentrated assaults. But it ended in the discomfiture of the Confederates, and established Islam firmer than ever. It was a well-organised and formidable attack, but the Muslims had made preparations to meet it. One of the preparations, which took the enemy by surprise, was the Trench (*Khandaq)* dug round Madīnah by the Prophet's order and under the supervision of Salmān the Persian. The siege and battle are therefore known as the Battle of the Trench or the Battle of the Confederates.

As regards the position and dignity of the ladies of the Prophet's Household and the Muslim women generally, salutary principles are laid down to safeguard their homes and protect them from slander and insult. The ladies of the Household interested themselves in social work and work of instruction for the Muslim women, and Muslim women were being trained more and more in community service. Two of them (the two Zaynabs) devoted themselves to the poor. The nursing of the wounded on or by the battlefield was specially necessary in those days of warfare. The Prophet's daughter Fāṭimah, then aged about 19 to 20, lovingly nursed her father's wounds at Uḥud (A.H. 3); Rufaydah nursed Sa'd ibn Mu'ādh's wounds at the Siege of Madīnah by the Confederates (A.H. 5); and in the Khaybar expedition (A.H. 7) Muslim women went out from Madīnah for nursing service.

A portion of this Sūrah sums up the lessons of the Battle of the Trench and must have been revealed some time after that Battle (Shawwāl A.H. 5). The marriage with Zaynab referred to in verse 37 also took place in the same year. Some portions (*e.g.*, verse 27) were probably revealed in A.H. 7 after the Khaybar settlement.

Summary—The pagan customs in human relationships should be abandoned, and men and women should be held in honour according to natural relationships and spiritual positions (33:1-8).

The Battle of the Trench and its lessons: hypocrites and their fears: Truth and noble examples to be followed (33:9-27).

High position and seemly conduct for the Prophet's wives: unhappy marriages (like Zaynab's) not to be perpetuated on false scruples: Prophet's wives to be treated kindly and gently (33:28-52).

Respect due to Prophet and his family: slander to be avoided and punished: guard your words and your responsibilities (33:53-73).

*** *** ***

In the name of Allah,
Most Gracious, Most Merciful.

1 O Prophet! Fear Allah, and listen not to the Unbelievers and the
Hypocrites:[1] verily Allah is full of knowledge and wisdom. 2 But follow

---

1. The fifth year A.H. was a critical year in the external history of early Islam, and this Sūrah must be read in the light of the events that then took place. As explained in the Introduction, the Grand Confederacy against Islam came and invested Madīnah and failed utterly. It consisted of the Makkan Unbelievers, the desert Arabs of Central Arabia, the Jews previously expelled for treachery from Madīnah, the Jews remaining in Madīnah, and the Hypocrites led by 'Abdullāh ibn Ubayy, who have already been described in 9:43-110. Their bond of union was the common hatred of Islam and it snapped under the reverses

that which comes to you by inspiration from your Lord: for Allah is well acquainted with (all) that you do. 3 And put your trust in Allah, and enough is Allah as a Disposer of affairs.

4 Allah has not made for any man two hearts in his (one) body: nor has He made your wives whom you divorce by *Ẓihār*[2] your mothers: nor has He made your adopted sons[3] your sons. Such is (only) your (manner of) speech by your mouths. But Allah tells (you) the Truth, and He shows the (right) Way. 5 Call them by (the names of) their fathers: that is juster in the sight of Allah. But if you know not[4] their father's (names, call them) your Brothers in faith, or your *Mawlās*. But there is no blame on you if you make a mistake[5] therein: (what counts is) the intention of your

---

they met with. It is important to note three points: (1) The Jews as a body now lost their last chance of bearing the standard of Islam: the best of them had already accepted the renewal of Allah's Message; (2) A definite status was given to the Prophet's household, after the slanders on 'Ā'ishah had been stilled (24:11-26), and the true position of the Mothers of the Believers had been cleared; (3) A further exposition of the purity of sexual relations was given, based on the story of Zaynab, the "Mother of the Poor". These points will be referred to in later notes. [3666]

2. This was an evil Arab custom, by which the husband selfishly deprived his wife of her conjugal rights and yet kept her to himself like a slave without her being free to remarry. He pronounced words implying that she was like his mother. After that she could not demand conjugal rights but was not free from his control and could not contract another marriage. See also 58:1-5, where this is condemned in the strongest terms and punishment is promised for it. A man sometimes said such words in a fit of anger: they did not affect him, but they degraded her position. [3670]

3. If a man called another's son "his son", it might create complications with natural and normal relationships if taken too literally. It is pointed out that it is not only *facon de parler* in men's mouths, and should not be taken literally. The truth is the truth and cannot be altered by men's adopting "sons": "Adoption" in the technical sense is not allowed in Muslim Law. Those who have been "wives of your sons proceeding from your loins" are within the Prohibited Degrees of marriage; 4:23; but this does not apply to "adopted" sons. [3671]

4. Freedmen were often called after their master's name as the "son of so and so". When they were slaves, perhaps their fathers' names were lost altogether. It is more correct to speak of them as the *Mawlā* of so and so. But *Mawlā* in Arabic might also imply a close relationship of friendship: in that case, too, it is better to use the right term instead of the term "son". "Brother" is not objectionable because "Brotherhood" is used in a wider sense than "fatherhood", and is not likely to be misunderstood. [3672]

5. What is aimed at is to destroy the superstition of erecting false relationships to the detriment of blood relations. It is not intended to penalise an unintentional slip in the

hearts: and Allah is Oft-Returning, Most Merciful.
6 The Prophet is closer to the Believers than their own selves, and his wives are their mothers. Blood-relations among each other have closer personal ties, in the Decree of Allah, than (the Brotherhood of) Believers and Muhājirs: nevertheless do you what is just to your closest friends: such is the writing in the Decree (of Allah).

7 And remember We took from the Prophets their Covenant: as (We did) from you: from Noah, Abraham, Moses, and Jesus the son of Mary: We took from them a solemn Covenant:
8 That (Allah) may question the (Custodians) of Truth concerning the Truth they (were charged with): and He has prepared for the Unbelievers a grievous Penalty.

SECTION 2

9 O you who believe! Remember the Grace of Allah, (bestowed) on you, when there came down on you hosts (to overwhelm you):[6] but We sent against them[7] a hurricane and forces that you saw not: but Allah sees (clearly) all that you do.
10 Behold! They came on you from above you and from below you, and behold, the eyes became dim and the hearts

---

matter, and indeed, even if a man deliberately calls another his son or father, who is not his son or father, out of politeness or affection, 'Allah is Oft-forgiving, Most Merciful'. It is the action of mischievous parties which is chiefly reprehended, if they intend false insinuations. A mere mistake on their part does not matter. [3673]

6. In this verse is summed up the beginning and the end of the fateful struggle of the Siege of Madīnah in A.H. 5. The composition of the unhallowed Confederacy that came to destroy Islam is referred to in the Introduction. They came with a force of ten to twelve thousand fighting men, an unprecedented army for that time and country. The battle is known as the Battle of the Trench. [3679]

7. After a close investment of two to four weeks, during which the enemy were disheartened by their lack of success, there was a piercing blast of the cold east wind. It was a severe winter, and February can be a very cold month in Madīnah, which is about 3,000 feet above sea level. The enemy's tents were torn up, their fires were extinguished, the sand and rain beat in their faces, and they were terrified by the portents against them. They had already well nigh fallen out amongst themselves, and beating a hasty retreat, they melted away. The Madīnah fighting strength was no more than 3,000, and the Jewish tribe of the Banū Qurayzah who were in their midst was a source of weakness as they were treacherously intriguing with the enemy. And further there were the Hypocrites: see note to 33:1 above. But there were hidden forces that helped the Muslims. Besides the forces of nature there were angels, though invisible to them, who assisted the Muslims. [3680]

gaped[8] up to the throats, and you imagined various (vain) thoughts about
Allah! 11 In that situation were the Believers tried: they were shaken as by
a tremendous shaking.

12 And behold! The Hypocrites and those in whose hearts is a disease
(even) say: "Allah and His Messenger promised us nothing but
delusions!"[9] 13 Behold! A party among them said: "You men of Yathrib!
You cannot stand (the attack)! Therefore go back!" And a band of them
ask for leave of the Prophet, saying, "Truly our houses[10] are bare and
exposed," though they were not exposed: they intended nothing but to run
away. 14 And if an entry had been effected to them from the sides of the
(City), and they had been incited to sedition, they would certainly have
brought it to pass, with none but a brief delay! 15 And yet they had already
covenanted with Allah not to turn their backs, and a covenant[11] with
Allah must (surely) be answered for. 16 Say: "Running away will not
profit you if you are running away from death or slaughter; and even if
(you do escape), no more than a brief (respite) will you be allowed to
enjoy!" 17 Say: "Who is it that can screen you from Allah if it be His wish
to give you Punishment or to give you Mercy?" Nor will they find for

---

8. The psychology of the combatants is described with matchless vigour in the Holy Text. The onrush of the enemy was really tremendous. The Trench round Madīnah was between the defenders and the huge attacking force, which had some high ground behind them "above you": when any of them came through the valley or over the Trench they seemed to come from below. The showers of arrows and stones on both sides must also have seemed to come from the air.[3682]

9. Before this year's mass attack on Madīnah, the Muslims had successfully reached the Syrian border to the north, and there were hopes of reaching Yemen in the south. The Holy Prophet had seen signs of expansion and victory for the Muslims. Now that they were shut within the Trench on the defensive, the Hypocrites taunted them with having indulged in delusive hopes. But the event showed that the hopes were *not* delusive. They were realised beyond expectations in a few years. [3683]

10. All the fighting men of Madīnah had come out of the City and camped in the open space between the City and the Trench that had been dug all round. The disaffected Hypocrites sowed defeatist rumours and pretended to withdraw for the defence of their homes, though their homes were not exposed, and were fully covered by the vigilant defensive forces inside the Trench. [3684]

11. Apparently, after the Battle of Uḥud, certain men who had shown cowardice were forgiven on undertaking that they would behave better next time. A solemn promise made to the Messenger of Allah is a promise to Allah, and it cannot be broken with impunity. [3686]

themselves, besides Allah, any protector or helper. 18 Verily Allah knows
those among you who keep back (men) and those who say to their
brethren, "Come along to us", but come not to the fight except for just a
little while, 19 Covetous over you. Then when fear comes, you will see
them looking to you, their eyes revolving, like (those of) one over whom
hovers death: but when the fear is past, they will smite you with sharp
tongues, covetous of goods. Such men have no faith, and so Allah has
made their deeds of none effect: and that is easy for Allah. 20 They think
that the Confederates have not withdrawn; and if the Confederates should
come (again), they would wish they were in the deserts (wandering)
among the Bedouins, and seeking news about you (from a safe distance);
and if they were in your midst, they would fight but little.

SECTION 3

21 You have indeed in the Messenger of Allah a beautiful pattern (of
conduct) for anyone whose hope is in Allah and the Final Day, and who
engages much in the praise of Allah. 22 When the Believers saw the
Confederate forces, they said: "This is what Allah and His Messenger had
promised us, and Allah and His Messenger told us what was true." And
it only added to their faith and their zeal in obedience. 23 Among the
Believers are men who have been true to their Covenant with Allah: of
them some have completed their vow (to the extreme), and some (still)
wait: but they have never changed (their determination) in the least: 24
That Allah may reward the men of Truth for their Truth, and punish the
Hypocrites if that be His Will, or turn to them in Mercy: for Allah is Oft-
Forgiving, Most Merciful.

25 And Allah turned back the Unbelievers for (all) their fury: no
advantage did they gain; and enough is Allah for the believers in their
fight. And Allah is full of Strength, Able to enforce His Will. 26 And those
of the People[12] of the Book who aided them—Allah did take them down

---

12. The Banū Qurayẓah (the Jewish tribe, who were bound by solemn engagements to help the defence of the city but intrigued with the enemies and treacherously aided them—*Ed.*) were filled with terror and dismay when Madīnah was free from the Qurayshī danger. They shut themselves up in their castles about three or four miles to the east (or north east) of Madīnah, and sustained a siege of 25 days, after which they surrendered, stipulating that they would abide by the decision of their fate at the hands of Sa'd ibn Mu'ādh, chief of the Aws tribe, with which they had been in alliance. [3702]

from their strongholds and cast terror into their hearts. (So that)[13] some you slew,[14] and some you made prisoners. 27 And He made you heirs of their lands, their houses, and their goods, and of a land which you had not frequented (before). And Allah has power over all things.

SECTION 4

28 O Prophet! Say to your Consorts: "If it be that you desire the life of this world, and its glitter,—then come![15] I will provide for your enjoyment

---

13. Sa'ad applied to them the Jewish Law of the Old Testament, not as strictly as the case warranted. In Deut. xx. 10-18, the treatment of a city "which is very far off from thee" is prescribed to be comparatively more lenient than the treatment of a city "of the people, which the Lord thy God does give thee for an inheritance," *i.e.*, which is near enough to corrupt the religion of the Jewish people. The punishment for these is total annihilation: "thou shalt save alive nothing that breatheth" (Deut. xx. 16). The more lenient treatment for far off cities is described in the next note. According to the Jewish standard, then, the Banū Qurayẓah deserved total extermination—of men, women, and children. They were in the territory of Madīnah itself, and further they had broken their engagements and helped the enemy. [3703]

14. Sa'ad adjudged them the mildest treatment of the "far-off" cities which is thus described in the Jewish Law: "Thou shalt smite every male thereof with the edge of the sword: but the women and the little ones, and the cattle, and all that is in the city, even all the spoil thereof, shalt thou take unto thyself; and thou shalt eat the spoil of thine enemies, which the Lord thy God hath given thee" (Deut. xx. 13-14). The men of the Qurayẓah were slain: the women were sold as captives of war; and their lands and properties were divided among the Muhājirs. [3704]

15. We now come to the subject of the position of the Consorts of Purity (*azwāj muṭahharāt*), the wives of the Holy Prophet. Their position was not like that of ordinary women or ordinary wives. They had special duties and responsibilities. The only youthful marriage of the Holy Prophet was his first marriage—that with Khadījah, the best of women and the best of wives. He married her fifteen years before he received the call to Prophethood; their married life lasted for twenty-five years, and their mutual devotion was of the noblest, judged by spiritual as well as social standards. During her life he had no other wife, which was unusual for a man of his standing among his people. When she died, his age was 50, and but for two considerations, he would probably never have married again, as he was most abstemious in his physical life. The two considerations which governed his later marriages were: (1) compassion and clemency, as when he wanted to provide for suffering widows, who could not be provided for in any other way in that stage of society; some of them, like Sawdā', had issue by their former marriage, requiring protection; (2) help in his duties of leadership, with women, who had to be instructed and kept together in the large Muslim family, where women and men had similar social rights. 'Ā'ishah, daughter of Abū Bakr, was clever and learned, and in *Hadīth* she is an important authority on the life of the Prophet. Zaynab, daughter of Khuzaymah, was specially devoted to the poor: she was called the "Mother of the Poor". The other Zaynab, daughter

and set you free in a handsome manner. 29 But if you seek Allah and His
Messenger, and the Home of the Hereafter, verily Allah has prepared for
the well-doers amongst you a great reward. 30 O Consorts of the Prophet!
If any of you were guilty of evident unseemly conduct, the Punishment
would be doubled to her, and that is easy for Allah.

PART XXII

31 But any of you that is devout in the service of Allah and His
Messenger, and works righteousness,—to her shall We grant her reward
twice: and We have prepared for her a generous Sustenance. 32 O
Consorts of the Prophet! You are not like any of the (other) women: if
you do fear (Allah), be not too complacent of speech, lest one in whose
heart is a disease should be moved with desire: but speak you a speech
(that is) just. 33 And stay quietly in your houses, and make not a dazzling
display, like that of the former Times of Ignorance; and establish regular
prayer, and give regular charity; and obey Allah and His Messenger. And
Allah only wishes to remove all abomination from you, you Members of
the Family, and to make you pure and spotless. 34 And recite what is
rehearsed to you in your homes, of the Signs of Allah and His Wisdom:
for Allah understands the finest mysteries and is well-acquainted (with
them)."

SECTION 5

35 For Muslim men and women,—for believing men and women, for devout men and women, for true men and women, for men and women who are patient and constant, for men and women who humble themselves, for men and women who give in charity, for men and women who fast (and deny themselves), for men and women who guard their chastity, and for men and women who engage much in Allah's praise,—for them has Allah prepared forgiveness and great reward.

---

of Jaḥsh, also worked for the poor, for whom she provided from the proceeds of her anual work, as she was skilled in leather work. But all the Consorts in their high position had to work and assist as Mothers of the *Ummah*. Theirs were not idle lives, like those of Odalisques, either for their own pleasure or the pleasure of their husband. They are told here that they had no place in the sacred Household if they merely wished for ease or worldly glitter. If such were the case, they could be divorced and amply provided for. [3706]

36 It is not fitting for a Believer, man or woman, when a matter has been decided by Allah and His Messenger, to have any option about their decision: if anyone disobeys Allah and His Messenger, he is indeed on a clearly wrong Path. 37 Behold! You did say to one who had received the grace of Allah[16] and your favour: "Retain you (in wedlock) your wife, and fear Allah." But you did hide in your heart[17] that which Allah was about to make manifest: you did fear the people, but it is more fitting that you should[18] fear Allah. Then when Zayd had dissolved (his marriage) with her, with the necessary (formality), We joined her in marriage to you: in order that (in future) there may be no difficulty to the Believers in (the matter of) marriage with the wives[19] of their adopted sons, when the latter have dissolved with the necessary (formality) (their marriage) with them. And Allah's command must be fulfilled. 38 There can be no difficulty to the Prophet in what Allah has indicated to him as a duty. It was the practice (approved) of Allah amongst those of old that have passed away. And the command of Allah is a decree determined. 39 (It is the practice of those) who preach the Messages of Allah, and fear Him, and fear none but Allah. And enough is Allah to call (men) to account. 40 Muḥammad is not the father of any of your men, but (he is) the

---

16. This was Zayd, son of Hārithah, one of the first to accept the faith of Islam. He was a freedman of the Holy Prophet, who loved him as a son and gave him in marriage to his own cousin Zaynab. The marriage however was not a happy one. See next note. [3722]

17. Zayd's marriage with the Prophet's cousin Zaynab, daughter of Jahsh, did not turn out to be a happy one. Zaynab the high-born looked down upon Zayd the freedman who had been a slave. And he was not comely to look at. Both were good people in their own way, and both loved the Prophet, but there was mutual incompatibility, and this is fatal to married life. Zayd wished to divorce her, but the Prophet asked him to hold his hand, and he obeyed. She was closely related to the Prophet; he had given a handsome marriage gift on her marriage to Zayd and people would certainly talk if such a marriage was broken off. But marriages are made on earth, not in heaven, and it is no part of Allah's Plan to torture people in a bond which should be a source of happiness but actually is a source of misery. Zayd's wish—indeed the mutual wish of the couple— was for the time being put away, but it became eventually an established fact, and everybody came to know of it. [3723]

18. All actual facts are referred to Allah. When the marriage is an unhappy one, Islam permits the bond to be dissolved, provided that all interests concerned are safeguarded. Apparently there was no issue here to be considered. Zaynab had to be considered, and she obtained the dearest wish of her heart in being raised to be a Mother of the Believers, with all the dignity and responsibility of that position. See note to 33:28 above. [3724]

19. The Pagan superstition and taboo about adopted sons had to be destroyed. See 33:4-5 and notes above. [3726]

Messenger of Allah, and the Seal of the Prophets: and Allah has full
knowledge of all things.

SECTION 6

41 O you who believe! Celebrate the praises of Allah, and do this often;
42 And glorify Him morning and evening. 43 He it is Who sends blessings
on you, as do His angels, that He may bring you out from the depths of
Darkness into Light: and He is Full of Mercy to the Believers. 44 Their
salutation on the Day they meet Him will be "Peace!"; and He has
prepared for them a generous Reward.

45 O Prophet! Truly We have sent you as a Witness, a Bearer of Glad
Tidings, and Warner,—46 And as one who invites to Allah's (Grace) by
His leave, and as a Lamp spreading Light. 47 Then give the Glad Tidings
to the Believers, that they shall have from Allah a very great Bounty. 48
And obey not (the behests) of the Unbelievers and the Hypocrites, and
heed not their annoyances, but put your trust in Allah. For enough is
Allah as a Disposer of affairs.

49 O you who believe! When you marry believing women, and then
divorce them before you have touched them, no period of *'Iddah* have
you to count in respect of them: so give them a present, and set them free
in a handsome manner.

50 O Prophet! We have made lawful to you your wives to whom you have
paid their dowers; and those whom your right hand possesses out of the
prisoners of war whom Allah has assigned to you; and daughters of your
paternal uncles and aunts, and daughters of your maternal uncles and
aunts, who migrated (from Makkah) with you; and any believing woman
who dedicates her soul to the Prophet if the Prophet wishes to wed
her;—this only for you, and not for the Believers (at large); We know
what We have appointed for them as to their wives and the captives
whom their right hands possess;—in order that there should be no
difficulty for you. And Allah is Oft-Forgiving, Most Merciful. 51 You
may defer (the turn of) any of them that you please, and you may receive
any you please: and there is no blame on you if you invite one whose
(turn) you hadst set aside. This is closer to the cooling of their eyes, the
prevention of their grief, and their satisfaction—that of all of them—with
that which you have to give them: and Allah knows (all) that is in your

hearts: and Allah is All-Knowing, Most Forbearing. 52 It is not lawful for
you (to marry more) women[20] after this, nor to change them for (other)
wives, even though their beauty attract you, except any your right hand
should possess (as handmaidens): and Allah does watch over all things.

SECTION 7

53 O you who believe! Enter not the Prophet's houses,—until leave is
given you,—for a meal, (and then) not (so early as) to wait for its
preparation: but when you are invited, enter; and when you have taken
your meal, disperse, without seeking familiar talk. Such (behaviour)
annoys the Prophet: he is ashamed to dismiss you, but Allah is not
ashamed (to tell you) the truth.

And when you ask (his ladies) for anything you want, ask them from before a screen: that makes for greater purity for your hearts and for theirs.

Nor is it right for you that you should annoy Allah's Messenger, or that
you should marry his widows after him at any time. Truly such a thing is
in Allah's sight an enormity. 54 Whether you reveal anything or conceal
it, verily Allah has full knowledge of all things. 55 There is no blame (on
these ladies if they appear) before their fathers or their sons, their
brothers, or their brothers' sons, or their sisters' sons, or their women, or
the (slaves) whom their right hands possess. And, (ladies), fear Allah; for
Allah is Witness to all things.

56 Allah and His Angels send blessings on the Prophet: O you that
believe! Send you blessings on him, and salute him with all respect. 57
Those who annoy Allah and His Messenger—Allah has cursed them in
this world and in the Hereafter, and has prepared for them a humiliating
Punishment. 58 And those who annoy believing men and women
undeservedly, bear (on themselves) a calumny and a glaring sin.

SECTION 8

59 O Prophet! Tell your wives and daughters, and the believing women,
that they should cast their outer garments over their persons (when

---

20. This was revealed in A.H. 7. After that the Prophet did not marry again, except the handmaiden, Mary the Copt, who was sent as a present by the Christian Muqawqas of Egypt. She became the mother of Ibrāhīm, who died in his infancy. [3754]

abroad): that is most convenient, that they should be known (as such) and
not molested. And Allah is Oft-Forgiving, Most Merciful. 60 Truly, if the
Hypocrites, and those in whose hearts is a disease, and those who stir up
sedition in the City, desist not, We shall certainly stir you up against
them: then will they not be able to stay in it as your neighbours for any
length of time: 61 They shall have a curse[21] on them: wherever they are
found, they shall be seized and slain (without mercy). 62 (Such was) the
practice (approved) of Allah among those who lived aforetime: no change
will you find in the practice (approved) of Allah.[22]

63 Men ask you concerning the Hour: say, "The knowledge thereof is with
Allah (alone)": and what will make you understand?—perchance the
Hour is nigh! 64 Verily Allah has cursed the Unbelievers and prepared for
them a blazing Fire,—65 To dwell therein for ever: no protector will they
find, nor helper. 66 The Day that their faces will be turned upside down
in the Fire, they will say: "Woe to us! Would that we had obeyed Allah
and obeyed the Messenger!" 67 And they would say: "Our Lord! We
obeyed our chiefs and our great ones, and they misled us as to the (right)
Path. 68 Our Lord! Give them double Penalty and curse them with a very
great Curse!"

SECTION 9

69 O you who believe! Be you not like those who vexed and insulted
Moses, but Allah cleared him of the (calumnies) they had uttered: and he
was honourable in Allah's sight. 70 O you who believe! Fear Allah, and
(always) say a word directed to the Right: 71 That He may make your
conduct whole and sound and forgive you your sins: he that obeys Allah
and His Messenger, has already attained the highest achievement.

---

21. This clearly refers to traitors, who will be deprived of the blessing and guidance of Allah. They sought to cause disorder in Allah's world – moral as well as material; but they will themselves be destroyed by the Law. Capital punishment is the only adequate punishment for treason and crimes of sustained concerted violence – for the protection of the hearths and homes of innocent citizens and the honour of their women. [3769]-Ed.

22. The Torah (law) that Madīnian Jews claimed to follow was much more severe: see notes to 33:26. That severity is mitigated in Islam. But it is a universal principle that any element which deliberately refuses to obey law and deliberately tries to subvert all order in society, secretly and openly, must be effectively suppressed, for the preservation of the life and health of the general community. [3770]- Ed.

72 We did indeed offer the Trust to the Heavens and the Earth and the
Mountains; but they refused to undertake it, being afraid thereof: but man
undertook it;—he was indeed unjust and foolish;—73 (With the result) that
Allah has to punish the Hypocrites, men and women, and the
Unbelievers, men and women, and Allah turns in Mercy to the Believers,
men and women: for Allah is Oft-Forgiving, Most Merciful.□

Chapter 34

Sūrah Saba'
(The City of Saba')

Translator's Introduction

Now we begin a series of Sūrah 34 to Sūrah 39 which recapitulate some of the features of the spiritual world. This Sūrah leads off with emphasis on Allah's Mercy and Power and Truth. Then (in Sūrah 35) we are told how angels manifest the Power of Allah, and how different is Good from Evil and Truth from Falsehood. Sūrah 36 is devoted to the Holy Prophet and the Qur'an that came through him. In Sūrah 37 the emphasis is on the snares of the Evil One; in Sūrah 38, on the conquest of evil by wisdom and power as in the case of David and Solomon, and by Patience and Constancy as in the case of Job; and in Sūrah 39, on the Final Judgement, which will sort out Faith from Unfaith and give to each its due.

The chronology has here no significance. This Sūrah belongs to the early Makkan period.

Summary—No Good or Truth is ever lost: Human Power and Prosperity are fleeting; but Allah's Power and Justice endure, and will enforce personal responsibility on man on the Last Day (34:1-30).

Faith and Unfaith will eventually find their true places and true values; Falsehood has no power: Truth is with Allah (34:31-54).

*** *** ***

In the name of Allah,
Most Gracious, Most Merciful.

1 Praise be to Allah, to Whom belong all things in the heavens and on
earth: to Him be Praise in the Hereafter: and He is Full of Wisdom,
acquainted with all things. 2 He knows all that goes into the earth, and all
that comes out thereof; all that comes down from the sky and all that
ascends thereto and He is the Most Merciful, the Oft-Forgiving.

3 The Unbelievers say, "Never to us will come the Hour": say, "Nay! But
most surely, by my Lord, it will come upon you;—by Him Who knows
the unseen,—from Whom is not hidden the least little atom in the heavens
or on earth: nor is there anything less than that, or greater, but is in the

Record Perspicuous: 4 That He may reward those who believe and work
deeds of righteousness: for such is Forgiveness and a Sustenance Most
Generous." 5 But those who strive against Our Signs, to frustrate
them,—for such will be a Penalty,—a Punishment most humiliating.

6 And those to whom knowledge has come see that the (Revelation) sent down to you from your Lord—that is the Truth, and that it guides to the Path of the Exalted (in Might), Worthy of all praise.

7 The Unbelievers say (in ridicule): "Shall we point out to you a man that
will tell you, when you are all scattered to pieces in disintegration, that
you shall (then be raised) in a New Creation? 8 Has he invented a
falsehood against Allah, or has a spirit (seized) him?"—Nay, it is those
who believe not in the Hereafter, that are in (real) Penalty, and in farthest
error. 9 See they not what is before them and behind them, of the sky and
the earth? If We wished, We could cause the earth to swallow them up,
or cause a piece of the sky to fall upon them. Verily in this is a Sign for
every devotee that turns to Allah (in repentance).

SECTION 2

10 We bestowed Grace aforetime on David from Ourselves: "O you
Mountains! Sing you back the Praises of Allah with him! And you birds
(also)!" And We made the iron soft for him;—11 (Commanding), "Make
you coats of mail, balancing well the rings of chain armour, and work you
righteousness; for be sure I see (clearly) all that you do."

12 And to Solomon (We made) the Wind (obedient): its early morning
(stride) was a month's (journey), and its evening (stride) was a month's
(journey); and We made a Font of molten brass to flow for him; and there
were *Jinns* that worked in front of him, by the leave of his Lord, and if
any of them turned aside from Our command, We made him taste of the
Penalty of the blazing Fire. 13 They worked for him as he desired,
(making) arches, images, basons as large as reservoirs, and (cooking)
cauldrons fixed (in their places): "Work you, sons of David, with thanks!
But few of My servants are grateful!"

14 Then, when We decreed (Solomon's) death, nothing showed them his death except a little worm of the earth, which kept (slowly) gnawing away at his staff: so when he fell down, the *Jinns* saw plainly that if they had known the unseen, they would not have tarried in the humiliating

Penalty (of their Task).

15 There was, for Saba',[1] aforetime, a Sign in their homeland—two
Gardens to the right and to the left. "Eat of the Sustenance (provided) by
your Lord, and be grateful to Him: a territory fair and happy, and a Lord
Oft-Forgiving!" 16 But they turned away (from Allah), and We sent
against them the Flood (released) from the Dams, and We converted their
two garden (rows) into "gardens" producing bitter fruit, and tamarisks,
and some few (stunted) Lote trees. 17 That was the Requital We gave them
because they ungratefully rejected Faith: and never do We give (such)
requital except to such as are ungrateful rejecters. 18 Between them and
the Cities on which We had poured our blessings, We had placed cities
in prominent positions, and between them We had appointed stages of
journey in due proportion: "Travel therein, secure, by night and by day."
19 But they said: "Our Lord! Place longer distances between our journey-
stages":[2] but they wronged themselves (therein). At length We made
them as a tale (that is told), and We dispersed them all in scattered
fragments. Verily in this are Signs for every (soul that is) patiently
constant and grateful. 20 And on them did Satan prove true his idea, and
they followed him, all but a party that believed. 21 But he had no authority
over them,—except that We might test the man who believes in the
Hereafter from him who is in doubt concerning it: and your Lord does
watch over all things.

SECTION 3

22 Say: "Call upon other (gods) whom you fancy, besides Allah: they have

---

1. This is the same city and territory in Yemen as is mentioned in 27:22: see note there as to its location. There the period was the time of Solomon and Queen Bilqīs. Here it is some centuries later. It was still a happy and prosperous country, amply irrigated from the Ma'rīb dam. Its roads or perhaps its canals, were skirted by gardens on both sides, right and left: at any given point you always saw two gardens. It produced fruit, spices, and frankincense, and got the name of Araby the Blest for that part of the country. [3810]

2. The covetous Saba' people, in order to get more profit from travellers' supplies by concentrating them on a few stations which they could monopolise, tended to choke off traffic and ruin the big trade. Selfishness often runs counter to true self-interest. It is historical fact that the great Yemen-Syria route in Arabia declined with the decline of Yemen. There were no doubt physical causes, but supreme above all were the moral causes, the grasping nature of the people, and their departure from the highest standards of righteousness. [3818]

no power,—not the weight of an atom,—in the heavens or on earth: no
(sort of) share have they therein, nor is any of them a helper to Allah. 23
No intercession can avail in His Presence, except for those for whom He
has granted permission. So far (is this the case) that, when terror is
removed from their hearts (at the Day of Judgement, then) will they say,
'What is it that your Lord commanded?' They will say, 'That which is
true and just; and He is the Most High, Most Great'." 24 Say: "Who gives
you sustenance, from the heavens and the earth?" Say: "It is Allah; and
certain it is that either we or you are on right guidance or in manifest
error!" 25 Say: "You shall not be questioned as to our sins, nor shall we
be questioned as to what you do." 26 Say: "Our Lord will gather us
together and will in the end decide the matter between us (and you) in
truth and justice: and He is the One to decide, the One Who knows all."
27 Say: "Show me those whom you have joined with Him as partners: by
no means (can you). Nay, He is Allah, the Exalted in Power, the Wise."
28 We have not sent you but as a universal (Messenger) to men, giving
them glad tidings, and warning them (against sin), but most men
understand not. 29 They say: "When will this promise (come to pass) if
you are telling the truth?" 30 Say: "The appointment to you is for a Day,
which you cannot put back for an hour nor put forward."

SECTION 4

31 The Unbelievers say: "We shall neither believe in this scripture nor in
(any) that (came) before it." Could you but see when the wrong-doers
will be made to stand before their Lord, throwing back the word (of
blame) on one another! Those who had been despised will say to the
arrogant ones: "Had it not been for you, we should certainly have been
believers!" 32 The arrogant ones will say to those who had been despised:
"Was it we who kept you back from Guidance after it reached you? Nay,
rather, it was you who transgressed." 33 Those who had been despised will
say to the arrogant ones: "Nay! It was a plot (of yours) by day and by
night: behold! you (constantly) ordered us to be ungrateful to Allah and
to attribute equals to Him!" They will declare (their) repentance when
they see the Penalty: We shall put yokes on the necks of the Unbelievers:
it would only be a requital for their (ill) Deeds.

34 Never did We send a warner to a population, but the wealthy ones
among them said: "We believe not in the (Message) with which you have

been sent." 35 They said: "We have more in wealth and in sons, and we
cannot be punished." 36 Say: "Verily my Lord enlarges and restricts the
Provision to whom He pleases, but most men understand not."

SECTION 5

37 It is not your wealth nor your sons, that will bring you nearer to Us in
degree: but only those who believe and work righteousness—these are the
ones for whom there is a multiplied Reward for their deeds, while secure
they (reside) in the dwellings on high! 38 Those who strive against Our
Signs, to frustrate them, will be given over into Punishment. 39 Say:
"Verily my Lord enlarges and restricts the Sustenance to such of His
servants as He pleases: and nothing do you spend in the least (in His
Cause) but He replaces it: for He is the Best of those who grant
Sustenance.

40 One Day He will gather them all together, and say to the angels, "Was
it you that these men used to worship?" 41 They will say, "Glory to You!
our (tie) is with You—as Protector—not with them. Nay, but they
worshipped the *Jinns*: most of them believed in them." 42 So on that Day
no power shall they have over each other, for profit or harm: and We
shall say to the wrong-doers, "Taste you the Penalty of the Fire,—the
which you were wont to deny!"

43 When Our clear Signs are rehearsed to them, they say, "This is only a
man who wishes to hinder you from the (worship) which your fathers
practised." And they say, "This is only a falsehood invented!" and the
Unbelievers say of the Truth when it comes to them, "This is nothing but
evident magic!" 44 But We had not given them Books which they could
study, nor sent messengers to them before you as warners. 45 And their
predecessors rejected (the Truth); these have not received a tenth of what
We had granted to those: yet when they rejected My messengers, how
(terrible) was My rejection (of them)!

SECTION 6

46 Say: "I do admonish you on one point: that you do stand up before
Allah,—(it may be) in pairs, or (it may be) singly,—and reflect (within
yourselves): your Companion is not possessed: he is no less than a warner
to you, in face of a terrible Penalty." 47 Say: "No reward do I ask of you:
it is (all) in your interest: my reward is only due from Allah: and He is

witness to all things." 48 Say: "Verily my Lord does cast the (mantle of)
Truth (over His servants),—He that has full knowledge of (all) that is
hidden." 49 Say: "The Truth has arrived, and Falsehood neither creates
anything new, nor restores anything." 50 Say: "If I am astray, I only stray
to the loss of my own soul: but if I receive guidance, it is because of the
inspiration of my Lord to me: it is He Who hears all things, and is (ever)
near."

51 If you could but see when they will quake with terror; but then there
will be no escape (for them), and they will be seized from a position
(quite) near. 52 And they will say, "We do believe (now) in the (Truth)";
but how could they receive (Faith) from a position (so) far off,—53 Seeing
that they did reject Faith (entirely) before, and that they (continually) cast
(slanders) on the Unseen from a position far off? 54 And between them
and their desires, is placed a barrier, as was done in the past with their
partisans: for they were indeed in suspicious (disquieting) doubt.□

Chapter 35

Sūrah Fāṭir
(The Originator of Creation)

Translator's Introduction

See Introduction to the last Sūrah.

This Sūrah deals with the mystery of Creation and its maintenance, with various forces typified by the wings of Angels. Whether we look to outer nature or to man, Allah's Grace proclaims His Glory, and protects His votaries from Evil.

It is an early Makkan Sūrah, but its chronology has no significance.

Summary—The forces which maintain Creation, as typified by angels, were themselves created by Allah, to Whom alone all praise is due: all else is naught (35:1-26).

All good is from Allah: who then will choose Evil, and reach the doom that goes with Evil? (35:27-45).

*** *** ***

In the name of Allah,
Most Gracious, Most Merciful.

1 Praise be to Allah, Who created (out of nothing) the heavens and the
earth, Who made the angels messengers with wings,—two, or three, or
four (pairs): He adds to Creation as He pleases: for Allah has power over
all things. 2 What Allah out of His Mercy does bestow on mankind there
is none can withhold: what He does withhold, there is none can grant,
apart from Him: and He is the Exalted in Power, full of Wisdom.

3 O men! Call to mind the grace of Allah unto you! Is there a Creator,
other than Allah, to give you sustenance from heaven or earth? There is
no god but He: how then are you deluded away from the Truth? 4 And if
they reject you, so were messengers rejected before you: to Allah go back
for decision all affairs. 5 O men! Certainly the promise of Allah is true.
Let not then this present life deceive you, nor let the Chief Deceiver

deceive you about Allah. 6 Verily Satan is an enemy to you: so treat him
as an enemy. He only invites his adherents, that they may become
companions of the blazing Fire. 7 For those who reject Allah, is a terrible
Penalty: but for those who believe and work righteous deeds, is
Forgiveness, and a magnificent Reward.

SECTION 2

8 Is he, then, to whom the evil of his conduct is made alluring, so that he
looks upon it as good, (equal to one who is rightly guided)? For Allah
leaves to stray whom He wills, and guides whom He wills. So let not your
soul go out in (vainly) sighing after them: for Allah knows well all that
they do! 9 It is Allah Who sends forth the Winds, so that they raise up the
Clouds, and We drive them to a land that is dead, and revive the earth
therewith after its death: even so (will be) the Resurrection! 10 If any do
seek for glory and power,—to Allah belong all glory and power. To Him
mount up (all) Words of Purity: it is He Who exalts each Deed of
Righteousness. Those that lay Plots of Evil,—for them is a Penalty
terrible; and the plotting of such will be void (of result). 11 And Allah did
create you from dust; then from a sperm drop; then He made you in pairs.
And no female conceives, or lays down (her load), but with His
knowledge. Nor is a man long-lived granted length of days, nor is a part
cut off from his life, but is in a Decree (ordained). All this is easy to
Allah. 12 Nor are the two bodies of flowing water alike,—the one
palatable, sweet, and pleasant to drink, and the other, salt and bitter. Yet
from each (kind of water) do you eat flesh fresh and tender, and you
extract ornaments to wear; and you see the ships therein that plough the
waves, that you may seek (thus) of the Bounty of Allah that you may be
grateful.

13 He merges Night into Day, and He merges Day into Night, and He has
subjected the sun and the moon (to His Law): each one runs its course for
a term appointed. Such is Allah your Lord: to Him belongs all Dominion.
And those whom you invoke besides Him have not the least power.[1] 14

---

1. Arabic *Qiṭmīr*, translated here "the least power", literally means "the thin, white skin that covers the date stone". It has neither strength nor texture, and has no value whatever. Anyone relying on any power other than that of Allah relies on nothing whatever. The *Qiṭmīr* is worse than the proverbial "broken reed". *Cf* 4:53 and 4:124, where the word *naqīr*, 'the groove in a date stone', is used similarly for a thing of no value or significance[3894].

If you invoke them, they will not listen to your call, and if they were to
listen, they cannot answer your (prayer). On the Day of Judgement they
will reject your "Partnership". And none, (O man!) can tell you (the
Truth) like the One Who is acquainted with all things.

SECTION 3

15 O you men! It is you that have need of Allah: but Allah is the One Free
of all wants, Worthy of all praise. 16 If He so pleased, He could blot you
out and bring in a New Creation. 17 Nor is that (at all) difficult for Allah.
18 Nor can a bearer of burdens bear another's burden. If one heavily laden
should call another to (bear) his load, not the least portion of it can be
carried (by the other), even though he be nearly related. You can but
admonish such as fear their Lord unseen and establish regular prayer.
And whoever purifies himself does so for the benefit of his own soul; and
the destination (of all) is to Allah.

19 The blind and the seeing are not alike; 20 Nor are the depths of
Darkness and the Light; 21 Nor are the (chilly) shade and the (genial) heat
of the sun: 22 Nor are alike those[2] that are living and those that are dead.
Allah can make any that He wills to hear; but you cannot make those to
hear who are (buried) in graves. 23 You are no other than a warner.[3] 24
Verily We have sent you in truth, as a bearer of glad tidings, and as a
warner: and there never was a people, without a warner having lived
among them (in the past). 25 And if they reject you, so did their
predecessors, to whom came their messengers with clear Signs, Books of
dark prophecies, and the Book of Enlightenment. 26 In the end did I
punish those who rejected Faith: and how (terrible) was My rejection (of
them)!

---

2. The final contrast between the Living and the Dead; those whose future has in it the promise of growth and fulfilment, and those who are inert and on the road to perish. With Allah everything is possible: He can give Life to the Dead. But the human Teacher should not expect that people who are (spiritually) dead and buried will by any chance hear his call. [3905]

3. The function of a Prophet is to preach Allah's Truth, to point out the right Way, to show men the need of repentance, and to warn them against the dangers which they incur by living a life of evil. He cannot compel them to accept the Truth or listen to the Message. [3906].

SECTION 4

27 See you not that Allah sends down rain from the sky? With it We then
bring out produce of various colours. And in the mountains are tracts
white and red, of various shades of colour, and black intense in hue. 28
And so amongst men and crawling creatures and cattle, are they of
various colours. Those truly fear Allah, among His Servants, who have
knowledge: for Allah is Exalted in Might, Oft-Forgiving. 29 Those who
rehearse the Book of Allah, establish regular prayer, and spend (in
charity) out of what We have provided for them, secretly and openly,
hope for a commerce that will never fail: 30 For He will pay them their
reward, nay, He will give them (even) more out of His Bounty: for He is
Oft-Forgiving, Most Ready to appreciate (service).

31 That which We have revealed to you of the Book is the
Truth,—confirming what was (revealed) before it: for Allah is
assuredly—with respect to His servants—well acquainted and Fully
Observant. 32 Then We have given the Book for inheritance to such of
Our servants as We have chosen: but there are among them some who
wrong their own souls; some who follow a middle course; and some who
are, by Allah's leave, foremost in good deeds; that is the highest Grace.
33 Gardens of Eternity will they enter: therein will they be adorned with
bracelets of gold and pearls; and their garments there will be of silk. 34
And they will say: "Praise be to Allah, Who has removed from us (all)
sorrow: for our Lord is indeed Oft-Forgiving, ready to appreciate (service):
35 Who has, out of His Bounty, settled us in a Home that will last: no toil nor
sense of weariness shall touch us therein."

36 But those who reject (Allah)—for them will be the Fire of Hell: no term
shall be determined for them, so they should die, nor shall its Penalty be
lightened for them. Thus do We reward every ungrateful one! 37 Therein
will they cry aloud (for assistance): "Our Lord! Bring us out: we shall
work righteousness, not the (deeds) we used to do!"—"Did We not give
you long enough life so that he that would should receive admonition?
And (moreover) the warner came to you. So taste you (the fruits of your
deeds): for the wrong-doers there is no helper."

SECTION 5

38 Verily Allah knows (all) the hidden things of the heavens and the earth:

verily He has full knowledge of all that is in (men's) hearts. 39 He it is that
has made you inheritors in the earth: if, then, any do reject (Allah), their
rejection (works) against themselves: their rejection but adds to the odium
for the Unbelievers in the sight of their Lord: their rejection but adds to
(their own) undoing. 40 Say: "Have you seen (these) 'Partners' of yours
whom you call upon besides Allah? Show Me what it is they have created
in the (wide) earth. Or have they a share in the heavens?" Or have We
given them a Book from which they (can derive) clear (evidence)?—Nay,
the wrong-doers promise each other nothing but delusions. 41 It is Allah
Who sustains the heavens and the earth, lest they cease (to function): and
if they should fail, there is none—not one—can sustain them thereafter:
verily He is Most Forbearing, Oft-Forgiving.

42 They swore their strongest oaths by Allah that if a warner came to
them, they would follow his guidance better than any (other) of the
Peoples: but when a warner came to them, it has only increased their
flight (from righteousness),—43 On account of their arrogance in the land
and their plotting of Evil, but the plotting of Evil will hem in only the
authors thereof. Now are they but looking for the way the ancients were
dealt with? But no change will you find in Allah's way (of dealing): no
turning off will you find in Allah's way (of dealing). 44 Do they not travel
through the earth, and see what was the End of those before
them,—though they were superior to them in strength? Nor is Allah to be
frustrated by anything whatever in the heavens or on earth: for He is All-
Knowing, All-Powerful. 45 If Allah were to punish men according to what
they deserve, He would not leave on the back of the (earth) a single living
creature: but He gives them respite for a stated Term: when their Term
expires, verily Allah has in His sight all His servants.□

Chapter 36

Sūrah Yā Sīn

Translator's Introduction

See Introduction to Sūrah 34. This particular Sūrah is devoted to the Holy Prophet and the Revelation which he brought. The Abbreviated Letters *Yā Sīn* are usually construed as a title of the Holy Prophet. But it is not permissible to be dogmatic about the meaning of Abbreviated Letters. This Sūrah is considered to be "the heart of the Qur'an", as it concerns the central figure in the teaching of Islam and the central doctrine of Revelation and the Hereafter. As referring to the Hereafter, it is appropriately read in solemn ceremonies after death.

In chronology it belongs to the middle or early Makkan period.

In Sūrah 37:130 (a cognate Sūrah) occurs the word *Ilyāsīn*.

Summary—The Qur'an is full of wisdom, and those are unfortunate who cannot profit by it: Parable of the City that defied—all but one—the Messengers of Grace and Mercy (36:1-32).

Various Signs of Allah in nature and Revelation (36:33-50).

The Resurrection and the Hereafter (36:51-83).

*** *** ***

In the name of Allah,
Most Gracious, Most Merciful.

1 *Yā Sīn.*[1] 2 By the Qur'an, full of Wisdom,—3 You are indeed one of the
messengers, 4 On a straight Way. 5 It is a Revelation sent down by (Him),
the Exalted in Might, Most Merciful. 6 In order that you may admonish

1. Some Commentators take *Yā* to be the vocative article, and *Sīn* to be the abbreviation of *Insān, Sīn* being the only "Firm Letter" in the word. In that case it would be an address to man. "O man!" But 'man' in this connection is understood to mean the Leader of man, the noblest of mankind, Muḥammad, the Prophet of Allah. For this Sūrah deals mainly with the Holy Prophet and his Message. But no dogmatic assertion can be made about the Abbreviated Letters, for which see note to Sūrah 2:1. *Yā Sīn* is usually treated as a title of the Holy Prophet. [3943]

a people, whose fathers had received[2] no admonition, and who therefore
remain heedless (of the Signs of Allah).

7 The Word is proved true against the greater part of them: for they do not
believe. 8 We have put yokes round their necks right up to their chins, so
that their heads are forced up (and they cannot see). 9 And We have put
a bar in front of them and a bar behind them, and further, We have
covered them up; so that they cannot see. 10 The same is it to them
whether you admonish them or you do not admonish them: they will not
believe.

11 You can but admonish such a one as follows the Message and fears the
(Lord) Most Gracious, unseen: give such a one, therefore, good tidings,
of Forgiveness and a Reward most generous. 12 Verily We shall give life
to the dead, and We record that which they send before and that which
they leave behind, and of all things have We taken account in a clear
Book (of evidence).

SECTION 2

13 Set forth to them, by way of a parable, the (story of) the Companions
of the City. Behold, there came messengers to it. 14 When We (first) sent
to them two messengers, they rejected them: but We strengthened them
with a third: they said, "Truly, we have been sent on a mission to you."
15 The (people) said: "You are only men like ourselves; and (Allah) Most
Gracious sends no sort of revelation: you do nothing but lie." 16 They
said: "Our Lord does know that we have been sent on a mission to you:
17 And our duty is only to proclaim the clear Message." 18 The (people)
said: "For us, we augur an evil omen from you: if you desist not, we will
certainly stone you. And a grievous punishment indeed will be inflicted
on you by us." 19 They said: "Your evil omens are with yourselves: (deem
you this an evil omen), if you are admonished? Nay, but you are a people
transgressing all bounds!" 20 Then there came running, from the farthest
part of the City, a man, saying, "O my people! Obey the messengers: 21
Obey those who ask no reward of you (for themselves), and who have
themselves received Guidance." 22 "It would not be reasonable in me if

---

2. The Quraysh had received no Prophet before, and therefore one of themselves was made the vehicle for the universal Message to the whole world. [3946]

I did not serve Him Who created me, and to Whom you shall (all) be
brought back. 23 Shall I take (other) gods besides Him? If (Allah) Most
Gracious should intend some adversity for me, of no use whatever will
be their intercession for me, nor can they deliver me. 24 I would indeed,
if I were to do so, be in manifest Error. 25 For me, I have faith in the Lord
of you (all): listen, then, to me!" 26 It was said: "Enter you the Garden."
He said: "Ah me! Would that my People knew (what I know)!—27 For
that my Lord[3] has granted me Forgiveness and has enrolled me among
those held in honour!"

PART XXIII

28 And We sent not down against his People, after him, any hosts from
heaven, nor was it needful for Us so to do. 29 It was no more than a single
mighty Blast, and behold! they were (like ashes) quenched and silent. 30
Ah! Alas for (My) servants! There comes not a messenger to them but
they mock him! 31 See they not how many generations before them We
destroyed? Not to them will they return: 32 But each one of them all—will
be brought before Us (for judgement).

SECTION 3

33 A Sign for them is the earth that is dead: We do give it life, and
produce grain therefrom, of which you do eat. 34 And We produce therein
orchards with date palms and vines, and We cause springs to gush forth
therein: 35 That they may enjoy the fruits of this (artistry): it was not their
hands that made this: will they not then give thanks? 36 Glory to Allah,
Who created in pairs all things that the earth produces, as well as their
own (human) kind and (other) things of which they have no knowledge.

37 And a Sign for them is the Night: We withdraw therefrom the Day, and
behold they are plunged in darkness; 38 And the Sun runs his course for
a period determined for him: that is the decree of (Him), the Exalted in
Might, the All-Knowing. 39 And the Moon,—We have measured for her

---

3. This man was just a simple honest soul, but he heard and obeyed the call of the prophets and obtained his spiritual desire for himself and did his best to obtain salvation for his people. For he loved his people and respected his ancestral traditions as far as they were good, but had no hesitation in accepting the new Light when it came to him. All his past was forgiven him and he was raised to dignity and honour in the Kingdom of Heaven. [3972]

mansions (to traverse) till she returns like the old (and withered) lower
part of a date stalk. 40 It is not permitted to the Sun to catch up the Moon,
nor can the Night outstrip the Day: each (just) swims along in (its own)
orbit (according to Law).

41 And a Sign for them is that We bore their race (through the Flood) in
the loaded Ark; 42 And We have created for them similar (vessels) on
which they ride. 43 If it were Our Will, We could drown them: then would
there be no helper (to hear their cry), nor could they be delivered, 44
Except by way of Mercy from Us, and by way of (worldly) convenience
(to serve them) for a time.

45 When they are told, "Fear you that which is before you and that which
will be after you, in order that you may receive Mercy," (they turn back).
46 Not a Sign comes to them from among the Signs of their Lord, but they
turn away therefrom. 47 And when they are told, "Spend you of (the
bounties) with which Allah has provided you," the Unbelievers say to
those who believe: "Shall we then feed those whom, if Allah had so
willed, He would have fed, (Himself)?—you are in nothing but manifest
error." 48 Further, they say, "When will this promise (come to pass), if
what you say is true?" 49 They will not (have to) wait for aught but a
single Blast: it will seize them while they are yet disputing among
themselves! 50 No (chance) will they then have, by will, to dispose (of
their affairs), nor to return to their own people!

SECTION 4

51 The trumpet shall be sounded, when behold! from the sepulchres (men)
will rush forth to their Lord! 52 They will say: "Ah! Woe unto us! Who
has raised us up from our beds of repose?" . . . (A voice will say:) "This
is what (Allah) Most Gracious had promised. And true was the word of
the messengers!" 53 It will be no more than a single Blast, when lo! they
will all be brought up before Us! 54 Then, on that Day, not a soul will be
wronged in the least, and you shall but be repaid the meeds of your past
Deeds.

55 Verily the Companions of the Garden shall that Day have joy in all that
they do; 56 They and their associates will be in groves of (cool) shade,
reclining on Thrones (of dignity); 57 (Every) fruit (enjoyment) will be
there for them; they shall have whatever they call for; 58 "Peace!"—a

word (of salutation) from a Lord Most Merciful!

59 "And O you in sin! Get you apart this Day! 60 Did I not enjoin on you,
O you Children of Adam, that you should not worship Satan; for that he
was to you an enemy avowed?—61 And that you should worship Me, (for
that) this was the straight Way? 62 But he did lead astray a great multitude
of you. Did you not, then, understand? 63 This is the Hell of which you
were (repeatedly) warned! 64 Embrace you the (Fire) this Day, for that
you (persistently) rejected (Truth)."

65 That Day shall We set a seal on their mouths. But their hands will
speak to Us, and their feet bear witness, to all that they did. 66 If it had
been Our Will, We could surely have blotted out their eyes; then should
they have run about groping for the Path, but how could they have seen?
67 And if it had been Our Will, We could have transformed them (to
remain) in their places; then should they have been unable to move about,
nor could they have returned (after error).

SECTION 5

68 If We grant long life to any, We cause him to be reversed in nature:
will they not then understand?

69 We have not instructed the (Prophet) in Poetry, nor is it meet for him:
this is no less than a Message and a Qur'an making things clear: 70 That
it may give admonition to any (who are) alive, and that the charge may
be proved against those who reject (Truth). 71 See they not that it is We
Who have created for them—among the things which Our hands have
fashioned—cattle, which are under their dominion?—72 And that We have
subjected them to their (use)? Of them some do carry them and some they
eat: 73 And they have (other) profits from them (besides), and they get
(milk) to drink. Will they not then be grateful? 74 Yet they take (for
worship) gods other than Allah, (hoping) that they might be helped! 75
They have not the power to help them: but they will be brought up
(before Our Judgement Seat) as a troop (to be condemned). 76 Let not
their speech, then, grieve you. Verily We know what they hide as well as
what they disclose.

77 Does not man see that it is We Who created him from sperm? Yet
behold! he (stands forth) as an open adversary! 78 And he makes
comparisons for Us, and forgets his own (origin and) creation: he says,

"Who can give life to (dry) bones and decomposed ones (at that)?" 79 Say, "He will give them life Who created them for the first time! For He is well-versed in every kind of creation!—80 The same Who produces for you fire out of[4] the green tree, when behold! you kindle therewith (your own fires)! 81 Is not He Who created the heavens and the earth able to create the like thereof?"—Yes, indeed! For He is the Creator Supreme, of skill and knowledge (infinite)! 82 Verily, when He intends a thing, His Command is, "be", and it is! 83 So glory to Him in Whose hands is the dominion of all things: and to Him will you all be brought back.□

---

4. Even older and more primitive than the method of striking fire against steel and flint is the method of using twigs of trees for the purpose. In the *E.B.*, 14th edition, 9:262, will be found a picture of British Guyana boys making a fire by rotating a stick in a round hole in a piece of wood lying on the ground. The Arab method was to use a wooden instrument called the *Zinād*. It consisted of two pieces to be rubbed together. The upper was called the *'Afār* or *Zand*, and the lower the *Markh*. The *markh* is a twig from a kind of spreading tree, the *Cynanchuin viminale*, of which the branches are bare, without leaves or thorns. When they are tangled together, and a wind blows, they get ignited and strike fire (Lane's Arabic Lexicon). In modern Arabic *Zand* is by analogy applied to the flint piece used for striking fire with steel. [4026]

Chapter 37

Sūrah Al-Ṣāffāt
(Those Ranged in Ranks)

Translator's Introduction

As explained in the Introduction to Sūrah 34, this is the fourth of a series of Sūrahs in which the mysteries of the spiritual world are manifested in different ways, tending to the defeat and final extirpation of Evil. The defeat of Evil is throughout connected with Revelation, and here the ranged fight is illustrated by a reference to the angels in heaven and to the earlier Prophets in our earthly history, from Noah to Jonah. In chronology, this Sūrah belongs to the early middle Makkan period.

Summary—Through all the mysteries of the heavens and the earth, there is a sorting out of the evil against the good: their final destinations contrasted (37:1-74).

Peace and victory came to Noah, Abraham, Moses and Aaron, Ilyās and Lūṭ, in their conflict with Evil (37:75-138).

So was it with Jonah when he glorified Allah. But men will ascribe to Allah what is unworthy of Him: Allah's Prophets strive for His glory, and shall be victorious (37:139-182).

*** *** ***

In the name of Allah,
Most Gracious, Most Merciful.

1 By[1] those who range themselves in ranks, 2 And so are strong in
repelling (evil), 3 And thus proclaim the Message (of Allah)![2] 4 Verily,

---

1. At a later stage, we shall study the general meaning of the adjurations in the Qur'an indicated by the particle *wa*. Here we may note that the last Sūrah (*Yā Sīn*) practically began with the adjuration "by the Qur'an, full of wisdom": emphasising the fact that Revelation was the evidence by which we could learn the highest wisdom of the spiritual world. Here our attention is called in three verses or clauses, to three definite attitudes which illustrate the triumph of Good and the frustration of Evil. See the notes following. [4030]

2. Two questions arise: (1) are the doers of the three things noted in verses 1-3 the same persons, whose actions or qualities are differently described, or are they three distinct sets of persons? (2) in either case, who are they? As to (1) the most authoritative view is

verily, your Allah is One!—5 Lord of the heavens and of the earth and all
between them, and Lord of every point at the rising of the sun!

6 We have indeed decked the lower heaven with beauty (in) the stars,—7
(For beauty) and for guard against all obstinate rebellious evil spirits, 8
(So) they should not strain their ears in the direction of the Exalted
Assembly but be cast away from every side, 9 Repulsed, for they are
under a perpetual penalty, 10 Except such as snatch away something by
stealth, and they are pursued by a flaming fire, of piercing brightness.

11 Just ask their[3] opinion: are they the more difficult to create, or the
(other) beings We have created? Them have We created out of a sticky
clay! 12 Truly do you marvel, while they ridicule, 13 And, when they are
admonished, pay no heed,—14 And, when they see a Sign, turn it to
mockery, 15 And say, "This is nothing but evident sorcery! 16 What! When
we die, and become dust and bones, shall we (then) be raised up (again)?
17 And also our fathers of old?" 18 Say you: "Indeed, and you shall then
be humiliated (on account of your evil)." 19 Then it will be a single
(compelling) cry; and behold, they will begin to see! 20 They will say,
"Ah! Woe to us! This is the Day of Judgement!" 21 (A voice will say,)
"This is the Day of Sorting Out, whose truth you (once) denied!"

SECTION 2

22 "Bring you up", it shall be said, "the wrong-doers and their wives, and
the things they worshipped—23 Besides Allah, and lead them to the Way
to the (fierce) Fire! 24 But stop them, for they must be asked: 25 'What is
the matter with you that you help not each other?'"

26 Nay, but that day they shall submit (to Judgement); 27 And they will

---

that the three clauses describe the same set of persons in different aspects. As to (2) some take them to refer to angels, and others understand by them the good men, the men of Allah, who strive and range themselves in Allah's service. The words are perfectly general, and I interpret them to refer to both classes. The feminine form is grammatically used in Arabic idiom for the indefinite plural. In 37:165 below, the word *ṣāffūn* is used in the definite plural, and seems to be spoken by these beings, angels or men of Allah or both, according to how we interpret this verse. [4031]

3. *Their*: "they" are the doubters, the evil ones, the deniers of Allah's grace and mercy, who laugh at Revelation and disbelieve in a Hereafter. Are they more important or more difficult to create than the wonderful variety of beings in Allah's spacious Creation? Do they forget their own lowly state, as having been created from muddy clay? [4040]

turn to one another, and question one another. 28 They will say: "It was
you who used to come to us from the right hand (of power and
authority)!"[4] 29 They will reply: "Nay, you yourselves had no Faith! 30
Nor had we any authority over you. Nay, it was you who were a people
in obstinate rebellion! 31 So now has been proved true, against us, the
Word of our Lord that we shall indeed (have to) taste (the punishment of
our sins). 32 We led you astray: for truly we were ourselves astray."

33 Truly, that Day, they will (all) share in the Penalty. 34 Verily that is how
We shall deal with Sinners. 35 For they, when they were told that there is
no god except Allah, would puff themselves up with Pride, 36 And say:
"What! Shall we give up our gods for the sake of a Poet possessed?"[5] 37
Nay! He has come with the (very) Truth, and he confirms (the Message
of) the messengers (before him). 38 You shall indeed taste of the grievous
Penalty;—39 But it will be no more than the retribution of (the Evil) that
you have wrought;—40 But the sincere (and devoted) Servants of
Allah,—41 For them is a Sustenance determined, 42 Fruits (Delights); and
they (shall enjoy) honour and dignity, 43 In Gardens of Felicity, 44 Facing
each other on Thrones (of dignity): 45 Round will be passed to them a Cup
from a clear-flowing fountain, 46 Crystal-white, of a taste delicious to
those who drink (thereof), 47 Free from headiness; nor will they suffer
intoxication therefrom. 48 And besides them will be chaste women,
restraining their glances, with big eyes (of wonder and beauty). 49 As if
they were (delicate) eggs closely guarded.

50 Then they will turn to one another and question one another. 51 One of
them will start the talk and say: "I had an intimate companion (on the
earth), 52 Who used to say, 'What! Are you amongst those who bear
witness to the truth (of the Message)? 53 When we die and become dust
and bones, shall we indeed receive rewards and punishments?'" 54 (A
voice) said: "Would you like to look down?" 55 He looked down and saw

---

4. This is the mutual recrimination of the sinners—those who sinned, against those whose instigation or evil example led them into sin. The misleaders in the life here below often used their power and influence to spread evil. The "right hand" is the hand of power and authority. Instead of using it for righteous purposes, they used it for evil,—selfishly for their own advantage, and mischievously for the degradation of others. [4052]

5. Possessed of an evil spirit, or mad. Such was the charge which the Unbelievers sometimes levelled at the Holy Prophet in the early stages of his preaching. [4057]

him in the midst of the Fire. 56 He said: "By Allah! You were little short
of bringing me to perdition! 57 Had it not been for the Grace of my
Lord,[6] I should certainly have been among those brought (there)! 58 Is it
(the case) that we shall not die, 59 Except our first death, and that we[7]
shall not be punished?" 60 Verily this is the supreme achievement! 61 For
the like of this let all strive, who wish to strive.

62 Is that the better entertainment or the Tree of *Zaqqūm*?[8] 63 For We
have truly made it (as) a trial for the wrong-doers. 64 For it is a tree that
springs out of the bottom of Hell-Fire: 65 The shoots of its fruit-stalks are
like the heads of devils: 66 Truly they will eat thereof and fill their bellies
therewith. 67 Then on top of that they will be given a mixture made of
boiling water. 68 Then shall their return be to the (blazing) Fire. 69 Truly
they found their fathers on the wrong Path; 70 So they (too) were rushed
down on their footsteps! 71 And truly before them, many of the ancients
went astray;—72 But We sent aforetime, among them, (messengers) to
admonish them;—73 Then see what was the end of those who were
admonished (but heeded not),—74 Except the sincere (and devoted)
Servants of Allah.

SECTION 3

75 (In the days of old), Noah cried to Us, and We are the best to hear
prayer. 76 And We delivered him and his people from the Great Calamity,
77 And made his progeny to endure (on this earth); 78 And We left (this
blessing) for him among generations to come in later times: 79 "Peace and
salutation to Noah among the nations!" 80 Thus indeed do We reward
those who do right. 81 For he was one of Our believing Servants. 82 Then
the rest We overwhelmed in the Flood.

---

6. And he gratefully acknowledges his shortcomings: "I should have been a sinner just like this, but for the grace of Allah!" He sees that if he had erred it would have been no excuse to plead the other man's example. He had Faith and was saved, to walk in the path of righteousness. [4069]

7. After he realises the great danger from which he narrowly escaped, his joy is so great that he can hardly believe it! Is the danger altogether past now? Are the portals of death closed for ever? Is he safe now from the temptations which will bring him to ruin and punishment? [4070]

8. *Cf.* 17:60. This bitter tree of Hell is a symbol of the contrast with the beautiful Garden of heaven with its delicious fruits. [4072]

83 Verily among those who followed His Way was Abraham. 84 Behold!
he approached his Lord with a sound heart. 85 Behold! he said to his
father and to his people, "What is that which you worship? 86 Is it a
Falsehood—gods other than Allah—that you desire? 87 Then what is your
idea about the Lord of the Worlds?" 88 Then did he cast a glance at the
Stars. 89 And he said, "I am indeed sick (at heart)!" 90 So they turned away
from him, and departed.

91 Then did he turn to their gods and said, "Will you not eat (of the
offerings before you)? 92 What is the matter with you that you speak not
(intelligently)?" 93 Then did he turn upon them, striking (them) with the
right hand. 94 Then came (the worshippers) with hurried steps, and faced
(him). 95 He said: "Worship you that which you have (yourselves) carved?
96 But Allah has created you and your handiwork!" 97 They said, "Build
him a furnace, and throw him into the blazing fire!" 98 (This failing), they
then sought a stratagem against him, but We made them the ones most
humiliated!

99 He said: "I will go to my Lord! He will surely guide me![9] 100 O my
Lord! Grant me a righteous (son)!" 101 So We gave him the good news[10]
of a boy ready to suffer and forbear. 102 Then, when (the son) reached (the
age of) (serious) work with him, he said: "O my son! I see in vision that
I offer you in sacrifice: now see what is your view!" (The son) said: "O
my father! Do as you are commanded: you will find me, if Allah so wills
one practising Patience and Constancy!" 103 So when they had both
submitted their wills (to Allah), and he had laid him prostrate on his
forehead (for sacrifice),[11] 104 We called out to him "O Abraham! 105 You

---

9. This was the *Hijrah* of Abraham. He left his people and his land, because the Truth was dearer to him than the ancestral falsehoods of his people. He trusted himself to Allah, and under Allah's guidance he laid the foundations of great peoples. See 21:69. [4095]

10. This was in the fertile land of Syria and Palestine. The boy thus born was, according to Muslim tradition, (which however is not unanimous on this point), the first-born son of Abraham, *viz.*, Ismā'īl. The name itself is from the root *Sami'a,* to hear, because Allah had heard Abraham's prayer (verse 100). Abraham's age when Ismā'īl was born was 86 (Gen. xvi. 16). [4096]

11. Our version may be compared with the Jewish-Christian version of the present Old Testament. The Jewish tradition, in order to glorify the younger branch of the family, descended from Isaac, ancestor of the Jews, as against the elder branch, descended from Ismā'īl, ancestor of the Arabs, refers this sacrifice to Isaac (Gen. xxii. 1-18). Now Isaac

have already fulfilled the vision!"—thus indeed do We reward those who
do right. 106 For this was obviously a trial—107 And We ransomed him
with a momentous sacrifice: 108 And We left (this blessing) for him
among generations (to come) in later times: 109 "Peace and salutation to
Abraham!" 110 Thus indeed do We reward those who do right. 111 For he
was one of Our believing Servants. 112 And We gave him the good news
of Isaac—a prophet,—one of the Righteous. 113 We blessed him and
Isaac: but of their progeny are (some) that do right, and (some) that
obviously do wrong, to their own souls.

SECTION 4

114 Again (of old) We bestowed Our favour on Moses and Aaron, 115 And
We delivered them and their people from (their) Great Calamity; 116 And
We helped them, so they overcame (their troubles); 117 And We gave them
the Book which helps to make things clear; 118 And We guided them to
the straight Way. 119 And We left (this blessing) for them among
generations (to come) in later times: 120 "Peace and salutation to Moses
and Aaron!" 121 Thus indeed do We reward those who do right. 122 For
they were two of Our believing Servants.

123 So also was Elias[12] among those sent (by Us). 124 Behold, he said to

---

was born when Abraham was 100 years old (Gen. xxi. 5), while Ismā'īl was born to Abraham when Abraham was 86 years old (Gen. xvi. 16) Ismā'īl was therefore 14 years older than Isaac. During his first 14 years Ismā'īl was the *only* son of Abraham; at no time was Isaac the only son of Abraham. Yet, in speaking of the sacrifice, the Old Testament says (Gen. xxii. 2): "And He said, Take now thy son, thine only son Isaac, whom thou lovest, and get thee into the land of Moriah: and offer him there for a burnt offering..." This slip shows at any rate which was the older version, how it was overlaid, like the present Jewish records, in the interests of a tribal religion. The "land of Moriah" is not clear: it was three days' journey from Abraham's place (Gen. xxii. 4). There is less warrant for identifying it with the hill of Moriah on which Jerusalem was afterwards built than with the hill of Marwah which is identified with the Arab tradition about Ismā'īl. [4101]

12. See 6:85. Elias is the same as Elijah, whose story will be found in the Old Testament in 1 Kings xvii-xix and 2 Kings i-ii. Elijah lived in the reign of Ahab (896-874 B.C.) and Ahaziah 874-872 B.C.), kings of the (northern) kingdom of Israel or Samaria. He was a prophet of the desert, like John the Baptist—unlike our Holy Prophet, who took part in, controlled, and guided all the affairs of his people. Both Ahab and Ahaziah were prone to lapse into the worship of Ba'l, the sun-god worshipped in Syria. That worship also included the worship of nature-powers and procreative powers, as in the Hindu worship of the Lingam, and led to many abuses. King Ahab had married a princess of Sidon, Jezebel, a wicked woman who led her husband to forsake God and adopt Ba'l worship.

his people, "Will you not fear (Allah)? 125 Will you call upon Ba'l and
forsake the Best of Creators,—126 Allah, your Lord and Cherisher and the
Lord and Cherisher of your fathers of old?" 127 But they rejected him, and
they will certainly be called up (for punishment),—128 Except the sincere
and devoted Servants of Allah (among them). 129 And We left (this
blessing) for him among generations (to come) in later times: 130 "Peace
and salutation to such as Elias!" 131 Thus indeed do We reward those who
do right. 132 For he was one of Our believing Servants.

133 So also was Lūṭ among those sent (by Us). 134 Behold, We delivered
him and his adherents, all, 135 Except an old woman who was among
those who lagged behind: 136 Then We destroyed the rest. 137 Verily, you
pass by their (sites), by day—138 And by night: will you not understand?

SECTION 5

139 So also was Jonah among those sent (by Us). 140 When he ran away (like
a slave from captivity) to the ship (fully) laden, 141 He (agreed to) cast
lots, and he was condemned: 142 Then the big Fish did swallow him, and
he had done acts worthy of blame. 143 Had it not been that he (repented
and) glorified Allah, 144 He would certainly have remained inside the Fish
till the Day of Resurrection. 145 But We cast him forth on the naked shore
in a state of sickness, 146 And We caused to grow, over him, a spreading
plant of the Gourd kind. 147 And We sent him (on a mission) to a hundred
thousand (men) or more. 148 And they believed; so We permitted them to
enjoy (their life) for a while.

149 Now ask them their opinion: is it that your Lord has (only) daughters,
and they have sons?—150 Or that We created the angels female, and they
are witnesses (thereto)? 151 Is it not that they say, from their own
invention, 152 "Allah has begotten children"? But they are liars! 153 Did He
(then) choose daughters rather than sons? 154 What is the matter with you?
How judge you? 155 Will you not then receive admonition? 156 Or have
you an authority manifest? 157 Then bring you your Book (of authority)
if you be truthful!

Elijah denounced all Ahab's sins as well as the sins of Ahaziah and had to flee for his life. Eventually, according to the Old Testament (2 Kings, ii. 11) he was taken up in a whirlwind to heaven in a chariot of fire after he had left his mantle with Elisha the Prophet. [4112]

158 And they have invented a blood-relationship between Him and the
Jinns: but the *Jinns* know (quite well) that they have indeed to appear
(before His Judgement Seat)! 159 Glory to Allah! (He is free) from the
things they ascribe (to Him)! 160 Not (so do) the Servants of Allah, sincere
and devoted. 161 For, verily, neither you nor those you worship—162 Can
lead (any) into temptation concerning Allah, 163 Except such as are
(themselves) going to the blazing Fire!

164 (Those ranged in ranks say): "Not one of us but has a place appointed;
165 And we are verily ranged in ranks (for service); 166 And we are verily
those who declare (Allah's) glory!"

167 And there were those who said, 168 "If only we had had before us a
Message from those of old, 169 We should certainly have been Servants
of Allah, sincere (and devoted)!" 170 But (now that the Qur'an has come),
they reject it: but soon will they know! 171 Already has Our Word been
passed before (this) to Our Servants sent (by Us), 172 That they would
certainly be assisted, 173 And that Our forces,—they surely must conquer.
174 So turn you away from them for a little while, 175 And watch them
(how they fare), and they soon shall see (how you fare)!

176 Do they wish (indeed) to hurry on Our Punishment? 177 But when it
descends into the open space before them, evil will be the morning for
those who were warned (and heeded not)! 178 So turn you away from them
for a little while, 179 And watch (how they fare) and they soon shall see
(how you fare)! 180 Glory to your Lord, the Lord of Honour and Power!
(He is free) from what they ascribe (to Him)! 181 And Peace on the
messengers! 182 And Praise to Allah, the Lord and Cherisher of the
Worlds.□

Chapter 38

Sūrah Ṣād

Translator's Introduction

For the place of this Sūrah in the series of six, dealing with some of the mysteries of the spiritual world, see Introduction to Sūrah 34.

This Sūrah, both in chronology and subject matter, is cognate to Sūrah 37, and carries forward the same argument. But here the emphasis is laid on the working of earthly power when combined with spiritual power, and it is pointed out how much more significant (and real) spiritual power is. For this reason the illustrative stories are mainly those of David and Solomon who were kings as well as prophets, and a parallel is suggested with the unfolding public life of our Holy Prophet.

Summary—Worldly and evil men are surprised at the renewal of Truth and Righteousness: but righteousness has more power than worldly strength, as is seen in the story of kings like David, who had both (38:1-26).

So also Solomon loved the Lord more than worldly power, which may be good but may be misused by evil men; so also Job and other men of power and insight, chose the path of final bliss rather than final misery (38:27-64).

So also in the case of the final Messenger; his Gospel of Unity must triumph over all Jealousy and Arrogance in Allah's good time (38:65-88).

*** *** ***

In the name of Allah,
Most Gracious, Most Merciful.

1 *Ṣād.*[1] By the Qur'an, full of Admonition: (this is the Truth). 2 But the
Unbelievers (are steeped) in Self-glory and Separatism. 3 How many
generations before them did We destroy? In the end they cried (for

---

1. *Ṣād* is a letter of the Arabic alphabet. It is used here as an Abbreviated Letter, for which see note to 2:1. See also the second paragraph of note 206 to 7:1 for this particular letter. No dogmatism is permissible in trying to interpret Abbreviated Letters. But it is suggested that it may stand for *Qaṣaṣ* ('Stories'), in which the dominant consonant is *ṣ*. For this Sūrah is concerned mainly with the stories of David and Solomon as illustrative of the relative positions of spiritual and worldly power. Sale's note: "It may stand for Solomon" is a real howler, for in Arabic the letter *Ṣād* does not occur at all in the name of Solomon. [4146]

mercy)—when there was no longer time for being saved!

4 So they wonder that a Warner has come to them from among them-
selves! And the Unbelievers say, "This is a sorcerer telling lies! 5 Has he
made the gods (all) into one Allah? Truly this is a wonderful thing!" 6
And the leaders among them go away (impatiently), (saying), "Walk you
away, and remain constant to your gods! For this is truly a thing designed
(against you)! 7 We never heard (the like) of this among the people of
these latter days: this is nothing but a made-up tale!" 8 "What! Has the
Message been sent to him—(of all persons) among us?" But they are in
doubt concerning My (Own) Message! Nay, they have not yet tasted My
Punishment! 9 Or have they the Treasures of the Mercy of your
Lord,—the Exalted in Power, the Grantor of Bounties without measure?
10 Or have they the dominion of the heavens and the earth and all
between? If so, let them mount up with the ropes and means (to reach that
end)! 11 But there—will be put to flight even a host of confederates. 12
Before them (were many who) rejected messengers,—the people of Noah,
and 'Ād, and Pharaoh, the Lord of Stakes, 13 And Thamūd, and the people
of Lūṭ, and the Companions of the Wood;—such were the Confederates.
14 Not one (of them) but rejected the messengers, but My Punishment
came justly and inevitably (on them).

SECTION 2

15 These (today) only wait for a single mighty Blast, which (when it
comes) will brook no delay. 16 They say: "Our Lord! Hasten to us our
sentence (even) before the Day of Account!" 17 Have patience at what they
say, and remember Our servant David, the man of strength: for he ever
turned (to Allah). 18 It was We that made the hills declare, in unison with
him, Our Praises, at eventide and at break of day, 19 And the birds
gathered (in assemblies): all with him did turn (to Allah). 20 We
strengthened his kingdom, and gave him wisdom and sound judgement
in speech and decision.

21 Has the Story of the Disputants reached you? Behold, they climbed
over the wall of the private chamber; 22 When they entered the presence
of David, and he was terrified of them, they said: "Fear not: we are two
disputants, one of whom has wronged the other: decide now between us
with truth, and treat us not with injustice, but guide us to the even Path.
23 This man is my brother: he has nine and ninety ewes, and I have (but)

one. Yet he says, 'Commit her to my care,' and is (moreover) harsh to me
in speech." 24 (David) said: "He has undoubtedly wronged you[2] in
demanding your (single) ewe to be added to his (flock of) ewes: truly
many are the Partners (in business)[3] who wrong each other: not so do
those who believe and work deeds of righteousness, and how few are
they?" And David gathered that We had tried him: he asked forgiveness
of his Lord,[4] fell down, bowing (in prostration), and turned (to Allah in
repentance). 25 So We forgave him this (lapse): he enjoyed, indeed, a Near
Approach to Us, and a beautiful Place of (final) Return. 26 O David! We
did indeed make you a vicegerent on earth: so judge you between men in
truth (and justice): nor follow you the lusts (of your heart), for they will
mislead you from the Path of Allah: for those who wander astray from the
Path of Allah, is a Penalty grievous, for that they forget the Day of
Account.

SECTION 3

27 Not without purpose did We create heaven and earth and all between!
That were the thought of Unbelievers! But woe to the Unbelievers
because of the Fire (of Hell)! 28 Shall We treat those who believe and
work deeds of righteousness, the same as those who do mischief on earth?
Shall We treat those who guard against evil, the same as those who turn
aside from the right? 29 (Here is) a Book which We have sent down unto

---

2. The circumstances were mysterious, the accusation was novel; it was not clear why the unjust brother should also have come with the complainant, risking his life in climbing the wall to evade the guard, and he certainly said nothing. David took them literally, and began to preach about the falsehood and the fraud of men, who should be content with what they have, but who always covet more. [4174]

3. Especially, said David, is it wrong for brothers or men in partnership to take advantage of each other; but how few are the men who are righteous? He had in mind his own devotion and justice. But lo and behold! the men disappeared as mysteriously as they had come. It was then that David realised that his vision had been a trial or temptation—a test of his moral or spiritual fibre! Great though he was as a king, and just though he was as a judge, the moment that he thought of these things in self-pride, his merit vanished. In himself he was as other men; it was Allah's grace that gave him wisdom and justice, and he should have been humble in the sight of Allah. [4175]

4. Judged by ordinary standards, David had done no wrong; he was a good and just king. Judged by the highest standard of those nearest to Allah (*Muqarrabūn,* 56:11), the thought of self-pride and self-righteousness had to be washed off from him by his own act of self-realisation and repentance. This was freely accepted by Allah, as the next verse shows. [4176]

you, full of blessings, that they may mediate on its Signs, and that men of understanding may receive admonition.

30 To David We gave Solomon (for a son),—[5] how excellent in Our
service! Ever did he turn (to Us)! 31 Behold, there were brought[6] before
him, at eventide, coursers of the highest breeding, and swift of foot; 32
And he said, "Truly do I love[7] the love of good, with a view to the glory
of my Lord,"—until (the sun) was hidden in the veil (of night): 33 "Bring
them back to me." Then began he to pass his hand over (their) legs and
their necks.

34 And We did try Solomon: We placed on his throne a body (without
life); but he did turn (to Us in true devotion): 35 He said, "O my Lord!
Forgive me, and grant me a Kingdom which, (it may be), suits not
another after me: for You are the Grantor of Bounties (without measure)."
36 Then We subjected the Wind to his power, to flow gently to his order,
however he willed,—37 As also the evil ones,[8] (including) every kind of
builder and diver,—38 As also others bound[9] together in fetters. 39 "Such
are Our Bounties: whether you bestow them (on others) or withhold them,
no account will be asked." 40 And he enjoyed, indeed, a Near Approach
to Us, and a beautiful Place of (final) Return.

---

5. The greatest in this life have yet need of this spiritual blessing: without it all worldly good is futile. Referring back to the story of David, we are now introduced to Solomon, who was a great king but greater still because he served Allah and turned to Him. The Qur'an, unlike the Old Testament, represents Solomon as a righteous king, not as an idolater, doing "evil in the sight of the Lord" (1 Kings, xi. 6). [4182]

6. The passages about David and Solomon have been variously interpreted by the Commentators. The versions which I have suggested have good authority behind them, though I have followed my own judgement in filling in the details. [4183]

7. The story is not found in the Old Testament. I interpret it to mean that, like his father David, Solomon was also most meticulous in not allowing the least motive of self to be mixed up with his spiritual virtues. He was fond of horses: he had great armies and wealth, but he used them all in Allah's service. *Cf.* 27:19; 27:40, etc. His battles were not fought for lust of blood, but as *Jihād* in the cause of righteousness. His love of horses was not like that of a mere race-goer or of a warrior: there was a spiritual element in it. He loved by a kind of love which was spiritual—the love of the highest Good. [4185]

8. *Cf.* 21:82 and also 34:12-13: in the latter passage the spirits mentioned are called *Jinns*. The divers were probably those employed in pearl fisheries. [4194]

9. *Cf.* 14:49, where the same expression "bound together in fetters" is applied to Sinners on the Day of Judgement. [4195]

SECTION 4

41 Commemorate Our servant Job. Behold he cried to his Lord: "The Evil
One has afflicted me with distress[10] and suffering!" 42 (The command
was given:) "Strike with your foot: here is (water) wherein to wash, cool
and refreshing, and (water) to drink." 43 And We gave him (back) his
people, and doubled their number,—as a Grace from Ourselves, and a
thing for commemoration, for all who have Understanding. 44 "And take
in your hand a little grass, and strike[11] therewith: and break not (your
oath)." Truly We found him full of patience and constancy. How
excellent in Our service! Ever did he turn (to Us)!

45 And commemorate Our servants Abraham, Isaac, and Jacob, possessors
of Power and Vision. 46 Verily We did choose them for a special
(purpose)—proclaiming the Message of the Hereafter. 47 They were, in
Our sight, truly, of the company of the Elect and the Good.

48 And commemorate Ismā'īl, Elisha, and Dhū al-Kifl: each of them was
of the company of the Good.

49 This is a Message (of admonition): and verily, for the Righteous, is a
beautiful Place of (final) Return,—50 Gardens of Eternity, whose doors
will (ever) be open to them; 51 Therein will they recline (at ease): therein
can they call (at pleasure) for fruit in abundance, and (delicious) drink;
52 And beside them will be chaste women restraining[12] their glances,

---

10. The distress was of many kinds, physical, mental, and spiritual. See 21:83. He suffered from loathsome sores; he lost his home, his possessions, and his family; and almost his balance of mind. But he did not lose Faith but turned to Allah (see verse 44 below), and the recuperative process began. [4199]

11. In his worst distress Job was patient and constant in faith, but apparently his wife was not. According to the book of Job (ii. 9-10), "Then said his wife unto him, Dost thou still retain thine integrity? Curse God, and die. But he said unto her, Thou speakest as one of the foolish women speaketh. What? Shall we receive good at the hand of God, and shall we not receive evil? In all this did not Job sin with his lips." He must have said in his haste to the woman that he would beat her: he is asked now to correct her with only a wisp of grass, to show that he was gentle and humble as well as patient and constant. [4202]

12. *Cf.* 37:48 and 36:56. As we conceive happiness in this life, it is not complete if it is only solitary. How we hanker after someone who can share in our highest joy! That feeling is also figured here. [4209]

(companions) of equal age.[13] 53 Such is the Promise made to you for the
Day of Account! 54 Truly such will be Our Bounty (to you); it will never
fail;—

55 Indeed, such! But—for the wrong-doers will be an evil Place of (final)
Return!— 56 Hell!—they will burn therein,—an evil bed (indeed, to lie
on)!—57 Indeed, such!—then shall they taste it,—a boiling fluid, and a
fluid dark, murky, intensely cold!—58 And other Penalties of a similar
kind, to match them! 59 Here is a troop rushing headlong with you! No
welcome for them! Truly, they shall burn in the Fire! 60 (The followers
shall cry to the misleaders:) "Nay, you (too)! No welcome for you! It is
you who have brought this upon us! Now evil is (this) place to stay in!"
61 They will say: "Our Lord! Whoever brought this upon us,—add to him
a double Penalty in the Fire!" 62 And they will say: "What has happened
to us that we see not men whom we used to number among the bad ones?
63 Did we treat them (as such) in ridicule, or have (our) eyes failed to
perceive them?" 64 Truly that is just and fitting,—the mutual
recriminations of the People of the Fire!

SECTION 5

65 Say: "Truly am I a Warner: no god is there but the One Allah, Supreme
and Irresistible,—66 The Lord of the heavens and the earth, and all
between,—Exalted in Might, able to enforce His Will, forgiving again
and again." 67 Say: "That is a Message supreme (above all),—68 From
which you do turn away! 69 No knowledge have I of the Chiefs on high,
when they discuss (matters) among themselves. 70 Only this has been
revealed to me: that I am to give warning plainly and publicly."

71 Behold, your Lord said to the angels: "I am about to create man from
clay: 72 When I have fashioned him (in due proportion) and breathed into
him of My spirit, fall you down in obeisance unto him." 73 So the angels
prostrated themselves, all of them together: 74 Not so Iblīs: he was
haughty, and became one of those who reject Faith. 75 (Allah) said: "O
Iblīs! What prevents you from prostrating yourself to one whom I have

---

13. To make the metaphor of social happiness complete, we want companionship of equal age. Age and youth cannot be happy together. It is not suggested that in the Timeless state figured here, there will be old age; but if it is possible to conceive of temperamental differences then, the company will be so arranged that it will be congenial. Or we can accept the type of youth and freshness as common to all in that happy state. [4210]

created with My hands? Are you haughty? Or are you one of the high
(and mighty) ones?" 76 (Iblīs) said: "I am better than he: You created me
from fire, and him You created from clay." 77 (Allah) said: "Then get you
out from here: for you are rejected, accursed. 78 And My Curse shall be
on you till the Day of Judgement." 79 (Iblīs) said: "O my Lord! Give me
then respite till the Day the (dead) are raised." 80 (Allah) said: "Respite
then is granted you—81 Till the Day of the Time Appointed." 82 (Iblīs)
said: "Then, by Your Power, I will put them all in the wrong,—83 Except
Your Servants amongst them, sincere and purified (by Your grace)." 84
(Allah) said: "Then it is just and fitting—and I say what is just and
fitting—85 That I will certainly fill Hell with you and those that follow
you,—every one."

86 Say: "No reward do I ask[14] of you for this (Qur'an), nor am I a
pretender. 87 This is no less than a Message to (all) the Worlds. 88 And you
shall certainly know the truth of it (all) after a while."□

14. *Cf.* 25:57; 26:109; and many other passages. The prophet of Allah neither seeks nor expects any reward from men. On the contrary he suffers much at their hands. He is unselfish and offers his services under Allah's inspiration. He is satisfied with the hope "that each one who will may take a straight Path to his Lord." That is his reward. And the reward he hopes for from Allah is similarly unselfish. He earnestly hopes to win His Good Pleasure—or, to use another metaphor, "to see His Face". [4238]

Chapter 39

Sūrah Al-Zumar
(The Crowds)

Translator's Introduction

This is the last of the series of six Sūrahs beginning with Sūrah 34, which deal with the mysteries of the spiritual world, as leading up to the *Ma'ād,* or the Hereafter. See Introduction to Sūrah 34.

Its subject matter is how Creation in its great variety is yet sorted out in Groups or Classes, all governed by one Plan, and created and sustained by One Allah, Who will separate Good from Evil at the last Day. The word *zumar* occurs in verses 71 and 73.

Its chronology has no significance. It belongs to the later Makkan period.

Summary—The variety in Creation yet points to the unity of Plan: there is only One Allah: to Him is due all worship and from Him flow all Justice and Grace (39:1-21).

There is unity in Revelation, and guidance comes from Allah alone: turn to Him only, for all else is false (39:22-52).

Allah's Mercy is all-embracing: despair not: seek it before it is too late: for Judgement and Justice will come for certain (39:53-75).

*** *** ***

In the name of Allah,
Most Gracious, Most Merciful.

1 The revelation of this Book is from Allah, the Exalted in Power, Full of
Wisdom. 2 Verily it is We Who have revealed the Book to you in Truth:
so serve Allah, offering Him sincere devotion. 3 Is it not to Allah that
sincere devotion is due? But those who take for protectors other than
Allah (say): "We only serve them in order that they may bring us nearer
to Allah." Truly Allah will judge between them in that wherein they
differ. But Allah guides not such as are false and ungrateful.

4 Had Allah wished to take to Himself a son, He could have chosen whom

He pleased out of those whom He[1] does create: but Glory be to Him!
(He is above such things.) He is Allah, the One, the Irresistible. 5 He
created the heavens and the earth in true (proportions): He makes the
Night overlap the Day, and the Day overlap the Night: He has subjected
the sun and the moon (to His law): each one follows a course for a time
appointed. Is not He the Exalted in Power—He Who forgives again and
again? 6 He created you (all) from a single Person: then created, of like
nature, his mate; and He sent down for you eight head[2] of cattle in pairs:
He makes you, in the wombs of your mothers, in stages, one after
another, in three veils of darkness.[3] Such is Allah, your Lord and
Cherisher: to Him belongs (all) dominion. There is no god but He: then
how are you turned away (from your true Centre)?

7 If you reject (Allah), truly Allah has no need of you; but He likes not
ingratitude from His servants: if you are grateful, He is pleased with you.
No bearer of burdens can bear the burden of another. In the end, to your
Lord is your Return, when He will tell you the truth of all that you did (in
this life). For He knows well all that is in (men's) hearts. 8 When some
trouble touches man, he cries unto his Lord, turning to Him in repentance:
but when He bestows a favour upon him as from Himself, (man) does
forget what he cried and prayed for before, and he does set up rivals unto
Allah, thus misleading others from Allah's Path. Say, "Enjoy your

---

1. It is blasphemy to say that God begot a son. If that were true, He should have had a wife (6:101), and His son would have been of the same kind as Himself; whereas God is One, with no one else like unto Him (112:4). Begetting is an animal act which goes with sex. How can it be consistent with our conception of One Who is above all Creatures? If such a blasphemous thought were possible, as that God wanted someone else to help Him, He could have chosen the best of His creatures instead of lowering Himself to an animal act. But glory to God! He is above such things! His Unity is the first thing that we have to learn about Him. As He is Omnipotent, He requires no creatures to help Him or bring other creatures to Him. [4246]

2. See 6:143-4, where four kinds of cattle are mentioned in pairs in connection with certain Arab superstitions which are there condemned. Here the same four kinds are mentioned as representative of domesticated cattle given by God as useful to man. These are sheep, goats, camels, and oxen. In Arab idiom the horse is not included among "cattle".

For the wisdom and goodness of God in granting man dominion over cattle, see 36:71-73. [4250]

3. The three veils of darkness which cover the unborn child are: the caul or membrane, the womb, and the hollow in which the womb is enclosed. But we might understand "three" in a cumulative rather than a numerical sense. [4252]

blasphemy for a little while: verily you are (one) of the Companions of
the Fire!"

9 Is one who worships devoutly during the hours of the night prostrating
himself or standing (in adoration), who takes heed of the Hereafter, and
who places his hope in the Mercy of his Lord—(like one who does not)?
Say: "Are those equal, those who know and those who do not know? It
is those who are endued with understanding that receive admonition."

SECTION 2

10 Say: "O you My servants who believe! Fear your Lord. Good is (the
reward) for those who do good in this world. Spacious is Allah's earth!
Those who patiently persevere will truly receive a reward without
measure!"

11 Say: "Verily, I am commanded to serve Allah with sincere devotion; 12
And I am commanded to be the first of those who bow to Allah in Islam."
13 Say: "I would, if I disobeyed my Lord, indeed have fear of the Penalty
of a Mighty Day." 14 Say: "It is Allah I serve, with my sincere (and
exclusive) devotion: 15 Serve you what you will besides Him." Say:
"Truly, those in loss are those who lose their own souls and their people
on the Day of Judgement: Ah! That is indeed the (real and) evident
Loss!" 16 They shall have Layers of Fire above them, and Layers (of Fire)
below them: with this does Allah warn off His Servants: "O My Servants!
then fear you Me!"

17 Those who eschew Evil,—and fall not into its worship,—and turn to
Allah (in repentance),—for them is Good News: so announce the Good
News to My Servants,—18 Those who listen to the Word, and follow the
best (meaning) in it: those are the ones whom Allah has guided, and those
are the ones endued with understanding. 19 Is, then, one against whom the
decree of Punishment is justly due (equal to one who eschews evil)?
Would you, then, deliver one (who is) in the Fire? 20 But it is for those
who fear their Lord, that lofty mansions, one above another, have been
built: beneath them flow rivers (of delight): (such is) the Promise of
Allah: never does Allah fail in (His) promise. 21 See you not that Allah

sends down rain from the sky, and leads it through springs in the earth?[4] Then He causes to grow, therewith, produce of various colours: then it withers; you will see it grow yellow; then He makes it dry up and crumble away. Truly, in this, is a Message of remembrance to men of understanding.

SECTION 3

22 Is one whose heart Allah has opened to Islam, so that he has received Enlightenment from Allah, (no better than one hardhearted)? Woe to those whose hearts are hardened against celebrating the praises of Allah! They are manifestly wandering (in error)! 23 Allah has revealed (from time to time) the most beautiful Message in the form of a Book, consistent with itself, (yet) repeating (its teaching in various aspects): the skins of those who fear their Lord tremble thereat; then their skins and their hearts do soften to the celebration of Allah's praises. Such is the guidance of Allah: He guides therewith whom He pleases, but such as Allah leaves to stray, can have none to guide. 24 Is, then, one who has to fear the brunt of the Penalty on the Day of Judgement (and receive it) on his face, (like one guarded therefrom)? It will be said to the wrong-doers: "Taste you (the fruits of) what you earned!" 25 Those before them (also) rejected (revelation), and so the Punishment came to them from directions they did not perceive. 26 So Allah gave them a taste of humiliation in the present life, but greater is the Punishment of the Hereafter, if they only knew!

27 We have put forth for men, in this Qur'an every kind of Parable, in order that they may receive admonition. 28 (It is) a Qur'an in Arabic,[5] without any crookedness (therein): in order that they may guard against

---

4. The circuit of water, by which the rain falls from the clouds, is absorbed through the earth, and flows through rivers or underground streams to the sea, where it again rises as vapour and forms clouds, was explained in notes to 25:53. Here our attention is drawn to one portion of the process. The rain fructifies the soil and the seeds. Produce of various kinds is raised. The harvest ripens and is gathered in. The plants wither, dry up, and crumble away. Men and animals are fed. And the circuit starts again in another season. Here is a Sign of the Grace and Goodness of God, clear to those who understand. [4273]

5. Previous revelations had been in other languages. Now the revelation was given in Arabia in Arabic itself, the language of the country which all could understand. And it is a beautiful language, straight and flexible, and fit to be the vehicle of sublime truths. [4285]

Evil. 29 Allah puts forth a Parable—a man belonging to many partners at
variance with each other, and a man belonging entirely to one master: are
those two equal in comparison? Praise be to Allah! But most of them
have no knowledge. 30 Truly you will die (one day), and truly they (too)
will die (one day). 31 In the End will you (all), on the Day of Judgment,
settle your disputes in the presence of your Lord.

PART XXIV

SECTION 4

32 Who, then, does more wrong than one who utters a lie concerning
Allah, and rejects the Truth when it comes to him; is there not in Hell an
abode for blasphemers? 33 And he who brings the Truth and he who
confirms (and supports) it—such are the men who do right. 34 They shall
have all that they wish for, in the presence of their Lord: such is the
reward of those who do good: 35 So that Allah will turn off from them
(even) the worst in their deeds and give them their reward according to
the best of what they have done.

36 Is not Allah enough for his servant? But they try to frighten you with
other (gods) besides Him! For such as Allah leaves to stray, there can be
no guide. 37 And such as Allah does guide there can be none to lead
astray. Is not Allah Exalted in Power, (able to enforce His Will), Lord of
Retribution? 38 If indeed you ask them who it is that created[6] the heavens
and the earth, they would be sure to say, "Allah". Say: "See you then? the
things that you invoke besides Allah,—can they, if Allah wills some
Penalty for me, remove His Penalty?—or if He wills some Grace for me,
can they keep back His Grace?" Say: "Sufficient is Allah for me! In Him
trust those who put their trust." 39 Say: "O my people! Do whatever you
can: I will do (my part): but soon will you know—40 Who it is to whom
comes a Penalty of ignominy, and on whom descends a Penalty that

---

6. *Cf.* 29:61; and also 23:85. Most worshippers of false gods are neither atheists nor sceptics. They admit the existence of God as an abstract proposition, but it has not come into their hearts and souls: it has not been translated into their lives. They run after false worship on account of ancestral custom or on account of their thoughtlessness or false environment, or on account of their selfish desires or limited outlook. To them is addressed the argument: Ultimately your false gods can do nothing for you: why not turn to the One True God, on Whom you depend, and Who can give you Grace and Mercy, Justice and Punishment?[4299]

abides."

41 Verily We have revealed the Book to you in Truth, for (instructing) mankind. He, then, that receives guidance benefits his own soul: but he that strays injures his own soul. Nor are you set over them to dispose of their affairs.

SECTION 5

42 It is Allah that takes the souls (of men) at death; and those that die not (He takes) during their sleep: those on whom He has passed the decree of death, He keeps back (from returning to life), but the rest He sends (to their bodies) for a term appointed. Verily in this are Signs for those who reflect. 43 What! Do they take for intercessors others besides Allah? Say: "Even if they have no power whatever and no intelligence?" 44 Say: "To Allah belongs exclusively (the right to grant) Intercession:[7] to Him belongs the dominion of the heavens and the earth: in the End, it is to Him that you shall be brought back." 45 When Allah, the One and Only, is mentioned, the hearts of those who believe not in the Hereafter are filled with disgust and horror; but when (gods) other than He are mentioned, behold, they are filled with joy! 46 Say: "O Allah! Creator of the heavens and the earth! Knower of all that is hidden and open! It is You that will judge between Your Servants in those matters about which they have differed."

47 Even if the wrong-doers had all that there is on earth, and as much more, (in vain) would they offer it for ransom from the pain of the Penalty on the Day of Judgement: but something will confront them from Allah, which they could never have counted upon! 48 For the evils of their deeds will confront them, and they will be (completely) encircled by that which they used to mock at! 49 Now, when trouble touches man, he cries to Us: but when We bestow a favour upon him as from Ourselves, he says, "This has been given to me because of a certain knowledge (I

---

7. For *Shafā'ah* (Intercession, Advocacy) see 2:255; 10:3; 20:109, and 21:28. It follows that do no one can intercede with God, except (1) by God's permission, and (2) for those who have prepared themselves by penitence for God's acceptance. Even in earthly Courts, Advocacy is not permitted to anyone; the Advocate must be granted the position of Advocate before he can plead before the judge. Nor can it be supposed that a plea for forgiveness or mercy can be put forward except on grounds recognised by equity and justice. [4311]

have)!" Nay, but this is but a trial, but most of them understand not! 50
Thus did the (generations) before them say! But all that they did was of
no profit to them. 51 Nay, the evil results of their deeds overtook them.
And the wrong-doers of this (generation)—the evil results of their deeds
will soon overtake them (too), and they will never be able to frustrate
(Our Plan)! 52 Know they not that Allah enlarges the provision or restricts
it, for any He pleases? Verily, in this are Signs for those who believe!

SECTION 6

53 Say: "O my servants who have transgressed against their souls! Despair
not of the Mercy of Allah: for Allah forgives all sins: for He is
Oft-Forgiving, Most Merciful. 54 Turn you to your Lord (in repentance)
and bow to His (Will), before the Penalty comes on you: after that you
shall not be helped. 55 And follow the best of (the courses) revealed to
you from your Lord, before the Penalty comes on you—of a sudden,
while you perceive not!—56 Lest the soul should (then) say: 'Ah! Woe is
me!—In that I neglected (my duty) towards Allah, and was but among
those who mocked!'—57 Or (lest) it should say: 'If only Allah had guided
me, I should certainly have been among the righteous!'—58 Or (lest) it
should say when it (actually) sees the Penalty: 'If only I had another
chance, I should certainly be among those who do good!' 59 (The reply
will be:) 'Nay, but there came to you My Signs, and you did reject them:
you were haughty, and became one of those who reject Faith!'"

60 On the Day of Judgement will you see those who told lies against
Allah;—their faces will be turned black; is there not in Hell an abode for
the Haughty? 61 But Allah will deliver the righteous to their place of
salvation: no evil shall touch them, nor shall they grieve. 62 Allah is the
Creator of all things, and He is the Guardian and Disposer of all affairs.
63 To Him belong the keys of the heavens and the earth: and those who
reject the Signs of Allah,—it is they who will be in loss.

SECTION 7

64 Say: "Is it someone other than Allah that you order me to worship, O
you ignorant ones?" 65 But it has already been revealed to you,—as it was
to those before you,—"If you were to join (gods with Allah), truly
fruitless will be your work (in life), and you will surely be in the ranks of
those who lose (all spiritual good)." 66 Nay, but worship Allah, and be of
those who give thanks. 67 No just estimate have they made of Allah, such

as is due to Him: on the Day of Judegment the whole of the earth will be
but His handful, and the heavens will be rolled up in His right hand:
Glory to Him! High is He above the Partners they attribute to Him! 68 The
Trumpet will (just) be sounded, when all that are in the heavens and on
earth will swoon, except such as it will please Allah (to exempt). Then
will a second one be sounded, when, behold, they will be standing and
looking on! 69 And the Earth will shine with the glory of its Lord: the
Record (of deeds) will be placed (open); the prophets and the witnesses
will be brought forward and a just decision[8] pronounced between them;
and they will not be wronged (in the least). 70 And to every soul will be
paid in full (the fruit) of its deeds; and (Allah) knows best all that they do.

SECTION 8

71 The Unbelievers will be led to Hell in a crowd:[9] until, when they arrive there, its gates will be opened. And its keepers will say,[10] "Did not messengers come to you from among yourselves, rehearsing to you the Signs of your Lord, and warning you of the Meeting of this Day of yours?" The answer will be: "True: but the Decree of Punishment has
been proved true against the Unbelievers!" 72 (To them) will be said:
"Enter you the gates of Hell, to dwell therein: and evil is (this) abode of the arrogant!"

73 And those who feared their Lord will be led to the Garden in crowds: until behold, they arrive there; its gates will be opened; and its keepers will say: "Peace be upon you! Well have you done! Enter you here, to
dwell therein." 74 They will say: "Praise be to Allah, Who has truly
fulfilled His Promise to us, and has given us (this) land in heritage: we

---

8. It is in such a scene of Reality that Judgement will be held. Before the Throne of God, the book of each man's deeds and motives will be placed wide open, which all may see; the Prophets and the Preachers of Truth and the martyrs who gave their lives or made their real sacrifices in the cause of Truth, will be in the Court, to give evidence; and the decision pronounced will be absolutely just, for the Judge will not only be just, and He will know every fact and circumstance, and His wisdom will give due weight to everything, great or small. [4345]

9. *Crowds*: this is the word which gives the keynote to the Sūrah. If the soul does not stand to its own convictions or search out the Truth by itself, it will be classed with the crowds that go to Perdition! [4347]

10. The Keepers may be supposed to be angels, who know nothing of the conditions of evil on this earth, and are surprised at such crowds coming to the "Evil Abode". [4348]

can dwell in the Garden as we will: how excellent a reward for those who work (righteousness)!" 75 And you will see the angels surrounding the Throne (Divine) on all sides, singing Glory and Praise to their Lord. The Decision between them (at Judgement) will be in (perfect) justice, and the cry (on all sides) will be, "Praise be to Allah,[11] the Lord of the Worlds!"□

---

11. These are the opening words of the first Sūrah, and they describe the atmosphere of the final Bliss in Heaven, in the Light of the Countenance of their Lord, The Universal Lord of all! [4355]

Chapter 40

Sūrah Ghāfir or *Al-Mu'min* (Forgiver or The Believer)

Translator's Introduction

This Sūrah is called Ghāfir (Forgiver, see verse 3). It is also called "The Believer" (*Mu'min*) from the story of the individual Believer among the people of Pharaoh, who declares his faith and looks to the Future (verses 28-45). In Sūrah 23, called "The Believers" (*Mu'minūn*), the argument was about the collective force of Faith and virtue. Here it is about the individual's witness to Faith and Virtue, and his triumph in the End.

We now begin a series of seven Sūrahs (40-46) to which are affixed the Abbreviated Letters *Ḥā Mīm*. Chronologically they all belong to the same period, the later Makkan Period, and they immediately follow the last Sūrah in time. About the Abbreviated Letters generally, see note to Sūrah 2:1. As to the precise meaning of *Ḥā Mīm* no authoritative explanation is available. If *Mīm* here has a signification similar to *Mīm* in *Alif, Lām, Mīm* (see note to Sūrah 2:1), it means the End of things, the Last Day, and all these Sūrahs direct our special attention to that *Ḥā*, the emphatic guttural, in contrast with the softer breathing of *Alif,* may be meant to suggest that the Beginning (see note to 2:1, last paragraph) is only for the End, the Present for the Future, and to emphasise the eschatological element in Faith. But this is mere conjecture, and should be taken for no more than it is worth.

The general theme of the whole series is the relation of Faith to Unfaith, Revelation to Rejection, Goodness to Evil, Truth to Falsehood. It is shown that the first in each of these pairs is the real friend, helper, and protector of man, while the second is his enemy. The very word *Ḥamīm* in that sense is used in Sūrahs 40 and 41 (40:18 and 41:34), while in the other Sūrahs we have words of equivalent import, *e.g.*, *walī* or *naṣīr* (42:8 and 31); *qarīn* (43:36, 38); *mawlā* (44:41); *awliyā'* or *nāṣirīn* (45:19, 34); and *awliyā'* (46:32). Is it permissible to connect the Abbreviated Letters *Ḥā Mīm* with these ideas as expressed in the word *Ḥamīm*?

Another suggestion worthy of consideration is that *Ḥā* stands for *Ḥayy,* and *Mīm* for *Qayyūm.* These are two attributes of Allah, meaning, (1) the Living, and (2) the Self-Subsisting, Eternal. The one points to Life, and Revelation, and the other to the Hereafter and Eternity; and both these matters are specially dealt with in the seven *Ḥā Mīm* Sūrahs. The first letter of Ḥayy (*Ḥā*) is appropriate for life, and the last letter of *Qayyūm* is appropriate for the Last Days, the *Ma'ād,* the Hereafter. Again, this is mere conjecture, and should not be taken for more than it is worth.

Summary—Faith is ever justified, for Allah forgives: but evil deeds must have evil fruits, for Allah knows and is just (40:1-20).

In all history Evil came to evil; the protest of Faith, in the midst of Evil, may be ignored; but Faith is protected by Allah, while Evil perishes (40:21-50).

No doubt is there of the Future Judgement; the Power, Goodness, and Justice of Allah are manifest; will man dispute, or will he accept the Signs before it is too late? (40:51-85).

*** *** ***

In the name of Allah,
Most Gracious, Most Merciful.

1 *Ḥā Mīm.*[1] 2 The revelation of this Book is from Allah, Exalted in
Power, Full of Knowledge,—3 Who forgives Sin, accepts Repentance, is
Strict in Punishment, and has a Long Reach (in all things). There is no
god but He: to Him is the Final Goal.

4 None can dispute about the Signs of Allah but the Unbelievers. Let not,
then, their strutting about through the land deceive you! 5 But (there were
people) before them, who denied (the Signs),—the people of Noah, and
the Confederates (of Evil) after them; and every people plotted against
their prophet, to seize him, and disputed by means of vanities, therewith
to condemn the Truth; but it was I that seized them! And how (terrible)
was My Requital! 6 Thus was the Decree of your Lord proved true against
the Unbelievers; that truly they are Companions of the Fire!

7 Those who sustain the Throne (of Allah) and those around it sing Glory
and Praise to their Lord; believe in Him; and implore Forgiveness for
those who believe: "Our Lord! Your Reach is over all things, in Mercy
and Knowledge. Forgive, then, those who turn in Repentance, and follow
Your Path; and preserve them from the Penalty of the blazing Fire! 8 And
grant, our Lord! that they enter the Gardens of Eternity, which You have
promised to them, and to the righteous among their fathers, their wives,
and their posterity! For You are (He), the Exalted in Might, Full of
Wisdom. 9 And preserve them from (all) ills; and any whom You do
preserve from ills that Day,—on them will You have bestowed Mercy
indeed: and that will be truly (for them) the highest Achievement."

---

1. See paragraphs 2-4 of the Introduction to this Sūrah. [4356]

SECTION 2

10 The Unbelievers will be addressed: "Greater was the aversion of Allah
to you than (is) your aversion to yourselves, seeing that you were called
to the Faith and you used to refuse." 11 They will say: "Our Lord! Twice
have You made us without life, and twice have You given us Life! Now
have we recognised our sins: is there any way out (of this)?" 12 (The
answer will be:) "This is because, when Allah was invoked as the Only
(object of worship), you did reject Faith, but when partners were joined
to Him, you believed! The Command is with Allah, Most High, Most
Great!"

13 He it is Who shows you His Signs, and sends down sustenance for you
from the sky: but only those receive admonition who turn (to Allah). 14
Call you, then, upon Allah with sincere devotion to Him, even though the
Unbelievers may detest it. 15 Raised high above ranks (or degrees), (He
is) the Lord of the Throne (of authority): by His Command does He send
the spirit (of inspiration) to any of His servants He pleases, that it may
warn (men) of the Day of Mutual Meeting,—16 The Day whereon they
will (all) come forth: not a single thing concerning them is hidden from
Allah. Whose will be the dominion that Day? That of Allah, the One, the
Irresistible! 17 That Day will every soul be requited for what it earned; no
injustice will there be that Day, for Allah is Swift in taking account.

18 Warn them of the Day that is (ever) drawing near, when the hearts will
(come) right up to the throats to choke (them); no intimate friend nor
intercessor will the wrong-doers have, who could be listened to. 19 (Allah)
knows of (the tricks) that deceive with the eyes, and all that the hearts (of
men) conceal. 20 And Allah will judge with (Justice and) Truth: but those
whom (men) invoke besides Him, will not (be in a position) to judge at
all. Verily it is Allah (alone) Who hears and sees (all things).

SECTION 3

21 Do they not travel through the earth and see what was the End of those
before them? They were even superior to them in strength, and in the
traces (they have left) in the land: but Allah did call them to account for
their sins, and none had they to defend them against Allah. 22 That was
because there came to them their messengers with clear (Signs), but they
rejected them: so Allah called them to account: for He is Full of Strength,
Strict in Punishment.

23 Of old We sent Moses, with Our Signs and an Authority manifest, 24 To
Pharaoh, Hāmān, and Qārūn; but they called (him) "a sorcerer telling
lies!" 25 Now, when he came to them in Truth, from Us, they said, "Slay
the sons of those who believe with him, and keep alive their females," but
the plots of Unbelievers (end) in nothing but errors (and delusions)! 26
Said Pharaoh: "Leave me to slay Moses; and let him call on his Lord!
What I fear is lest he should change your religion, or lest he should cause
mischief to appear in the land!" 27 Moses said: "I have indeed called upon
my Lord and your Lord (for protection) from every arrogant one who
believes not in the Day of Account!"

SECTION 4

28 A Believer, a man from among the people of Pharaoh, who had
concealed his faith, said: "Will you slay a man because he says, 'My Lord
is Allah'?[2] —when he has indeed come to you with clear (Signs) from
your Lord? And if he be a liar, on him is (the sin of) his lie: but, if he is
telling[3] the Truth, then will fall on you something of the (calamity) of
which he warns you: truly Allah guides not one who transgresses and
lies! 29 O my people! Yours is the dominion this day: you have the upper
hand in the land: but who will help us from the Punishment of Allah,
should it befall us?" Pharaoh said: "I but point out to you that which I see
(myself);[4] nor do I guide you but to the Path of Right!"

---

2. There is nothing to justify the identification of this man with the man mentioned in 28:20, who warned Moses long before Moses had received his mission. On the contrary, in this passage, the man is evidently speaking after Moses had received his mission, preached to Pharaoh, and got a certain amount of success, for which Pharaoh and his people were trying to seek his life. Moses had evidently already brought his Clear Signs. [4396]

3. A commonsense view is put before them by an Egyptian who loves his own people and does not wish them to perish in sin. "Will you kill this man for calling on God? Have you not seen his character and behaviour? Do you not see the 'Clear Signs' about him that bespeak his credentials? Suppose for a moment that he is a liar and pretender: he will suffer for his falsehood, but why should you turn against God? But suppose that he is really inspired by God to tell you the truth and warn you against evil, what will be your fate when God's Wrath descends? For it must descend if he is a true Messenger sent by God." [4397]

4. Pharaoh's egotism and arrogance come out. 'I can see and understand everything. As I see things, so do I direct you. The Path which I see must be right and you must follow it.' [4400]

30 Then said the man who believed: "O my people! Truly I do fear for you
something like the Day (of disaster) of the Confederates (in sin)![5]—31
Something like the fate of the people of Noah, the 'Ād, and the Thamūd,
and those who came after them: but Allah never wishes injustice to His
Servants. 32 And O my people! I fear for you a Day when there will be
mutual calling (and wailing),—33 A Day when you shall turn your backs
and flee: no defender shall you have from Allah: any whom Allah leaves
to stray, there is none to guide. 34 And to you there came Joseph in times
gone by, with clear Signs, but you ceased not to doubt of the (mission)
for which he had come: at length, when he died, you said: 'No messenger
will Allah send after him.' Thus does Allah leave to stray such as
transgress and live in doubt,—35 (Such) as dispute about the Signs of
Allah, without any authority that has reached them. Grievous and odious
(is such conduct) in the sight of Allah and of the Believers. Thus does
Allah seal up every heart—of arrogant and obstinate transgressors."

36 Pharaoh said: "O Hāmān! Build me a lofty palace, that I may attain the
ways and means,—37 The ways and means of (reaching) the heavens, and
that I may mount up to the Allah of Moses: but as far as I am concerned,
I think (Moses) is a liar!" Thus was made alluring, in Pharaoh's eyes, the
evil of his deeds, and he was hindered from the Path; and the plot of
Pharaoh led to nothing but perdition (for him).

SECTION 5

38 The man who believed said further: "O my people! Follow me: I will
lead you to the Path of Right. 39 O my people! This life of the present is
nothing but (temporary) convenience: it is the Hereafter that is the Home
that will last. 40 He that works evil will not be requited but by the like
thereof: and he that works a righteous deed—whether man or
woman—and is a Believer—such will enter the Garden (of bliss): therein
will they have abundance without measure. 41 And O my people! How
(strange) it is for me to call you to Salvation while you call me to the
Fire! 42 You do call upon me to blaspheme against Allah, and to join with
Him partners of whom I have no knowledge; and I call you to the Exalted
in Power, Who forgives again and again!" 43 "Without doubt you do call
me to one who is not fit to be called to, whether in this world, or in the

5. *Cf.* 38:11-13, and 40:5. [4402]

Hereafter; our Return will be to Allah; and the Transgressors will be
Companions of the Fire! 44 Soon will you remember what I say to you
(now). My (own) affair I commit to Allah: for Allah (ever) watches over
His Servants."

45 Then Allah saved him from (every) ill that they plotted (against him),
but the brunt of the Penalty encompassed on all sides the people of
Pharaoh. 46 In front of the Fire will they be brought, morning and
evening: and (the sentence will be) on the Day that Judgement will be
established: "Cast you the people of Pharaoh into the severest Penalty!"

47 Behold, they will dispute with each other in the Fire! The weak ones
(who followed) will say to those who had been arrogant, "We but
followed you: can you then take (on yourselves) from us some share of
the Fire?" 48 Those who had been arrogant will say: "We are all in this
(Fire)! Truly, Allah has judged between (His) Servants!" 49 Those in the
Fire will say to the Keepers of Hell: "Pray to your Lord to lighten us the
Penalty for a day (at least)!" 50 They will say: "Did there not come to you
your messengers with clear Signs?" They will say, "Yes". They will.
reply, "Then pray (as you like)! But the prayer of those without Faith is
nothing but (futile wandering) in (mazes of) error!"

SECTION 6

51 We will, without doubt, help Our messengers and those who believe,
(both) in this world's life and on the Day when the Witnesses will stand
forth,—52 The Day when no profit will it be to Wrong-doers to present
their excuses, but they will (only) have the Curse and the Home of
Misery. 53 We did aforetime give Moses the (Book of) Guidance, and We
gave the Book in inheritance to the Children of Israel,—54 A Guide and
a Message to men of understanding. 55 Patiently, then, persevere: for the
Promise of Allah is true: and ask forgiveness for your fault, and celebrate
the Praises of your Lord in the evening and in the morning. 56 Those who
dispute about the Signs of Allah without any authority bestowed on
them,—there is nothing in their breasts but (the quest of) greatness, which
they shall never attain to: seek refuge, then, in Allah: it is He Who hears
and sees (all things).

57 Assuredly the creation of the heavens and the earth is a greater (matter)
than the creation of men: yet most men understand not. 58 Not equal are

the blind and those who (clearly) see: nor are (equal) those who believe
and work deeds of righteousness, and those who do evil. Little do you
learn by admonition! 59 The Hour will certainly come: therein is no doubt:
yet most men believe not. 60 And your Lord says: "Call on Me; I will
answer your (prayer): but those who are too arrogant to serve Me will
surely find themselves in Hell—in humiliation!"

SECTION 7

61 It is Allah Who has made the Night for you, that you may rest therein,
and the Day as that which helps (you) to see. Verily Allah is full of Grace
and Bounty to men: yet most men give no thanks. 62 Such is Allah, your
Lord, the Creator of all things; there is no god but He: then how you are
deluded away from the Truth! 63 Thus are deluded those who are wont to
reject the Signs of Allah.

64 It is Allah Who has made for you the earth as a resting place, and the
sky as a canopy, and has given you shape—and made your shapes
beautiful,—and has provided for you Sustenance, of things pure and
good;—such is Allah your Lord. So Glory to Allah, the Lord of the
Worlds! 65 He is the Living (One): there is no god but He: call upon Him,
giving Him sincere devotion. Praise be to Allah, Lord of the Worlds!

66 Say: "I have been forbidden to invoke those whom you invoke besides
Allah,—seeing that the clear Signs have come to me from my Lord; and
I have been commanded to bow (in Islam) to the Lord of the Worlds." 67
It is He Who has created you from dust, then from a sperm-drop, then
from a leech-like clot; then does he get you out (into the light) as a child:
then lets you (grow and) reach your age of full strength; then lets you
become old,—though of you there are some who die before;—and lets
you reach a Term appointed; in order that you may learn wisdom. 68 It is
He Who gives Life and Death; and when He decides upon an affair, He
says to it, "Be", and it is.

SECTION 8

69 See you not those that dispute concerning the Signs of Allah? How are
they turned away (from Reality)?—70 Those who reject the Book and the
(revelations) with which We sent Our messengers: but soon shall they
know,—71 When the yokes (shall be) round their necks, and the chains;
they shall be dragged along,—72 In the boiling fetid fluid; then in the Fire

shall they be burned, 73 Then shall it be said to them: "Where are the
(deities) to which you gave part-worship,—74 In derogation of Allah?"
They will reply: "They have left us in the lurch: nay, we invoked not, of
old, anything (that had real existence)." Thus does Allah leave the
Unbelievers to stray. 75 "That was because you were wont to rejoice on
the earth in things other than the Truth, and that you were wont to be
insolent. 76 Enter you the gates of Hell, to dwell therein: and evil is (this)
abode of the arrogant!"

77 So persevere in patience; for the Promise of Allah is true: and whether
We show you (in this life) some part of what We promise them,—or We
take your soul (to Our Mercy) (before that),—(in any case) it is to Us that
they shall (all) return. 78 We did aforetime send messengers before you:
of them there are some whose story We have related to you, and some
whose story We have not related to you. It was not (possible) for any
messenger to bring a Sign except by the leave of Allah: but when the
Command of Allah was issued, the matter was decided in truth and
justice, and there perished, there and then, those who stood on
Falsehoods.

SECTION 9

79 It is Allah Who made cattle for you, that you may use some for riding
and some for food; 80 And there are (other) advantages in them for you
(besides); that you may through them attain to any need (there may be)
in your hearts; and on them and on ships you are carried. 81 And He
shows you (always) His Signs: then which of the Signs of Allah will you
deny? 82 Do they not travel through the earth and see what was the End
of those before them? They were more numerous than these and superior
in strength and in the traces (they have left) in the land: yet all that they
accomplished was of no profit to them. 83 For when their messengers
came to them with clear Signs, they exulted in such knowledge (and skill)
as they had; but that very (Wrath) at which they were wont to scoff
hemmed them in. 84 But when they saw Our Punishment, they said: "We
believe in Allah,—the one Allah—and we reject the partners we used to
join with Him." 85 But their professing the Faith when they (actually) saw
Our Punishment was not going to profit them. (Such has been) Allah's
way of dealing with His servants (from the most ancient times). And even
thus did the Rejecters of Allah perish (utterly)!□

Chapter 41

Sūrah Fuṣṣilat or *Ḥā Mīm*
(Expounded)

Translator's Introduction

This is the second of the series of seven Sūrahs bearing the Abbreviated Letters *Ḥā Mīm*, as explained in the Introduction to Sūrah 40. To prevent confusion with other Sūrahs of the *Ḥā Mīm* series, the word *Sajdah* is sometimes added to the title, making it *Ḥā Mīm al-Sajdah*, the double title being necessary as there is another Sūrah called *Sajdah* (Sūrah 32). To avoid the double title, it is sometimes called *Fuṣṣilat,* from the occurrence of the word in verse 3.

The meaning of *Ḥā Mīm* has been explained in the Introduction to Sūrah 40., where will also be found a note on the chronology and general theme of the seven *Ḥā Mīm* Sūrahs.

For this particular Sūrah the theme is that the basis of Faith and Revelation is Allah's Power and Goodness, and the fruit of both is man's righteousness and healing.

Summary—What is Revelation and Faith, and what is man's attitude to both, and what are its consequences? (41:1-32).

The fruits of Faith and Unfaith, Truth and Falsehood (41:33-54).

*** *** ***

In the name of Allah,
Most Gracious, Most Merciful.

1 *Ḥā Mīm.*[1] 2 A revelation from (Allah), Most Gracious, Most
Merciful—3 A Book, whereof the verses are explained in detail;—a
Qur'an in Arabic, for people who understand—4 Giving Good News and
Admonition: yet most of them turn away, and so they hear not.

5 They say: "Our hearts are under veils, (concealed) from that to which
you do invite us, and in our ears is a deafness, and between us and you
is a screen: so do you (what you will); for us, we shall do (what we
will!)" 6 Say you: "I am but a man like you: it is revealed to me by

1. Abbreviated Letters: See Introduction to Sūrah 40. See also 40:8 and 41:34. [4462]

inspiration, that your God is one God: so stand true to Him, and ask for His forgiveness." And woe to those who join gods with Allah,—7 Those who practise not regular charity, and who even deny the Hereafter. 8 For those who believe and work deeds of righteousness is a reward that will never fail.

SECTION 2

9 Say: Is it that you deny Him Who created the earth in two Days?[2] And do you join equals with Him? He is the Lord of (all) the Worlds. 10 He set on the (earth), mountains standing firm, high above it, and bestowed blessings on the earth, and measured therein all things to give them nourishment in due proportion, in four Days, in accordance with (the needs of) those who seek (sustenance). 11 Moreover He comprehended in His design the sky, and it had been (as) smoke: He said to it and to the earth: "Come you together, willingly or unwillingly." They said: "We do come (together), in willing obedience." 12 So He completed them as seven firmaments in two Days,[3] and He assigned to each heaven its duty and

---

2. This is a difficult passage, describing the primal creation of our physical earth and the physical heavens around us. If we count the two Days mentioned in this verse, the four Days mentioned in verse 10, and the two Days mentioned in verse 12, we get a total of eight Days, while in many passages the creation is stated to have taken place in six Days: see 7:54 and 32:4. Commentators understand the "four Days" in verse 10 to include the two Days in verse 9, so that the total for the universe comes to six Days. This is reasonable, because the processes described in verses 9 and 10 form really one series. In the one case it is the creation of the formless matter of the earth; in the other case it is the gradual evolution of the form of the earth, its mountains and seas, and its animal and vegetable life, with the "nourishment in due proportion", proper to each. *Cf.* also 15:19-20. [4470]

3. For "*Days*", which may include thousands of years, see 7:54. They refer to stages in the evolution of physical nature. In the Biblical cosmogony, (Gen. i, and ii. 1-7), which reflects old Babylonian cosmogony, the scheme is apparently to be taken literally as to days and is as follows: the first day God created light; the second, the firmament; the third, the earth and vegetation; the fourth, the stars and planets: the fifth, fish and fowl from the sea; and the sixth, cattle, creeping things, beasts on land, and man: on the seventh day He ended His work and rested. Our scheme is wholly different. (1) God did not rest, and never rests. "His Throne doth extend over the heavens and the earth, and He feeleth no fatigue in guarding and preserving them"; (2) God's work has not ended; His activity still goes on, 32:5; 7:54; (3) man in our scheme does not come in with land animals; his advent is much later; (4) our stages are not sharply divided from each other, as in the above scheme, where the stars and planets having been created on the fourth day, it is not intelligible how the first three days were counted, nor how vegetation grew on the third day. Our stages for

command. And We adorned the lower heaven with lights, and (provided it) with guard. Such is the Decree of (Him) the Exalted in Might, Full of Knowledge.

13 But if they turn away, say you: "I have warned you of a stunning
Punishment (as of thunder and lightning) like that which (overtook) the
'Ād and the Thamūd!" 14 Behold, the messengers came to them, from
before them and behind them, (preaching): "Serve none but Allah." They
said, "If our Lord had so pleased, He would certainly have sent down
angels (to preach): now we reject your mission (altogether)." 15 Now the
'Ād behaved arrogantly through the land, against (all) truth and reason,
and said: "Who is superior to us in strength?" What! Did they not see that
Allah, Who created them, was superior to them in strength? But they
continued to reject Our Signs! 16 So We sent against them a furious Wind
through days of disaster, that We might give them a taste of a Penalty of
humiliation in this life; but the Penalty of a Hereafter will be more
humiliating still: and they will find no help. 17 As to the Thamūd, We gave
them guidance, but they preferred blindness (of heart) to Guidance: so the
stunning Punishment of humiliation seized them, because of what they
had earned. 18 But We delivered those who believed and practised
righteousness.

SECTION 3

19 On the Day that the enemies of Allah will be gathered together to the
Fire, they will be marched in ranks. 20 At length, when they reach the
(Fire), their hearing, their sight, and their skins will bear witness against
them, as to (all) their deeds. 21 They will say to their skins: "Why bear
you witness against us?" They will say: "Allah has given us
speech,—(He) Who gives speech to everything: He created you for the
first time, and unto Him were you to return. 22 You did not seek to hide
yourselves, lest your hearing, your sight, and your skins should bear
witness against you! But you did think that Allah knew not many of the
things that you used to do! 23 But this thought of yours which you did
entertain concerning your Lord, has brought you to destruction, and

---

earth and heavens are not in sequence of time for the heavens and the earth. Our six stages are broadly speaking, (1) the throwing off of our planet from cosmic matter; (2) its cooling and condensing; (3) and (4) the growth of vegetable and animal life; (5) and (6) the parallel growth of the starry realm and our solar system. [4477]

(now) have you become of those utterly lost!" 24 If, then, they have
patience, the Fire will be a home for them! And if they beg to be received
into favour, into favour will they not (then) be received. 25 And We have
destined for them intimate companions (of like nature), who made
alluring to them what was before them and behind them; and the sentence
among the previous generations of *Jinns* and men, who have passed
away, is proved against them; for they are utterly lost.

SECTION 4

26 The Unbelievers say: "Listen not to this Qur'an, but talk at random in
the midst of its (reading), that you may gain the upper hand!" 27 But We
will certainly give the Unbelievers a taste of a severe Penalty, and We
will requite them for the worst of their deeds. 28 Such is the requital of the
enemies of Allah,—the Fire: therein will be for them the eternal Home:
a (fit) requital, for that they were wont to reject Our Signs. 29 And the
Unbelievers will say: "Our Lord! Show us those, among *Jinns* and men,
who misled us: we shall crush them beneath our feet, so that they become
the vilest (before all)."

30 In the case of those who say, "Our Lord is Allah", and, further, stand
straight and steadfast, the angels descend on them (from time to time):
"Fear you not!" (they suggest), nor grieve! But receive the Glad Tidings
of the Garden (of Bliss), that which you were promised! 31 We are your
protectors in this life and in the Hereafter: therein shall you have all that
your souls shall desire; therein shall you have all that you ask for!—32 A
hospitable gift from One Oft-Forgiving, Most Merciful!"

SECTION 5

33 Who is better in speech than one who calls (men) to Allah, works
righteousness, and says, "I am of those who bow in Islam"? 34 Nor can
Goodness and Evil be equal. Repel (Evil) with what is better: then will he
between whom and you was hatred become as it were your friend and
intimate! 35 And no one will be granted such goodness except those who
exercise patience and self-restraint,—none but persons of the greatest
good fortune. 36 And if (at any time) an incitement to discord is made to
you by the Evil One, seek refuge in Allah. He is the One Who hears and
knows all things.

37 Among His Signs are the Night and the Day, and the Sun and the

Moon. Adore not the sun and the moon, but adore Allah, Who created
them, if it is Him you wish to serve. 38 But if the (Unbelievers) are
arrogant, (no matter): for in the presence of your Lord are those who
celebrate His praises by night and by day. And they never flag (nor feel
themselves above it). 39 And among His Signs is this: you see the earth
barren and desolate; but when We send down rain to it, it is stirred to life
and yields increase. Truly, He Who gives life to the (dead) earth can
surely give life to (men) who are dead. For He has power over all things.

40 Those who pervert the Truth in Our Signs are not hidden from Us.
Which is better?—he that is cast into the Fire, or he that comes safe
through, on the Day of Judgement? Do what you will: verily He sees
(clearly) all that you do. 41 Those who reject the Message when it comes
to them (are not hidden from Us). And indeed it is a Book of exalted
power. 42 No falsehood can approach it from before or behind it: it is sent
down by One Full of Wisdom, Worthy of all Praise. 43 Nothing is said to
you that was not said to the messengers before you: that your Lord has at
His command (all) Forgiveness as well as a most grievous Penalty. 44 Had
We sent this as a Qur'an (in a language) other than Arabic, they would
have said: "Why are not its verses explained in detail? What! (a Book)
not in Arabic and (a Messenger) an Arab?" Say: "It is a guide and a
healing to those who believe; and for those who believe not, there is a
deafness in their ears, and it is blindness in their (eyes): they are (as it
were) being called from a place far distant!"

SECTION 6

45 We certainly gave Moses the Book aforetime: but disputes arose
therein. Had it not been for a Word that went forth before from your
Lord, (their differences) would have been settled between them: but they
remained in suspicious disquieting doubt thereon. 46 Whoever works
righteousness benefits his own soul; whoever works evil, it is against his
own soul: nor is your Lord ever unjust (in the least) to His servants.

PART XXV

47 To Him is referred the Knowledge of the Hour (of Judgement: He
knows all): no date-fruit comes out of its sheath, nor does a female
conceive (within her womb) nor bring forth (young) but by His
Knowledge. The Day that (Allah) will propound to them the (question),

"Where are the Partners (ye attributed) to Me?" they will say, "We do
assure You not one of us can bear witness!" 48 The (deities) they used to
invoke aforetime will leave them in the lurch, and they will perceive that
they have no way of escape.

49 Man does not weary of asking for good (things), but if ill touches him,
he gives up all hope (and) is lost in despair. 50 When We give him a taste
of some mercy from Ourselves, after some adversity has touched him, he
is sure to say, "This is due to my (merit): I think not that the Hour (of
Judgement) will (ever) be established; but if I am brought back to my
Lord, I have (much) good (stored) in His sight!" But We will show the
Unbelievers the truth of all that they did, and We shall give them the taste
of a severe Penalty.

51 When We bestow favours on man, he turns away, and gets himself
remote on his side (instead of coming to Us); and when evil seizes him,
(he comes) full of prolonged prayer!

52 Say: "See you if the (Revelation) is (really) from Allah, and yet do you
reject it? Who is more astray than one who is in a schism far (from any
purpose)?" **53** Soon will We show them Our Signs in the (furthest)
regions (of the earth), and in their own souls, until it becomes manifest
to them that this is the Truth. Is it not enough that your Lord does witness
all things? **54** Ah indeed! Are they in doubt concerning the Meeting with
their Lord? Ah indeed! It is He that does encompass all things!□

Chapter 42

Sūrah Al-Shūrā
(Consultation)

Translator's Introduction

This is the third Sūrah of the *Ḥā Mīm* series of seven Sūrahs, for which see the Introduction to Sūrah 40.

The theme is how evil and blasphemy can be cured by the Mercy and Guidance of Allah, which come through His Revelation. Men are asked to settle their differences in patience by mutual Consultation (42:38); which explains the title of the Sūrah.

Summary—The Contrast of blasphemy and disputation against Revelation, Unity, and Faith, as relying on the Signs and the Mercy of Allah (42:1-29).

Evil comes through men's own deeds, of which they cannot avoid the consequences, but Guidance comes through Allah's Mercy and Revelation (42:30-53).

*** *** ***

In the name of Allah,
Most Gracious, Most Merciful.

1 *Ḥā Mīm.*[1] 2 *'Ayn Sīn Qāf.*[2] 3 Thus does (He) send inspiration to you as
(He did) to those before you—Allah, Exalted in Power, Full of Wisdom.
4 To Him belongs all that is in the heavens and on earth: and He is Most
High, Most Great. 5 The heavens are almost rent asunder from above
them (by His Glory): and the angels celebrate the Praises of their Lord,
and pray for forgiveness for (all) beings on earth: Behold! Verily Allah
is He, the Oft-Forgiving, Most Merciful.

6 And those who take as protectors others besides Him—Allah does watch
over them; and you are not the disposer of their affairs. 7 Thus have We

---

1. See Introduction to Sūrah 40, paragraphs 2-4. [4526]

2. This Sūrah has a double set of Abbreviated Letters, one in the first verse, and one in this second verse. No authoritative explanation of this second set is available, and I refrain from speculation. [4527]

sent by inspiration to you an Arabic Qur'an: that you may warn the
Mother of Cities[3] and all around her—and warn (them) of the Day of
Assembly, of which there is no doubt: (when) some will be in the Garden,
and some in the blazing Fire. 8 If Allah had so willed, He could have
made them a single people; but He admits whom He will to His Mercy;
and the wrong-doers will have no protector nor helper. 9 What! Have they
taken (for worship) protectors besides Him? But it is Allah,—He is the
Protector, and it is He Who gives life to the dead: it is He Who has power
over all things.

SECTION 2

10 Whatever it be wherein you differ, the decision thereof is with Allah:
such is Allah my Lord: in Him I trust, and to Him I turn. 11 (He is) the
Creator of the heavens and the earth: He has made for you pairs from
among yourselves, and pairs among cattle: by this means does He
multiply you: there is nothing whatever like unto Him, and He is the One
that hears and sees (all things). 12 To Him belong the keys of the heavens
and the earth: He enlarges and restricts the Sustenance to whom He will:
for He knows full well all things. 13 The same religion has He established
for you as that which He enjoined on Noah—that which We have sent by
inspiration to thee—and that which We enjoined on Abraham, Moses, and
Jesus: namely, that you should remain steadfast in Religion, and make no
divisions therein: to those who worship other things than Allah, hard is
the (way) to which you call them. Allah chooses to Himself those whom
He pleases, and guides to Himself those who turn (to Him). 14 And they
became divided only after knowledge reached them,—through selfish
envy as between themselves. Had it not been for a Word that went forth
before from your Lord, (tending) to a Term appointed, the matter would
have been settled between them: but truly those who have inherited the
Book after them are in suspicious (disquieting) doubt concerning it.

15 Now then, for that (reason), call (them to the Faith), and stand steadfast
as you are commanded, nor follow you their vain desires; but say: "I
believe in the Book which Allah has sent down; and I am commanded to
judge justly between you. Allah is our Lord and your Lord: for us (is the

---

3. The City of Makkah. See 6:92. This is undoubtedly a Makkan verse. Even apart from the *Qiblah*, Makkah is the centre of Islam, and "all around her" is the whole world. [4534]

responsibility for) our deeds, and for you for your deeds. There is no
contention between us and you. Allah will bring us together, and to Him
is (our) final goal." 16 But those who dispute concerning Allah after He
has been accepted,—futile is their dispute in the sight of their Lord: on
them is Wrath, and for them will be a Penalty terrible. 17 It is Allah Who
has sent down the Book in Truth, and the Balance (by which to weigh
conduct). And what will make you realise that perhaps the Hour is close
at hand? 18 Only those wish to hasten it who believe not in it: those who
believe hold it in awe, and know that it is the Truth. Behold, verily those
that dispute concerning the Hour are far astray. 19 Gracious is Allah to His
servants: He gives Sustenance to whom He pleases: and He has Power
and can carry out His Will.

SECTION 3

20 To any that desires the tilth of the Hereafter, We give increase in his
tilth, and to any that desires the tilth of this world, We grant somewhat
thereof, but he has no share or lot in the Hereafter.

21 What! Have they partners (in godhead), who have established for them
some religion without the permission of Allah? Had it not been for the
Decree of Judgement, the matter would have been decided between them
(at once). But verily the wrong-doers will have a grievous Penalty. 22 You
will see the wrong-doers in fear on account of what they have earned, and
(the burden of) that must (necessarily) fall on them. But those who
believe and work righteous deeds will be in the luxuriant meads of the
Gardens: they shall have, before their Lord, all that they wish for. That
will indeed be the magnificent Bounty (of Allah). 23 That is (the Bounty)
whereof Allah gives Glad Tidings to His Servants who believe and do
righteous deeds. Say: "No reward do I ask of you for this except the love
of those near of kin." And if anyone earns any good, We shall give him
an increase of good in respect thereof: for Allah is Oft-Forgiving, Most
Ready to appreciate (service).

24 What! Do they say, "He has forged a falsehood against Allah"? But if
Allah willed, He could seal up your heart. And Allah blots out Vanity,
and proves the Truth by His Words. For He knows well the secrets of all
hearts. 25 He is the One that accepts repentance from His Servants and
forgives sins: and He knows all that you do. 26 And He listens to those
who believe and do deeds of righteousness, and gives them increase of

His Bounty: but for the Unbelievers there is a terrible Penalty. 27 If Allah
were to enlarge the provision for His Servants, they would indeed
transgress beyond all bounds through the earth; but He sends (it) down
in due measure as He pleases. For He is with His Servants
Well-Acquainted, Watchful. 28 He is the One that sends down rain (even)
after (men) have given up all hope, and scatters His Mercy (far and wide).
And He is the Protector, Worthy of all Praise. 29 And among His Signs is
the creation of the heavens and the earth, and the living creatures that He
has scattered through them: and He has Power to gather them together
when He wills.

SECTION 4

30 Whatever misfortune happens to you, is because of the things your
hands have wrought, and for many (of them) He grants forgiveness. 31
Nor can you frustrate (aught), (fleeing) through the earth; nor have you,
besides Allah, anyone to protect or to help. 32 And among His Signs are
the ships, smooth-running through the ocean, (tall) as mountains. 33 If it
be His Will, He can still the Wind: then would they become motionless
on the back of the (ocean). Verily in this are Signs for everyone who
patiently perseveres and is grateful. 34 Or He can cause them to perish
because of the (evil) which (the men) have earned; but much does He
forgive. 35 But let those know, who dispute about Our Signs, that there is
for them no way of escape.

36 Whatever you are given (here) is (but) a convenience of this life: but
that which is with Allah is better and more lasting: (it is) for those who
believe and put their trust in their Lord; 37 Those who avoid the greater
crimes and shameful deeds, and, when they are angry even then forgive;
38 Those who listen to their Lord, and establish regular prayer; who
(conduct) their affairs by mutual Consultation;[4] who spend out of what
We bestow on them for Sustenance; 39 And those who, when an

4. *Consultation*. This is the keyword of the Sūrah, and suggests the ideal way in which a good man should conduct his affairs, so that, on the one hand, he may not become too egotistical, and, on the other, he may not lightly abandon the responsibilities which devolve on him as a Personality whose development counts in the sight of God. This principle was applied to its fullest extent by the Holy Prophet in his private and public life, and was fully acted upon by the early rulers of Islam. Modern representative government is an attempt—by no means perfect—to apply this principle in State affairs. See my *Religious Polity of Islam*. [4579]

oppressive wrong is inflicted on them, (are not cowed but) help and
defend themselves.

40 The recompense for an injury is an injury equal thereto (in degree): but
if a person forgives and makes reconciliation, his reward is due from
Allah: for (Allah) loves not those who do wrong.[5] 41 But indeed if any
do help and defend themselves after a wrong (done) to them, against such
there is no cause of blame. 42 The blame is only against those who
oppress men with wrong-doing and insolently transgress beyond bounds
through the land, defying right and justice: for such there will be a
Penalty grievous. 43 But indeed if any show patience and forgive, that
would truly be an exercise of courageous will and resolution in the
conduct of affairs.

SECTION 5

44 For any whom Allah leaves astray, there is no protector thereafter. And
you will see the wrong-doers, when in sight of the Penalty, say: "Is there
any way (to effect) a return?" 45 And you will see them brought forward
to the (Penalty), in a humble frame of mind because of (their) disgrace,
(and) looking with a stealthy glance. And the Believers will say: "Those
are indeed in loss, who have given to perdition their own selves and those
belonging to them on the Day of Judgement. Behold! Truly the
wrong-doers are in a lasting Penalty!" 46 And no protectors have they to
help them, other than Allah. And for any whom Allah leaves to stray,
there is no way (to the Goal).

47 Listen you to your Lord, before there come a Day which there will be
no putting back, because of (the ordainment of) Allah! That Day there
will be for you no place of refuge nor will there be for you any room for
denial (of your sins)! 48 If then they turn away, We have not sent you as
a guard over them. Your duty is but to convey (the Message). And truly,
when We give man a taste of a Mercy from Ourselves, he does exult
thereat, but when some ill happens to him, on account of the deeds which
his hands have sent forth, truly then is man ungrateful!

49 To Allah belongs the dominion of the heavens and the earth. He creates

---

5. God does not love those who do wrong. If, therefore, we tolerate wrong, or encourage wrong by allowing it to run rampant when we can prevent it, we fail in our duty to God. [4583]

what He wills (and plans). He bestows (children) male or female according to His Will (and Plan),[6] 50 Or He bestows both males and females, and He leaves barren whom He will: for He is full of knowledge and power.

51 It is not fitting for a man that Allah should speak to him except by inspiration,[7] or from behind a veil,[8] or by the sending of a messenger[9] to reveal, with Allah's permission, what Allah wills: for He is Most High, Most Wise. 52 And thus have We, by Our command, sent inspiration to you: you knew not (before) what was Revelation, and what was Faith; but We have made the (Qur'an) a Light, wherewith We guide such of Our servants as We will; and verily you do guide (men) to the straight Way,—53 The Way of Allah, to Whom belongs whatever is in the heavens and whatever is on earth. Behold (how) all affairs tend towards Allah!□

---

6. Life is not confined to our one little planet. It is a very old speculation to imagine some life like human life on the planet Mars. Though no scientific demonstration is possible, it is reasonable to suppose that life in some form or other is scattered through some of the millions of heavenly bodies scattered through space. What a wonderful Sign of Allah! The Almighty Who created such countless beings has surely the power to bring them together. *cf* 65:12 [4569]

7. God is Most High, Most Wise: man is, in spite of his high destiny, often the lowest of the low (95:5). Yet God, out of His infinite Mercy and Grace, has bestowed His Revelation on man. How does it come about? Three ways are mentioned: (1) *Waḥyun,* Inspiration; (2) from behind a veil; and (3) by the sending of a Messenger: see the notes following.

Arabic *Waḥyun,* translated here "Inspiration", is interpreted to be of two kinds: (1) a suggestion thrown by God into the heart or mind of man, by which man understands the substance of the Message, whether it is a command or prohibition, or an explanation of a great truth; and (2) verbal or literal inspiration, by which the actual words of God are conveyed in human language. [4598]

8. *Behind a veil*: not of course a material veil, but the mystic veil of Light.

Ṣaḥīḥ Muslim relates a tradition that the Prophet said: "His veil is Light: were He to withdraw it, then would the august splendours of His countenance surely consume everything that comes within His Sight." [4599]

9. *Messenger*: *Rasūl*: the angel Gabriel, through whom the revelations were given to the Holy Prophet. These spiritual visions, conveying the message of Revelation, are the basis of the Qur'an. [4600]

Chapter 43

Sūrah Al-Zukhruf
(The Gold Adornments)

Translator's Introduction

This is the fourth Sūrah of the *Ḥā Mīm* series of seven Sūrahs. For their chronology and general theme see the Introduction to Sūrah 40.

This Sūrah deals with the contrasts between the real glory of Truth and Revelation and the false glitter of what people like to believe and worship. It cites the examples of Abraham, Moses, and Jesus, as exposing the False and holding up the Truth. The keyword (*Zukhruf,* Gold Adornments) occurs in verse 38, but the idea occurs all through the Sūrah.

Summary—The Book of Revelation makes things clear, even though the ignorant and foolish mock at it and ignore Allah's Signs: it will last, while its rejecters will perish (43:1-25).

Abraham exposed the falsehood of traditional worship: the glitter and adornments of this world will not last: what was the end of Pharaoh in his arrogant fight with Moses? (43:26-56).

Jesus was a servant of Allah, but his sectarian followers raised false disputations about him: all is known to Allah, Whose Truth will shine, in spite of unfaith (43:57-89).

*** *** ***

In the name of Allah,
Most Gracious, Most Merciful.

1 *Ḥā Mīm.*[1] 2 By the Book that makes things clear,—3 We have made it
a Qur'an in Arabic, that you may be able to understand (and learn
wisdom). 4 And verily, it is in the Mother of the Book, in Our Presence,
high (in dignity), full of wisdom.

5 Shall We then take away the Message from you and repel (you), for that
you are a people transgressing beyond bounds? 6 But how many were the
prophets We sent amongst the peoples of old? 7 And never came there a
prophet to them but they mocked him. 8 So We destroyed

1. Abbreviated Letters: see Introduction to Sūrah 40, paragraphs 2-4. [4604]

(them)—stronger in power than these;—and (thus) has passed on the Parable of the peoples of old.

9 If you were to question them, 'Who created the heavens and the earth?'
they would be sure to reply, 'They were created by (Him), the Exalted in
Power, Full of Knowledge'—10 (Indeed, the same that) has made for you
the earth (like a carpet) spread out, and has made for you roads (and
channels) therein, in order that you may find guidance (on the way); 11
That sends down (from time to time) rain from the sky in due
measure;—and We raise to life therewith a land that is dead; even so will
you be raised (from the dead);—12 That has created pairs in all things, and
has made for you ships and cattle on which you ride, 13 In order that you
may sit firm and square on their backs, and when so seated, you may
celebrate the (kind) favour of your Lord, and say, "Glory to Him Who has
subjected these to our (use), for we could never have accomplished this
(by ourselves), 14 And to our Lord, surely, must we turn back!" 15 Yet
they attribute to some of His servants a share with Him (in His godhead)!
Truly is man a blasphemous ingrate avowed!

SECTION 2

16 What! Has He taken daughters out of what He Himself creates, and
granted to you sons for choice? 17 When news is brought to one of them
of (the birth of) what he sets up as a likeness to (Allah) Most Gracious,
his face darkens, and he is filled with inward grief! 18 Is then one brought
up among trinkets, and unable to give a clear account in a dispute (to be
associated with Allah)? 19 And they make into females angels who
themselves serve Allah. Did they witness their creation? Their evidence
will be recorded, and they will be called to account!

20 ("Ah!") they say, "If it had been the Will of (Allah) Most Gracious, we
should not have worshipped such (deities)!" Of that they have no
knowledge! They do nothing but lie! 21 What! Have We given them a
Book before this, to which they are holding fast? 22 Nay! They say: "We
found our fathers following a certain religion, and we do guide ourselves
by their footsteps." 23 Just in the same way, whenever We sent a Warner
before you to any people, the wealthy ones among them said: "We found
our fathers following a certain religion, and we will certainly follow in
their footsteps." 24 He said: "What! Even if I brought you better guidance
than that which you found your fathers following?" They said: "For us,

we deny that you (prophets) are sent (on a mission at all)." 25 So We
exacted retribution from them: now see what was the end of those who
rejected (Truth)!

SECTION 3

26 Behold! Abraham said to his father and his people: "I do indeed clear
myself of what you worship: 27 (I worship) only Him Who made me, and
He will certainly guide me." 28 And he left it as a Word to endure among
those who came after him, that they may turn back (to Allah). 29 Indeed,
I have given the good things of this life to these (men) and their fathers,
until the Truth has come to them, and a messenger making things clear.
30 But when the Truth came to them, they said: "This is sorcery, and we
do reject it."

31 Also, they say: "Why is not this Qur'an sent down to some leading man
in either of the two (chief) cities?" 32 Is it they who would portion out the
Mercy of your Lord? It is We Who portion out between them their
livelihood in the life of this world: and We raise some of them above
others in ranks, so that some may command work from others. But the
Mercy of your Lord is better than the (wealth) which they amass. 33 And
were it not that (all) men might become of one (evil) way of life, We
would provide, for everyone that blasphemes against (Allah) Most
Gracious, silver roofs for their houses and (silver) stairways on which to
go up, 34 And (silver) doors to their houses, and thrones (of silver) on
which they could recline, 35 And also adornments[2] of gold. But all this
were nothing but conveniences of the present life: the Hereafter, in the
sight of your Lord is for the Righteous.

SECTION 4

36 If anyone withdraws himself from remembrance of (Allah) Most
Gracious, We appoint for him an evil one, to be an intimate companion
to him. 37 Such (evil ones) really hinder them from the Path, but they
think that they are being guided aright! 38 At length, when (such a one)
comes to Us, he says (to his evil companion): "Would that between me
and you were the distance of East and West!" Ah! Evil is the companion
(indeed)! 39 When you have done wrong, it will avail you nothing, that

2. *Adornments of gold*: the keyword to this Sūrah. All false glitter and adornments of this world are as nothing. They more often hinder than help. [4637]

Day, that you shall be partners in Punishment!

40 Can you then make the deaf to hear, or give direction to the blind or to
such as (wander) in manifest error? 41 Even if We take you away, We
shall be sure to exact retribution from them, 42 Or We shall show you that
(accomplished) which We have promised them: for verily We shall
prevail over them. 43 So hold you fast to the Revelation sent down to you;
verily you are on a straight Way. 44 The (Qur'an) is indeed the Message,
for you and for your people; and soon shall you (all) be brought to
account. 45 And question you Our messengers whom We sent before you;
did We appoint any deities other than (Allah) Most Gracious, to be
worshipped?

SECTION 5

46 We did send Moses aforetime, with Our Signs, to Pharaoh and his
Chiefs: He said, "I am a messenger of the Lord of the Worlds." 47 But
when he came to them with Our Signs, behold, they ridiculed them. 48 We
showed them Sign after Sign, each greater than its fellow, and We seized
them with Punishment, in order that they might turn (to Us). 49 And they
said, "O you sorcerer! Invoke your Lord for us according to His covenant
with you; for we shall truly accept guidance." 50 But when We removed
the Penalty from them, behold, they broke their word. 51 And Pharaoh
proclaimed among his people, saying: "O my people! Does not the
dominion of Egypt belong to me, (witness) these streams flowing
underneath my (palace)? What! See you not then? 52 Am I not better than
this (Moses), who is a contemptible wretch and can scarcely express
himself clearly? 53 Then why are not gold bracelets bestowed on him, or
(why) come (not) with him angels accompanying him in procession?" 54
Thus did he make fools of his people, and they obeyed him: truly were
they a people rebellious (against Allah). 55 When at length they provoked
Us, We exacted retribution from them, and We drowned them all. 56 And
We made them (a people) of the Past and an Example to later ages.

SECTION 6

57 When (Jesus) the son of Mary is held up as an example, behold, your
people raise a clamour thereat (in ridicule)! 58 And they say, "Are our
gods best, or he?" This they set forth to you, only by way of disputation:
indeed, they are a contentious people. 59 He was no more than a servant:
We granted Our favour to him, and We made him an example to the

Children of Israel. 60 And if it were Our Will, We could make angels from
amongst you, succeeding each other on the earth. 61 And (Jesus) shall be
a Sign (for the coming of) the Hour (of Judgment): therefore have no
doubt about the (Hour), but follow you Me: this is a straight Way. 62 Let
not the Evil One hinder you: for he is to you an enemy avowed.

63 When Jesus came with clear Signs, he said: "Now have I come to you
with Wisdom, and in order to make clear to you some of the (points) on
which you dispute: therefore fear Allah and obey me. 64 For Allah, He is
my Lord and your Lord: so worship you Him: this is a straight Way." 65
But sects from among themselves fell into disagreement: then woe to the
wrong-doers, from the Penalty of a Grievous Day! 66 Do they only wait
for the Hour—that it should come on them suddenly, while they perceive
not? 67 Friends on that day will be foes, one to another,—except the
Righteous.

SECTION 7

68 My devotees! No fear shall be on you that Day, nor shall you
grieve,—69 (Being) those who have believed in Our Signs and bowed
(their wills to Ours) in Islam. 70 Enter you the Garden, you and your
wives, in (beauty and) rejoicing. 71 To them will be passed round, dishes
and goblets of gold: there will be there all that the souls could desire, all
that the eyes could delight in: and you shall abide therein (for ever). 72
Such will be the Garden of which you are made heirs for your (good)
deeds (in life). 73 You shall have therein abundance of fruit, from which
you shall have satisfaction.

74 The Sinners will be in the Punishment of Hell, to dwell therein (for
ever): 75 Nowise will the (punishment) be lightened for them, and in
despair will they be there overwhelmed. 76 Nowise shall We be unjust to
them: but it is they who have been unjust themselves. 77 They will cry: "O
Mālik![3] Would that your Lord put an end to us!" He will say, "Nay, but
you shall abide!"

78 Verily We have brought the Truth to you: but most of you have a
hatred for Truth. 79 What! Have they settled some Plan (among

3. *Mālik*: one who is lord or possessor; one who is in charge; applied to the Angel in charge of Hell. [4674]

themselves)? But it is We Who settle things. 80 Or do they think that We
hear not their secrets and their private counsels? Indeed (We do), and Our
messengers are by them, to record.

81 Say: "If (Allah) Most Gracious had a son, I would be the first to
worship." 82 Glory to the Lord of the heavens and the earth, the Lord of
the Throne (of Authority)! (He is free) from the things they attribute (to
Him)! 83 So leave them to babble and play (with vanities) until they meet
that Day of theirs, which they have been promised. 84 It is He Who is
Allah in heaven and Allah on earth; and He is Full of Wisdom and
Knowledge. 85 And blessed is He to Whom belongs the dominion of the
heavens and the earth, and all between them: with Him is the knowledge
of the Hour (of Judgement): and to Him shall you be brought back. 86
And those whom they invoke besides Allah have no power of
intercession;—only he who bears witness to the Truth, and they know
(him). 87 If you ask them, who created them, they will certainly say,
Allah: How then are they deluded away (from the Truth)? 88 (Allah has
knowledge) of the (Prophet's) cry, "O my Lord! Truly these are people
who will not believe!" 89 But turn away from them, and say "Peace!" But
soon shall they know!□

Chapter 44

Sūrah Al-Dukhān
(The Smoke)

Translator's Introduction

For the chronology and the general theme of the Sūrahs of the *Hā Mīm* series of which this is the fifth, see the Introduction to Sūrah 40.

The theme of this particular Sūrah is how worldly pride and power are humbled in the dust if they resist spiritual forces, and how Evil and Good find their true setting in the Hereafter.

The title word *Dukhān* occurs in verse 10. It means smoke or mist, and may refer to a drought or famine.

Summary—Revelation explains clearly how worldly pride and arrogance may come to naught, even at long odds, against spiritual truths (44:1-29).

A people may be given all blessings and may fail in its trust, as did Israel: will the Quraysh learn the lesson of Good and Evil? (44:30-59).

*** *** ***

In the name of Allah,
Most Gracious, Most Merciful.

1 *Hā Mīm*.[1] 2 By the Book that makes things clear;—3 We sent it down
during a blessed night: for We (ever) wish to warn (against Evil). 4 In that
(night) is made distinct every affair of wisdom, 5 By command, from Our
Presence. For We (ever) send (revelations), 6 As a Mercy from your Lord:
for He hears and knows (all things); 7 The Lord of the heavens and the
earth and all between them, if you (but) have an assured faith. 8 There is
no god but He: it is He Who gives life and gives death,—the Lord and
Cherisher to you and your earliest ancestors.

9 Yet they play about in doubt. 10 Then watch you for the Day that the sky
will bring forth a kind of smoke (or mist) plainly visible, 11 Enveloping
the people: this will be a Penalty grievous. 12 (They will say): "Our Lord!

---

1. These Abbreviated Letters are discussed in the Introduction to Sūrah 40, paragraphs 2-4. [4688]

Remove the Penalty from us, for we do really believe!" 13 How shall the
Message be (effectual) for them, seeing that a messenger explaining
things clearly has (already) come to them,—14 Yet they turn away from
him and say: "Tutored (by others), a man possessed!" 15 We shall indeed
remove the Penalty for a while, (but) truly you will revert (to your ways).
16 One day We shall seize you with a mighty onslaught: We will indeed
(then) exact Retribution!

17 We did, before them, try the people of Pharaoh: there came to them a
messenger most honourable, 18 Saying: "Restore to me the servants of
Allah: I am to you a messenger worthy of all trust; 19 And be not arrogant
as against Allah: for I come to you with authority manifest. 20 For me, I
have sought safety with my Lord and your Lord, against your injuring
me. 21 If you believe me not, at least keep yourselves away from me." 22
(But they were aggressive): then he cried to his Lord: "These are indeed
a people given to sin." 23 (The reply came): "March forth with My
servants by night: for you are sure to be pursued. 24 And leave the sea as
a furrow (divided): for they are a host (destined) to be drowned." 25 How
many were the gardens and springs they left behind, 26 And cornfields and
noble buildings, 27 And wealth (and conveniences of life), wherein they
had taken such delight! 28 Thus (was their end)! And We made other
people inherit (those things)! 29 And neither heaven nor earth shed a tear
over them: nor were they given a respite (again).

SECTION 2

30 We did deliver aforetime the Children of Israel from humiliating
Punishment, 31 Inflicted by Pharaoh, for he was arrogant (even) among
inordinate transgressors. 32 And We chose them aforetime above the
nations, knowingly, 33 And granted them Signs in which there was a
manifest trial.

34 As to these (Quraysh), they say forsooth: 35 "There is nothing beyond
our first death, and we shall not be raised again. 36 Then bring (back) our
forefathers, if what you say is true!" 37 What! Are they better than the
people of Tubba'[2] and those who were before them? We destroyed them

---

2. *Tubba'* is understood to be a title or family name of the Ḥimyar kings in Yemen, of the tribe of Ḥamdān. The Ḥimyar were an ancient race. At one time they seem to have extended their hegemony over all Arabia and perhaps beyond, to the East African Coast.

because they were guilty of sin.

38 We created not the heavens, the earth, and all between them, merely in
(idle) sport; 39 We created them not except for just ends: but most of them
do not understand. 40 Verily the Day of Sorting Out is the time appointed
for all of them,—41 The Day when no protector can avail his client in
aught, and no help can they receive, 42 Except such as receive Allah's
Mercy: for He is Exalted in Might, Most Merciful.

SECTION 3

43 Verily the tree of Zaqqūm,[3] 44 Will be the food of the Sinful,—45 Like
molten brass; it will boil in their insides, 46 Like the boiling of scalding
water. 47 (A voice will cry): "Seize you him and drag him into the midst
of the blazing Fire! 48 Then pour over his head the Penalty of Boiling
Water. 49 Taste you (this)! Truly were you mighty, full of honour! 50 Truly
this is what you used to doubt!"

51 As to the Righteous (they will be) in a position of Security, 52 Among
Gardens and Springs; 53 Dressed in fine silk and in rich brocade, they will
face each other; 54 So; and We shall join them to Companions with
beautiful, big, and lustrous eyes. 55 There can they call for every kind of
fruit in peace and security; 56 Nor will they there taste Death, except the
first death; and He will preserve them from the Penalty of the blazing
Fire,—57 As a Bounty from your Lord! That will be the supreme
achievement!

58 Verily, We have made this (Qur'an) easy, in your tongue, in order that
they may give heed. 59 So wait you and watch; for they (too) are
waiting.□

Their earliest religion seems to have been Sabianism, or the worship of the heavenly bodies. They seem at different times, later on, to have professed the Jewish and the Christian religion. Among the Embassies sent by the Holy Prophet in A.H. 9 -10 was one to the Ḥimyar of Yemen, which led to their coming into Islam. This was of course much later than the date of this Sūrah. [4715]

3. The opposite of "delicious Fruits" is the terrible tree of *Zaqqūm,* which is further described in 37:62-68. Also see 17:60. [4722]

Chapter 45

Sūrah Al-Jāthiyah
(The Kneeling Down)

Translator's Introduction

This is the sixth Sūrah of the *Hā Mīm* series: for their general theme and chronology, see the Introduction to S. 40.

Summary—The title, *Al-Jāthiyah* (The Kneeling Down, or Bowing the Knee), taken from verse 28, expresses the leading idea in the Sūrah. In this life, in spite of the Signs of Allah, and the evidences of His goodness all around, men go about in Unfaith, and mocking at Faith; but the End will bring them all to their knees.

*** *** ***

In the name of Allah,
Most Gracious, Most Merciful.

1 *Ḥā Mīm.*[1] 2 The revelation of the Book is from Allah the Exalted in
Power, Full of Wisdom. 3 Verily in the heavens and the earth, are Signs
for those who believe. 4 And in the creation of yourselves and the fact that
animals are scattered (through the earth), are Signs for those of assured
Faith. 5 And in the alternation of Night and Day, and the fact that Allah
sends down Sustenance from the sky, and revives therewith the earth after
its death, and in the change of the winds—are Signs for those that are
wise. 6 Such are the Signs of Allah, which We rehearse to you in Truth:
then in what exposition will they believe after (rejecting) Allah and His
Signs?

7 Woe to each sinful dealer in Falsehoods: 8 He hears the Signs of Allah
rehearsed to him, yet is obstinate and lofty, as if he had not heard them:
then announce to him a Penalty grievous! 9 And when he learns
something of Our Signs, he takes them in jest: for such there will be a
humiliating Penalty. 10 In front of them is Hell: and of no profit to them
is anything they may have earned, nor any protectors they may have

---

1. See Introduction to Sūrah 40, paragraphs 2-4. [4735]

taken to themselves besides Allah: for them is a tremendous Penalty.

11 This is (true) Guidance and for those who reject the Signs of their Lord,
is a grievous Penalty of abomination.

SECTION 2

12 It is Allah Who has subjected the sea to you, that ships may sail
through it by His command, that you may seek of His Bounty, and that
you may be grateful. 13 And He has subjected to you, as from Him, all that
is in the heavens and on earth: behold, in that are Signs indeed for those
who reflect. 14 Tell those who believe, to forgive those who do not look
forward to the Days of Allah: it is for Him to recompense (for good or ill)
each people according to what they have earned. 15 If anyone does a
righteous deed, it ensures to the benefit of his own soul; if he does evil,
it works against (his own soul). In the end will you (all) be brought back
to your Lord.

16 We did aforetime grant to the Children of Israel the Book, the Power
of Command, and Prophethood; We gave them, for Sustenance, things
good and pure; and We favoured them above the nations. 17 And We
granted them clear Signs in affairs (of Religion): it was only after
knowledge had been granted to them that they fell into schisms, through
insolent envy among themselves. Verily your Lord will judge between
them on the Day of Judgement as to those matters in which they set up
differences. 18 Then We put you on the (right) Way[2] of Religion: so
follow you that (Way), and follow not the desires of those who know not.
19 They will be of no use to you in the sight of Allah: it is only
wrong-doers (that stand as) protectors, one to another: but Allah is the
Protector of the Righteous. 20 These are clear evidences to men and a
Guidance and Mercy to those of assured Faith. 21 What! Do those who
seek after evil ways think that We shall hold them equal with those who
believe and do righteous deeds—that equal will be their life and their
death? Ill is the judgement that they make.

---

2. Sharī'ah is best translated the "right Way of Religion": which is wider than the mere formal rites and legal provisions, which mostly came in the Madīnah period, long after this Makkan verse had been revealed. [4756]

SECTION 3

22 Allah created the heavens and the earth for just ends, and in order that
each soul may find the recompense of what it has earned, and none of
them be wronged. 23 Then see you such a one as takes as his god his own
vain desire? Allah has, knowing (him as such), left him astray, and sealed
his hearing and his heart (and understanding), and put a cover on his
sight. Who, then, will guide him after Allah (has withdrawn Guidance)?
Will you not then receive admonition? 24 And they say: "What is there but
our life in this world? We shall die and we live, and nothing but Time can
destroy us." But of that they have no knowledge: they merely conjecture:
25 And when Our clear Signs are rehearsed to them, their argument is
nothing but this: they say, "Bring (back) our forefathers, if what you say
is true!" 26 Say: "It is Allah Who gives you life, then gives you death;
then He will gather you together for the Day of Judgement about which
there is no doubt": but most men do not understand.

SECTION 4

27 To Allah belongs the dominion of the heavens and the earth, and the
Day that the Hour of Judgement is established,—that Day will the dealers
in Falsehood perish! 28 And you will see every sect bowing the knee:
every sect will be called to its Record: "This Day shall you be
recompensed for all that you did! 29 This Our Record speaks about you
with truth: for We were wont to put on record all that you did."

30 Then, as to those who believed and did righteous deeds, their Lord will
admit them to His Mercy: that will be the Achievement for all to see. 31
But as to those who rejected Allah, (to them will be said): "Were not Our
Signs rehearsed to you? But you were arrogant, and were a people given
to sin! 32 And when it was said that the promise of Allah was true, and
that the Hour—there was no doubt about its (coming), you used to say,
'We know not what is the Hour: we only think it is an idea, and we have
no firm assurance.'" 33 Then will appear to them the evil (fruits) of what
they did, and they will be completely encircled by that which they used
to mock at!

34 It will also be said: "This Day We will forget you as you forgot the
meeting of this Day of yours! And your abode is the Fire, and no helpers
have you! 35 This, because you used to take the Signs of Allah in jest, and
the life of the world deceived you:" (from) that Day, therefore, they shall

not be taken out thence, nor shall they be received into Grace.

36 Then Praise be to Allah, Lord of the heavens and Lord of the
earth—Lord and Cherisher of all the Worlds! 37 To Him be glory
throughout the heavens and the earth: and He is Exalted in Power, Full
of Wisdom!□

Chapter 46

Sūrah Al-Aḥqāf
(Winding Sand-tracts)

Translator's Introduction

This is the seventh and last Sūrah of the *Ḥā Mīm* series. For the general theme and chronological place of these Sūrahs see the Introduction to Sūrah 40.

The *Aḥqāf* (mentioned in verse 21) are the long and winding crooked tracts of sandhills, characteristic of the country of the 'Ād people, adjoining Ḥaḍramawt and Yemen: see 7:65. These people had, at that time, probably a fertile irrigated country, but their sins brought on the calamity mentioned in 46:24-25. The lesson of this Sūrah is that if the Truth is challenged, the challenge will be duly answered, and Truth vindicated.

Summary—All Creation has a Purpose behind it: Truth and Revelation will be vindicated, and those who question it will be undone by the very means by which they set such store: the righteous should wait in patience and constancy (46:1-35).

*** *** ***

PART XXVI

In the name of Allah,
Most Gracious, Most Merciful.

1 *Ḥā Mīm.*[1] 2 The revelation of the Book is from Allah the Exalted in
Power, Full of Wisdom. 3 We created not the heavens and the earth and
all between them but for just ends, and for a term appointed: but those
who reject Faith turn away from that whereof they are warned. 4 Say: "Do
you see what it is you invoke besides Allah? Show me what it is they
have created on earth, or have they a share in the heavens? Bring me a
Book (revealed) before this, or any remnant of knowledge (you may
have), if you are telling the truth!" 5 And who is more astray than one
who invokes besides Allah, such as will not answer him to the Day of
Judgement, and who (in fact) are unconscious of their call (to them)? 6

1. See Introduction to Sūrah 40, paragraphs 2-4. [4774]

And when mankind are gathered together (at the Resurrection), they will be hostile to them and reject their worship (altogether)!

7 When Our clear Signs are rehearsed to them, the Unbelievers say, of the
Truth when it comes to them: "This is evident sorcery!" 8 Or do they say,
"He has forged it"? Say: "Had I forged it, then can you obtain no single
(blessing) for me from Allah. He knows best of that whereof you talk (so
glibly)! Enough is He for a witness between me and you! And He is
Oft-Forgiving, Most Merciful." 9 Say: "I am no bringer of new-fangled
doctrine among the messengers, nor do I know what will be done with me
or with you. I follow but that which is revealed to me by inspiration; I am
but a Warner open and clear." 10 Say: "See you? If (this teaching) be
from Allah, and you reject it, and a witness from among the Children of
Israel testifies to its similarity (with earlier scripture), and has believed
while you are arrogant, (how unjust you are!) Truly, Allah guides not a
people unjust."

SECTION 2

11 The Unbelievers say of those who believe: "If (this Message) were a
good thing, (such men) would not have gone to it first, before us!" And
seeing that they guide not themselves thereby, they will say, "This is an
(old,) falsehood!" 12 And before this, was the Book of Moses as a guide
and a mercy: and this Book confirms (it) in the Arabic tongue; to
admonish the unjust, and as Glad Tidings to those who do right. 13 Verily
those who say, "Our Lord is Allah," and remain firm (on that Path),—on
them shall be no fear, nor shall they grieve. 14 Such shall be Companions
of the Garden, dwelling therein (for ever): a recompense for their (good)
deeds.

15 We have enjoined on man kindness to his parents: in pain did his
mother bear him, and in pain did she give him birth. The carrying of the
(child) to his weaning is (a period of) thirty months.[2] At length, when he

---

2. In 31:14 the time of weaning was stated to be at the age of two years, *i.e.*, 24 months. See also 2:233. That leaves six months as the *minimum* period of human gestation after which the child is known to be viable. This is in accordance with the latest ascertained scientific facts. The *average* period is 280 days, or ten times the inter-menstrual period, and of course the average period of weaning is much less than 24 months.

The maximum period of breast-feeding (2 years) is again in accordance with the

reaches the age of full strength[3] and attains forty years, he says, "O my
Lord! Grant me that I may be grateful for Your favour which You have
bestowed upon me, and upon both my parents, and that I may work
righteousness such as You may approve; and be gracious to me in my
issue. Truly have I turned to You and truly do I bow (to You) in Islam."
16 Such are they from whom We shall accept the best of their deeds and
pass by their ill deeds: (they shall be) among the Companions of the
Garden: a promise of truth, which was made to them (in this life).

17 But (there is one) who says to his parents, "Fie on you! Do you hold
out the promise to me that I shall be raised up, even though generations
have passed before me (without rising again)?" And the two seek Allah's
aid, (and rebuke the son): "Woe to you! Have faith! For the promise of
Allah is true." But he says, "This is nothing but tales of the ancients!" 18
Such are they against whom is proved the Sentence among the previous
generations of *Jinns* and men, that have passed away; for they will be
(utterly) lost. 19 And to all are (assigned) degrees according to the deeds
which they (have done), and in order that (Allah) may recompense their
deeds, and no injustice be done to them. 20 And on the Day that the
Unbelievers will be placed before the Fire, (it will be said to them): "You
received your good things in the life of the world, and you took your
pleasure out of them: but today shall you be recompensed with a Penalty
of humiliation: for that you were arrogant on earth without just cause, and
that you (ever) transgressed."

---

time that the first dentition is ordinarily completed in a human child. The lower milk incisors in the centre come out between the 6th and 9th month; then come out the milk teeth at intervals, until the canines appear. The second molars come out at about 24 months, and with them the child has a complete apparatus of milk teeth. Nature now expects him to chew and masticate and be independent of his mother's milk completely. On the other hand it hurts the mother to feed from the breast after the child has a complete set of milk teeth. The permanent teeth begin at the sixth year, and the second molars come at 12 years. The third molars are the wisdom teeth, which may appear at 18 to 20 years, or not at all. [4790]

3. The age of full strength (*ashudd*) is held to be between 18 and 30 or 32. Between 30 and 40 the man is in his best manhood. After that he begins to look to his growing issue, and rightly commends the new generation to Allah. Perhaps his spiritual faculties also gain the upper hand after 40. [4791]

SECTION 3

21 Mention (Ḥūd) one of 'Ād's (own) brethren: behold, he warned his
people about the winding Sand-tracts: but there have been warners before
him and after him: "Worship you none other than Allah: truly I fear for
you the Penalty of a Mighty Day." 22 They said: "Have you come in order
to turn us aside from our gods? Then bring upon us the (calamity) with
which you do threaten us, if you are telling the truth!" 23 He said: "The
Knowledge (of when it will come) is only with Allah: I proclaim to you
the mission on which I have been sent: but I see that you are a people in
ignorance!" 24 Then, when they saw the (Penalty in the shape of) a cloud
traversing the sky, coming to meet their valleys, they said, "This cloud
will give us rain!" "Nay, it is the (calamity) you were asking to be
hastened!—a wind wherein is a grievous Penalty! 25 Everything will it
destroy by the command of its Lord!" Then by the morning
they—nothing was to be seen but (the ruins of) their houses! Thus do We
recompense those given to sin! 26 And We had firmly established them in
a (prosperity and) power which We have not given to you (you Quraysh!)
And We had endowed them with (faculties of) hearing, seeing, heart and
intellect: but of no profit to them were their (faculties of) hearing, sight,
and heart and intellect, when they went on rejecting the Signs of Allah;
and they were (completely) encircled by that which they used to mock at!

SECTION 4

27 We destroyed aforetime populations round about you; and We have
shown the Signs in various ways, that they may turn (to Us). 28 Why then
was no help forthcoming to them from those whom they worshipped as
gods, besides Allah, as a means of access (to Allah)? Nay, they left them
in the lurch: but that was their falsehood and their invention.

29 Behold, We turned towards you a company[4] of *Jinns* (quietly)
listening to the Qur'an: when they stood in the presence thereof, they
said, "Listen in silence!" When the (reading) was finished, they returned
to their people, to warn (them of their sins). 30 They said, "O our people!

---

4. *A company of Jinns. Nafar* (company) may mean a group of from three to ten persons. For *Jinns*, see 6:100. They listened to the reading of the Qur'an with great respect. The next verse shows that they had heard of the Jewish religion, but they were impressed with the Message of Islam, and they seem to have gone back to their people to share the Good News with them. [4809]

We have heard a Book revealed after Moses, confirming what came
before it: it guides (men) to the Truth and to a straight Path. 31 O our
people, listen to the one who invites (you) to Allah, and believe in him:
He will forgive you your faults, and deliver you from a Penalty grievous.
32 If any does not listen to the one who invites (us) to Allah, he cannot
frustrate (Allah's Plan) on earth, and no protectors can he have besides
Allah: such men (wander) in manifest error."

33 See they not that Allah, Who created the heavens and the earth, and
never wearied with their creation, is able to give life to the dead? Indeed,
verily He has power over all things. 34 And on the Day that the
Unbelievers will be placed before the Fire, (they will be asked,) "Is this
not the Truth?" They will say, "Indeed, by our Lord!" (One will say:)
"Then taste you the Penalty, for that you were wont to deny (Truth)!"

35 Therefore patiently persevere, as did (all) messengers of inflexible
purpose; and be in no haste about the (Unbelievers). On the Day that they
see the (Punishment) promised them, (it will be) as if they had not tarried
more than an hour in a single day. (Yours but) to proclaim the Message:
but shall any be destroyed except those who transgress?□

Chapter 47

Sūrah Muḥammad

Translator's Introduction

We have examined and followed the current arrangement of the Sūrahs according to subject matter and independently of chronology, and we have found that a logical thread runs through them. We have now finished more than five-sixths of the Qur'an. The remaining sixth consists of short Sūrahs, but these are again grouped according to subject matter.

We begin the first of such groups with a group of three Sūrahs (47-49), which deal with the organisation of the Muslim *Ummah* or community both for external defence and in internal relations. The present Sūrah deals with the necessity of defence against external foes by courage and strenuous fighting, and dates from about the first year of the Hijrah, when the Muslims were under threat of extinction by invasion from Makkah.

Summary—Aggressive hostility to Faith and Truth should be fought firmly, and Allah will guide (47:1-19).

Faint-heartedness condemned; those who strive and those who turn away will be sorted out (47:20-38).

*** *** ***

In the name of Allah,
Most Gracious, Most Merciful.

1 Those who reject Allah and hinder (men) from the Path of Allah,—their
deeds will Allah render astray (from their mark). 2 But those who believe
and work deeds of righteousness, and believe in the (Revelation) sent
down to Muḥammad—for it is the Truth from their Lord—He will
remove from them their ills and improve their condition. 3 This because
those who reject Allah follow vanities, while those who believe follow
the Truth from their Lord: thus does Allah set forth for men their lessons
by similitudes. 4 Therefore, when you meet the Unbelievers (in fight),
smite at their necks; at length, when you have thoroughly subdued them,
bind a bond firmly (on them): thereafter (is the time for) either generosity
or ransom: until the war lays down its burdens. Thus (are you
commanded): but if it had been Allah's Will, He could certainly have

exacted retribution from them (Himself); but (He lets you fight) in order
to test you, some with others. But those who are slain in the Way of
Allah,—He will never let their deeds be lost. 5 Soon will He guide them
and improve their condition, 6 And admit them to the Garden which He
has announced for them.

7 O you who believe! If you will aid (the cause of) Allah, He will aid you,
and plant your feet firmly. 8 But those who reject (Allah),—for them is
destruction, and (Allah) will render their deeds astray (from their mark).
9 That is because they hate the Revelation of Allah; so He has made their
deeds fruitless. 10 Do they not travel through the earth, and see what was
the End of those before them (who did evil)? Allah brought utter
destruction on them, and similar (fates await) those who reject Allah. 11
That is because Allah is the Protector of those who believe, but those who
reject Allah have no protector.

SECTION 2

12 Verily Allah will admit those who believe and do righteous deeds, to
Gardens beneath which rivers flow; while those who reject Allah will
enjoy (this world)[1] and eat as cattle eat; and the Fire will be their abode.
13 And how many cities, with more power than your city which has driven
you out, have We destroyed (for their sins)? And there was none to aid
them. 14 Is then one who is on a clear (Path) from his Lord, no better than
one to whom the evil of his conduct seems pleasing, and such as follow
their own lusts?

15 (Here is) a Parable of the Garden which the righteous are promised: in
it are rivers of water incorruptible; rivers of milk of which the taste never
changes; rivers of wine, a joy to those who drink; and rivers of honey
pure and clear. In it there are for them all kinds of fruits; and Grace from
their Lord. (Can those in such Bliss) be compared to such as shall dwell
for ever in the Fire, and be given, to drink, boiling water, so that it cuts
up their bowels (to pieces)?

---

1. An apt simile. Beasts of the field eat their fill, but have no higher interests. Men who worship the world exclusively are no better: their pleasures and enjoyments rise no higher than those of the beasts of the field. They have no inkling of spiritual happiness. On the contrary, as they were endowed with spiritual faculties which they misused, they will not escape the Fire of Punishment, the Penalty of Sin. [4830]

16 And among them are men who listen to you, but in the end, when they
go out from you, they say to those who have received Knowledge, "What
is it he said just then?" Such are men whose hearts Allah has sealed, and
who follow their own lusts. 17 But to those who receive Guidance, He
increases the (light of) Guidance, and bestows on them their Piety and
Restraint (from evil). 18 Do they then only wait[2] for the Hour,—that it
should come on them suddenly? But already have come some tokens
thereof, and when it (actually) is on them, how can they benefit then by
their admonition? 19 Know, therefore, that there is no god but Allah, and
ask forgiveness for your fault, and for the men and women who believe:
for Allah knows how you move about and how you dwell in your homes.

SECTION 3

20 Those who believe say, "Why is not a Sūrah sent down (for us)?" But
when a Sūrah of basic or categorical meaning is revealed, and fighting is
mentioned therein, you will see those in whose hearts is a disease looking
at you with a look of one in a swoon at the approach of death. But more
fitting for them—21 Were it to obey and say what is just, and when a
matter is resolved on, it were best for them if they were true to Allah. 22
Then, is it to be expected of you, if you were put in authority, that you
will do mischief in the land, and break your ties of kith and kin?

23 Such are the men whom Allah has cursed for He has made them deaf
and blinded their sight. 24 Do they not then earnestly seek to understand
the Qur'an, or are their hearts locked up by them? 25 Those who turn back
as apostates after Guidance was clearly shown to them,—the Evil One has
instigated them and buoyed them up with false hopes. 26 This, because
they said to those who hate what Allah has revealed, "We will obey you
in part of (this) matter"; but Allah knows their (inner) secrets. 27 But how
(will it be) when the angels take their souls at death, and smite their faces

---

2. The sands of time are always running, and when a wrong is done, the time for its punishment is approaching every moment. No one should therefore wait. The time for repentance is *Now* at any given time. When the punishment comes, it is too late for repentance, and all admonition would be useless.

Looking to the particular time when this Sūrah was revealed, *viz*., about a year after the Hijrah, already there were Signs that the plans of the Pagans to crush Islam were crumbling to pieces. The Hijrah showed how much goo- will there was in Madīnah for the Holy Prophet of Allah, and how many people from Makkah adhered to him. The battle of Badr showed that they could hold their own against odds of three to one. [4840]

and their backs? 28 This because they followed that which called forth the
Wrath of Allah, and they hated Allah's good pleasure; so He made their
deeds of no effect.

SECTION 4

29 Or do those in whose hearts is a disease, think that Allah will not bring
to light all their rancour? 30 Had We so willed, We could have shown
them up to you, and you should have known them by their marks: but
surely you will know them by the tone of their speech! And Allah knows
all that you do. 31 And We shall try you until We test those among you
who strive their utmost and persevere in patience; and We shall try your
reported (mettle). 32 Those who reject Allah, hinder (men) from the Path
of Allah, and resist the Messenger, after Guidance has been clearly shown
to them, will not injure Allah in the least, but He will make their deeds of
no effect. 33 O you who believe! Obey Allah, and obey the Messenger,
and make not vain your deeds! 34 Those who reject Allah, and hinder
(men) from the Path of Allah, then die rejecting Allah,—Allah will not
forgive them.

35 Be not weary and faint-hearted, crying for peace, when you should be
uppermost: for Allah is with you, and will never put you in loss for your
(good) deeds. 36 The life of this world is but play and amusement: and if
you believe and guard against Evil, He will grant you your recompense,
and will not ask you (to give up) your possessions. 37 If He were to ask
you for all of them, and press you, you would covetously withhold, and
He would bring out all your ill-feeling. 38 Behold, you are those invited
to spend (of your substance) in the Way of Allah: but among you are
some that are niggardly. But any who are niggardly are so at the expense
of their own souls. But Allah is free of all wants, and it is you that are
needy. If you turn back (from the Path), He will substitute in your stead
another people; then they would not be like you!□

Chapter 48

Sūrah Al-Fatḥ (The Victory)

Translator's Introduction

1. This is the second of the group of three Madīnah Sūrahs described in the Introduction to Sūrah 47. Its date is fixed by the mention of the Treaty of Ḥudaybiyah, Dhū al-Qa'dah A.H. 6 = February 628 (see 9:13).

2. Ḥudaybīyah is a plain, a short day's march to the north of Makkah, a little to the west of the Madīnah-Makkah road, as used in the Prophet's time. Six years had passed since the Prophet had left his beloved City, and it had been in the hands of the Pagan autocracy. But Islam had grown during these six years. Its *Qiblah* was towards the Ka'bah. The Pagans had tried to attack Islam at various times and had been foiled. By Arab custom every Arab was entitled to visit the Sacred Enclosure unarmed, and fighting of any kind was prohibited during the Sacred Months (see 2:194), which included the month of Dhū al-Qa'dah. In Dhū al-Qa'dah A.H. 6, therefore, the Prophet desired to perform the *Umrah* or lesser pilgrimage (2:196), unarmed, but accompanied by his followers. A large following joined him, to the number of fourteen to fifteen hundred.

3. This was not to the liking of the Pagan autocracy at Makkah, which became alarmed, and in breach of all Arab tradition and usage, prepared to prevent the peaceful party from performing the rites of pilgrimage. They marched out to fight the unarmed party. The Prophet turned a little to the west of the road, and encamped at Ḥudaybiyah, where negotiations took place. On the one hand, the Prophet was unwilling to give the Quraysh any pretended excuse for violence in the Sacred Territory; on the other, the Quraysh had learnt, by six years' bitter experience, that their power was crumbling on all sides, and Islam was growing with its moral and spiritual forces, which were also reflected in its powers of organisation and resistance. The enthusiasm with which the Covenant of Fealty was entered into under a tree in Ḥudaybiyah (48:18) by that great multitude united in devotion to their great leader, was evidence of the great power which he commanded even in a worldly sense if the Quraysh had chosen to confront him.

4. A peaceful Treaty was therefore concluded, known as the Treaty of Ḥudaybiyah. It stipulated: (1) that there was to be peace between the parties for ten years; (2) that any tribe or person was free to join either party or make an alliance with it; (3) that if a Quraysh person from Makkah, under guardianship, should join the Prophet without the guardian's permission, he (or she) should be sent back to the guardian, but in the contrary case, they should not be sent back; and (4) that the Prophet and his party were not to enter Makkah that year, but that

they could enter unarmed the following year.

5. Item 3, not being reciprocal, was objected to in the Muslim camp, but it really was of little importance. Muslims under guardianship, sent back to Makkah, were not likely to renounce the blessings of Islam; on the other hand Muslims going to Makkah would be centres of influence for Islam, and it was more important that they should be allowed to remain there than that they should be sent back to Madīnah. It was impossible to think that there would be apostates or renegades to Paganism! "Look on this picture, and on that!"

6. The Muslims faithfully observed the terms of the Treaty. The following year (A.H. 7) they performed the lesser Pilgrimage in great state for three days. It is true that the Makkans later on broke the Peace in the attack which one of their allied tribes (the Banū Bakr) made on the Muslim Banū Khuzā'ah (who were in alliance with the Prophet), but this led to the conquest of Makkah and the sweeping away of the autocracy. Meanwhile Ḥudaybiyah was a great victory, morally and socially, as well as politically, and its lessons are expounded in this Sūrah, as the lessons of Badr were expounded in 8:42-48, and of Uḥud in 3:121-129, 149-180.

Summary—Victory comes from cool courage, devotion, faith, and patience, as shown at Ḥudaybiyah; therefore remember Allah, and follow His Prophet (48:1-29).

*** *** ***

In the name of Allah,
Most Gracious, Most Merciful.

1 Verily We have granted you a manifest Victory:[1] 2 That Allah may
forgive you your faults of the past and those to follow; fulfil His favour
to you; and guide you on the straight Way; 3 And that Allah may help you
with powerful help. 4 It is He Who sent down Tranquillity into the hearts
of the Believers, that they may add faith to their Faith;—for to Allah
belong the Forces of the heavens and the earth; and Allah is Full of
Knowledge and Wisdom;— 5 That He may admit the men and women
who believe, to Gardens beneath which rivers flow, to dwell therein for

1. This is best referred to the Treaty of Ḥudaybiyah, for which see the Introduction to this Sūrah. By this Treaty the Makkan Quraysh, after many years of unrelenting conflict with Islam, at length recognised Islam as (what they thought) an equal power with themselves. In reality the door was then opened for the free spread of Islam throughout Arabia and thence through the world. [4866]

ever, and remove their ills from them;—and that is, in the sight of Allah,
the highest achievement (for man),—6 And that He may punish the
Hypocrites, men and women, and the Polytheists, men and women, who
imagine an evil opinion of Allah. On them is a round of Evil: the Wrath
of Allah is on them: He has cursed them and got Hell ready for them: and
evil is it for a destination. 7 For to Allah belong the Forces of the heavens
and the earth; and Allah is Exalted in Power, Full of Wisdom.

8 We have truly sent you as a witness, as a bringer of Glad Tidings, and
as a Warner: 9 In order that you (O men) may believe in Allah and His
Messenger, that you may assist and honour Him, and celebrate His
praises morning and evening. 10 Verily those who pledge[2] their fealty to
you do no less than pledge their fealty to Allah: the Hand of Allah is over
their hands: then anyone who violates his oath, does so to the harm of his
own soul, and anyone who fulfils what he has covenanted with
Allah,—Allah will soon grant him a great Reward.

SECTION 2

11 The desert Arabs who[3] lagged behind will say to you: "We were
engaged in (looking after) our flocks and herds, and our families: do you
then ask forgiveness for us."[4] They say with their tongues what is not in
their hearts. Say: "Who then has any power at all (to intervene) on your

---

2. In the Ḥudaybiyah negotiations, when it was uncertain whether the Quraysh would treat well or ill the Prophet's delegate to Makkah, there was a great wave of feeling in the Muslim camp of 1400 to 1500 men. They came with great enthusiasm and swore their fealty to the Prophet, by placing hand on hand according to the Arab custom: see paragraph 3 of the Introduction to this Sūrah. This in itself was a wonderful demonstration of moral and material strength, a true Victory; it is called *Bay'ah al-Riḍwān* (Fealty of Allah's Good Pleasure) in Islamic History. They placed their hands on the Prophet's hand, but the Hand of Allah was above them, and He accepted their Fealty.

'Alayhu is an archaic form for *'Alayhi.* [4877]

3. When the Prophet started from Madīnah on the Makkah journey which ended in Ḥudaybiyah, he asked all Muslims to join him in the pious undertaking, and he had a splendid response. But some of the desert tribes hung back and made excuses. Their faith was but lukewarm, and they did not want to share in any trouble which the Makkans might give to the unarmed Muslims on pilgrimage. Their excuse that they were engaged in looking after their flocks and herds and their families was an afterthought, and in any case made after the return of the Prophet and his party with enhanced prestige to Madīnah. [4878]

4. They said this with their tongues, but no thought of piety was in their hearts. [4879]

behalf with Allah, if His Will is to give you some loss[5] or to give you some profit? But Allah is well acquainted with all that you do. 12 Nay, you thought that the Messenger and the Believers would never return to their families; this seemed pleasing in your hearts,[6] and you conceived an evil thought, for you are a people lost (in wickedness)." 13 And if any believe not in Allah and His Messenger, We have prepared, for those who reject Allah, a blazing Fire! 14 To Allah belongs the dominion of the heavens and the earth: He forgives whom He wills, and He punishes whom He wills: but Allah is Oft-Forgiving, Most Merciful.

15 Those who lagged behind[7] (will say), when you (are free to) march and take booty (in war): "Permit us to follow you." They wish to change Allah's decree: Say: "Not thus will you follow us: Allah has already declared (this) beforehand": then they will say, "But you are[8] jealous of us." Nay, but little do they understand (such things). 16 Say to the desert Arabs who lagged behind: "You shall be summoned (to fight) against a people given to vehement war: then shall you fight, or they shall submit. Then if you show obedience, Allah will grant you a goodly reward, but if you turn back as you did before, He will punish you with a grievous Penalty." 17 No blame is there on the blind, nor is there blame on the lame, nor on one ill (if he joins not the war): but he that obeys Allah and

---

5. Their false excuse was based on a calculation of worldly profit and loss. But what about the spiritual loss in detaching themselves from the Holy Prophet or spiritual profit in joining in the splendidly loyal feelings of service and obedience which were demonstrated at Ḥudaybiyah? And in any case they need not think that all their real and secret motives were not known to Allah. [4880]

6. Their faith was so shaky that they thought the worst would happen, and that the Makkan Quraysh would destroy the unarmed band. In their heart of hearts they would not have been sorry, because they were steeped in wickedness and rejoiced in the sufferings of others. But such persons will burn in the fire of their own disappointment. [4881]

7. Now comes out another motive behind the minds of the laggards. The journey for pilgrimage had no promise of war booty. If at any future time there should be a promise of booty they would come! But that is to reverse Allah's law and decree. *Jihād* is not for personal gain or booty: see Sūrah 8 and Introduction to Sūrah 8, paragraph 2. On the contrary *Jihād* is hard striving, in war and peace, in the Cause of Allah. [4883]

8. The desert Arabs loved fighting and plunder, and understood such motives for war. The higher motives seemed to be beyond them. Like ignorant men they attributed petty motives or motives of jealousy if they were kept out of the vulgar circle of fighting for plunder. But they had to be schooled, and they were schooled to higher ideas of discipline, self-sacrifice, and striving hard for a Cause. [4886]

His Messenger,—(Allah) will admit him to Gardens beneath which rivers flow; and he who turns back, (Allah) will punish him with a grievous Penalty.

SECTION 3

18 Allah's Good Pleasure[9] was on the Believers when they swore Fealty to you under the Tree: He knew what was in their hearts, and He sent down Tranquillity to them; and He rewarded them with a speedy
Victory;[10] 19 And many gains will they acquire (besides): and Allah is
Exalted in Power, Full of Wisdom. 20 Allah has promised you many gains that you shall[11] acquire, and He has given[12] you these beforehand; and He has restrained the hands of men from you; that it may be a Sign for[13]
the Believers, and that He may guide you to a straight Path; 21 And other
gains (there are), which are not within your power, but which Allah has compassed: and Allah has power over all things.

22 If the Unbelievers should fight you, they would certainly turn their
backs; then would they find neither protector nor helper. 23 (Such has
been) the practice (approved) of Allah already in the past: no change will
you find in the practice (approved) of Allah. 24 And it is He Who has
restrained their hands from you and your hands from them in the midst of Makkah, after that He gave you the victory over them. And Allah sees
well all that you do. 25 They are the ones who denied Revelation and

9. The great ceremony of the Fealty of Allah's Good Pleasure took place while the Holy Prophet sat under a tree in the plain of Ḥudaybiyah. [4892]

10. The Treaty of Ḥudaybīyah itself was a "speedy Victory": it followed immediately after the *Bay'ah*. [4895]

11. The gains so far seen from the *Bay'ah* and their calm and disciplined behaviour were certainly great; but greater still were to follow in the spiritual sense, in the rapid spread of Islam, in the clearance from the Sacred House of the idolatrous autocracy, and in the universal acceptance of the Message of Allah in Arabia. [4896]

12. The first fruits of the *Bay'ah* were the victory or treaty of Ḥudaybiyah, the cessation for the time being of the hostility of the Makkan Quraysh, and the opening out of the way to Makkah. These things are implied in the phrase "He has restrained the hands of men from you." [4897]

13. Ḥudaybiyah (in both the *Bay'ah* and the Treaty) was truly a signpost for the Believers: it showed the solidarity of Islam, and the position which the Muslims had won in the Arab world. [4898]

hindered you from the Sacred Mosque and the sacrificial animals,[14]
detained from reaching their place of sacrifice. Had there not been
believing men and believing women whom you did not know that[15] you
were trampling down and on whose account a crime would have accrued
to you without (your) knowledge, (Allah would have allowed you to
force your way, but He held back your hands) that He may admit to His
Mercy whom He will. If they had been apart, We should certainly have
punished the Unbelievers among them with a grievous punishment. 26
While the Unbelievers got up in their hearts heat and cant—the heat[16]
and cant of Ignorance,—Allah sent down His Tranquillity to His
Messenger and to the Believers, and made them stick close to the
command of self-restraint; and well were they entitled to it and worthy of
it. And Allah has full knowledge of all things.

SECTION 4

27 Truly did Allah fulfil the vision for His Messenger: you shall enter the
Sacred Mosque, if Allah wills, with minds secure, heads shaved, hair cut
short, and without fear. For He knew what you knew not, and He granted,
besides this, a speedy victory. 28 It is He Who has sent His Messenger
with Guidance and the Religion of Truth, to proclaim it over all religion:
and enough is Allah for a Witness. 29 Muḥammad is the Messenger of
Allah; and those who are with him are strong against Unbelievers, (but)

---

14. The Muslims from Madīnah had brought the animals for sacrifice with them, and had put on the *Iḥrām* or pilgrim's garb (see 2:197), but they were not only prevented from entering Makkah, but were also prevented from sending the sacrificial animals to the place of sacrifice in Makkah, as they could have done under 2:196. The sacrifice was therefore actually offered at Ḥudaybiyah. [4903]

15. There were at the time in Makkah believing Muslims, men and women, and the faith of some of them was unknown to their brethren from Madīnah. Had a fight taken place in Makkah, even though the Muslims had been successful, they would unwittingly have killed some of these unknown Muslims, and thus would unwittingly have been guilty of shedding Muslim blood. This was prevented by the Treaty. [4904]

16. While the Unbelievers were blustering and excited, and meticulously objected to introductory words such as "In the name of Allah, Most Gracious, Most Merciful, from Muḥammad, the Prophet of God" (they did not like the titles), the Prophet remained calm and collected, and got the substance of their demands embodied in the Treaty without worrying about words. Even though the terms of the Treaty appeared to the Companions, at first, to be unfair to Muslims, they remained faithful to their Leader and showed trust in his better judgement, a trust that was vindicated by the events that followed. [4907]

compassionate amongst each other. You will see them bow and prostrate themselves (in prayer), seeking Grace from Allah and (His) Good Pleasure. On their faces are their marks, (being) the traces of their prostration. This is their similitude in the Torah; and their similitude in the Gospel is like a seed which sends forth its blade, then makes it strong; it then becomes thick, and it stands on its own stem, (filling) the sowers with wonder and delight. As a result, it fills the Unbelievers with rage at them. Allah has promised those among them who believe and do righteous deeds forgiveness, and a great Reward.□

Chapter 49

Sūrah Al-Ḥujurāt
(The Inner Apartments)

Translator's Introduction

This is the third of the group of three Madīnan Sūrahs, which began with Sūrah 47. See the Introduction to that Sūrah.

Its subject matter is the manners to be observed by the members of the rapidly-growing Muslim community, among themselves and towards its Leader. The keyword "*Ḥujurāt*" (Inner Apartments) occurs in verse 4.

Its date is referred to the Year of Deputations, A.H. 9, when a large number of deputations of all kinds visited Madīnah to offer their allegiance to Islam.

Summary—A community must show its respect to its Leader in all forms of behaviour; quarrels are unseemly and should be composed; manners spring from morals; and mutual respect and confidence are a duty and a privilege in Islam (49:1-18).

*** *** ***

In the name of Allah,
Most Gracious, Most Merciful.

1 O you who believe! Put not yourselves forward[1] before Allah and His Messenger; but fear Allah: for Allah is He Who hears and knows all things.

2 O you who believe! Raise not your voices[2] above the voice of the Prophet, nor speak aloud to him in talk, as you may speak aloud to one

---

1. Several shades of meaning are implied: (1) do not make yourselves conspicuous in word or deed when in the presence of Allah (*e.g.*, in a Mosque, or at Prayers or religious assemblies); (2) do not anticipate in word or deed what your Leader (Allah's Messenger) may say or do; (3) do not be impatient, trying to hasten things before the time is ripe, of which the best Judge is Allah, Who speaks through His Messenger. Be reverent in all things, as in the presence of Allah: for He hears and sees all things; (4) Look to the Qur'an and the *Sunnah* of the Prophet (peace be on him) for guidance and let nothing else take precedence over them. [4919]

2. It is bad manners to talk loudly before your Leader. Some ill-mannered people so raise their voices as to drown the voice of their Leader, in conversation or in Council. [4920]

another, lest your deeds become[3] vain and you perceive not. 3 Those that
lower their voice in the presence of Allah's Messenger,—their hearts has
Allah tested for piety: for them is Forgiveness and a great Reward.

4 Those who shout out[4] to you from without the Inner Apartments—
most of them lack understanding. 5 If only they had patience until you
could come out to them, it would be best for them: but Allah is
Oft-Forgiving, Most Merciful.

6 O you who believe! If a wicked person comes to you with any news, ascertain the truth, lest you harm people unwittingly, and afterwards become full of repentance for what you have done.

7 And know that among you is Allah's Messenger: were he, in many
matters, to follow your (wishes), you would certainly fall into misfortune:
but Allah has endeared the Faith to you, and has made it beautiful in your
hearts, and He has made hateful to you unbelief, wickedness, and
rebellion: such indeed are those who walk in righteousness;— 8 A grace
and favour from Allah; and Allah is Full of Knowledge and Wisdom.

9 If two parties among the Believers fall into a quarrel, make you peace
between them: but if one of them transgresses beyond bounds against the
other, then fight you (all) against the one that transgresses until it
complies with the command of Allah; but if it complies, then make peace
between them with justice, and be fair: for Allah loves those who are fair
(and just). 10 The Believers are but a single Brotherhood: so make peace
and reconciliation between your two (contending) brothers; and fear
Allah, that you may receive Mercy.

---

3. Such rudeness may even destroy the value of such services as they may otherwise have been able to render, and all this without their even realising the harm they were doing to the Cause. [4921]

4. To shout aloud to your Leader from outside his Chambers shows disrespect both for his person, his time, and his engagements. Only ignorant fools would be guilty of such unseemly behaviour. It is more seemly for them to wait and bide their time until he is free to come out and attend to them. But, in the Court of a spiritual King, much is forgiven that is due to lack of knowledge and understanding. In the earthly Court, ignorance of the Law excuses no man. If a man behaved in that way to the General of an army or the Governor of a Province, not to speak of an earthly King, he would be laid hands on by the Guard, and could never gain the access he desires. [4923]

SECTION 2

11 O you who believe! Let not some men among you laugh at others: it may be that the (latter) are better than the (former): nor let some women laugh at others: it may be that the (latter) are better than the (former): nor defame nor be sarcastic to each other, nor call each other by (offensive) nicknames: ill-seeming is a name connoting wickedness, (to be used of one) after he has believed: and those who do not desist are (indeed) doing wrong.

12 O you who believe! Avoid suspicion as much (as possible): for suspicion in some cases is a sin: and spy not on each other, nor speak ill of each other behind their backs. Would any of you like to eat the flesh of his dead[5] brother? Nay, you would abhor it . . . But fear Allah: for Allah is Oft-Returning, Most Merciful.

13 O mankind! We created you from a single (pair) of a male and a female, and made you into nations and tribes, that you may know each other (not that you may despise each other). Verily the most honoured of you in the sight of Allah is (he who is) the most righteous of you. And Allah has full knowledge and is well-acquainted (with all things).

14 The desert Arabs say, "We believe." Say, "You have no faith; but you
(only) say, 'We have submitted our wills to Allah,' for not yet has Faith
entered your hearts. But if you obey Allah and His Messenger, He will not
belittle aught of your deeds: for Allah is Oft-Forgiving, Most Merciful." 15
Only those are Believers who have believed in Allah and His Messenger, and
have never since doubted, but have striven with their belongings and their
persons in the Cause of Allah: such are the sincere ones. 16 Say: "What! Will
you instruct Allah about your religion? But Allah knows all that is in the
heavens and on earth: He has full knowledge of all things." 17 They impress
on you as a favour that they have embraced Islam. Say, "Count not your
Islam as a favour upon me: nay, Allah has conferred a favour upon you that He
has guided you to the Faith, if you be true and sincere. 18 Verily Allah knows the
secrets of the heavens and the earth: and Allah sees well all that you do."□

---

5. No one would like even to think of such an abomination as eating the flesh of his brother. But when the brother is dead, and the flesh is carrion, abomination is added to abomination. In the same way we are asked to refrain from hurting people's feelings when they are present; how much worse is it when we say things, true or false, when they are absent! [4932]

Chapter 50

Sūrah Qāf

Translator's Introduction

We now come to a group of seven Makkan Sūrahs (50-56), dealing with Allah's revelation through nature, through history, and through the mouths of the Prophets, and pointing to the Hereafter. We saw that the last group of three (47-49) dealt with the external and internal relations of the *Ummah* when formed. In the present group our attention is more particularly directed to aspects eschatological—the Future before us when this life is done.

This particular Sūrah belongs to the early Makkan period. After an appeal to nature and to the fate of wicked peoples in history, it removes as it were the veil (verse 22) from the Future after death.

Summary—Sceptics can look up to the heavens above and to Nature around them, as well as to the fate of sin in the history of the past: will they doubt Allah's Revelation when the veil is lifted? (59:1-29).

A vision of the Day of Recompense and the Day of Reality (50:30-45).

******

In the name of Allah,
Most Gracious, Most Merciful.

1 *Qāf*:[1] By the Glorious Qur'an (you are Allah's Messenger). 2 But they
wonder that there has come to them a Warner from among themselves.
So the Unbelievers say: "This is a wonderful thing! 3 What! When we die
and become dust, (shall we live again)? That is a (sort of) Return far
(from our understanding)."

4 We already know how much of them the earth takes away: with Us is
a Record guarding (the full account). 5 But they deny the truth when it

---

1. This is an Abbreviated Letter. For Abbreviated Letters generally, see note to 2:1. This particular Abbreviated Letter *Qāf* occurs only here as a single letter, and in combination at the beginning of Sūrah 42, where I was unable to explain the full combination. Here the *Qāf* is taken by several Commentators to represent *Quḍiyah al-Amr,* "the matter has been decreed," with reference to the eschatological trend of the Sūrah. Allah knows best. [4939]

comes to them: so they are in a confused state. 6 Do they not look at the
sky above them?—how We have made it and adorned it, and there are no
flaws in it? 7 And the earth—We have spread it out, and set thereon
mountains standing firm, and produced therein every kind of beautiful
growth (in pairs)—8 To be observed and commemorated by every
devotee turning (to Allah). 9 And We send down from the sky rain
charged with blessing, and We produce therewith gardens and grain for
harvests; 10 And tall (and stately) palm trees, with shoots of fruit stalks,
piled one over another;—11 As sustenance for (Allah's) Servants;—and
We give (new) life therewith to land that is dead: thus will be the
Resurrection.

12 Before them was denied (the Hereafter) by the people of Noah, the
Companions of the Rass, the Thamūd, 13 The 'Ād, Pharaoh, the Brethren
of Lūṭ, 14 The Companions of the Wood, and the people of Tubba'; each
one (of them) rejected the messengers, and My warning was duly fulfilled
(in them). 15 Were We then weary with the first Creation, that they should
be in confused doubt about a new Creation?

SECTION 2

16 It was We Who created man, and We know what dark suggestions his
soul makes to him: for We are nearer to him than (his) jugular vein. 17
Behold, two (guardian angels) appointed to learn (his doings) learn (and
note them), one sitting on the right and one on the left. 18 Not a word does
he utter but there is a sentinel by him, ready (to note it). 19 And the stupor
of death will bring truth (before his eyes): "This was the thing which you
were trying to escape!"

20 And the Trumpet shall be blown: that will be the Day whereof Warning
(had been given). 21 And there will come forth every soul: with each will
be an (angel) to drive, and an (angel) to bear witness. 22 (It will be said:)
"You were heedless of this; now have We removed your veil, and sharp
is your sight this Day!" 23 And his Companion will say: "Here is (his
record) ready with me!" 24 (The sentence will be:) "Throw, throw into
Hell every contumacious Rejecter, (of Allah)!—25 Who forbade what was
good, transgressed all bounds, cast doubts and suspicions; 26 Who set up
another god beside Allah: throw him into a severe Penalty." 27 His
Companion will say: "Our Lord! I did not make him transgress, but he
was (himself) far astray." 28 He will say: "Dispute not with each other in

My Presence: I had already in advance sent you Warning. 29 The Word
changes not before Me, and I do not the least injustice to My Servants."

SECTION 3

30 One Day We will ask Hell, "Are you filled to the full?" It will say,
"Are there any more (to come)?"

31 And the Garden will be brought near to the Righteous,—no more a
thing distant. 32 (A voice will say:) "This is what was promised for
you,—for everyone who turned (to Allah) in sincere repentance, who kept
(His Law), 33 Who feared (Allah) Most Gracious unseen, and brought a
heart turned in devotion (to Him): 34 Enter you therein in Peace and
Security; this is a Day of Eternal Life!" 35 There will be for them therein
all that they wish,—and more besides in Our Presence.

36 But how many generations before them did We destroy (for their
sins),—stronger in power than they? Then did they wander through the
land: was there any place of escape (for them)? 37 Verily in this is a
Message for any that has a heart and understanding or who gives ear and
earnestly witnesses (the truth).

38 We created the heavens and the earth and all between them in six Days,
nor did any sense of weariness touch Us. 39 Bear, then, with patience, all
that they say, and celebrate the praises of your Lord, before the rising of
the sun and before (its) setting. 40 And during part of the night, (also,)
celebrate His praises, and (so likewise) after the postures of adoration. 41
And listen for the Day when the Caller will call out from a place quite
near,—42 The Day when they will hear a (mighty) Blast in (very) truth:
that will be the Day of Resurrection. 43 Verily it is We Who give Life and
Death; and to Us is the Final Goal—44 The Day when the Earth will be
rent asunder, from (men) hurrying out: that will be a gathering
together,—quite easy for Us.

45 We know best what they say; and you are not one to overawe them by
force. So admonish with the Qur'an such as fear My Warning!□

Chapter 51

Sūrah Al-Dhāriyāt
(The Winds That Scatter)

Translator's Introduction

This is an early Makkan Sūrah, the second of the seven Sūrahs forming a group dealing with Revelation and the Hereafter. See Introduction to Sūrah 50. This Sūrah deals with the varying ways in which Truth prevails irresistibly even against all human probabilities.

Summary—The winds may blow and scatter, lift and rush, or divide in all directions; but the Truth and Promise of Allah are sure and stable, whereof you may see Signs both around and within you (51:1-23).

Past events and what you see before you point to the unfailing consequences of all you do: Allah, of His Grace, sends you a Reminder: the loss is your own if you reject and deny (51:24-60).

*** *** ***

In the name of Allah,
Most Gracious, Most Merciful.

1 By the (Winds) that scatter broadcast; 2 And those that lift and bear
away heavy weights; 3 And those that flow with ease and gentleness; 4
And those that distribute and apportion by Command;—5 Verily that
which you are promised is true; 6 And verily Judgement and Justice must
indeed come to pass.

7 By the Sky with (its) numerous Paths, 8 Truly you are in a doctrine
discordant, 9 Through which are deluded (away from the Truth) such as
would be deluded. 10 Woe to the falsehood-mongers,—11 Those who
(flounder) heedless in a flood of confusion: 12 They ask, "When will be
the Day of Judgment and Justice?" 13 (It will be) a Day when they will be
tried (and tested) over the Fire! 14 "Taste you your trial! This is what you
used to ask to be hastened!"

15 As to the Righteous, they will be in the midst of Gardens and Springs,
16 Taking joy in the things which their Lord gives them, because, before
then, they lived a good life. 17 They were in the habit of sleeping but little

by night, 18 And in the hours of early dawn, they (were found) praying for
Forgiveness; 19 And in their wealth and possessions (was remembered)
the right of the (needy), him who asked, and him who (for some reason)
was[1] prevented (from asking).

20 On the earth are Signs for those of assured Faith, 21 As also in your own
selves: will you not then see? 22 And in heaven is your Sustenance, as
(also) that which you are promised. 23 Then, by the Lord of heaven and
earth, this is the very Truth, as much as the fact that you can speak
intelligently to each other.

SECTION 2

24 Has the story[2] reached you, of the honoured guests of Abraham? 25
Behold, they entered his presence, and said: "Peace!" He said, "Peace!"
(and thought, "These seem) unusual people." 26 Then he turned quickly
to his household, brought out a fatted calf, 27 And placed it before them
... he said, "Will you not eat?" 28 (When they did not eat), he conceived
a fear of them. They said, "Fear not," and they gave him glad tidings of
a son endowed with knowledge. 29 But his wife came forward (laughing)
aloud: she smote her forehead and said: "A barren old woman!" 30 They
said, "Even so has your Lord spoken: and He is full of Wisdom and
Knowledge."

PART XXVII

31 (Abraham) said: "And what, O you Messengers, is your errand (now)?"
32 They said, "We have been sent to a people (deep) in sin;—33 To bring

---

1. True charity remembers not only those in need who ask, but also those who are prevented by some reason from asking. The man of true charity seeks out the latter. There may be various reasons which prevent a man from asking for help: (1) he may be ashamed to ask, or his sense of honour may prevent him from asking; (2) he may be so engrossed in some great ideal that he may not think of asking; (3) he may even not know that he is in need, especially when we think of wealth and possessions in a spiritual sense, as including spiritual gifts and talents; (4) he may not know that you possess the things that can supply his needs; and (5) he may be a dumb and helpless creature, whether a human being or a dumb animal, or any creature within your ken or power. Charity in the higher sense includes all help, from one better endowed to one less well endowed. *Cf.* 2:177; also 2:273-274. [5001]

2. *Cf.* 11:69-73, where further details of the story will be found. *Cf.* also 15:51-56. [5005]

on, on them, (a shower of) stones of clay (brimstone), 34 Marked as from
your Lord for those who trespass beyond bounds." 35 Then We evacuated
those of the Believers who were there, 36 But We found not there any just
(Muslim) persons except in one house:[3] 37 And We left there a Sign for
such as fear the grievous Penalty.

38 And in Moses (was another Sign): behold, We sent him to Pharaoh,
with authority manifest. 39 But (Pharaoh) turned back with his Chiefs, and
said, "A sorcerer, or one possessed!" 40 So We took him and his forces,
and threw them into the sea; and his was the blame.

41 And in the 'Ād (people) (was another Sign): behold, We sent against
them the devastating Wind: 42 It left nothing whatever that it came up
against, but reduced it to ruin and rottenness.

43 And in the Thamūd (was another Sign): behold, they were told, "Enjoy
(your brief day) for a little while!" 44 But they insolently defied the
Command of their Lord: so the stunning noise (of an earthquake) seized
them, even while they were looking on. 45 Then they could not even stand
(on their feet), nor could they help themselves.

46 So were the people of Noah before them: for they wickedly
transgressed.

SECTION 3

47 With power and skill did We construct the Firmament: for it is We Who
create the vastness of Space.[4] 48 And We have spread out the (spacious)
earth: how excellently We do spread out! 49 And of everything We have
created pairs: that you may receive instruction. 50 Hasten you then (at
once) to Allah: I am from Him a Warner to you, clear and open! 51 And
make not another an object of worship with Allah: I am from Him a
Warner to you, clear and open!

52 Similarly, no messenger came to the peoples before them, but they said

---

3. That was the house of Lūṭ: and even there, his wife had no faith: she disobeyed the Command and perished: 11:81. [5014]

4. An alternative rendering of this verse is; "And it is We who built the universe with (Our creative) power; and, verily, it is We who are steadily expanding it." (*The Message of the Qur'an*, Translated and Explained by Muhammad Asad).- Ed.

(of him) in like manner, "A sorcerer, or one possessed!" 53 Is this the
legacy they have transmitted, one to another? Nay, they are themselves
a people transgressing beyond bounds! 54 So turn away from them: not
thine is the blame. 55 But teach (thy Message): for teaching benefits the
Believers.

56 I have only created *Jinns* and men, that they may serve Me. 57 No
Sustenance do I require of them, nor do I require that they should feed
Me. 58 For Allah is He Who gives (all) Sustenance,—Lord of
Power,—Steadfast (forever). 59 For the wrong-doers, their portion is like
unto the portion of their fellows (of earlier generations): then let them not
ask Me to hasten (that portion)! 60 Woe, then, to the Unbelievers, on
account of that Day of theirs which they have been promised!□

Chapter 52

Sūrah Al-Ṭūr
(The Mount)

Translator's Introduction

This is the third of the group of seven Makkan Sūrahs described in the Introduction to Sūrah 50.

It is, like its predecessor, an early Makkan Sūrah. The points here emphasised are: that Revelation is in accord with all Allah's Signs, including previous Revelations, and that the Hereafter is inevitable, and we must prepare for it.

Summary—All Signs of Allah, including previous Revelations, point to the inevitable consequences of ill-deeds and good deeds: how can people deny or ignore the Message of Revelation? (52:1-49).

******

In the name of Allah,
Most Gracious, Most Merciful.

1 By the Mount (of Revelation); 2 By a Decree inscribed; 3 In a Scroll
unfolded; 4 By the much-frequented House; 5 By the Canopy Raised
High; 6 And by the Ocean filled with Swell;—7 Verily, the Doom of your
Lord will indeed come to pass;—8 There is none can avert it;—9 On the
Day when the firmament will be in dreadful commotion. 10 And the
mountains will fly hither and thither.

11 Then woe that Day to those that treat (Truth) as Falsehood;—12 That
play (and paddle) in shallow trifles. 13 That Day shall they be thrust down
to the Fire of Hell, irresistibly. 14 "This", it will be said, "is the
Fire,—which you were wont to deny! 15 Is this then a fake, or is it you
that do not see? 16 Burn you therein: the same is it to you whether you
bear it with patience, or not: you but receive the recompense of your
(own) deeds."

17 As to the Righteous, they will be in Gardens, and in Happiness,—18
Enjoying the (Bliss) which their Lord has bestowed on them, and their

Lord shall deliver them from the Penalty of the Fire. 19 (To them will be
said:) "Eat and drink you, with profit and health, because of your (good)
deeds." 20 They will recline (with ease) on Thrones (of dignity) arranged
in ranks; and We shall join them to Companions, with beautiful big and
lustrous eyes.

21 And those who believe and whose families follow them in Faith,—to
them shall We join their families: nor shall We deprive them (of the fruit)
of aught of their works: (yet) is each individual in pledge for his deeds.
22 And We shall bestow on them, of fruit and meat, anything they shall
desire. 23 They shall there exchange, one with another, a (loving) cup free
of frivolity, free of all taint of ill. 24 Round about them will serve,
(devoted) to them. Youths (handsome) as Pearls well-guarded.

25 They will advance to each other, engaging in mutual enquiry. 26 They
will say: "Aforetime, we were not without fear for the sake of our people.
27 But Allah has been good to us, and has delivered us from the Penalty
of the Scorching Wind. 28 Truly, we did call unto Him from of old: truly
it is He, the Beneficent, the Merciful!"

SECTION 2

29 Therefore proclaim you the praises (of your Lord): for by the Grace of
your Lord, you are no (vulgar) soothsayer, nor are you one possessed. 30
Or do they say:—"A Poet! We await for him some calamity (hatched) by
Time!" 31 Say you: "Await you!—I too will wait along with you!" 32 Is it
that their faculties of understanding urge them to this, or are they but a
people transgressing beyond bounds? 33 Or do they say, "He fabricated
the (Message)"? Nay, they have no faith! 34 Let them then produce a
recital like unto it,—if (it be) they speak the Truth!

35 Were they created of nothing, or were they themselves the creators? 36
Or did they create the heavens and the earth? Nay, they have no firm
belief. 37 Or are the Treasures of your Lord with them, or are they the
managers (of affairs)? 38 Or have they a ladder, by which they can (climb
up to heaven and) listen (to its secrets)? Then let (such a) listener of theirs
produce a manifest proof. 39 Or has He only daughters and you have
sons? 40 Or is it that you do ask for a reward, so that they are burdened
with a load of debt?—41 Or that the Unseen is in their hands, and they
write it down? 42 Or do they intend a plot (against you)? But those who

defy Allah are themselves involved in a Plot! 43 Or have they a god other than Allah? Exalted is Allah far above the things they associate with Him!

44 Were they to see a piece of the sky falling (on them), they would (only)
say: "Clouds gathered in heaps!" 45 So leave them alone until they
encounter that Day of theirs, wherein they shall (perforce) swoon (with
terror),—46 The Day when their plotting will avail them nothing and no
help shall be given them. 47 And verily, for those who do wrong, there is
another punishment besides this: but most of them understand not. 48 Now
await in patience the command of your Lord: for verily you are in Our
eyes: and celebrate the praises of your Lord the while you stand forth, 49
And for part of the night also praise you Him,—and at the retreat of the
stars!□

Chapter 53

Sūrah Al-Najm
(The Star)

Translator's Introduction

This is an early Makkan Sūrah, and is the fourth of the series of seven which were described in the Introduction to Sūrah 50.

The particular theme of this Sūrah is that Revelation is not an illusion: the illusion is in the minds of those who doubt and have false ideas of Allah: Allah is the source and goal of all things.

In some Sūrahs the consecutive arrangement is shown or suggested by a cue-word. Here the cue-word is "star", corresponding to "stars" in the last verse of the last Sūrah. So in 46:1, the words: "Exalted in Power, Full of Wisdom", are carried forward from the last verse of Sūrah 45, and indeed the same words occur in the first verse of Sūrah 45. So, again the words: "Most Merciful, Oft-Forgiving"; in 34:2, refer back to the words: "Oft-Forgiving, Most Merciful": in the last line of Sūrah 33. In 54:1, the nearness of Judgement recalls the same idea at the end of the previous Sūrah (53:57). Other examples will also be found.

Summary—The impression received by the Prophet in revelation is neither error on his part nor deception by others, nor does he speak from selfish motives: it comes clearly from Allah, Who is not what the vain imaginations of men conceive: He is All-in-All, First and Last, Lord of all, Ample in forgiveness (53:1-32).

Those who turn away are petty and ignorant, not knowing that Allah is the source and goal of all things—in men, in nature, and in the events of history: therefore serve you Him (53:33-62).

*** *** ***

In the name of Allah,
Most Gracious, Most Merciful.

1 By the Star when it goes down,—2 Your Companion is neither astray[1]

---

1. "Your Companion" is the Holy Prophet Muḥammad, who had lived among the Quraysh all his life. He is defended from three kinds of charges that the Unbelievers brought against him: (1) that he was going astray, either through defect of intelligence or through carelessness; (2) that he was being misled or deceived by evil spirits; and (3) that

nor being misled. 3 Nor does he say (aught) of (his own) Desire. 4 It is no
less than inspiration sent down to him: 5 He was taught by one[2] Mighty
in Power, 6 Endued with Wisdom: for he appeared (in stately form); 7
While he was in the highest part of the horizon: 8 Then he approached and
came closer, 9 And was at a distance of but two bow-lengths[3] or (even)
nearer; 10 So did (Allah) convey the inspiration to His
Servant—(conveyed) what He (meant) to convey. 11 The (Prophet's)
(mind and) heart in no way falsified that which he saw.

12 Will you then dispute with him concerning what he saw? 13 For indeed
he saw him at a second descent,[4] 14 Near the Lote-tree[5] beyond which
none may pass: 15 Near it is the Garden of Abode. 16 Behold, the Lote-tree
was shrouded (in mystery unspeakable!) 17 (His) sight never swerved, nor
did it go wrong! 18 For truly did he see, of the Signs of his Lord, the
Greatest!

19 Have you seen Lāt, and 'Uzzā, 20 And another, the third (goddess),
Manāt? 21 What! For you the male sex, and for Him, the female? 22
Behold, such would be indeed a division most unfair! 23 These are
nothing but names which you have devised,—you and your fathers,—for
which Allah has sent down no authority (whatever). They follow nothing
but conjecture and what their own souls desire!—Even though there has
already come to them Guidance from their Lord! 24 Nay, shall man have
(just) anything he hankers after? 25 But it is to Allah that the End and the
Beginning (of all things) belong.

---

he spoke out of a whim or impulse, or from a selfish desire to impress his own personality. None of these charges were true. On the contrary he had direct inspiration from Allah. [5086]

2. This is referred by the Commentators to the angel Gabriel, through whom the inspiration came. *Cf.* 81:20. [5087]

3. Two bow-shots (counting 100 to 150 yards to a bow-shot) would be a clearly visible distance. [5089]

4. The first occasion when Gabriel appeared in a visible form was at the Mountain of Light, when he brought his first revelation beginning with *Iqra'*. The second was at the Prophet's *Mi'rāj* or Ascension: see Introduction to Sūrah 17, paragraphs 2-4. These were the only two occasions when Gabriel appeared in visible form. [5092]

5. For the Lote-tree in its literal meaning, see 24:16. The wild Lote is thorny; under cultivation it yields good fruit and shade, and is symbolic of heavenly bliss, as here and in 56:28. [5093]

SECTION 2

26 How many so ever be the angels in the heavens, their intercession will
avail nothing except after Allah has given leave for whom He pleases and
that he is acceptable to Him. 27 Those who believe not in the Hereafter,
name the angels with female names. 28 But they have no knowledge
therein. They follow nothing but conjecture; and conjecture avails
nothing against Truth. 29 Therefore shun those who turn away from Our
Message and desire nothing but the life of this world. 30 That is as far as
knowledge will reach them. Verily your Lord knows best those who stray
from His Path, and He knows best those who receive guidance.

31 Indeed, to Allah belongs all that is in the heavens and on earth: so that
He rewards those who do evil, according to their deeds, and He rewards
those who do good, with what is best. 32 Those who avoid great sins and
shameful deeds, only (falling into) small faults,—verily your Lord is
ample in forgiveness. He knows you well when He brings you out of the
earth, and when you are hidden in your mothers' wombs. Therefore
justify not yourselves: He knows best who it is that guards against evil.

SECTION 3

33 See you one who turns back, 34 Gives a little, then hardens (his heart)?[6]
35 What! Has he knowledge of the Unseen so that he can see? 36 Nay, is
he not acquainted with what is in the books of Moses—37 And of
Abraham who fulfilled his engagements?—38 Namely, that no bearer of
burdens can bear the burden of another; 39 That man can have nothing but
what he strives for; 40 That (the fruit of) his striving will soon come in
sight: 41 Then will he be rewarded with a reward complete; 42 That to your
Lord is the final Goal; 43 That it is He Who grants Laughter and Tears; 44
That it is He Who grants Death and Life; 45 That He did create in
pairs,—male and female, 46 From a seed when lodged (in its place); 47

---

6. The particular reference in this passage, according to Bayḍāwī is to Walīd ibn Mughīrah, who bargained with a Quraysh Pagan for a certain sum if the latter would take upon himself the sins of Walīd. He paid a part of the sum but withheld the rest. The general application that concerns us is threefold: (1) if we accept Islam, we must accept it whole-heartedly and not look back to Pagan superstitions; (2) we cannot play fast and loose with our promises; and (3) no man can bargain about spiritual matters for he cannot see what his end will be unless he follows the law of Allah, which is the law of righteousness. [5108]

That He has promised a Second Creation (Raising of the Dead); 48 That
it is He Who gives wealth and satisfaction; 49 That He is the Lord of
Sirius (the Mighty Star); 50 And that it is He Who destroyed the
(powerful) ancient 'Ād (people), 51 And the Thamūd, nor gave them a
lease of perpetual life. 52 And before them, the people of Noah, for that
they were (all) most unjust and most insolent transgressors.

53 And He destroyed the Overthrown Cities (of Sodom and Gomorrah), 54
So that (ruins unknown) have covered them up. 55 Then which of the gifts
of your Lord, (O man,) will you dispute about? 56 This is a Warner, of the
(series of) Warners of old! 57 The (Judgement) ever approaching draws
near: 58 No (soul) but Allah can lay it bare. 59 Do you then wonder at this
recital? 60 And will you laugh and not weep,—61 Wasting your time in
vanities? 62 But fall you down in prostration to Allah, and adore (Him)!□

Chapter 54

Sūrah Al-Qamar
(The Moon)

Translator's Introduction

This is an early Makkan Sūrah, the fifth in the series dealing with Judgement, and the truth of Revelation, as explained in the Introduction to Sūrah 50.

The theme of the Sūrah is explained by the refrain: "Is there any that will receive admonition?" which occurs six times, at the end of each reference to a past story of sin and rejection of warnings and in the appeal to the simplicity of the Qur'an (verses 15, 17, 22, 32, 40, and 51). There is an invitation to listen to the Message and turn to Truth and Righteousness.

Summary—The Hour of Judgement is near, but men forget or reject the Message, as did the people of Noah, of 'Ād, of Thamūd, of Lot, and of Pharaoh. Is there any that will receive admonition? (54:1-55).

*** *** ***

In the name of Allah,
Most Gracious, Most Merciful.

1 The Hour (of Judgement) is near, and the moon is cleft asunder. 2 But if
they see a Sign, they turn away, and say, "This is (but) transient magic."
3 They reject (the warning) and follow their (own) lusts but every matter
has its appointed time. 4 There have already come to them Recitals
wherein there is (enough) to check (them), 5 Mature wisdom;—but (the
preaching of) Warners profits them not.

6 Therefore, (O Prophet,) turn away from them. The Day that the Caller
will call (them) to a terrible affair, 7 They will come forth,—their eyes
humbled—from (their) graves, (torpid) like locusts scattered abroad, 8
Hastening, with eyes transfixed, towards the Caller!—"Hard is this Day!"
the Unbelievers will say.

9 Before them the people of Noah rejected (their messenger): they
rejected Our servant, and said, "Here is one possessed!", and he was
driven out. 10 Then he called on his Lord: "I am one overcome: do You

then help (me)!" 11 So We opened the gates of heaven, with water pouring
forth. 12 And We caused the earth to gush forth with springs, so the waters
met (and rose) to the extent decreed. 13 But We bore him on an (Ark)
made of broad planks and caulked with palm-fibre: 14 She floats under
Our eyes (and care): a recompense to one who had been rejected (with
scorn)! 15 And We have left this as a Sign (for all time): then is there any
that will receive admonition?

16 But how (terrible) was My Penalty and My Warning? 17 And We have
indeed made the Qur'an easy to understand and remember: then is there
any that will receive admonition?

18 The 'Ād (people) (too) rejected (Truth): then how terrible was My
Penalty and My Warning? 19 For We sent against them a furious wind, on
a Day of violent Disaster, 20 Plucking out men as if they were roots of
palm-trees torn up (from the ground). 21 Indeed, how (terrible) was My
Penalty and My Warning! 22 But We have indeed made the Qur'an easy
to understand and remember: then is there any that will receive
admonition?

SECTION 2

23 The Thamūd (also) rejected (their) Warners. 24 For they said: "What! A
man! A solitary one from among ourselves! Shall we follow such a one?
Truly should we then be straying in mind, and mad! 25 Is it that the
Message is sent to *him*, of all people amongst us? Nay, he is a liar, an
insolent one!" 26 Ah! They will know on the morrow, which is the liar, the
insolent one! 27 For We will send the she-camel by way of trial for them.
So watch them, (O Ṣāliḥ), and possess yourself in patience! 28 And tell
them that the water is to be divided between them: each one's right to
drink being brought forward (by suitable turns). 29 But they called to their
companion, and he took a sword in hand, and hamstrung (her). 30 Ah!
How (terrible) was My Penalty and My Warning! 31 For We sent against
them a single mighty Blast, and they became like the dry stubble used by
one who pens cattle. 32 And We have indeed made the Qur'an easy to
understand and remember: then is there any that will receive admonition?

33 The people of Lūṭ rejected (his) Warning. 34 We sent against them a
violent tornado with showers of stones, (which destroyed them), except
Lūṭ's household: them We delivered by early Dawn,—35 As a Grace from

Us: thus do We reward those who give thanks. 36 And (Lūṭ) did warn
them of Our Punishment, but they disputed about the Warning. 37 And
they even sought to snatch away his guests from him, but We blinded
their eyes. (They heard:) "Now taste you My Wrath and My Warning."
38 Early on the morrow an abiding Punishment seized them: 39 "So taste
you My Wrath and My Warning." 40 And We have indeed made the
Qur'an easy to understand and remember: then is there any that will
receive admonition?

SECTION 3

41 To the people of Pharaoh, too, aforetime, came Warners (from Allah).
42 The (people) rejected all Our Signs; but We seized them with such
Penalty (as comes) from One Exalted in Power, able to carry out His
Will. 43 Are your Unbelievers, (O Quraysh), better than they? Or have you
an immunity in the Sacred Books? 44 Or do they say: "We acting together
can defend ourselves"? 45 Soon will their multitude be put to flight, and
they will show their backs. 46 Nay, the Hour (of Judgement) is the time
promised them (for their full recompense): and that Hour will be most
grievous and most bitter. 47 Truly those in sin are the ones straying in
mind, and mad. 48 The Day they will be dragged through the Fire on their
faces, (they will hear:) "Taste you the touch of Hell!" 49 Verily, all things
have We created in proportion and measure. 50 And Our Command is but
a single (Act),—like the twinkling of an eye. 51 And (oft) in the past, have
We destroyed gangs like unto you: then is there any that will receive
admonition?

52 All that they do is noted in (their) Books (of Deeds): 53 Every matter,
small and great, is on record.

54 As to the Righteous, they will be in the midst of Gardens and Rivers,
55 In an Assembly of Truth, in the Presence of a Sovereign Omnipotent.□

Chapter 55

Sūrah Al-Raḥmān
(The Most Gracious)

Translator's Introduction

The majority of Commentators consider this an early Makkan Sūrah, though some consider at least a part of it as dating from Madīnah. The greater part of it is undoubtedly early Makkan.

It is highly poetical and most sublime, and the refrain "Then which of the favours of your Lord will you deny?" is interspersed 31 times among its 78 verses.

It is the sixth of the series of seven dealing with Revelation, the favours of Allah, and the Hereafter: see Introduction to Sūrah 50.

Here the special theme is indicated by the refrain. The rhyme in most cases is in the dual grammatical form, and the argument implies that though things are created in pairs, there is an underlying Unity, through the Creator, in the favours which He bestows, and in the goal to which they are marching.

Summary—Allah Most Gracious has sent Revelation, one of His greatest favours to man; His creation is in pairs, well-balanced; all created things receive His favours, but they will all pass away, and only Allah will endure through the ages (55:1-34).

Ultimately all evil shall return to its destination, as well as all Good, but ever blessed is the name of Allah, Lord of Glory, Honour and Bounty (55:35-78).

*** *** ***

In the name of Allah,
Most Gracious, Most Merciful.

1 (Allah) Most Gracious! 2 It is He Who has taught the Qur'an.

3 He has created man: 4 He has taught him speech (and Intelligence). 5 The
sun and the moon follow courses (exactly) computed; 6 And the herbs and
the trees—both (alike) bow in adoration. 7 And the Firmament has He
raised high, and He has set up the Balance (of Justice), 8 In order that you
may not transgress (due) balance. 9 So establish weight with justice and
fall not short in the balance. 10 It is He Who has spread out the earth for
(His) creatures: 11 Therein is fruit and date palms, producing spathes

(enclosing dates); 12 Also corn, with (its) leaves and stalk for fodder, and sweet-smelling plants. 13 Then which of the favours of your Lord will you deny?

14 He created man from sounding clay like unto pottery, 15 And He created *Jinns* from fire free of smoke: 16 Then which of the favours of your Lord will you deny?

17 (He is) Lord of the two Easts[1] and Lord of the two Wests: 18 Then which of the favours of your Lord will you deny?

19 He has let free the two bodies of flowing water, meeting together: 20 Between them is a Barrier which they do not transgress: 21 Then which of the favours of your Lord will you deny?

22 Out of them come Pearls and Coral: 23 Then which of the favours of your Lord will you deny?

24 And His are the Ships sailing smoothly through the seas, lofty as mountains: 25 Then which of the favours of your Lord will you deny?

SECTION 2

26 All that is on earth will perish: 27 But will abide (forever) the Face of your Lord,—full of Majesty, Bounty and Honour. 28 Then which of the favours of your Lord will you deny?

29 Of Him seeks (its need) every creature in the heavens and on earth: every day in (new) Splendour does He (shine)! 30 Then which of the favours of your Lord will you deny?

31 Soon shall We settle your affairs, O both you worlds! 32 Then which of the favours of your Lord will you deny?

33 O you assembly of *Jinns* and men! If it be you can pass beyond the zones of the heavens and the earth, pass you! Not without authority shall you be able to pass! 34 Then which of the favours of your Lord will you deny?

---

1. *The two Easts* are the two extreme points where the sun rises during the year, and includes all the points between. Similarly *the two Wests* include the two extreme points of the sun's setting and all the points between. The Dual number fits with the general atmosphere of Duality in this Sūrah. Allah is Lord of every region of the earth and sky, and He scatters His bounties everywhere. [5184]

35 On you will be sent (O you evil ones both!) a flame of fire (to burn)
and a smoke (to choke): no defence will you have: 36 Then which of the
favours of your Lord will you deny? 37 When the sky is rent asunder, and
it becomes red like ointment: 38 Then which of the favours of your Lord
will you deny? 39 On that Day no question will be asked of man or *Jinn*
as to his sin, 40 Then which of the favours of your Lord will you deny? 41
(For) the sinners will be known by their Marks: and they will be seized
by their forelocks and their feet. 42 Then which of the favours of your
Lord will you deny? 43 This is the Hell which the Sinners deny: 44 In its
midst and in the midst of boiling hot water will they wander round! 45
Then which of the favours of your Lord will you deny?

SECTION 3

46 But for such as fear the time when they will stand before (the
Judgement Seat of) their Lord, there will be two Gardens—47 Then which
of the favours of your Lord will you deny?—48 Containing all kinds (of
trees and delights);—49 Then which of the favours of your Lord will you
deny?—50 In them (each) will be two Springs flowing (free); 51 Then
which of the favours of your Lord will you deny?—52 In them will be
Fruits of every kind, two and two. 53 Then which of the favours of your
Lord will you deny? 54 They will recline on Carpets, whose inner linings
will be of rich brocade: the Fruit of the Gardens will be near (and easy of
reach). 55 Then which of the favours of your Lord will you deny? 56 In
them will be (Maidens), chaste, restraining their glances, whom no man
or *Jinn* before them has touched;—57 Then which of the favours of your
Lord will you deny?—58 Like unto rubies and coral. 59 Then which of the
favours of your Lord will you deny? 60 Is there any Reward for
Good—other than Good? 61 Then which of the favours of your Lord will
you deny?

62 And besides these two, there are two other Gardens,—63 Then which of
the favours of your Lord will you deny?—64 Dark-green in colour (from
plentiful watering). 65 Then which of the favours of your Lord will you
deny? 66 In them (each) will be two Springs pouring forth water in
continuous abundance: 67 Then which of the favours of your Lord will
you deny? 68 In them will be Fruits, and dates and pomegranates: 69 Then
which of the favours of your Lord will you deny? 70 In them will be fair
(Companions), good, beautiful;—71 Then which of the favours of your

Lord will you deny?—
72 Companions restrained (as to their glances), in (goodly) pavilions;—
73 Then which of the favours of your Lord will you deny?—
74 Whom no man or *Jinn* before them has touched;—
75 Then which of the favours of your Lord will you deny?—
76 Reclining on green Cushions and rich Carpets of beauty.
77 Then which of the favours of your Lord will you deny?

78 Blessed be the name of your Lord, full of Majesty, Bounty and Honour.□

Chapter 56

Sūrah Al-Wāqi'ah
(The Inevitable Event)

Translator's Introduction

This is the seventh and last Sūrah of the series devoted to Revelation and the Hereafter, as explained in the Introduction to Sūrah 50.

It belongs to the early Makkan period, with the possible exception of one or two verses.

The theme is the certainty of the Day of Judgement and its adjustment of true Values (56:1-56); Allah's Power, Goodness and Glory (56:57-74); and the truth of Revelation (56:75-96).

Summary—When the Day of Judgement comes, the world as we know it will be shaken to its foundations, and men shall be sorted out into three sorts: those nearest to Allah, in exalted Bliss; the Companions of the Right Hand, in Bliss; and the Companions of the Left Hand, in Misery (56:1-56).

Surely the Power and Goodness of Allah, of which Revelation is a Sign, should lead man to accept the Message and glorify Him (56:57-96).

*** *** ***

In the name of Allah,
Most Gracious, Most Merciful.

1 When the Event Inevitable comes to pass, 2 Then will no (soul) entertain
falsehood concerning its coming. 3 (Many) will it bring low; (many) will
it exalt; 4 When the earth shall be shaken to its depths, 5 And the
mountains shall be crumbled to atoms, 6 Becoming dust scattered abroad,
7 And you shall be sorted out into three classes.

8 Then (there will be) the Companions of the Right Hand;—what will be
the Companions of the Right Hand? 9 And the Companions of the Left
Hand,—what will be the Companions of the Left Hand? 10 And those
Foremost (in Faith) will be Foremost (in the Hereafter).

11 These will be those Nearest to Allah: 12 In Gardens of Bliss: 13 A
number of people from those of old, 14 And a few from those of later
times. 15 (They will be) on Thrones encrusted (with gold and precious

stones), 16 Reclining on them, facing each other. 17 Round about them will
(serve) youths of perpetual (freshness), 18 With goblets, (shining) beakers,
and cups (filled) out of clear-flowing fountains: 19 No after-ache will they
receive therefrom, nor will they suffer intoxication: 20 And with fruits,
any that they may select: 21 And the flesh of fowls, any that they may
desire. 22 And (there will be) Companions with beautiful, big, and lustrous
eyes,—23 Like unto Pearls well-guarded. 24 A Reward for the deeds of
their past (life). 25 No frivolity will they hear therein, nor any taint of
ill,—26 Only the saying, "Peace! Peace".

27 The Companions of the Right Hand,—what will be the Companions of
the Right Hand? 28 (They will be) among Lote trees without thorns, 29
Among Ṭalḥ trees with flowers (or fruits) piled one above another,—30 In
shade long-extended, 31 By water flowing constantly, 32 And fruit in
abundance. 33 Whose season is not limited, nor (supply) forbidden, 34 And
on Thrones (of Dignity), raised high. 35 We have created (their
Companions) of special creation, 36 And made them virgin-pure (and
undefiled),—37 Beloved (by nature), equal in age,—38 For the
Companions of the Right Hand.

SECTION 2

39 A (goodly) number from those of old, 40 And a (goodly) number from
those of later times.

41 The Companions of the Left Hand,—what will be the Companions of
the Left Hand? 42 (They will be) in the midst of a fierce Blast of Fire and
in Boiling Water, 43 And in the shades of Black Smoke: 44 Nothing (will
there be) to refresh, nor to please: 45 For that they were wont to be
indulged, before that, in wealth (and luxury), 46 And persisted obstinately
in wickedness supreme! 47 And they used to say, "What! When we die
and become dust and bones, shall we then indeed be raised up again?—48
(We) and our fathers of old?" 49 Say: "Indeed, those of old and those of
later times, 50 All will certainly be gathered together for the meeting
appointed for a Day well-known. 51 Then will you truly,—O you that go
wrong, and treat (Truth) as Falsehood!—52 You will surely taste of the
Tree of Zaqqūm. 53 Then will you fill your insides therewith, 54 And drink
Boiling Water on top of it: 55 Indeed you shall drink like diseased camels
raging with thirst!" 56 Such will be their entertainment on the Day of
Requital!

57 It is We Who have created you: why will you not witness the Truth? 58
Do you then see?—the (human Seed) that you throw out,—59 Is it you
who create it, or are We the Creators? 60 We have decreed Death to be
your common lot, and We are not to be frustrated, 61 From changing your
Forms and creating you (again) in (Forms) that you know not. 62 And you
certainly know already the first form of creation: why then do you not
celebrate His praises?

63 See you the seed that you sow in the ground? 64 Is it you that cause it
to grow, or are We the Cause? 65 Were it Our Will, We could crumble it
to dry powder, and you would be left in wonderment, 66 (Saying), "We
are indeed left with debts (for nothing): 67 Indeed are we shut out (of the
fruits of our labour)"

68 See you the water which you drink? 69 Do you bring it Down (in rain)
from the Cloud or do We? 70 Were it Our Will, We could make it salt
(and unpalatable): then why do you not give thanks?

71 See you the Fire which you kindle? 72 Is it you who grow the tree which
feeds the fire, or do We grow it? 73 We have made it a memorial (of Our
handiwork), and an article of comfort and convenience for the denizens
of deserts. 74 Then celebrate with praises the name of your Lord, the
Supreme!

SECTION 3

75 Furthermore I call to witness the setting of the Stars,—76 And that is
indeed a mighty adjuration if you but knew,—77 That this is indeed a
Qur'an most honourable, 78 In a Book well-guarded, 79 Which none shall
touch but those who are clean: 80 A Revelation from the Lord of the
Worlds.

81 Is it such a Message that you would hold in light esteem? 82 And have
you made it your livelihood that you should declare it false? 83 Then why
do you not (intervene) when (the soul of the dying man) reaches the
throat,—84 And you the while (sit) looking on,—85 But We are nearer to
him than you, and yet see not,—86 Then why do you not—if you are
exempt from (future) account,—87 Call back the soul, if you are true (in
the claim of Independence)?

88 Thus, then, if he be of those Nearest to Allah, 89 (There is for him) Rest

and Satisfaction, and a Garden of Delights. 90 And if he be of the
Companions of the Right Hand, 91 (For him is the salutation), "Peace be
unto you", from the Companions of the Right Hand. 92 And if he be of
those who treat (Truth) as Falsehood, who go wrong, 93 For him is
Entertainment with Boiling Water. 94 And burning in Hell-Fire. 95 Verily,
this is the very Truth and Certainty.

96 So celebrate with praises the name of your Lord, the Supreme.□

Chapter 57

Sūrah Al-Ḥadīd
(Iron)

Translator's Introduction

We have now studied the contents of nearly nine-tenths of the Qur'an. We have found that the arrangement of the Sūrahs in the present Text is not haphazard, but that they follow a distinct logical order more helpful for study than the chronological order. The comprehensive scheme of building up the new *Ummah* or Brotherhood and its spiritual implications is now complete. The remaining tenth of the Qur'an may be roughly considered in two parts. The first contains ten Sūrahs (Sūrah 57 to Sūrah 66), all revealed in Madīnah, and each dealing with some special point which needs emphasis in the social life of the *Ummah*. The second (Sūrah 67 to 94) contains short Makkan lyrics, each dealing with some aspect of spiritual life, expressed in language of great mystic beauty.

The present Madīnan Sūrah is chiefly concerned with spiritual humility and the avoidance of arrogance, and a warning that retirement from the world may not be the best way of seeking the good pleasure of Allah. Its probable date is after the Conquest of Makkah, A.H. 8.

Summary—Allah's Power and Knowledge extend to all things: follow His Light direct, without doubt or fear or half-heartedness, but with humility, generous charity, and faith, and not in a life of isolation from the world (57:1-29).

******

In the name of Allah,
Most Gracious, Most Merciful.

1 Whatever is in the heavens and on earth,—let it declare the Praises and
Glory of Allah: for He is the Exalted in Might, the Wise. 2 To Him
belongs the dominion of the heavens and the earth: it is He Who gives
Life and Death; and He has Power over all things. 3 He is the First and the
Last, the Evident and the Immanent: and He has full knowledge of all
things. 4 He it is Who created the heavens and the earth in six Days, and
is moreover firmly established on the Throne (of authority). He knows
what enters within the earth and what comes forth out of it, what comes
down from heaven and what mounts up to it. And He is with you

wherever you may be. And Allah sees well all that you do. 5 To Him
belongs the dominion of the heavens and the earth: and all affairs are
referred back to Allah. 6 He merges Night into Day, and He merges Day
into Night; and He has full knowledge of the secrets of (all) hearts.

7 Believe in Allah and His Messenger, and spend (in charity) out of the
(substance) whereof He has made you heirs. For, those of you who
believe and spend (in charity),—for them is a great Reward. 8 What cause
have you why you should not believe in Allah?—and the Messenger
invites you to believe in your Lord, and has indeed taken your Covenant,
if you are men of Faith. 9 He is the One Who sends to His Servant
manifest Signs, that He may lead you from the depths of Darkness into
the Light. And verily Allah is to you Most Kind and Merciful. 10 And
what cause have you why you should not spend in the cause of
Allah?—for to Allah belongs the heritage of the heavens and the earth.
Not equal among you are those who spent (freely) and fought, before the
Victory, (with those who did so later). Those are higher in rank than those
who spent (freely) and fought afterwards. But to all has Allah promised
a goodly (reward). And Allah is well-acquainted with all that you do.

SECTION 2

11 Who is he that will loan to Allah a beautiful loan? For (Allah) will
increase it manifold to his credit, and he will have (besides) a liberal
reward. 12 One Day shall you see the believing men and the believing
women—how their Light runs forward before them and by their right
hands: (their greeting will be): "Good News for you this Day! Gardens
beneath which flow rivers! to dwell therein for ever! This is indeed the
highest Achievement!" 13 One Day will the Hypocrites—men and
women—say to the Believers: "Wait for us! Let us borrow (a light) from
your Light!" It will be said: "Turn you back to your rear! Then seek a
light (where you can)!" So a wall will be put up between them, with a
gate therein. Within it will be Mercy throughout, and without it, all
alongside, will be (Wrath and) Punishment! 14 (Those without) will call
out, "Were we not with you?" (The others) will reply, "True! But you led
yourselves into temptation; you looked forward (to our ruin); you
doubted (Allah's Promise); and (your false) desires deceived you; until
there issued the Command of Allah. And the Deceiver deceived you in
respect of Allah. 15 This Day shall no ransom be accepted of you, nor of

those who rejected Allah. Your abode is the Fire: that is the proper place
to claim you: and an evil refuge it is!"

16 Has not the time arrived for the Believers that their hearts in all
humility should engage in the remembrance of Allah and of the Truth
which has been revealed (to them), and that they should not become like
those to whom was given Revelation aforetime, but long ages passed over
them and their hearts grew hard? For many among them are rebellious
transgressors. 17 Know you (all) that Allah gives life to the earth after its
death! Already have We shown the Signs plainly to you, that you may
learn wisdom. 18 For those who give in charity, men and women, and loan
to Allah a Beautiful Loan, it shall be increased manifold (to their credit),
and they shall have (besides) a liberal reward. 19 And those who believe
in Allah and His messengers—they are the Sincere (lovers of Truth), and
the Witnesses (who testify), in the eyes of their Lord: they shall have their
Reward and their Light. But those who reject Allah and deny Our
Signs,—they are the Companions of Hell-Fire.

SECTION 3

20 Know you (all), that the life of this world is but play and amusement,
pomp and mutual boasting and multiplying, (in rivalry) among
yourselves, riches and children. Here is a similitude: how rain and the
growth which it brings forth, delight (the hearts of) the tillers; soon it
withers; you will see it grow yellow; then it becomes dry and crumbles
away. But in the Hereafter is a Penalty severe (for the devotees of
wrong). And Forgiveness from Allah and (His) Good Pleasure (for the
devotees of Allah). And what is the life of this world, but goods and
chattels of deception? 21 Be you foremost (in seeking) Forgiveness from
your Lord, and a Garden (of Bliss), the width whereof is as the width of
heaven and earth, prepared for those who believe in Allah and His
messengers: that is the Grace of Allah, which He bestows on whom He
pleases: and Allah is the Lord of Grace abounding.

22 No misfortune can happen on earth or in your souls but is recorded in
a decree before We bring it into existence: that is truly easy for Allah: 23
In order that you may not despair over matters that pass you by, nor exult
over favours bestowed upon you. For Allah loves not any vainglorious
boaster,—24 Such persons as are covetous and commend covetousness to
men, and if any turn back (from Allah's Way), verily Allah is free of all

needs, Worthy of all praise.

25 We sent aforetime Our messengers with clear Signs and sent down with
them the Book and the Balance (of Right and Wrong), that men may
stand forth in justice; and We sent down Iron, in which is (material for)
mighty war, as well as many benefits for mankind, that Allah may test
who it is that will help, unseen, Him and His messengers: for Allah is Full
of Strength, Exalted in Might (and able to enforce His Will).

SECTION 4

26 And We sent Noah and Abraham, and established in their line
Prophethood and Revelation: and some of them were on right guidance,
but many of them became rebellious transgressors. 27 Then, in their wake,
We followed them up with (others of) Our messengers: We sent after
them Jesus the son of Mary, and bestowed on him the Gospel; and We
ordained in the hearts of those who followed him Compassion and Mercy.
But the Monasticism which they invented for themselves, We did not
prescribe for them: (We commanded) only the seeking for the Good
Pleasure of Allah; but that they did not foster as they should have done.
Yet We bestowed, on those among them who believed, their (due)
reward, but many of them are rebellious transgressors.

28 O you that believe! Fear Allah, and believe in His Messenger, and He
will bestow on you a double portion of His Mercy: He will provide for
you a Light by which you shall walk (straight in your path), and He will
forgive you (your past): for Allah is Oft-Forgiving, Most Merciful. 29 That
the People of the Book may know that they have no power whatever over
the Grace of Allah, that (His) Grace is (entirely) in His Hand, to bestow
it on whoever He wills. For Allah is the Lord of Grace abounding.□

Chapter 58

Sūrah Al-Mujādilah
(The Woman Who Pleads)

Translator's Introduction

This is the second of the ten Madīnan Sūrahs referred to in the Introduction to the last Sūrah. Its subject matter is the acceptance of a woman's plea on behalf of herself and her children (see 58:1 below), and a condemnation of all secret counsels and intrigues in the Muslim Brotherhood.

The date is somewhat close to that of Sūrah 33, say between A.H. 5 and A.H. 7.

Summary—All false pretences, especially those that degrade a woman's position, are condemned—as well as secret consultations between men and intrigues with falsehood, mischief, and sedition (58:1-22).

*** *** ***

PART XXVIII

In the name of Allah,
Most Gracious, Most Merciful.

1 Allah has indeed heard (and accepted) the statement of the woman who pleads[1] with you concerning her husband and carries her complaint (in prayer) to Allah: and Allah (always) hears the arguments between both sides among you: for Allah hears and sees (all things). 2 If any men among you divorce their wives by *Ẓihār* (calling them mothers), they

---

1. The immediate occasion was what happened to Khawlah bint Tha'labah, wife of Aws the son of Ṣāmit. Though in Islam, he divorced her by an old pagan custom: the formula was known as *Ẓihār*, and consisted of the words "Thou art to me as the back of my mother". This was held by pagan custom to imply a divorce and freed the husband from any responsibility for conjugal duties, but did not leave the wife free to leave the husband's home, or to contract a second marriage. Such a custom was in any case degrading to a woman. It was particularly hard on Khawlah, for she loved her husband and pleaded that she had little children who she had no resources herself to support and whom under *Ẓihār* her husband was not bound to support. She urged her plea to the Prophet and in prayer to Allah. Her just plea was accepted, and this iniquitous custom, based on false words, was abolished. See 33:4. [5330]

cannot be their mothers: none can be their mothers except those who gave
them birth. And in fact they use words (both) iniquitous and false: but
truly Allah is One that blots out (sins), and forgives (again and again). 3
But those who divorce their wives by *Ẓihār*, then wish to go back on the
words they uttered,—(it is ordained that such a one) should free a slave
before they touch each other: this are you admonished to perform: and
Allah is well-acquainted with (all) that you do. 4 And if any has not (the
wherewithal), he should fast for two months consecutively before they
touch each other. But if any is unable to do so, he should feed sixty
indigent ones. This, that you may show your faith in Allah and His
Messenger. Those are limits (set by) Allah. For those who reject (Him),
there is a grievous penalty. 5 Those who resist Allah and His Messenger
will be humbled to dust, as were those before them: for We have already
sent down clear Signs. And the Unbelievers (will have) a humiliating
penalty,—6 On the Day that Allah will raise them all up (again) and show
them the Truth (and meaning) of their conduct. Allah has reckoned its
(value), though they may have forgotten it, for Allah is Witness to all
things.

SECTION 2

7 See you not that Allah does know (all) that is in the heavens and on
earth? There is not a secret consultation between three, but He makes the
fourth among them,—nor between five but He makes the sixth,—nor
between fewer nor more, but He is in their midst, wherever they be: in the
end will He tell them the truth of their conduct, on the Day of Judgement.
For Allah has full knowledge of all things. 8 Turn you not your sight
towards those who were forbidden secret counsels yet revert to that which
they were forbidden (to do)? And they hold secret counsels among
themselves for iniquity and hostility, and disobedience to the Messenger.
And when they come to you, they salute you, not as Allah salutes you,
(but in crooked ways): and they say to themselves, "Why does not Allah
punish us for our words?" Enough for them is Hell: in it will they burn,
and evil is that destination!

9 O you who believe! When you hold secret counsel, do it not for iniquity
and hostility, and disobedience to the Prophet; but do it for righteousness
and self-restraint; and fear Allah, to Whom you shall be brought back. 10
Secret counsels are only (inspired) by the Evil One, in order that he may

cause grief to the Believers; but he cannot harm them in the least, except as Allah permits; and on Allah let the Believers put their trust.

11 O you who believe! When you are told to make room in the assemblies, (spread out and) make room: (ample) room will Allah provide for you. And when you are told to rise up, rise up: Allah will raise up, to (suitable) ranks (and degrees), those of you who believe and who have been granted (mystic) knowledge. And Allah is well-acquainted with all you do.

12 O you who believe! When you consult the Messenger in private, spend
something in charity before your private consultation. That will be best
for you, and most conducive to purity (of conduct). But if you find not
(the wherewithal), Allah is Oft-Forgiving, Most Merciful. 13 Is it that you
are afraid of spending sums in charity before your private consultation
(with him)? If, then, you do not so, and Allah forgives you, then (at least)
establish regular prayer; practise regular charity; and obey Allah and His
Messenger. And Allah is well-acquainted with all that you do.

SECTION 3

14 Turn you not your attention to those who turn (in friendship) to such as
have the wrath of Allah upon them? They are neither of you nor of them,
and they swear to falsehood knowingly. 15 Allah has prepared for them a
severe penalty: evil indeed are their deeds. 16 They have made their oaths
a screen (for their misdeeds): thus they obstruct (men) from the path of
Allah: therefore shall they have a humiliating penalty. 17 Of no profit
whatever to them, against Allah, will be their riches nor their sons: they
will be Companions of the Fire, to dwell therein (for ever)! 18 One day
will Allah raise them all up (for judgement): then will they swear to Him
as they swear to you: and they think that they have something (to stand
upon). No, indeed! they are but liars! 19 The Evil One has got the better
of them: so he has made them lose the remembrance of Allah. They are
the party of the Evil One. Truly, it is the party of the Evil One that will
perish!

20 Those who resist Allah and His Messenger will be among those most
humiliated. 21 Allah has decreed: "It is I and My messengers who must
prevail": for Allah is One full of strength, able to enforce His Will. 22 You
will not find any people who believe in Allah and the Last Day, loving
those who resist Allah and His Messenger, even though they were their

fathers or their sons, or their brothers, or their kindred. For such He has written Faith in their hearts, and strengthened them with a spirit from Himself. And He will admit them to Gardens beneath which rivers flow, to dwell therein (for ever). Allah will be well pleased with them, and they with Him. They are the party of Allah. Truly it is the party of Allah that will achieve felicity.□

Chapter 59

Sūrah Al-Ḥashr
(The Gathering *or* Banishment)

Translator's Introduction

This is the third of the series of ten short Madīnan Sūrahs, dealing each with a special point in the life of the *Ummah*: see Introduction to Sūrah 57. The special theme here is how treachery to the *Ummah* on the part of its enemies recoils on the enemies themselves, while it strengthens the bond between the different sections of the *Ummah* itself, and this is illustrated by the story of the expulsion of the Jewish tribe of the Banū Naḍīr in Rabī' al-Awwal, A.H. 4.

This fixes the date of the Sūrah.

Summary—The expulsion of the treacherous Jews from the neighbourhood of Madīnah was smoothly accomplished: their reliance on their fortified positions and on the faith of their allies in treachery proved futile. But the internal bonds in the *Ummah* were strengthened. Such is the wisdom of Allah, Lord of the Most Beautiful Names (59:1-24).

*** *** ***

In the name of Allah,
Most Gracious, Most Merciful.

1 Whatever is in the heavens and on earth, let it declare the Praises and Glory of Allah: for He is the Exalted in Might, the Wise.

2 It is He Who got out the Unbelievers among the People of the Book[1]

---

1. This refers to the Jewish tribe of the Banū Naḍīr whose intrigues and treachery nearly undid the Muslim cause during the perilous days of the battle of Uḥud in Shawwāl, A.H. 3. Four months after, in Rabī' al-Awwal, A.H. 4, steps were taken against them. They were asked to leave the strategic position which they occupied, about three miles south of Madīnah, endangering the very existence of the *Ummah* in Madīnah. At first they demurred, relying on their fortresses and on their secret alliances with the Pagans of Makkah and the Hypocrites of Madīnah. But when the Muslim army was gathered to punish them and actually besieged them for some days, their allies stirred not a finger in their aid, and they were wise enough to leave. Most of them joined their brethren in Syria, which they were permitted to do, after being disarmed. Some of them joined their brethren in Khaybar: see 33:27. The Banū Naḍīr richly deserved punishment, but their lives were

from their homes at the first gathering (of the forces). Little did you think that they would get out: and they thought that their fortresses would defend them from Allah! But the (Wrath of) Allah came to them from quarters[2] from which they little expected (it), and cast terror into their hearts, so that they destroyed their dwellings by their own[3] hands and the hands of the Believers. Take warning, then, O you with eyes (to see)!
3 And had it not been that Allah had decreed banishment for them, He would certainly have punished them in this world: and in the Hereafter they shall (certainly) have the Punishment of the Fire.
4 That is because they resisted Allah and His Messenger: and if anyone resists Allah, verily Allah is severe in Punishment.
5 Whether you cut down (O you Muslims!) the tender palm trees, or you left them standing on their roots, it was by leave of Allah, and in order that He might cover with shame the rebellious transgressors.

6 What Allah has bestowed on His Messenger (and taken away) from them—for this you made no expedition with either cavalry or camelry: but Allah gives power to His messengers over any He pleases: and Allah has power over all things.
7 What Allah has bestowed[4] on His Messenger

---

spared, and they were allowed to carry away their goods and chattels. [5369]

2. They had played a double game. Originally they were sworn allies of the Madīnan Muslims under the Holy Prophet, but they secretly intrigued with the Makkan Pagans under Abū Sufyān and the Madīnan Hypocrites. They even tried treacherously to take the life of the Prophet while he was on a visit to them, breaking both the laws of hospitality and their own sworn alliance. They thought the Pagan Quraysh of Makkah and the Hypocrites of Madīnah would help them, but they did not help them. On the contrary the eleven day siege showed them their own helplessness. Their supplies were cut off: the exigencies of the siege necessitated the destruction of their outlying palm trees; and the unexpected turn in their fortunes disheartened them. Their hearts were struck with terror and they capitulated. But they laid waste their homes before they left: see next note. [5371]

3. Their lives were spared, and they were allowed ten days in which to remove themselves, their families, and such goods as they could carry. In order to leave no habitations for the Muslims they demolished their own houses and laid waste their property, to complete the destruction which the operations of war had already caused at the hands of the besieging Muslim forces. [5372]

4. The Jews had originally come from outside Arabia, and seized the land near Madīnah. They refused to adapt themselves to the people of Arabia, and were in fact a thorn in the side of the genuine Arabs of Madīnah. Their dispossession is therefore a restoration of the land to its original people. But the word *Afā'* is here understood in a technical sense, as meaning property abandoned by the enemy or taken from him without

(and taken away) from the people[5] of the townships,—belongs to Allah,—to His Messenger and to kindred and orphans, the needy and the wayfarer; in order that it may not (merely) make a circuit between the wealthy among you. So take what the Messenger assigns to you, and deny yourselves that which he withholds from you. And fear Allah; for Allah is strict in punishment.

8 (Some part is due) to the indigent Muhājirs,[6] those who were expelled from their homes and their property, while seeking Grace from Allah and (His) Good Pleasure, and aiding Allah and His Messenger: such are indeed the sincere ones;—
9 But those who before them, had homes[7] (in Madīnah) and had adopted the Faith,—show their affection to such as came to them for refuge, and entertain no desire in their hearts for things given to the (latter), but give them preference over themselves, even though poverty was their (own lot). And those saved from the covetousness of their own souls—they are the ones that achieve

---

a formal war. In that sense it is distinguished from *Anfāl,* or spoils, taken after actual fighting, about which see 8:1 and 41. [5379]

5. *The people of the townships*: the townships were the Jewish settlements round Madīnah, of the Banū Naḍīr, and possibly of other tribes. *Cf.* the "townships" mentioned in 59:14 below. The reference cannot be to the Wādī al Qurā (Valley of Towns), now Madā'in Ṣāliḥ, which was subjugated after Khaybar and Fadak in A.H. 7, unless this verse is later than the rest of the Sūrah. [5380]

6. The *Muhājirs* are those who forsook their homes and property in Makkah in order to assist the Holy Prophet in his migration to Madīnah (*Hijrah*). Their devotion and sincerity were proved beyond doubt by their self-denial, and they were now to be rewarded. [5382]

7. This refers to the *Anṣār* (the Helpers), the people of Madīnah, who accepted Islam when it was persecuted in Makkah, and who invited the Holy Prophet to join them and become their Leader in Madīnah. The *Hijrah* was possible because of their good-will and their generous hospitality. They entertained the Prophet and all the refugees (*Muhājirs*) who came with him. The most remarkable ties of full brotherhood were established between individual members of the one group and the other. Until the *Ummah* got its own resources, the Helpers regularly gave and the Refugees regularly received. The Helpers counted it a privilege to entertain the Refugees, and even the poor vied with the rich in their spirit of self-sacrifice. When the confiscated land and property of the Banū Naḍīr was divided, and the major portion was assigned to the Refugees, there was not the least jealousy on the part of the Helpers. They rejoiced in the good fortune of their brethren. And incidentally they were themselves relieved of anxiety and responsibility on their behalf. [5383]

prosperity. 10 And those who came after them say: "Our Lord! Forgive us,
and our brethren who came before us into the Faith, and leave not, in our
hearts, rancour (or sense of injury) against those who have believed. Our
Lord! You are indeed full of Kindness, Most Merciful."

SECTION 2

11 Have you not observed the Hypocrites say to their misbelieving
brethren among the People of the Book?—"If you are expelled, we too
will go out with you, and we will never listen to anyone in your affair;
and if you are attacked (in fight) we will help you." But Allah is witness
that they are indeed liars. 12 If they are expelled, never will they go out
with them; and if they are attacked (in fight), they will never help them;
and if they do help them, they will turn their backs; so they will receive
no help. 13 Of a truth you are stronger (than they) because of the terror in
their hearts, (sent) by Allah. This is because they are men devoid of
understanding. 14 They will not fight you (even) together, except in
fortified townships, or from behind walls. Strong is their fighting (spirit)
amongst themselves: you would think they were united, but their hearts
are divided: that is because they are a people devoid of wisdom.

15 Like those who lately[8] preceded them, they have tasted the evil result
of their conduct; and (in the Hereafter there is) for them a grievous
penalty;—16 (Their allies deceived them), like the Evil One, when he says
to man, "Deny Allah": but when (man) denies Allah, (the Evil One) says,
"I am free of you: I do fear Allah, the Lord of the Worlds!" 17 The end of
both will be that they will go into the Fire, dwelling therein for ever. Such
is the reward of the wrong-doers.

SECTION 3

18 O you who believe! Fear Allah, and let every soul look to what
(provision) he has sent forth for the morrow. Indeed, fear Allah: for Allah

---

8. The immediate reference was probably to the Jewish goldsmith tribe of the Qaynuqā', who were also settled in a fortified township near Madīnah. They were also punished and banished for their treachery, about a month after the battle of Badr, in which the Makkan Pagans had suffered a signal defeat, in Shawwāl, A.H. 2. The Naḍīr evidently did not take that lesson to heart. The general meaning is that we must learn to be on our guard against the consequences of treachery and sin. No fortuitous alliances with other men of iniquity will save us. [5392]

is well-acquainted with (all) that you do. 19 And be you not like those who
forgot Allah; and He made them forget their own souls! Such are the
rebellious transgressors! 20 Not equal are the Companions of the Fire and
the Companions of the Garden: it is the Companions of the Garden, that
will achieve Felicity.

21 Had We sent down this Qur'an on a mountain, verily, you would have
seen it humble itself and cleave asunder for fear of Allah. Such are the
similitudes which We propound to men, that they may reflect.

22 Allah is He, than Whom there is no other god;—Who knows (all
things) both secret and open; He, Most Gracious, Most Merciful. 23 Allah
is He, than Whom there is no other god;—the Sovereign, the Holy One,
the Source of Peace (and Perfection), the Guardian of Faith, the Preserver
of Safety, the Exalted in Might, the Irresistible, the Supreme: Glory to
Allah! (High is He) above the partners they attribute to Him. 24 He is
Allah, the Creator, the Evolver, the Bestower of Forms (or Colours). To
Him belong the Most Beautiful Names: whatever is in the heavens and on
earth, does declare His Praises and Glory: and He is the Exalted in Might,
the Wise.□

Chapter 60

Sūrah Al-Mumtaḥanah
(The Woman To Be Examined)

Translator's Introduction

This is the fourth of the ten Madīnan Sūrahs, each dealing with a special point in the life of the *Ummah*.

Here the point is: what social relations are possible with the unbelievers? A distinction is made between those who persecute you for your Faith and want to destroy you and your Faith, and those who have shown no such rancour. For the latter there is hope of mercy and forgiveness. The question of women and cross-marriages is equitably dealt with.

The date is after the pagans had broken the treaty of Hudaybīyah, for which see Introduction to Sūrah 48—say about A.H. 8, not long before the conquest of Makkah.

Summary—The enemies of your Faith, who would exterminate you and your Faith, are not fit objects of your love: follow Abraham's example: but with those unbelievers who show no rancour, you should deal with kindness and justice: marriages between believers and unbelievers (60:1-13).

*** *** ***

In the name of Allah,
Most Gracious, Most Merciful.

1 O you who believe! Take not My enemies and yours as friends (or protectors),—offering them (your) love,[1] even though they have rejected the Truth that has come to you, and have (on the contrary) driven out the

---

1. The immediate occasion for this was a secret letter sent by one Hātib, a *Muhājir*, from Madīnah, to the Pagans at Makkah, in most friendly terms, seeking their protection on behalf of his children and relatives left behind in Makkah. The letter was intercepted, and he confessed the truth. He was forgiven as he told the truth and his motive did not appear to be heinous, but the instruction was given for future guidance. This was shortly before the conquest of Makkah, but the principle is of universal application. You cannot be on terms of secret intimacy with the enemies of your Faith and people, who are persecuting your Faith and seeking to destroy your Faith and you. You may not do so even for the sake of your relatives, as it compromises the life and existence of your whole community. [5409]

Prophet and yourselves (from your homes), (simply) because you believe
in Allah your Lord! If you have come out to strive in My Way and to
seek My Good Pleasure, (take them not as friends), holding secret
converse of love (and friendship) with them: for I know full well all that
you conceal and all that you reveal. And any of you that does this has
strayed from the straight Path. 2 If they were to get the better of you,[2]
they would behave to you as enemies, and stretch forth their hands and
their tongues against you for evil; and they desire that you should reject
the Truth. 3 Of no profit to you will be your relatives and your children on
the Day of Judgement: He will judge between you: for Allah sees well all
that you do.

4 There is for you an excellent example (to follow) in Abraham and those
with him, when they said to their people: "We are clear of you and of
whatever you worship besides Allah: we have rejected you, and there has
arisen, between us and you, enmity and hatred for ever,—unless you
believe in Allah and Him alone": but not when Abraham said to his
father: "I will pray for forgiveness for you, though I have no power (to
get) aught on your behalf from Allah." (They prayed): "Our Lord! In You
do we trust, and to You do we turn in repentance: to You is (our) final
Goal. 5 Our Lord! Make us not a (test and) trial for the Unbelievers, but
forgive us, our Lord! For You are the Exalted in Might, the Wise." 6
There was indeed in them an excellent example for you to follow,—for
those whose hope is in Allah and in the Last Day. But if any turn away,
truly Allah is Free of all Wants, Worthy of all Praise.

SECTION 2

7 It may be that Allah will grant love (and friendship) between you and
those whom you (now) hold as enemies. For Allah has power (over all
things); and Allah is Oft-Forgiving, Most Merciful. 8 Allah forbids you
not, with regard to those who fight you not for (your) Faith nor drive you

2. Besides the question of your fidelity to your own people, even your own selfish interests require you to beware of secret intrigues with your enemies. They will welcome you as cat's paws. But what will happen when they have used you and got the better of you and your people? Then they will show you their hand; and a heavy hand it will be! Not only will they injure you with their hands but with their tongues! The only words they will use for you will be "Traitors to their own"! If they intrigue with you now, it is to pervert you from the Path of Truth and righteousness and to win you over to their evil ways. [5411]

out of your homes, from dealing kindly and justly with them: for Allah loves those who are just.
9 Allah only forbids you, with regard to those who fight you for (your) Faith, and drive you out of your homes, and support (others) in driving you out, from turning to them (for friendship and protection). It is such as turn to them (in these circumstances), that do wrong.

10 O you who believe! When there come to you believing women refugees, examine (and test) them: Allah knows best as to their Faith: if you ascertain that they are Believers, then send them not back to the Unbelievers. They are not lawful (wives) for the Unbelievers, nor are the (Unbelievers) lawful (husbands) for them. But pay the Unbelievers what they have spent (on their dower), and there will be no blame on you if you marry them on payment of their dower to them. But hold not to the guardianship of unbelieving women: ask for what you have spent on their dowers, and let the (Unbelievers) ask for what they have spent (on the dowers of women who come over to you). Such is the command of Allah: He judges (with justice) between you. And Allah is full of Knowledge and Wisdom.
11 And if any of your wives deserts you to the Unbelievers, and you have an accession (by the coming over of a woman from the other side), then pay to those whose wives have deserted the equivalent of what they had spent (on their dower). And fear Allah, in Whom you believe.

12 O Prophet! When believing women come to you to take the oath of fealty to you, that they will not associate in worship any other thing whatever with Allah, that they will not steal, that they will not commit adultery (or fornication), that they will not kill their children, that they will not utter slander, intentionally forging falsehood, and that they will not disobey you in any just matter,—then do you receive their fealty, and pray to Allah for the forgiveness (of their sins): for Allah is Oft-Forgiving, Most Merciful.

13 O you who believe! Turn not (for friendship) to people on whom is the wrath of Allah. Of the Hereafter they are already in despair, just as the unbelievers are in despair about those (buried) in graves.□

Chapter 61

Sūrah Al-Ṣaff
(The Battle Array)

Translator's Introduction

This is the fifth Sūrah of the series of short Madīnan Sūrahs beginning with Sūrah 57. Its subject matter is the need for discipline, practical work, and self-sacrifice in the cause of the *Ummah*. Its date is uncertain, but it was probably revealed shortly after the battle of Uḥud, which was fought in Shawwāl, A.H. 3.

Summary—Allah's Glory shines through all Creation: but what discipline can you show to back your words with action? What lessons can you learn from the stories of Moses and Jesus? Help the Cause, and Allah's help will come with glorious results (61:1-14).

*** *** **

In the name of Allah,
Most Gracious, Most Merciful.

1 Whatever is in the heavens and on earth, let it declare the Praises and Glory of Allah: for He is the Exalted in Might, the Wise.

2 O you who believe! Why say you that which you do not? 3 Grievously
odious is it in the sight of Allah that you say that which you do not. 4
Truly Allah loves those who fight in His Cause in battle array, as if they
were a solid cemented structure.[1]

5 And remember, Moses said to his people: "O my people! Why do you vex and insult me, though you know that I am the messenger of Allah (sent) to you?" Then when they went wrong, Allah let their hearts go

---

1. A battle array, in which a large number of men stand, march, or hold together against assault as if they were a solid wall, is a striking example of order, discipline, cohesion and courage. *"A solid cemented structure"* is even a better simile than the usual "solid wall" as the "structure" or building implies a more diversified organisation held together in unity and strength, each part contributing strength in its own way, and the whole held together not like a mass but like a differing cells of a living body, united in one cause. *Cf* [4031] to 37:1. [5433] – Ed.

wrong. For Allah guides not those who are rebellious transgressors.

6 And remember, Jesus, the son of Mary, said: "O Children of Israel! I am the messenger of Allah (sent) to you, confirming the Law (which came) before me, and giving glad Tidings of a Messenger to come after me, whose name shall be Aḥmad."[2] But when he came to them with clear Signs,[3] they said, "This is evident sorcery!"

7 Who does greater wrong than one who invents falsehood against Allah, even as he is being invited to Islam? And Allah guides not those who do
wrong. 8 Their intention is to extinguish Allah's Light (by blowing) with their mouths: but Allah will complete (the revelation of) His Light, even
though the Unbelievers may detest (it). 9 It is He Who has sent His Messenger with Guidance and the Religion of Truth, that he may proclaim it over all religion, even though the Pagans may detest (it).

SECTION 2

10 O you who believe! Shall I lead you to a bargain that will save you
from a grievous penalty?—11 That you believe in Allah and His Messenger, and that you strive (your utmost) in the Cause of Allah, with your property and your persons: that will be best for you, if you but
knew! 12 He will forgive you your sins, and admit you to Gardens beneath which rivers flow, and to beautiful mansions in Gardens of Eternity: that
is indeed the supreme achievement. 13 And another (favour will He bestow,) which you do love,—help from Allah and a speedy victory. So

---

2. "Aḥmad" or "Muḥammad": the Praised One, is almost a translation of the Greek word *Periclytos*. In the present Gospel of John, xiv. 16, xv. 26, and xvi. 7, the word "Comforter" in the English version is for the Greek word "Paracletos", which means "Advocate", "one called to the help of another, a kind friend", rather than "Comforter". Our scholars contend that Paracletos is a corrupt reading for Periclytos, and that in the original saying of Jesus there was a prophecy of our Holy Prophet *Aḥmad* by name. Even if we read Paraclete, it would apply to the Holy Prophet, who is "a Mercy for all creatures" (21:107) and "most kind and merciful to the Believers" (9:128). See also 3:81. [5438]

3. Our Holy Prophet was foretold in many ways; and when he came, he showed forth many Clear Signs, for his whole life from beginning to end was one vast miracle. He fought and won against odds. Without learning from men he taught the highest wisdom. He melted hearts that were hard, and he strengthened hearts that were tender and required support. In all his sayings and doings men of discernment could see the working of Allah's hand; yet the ignorant Unbelievers called it all Sorcery!—called that unreal which became the most solid fact of human history! [5439]

give the Glad Tidings to the Believers.

14 O you who believe! Be you helpers of Allah: as said Jesus the son of Mary to the Disciples, "Who will be my helpers to (the work of) Allah?" Said the Disciples, "We are Allah's helpers!" Then a portion of the Children of Israel believed, and a portion disbelieved: but We gave power to those who believed, against their enemies, and they became the ones that prevailed.□

Chapter 62

Sūrah Al-Jumu'ah
(Congregation)

Translator's Introduction

This is the sixth Sūrah in the Madīnan series of short Sūrahs which began with Sūrah 57.

The special theme here is the need for mutual contact in the Community for worship and understanding: for the spirit of the Message is for all, ignorant and learned, in order that they may be purified and may learn wisdom.

The date has no special significance: it may be placed in the early Madīnan period, say between A.H. 2 and 3.

Summary—The Revelation has come among unlearned men, to teach purity and wisdom not only to them but to others, including those who may have an older Message but do not understand it: meet solemnly for the Assembly (Friday) Prayer, and let not worldly interests deflect you therefrom (62:1-11).

*** *** ***

In the name of Allah,
Most Gracious, Most Merciful.

1 Whatever is in the heavens and on earth, does declare the Praises and
Glory of Allah,—the Sovereign, the Holy One, the Exalted in Might, the
Wise. 2 It is He Who has sent amongst the Unlettered a messenger from
among themselves, to rehearse to them His Signs, to sanctify them, and
to instruct them in Scripture and Wisdom—although they had been,
before, in manifest error;—3 As well as (to confer all these benefits upon)
others of them, who have not already joined them: and He is Exalted in
Might, Wise. 4 Such is the Bounty of Allah, which He bestows on whom
He will: and Allah is the Lord of the highest bounty.

5 The similitude of those who were charged with the (obligations of the)
Mosaic Law, but who subsequently failed in those (obligations), is that
of a donkey which carries huge tomes (but understands them not). Evil
is the similitude of people who falsify the Signs of Allah: and Allah

guides not people who do wrong. 6 Say: "O you that stand on Judaism!
If you think that you are friends to Allah, to the exclusion of (other) men,
then express your desire for death, if you are truthful!" 7 But never will
they express their desire (for death), because of the (deeds) their hands
have sent on before them! And Allah knows well those that do wrong! 8
Say: "The death from which you flee will truly overtake you: then will
you be sent back to the Knower of things secret and open: and He will tell
you (the truth of) the things that you did!"

SECTION 2

9 O you who believe! When the call is proclaimed to prayer on Friday (the
Day of Assembly), hasten earnestly to the remembrance of Allah, and
leave off business (and traffic): that is best for you if you but knew! 10
And when the Prayer is finished, then may you disperse through the land,
and seek of the bounty of Allah: and celebrate the Praises of Allah often
(and without stint): that you may prosper.

11 But when they see some bargain or some amusement, they disperse
headlong to it, and leave you standing. Say: "The (blessing) from the
Presence of Allah is better than any amusement or bargain! And Allah is
the Best to provide (for all needs)."□

Chapter 63

Sūrah Al-Munāfiqūn (The Hypocrites)

Translator's Introduction

This is the seventh of the ten short Madīnan Sūrahs dealing with a special feature in the social life of the Brotherhood.

The special feature here dealt with is the wiles and mischief of the Hypocrite element in any community, and the need of guarding against it and against the temptation it throws in the way of the Believers.

The battle of Uḥud (Shawwāl A.H. 3) unmasked the Hypocrites in Madīnah: see 3:167. This Sūrah may be referred to some time after that event, say about A.H. 4 or possibly A.H. 5 if the words reported in verse 8 were uttered in the expedition against the Banū Muṣṭaliq, A.H. 5.

Summary—False are the oaths of the Hypocrites: they only seek selfish ends: Believers should beware of their wiles and strive devotedly always for the Cause (63:1-11).

*** *** ***

In the name of Allah,
Most Gracious, Most Merciful.

1 When the Hypocrites come to you, they say, "We bear witness that you
are indeed the Messenger of Allah." Certainly, Allah knows that you are
indeed His Messenger, and Allah bears witness that the Hypocrites are
indeed liars. 2 They have made their oaths a screen (for their misdeeds):
thus they obstruct (men) from the Path of Allah: truly evil are their deeds.
3 That is because they believed, then they rejected Faith: so a seal was set
on their hearts: therefore they understand not.

4 When you look at them, their exteriors please you; and when they speak,
you listen to their words. They are as (worthless as hollow) pieces of
timber propped up, (unable to stand on their own). They think that every
cry is against them. They are the enemies; so beware of them. The curse
of Allah be on them! How are they deluded (away from the Truth)! 5 And
when it is said to them, "Come, the Messenger of Allah will pray for your

forgiveness", they turn aside their heads, and you would see them turning away their faces in arrogance.

6 It is equal to them whether you pray for their forgiveness or not. Allah will not forgive them. Truly Allah guides not rebellious transgressors. 7
They are the ones who say, "Spend nothing on those who are with Allah's Messenger,[1] to the end that they may disperse (and quit Madīnah)." But to Allah belong the treasures of the heavens and the earth; but the Hypocrites understand not. 8 They say, "If we return to Madīnah, surely the more honourable (element) will expel therefrom the meaner."[2] But honour belongs to Allah and His Messenger, and to the Believers; but the Hypocrites know not.

SECTION 2

9 O you who believe! Let not your riches or your children divert you from the remembrance of Allah. If any act thus, the loss is their own. 10 And spend something (in charity) out of the substance which We have bestowed on you, before Death should come to any of you and he should say, "O my Lord! Why did You not give me respite for a little while? I should then have given (largely) in charity, and I should have been one of the doers of good." 11 But to no soul will Allah grant respite when the time appointed (for it) has come; and Allah is well acquainted with (all) that you do.□

---

1. The *Muhājirūn*, who had come to be with the Holy Prophet in Madīnah in exile, were received, helped, entertained by the *Anṣār* (Helpers). The Hypocrites in Madīnah did not like this, and tried in underhand ways to dissuade the good folk of Madīnah from doing all they could for the exiles. But their tricks did not succeed. [5474]

2. Words of this import were spoken by 'Abdullāh Ibn Ubayy, the leader of the Madīnah Hypocrites to or about the Exiles, in the course of the expedition against the Banū Muṣṭaliq in the fourth or fifth year of the *Hijrah*. He had hopes of leadership which were disappointed by the coming to Madīnah of a man far greater than he. So he arrogated to himself and his clique the title of "the more honourable (element)" and slightingly spoke of the Emigrants as the "meaner" element that had intruded from outside.[5475]

Chapter 64

Sūrah Al-Taghābun
(The Mutual Loss and Gain)

Translator's Introduction

This is the eighth of the short Madīnan Sūrahs, each dealing with a special aspect of the life of the Community.

The special aspect spoken of here is the mutual gain and loss of Good and Evil, contrasted in this life and in the Hereafter.

It is an early Madīnan Sūrah, of the year 1 of the Hijrah or possibly even of the Makkan period just before the Hijrah.

Summary—Both the Unbelievers and the Believers were created by the One True Allah, Who created all and knows all: why should Unbelief and Evil exult in worldly gain when their loss will be as manifest in the Hereafter as will be the gains of the Believers? (64:1-18).

*** *** ***

In the name of Allah,
Most Gracious, Most Merciful.

1 Whatever is in the heavens and on earth, does declare the Praises and
Glory of Allah: to Him belongs dominion, and to Him belongs praise: and
He has power over all things. 2 It is He Who has created you; and of you
are some that are Unbelievers, and some that are Believers: and Allah
sees well all that you do. 3 He has created the heavens and the earth in just
proportions, and has given you shape, and made your shapes beautiful:
and to Him is the final Goal. 4 He knows what is in the heavens and on
earth; and He knows what you conceal and what you reveal: indeed,
Allah knows well the (secrets) of (all) hearts.

5 Has not the story reached you, of those who rejected Faith aforetime?
So they tasted the evil result of their conduct; and they had a grievous
Penalty. 6 That was because there came to them messengers with clear
Signs, but they said: "Shall (mere) human beings direct us?" So they
rejected (the Message) and turned away. But Allah can do without
(them): and Allah is free of all needs, Worthy of all praise.

7 The Unbelievers think that they will not be raised up (for Judgement).
Say: "Indeed, by my Lord, you shall surely be raised up: then shall you
be told (the truth) of all that you did. And that is easy for Allah." 8
Believe, therefore, in Allah and His Messenger, and in the Light which
We have sent down. And Allah is well acquainted with all that you do. 9
The Day that He assembles you (all) for a Day of Assembly,—that will
be a Day of mutual loss and gain (among you), and those who believe in
Allah and work righteousness—He will remove from them their ills, and
He will admit them to Gardens beneath which Rivers flow, to dwell
therein for ever: that will be the supreme Achievement. 10 But those who
reject Faith and treat Our Signs as falsehoods, they will be Companions
of the Fire, to dwell therein for ever: and evil is that Goal.

SECTION 2

11 No kind of calamity can occur, except by the leave of Allah: and if
anyone believes in Allah, (Allah) guides his heart (aright): for Allah
knows all things. 12 So obey Allah, and obey His Messenger: but if you
turn back, the duty of Our Messenger is but to proclaim (the Message)
clearly and openly. 13 Allah! There is no god but He: and on Allah,
therefore, let the Believers put their trust.

14 O you who believe! Truly, among your wives and your children are
(some that are) enemies to yourselves: so beware of them! But if you
forgive and overlook, and cover up (their faults), verily Allah is
Oft-Forgiving, Most Merciful. 15 Your riches and your children may be
but a trial: but in the Presence of Allah, is the highest Reward.

16 So fear Allah as much as you can; listen and obey; and spend in charity
for the benefit of your own soul. And those saved from the covetousness
of their own souls,—they are the ones that achieve prosperity. 17 If you
loan to Allah, a beautiful loan, He will double it to your (credit), and He
will grant you Forgiveness: for Allah is Most Ready to appreciate
(service), Most Forbearing,—18 Knower of what is hidden and what is
open, Exalted in Might, Full of Wisdom.□

Chapter 65

Sūrah Al-Ṭalāq
(Divorce)

Translator's Introduction

This is the ninth of the ten short Madīnan Sūrahs dealing with the social life of the Community. The aspect dealt with here is Divorce, and the necessity of precautions to guard against its abuse. The relations of the sexes are an important factor in the social life of the Community, and this and the following Sūrah deal with certain aspects of it. "Of all things permitted by Law", said the Prophet, "divorce is the most hateful in the sight of Allah" (Abū Dāwūd, *Sunan,* xiii. 3). While the sanctity of marriage is the essential basis of family life, the incompatibility of individuals and the weaknesses of human nature require certain outlets and safeguards if that sanctity is not to be made into a fetish at the expense of human life. That is why the question of Divorce is in this Sūrah linked with the question of insolent impiety and its punishment.

The date is somewhere about A.H. 6, but the chronology has no significance.

Summary—Provision to be made for women in case of Divorce; insolent impiety always leads to punishment (65:1-12).

*** *** ***

In the name of Allah,
Most Gracious, Most Merciful

1 O Prophet! When you do divorce women,[1] divorce them at their prescribed periods, and count (accurately) their prescribed periods: and fear Allah your Lord:[2] and turn them not out of their houses,[3] nor shall

---

1. Note that in the first instance the Prophet is himself addressed individually, as the Teacher and representative of the Community. Then the actual directions: "when you...": are addressed to the Community collectively.[5503]

2. *'Iddah*, as a technical term in divorce law, is explained in 2:228. Its general meaning is "a prescribed period": in that general sense it is used in 2:185 for a prescribed period of fasting. [5505]

3. The prescribed period (see last note) is in the interests of the wife, of the husband, of an unborn child (if there is any), and of sex laws in nature, and therefore the elementary

they (themselves) leave,[4] except in case they are guilty of some open lewdness, those are limits set by Allah: and any who transgresses the limits of Allah, does verily wrong his (own) soul: you know not if
perchance Allah will bring about thereafter some new situation. 2 Thus
when they fulfil their term appointed, either take them back on equitable terms or part with them on equitable terms; and take for witness two persons from among you, endued with justice, and establish the evidence (as) before Allah. Such is the admonition given to him who believes in Allah and the Last Day. And for those who fear Allah, He (ever) prepares
a way out, 3 And He provides for him from (sources) he never could
imagine. And if anyone puts his trust in Allah, sufficient is (Allah) for him. For Allah will surely accomplish His purpose: verily, for all things has Allah appointed a due proportion.

4 Such of your women as have passed the age of monthly courses, for
them the prescribed period, if you have any doubts, is three months, and for those who have no courses (it is the same): for those who carry (life within their wombs), their period is until they deliver their burdens: and for
those who fear Allah, He will make their path easy. 5 That is the Command
of Allah, which He has sent down to you: and if anyone fears Allah, He will remove his ills from him, and will enlarge his reward.

6 Let the women live (in *'iddah*) in the same style as you live, according
to your means: annoy them not, so as to restrict them. And if they carry (life in their wombs), then spend (your substance) on them until they

---

dictates of refined human society. In English Law the six months' interval between the decree *nisi* and the decree absolute in divorce attains the same purpose in a roundabout way. Commentators suggest that the divorce should not be pronounced during the courses. Read with 2:222, this implies that any incipient differences between husband and wife should not be forced to an issue at a time when sex is least attractive and almost repulsive. Everything should be done to strengthen the social and spiritual aspects of marriage and keep down stray impulses of animal instinct. The parties are to think seriously in a mood of piety, keeping the fear of Allah in their minds. [5506]

4. As Islam treats the married woman as a full juristic personality in every sense of the term, a married woman has a right, in the married state, to a house or apartment of her own. And a house or apartment implies the reasonable expenses for its upkeep and for her own and her children's maintenance. And this is obligatory not only in the married state, but during the *'iddah,* which is necessarily a most trying period for the woman. During this period she must not only not be turned out, but it is not decent for her to leave of her own accord, lest the chances of reconciliation should be diminished: see the next note. [5507]

deliver their burden: and if they suckle your (offspring), give them their
recompense: and take mutual counsel together, according to what is just
and reasonable. And if you find yourselves in difficulties, let another
woman suckle (the child) on the (father's) behalf. 7 Let the man of means
spend according to his means: and the man whose resources are
restricted, let him spend according to what Allah has given him. Allah
puts no burden on any person beyond what He has given him. After a
difficulty, Allah will soon grant relief.

SECTION 2

8 How many populations that insolently opposed the command of their
Lord and of His messengers, did We not then call to account—to severe
account?—and We imposed on them an exemplary Punishment. 9 Then
did they taste the evil result of their conduct, and the End of their conduct
was Perdition. 10 Allah has prepared for them a severe Punishment (in the
Hereafter). Therefore fear Allah, O you men of understanding—who have
believed!—for Allah has indeed sent down to you a Message,—11 A
Messenger, who rehearses to you the Signs of Allah containing clear
explanations, that he may lead forth those who believe and do righteous
deeds from the depths of Darkness into Light. And those who believe in
Allah and work righteousness, He will admit to Gardens beneath which
Rivers flow, to dwell therein for ever: Allah has indeed granted for them
a most excellent Provision. 12 Allah is He Who created seven Firmaments
and of the earth a similar number. Through the midst of them (all)
descends His Command: that you may know that Allah has power over
all things, and that Allah comprehends all things in (His) Knowledge.□

Chapter 66

Sūrah Al-Taḥrīm
(Prohibition)

Translator's Introduction

This is the tenth and last of the series of short Madīnan Sūrahs which began with Sūrah 57: see Introduction to that Sūrah. The point dealt with here is: how far the turning away from sex or the opposition of one sex against another or a want of harmony between the sexes may injure the higher interests of society.

The date may be taken to be somewhere about A.H. 7.

Summary—The failings of the weaker sex should not turn away men from normal social life: harmony and mutual confidence should be taught and enforced, and Allah's blessing will descend on the virtuous even if their lot is cast with the wicked (66:1-12).

*** *** ***

In the name of Allah,
Most Gracious, Most Merciful.

1 O Prophet! Why hold you to be forbidden that which Allah has made lawful to you? You seek to please your consorts. But Allah is Oft-Forgiving, Most Merciful.[1] 2 Allah has already ordained for you, (O

---

1. The Prophet's household was not like other households. The Consorts of Purity were expected to hold a higher standard in behaviour and reticence than ordinary women, as they had higher work to perform. See 33:28. But they were human beings after all, and were subject to the weaknesses of their sex, and they sometimes failed. The imprudence of 'Ā'ishah (see 24:11) once caused serious difficulties: the Holy Prophet's mind was sorely distressed, and he renounced the society of his wives for some time. This renunciation seems to be referred to here. The situation was none the less difficult for him because 'Ā'ishah was a daughter of Abū Bakr, one of the truest and most intimate of his Companions and lieutenants. The Commentators usually cite the following incident in connection with the revelation of these verses. It is narrated from 'Ā'ishah, the wife of the Holy Prophet (peace be on him) by Bukhārī, Muslim, Nasā'ī, Abū Dāwūd and others that the Holy Prophet usually visited his wives daily after *'Asr* Prayer. Once it so happened that he stayed longer than usual at the quarters of Zaynab bint Jahsh, for she had received from somewhere some honey which the Holy Prophet liked very much. "At this", said 'Ā'ishah, "I felt jealous, and I, Ḥafṣah, Sawdah and Ṣafīyah agreed among ourselves that when he

men), the dissolution of your oaths (in some cases): and Allah is your Protector, and He is Full of Knowledge and Wisdom.

3 When the Prophet disclosed a matter in confidence[2] to one of his consorts, and she then divulged it (to another), and Allah made it known to him, he confirmed[3] part thereof and repudiated a part. Then when he told her thereof, she said, "Who told you this?" He said, "He told me Who knows and is well-acquainted (with all things)." 4 If you two turn in repentance to Him, your hearts are indeed so inclined; but if you back up each other against him, truly Allah is his Protector, and Gabriel, and (every) righteous one among those who believe,—and furthermore, the angels—will back (him) up.

5 It may be, if he divorced you (all), that Allah will give him in exchange Consorts better than you,—who submit (their wills), who believe, who are devout, who turn to Allah in repentance, who worship (in humility), who travel (for Faith) and fast,—previously married or virgins. 6 O you who believe! Save yourselves and your families from a Fire whose fuel is Men and Stones, over which are (appointed) angels stern (and) severe, who flinch not (from executing) the Commands they receive from Allah,

---

visits us each of us would tell him that a peculiar odour came from his mouth as a result of what he had eaten, for we knew that he was particularly sensitive to offensive smells." So when his wives hinted at it, he vowed that he would never again use honey. Thereupon these verses were revealed, reminding him that he should not declare to himself unlawful that which Allah had made lawful to him. The important point to bear in mind is that he was at once rectified by revelation, which reinforces the fact that the prophets are always under divine protection, and even the slightest lapse on their part is never left uncorrected. [5529]

2. Who these two consorts were, and what was the matter in confidence which was disclosed, we are not expressly told, but the facts mentioned in note 1 above will help us to understand this passage. The sacred words imply that the matter was of great importance to the principle involved, but that the details were not of sufficient importance for permanent record. For the lessons to be drawn, see the notes following. [5532]

3. The moral we have to draw is manifold: (1) If anything is told to us in confidence, especially by one at the head of affairs, we must not divulge it even to our closest friend. (2) If such divulgence is made in the most secret whispers, Allah's Plan is such that it will come to light and expose those guilty of breach of confidence. (3) When the whispered version is compared with the true version and the actual facts, it will be found that the whispered version is in great part untrue, due to the misunderstanding and exaggeration inevitable in the circumstances. (4) The breach of confidence must inevitably rebound to the shame of the guilty party, whose surprise only covers a sense of humiliation. [5533]

but do (precisely) what they are commanded. 7 (They will say), "O you
Unbelievers! Make no excuses this Day! You are being but requited for
all that you did!"

SECTION 2

8 O you who believe! Turn to Allah with sincere repentance: in the hope
that your Lord will remove from you your ills and admit you to Gardens
beneath which Rivers flow,—the Day that Allah will not permit to be
humiliated the Prophet and those who believe with him. Their Light will
run forward before them and by their right hands, while they say, "Our
Lord! Perfect our Light for us, and grant us Forgiveness: for You have
power over all things."

9 O Prophet! Strive hard against the Unbelievers and the Hypocrites, and
be firm against them. Their abode is Hell—an evil refuge (indeed).

10 Allah sets forth, for an example to the Unbelievers, the wife of Noah
and the wife of Lūṭ: they were (respectively) under two of our righteous
Servants, but they were false to their (husbands), and they profited
nothing before Allah on their account, but were told: "Enter you the Fire
along with (others) that enter!" 11 And Allah sets forth, as an example to
those who believe, the wife of Pharaoh: behold she said: "O my Lord!
Build for me, in nearness to You, a mansion in the Garden, and save me
from Pharaoh and his doings, and save me from those that do wrong"; 12
And Mary the daughter of 'Imrān, who guarded her chastity; and We
breathed into (her body) of Our spirit; and she testified to the truth of the
words of her Lord and of His Revelations, and was one of the devout
(Servants).□

Chapter 67

Sūrah Al-Mulk
(The Dominion)

Translator's Introduction

We have now done fourteen-fifteenths of the Qur'an, and have followed step by step the development of its argument establishing the *Ummah* or Brotherhood of Islam.

There is a logical break here. The remaining fifteenth consists of short spiritual Lyrics, mostly of the Makkan period, dealing mainly with the inner life of man, and in its individual aspects. They may be compared to Hymns or Psalms in other religious literature. But these short Qur'anic Sūrahs have a grandeur, a beauty, a mystic meaning, and a force of earnestness under persecution, all their own. With their sources in the sublimest regions of heaven, their light penetrates into the darkest recesses of Life, into the concrete facts which are often mistaken for the whole of Reality, though they are but an insignificant portion and on the surface and fleeting. There is much symbolism in language and thought, in describing the spiritual in terms of the things we see and understand.

It is the contrast between the shadows of Reality here and the eternal Reality, between the surface world and the profound inner World, that is urged on our attention here.

This Sūrah of 30 verses belongs to the Middle Makkan period, just before Sūrah 69 and Sūrah 70. Allah is mentioned here by the name *Raḥmān* (Most Gracious), as He is mentioned by the names of *Rabb* (Lord and Cherisher) and *Raḥmān* (Most Gracious) in Sūrah 19.

*** *** ***

PART XXIX

In the name of Allah,
Most Gracious, Most Merciful.

1 Blessed be He in Whose hands is Dominion; and He over all things has
Power;—2 He Who created Death and Life, that He may try which of you
is best in deed: and He is the Exalted in Might, Oft-Forgiving;—3 He
Who created the seven heavens one above another: no want of proportion
will you see in the Creation of (Allah) Most Gracious. So turn your vision
again: see you any flaw? 4 Again turn your vision a second time: (your)
vision will come back to you dull and discomfited, in a state worn out. 5

And We have, (from of old), adorned the lowest heaven with Lamps, and
We have made such (Lamps) (as) missiles to drive away the Evil Ones,
and have prepared for them the Penalty of the blazing Fire.

6 For those who reject their Lord (and Cherisher) is the Penalty of Hell:
and evil is (such) destination. 7 When they are cast therein, they will hear
the (terrible) drawing in of its breath even as it blazes forth, 8 Almost
bursting with fury: every time a Group is cast therein, its Keepers will
ask, "Did no Warner come to you?" 9 They will say: "Yes indeed; a
Warner did come to us, but we rejected him and said, 'Allah never sent
down any (Message): you are nothing but an egregious delusion!'" 10
They will further say: "Had we but listened or used our intelligence, we
should not (now) be among the Companions of the blazing Fire!" 11 They
will then confess their sins: but far will be (Forgiveness) from the
Companions of the blazing Fire!

12 As for those who fear their Lord unseen, for them is Forgiveness and
a great Reward. 13 And whether you hide your word or publish it, He
certainly has (full) knowledge, of the secrets of (all) hearts. 14 Should He
not know—He that created? And He is the One that understands the finest
mysteries (and) is well-acquainted (with them).

SECTION 2

15 It is He Who has made the earth manageable for you, so traverse you
through its tracts and enjoy of the Sustenance which He furnishes: but
unto Him is the Resurrection. 16 Do you feel secure that He Who is in
Heaven will not cause you to be swallowed up by the earth when it
shakes (as in an earthquake)? 17 Or do you feel secure that He Who is in
Heaven will not send against you a violent tornado (with showers of
stones), so that you shall know how (terrible) was My warning? 18 But
indeed men before them rejected (My warning): then how (terrible) was
My rejection (of them)?

19 Do they not observe the birds above them, spreading their wings and
folding them in? None can uphold them except (Allah) Most Gracious:
truly it is He that watches over all things. 20 Nay, who is there that can
help you, (even as) an army, besides (Allah) Most Merciful? In nothing
but delusion are the Unbelievers. 21 Or who is there that can provide you
with Sustenance if He were to withhold His provision? Nay, they
obstinately persist in insolent impiety and flight (from the Truth).

22 Is then one who walks headlong, with his face grovelling, better
guided,—or one who walks evenly on a straight Way? 23 Say: "It is He
Who has created you (and made you grow), and made for you the
faculties of hearing, seeing, feeling and understanding: little thanks it is
you give." 24 Say: "It is He Who has multiplied you through the earth, and
to Him shall you be gathered together."

25 They ask: When will this promise be (fulfilled)?—if you are telling the
truth. 26 Say: "As to the knowledge of the time, it is with Allah alone: I
am (sent) only to warn plainly in public." 27 At length, when they see it
close at hand, grieved will be the faces of the Unbelievers, and it will be
said (to them): "This is (the promise fulfilled), which you were calling
for!"

28 Say: "See you?—If Allah were to destroy me, and those with me, or if
He bestows His Mercy on us,—yet who can deliver the Unbelievers from
a grievous Penalty?" 29 Say: "He is (Allah) Most Gracious: we have
believed in Him, and on Him have we put our trust: so, soon will you
know which (of us) it is that is in manifest error." 30 Say: "See you?—If
your stream be some morning lost (in the underground earth), who then
can supply you with clear-flowing water?"□

Chapter 68

Sūrah Al-Qalam or *Nūn*
(The Pen)

Translator's Introduction

This is a very early Makkan revelation. The general opinion of Muslim Commentary is that a great part of it was second in order of revelation, the first being Sūrah 96 (*Iqra'*), verses 1-5: see *Itqān*, Chapter 7.

The last Sūrah having defined the true Reality in contrast with the false standards set up by men, this illustrates the theme by an actual historical example. Our Holy Prophet was the sanest and wisest of men: those who could not understand him called him mad or possessed. So, in every age, it is the habit of the world to call Truth Falsehood and Wisdom Madness, and, on the other hand, to exalt Selfishness as Planning, and Arrogance as Power. The contrast is shown up between the two kinds of men and their real inner worth.

Summary—Let the good carry on their work, in spite of the abuse of the Companions of Evil: let all remember Allah, before Whom all men are on trial (68:1-33).
True Judgement comes from Allah, and not from the false standards of men (68:34-52).

*** *** ***

In the name of Allah,
Most Gracious, Most Merciful.

1 *Nūn*.[1] By the Pen[2] and by the (Record) which (men) write,—2 You are

---

1. *Nūn* is an Abbreviated Letter. *Nūn* may mean a fish, or an ink holder, or it may be just the Arabic letter of the alphabet *N*. In the last case, it may refer to either or both of the other meanings. Note also that the Arabic rhyme in this Sūrah ends in *N*. The reference to ink would be an appropriate link with the 'Pen' in verse 1. The reference to the fish would be appropriate with reference to the story of Jonah in verses 48-50. Jonahs title is "the Companion of the Fish", (Dhū al-Nūn, 21:87), as he was, in the story, swallowed by the Fish. The letter *N* could also symbolically represent Jonah in the Arabic form Yūnus, where the characteristic "Firm Letter" is *N*. [5592]

2. The mystic 'Pen and the mystic `Record' are the symbolical foundation of the Revelation to man. The adjuration by the Pen disposes of the flippant charge that Allah's

not, by the Grace of your Lord, mad or possessed. 3 Nay, verily for you
is a Reward unfailing: 4 And you (stand) on an exalted standard of
character. 5 Soon will you see, and they will see, 6 Which of you is
afflicted with madness. 7 Verily it is your Lord that knows best, which
(among men) has strayed from His Path: and He knows best those who
receive (true) Guidance.

8 So listen not to those who deny (the Truth). 9 Their desire is that you
should be pliant: so would they be pliant.

10 Heed not the type of despicable men—ready with oaths, 11 A slanderer,
going about with calumnies, 12 (Habitually) hindering (all) good,
transgressing beyond bounds, deep in sin, 13 Violent (and cruel),—with
all that, base-born,—14 Because he possesses wealth and (numerous)
sons. 15 When to him are rehearsed Our Signs, "Tales of the Ancients",
he cries! 16 Soon shall We brand (the beast) on the snout!

17 Verily We have tried them as We tried the People of the Garden, when
they resolved to gather the fruits of the (garden) in the morning. 18 But
made no reservation, ("If it be Allah's Will"). 19 Then there came on the
(garden) a visitation from your Lord, (which swept away) all around,
while they were asleep. 20 So the (garden) became, by the morning, like
a dark and desolate spot, (whose fruit had been gathered). 21 As the
morning broke, they called out, one to another,—22 "Go you to your tilth
(betimes) in the morning, if you would gather the fruits." 23 So they
departed, conversing in secret low tones, (saying)—24 "Let not a single
indigent person break in upon you into the (garden) this day." 25 And they
opened the morning, strong in an (unjust) resolve. 26 But when they saw
the (garden), they said: "We have surely lost our way: 27 Indeed we are
shut out (of the fruits of our labour)!" 28 Said one of them, more just (than
the rest): "Did I not say to you, 'Why not glorify (Allah)?'" 29 They said:
"Glory to our Lord! Verily we have been doing wrong!" 30 Then they
turned, one against another, in reproach. 31 They said: "Alas for us! We
have indeed transgressed! 32 It may be that our Lord will give us in
exchange a better (garden) than this: for we do turn to Him (in

---

Messenger was mad or possessed. For he spoke words of power, not incoherent, but full of meaning, and through the Record of the Pen, that meaning unfolds itself, in innumerable aspects to countless generations. Muḥammad was the living Grace and Mercy of Allah, and his very nature exalted him above abuse and persecution. [5593]

repentance)!" 33 Such is the Punishment (in this life); but greater is the
Punishment in the Hereafter—if only they knew!

SECTION 2

34 Verily, for the Righteous, are Gardens of Delight, in the Presence of
their Lord. 35 Shall We then treat the People of Faith like the People of
Sin? 36 What is the matter with you? How judge you? 37 Or have you a
Book through which you learn—38 That you shall have, through it
whatever you choose? 39 Or have you Covenants with Us on oath,
reaching to the Day of Judgement, (providing) that you shall have
whatever you shall demand? 40 Ask you of them, which of them will stand
surety for that! 41 Or have they some "Partners" (in Godhead)? Then let
them produce their "partners", if they are truthful!

42 The Day that the Shin shall be laid bare, and they shall be summoned
to bow in adoration, but they shall not be able,—43 Their eyes will be cast
down,—ignominy will cover them; seeing that they had been summoned
aforetime to bow in adoration, while they were whole, (and had refused).
44 Then leave Me alone with such as reject this Message: by degrees shall
We punish them from directions they perceive not. 45 A (long) respite will
I grant them: truly powerful is My Plan. 46 Or is it that you do ask them
for a reward, so that they are burdened with a load of debt?—47 Or that
the Unseen is in their hands, so that they can write it down?

48 So wait with patience for the Command of your Lord, and be not like
the Companion of the Fish—when he cried out in agony. 49 Had not Grace
from his Lord reached him, he would indeed have been cast off on the
naked shore, in disgrace. 50 Thus did his Lord choose him and make him
of the Company of the Righteous.

51 And the Unbelievers would almost trip you up with their eyes when
they hear the Message; and they say: "Surely he is possessed!" 52 But it
is nothing less than a Message to all the worlds.□

Chapter 69

Sūrah Al-Ḥāqqah
(The Sure Reality)

Translator's Introduction

This Sūrah belongs to the early middle period of Makkan Revelation. The eschatological argument is pressed home: the absolute Truth cannot fail; it must prevail; therefore be not lured by false appearances in this life; it is Revelation that points to the sure and certain Reality.

*** *** ***

In the name of Allah,
Most Gracious, Most Merciful.

1 The Sure Reality! 2 What is the Sure Reality? 3 And what will make you
realise what the Sure Reality is?

4 The Thamūd and the 'Ād people (branded) as false the Stunning
Calamity! 5 But the Thamūd,—they were destroyed by a terrible Storm of
thunder and lightning! 6 And the 'Ād, they were destroyed by a furious
Wind, exceedingly violent; 7 He made it rage against them seven nights
and eight days in succession: so that you could see the (whole) people
lying prostrate in its (path), as if they had been roots of hollow palm trees
tumbled down! 8 Then see you any of them left surviving?

9 And Pharaoh, and those before him, and the Cities Over-
thrown,[1]committed habitual Sin. 10 And disobeyed (each) the messenger
of their Lord; so He punished them with an abundant Penalty. 11 We,
when the water (of Noah's Flood) overflowed beyond its limits, carried
you (mankind), in the floating (Ark), 12 That We might make it a Message
unto you, and that ears (that should hear the tale and) retain its memory
should bear its (lessons) in remembrance.

1. *The Cities Overthrown*: Sodom and Gomorrah, Cities of the Plain, to whom Lot preached. See 9:70 and 7:80-84. [5644]

13 Then, when one blast is sounded on the Trumpet, 14 And the earth is
moved, and its mountains, and they are crushed to powder at one
stroke,—15 On that Day shall the (Great) Event come to pass. 16 And the
sky will be rent asunder, for it will that Day be flimsy, 17 And the angels
will be on its sides, and eight will, that Day, bear the Throne of your Lord
above them.

18 That Day shall you be brought to Judgement: not an act of yours that
you hide will be hidden. 19 Then he that will be given his Record in his
right hand will say: "Ah here! Read you my Record! 20 I did really
understand that my Account would (one Day) reach me!" 21 And he will
be in a life of Bliss, 22 In a Garden on high, 23 The Fruits whereof (will
hang in bunches) low and near. 24 "Eat you and drink you, with full
satisfaction; because of the (good) that you sent before you, in the days
that are gone!"

25 And he that will be given his Record in his left hand, will say: "Ah!
Would that my Record had not been given to me! 26 And that I had never
realised how my account (stood)! 27 Ah! Would that (Death) had made an
end of me! 28 Of no profit to me has been my wealth! 29 My power has
perished from me!"

30 (The stern command will say): "Seize you him, and bind you him, 31
And burn you him in the blazing Fire. 32 Further, make him march in a
chain, whereof the length is seventy cubits! 33 This was he that would not
believe in Allah Most High, 34 And would not encourage the feeding of
the indigent! 35 So no friend has he here this Day. 36 Nor has he any food
except the corruption from the washing of wounds, 37 Which none do eat
but those in sin."

SECTION 2

38 So I do call to witness what you see, 39 And what you see not, 40 That
this is verily the word of an honoured messenger; 41 It is not the word of
a poet: little it is you believe! 42 Nor is it the word of a soothsayer: little
admonition it is you receive. 43 (This is) a Message sent down from the
Lord of the Worlds.

44 And if the messenger were to invent any sayings in Our name, 45 We
should certainly seize him by his right hand, 46 And We should certainly
then cut off the artery of his heart: 47 Nor could any of you withhold him

(from Our wrath).

48 But verily this is a Message for the God-fearing. 49 And We certainly
know that there are amongst you those that reject (it). 50 But truly
(Revelation) is a cause of sorrow for the Unbelievers. 51 But verily it is
Truth of assured certainty. 52 So glorify the name of your Lord Most
High.□

Chapter 70

Sūrah Al-Ma'ārij
(The Ways of Ascent)

Translator's Introduction

This is another eschatological Sūrah closely connected in subject matter with the last one. Patience and the mystery of Time will show the ways that climb to Heaven. Sin and Goodness must each eventually come to its own.

Chronologically it belongs to the late early or early middle Makkan period, possibly soon after S. 49.

*** *** ***

In the name of Allah,
Most Gracious, Most Merciful.

1 A questioner asked about a Penalty to befall—2 The Unbelievers, the
which there is none to ward off,—3 (A Penalty) from Allah, Lord of the
Ways of Ascent.

4 The angels and the Spirit ascend unto Him in a Day the measure
whereof is (as) fifty thousand years: 5 Therefore do you hold Patience,—a
Patience of beautiful (contentment). 6 They see the (Day) indeed as a
far-off (event): 7 But We see it (quite) near.

8 The Day that the sky will be like molten brass, 9 And the mountains will
be like wool, 10 And no friend will ask after a friend, 11 Though they will
be put in sight of each other—the sinner's desire will be: would that he
could redeem himself from the Penalty of that Day by (sacrificing) his
children, 12 His wife and his brother, 13 His kindred who sheltered him, 14
And all, all that is on earth,—so it could deliver him: 15 By no means! for
it would be the Fire of Hell!—16 Plucking out (his being) right to the
skull!—17 Inviting (all) such as turn their backs and turn away their faces
(from the Right). 18 And collect (wealth) and hide it (from use)!

19 Truly man was created very impatient;—20 Fretful when evil touches
him; 21 And niggardly when good reaches him;—22 Not so those devoted
to prayer;—23 Those who remain steadfast to their prayer; 24 And those in

whose wealth is a recognised right. 25 For the (needy) who asks and him
who is prevented (for some reason from asking); 26 And those who hold
to the truth of the Day of Judgment; 27 And those who fear the displeasure
of their Lord,—28 For their Lord's displeasure is the opposite of Peace and
Tranquillity;—29 And those who guard their chastity, 30 Except with their
wives and the (captives) whom their right hands possess—for (then) they
are not to be blamed, 31 But those who trespass beyond this are
transgressors;—32 And those who respect their trusts and covenants; 33
And those who stand firm in their testimonies; 34 And those who guard
(the sacredness) of their worship;—35 Such will be the honoured ones in
the Gardens (of Bliss).

SECTION 2

36 Now what is the matter with the Unbelievers that they rush madly
before thee—37 From the right and from the left, in crowds? 38 Does every
man of them long to enter the Garden of Bliss? 39 By no means! for We
have created them out of the (base matter) they know!

40 Now I do call to witness the Lord of all points in the East and the West
that We can certainly— 41 Substitute for them better (men) than they; and
We are not to be defeated (in Our Plan). 42 So leave them to plunge in
vain talk and play about, until they encounter that Day of theirs which
they have been promised!— 43 The Day whereon they will issue from
their sepulchres in sudden haste as if they were rushing to a goalpost
(fixed for them)—44 Their eyes lowered in dejection, —ignominy
covering them (all over)! Such is the Day the which they are promised!□

Chapter 71

Sūrah Nūḥ
(Noah)

Translator's Introduction

This is another early Makkan Sūrah, of which the date has no significance. The theme is that while Good must uphold the standard of Truth and Righteousness, a stage is reached when it must definitely part company with Evil, lest Evil should spread its corruption. The story of Noahs agony is almost a Parable for the Holy Prophets persecution in the Makkan period.

*** *** ***

In the name of Allah,
Most Gracious, Most Merciful.

1 We sent Noah to his people (with the Command): "Do you warn your
people before there comes to them a grievous Penalty." 2 He said: "O my
people! I am to you a Warner, clear and open: 3 That you should worship
Allah, fear Him and obey me: 4 So He may forgive you your sins and
give you respite for a stated Term: for when the Term given by Allah is
accomplished, it cannot be put forward: if you only knew."

5 He said: "O my Lord! I have called to my people night and day: 6 But
my call only increases (their) flight (from the Right). 7 And every time I
have called to them, that You might forgive them, they have (only) thrust
their fingers into their ears, covered themselves up with their garments,
grown obstinate, and given themselves up to arrogance. 8 So I have called
to them aloud;" 9 "Further I have spoken to them in public and secretly
in private, 10 Saying, 'Ask forgiveness from your Lord; for He is
Oft-Forgiving; 11 He will send rain to you in abundance; 12 Give you
increase in wealth and sons; and bestow on you gardens and bestow on
you rivers (of flowing water). 13 What is the matter with you, that you
place not your hope for kindness and long-suffering in Allah,—14 Seeing
that it is He that has created you in diverse stages? 15 See you not how
Allah has created the seven heavens one above another, 16 And made the
moon a light in their midst, and made the sun as a (Glorious) Lamp? 17

And Allah has produced you from the earth, growing (gradually), 18 And
in the end He will return you into the (earth), and raise you forth (again
at the Resurrection)? 19 And Allah has made the earth for you as a carpet
(spread out), 20 That you may go about therein, in spacious roads."

SECTION 2

21 Noah said: "O my Lord! They have disobeyed me, but they follow
(men) whose wealth and children give them no increase but only Loss. 22
And they have devised a tremendous Plot. 23 And they have said (to each
other), 'Abandon not your gods: abandon neither Wadd nor Suwā',
neither Yaghūth nor Ya'ūq, nor Nasr';—24 They have already misled
many; and grant You no increase to the wrong-doers but in straying (from
their mark)." 25 Because of their sins they were drowned (in the flood),
and were made to enter the Fire (of Punishment): and they found—in lieu
of Allah—none to help them.

26 And Noah, said: "O my Lord! Leave not of the Unbelievers, a single
one on earth! 27 For, if You do leave (any of) them, they will but mislead
Your devotees, and they will breed none but wicked ungrateful ones. 28
O my Lord! Forgive me, my parents, all who enter my house in Faith, and
(all) believing men and believing women: and to the wrong-doers grant
You no increase but in Perdition!"□

Chapter 72

Sūrah Al-Jinn
(The Spirits)

Translator's Introduction

This is a late Makkan Sūrah, of which we can be tolerably certain of the date. It was two years before the Hijrah, when the Prophet, despised and rejected in his native city of Makkah, went to evangelise the lordly men of Ṭā'if. They maltreated him and nearly killed him; what caused him even greater pain was the maltreatment of the humble and lowly men who went with him. Ṭabarī has handed down that memorable Prayer of faith and humility which he offered in the midst of his suffering. On his return journey to Makkah, a glorious vision was revealed to him—hidden spiritual forces working for him—people not known to him accepting his mission while his own people were still rejecting him. Within two months some strangers from Madīnah had privately met him and laid the foundations of that *Hijrah* which was to change the fate of Arabia and the course of world history.

*** *** ***

In the name of Allah,
Most Gracious, Most Merciful.

1 Say: "It has been revealed to me that a company of *Jinns*[1] listened (to
the Qur'an). They said, 'We have really heard a wonderful Recital! 2 It
gives guidance to the Right, and we have believed therein: we shall not
join (in worship) any (gods) with our Lord. 3 And exalted is the Majesty
of our Lord: He has taken neither a wife nor a son. 4 There were some
foolish ones among us, who used to utter extravagant lies against Allah;
5 But we do think that no man or spirit should say aught that is untrue
against Allah.

6 'True, there were persons among mankind who took shelter with
persons among the *Jinns*, but they increased them in folly. 7 And they
(came to) think as you thought, that Allah would not raise up anyone (to
Judgement). 8 And we pried into the secrets of heaven; but we found it

1. For *Jinns*, see 6:100 and accompanying note. [5728]

filled with stern guards and flaming fires. 9 We used, indeed, to sit there
in (hidden) stations, to (steal) a hearing; but any who listens now will find
a flaming fire watching him in ambush. 10 And we understand not
whether ill is intended to those on earth, or whether their Lord (really)
intends to guide them to right conduct.

11 'There are among us some that are righteous, and some the contrary:
we follow divergent paths. 12 But we think that we can by no means
frustrate Allah throughout the earth, nor can we frustrate Him by flight.
13 And as for us, since we have listened to the Guidance, we have
accepted it: and any who believes in his Lord has no fear, either of a short
(account) or of any injustice. 14 Amongst us are some that submit their
wills (to Allah), and some that swerve from justice. Now those who
submit their wills—they have sought out (the path) of right conduct: 15
But those who swerve,—they are (but) fuel for Hell-fire'"—

16 (And Allah's Message is): "If they (the Pagans) had (only) remained on
the (right) Way, We should certainly have bestowed on them rain in
abundance. 17 That We might try them by that (means). But if any turns
away from the remembrance of his Lord, He will cause him to undergo
a severe Penalty. 18 And the places of worship are for Allah (alone): so
invoke not anyone along with Allah; 19 Yet when the Devotee of Allah[2]
stands forth to invoke Him, they just make round him a dense crowd."

SECTION 2

20 Say: "I do no more than invoke my Lord, and I join not with Him any
(false god)." 21 Say: "It is not in my power to cause you harm, or to bring
you to right conduct." 22 Say: "No one can deliver me from Allah (if I
were to disobey Him), nor should I find refuge except in Him, 23 Unless
I proclaim what I receive from Allah and His Messages: for any that
disobey Allah and His Messenger—for them is Hell: they shall dwell
therein for ever."

24 At length, when they see (with their own eyes) that which they are
promised,—then will they know who it is that is weakest in (his) helper
and least important in point of numbers. 25 Say: "I know not whether the
(Punishment) which you are promised is near, or whether my Lord will

---

2. *The Devotee of Allah*: the Holy Prophet Muḥammad. [5743]

appoint for it a distant term. 26 He (alone) knows the Unseen, nor does He make anyone acquainted with His Mysteries,—27 Except a messenger whom He has chosen: and then He makes a band of watchers march before him and behind him, 28 That He may know that they have (truly) brought and delivered the Messages of their Lord: and He surrounds (all the mysteries) that are with them, and takes account of every single thing."□

Chapter 73

Sūrah Al-Muzzammil (Folded in Garments)

Translator's Introduction

This is one of the earliest Sūrahs to have been revealed. The first was Sūrah 96:1-5 (*Iqra'*), in the fortieth year of the Prophet's life, say about 12 years before the Hijrah. Then there was an interruption (*Fatrah*), of which the duration cannot be exactly ascertained, as there was no external history connected with it. The usual estimate puts it at about six months, but it may have been a year or two years. The years were then counted by the luni-solar calendar. The second Sūrah in chronological order was probably a great portion of Sūrah 68. (*Al-Qalam*), which came after the *Fatrah* was over. About the same time came this Sūrah (say third) and Sūrah 74, which follows (say fourth), and the remainder of Sūrah 96. We may roughly put the date of this Sūrah at about 11 to 10 years before the Hijrah.

The subject matter is the significance of Prayer and Humility in spiritual life and the terrible fate of those who reject Faith and Revelation.

*** *** ***

In the name of Allah,
Most Gracious, Most Merciful.

1 O you folded in garments![1] 2 Stand (to prayer) by night, but not all
night,[2]—3 Half of it—or a little less, 4 Or a little more; and recite the
Qur'an in slow, measured rhythmic tones.

---

1. *Muzzammil*: Some Commentators understand by this, "properly dressed for prayer", or "folded" in a sheet, as one renouncing the vanities of this world. *Muzzammil* is one of the titles of our Holy Prophet. But there is a deeper mystic meaning in this and the address "you wrapped up" of the next Sūrah. Human nature requires warm garments and wrappings to protect the body from cold or heat or rain. But in the spiritual world these wrappings are useless; the soul must stand bare and open before Allah, in the silence of the night, but not too austerely, as the following verses show. [5754]

2. The Prophet was prone to austerities in the cave of Ḥirā, both before and after he received his mission, spending days and nights in prayer and contemplation. Midnight and after midnight prayers have technically received the name of *Tahajjud*. See also verse 20 below; also 17:79. [5755]

5 Soon shall We send down to you a weighty Message. 6 Truly the rising
by night is most potent for governing (the soul), and most suitable for
(framing) the Word (of prayer and praise). 7 True, there is for you by day
prolonged occupation with ordinary duties: 8 But keep in remembrance
the name of your Lord and devote yourself to Him wholeheartedly. 9 (He
is) Lord of the East and the West: there is no god but He: take Him
therefore for (thy) Disposer of Affairs.

10 And have patience with what they say, and leave them with noble
(dignity). 11 And leave Me (alone to deal with) those in possession of the
good things of life, who (yet) deny the Truth; and bear with them for a
little while. 12 With Us are Fetters (to bind them), and a Fire (to burn
them), 13 And a Food that chokes, and a Penalty grievous. 14 One Day the
earth and the mountains will be in violent commotion. And the mountains
will be as a heap of sand poured out and flowing down.

15 We have sent to you, (O men!) a messenger, to be a witness concerning
you, even as We sent a messenger to Pharaoh. 16 But Pharaoh disobeyed
the messenger; so We seized him with a heavy Punishment. 17 Then how
shall you, if you deny (Allah), guard yourselves against a Day that will
make children hoary-headed?—18 Whereon the sky will be cleft asunder?
His Promise needs must be accomplished. 19 Verily this is an Admonition;
therefore, whoever will, let him take a (straight) path to his Lord!

SECTION 2

20 Your Lord does know that you stand forth (to prayer) almost two-thirds of the night, or half the night, or a third of the night, and so do a party of those with you. But Allah does appoint night and day in due measure. He knows that you are unable to keep count thereof. So He has turned to you (in mercy): read you, therefore, of the Qur'an as much as may be easy for you. He knows that there may be (some) among you in ill-health; others travelling through the land, seeking of Allah's bounty; yet others fighting in Allah's Cause. Read you, therefore, as much of the Qur'an as may be easy (for you); and establish regular prayer and give regular charity; and loan to Allah a Beautiful Loan. And whatever good you send forth for your souls you shall find it in Allah's Presence,—indeed, better and greater, in Reward, and seek you the Grace of Allah: for Allah is Oft-forgiving, Most Merciful.□

Chapter 74

Sūrah Al-Muddaththir
(The One Wrapped Up)

Translator's Introduction

This Sūrah dates from about the same time as the last one. Its subject matter is also similar: Prayer and Praise, and the need of patience in a period of great spiritual stress: the unjust who cause sorrow and suffering now will themselves experience agony in the Hereafter.

*** *** ***

In the name of Allah,
Most Gracious, Most Merciful.

1 O you wrapped up[1] (in a mantle)! 2 Arise and deliver your warning! 3
And your Lord do you magnify! 4 And your garments keep free from
stain! 5 And all abomination shun! 6 Nor expect, in giving, any increase
(for yourself)! 7 But, for your Lord's (Cause), be patient and constant!

8 Finally, when the Trumpet is sounded, 9 That will be—that Day—a Day
of Distress,—10 Far from easy for those without Faith.

11 Leave Me alone, (to deal) with the (creature) whom I created (bare and)
alone!—12 To whom I granted resources in abundance, 13 And sons to be
by his side!—14 To whom I made (life) smooth and comfortable! 15 Yet
is he greedy—that I should add (yet more);—16 By no means! For to Our
Signs he has been refractory! 17 Soon will I visit him with a mount of

---

1. In these wonderful early mystic verses there is a double thread of thought: (1) A particular occasion or person is referred to; (2) a general spiritual lesson is taught. As to (1), the Prophet was now past the stage of personal contemplation, lying down or sitting in his mantle; he was now to go forth, boldly to deliver his Message and publicly proclaim the Lord; his heart had always been purified, but now all his outward doings must be dedicated to Allah, and conventional respect for ancestral customs or worship must be thrown aside; his work as a Messenger was the most generous gift that could flow from his personality, but no reward or appreciation was to be expected from his people, but quite the contrary; there would be much call on his patience, but his contentment would arise from the good pleasure of Allah. As to (2), similar stages arise in a minor degree in the life of every good man, for which the Prophet's life is to be a universal pattern. [5778]

calamities!

18 For he thought and he plotted;—19 And woe to him! How he
plotted!—20 Indeed, woe to him; how he plotted!—21 Then he looked
round; 22 Then he frowned and he scowled; 23 Then he turned back and
was haughty; 24 Then said he: "This is nothing but magic, derived from
of old; 25 This is nothing but the word of a mortal!"

26 Soon will I cast him into Hell-fire! 27 And what will explain to you what
Hell-fire is? 28 Naught does it permit to endure, and naught does it leave
alone!—29 Darkening and changing the colour of man!

30 Over it are Nineteen.[2] 31 And We have set none but angels as guardians
of the Fire; and We have fixed their number only as a trial for
Unbelievers,—in order that the People of the Book may arrive at
certainty, and the Believers may increase in Faith,—and that no doubts
may be left for the People of the Book and the Believers, and that those
in whose hearts is a disease and the Unbelievers may say, "What symbol
does Allah intend by this?" Thus does Allah leave to stray whom He
pleases, and guide whom He pleases: and none can know the forces of
your Lord, except He. And this is no other than a warning to mankind.

SECTION 2

32 Nay, verily: by the Moon, 33 And by the Night as it retreats, 34 And by
the Dawn as it shines forth,—35 This is but one of the mighty (Portents),
36 A warning to mankind,—37 To any of you that chooses to press
forward, or to follow behind;—

38 Every soul will be (held) in pledge for its deeds. 39 Except the
Companions of the Right Hand. 40 (They will be) in Gardens (of Delight):
they will question each other, 41 And (ask) of the Sinners: 42 "What led
you into Hell-fire?" 43 They will say: "We were not of those who prayed;
44 Nor were we of those who fed the indigent; 45 But we used to talk
vanities with vain talkers; 46 And we used to deny the Day of Judgment,

---

2. The figure nineteen refers to angels appointed to guard Hell. The mystic significance of numbers is a favourite theme with some writers, but I lay no stress on it. In Christian theology the number of the Beast, 666, in Rev. xiii.18 has given rise to much controversy, and may refer only to the numerical value of the letters in the name of the Roman Emperor Nero. In our own literature I think that we ought to avoid too much insistence on speculative conjectures. [5795]

47 Until there came to us (the Hour) that is certain." 48 Then will no
intercession of (any) intercessors profit them.

49 Then what is the matter with them that they turn away from
admonition?—50 As if they were frightened asses, 51 Fleeing from a lion!
52 In fact, each one of them wants to be given scrolls (of revelation)
spread out! 53 By no means! But they fear not the Hereafter, 54 Nay, this
surely is an admonition: 55 Let any who will, keep it in remembrance! 56
But none will keep it in remembrance except as Allah wills: He is the
Lord of Righteousness, and the Lord of Forgiveness.□

Chapter 75

Sūrah Al-Qiyāmah
(The Resurrection)

Translator's Introduction

This Sūrah belongs to the early Makkan period, but comes chronologically a good deal later than the last Sūrahs.
Its subject matter is the Resurrection, viewed from the point of view of Man, especially unregenerate Man, as he is now, and as he will be then—his inner and psychological history.

*** *** ***

In the name of Allah,
Most Gracious, Most Merciful.

1 I do call to witness the Resurrection Day; 2 And I do call to witness the
self-reproaching spirit; (eschew Evil).

3 Does man think that We cannot assemble his bones? 4 Nay, We are able
to put together in perfect order the very tips of his fingers. 5 But man
wishes to do wrong (even) in the time in front of him. 6 He questions:
"When is the Day of Resurrection?"

7 At length, when the Sight is dazed, 8 And the moon is buried in
darkness. 9 And the sun and moon are joined together,—10 That Day will
Man say: "Where is the refuge?" 11 By no means! No place of safety! 12
Before your Lord (alone), that Day will be the place of rest. 13 That Day
will Man be told (all) that he put forward, and all that he put back. 14 Nay,
man will be evidence against himself, 15 Even though he were to put up
his excuses.

16 Move not your tongue concerning the (Qur'an) to make haste
therewith. 17 It is for Us to collect it and to promulgate it: 18 But when We
have promulgated it, follow you its recital (as promulgated): 19 Nay more,
it is for Us to explain it (and make it clear):

20 Nay, (you men!) but you love the fleeting life, 21 And leave alone the
Hereafter. 22 Some faces, that Day, will beam (in brightness and
beauty);—23 Looking towards their Lord; 24 And some faces, that Day,
will be sad and dismal, 25 In the thought that some backbreaking calamity
was about to be inflicted on them; 26 Indeed, when (the soul) reaches to
the collarbone (in its exit), 27 And there will be a cry, "Who is a magician
(to restore him)?" 28 And he will conclude that it was (the Time) of
Parting; 29 And one leg will be joined with another: 30 That Day the Drive
will be (all) to your Lord!

SECTION 2

31 So he gave nothing in charity, nor did he pray!—32 But on the contrary,
he rejected Truth and turned away! 33 Then did he stalk to his family in
full conceit! 34 Woe to you, (O men!), indeed, woe! 35 Again, Woe to you,
(O men!), indeed, woe!

36 Does man think that he will be left uncontrolled, (without purpose)? 37
Was he not a drop of sperm emitted (in lowly form)? 38 Then did he
become a leech-like clot; then did (Allah) make and fashion (him) in due
proportion. 39 And of him He made two sexes, male and female. 40 Has
not He, (the same), the power to give life to the dead?□

Chapter 76

Sūrah Al-Insān
(Man)

Translator's Introduction

The revelation of this Sūrah was probably in the early Makkan period, with the possible exception of some verses, but its date has no particular significance. This Sūrah is also called *Al-Dahr* (The Time).

Its theme is the contrast between the two classes of men, those who choose good and those who choose evil, with special reference to the former.

The title of the Sūrah recalls a Pagan Arab idea, which personified Time as existing spontaneously from eternity to eternity and responsible for the misery or the happiness of mankind. In 45:24 we read: "They say ... 'nothing but Time can destroy us'." This attitude is of course wrong. Time is a created thing: it has its mysteries, but it is no more eternal than matter. It is also relative to our conceptions and not absolute, as Einstein has proved. It is only Allah Who is Self-Subsisting, Eternal from the beginning and Eternal to the end, the absolute Existence and Reality. We must not transfer His attributes to any figments of our imagination.

This deification of Time (*Dahr*) as against a living personal Allah has given rise to the term *dahrīyah,* as applied to an atheist or a materialist.

The whole of the Sūrah is full of the highest symbolism, as is generally the case with Makkan Sūrahs, and this should always be remembered in their interpretation.

*** *** ***

In the name of Allah,
Most Gracious, Most Merciful.

1 Has there not been over Man a long period of Time, when he was
nothing—(not even) mentioned? 2 Verily We created Man from a drop of
mingled sperm, in order to try him: so We gave him (the gifts), of
Hearing and Sight. 3 We showed him the Way: whether he be grateful or
ungrateful (rests on his will).

4 For the Rejecters we have prepared Chains, Yokes, and a blazing Fire.
5 As to the Righteous, they shall drink of a Cup (of Wine) mixed with

Kāfūr,[1]—6 A Fountain where the Devotees of Allah do drink, making it
flow in unstinted abundance.

7 They perform (their) vows, and they fear a Day whose evil flies far and
wide. 8 And they feed, for the love of Allah, the indigent, the orphan, and
the captive,—9 (Saying), "We feed you for the sake of Allah alone: no
reward do we desire from you, nor thanks. 10 We only fear a Day of
distressful Wrath from the side of our Lord." 11 But Allah will deliver
them from the evil of that Day, and will shed over them a Light of Beauty
and (blissful) Joy.

12 And because they were patient and constant, He will reward them with
a Garden and (garments of) silk. 13 Reclining in the (Garden) on raised
thrones, they will see there neither the sun's (excessive heat) nor (the
moon's) excessive cold. 14 And the shades of the (Garden) will come low
over them, and the bunches (of fruit), there, will hang low in humility.

15 And amongst them will be passed round vessels of silver and goblets
of crystal,—16 Crystal-clear, made of silver: they will determine the
measure thereof (according to their wishes). 17 And they will be given to
drink thereof a Cup (of Wine) mixed with *Zanjabīl*,[2]—18 A fountain
there, called *Salsabīl*.[3] 19 And round about them will (serve) youths of
perpetual (freshness): if you see them, you would think them scattered
Pearls. 20 And when you look, it is there you will see a Bliss and a Realm
Magnificent. 21 Upon them will be green Garments of fine silk and heavy
brocade, and they will be adorned with Bracelets of silver; and their Lord
will give to them to drink of a Wine Pure and Holy. 22 "Verily this is a
Reward for you, and your Endeavour is accepted and recognised."

---

1. *Kāfūr* is literally Camphor. It is a fountain in the Realms of Bliss. It is a seasoning added to the Cup of pure, beatific Wine, which causes no intoxication (56:18-19), but stands for all that is wholesome, agreeable, and refreshing. Camphor is cool and refreshing, and is given as a soothing tonic in Eastern medicine. In minute doses its odour and flavour are also agreeable. [5835]

2. *Zanjabīl* literally means Ginger. In Eastern medicine Ginger is administered to give warmth to the body and zest to the taste; this is appropriate for the Royal Feast which is now figured forth. [5849]

3. *Salsabīl* literally means: "Seek the Way". The Way is now open to the presence of the Most High. The Banquet is spread. Get thyself ready. It is a "Realm Magnificent" (verse 20) in a new spiritual world. [5850]

SECTION 2

23 It is We Who have sent down the Qur'an to you by stages. 24 Therefore
be patient with constancy to the Command of your Lord, and listen not
to the sinner or the ingrate among them. 25 And celebrate the name or
your Lord morning and evening, 26 And part of the night, prostrate
yourself to Him; and glorify Him a long night through.

27 As to these, they love the fleeting life, and put away behind them a Day
(that will be) hard. 28 It is We Who created them, and We have made their
joints strong; but, when We will, We can substitute the like of them by a
complete change. 29 This is an admonition: whoever will, let him take a
(straight) Path to his Lord. 30 But you will not, except as Allah wills; for
Allah is full of Knowledge and Wisdom. 31 He will admit to His Mercy
whom He will; but the wrong-doers—for them has He prepared a
grievous Penalty.□

Chapter 77

Sūrah Al-Mursalāt
(Those Sent Forth)

Translator's Introduction

This Sūrah belongs to the early Makkan period, somewhere near to Sūrah 75 (*Al-Qiyāmah*). The theme is somewhat similar. It denounces the horrors of the Hereafter, for those who rejected Truth. The refrain, "Ah! woe, that Day, to the Rejecters of Truth!" which occurs ten times in its fifty verses, or, on an average, once in every five verses, indicates the *leitmotif.*

*** *** ***

In the name of Allah,
Most Gracious, Most Merciful.

1 By the (Winds) Sent Forth one after another (to man's profit); 2 Which
then blow violently in tempestuous Gusts, 3 And scatter (things) far and
wide; 4 Then separate them, one from another, 5 Then spread abroad a
Message, 6 Whether of Justification or of Warning;—7 Assuredly, what
you are promised must come to pass.

8 Then when the stars become dim; 9 When the heaven is cleft asunder; 10
When the mountains are scattered (to the winds) as dust; 11 And when the
messengers are (all) appointed a time (to collect);—12 For what Day are
these (portents) deferred? 13 For the Day of Sorting Out. 14 And what will
explain to you what is the Day of Sorting Out? 15 Ah! woe, that Day, to
the Rejecters of Truth!

16 Did We not destroy the men of old (for their evil)? 17 So shall We make
later (generations) follow them. 18 Thus do We deal with men of sin. 19
Ah! woe, that Day, to the Rejecters of Truth!

20 Have We not created you from a fluid (held) despicable?—21 The which
We placed in a place of rest, firmly fixed, 22 For a period (of gestation),
determined (according to need)? 23 For We do determine (according to
need); for We are the Best to determine (things). 24 Ah! woe, that Day, to
the Rejecters of Truth!

25 Have We not made the earth (as a place) to draw together, 26 The living
and the dead, 27 And made therein mountains standing firm, lofty (in
stature); and provided for you water sweet (and wholesome)? 28 Ah! woe,
that Day, to the Rejecters of Truth!

29 (It will be said:) "Depart you to that which you used to reject as false!
30 Depart you to a Shadow (of smoke ascending) in three columns, 31
(Which yields) no shade of coolness, and is of no use against the fierce
Blaze. 32 Indeed it throws about sparks (huge) as Forts, 33 As if there were
(a string of) yellow camels (marching swiftly)." 34 Ah! woe, that Day, to
the Rejecters of Truth!

35 That will be a Day when they shall not be able to speak. 36 Nor will it
be open to them to put forth pleas. 37 Ah! woe, that Day, to the Rejecters
of Truth!

38 That will be a Day of Sorting Out! We shall gather you together and
those before (you)! 39 Now, if you have a trick (or plot), use it against Me!
40 Ah! woe, that Day, to the Rejecters of Truth!

SECTION 2

41 As to the Righteous, they shall be amidst (cool) shades and springs (of
water). 42 And (they shall have) fruits—all they desire. 43 Eat you and
drink you to your heart's content: for that you worked (Righteousness).
44 Thus do We certainly reward the Doers of Good. 45 Ah! woe, that Day,
to the Rejecters of Truth!

46 (O you Unjust!) Eat you and enjoy yourselves (but) a little while, for
that you are Sinners. 47 Ah! woe, that Day, to the Rejecters of Truth!

48 And when it is said to them, "Prostrate yourselves!" they do not so. 49
Ah! woe, that Day, to the Rejecters of Truth! 50 Then what Message, after
that, will they believe in?□

Chapter 78

Sūrah Al-Naba'
(The Great News)

Translator's Introduction

This beautiful Makkan Sūrah is not quite so early as the last (Sūrah 77) nor quite so late as Sūrah 76, but nearer in time to the latter.

It sets forth Allah's loving care in a fine nature passage, and deduces from it the Promise of the Future, when Evil will be destroyed and Good will come to its own; and invites all who have the will, to seek refuge with their Lord.

*** *** ***

PART XXX

In the name of Allah,
Most Gracious, Most Merciful.

1 Concerning what are they disputing? 2 Concerning the Great News, 3
About which they cannot agree. 4 Verily, they shall soon (come to) know!
5 Verily, verily they shall soon (come to) know![1]

6 Have We not made the earth as a wide expanse, 7 And the mountains as
pegs? 8 And (have We not) created you in pairs, 9 And made your sleep
for rest, 10 And made the night as a covering, 11 And made the day as a
means of subsistence? 12 And (have We not) built over you the seven
firmaments, 13 And placed (therein) a light of splendour? 14 And do We

---

1. *Great News*: usually understood to mean the News or Message of the Resurrection or the Hereafter, about which there are various schools of thought among the Jews and Christians and other nations. There is practically nothing about the Resurrection in the Old Testament, and the Jewish sect of Sadducees even in the time of Christ denied the Resurrection altogether. The Pagan ideas of a future life—if any—varied from place to place and from time to time. Even in the early Christian Church, as we learn from Paul's First Epistle to the Corinthians, there were contentions in that little community (I. Corinthians, i.11), and some definitely denied the resurrection of the dead (*ib.*, xv. 12).

Great News may also be translated Great Message or a Message Supreme as I have translated at 38:67. In that case it would refer to the Qur'an, or the Message of Revelation, or the Message of the Holy Prophet, about which there was great contention in those days. As this Message also lays great stress on the Day of Judgement and the Resurrection, the practical result by either mode of interpretation amounts to the same. [5889]

not send down from the clouds water in abundance, 15 That We may
produce therewith corn and vegetables, 16 And gardens of luxurious
growth?

17 Verily the Day of Sorting Out is a thing appointed, 18 The Day that the
trumpet shall be sounded, and you shall come forth in crowds; 19 And the
heavens shall be opened as if there were doors, 20 And the mountains shall
vanish, as if they were a mirage.

21 Truly Hell is as a place of ambush, 22 For the transgressors a place of
destination: 23 They will dwell therein for ages. 24 Nothing cool shall they
taste therein, nor any drink, 25 Save a boiling fluid and a fluid, dark,
murky, intensely cold—26 A fitting recompense (for them). 27 For that they
used not to fear any account (for their deeds), 28 But they (impudently)
treated Our Signs as false. 29 And all things have We preserved on record.
30 "So taste you (the fruits of your deeds); for no increase shall We grant
you, except in Punishment."

SECTION 2

31 Verily for the Righteous there will be a fulfilment of (the Heart's)
desires; 32 gardens enclosed, and grapevines; 33 companions of equal age;
34 And a cup full (to the brim). 35 No vanity shall they hear therein, nor
untruth—36 Recompense from your Lord, a gift, (amply) sufficient—37
(From) the Lord of the heavens and the earth, and all between—(Allah)
Most Gracious: none shall have power to argue with Him.

38 The Day that the Spirit and the angels will stand forth in ranks, none
shall speak except any who is permitted by (Allah) Most Gracious, and
He will say what is right. 39 That Day will be the sure Reality: therefore,
whoever will, let him take a (straight) Return to his Lord! 40 Verily, We
have warned you of a penalty near—the Day when man will see (the
Deeds) which his hands have sent forth, and the unbeliever will say,
"Woe unto me! Would that I were (mere) dust!"□

Chapter 79

Sūrah Al-Nāzi'āt
(Those Who Tear Out)

Translator's Introduction

This is also an early Makkan Sūrah, of about the same date as the last, and deals with the theme of Judgement from the point of view of Pride and its Fall. The parable of Pharaoh occupies a central place in the argument: for he said, "I am your Lord Most High" and perished with his followers.

*** *** ***

In the name of Allah,
Most Gracious, Most Merciful.

1 By the (angels) who tear out (the souls of the wicked) with violence; 2
By those who gently draw out (the souls of the blessed); 3 And by those
who glide along (on errands of mercy), 4 Then press forward as in a race,
5 Then arrange to do (the Commands of their Lord), 6 One Day everything
that can be in commotion will be in violent commotion, 7 Followed by
oft-repeated (commotions): 8 Hearts that Day will be in agitation; 9 Cast
down will be (their owners') eyes.

10 They say (now): "What! Shall we indeed be returned to (our) former
state? 11 What!—when we shall have become rotten bones?" 12 They say:
"It would, in that case, be a return with loss!"

13 But verily, it will be but a single (compelling) Cry, 14 When, behold,
they will be in the (full) awakening (to Judgement).

15 Has the story of Moses reached you? 16 Behold, your Lord did call to
him in the sacred valley of Ṭuwā—17 "Go you to Pharaoh, for he has
indeed transgressed all bounds. 18 And say to him, 'Would you that you
should be purified (from sin)?—19 And that I guide you to your Lord, so
you should fear Him?'" 20 Then did (Moses) show him the Great Sign. 21
But (Pharaoh) rejected it and disobeyed (guidance); 22 Further, he turned
his back, striving hard (against Allah). 23 Then he collected (his men) and
made a proclamation, 24 Saying, "I am your Lord, Most High." 25 But

Allah did punish him, (and made an) example of him—in the Hereafter,
as in this life. 26 Verily in this is an instructive warning for whoever fears
(Allah).

SECTION 2

27 What! Are you the more difficult to create or the heaven (above)?
(Allah) has constructed it: 28 On high has He raised its canopy, and He has
given it order and perfection. 29 Its night does He endow with darkness,
and its splendour does He bring out (with light). 30 And the earth,
moreover, has He extended (to a wide expanse);[1] 31 He draws out
therefrom its moisture and its pasture; 32 And the mountains has He firmly
fixed;—33 For use and convenience to you and your cattle.

34 Therefore, when there comes the great, overwhelming (Event),—35 The
Day when man shall remember (all) that he strove for, 36 And Hell-Fire
shall be placed in full view for (all) to see,—37 Then, for such as had
transgressed all bounds, 38 And had preferred the life of this world, 39 The
Abode will be Hell-Fire; 40 And for such as had entertained the fear of
standing before their Lord's (tribunal) and had restrained (their) soul from
lower desires, 41 Their Abode will be the Garden.

42 They ask you about the Hour,—'When will be its appointed time? 43
Wherein are you (concerned) with the declaration thereof? 44 With your
Lord is the Limit fixed therefor. 45 You are but a Warner for such as fear
it. 46 The Day they see it, (it will be) as if they had tarried but a single
evening, or (at most till) the following morn!□

1. An alternative rendering of this verse is; "And the earth, moreover hath He made oval (ostrich egg) shaped". Please refer to "*Min Ilm Alfalak Al-Qurani*", by Dr Adrian Sharif, published by Darul Al-Ilm Lil-Malayeen, Lebanon (pages 114-116). Ed.

Chapter 80

Sūrah 'Abasa
(He Frowned)

Translator's Introduction

This is an early Makkan Sūrah, and is connected with an incident which reflects the highest honour on the Prophet's sincerity in the Revelations that were vouchsafed to him even if they seemed to reprove him for some natural and human zeal that led him to a false step in his mission according to his own high standards.

He was once deeply and earnestly engaged in trying to explain the Holy Qur'an to Pagan Quraysh leaders, when he was interrupted by a blind man, 'Abdullāh ibn Umm Maktūm, one who was also poor, so that no one took any notice of him. He wanted to learn the Qur'an. The Holy Prophet naturally disliked the interruption and showed impatience. Perhaps the poor man's feelings were hurt. But he whose gentle heart ever sympathised with the poor and the afflicted, got new Light from above, and without the least hesitation published this revelation, which forms part of the sacred scripture of Islam, as described in verses 13-16. And the Prophet always afterwards held the man in high honour.

The incident was only a passing incident, but after explaining the eternal principles of revelation, the Sūrah recapitulates the Mercies of Allah to man, and the consequences of a good or a wicked life here, as seen in the spiritual world to come, in the Hereafter.

*** *** ***

In the name of Allah,
Most Gracious, Most Merciful.

1 (The Prophet) frowned and turned away, 2 Because there came to him
the blind man (interrupting). 3 But what could tell you but that perchance
he might grow (in spiritual understanding)?—4 Or that he might receive
admonition, and the teaching might profit him? 5 As to one who regards
himself as self-sufficient, 6 To him do you attend; 7 Though it is no blame
to you if he grow not (in spiritual understanding). 8 But as to him who
came to you striving earnestly, 9 And with fear (in his heart), 10 Of him
were you unmindful.

11 By no means (should it be so)! For it is indeed a Message of

instruction: 12 Therefore let whoever will, keep it in remembrance.

13 (It is) in Books held (greatly) in honour, 14 Exalted (in dignity), kept
pure and holy, 15 (Written) by the hands of scribes—16 Honourable and
Pious and Just.

17 Woe to man! What has made him reject Allah; 18 From what stuff has
He created him? 19 From a sperm-drop: He has created him, and then
moulded him in due proportions; 20 Then does He make his path smooth
for him; 21 Then He causes him to die, and puts him in his Grave; 22 Then,
when it is His Will, He will raise him up (again). 23 By no means has he
fulfilled what Allah has commanded him.

24 Then let man look at his food, (and how We provide it): 25 For that We
pour forth water in abundance, 26 And We split the earth in fragments, 27
And produce therein Corn, 28 And Grapes and nutritious Plants, 29 And
Olives and Dates, 30 And enclosed Gardens, dense with lofty trees, 31 And
Fruits and Fodder,—32 For use and convenience to you and your cattle.

33 At length, when there comes the Deafening Noise,—34 That Day shall
a man flee from his own brother, 35 And from his mother and his father,
36 And from his wife and his children. 37 Each one of them, that Day, will
have enough concern (of his own) to make him indifferent to the others.

38 Some faces that Day will be beaming, 39 Laughing, rejoicing. 40 And
other faces that Day will be dust-stained; 41 Blackness will cover them: 42
Such will be the Rejecters of Allah, the Doers of Iniquity.□

Chapter 81

Sūrah Al-Takwīr
(The Folding Up)

Translator's Introduction

This is quite an early Makkan Sūrah, perhaps the sixth or seventh in chronological order. It opens with a series of highly graphic images portraying the break-up of the world as we know it (verses 1-13) and the enforcement of complete personal responsibility for each soul (verse 14). This is followed by a passage showing how the Qur'anic Revelation was true, and revealed through the angel Gabriel, and not merely a rhapsody from one possessed. Revelation is given for man's spiritual guidance (verses 14-29).

Comparable with this Sūrah are Sūrahs 82 and 84 which may be read with this.

*** *** ***

In the name of Allah,
Most Gracious, Most Merciful.

1 When the sun (with its spacious light) is folded up; 2 When the stars fall,
losing their lustre; 3 When the mountains vanish (like a mirage); 4 When
the she-camels, ten months with young, are left untended; 5 When the
wild beasts are herded together (in human habitations); 6 When the oceans
boil over with a swell; 7 When the souls are sorted out, (being joined, like
with like); 8 When the female (infant), buried alive, is questioned—9 For
what crime she was killed; 10 When the Scrolls are laid open; 11 When the
World on High is unveiled; 12 When the blazing Fire is kindled to fierce
heat; 13 And when the Garden is brought near;—14 (Then) shall each soul
know what it has put forward.

15 So verily I call to witness the Planets—that recede, 16 Go straight, or
hide; 17 And the Night as it dissipates; 18 And the Dawn as it breathes
away the darkness;—19 Verily this is the word of a most honourable
Messenger, 20 Endued with Power, with rank before the Lord of the
Throne, 21 With authority there, (and) faithful to his trust.

22 And (O people!) Your Companion is not one possessed; 23 And without
doubt he saw him in the clear horizon. 24 Neither does he withhold
grudgingly a knowledge of the Unseen. 25 Nor is it the word of an evil
spirit accursed.

26 When whither go you? 27 Verily this is no less than a Message to (all)
the Worlds: 28 (With profit) to whoever among you wills to go straight:
29 But you shall not will except as Allah wills—the Cherisher of the
Worlds.□

Chapter 82

Sūrah Al-Infiṭār
(The Cleaving Asunder)

Translator's Introduction

In subject matter this Sūrah is cognate to the last, though the best authorities consider it a good deal later in chronology in the early Makkan Period.

Its argument is subject to the threefold interpretation mentioned in 81:13, *viz.*, as referring (1) to the final Day of Judgement, (2) to the Lesser Judgement, on an individual's death, and (3) to the awakening of the Inner Light in the soul at any time, that being considered as Death to the Falsities of this life and a Rebirth to the true spiritual Reality.

*** *** ***

In the name of Allah,
Most Gracious, Most Merciful.

1 When the Sky is cleft asunder; 2 When the Stars are scattered; 3 When
the Oceans are suffered to burst forth; 4 And when the Graves are turned
upside down;—5 (Then) shall each soul know what it has sent forward
and (what it has) kept back.

6 O man! What has seduced you from your Lord Most Beneficent?—7
Him Who created you, fashioned you in due proportion, and gave you a
just bias; 8 In whatever Form He wills, does He put you together.

9 Nay! But you do reject Right and Judgement! 10 But verily over you (are
appointed angels) to protect you,—11 Kind and honourable—writing
down (your deeds): 12 They know (and understand) all that you do.

13 As for the Righteous, they will be in Bliss; 14 And the Wicked —they
will be in the Fire, 15 Which they will enter on the Day of Judgement, 16
And they will not be able to keep away therefrom.

17 And what will explain to you what the Day of Judgement is? 18 Again,
what will explain to you what the Day of Judgement is? 19 (It will be) the
Day when no soul shall have power (to do) aught for another: for the
Command, that Day, will be (wholly) with Allah.□

Chapter 83

Sūrah Al-Muṭaffifīn
(The Dealers in Fraud)

Translator's Introduction

This Sūrah is close in time to the last one and the next one.

It condemns all fraud—in daily dealings, as well as and especially in matters of Religion and higher spiritual Life.

*** *** ***

In the name of Allah,
Most Gracious, Most Merciful.

1 Woe to those that deal in fraud,—2 Those who, when they have to
receive by measure from men, exact full measure, 3 But when they have
to give by measure or weight to men, give less than due. 4 Do they not
think that they will be called to account?—5 On a Mighty Day, 6 A Day
when (all) mankind will stand before the Lord of the Worlds?

7 Nay! Surely the Record of the Wicked is (preserved) in *Sijjīn*.[1] 8 And
what will explain to you what *Sijjīn* is? 9 (There is) a Register (fully)
inscribed. 10 Woe, that Day, to those that deny—11 Those that deny the
Day of Judgement. 12 And none can deny it but the Transgressor beyond
bounds, the Sinner! 13 When Our Signs are rehearsed to him, he says,
"Tales of the Ancients!"

14 By no means! But on their hearts is the stain of the (ill) which they do!
15 Verily, from (the Light of) their Lord, that Day, will they be veiled. 16
Further, they will enter the Fire of Hell. 17 Further, it will be said to them:
"This is the (reality) which you rejected as false!"

---

1. This is a word from the same root as *Sijn,* a Prison. It rhymes with and is contrasted with *'Illīyīn* in verse 18 below. It is therefore understood by many Commentators to be a place, a Prison or a Dungeon in which the Wicked are confined pending their appearance before the Judgement Seat. The mention of the Inscribed register in verse 9 below may imply that *Sijjīn* is the name of the Register of Black Deeds, though verse 9 may be elliptical and may only describe the place by the significance of its contents. [6013]

18 Nay, verily the record of the Righteous is (preserved) in *'Illīyīn.*[2] 19
And what will explain to you what *'Illīyūn* is? 20 (There is) a Register
(fully) inscribed, 21 To which bear witness those Nearest (to Allah).

22 Truly the Righteous will be in Bliss: 23 On Thrones (of Dignity) will
they command a sight (of all things): 24 You will recognise in their faces
the beaming brightness of Bliss. 25 Their thirst will be slaked with Pure
Wine sealed: 26 The seal thereof will be Musk: and for this let those
aspire, who have aspirations: 27 With it will be (given) a mixture of
Tasnīm: 28 A spring, from (the waters) whereof drink those Nearest to
Allah.

29 Those in sin used to laugh at those who believed, 30 And whenever they
passed by them, used to wink at each other (in mockery); 31 And when
they returned to their own people, they would return jesting; 32 And
whenever they saw them, they would say, "Behold! These are the people
truly astray!" 33 But they had not been sent as Keepers over them! 34 But
on this Day the Believers will laugh at the Unbelievers: 35 On Thrones (of
Dignity) they will command (a sight) (of all things). 36 Will not the
Unbelievers have been paid back for what they did?□

---

2. *'Illīyīn*: the oblique form of the nominative *'illīyūn*, which occurs in the next verse. It is in contrast to the *Sijjīn* which occurs in verse 7 above, where see note above. Literally it means the 'High Places', but it is probably not the same as the 'Heights' (*A'rāf*) mentioned in 7:46. Nor need we necessarily identify it with the "dwellings on high" (*ghurufāt*) mentioned in 34:37. Applying the reasoning parallel to that which we applied to *Sijjīn*, we may interpret it as the Place where is kept the Register of the Righteous. [6019]

Chapter 84

Sūrah Al-Inshiqāq
(The Rending Asunder)

Translator's Introduction

Chronologically this Sūrah is closely connected with the last one. In subject matter it resembles more Sūrahs 82 and 81, with which it may be compared.

The Sūrah, which opens with a mention of some cataclysmic events, shows that the present phenomenal order will not last, and Allah's full Judgement will certainly be established: man should therefore strive for that World of Eternity and True Values.

*** *** ***

In the name of Allah,
Most Gracious, Most Merciful.

1 When the Sky is rent asunder, 2 And listens to (the Command of) its
Lord,—and it must needs (do so);—3 And when the earth is flattened out,
4 And casts forth what is within it, and becomes (clean) empty, 5 And
listens to (the Command of) its Lord,—and it must needs (do so);—(then
will come home the full Reality).

6 O you man! Verily you are ever toiling on towards your
Lord—painfully toiling,—but you shall meet Him. 7 Then he who is
given his Record in his right hand, 8 Soon will his account be taken by an
easy reckoning, 9 And he will turn to his people, rejoicing! 10 But he who
is given his Record behind his back,—11 Soon will he cry for Perdition,
12 And he will enter a blazing Fire. 13 Truly, did he go about among his
people, rejoicing! 14 Truly, did he think that he would not have to return
(to Us)! 15 Nay, nay! For his Lord was (ever) watchful of him!

16 So I do call to witness the ruddy glow of Sunset; 17 The Night and its
Homing; 18 And the Moon in her Fullness: 19 Allah shall surely travel from
stage to stage.

20 What then is the matter with them, that they believe not?—21 And when

the Qur'an is read to them, they fall not prostrate,[1] 22 But on the contrary the Unbelievers reject (it). 23 But Allah has full Knowledge of what they secrete (in their breasts). 24 So announce to them a Penalty grievous, 25 Except to those who believe and work righteous deeds: for them is a Reward that will never fail.□

---

1. *Prostrate*: out of respect and humble gratitude to Allah. [6049]

Chapter 85

Sūrah Al-Burūj
(The Zodiacal Signs)

Translator's Introduction

This is one of the earlier Makkan Sūrahs, chronologically cognate with Sūrah 91. The subject matter is the persecution of Allah's votaries. Allah watches over His own, and will deal with the enemies of Truth as He dealt with them in the past.

*** *** ***

In the name of Allah,
Most Gracious, Most Merciful.

1 By the sky, (displaying) the Zodiacal Signs; 2 By the promised Day (of
Judgement); 3 By one that witnesses, and the subject of the witness;—4
Woe to the makers of the pit (of fire),[1] 5 Fire supplied (abundantly) with
Fuel: 6 Behold! They sat over against the (fire), 7 And they witnessed (all)
that they were doing against the Believers. 8 And they ill-treated them for
no other reason than that they believed in Allah, Exalted in Power,
Worthy of all Praise!—9 Him to Whom belongs the dominion of the
heavens and the earth! And Allah is Witness to all things.

10 Those who persecute (or draw into temptation) the believers, men and
women, and do not turn in repentance, will have the penalty of Hell: they

---

1. Who were the makers of the pit of fire in which they burnt people for their Faith? The words are perfectly general, and we need not search for particular names, except by way of illustration. In ancient history, and in Medieval Europe, many lives were sacrificed at the stake because the victims did not conform to the established religion. In Arab tradition there is the story of Abraham: Nimrūd tries to burn him to death, but on account of Abraham's Faith, the fire became "a means of safety for Abraham": 21:69. Another case cited is that of Dhū Nuwās, the last Ḥimyarite King of Yemen, by religion a Jew, who persecuted the Christians of Najrān and is said to have burnt them to death. He seems to have lived in the latter half of the sixth Christian century, in the generation immediately preceding the Prophet's birth in A.D. 570. While the words are perfectly general, a reference is suggested to the persecution to which the early Muslims were subjected by the Pagan Quraysh. Among other cruelties, they were stripped, and their skins were exposed to the burning rays of the Arabian summer sun. [6055]

will have the penalty of the burning Fire. 11 For those who believe and do
righteous deeds, will be gardens; beneath which rivers flow: that is the
great Salvation, (the fulfilment of all desires),

12 Truly strong is the grip (and power) of your Lord. 13 It is He Who
creates from the very beginning, and He can restore (life). 14 And He is
the Oft-Forgiving, Full of loving-kindness, 15 Lord of the Throne of
Glory, 16 Doer (without let) of all that He intends.

17 Has the story reached you, of the Forces—18 Of Pharaoh and the
Thamūd? 19 And yet the Unbelievers (persist) in rejecting (the Truth)! 20
But Allah does encompass them from behind!

21 Nay, this is a Glorious Qur'an, 22 (Inscribed) in a Tablet Preserved!□

Chapter 86

Sūrah Al-Ṭāriq
(The Night-Visitant)

Translator's Introduction

This Sūrah also belongs to the early Makkan period, perhaps not far removed from the last Sūrah.

Its subject matter is the protection afforded to every soul in the darkest period of its spiritual history. The physical nature of man may be insignificant, but the soul given to him by Allah must win a glorious Future in the end.

*** *** ***

In the name of Allah,
Most Gracious, Most Merciful.

1 By the Sky and the Night-Visitant (therein);—2 And what will explain
to you what the Night-Visitant is?—3 (It is) the star of piercing
brightness;—4 There is no soul but has a protector over it.

5 Now let man but think from what he is created! 6 He is created from a
drop emitted—7 Proceeding from between the backbone and the ribs: 8
Surely (Allah) is able to bring him back (to life)!

9 The Day that (all) things secret will be tested, 10 (Man) will have no
power, and no helper.

11 By the Firmament which returns (in its round), 12 And by the Earth
which opens out (for the gushing of springs or the sprouting of
vegetation),—13 Behold this is the Word that distinguishes (Good from
Evil): 14 It is not a thing for amusement.

15 As for them, they are but plotting a scheme, 16 And I am planning a
scheme. 17 Therefore grant a delay to the Unbelievers: give respite to them
gently (for awhile).□

Chapter 87

Sūrah Al-A'lā
(The Most High)

Translator's Introduction

This is one of the earliest of the Makkan Sūrahs, being usually placed eighth in chronological order, and immediately after Sūrah 81.

The argument is that Allah has made man capable of progress by ordered steps, and by His Revelation will lead him still higher to purification and perfection.

*** *** ***

In the name of Allah,
Most Gracious, Most Merciful.

1 Glorify the name of your Guardian-Lord Most High, 2 Who has created,
and further, given order and proportion; 3 Who has ordained laws. And
granted guidance; 4 And Who brings out the (green and luscious) pasture,
5 And then does make it (but) swarthy stubble.

6 By degrees shall We teach you to declare (the Message), so you shall not
forget,[1] 7 Except as Allah wills: for He knows what is manifest and what
is hidden.

8 And We will make it easy for you (to follow) the simple (Path).[2] 9
Therefore give admonition in case the admonition profits (the hearer). 10
The admonition will be received by those who fear (Allah): 11 But it will

---

1. The particular occasion was an assurance to the Prophet, that though he was unlettered, the Message given to him would be preserved in his heart and in the hearts of men. The more general sense is that mankind, having once seized great spiritual truths, will hold fast to them, except as qualified in the following verse. [6085]

2. The path of Islam is simple and easy. It depends on no abstruse mysteries or self-mortifications, but on straight and manly conduct in accordance with the laws of man's nature as implanted in him by Allah (30:30). On the other hand, spiritual perfection may be most difficult, for it involves complete surrender on our part to Allah in all our affairs, thoughts, and desires: but after that surrender Allah's Grace will make our path easy. [6087]

be avoided by those most unfortunate ones, 12 Who will enter the Great
Fire, 13 In which they will then neither die nor live.

14 But those will prosper who purify themselves, 15 And glorify the name
of their Guardian-Lord, and (lift their hearts) in prayer.

16 Nay (behold), you prefer the life of this world; 17 But the Hereafter is
better and more enduring.

18 And this is in the Books of the earliest (Revelations),—19 The Books of
Abraham and Moses.□

Chapter 88

Sūrah Al-Ghāshiyah
(The Overwhelming Event)

Translator's Introduction

This is a late Sūrah of the early Makkan period, perhaps close in date to Sūrah 52. Its subject matter is the contrast between the destinies of the Good and the Evil in the Hereafter—on the Day when the true balance will be restored: the Signs of Allah even in this life should remind us of the Day of Account, for Allah is good and just, and His creation is for a just Purpose.

*** *** ***

In the name of Allah,
Most Gracious, Most Merciful.

1 Has the story reached you of the Overwhelming (Event)? 2 Some faces,
that Day, will be humiliated, 3 Labouring (hard), weary,—4 The while they
enter the blazing Fire,—5 The while they are given, to drink, of a boiling
hot spring, 6 No food will there be for them but a bitter *ḍarī'*,[1] 7 Which
will neither nourish nor satisfy hunger.

8 (Other) faces that Day will be joyful, 9 Pleased with their Striving,—10
In a Garden on high, 11 Where they shall hear no (word) of vanity: 12
Therein will be a bubbling spring: 13 Therein will be Thrones (of dignity),
raised on high, 14 Goblets placed (ready), 15 And Cushions set in rows, 16
And rich carpets (all) spread out.

17 Do they not look at the Camels, how they are made?—18 And at the
Sky, how it is raised high?—19 And at the Mountains, how they are fixed
firm?—20 And at the Earth, how it is spread out?

21 Therefore do you give admonition, for you are one to admonish. 22 You
are not one to manage (men's) affairs. 23 But if any turn away and reject
Allah,—24 Allah will punish him with a mighty punishment, 25 For to Us
will be their return; 26 Then it will be for Us to call them to account.□

---

1. It is a plant bitter and thorny, loathsome in smell and appearance. [6099]

Chapter 89

Sūrah Al-Fajr (The Break of Day)

Translator's Introduction

This is one of the earliest of the Sūrahs to be revealed—probably within the first ten in chronological order.

Its mystic meaning is suggested by contrasts—contrasts in nature and in man's long history. Thus does it enforce the lesson of Faith in the Hereafter to "those who understand". Man's history and legendary lore show that greatness does not last and the proudest are brought low. For enforcing moral and spiritual truths, the strictest history is no better than legend. Indeed all artistic history is legend, for it is written from a special point of view.

Man is easily cowed by contrasts in his own fortunes, and yet he does not learn from them the lesson of forbearance and kindness to others, and the final elevation of goodness in the Hereafter. When all the things on which his mind and heart are set on this earth shall be crushed to nothingness, he will see the real glory and power, love and beauty, of Allah, for these are the light of the Garden of Paradise.

*** *** ***

In the name of Allah,
Most Gracious, Most Merciful.

1 By the Break of Day; 2 By the Nights twice five; 3 By the Even and Odd
(contrasted); 4 And by the Night when it passes away;—5 Is there (not) in
these an adjuration (or evidence) for those who understand?

6 See you not how your Lord dealt with the 'Ād (people),—7 Of the (city
of) Iram, with lofty pillars, 8 The like of which were not produced in (all)
the land? 9 And with the Thamūd (people), who cut out (huge) rocks in
the valley?—10 And with Pharaoh, Lord of Stakes?[1] 11 (All) these

---

1. For "Lord of Stakes", see 38:12. For Pharaoh's arrogance and his fall, see 20:43, 78-79. The three examples given, the 'Ād, the Thamūd, and Pharaoh, show that neither nations nor individuals, however mighty, prosperous, or firmly established they may be, can live if they transgress the Law of Allah. The Law of Allah, which is also the law of the higher nature which He has bestowed on us, made them in the first place great and glorious: when they fell from it and "heaped mischief on mischief", they were swept away. [6117]

transgressed beyond bounds in the lands, 12 And heaped therein mischief
(on mischief). 13 Therefore did your Lord pour on them a scourge of
diverse chastisements: 14 For your Lord is (as a Guardian) on a
watchtower.

15 Now, as for man, when his Lord tries him, giving him honour and gifts,
then says he, (puffed up), "My Lord has honoured me." 16 But when He
tries him, restricting his subsistence for him, then says he (in despair),
"My Lord has humiliated me!"

17 Nay, nay! But you honour not the orphans! 18 Nor do you encourage
one another to feed the poor!—19 And you devour Inheritance—all with
greed, 20 And you love wealth with inordinate love!

21 Nay! When the earth is pounded to powder, 22 And your Lord comes,
and His angels, rank upon rank, 23 And Hell, that Day, is brought (face to
face),—on that Day will man remember, but how will that remembrance
profit him? 24 He will say: "Ah! Would that I had sent forth (Good Deeds)
for (this) my (Future) Life!" 25 For, that Day, His Chastisement will be
such as none (else) can inflict, 26 And His bonds will be such as none
(other) can bind.

27 (To the righteous soul will be said:) "O (you) soul, in (complete) rest
and satisfaction! 28 Come back you to your Lord,—well pleased
(yourself), and well-pleasing unto Him! 29 Enter you, then, among My
devotees! 30 Indeed, enter you My Heaven!"[2] □

---

2. The climax of the whole is: "Enter My Heaven!" Men may have imagined all kinds of heaven before, and many types and symbols are used in the sacred Word itself. But nothing can express the reality itself better than "My Heaven"—Allah's own Heaven! May we reach it through Allah's grace! [6129]

Chapter 90

Sūrah Al-Balad
(The City)

Translator's Introduction

This is an early Makkan revelation, and refers to the mystic relation (by divine sanction) of the Holy Prophet with the city of Makkah. He was born in that City, which had already been sacred for ages before. He was nurtured in that City and had (to use a modern phrase) the freedom of that City, belonging, as he did, to the noble family which held the government of its sacred precincts in its hands. But he was an orphan, and orphans in his day had a poor time. But his mind was turned to things divine. He protested against the prevailing idolatry and sin, and his parent City persecuted him and cast him out. He made another City, Yathrib, his own: it became the *Madīnah al-Nabī*, the City of the Prophet, and it has ever since been called Madīnah. We can speak of Madīnah as the Prophet's child. But the Prophet ever cherished in his heart the love of his parent City of Makkah, and in the fullness of time was received in triumph there. He purified it from all idols and abominations, re-established the worship of the One True Allah, overthrew the purse-proud selfish autocracy, restored the sway of the righteous (people of the Right Hand), the liberty of the slave, and the rights of the poor and downtrodden. What a wonderful career centring round a City? It becomes a symbol of the world's spiritual history.

*** *** ***

In the name of Allah,
Most Gracious, Most Merciful.

1 I do call to witness this City;—2 And you are a freeman of this City;—3
And (the mystic ties of) Parent and Child;—4 Verily We have created
man into toil and struggle.

5 Thinks he, that none has power over him? 6 He may say (boastfully):
"Wealth have I squandered in abundance!" 7 Thinks he that none beholds
him?

8 Have We not made for him a pair of eyes?—9 And a tongue, and a pair of

lips?—10 And shown him the two highways?[1] 11 But he has made no haste
on the path that is steep. 12 And what will explain to you the path that is
steep?—13 (It is:) freeing the bondman; 14 Or the giving of food in a day
of privation, 15 To the orphan with claims of relationship, 16 Or to the
indigent (down) in the dust.

17 Then will he be of those who believe, and enjoin patience, (constancy,
and self-restraint), and enjoin deeds of kindness and compassion. 18 Such
are the Companions of the Right Hand.

19 But those who reject Our Signs, they are the (unhappy) Companions of
the Left Hand. 20 On them will be Fire vaulted over (all round).□

---

1. The two highways of life are: (1) the steep and difficult path of virtue, which is further described in the verses following, and (2) the easy path of vice and the rejection of Allah, referred to in verses 19-20 below. Allah has given us not only the faculties implied in the eyes, the tongue, and the lips, but also given us the judgement by which we can choose our way; and He has sent us Teachers and Guides, with Revelation, to show us the right and difficult way. [6138]

Chapter 91

Sūrah Al-Shams
(The Sun)

Translator's Introduction

This is one of the early Makkan revelations. Beginning with a fine nature passage, and leading up to man's need of realising his spiritual responsibility, it ends with a warning of the terrible consequences for those who fear not the Hereafter.

*** *** ***

In the name of Allah,
Most Gracious, Most Merciful.

1 By the Sun and his (glorious) splendour; 2 By the Moon as she follows
him; 3 By the day as it shows up (the Sun's) glory; 4 By the Night as it
conceals it; 5 By the Firmament and its (wonderful) structure; 6 By the
Earth and its (wide) expanse: 7 By the Soul, and the proportion and order
given to it; 8 And its enlightenment as to its wrong and its right;—9 Truly
he succeeds that purifies it, 10 And he fails that corrupts it![1]

11 The Thamūd (people) rejected (their prophet) through their inordinate
wrong-doing, 12 Behold, the most wicked man among them was deputed
(for impiety).[2] 13 But the Messenger of Allah said to them: "It is a
She-camel of Allah! And (bar her not from) having her drink!" 14 Then
they rejected him (as a false prophet), and they hamstrung her. So their Lord,
on account of their crime, obliterated their traces and made them equal (in
destruction, high and low)! 15 And for Him is no fear of its consequences.□

---

1. This is the core of the Sūrah, and it is illustrated by a reference to the story of the Thamūd in the following verses. [6153]

2. The Prophet Ṣāliḥ made a certain she-camel a Sign or Symbol, a test case, "This she-camel of Allah is a Sign unto you: so leave her to graze in Allah's earth and let her come to no harm, or you shall be seized with grievous punishment" (7:73). But they plotted to kill her and sent the most wicked man among them to dare and do that deed of impiety. It was probably when she came to drink at the stream that she was hamstrung and killed. See 26:155, and 54:27. [6155]

Chapter 92

Sūrah Al-Layl (The Night)

Translator's Introduction

This was one of the first Sūrahs to be revealed—within the first ten; and may be placed in date close to Sūrah 89 and Sūrah 93. Note that in all these three Sūrahs the mystery and the contrast as between Night and Day are appealed to for the consolation of man in his spiritual yearning. Here we are told to strive our utmost towards Allah, and He will give us every help and satisfaction.

*** *** ***

In the name of Allah,
Most Gracious, Most Merciful.

1 By the Night as it conceals (the light); 2 By the Day as it appears in
glory; 3 By (the mystery of) the creation of male and female;—4 Verily,
(the ends) you strive for are diverse.

5 So he who gives (in charity) and fears (Allah), 6 And (in all sincerity)
testifies to the best,—7 We will indeed make smooth for him the path to
Bliss. 8 But he who is a greedy miser and thinks himself self-sufficient, 9
And gives the lie to the Best,—10 We will indeed make smooth for him
the path to Misery; 11 Nor will his wealth profit him when he falls
headlong (into the Pit).

12 Verily We take upon Ourselves to guide, 13 And verily unto Us (belong)
the End and the Beginning.

14 Therefore do I warn you of a Fire blazing fiercely; 15 None shall reach
it but those most unfortunate ones, 16 Who give the lie to Truth and turn
their backs.

17 But those most devoted to Allah shall be[1] removed far from it,—18
Those who spend their wealth for increase in self-purification, 19 And

1. "Those most devoted to Allah': (Arabic *Atqā*) the God-fearing men who live lives of purity, and seek only for the "Face of their Lord Most High". See the verses following. [6170]

have in their minds no favour from anyone for which a reward is expected in return, 20 But only the desire to seek for the Countenance of their Lord Most High;[2] 21 And soon will they attain (complete) satisfaction.□

---

2. The definition of Righteousness, Charity, or Self-sacrifice, becomes thus highly spiritualised. The *Atqā* (those most devoted to Allah) are so completely identified with Allah's Will that everything else is blotted out to them. What would seem to be sacrifice from other points of view, becomes their own highest pleasure and satisfaction—the "heaven" of the enlightened man. Every virtuous man will have his own bliss, for there are degrees in virtue and bliss. This supreme bliss is the portion—not the prize—of supreme virtue. [6174]

Chapter 93

Sūrah Al-Ḍuḥā
(The Glorious Morning Light)

Translator's Introduction

This Sūrah is close in date to Sūrahs 89 and 92, and the imagery drawn from the contrast of Night and Day is common to all three. In this Sūrah the vicissitudes of human life are referred to, and a message of hope and consolation is given to man's soul from Allah's past mercies, and he is bidden to pursue the path of goodness and proclaim the bounties of Allah. This is the general meaning. In particular, the Sūrah seems to have been revealed in a dark period in the outer life of the Holy Prophet, when a man of less resolute will might have been discouraged. But the Prophet is told to hold the present of less account than the glorious Hereafter which awaited him like the glorious morning after a night of stillness and gloom. The Hereafter was, not only in the Future Life, but his later life on this earth, full of victory and satisfaction.

*** *** ***

In the name of Allah,
Most Gracious, Most Merciful.

1 By the Glorious Morning Light, 2 And by the Night when it is still,—3
Thy Guardian-Lord has not forsaken you, nor is He displeased. 4 And
verily the Hereafter will be better for you than the present. 5 And soon
will your Guardian-Lord give you (that with which) you shall be
well-pleased.

6 Did He not find you an orphan and give you shelter (and care)? 7 And
He found you wandering, and He gave you guidance. 8 And He found you
in need, and made you independent. 9 Therefore, treat not the orphan with
harshness, 10 Nor repulse the petitioner (unheard); 11 But the Bounty of
your Lord—rehearse and proclaim!□

Chapter 94

Sūrah Al-Sharḥ
(The Expansion)

Translator's Introduction

This short Sūrah gives a message of hope and encouragement in a time of darkness and difficulty. It was revealed to the Holy Prophet soon after the last Sūrah (*Al-Ḍuḥā*), whose argument it supplements.

*** *** ***

In the name of Allah,
Most Gracious, Most Merciful.

1 Have We not expanded you your breast?—2 And removed from you
your burden, 3 The which did gall your back?—4 And raised high the
esteem (in which) you (are held)?

5 So, verily, with every difficulty, there is relief: 6 Verily, with every
difficulty there is relief. 7 Therefore, when you are free (from your
immediate task), still labour hard, 8 And to your Lord turn (all) your
attention.□

Chapter 95

Sūrah Al-Tīn
(The Fig)

Translator's Introduction

This is also a very early Sūrah. It appeals to the most sacred symbols to show that Allah created man in the best of moulds, but that man is capable of the utmost degradation unless he has Faith and leads a good life. In subject matter this Sūrah closely resembles Sūrah 103.

*** *** ***

In the name of Allah,
Most Gracious, Most Merciful.

1 By the Fig and the Olive, 2 And the Mount of Sinai, 3 And this City of
security,—4 We have indeed created man in the best of moulds, 5 Then do
We abase him (to be) the lowest of the low,—6 Except such as believe
and do righteous deeds: for they shall have a reward unfailing. 7 Then
what can, after this, contradict you, as to the Judgement (to come)? 8 Is
not Allah the wisest of Judges?□

Chapter 96

Sūrah Al-'Alaq
(The Clinging Clot)

Translator's Introduction

Verses 1-5 of this Sūrah were the first direct Revelation to the Holy Prophet. The circumstances, material and psychical, in which they came, are described in the notes which should be referred to.

After that there was an interval or break (*Fatrah*), extending over some months or perhaps over a year. Sūrah 68 is usually considered to have been the next revelation in point of time. But the remainder of this Sūrah (96:6-19) came soon after the *Fatrah,* and that portion is joined on to the first five verses containing the command to preach, because it explains the chief obstacle to the delivery of the message to man, *viz*.: man's own obstinacy, vanity, and insolence.

This Sūrah is also called *Iqra'* (Read!).

*** *** ***

In the name of Allah,
Most Gracious, Most Merciful.

1 Proclaim! (or Read!)[1] in the name of your Lord and Cherisher, Who
created—2 Created man, out of a (mere) clot of congealed blood: 3
Proclaim! And your Lord is Most Bountiful,—4 He Who taught (the use
of) the Pen,[2]—5 Taught man that which he knew not.

6 Nay, but man does transgress all bounds, 7 In that he looks upon himself
as self-sufficient. 8 Verily, to your Lord is the return (of all).

9 See you one who forbids—10 A votary when he (turns) to pray? 11 See

---

1. *Iqra'* (the Arabic word translated here "Proclaim" or "Read") may mean "read", or "proclaim aloud", the object understood as being Allah's Message. For an account of the circumstances in which this first revelation—the divine commission to preach and proclaim Allah's Message—came to the Holy Prophet, in the cave of Ḥirā (see the Translator's Introduction to the Book: C. 27-31). In worldly letters he was unversed, but with spiritual knowledge his mind and soul were filled, and now had come the time when he must stand forth to the world and declare his mission. [6203]

2. The symbol of a permanent revelation is the mystic Pen and the mystic Record. See note to Sūrah 68:1. [6206]

you if he is on (the road of) Guidance?—12 Or enjoins Righteousness? 13
See you if he denies (Truth) and turns away?

14 Knows he not that Allah does see? 15 Let him beware! If he desist not,
We will drag him by the forelock,—16 A lying, sinful forelock! 17 Then,
let him call (for help) to his council (of comrades): 18 We will call on the
angels of punishment (to deal with him)!
19 Nay, heed him not: but bow down in adoration, and bring yourself the
closer (to Allah)!□

Chapter 97

Sūrah Al-Qadr
(The Night of Power *or* Honour)

Translator's Introduction

The chronology of this Sūrah has no significance. It is probably Makkan, though some hold that it was revealed in Madīnah.

The subject matter is the mystic Night of Power (or Honour), in which Revelation comes down to a benighted world—it may be to the wonderful Cosmos of an individual—and transforms the conflict of wrong-doing into Peace and Harmony—through the agency of the angelic host, representing the spiritual powers of the Mercy of Allah.

*** *** ***

In the name of Allah,
Most Gracious, Most Merciful.

1 We have indeed revealed this (Message) in the Night of Power:[1] 2 And
what will explain to you what the Night of Power is? 3 The Night of
Power is better than a thousand Months. 4 Therein come down the angels
and the Spirit[2] by Allah's permission, on every errand: 5 Peace! This
until the rise of Morn!□

---

1. *Cf.* 44:3. The 23rd, 25th or 27th night of Ramaḍān, as well as other nights, have been suggested as the Night of Power. See, however, the Introduction to this Sūrah. It is best to take this in the mystic sense, which also accords with verse 3 below, which says that the Night of Power is better than a thousand months. It transcends Time: for it is Allah's Power dispelling the Darkness of Ignorance, by His Revelation, in every kind of affair. [6217]

2. *The Spirit*: usually understood to be the Angel Gabriel, the Spirit of Inspiration. [6219]

Chapter 98

Sūrah Al-Bayyinah
(The Clear Evidence)

Translator's Introduction

This Sūrah was probably an early Madīnan Sūrah, or possibly a late Makkan Sūrah.

In subject matter it carries forward the argument of the last Sūrah. The mystic night of revelation is indeed blessed: but those who reject Truth are impervious to Allah's Message, however clear may be the evidence in support of it.

*** *** ***

In the name of Allah,
Most Gracious, Most Merciful.

1 Those who reject (Truth), among the People of the Book[1] and among
the Polytheists, were not going to depart (from their ways) until there
should come to them Clear Evidence,—2 A messenger from Allah,
rehearsing scriptures kept pure and Holy: 3 Wherein are laws (or decrees)
right and straight.

4 Nor did the People of the Book make schisms, until after there came to

1. The People of the Book immediately referred to are the Jews and Christians, who had received scriptures in the same line of prophecy in which came our Holy Prophet. Their scriptures should have prepared them for the advent of the greatest and last of the Prophets. For the Jewish scriptures promised to the Jews, cousins or brethren to the Arabs, a prophet like Moses: "The Lord thy God will raise up unto thee a Prophet from the midst of thee, of thy brethren, like unto me; unto him ye shall hearken" (Deut. xviii,15). And Christ promised a Comforter (John, xiv,16; xv, 26; and xvi, 7; see 61:6) almost by name. The People of the Book fell from the true, straight, and standard religion, into devious ways, and would not come to the true Path until (they said) they were convinced by the arrival of the promised Prophet. But when the promised Prophet came in the person of Muḥammad, they rejected him, because they really did not seek for Truth but only followed their own fancies and desires. [6221]

them Clear Evidence.[2] 5 And they have been commanded no more than this: to worship Allah, offering Him sincere devotion, being true (in faith); to establish regular prayer; and to practise regular charity; and that is the Religion Right and Straight.

6 Those who reject (Truth), among the People of the Book and among the Polytheists, will be in Hell-Fire, to dwell therein (for ever). They are the worst of creatures. 7 Those who have faith and do righteous deeds,—they are the best of creatures. 8 Their reward is with Allah: Gardens of Eternity, beneath which rivers flow; they will dwell therein for ever; Allah well pleased with them, and they with Him: all this for such as fear their Lord and Cherisher.□

---

2. The Clear Evidence was the Holy Prophet himself, his life, his personality, and his teaching. [6223]

Chapter 99

Sūrah Al-Zilzāl
(The Convulsion)

Translator's Introduction

This Sūrah is close in date to the last: it is generally referred to the early Madīnan period, though it may possibly be of the late Makkan period.

It refers to the tremendous convulsion and uprooting which will take place when the present order of the world is dissolved and the new spiritual world of Justice and Truth takes its place. The symbol used is that of an earthquake which will shake our present material and phenomenal world to its very foundations. The mystic words in which the earthquake is described are remarkable for both power and graphic aptness. With that shaking all hidden mysteries will be brought to light.

*** *** ***

In the name of Allah,
Most Gracious, Most Merciful.

1 When the Earth is shaken to her (utmost) convulsion, 2 And the Earth
throws up her burdens (from within), 3 And man cries (distressed): `What
is the matter with her?'—4 On that Day will she declare her tidings: 5 For
that your Lord will have given her inspiration. 6 On that Day will men
proceed in companies sorted out, to be shown the Deeds that they (had
done). 7 Then shall anyone who has done an atom's weight of good, see
it! 8 And anyone who has done an atom's weight of evil, shall see it.□

Chapter 100

Sūrah Al-'Ādiyāt
(Those That Run)

Translator's Introduction

This is one of the earlier Makkan Sūrahs. In the depth of its mystery and the rhythm and sublimity of its language and symbolism, it may be compared with Sūrah 79. Its subject matter is the irresistible nature of spiritual power and knowledge, contrasted with unregenerate man's ingratitude, pettiness, helplessness, and ignorance.

*** *** ***

In the name of Allah,
Most Gracious, Most Merciful.

1 By the (Steeds) that run, with panting (breath), 2 And strike sparks of
fire, 3 And push home the charge in the morning, 4 And raise the dust in
clouds the while, 5 And penetrate forthwith into the midst (of the foe) *en*
masse;—6 Truly man is, to his Lord, ungrateful; 7 And to that (fact) he
bears witness (by his deeds); 8 And violent is he in his love of wealth.

9 Does he not know,—when that which is in the graves is scattered
abroad, 10 And that which is (locked up) in (human) breasts is made
manifest—11 That their Lord had been well-acquainted with them, (even
to) that Day?□

Chapter 101

Sūrah Al-Qāri'ah
(The Day of Noise and Clamour)

Translator's Introduction

This Makkan Sūrah describes the Judgement Day as the Day of Clamour, when men will be distracted and the landmarks of this world will be lost, but every deed will be weighed in a just balance, and find its real value and setting.

*** *** ***

In the name of Allah,
Most Gracious, Most Merciful.

1 The (Day) of Noise and Clamour: 2 What is the (Day) of Noise and
Clamour? 3 And what will explain to you what the (Day) of Noise and
Clamour is? 4 (It is) a Day whereon men will be like moths scattered
about, 5 And the mountains will be like carded wool. 6 Then, he whose
balance (of good deeds) will be (found) heavy, 7 Will be in a Life of good
pleasure and satisfaction. 8 But he whose balance (of good deeds) will be
(found) light,—9 Will have his home in a (bottomless) Pit. 10 And what
will explain to you what this is? 11 (It is) a Fire blazing fiercely!□

Chapter 102

Sūrah Al-Takāthur
(The Piling Up)

Translator's Introduction

This probably early Makkan Sūrah gives a warning against acquisitiveness, *i.e.*, the passion for piling up quantities or numbers, whether in the good things of this world, or in manpower or in other forms of megalomania, which leave no time or opportunity for pursuing the higher things of life.

*** *** ***

In the name of Allah,
Most Gracious, Most Merciful.

1 The mutual rivalry for piling up (the good things of this world) diverts
you (from the more serious things), 2 Until you visit the graves. 3 But no,
you soon shall know (the reality). 4 Again, you soon shall know! 5 Nay,
were you to know with certainty of mind, (you would beware!) 6 You
shall certainly see Hell-Fire! 7 Again, you shall see it with certainty of
sight! 8 Then, shall you be questioned that Day about the joy (you
indulged in!).□

Chapter 103

Sūrah Al-'Aṣr
(The Time)

Translator's Introduction

This early Makkan Sūrah refers to the testimony of Time through the Ages. All history shows that Evil came to an evil end. But Time is always in favour of those who have Faith, live clean and pure lives, and know how to wait, in patience and constancy. *Cf.* the theme of Sūrah 95.

*** *** ***

In the name of Allah,
Most Gracious, Most Merciful.

1 By (the token of) Time (through the Ages), 2 Verily Man is in loss, 3
Except such as have Faith, and do righteous deeds, and (join together) in
the mutual teaching of Truth, and of Patience and Constancy.□

Chapter 104

Sūrah Al-Humazah (The Scandalmonger)

Translator's Introduction

This Makkan Sūrah condemns all sorts of scandal, backbiting, and selfish hoarding of wealth, as destroying the hearts and affections of men.

*** *** ***

In the name of Allah,
Most Gracious, Most Merciful.

1 Woe to every (kind of) scandalmonger and backbiter,[1] 2 Who piles up
wealth and lays it by, 3 Thinking that his wealth would make him last for
ever!

4 By no means! He will be sure to be thrown into that which Breaks to
Pieces, 5 And what will explain to you that which Breaks to Pieces? 6 (It
is) the Fire of (the Wrath of) Allah kindled (to a blaze), 7 The which does
mount (Right) to the Hearts: 8 It shall be made into a vault over them, 9 In
columns outstretched.□

1. Three vices are here condemned in the strongest terms: (1) scandalmongering, talking or suggesting evil of men or women by word or innuendo, or behaviour, or mimicry, or sarcasm, or insult; (2) detracting from their character behind their backs, even if the things suggested are true, where the motive is evil; (3) piling up wealth, not for use and service to those who need it, but in miserly hoards, as if such hoards can prolong the miser's life or give him immortality: miserliness is itself a kind of scandal. [6266]

Chapter 105

Sūrah Al-Fīl
(The Elephant)

Translator's Introduction

This early Makkan Sūrah refers to an event that happened in the year of the birth of our Holy Prophet, say about A.D. 570. Yemen was then under the rule of the Abyssinians (Christians), who had driven out the Jewish Ḥimyarite rulers. Abrahah Ashram was the Abyssinian governor or viceroy. Intoxicated with power and fired by religious fanaticism, he led a big expedition against Makkah, intending to destroy the Ka'bah. He had an elephant or elephants in his train. But his sacrilegious intentions were defeated by a miracle. No defence was offered by the custodians of the Ka'bah as the army was too strong for them. But a shower of stones, thrown by flocks of birds, destroyed the invading army almost to a man. The stones produced sores and pustules on the skin, which spread like a pestilence.

*** *** ***

In the name of Allah,
Most Gracious, Most Merciful.

1 See you not how your Lord dealt with the Companions of the
Elephant?[1] 2 Did He not make their treacherous plan go astray? 3 And He
sent against them Flights of Birds,[2] 4 Striking them with stones[3] of
baked clay. 5 Then did He make them like an empty field of stalks and
straw, (of which the corn) has been eaten up.□

---

1. These were the troops of Abrahah the Abyssinian, who invaded Makkah with a large army, in which were some elephants. See Introduction to this Sūrah. [6271]

2. The miracle consisted in the birds coming in large flights and flinging stones at the army which caused a great pestilence to arise and destroy the whole of Abrahah's army. [6272]

3. *Sijjīl*: see 11:82. The word also occurs at 15:74. Stones of baked clay, or hard as baked clay, are part of the miracle in the story. [6273]

Chapter 106

Sūrah Quraysh
(The Tribe of Quraysh)

Translator's Introduction

This Makkan Sūrah may well be considered as a pendant to the last. If the Quraysh were fond of Makkah and proud of it, if they profited, by its central position and it guaranteed security, from their caravans of trade and commerce, let them be grateful, adore the One True God, and accept His Message.

*** *** ***

In the name of Allah,
Most Gracious, Most Merciful.

1 For the covenants (of security and safeguard enjoyed) by the Quraysh,[1] 2
Their covenants (covering) journeys by winter and summer,—3 Let them
adore the Lord of this House,[2] 4 Who provides them with food against
hunger, and with security against fear (of danger).□

---

1. The Quraysh were the noblest tribe of Arabia, the tribe to which belonged the Holy Prophet himself. They had the custody of the Ka'bah, the central shrine of Arabia, and their possession of Makkah gave them a triple advantage: (1) they had a commanding influence over other tribes; (2) their central position facilitated trade and intercourse, which gave them both honour and profit, and (3) the Makkah territory being, by Arabian custom, inviolable from the ravages of war and private feuds, they had a secure position, free from fear of danger. This honour and advantage they owed to their position as servants of the sacred shrine of the Ka'bah. They owed it to God. Was it not therefore right and fitting that they should adore the One True God, and listen to His Message of Unity and Purity, brought by His Prophet?

In those days of general insecurity, their prestige as custodians of Makkah enabled them to obtain Covenants of security and safeguard from the rulers of neighbouring countries on all sides—Syria, Persia, Yemen, and Abyssinia—protecting their trade journeys in all seasons. [6276]

2. The Ka'bah. [6278]

Chapter 107

Sūrah Al-Mā'ūn
(The Neighbourly Needs)

Translator's Introduction

This Sūrah—at least the first half of it—belongs to the early Makkan period. The subject matter is the meaning of true worship, which requires Faith, the practical and helpful love of those in need, and sincerity rather than show in devotion and charity.

*** *** ***

In the name of Allah,
Most Gracious, Most Merciful.

1 See you one who denies the Judgement (to come)? 2 Then such is the
(man) who repulses the orphan (with harshness), 3 And encourages not
the feeding of the indigent.

4 So woe to the worshippers, 5 Who are neglectful of their prayers, 6 Those
who (want but) to be seen (of men), 7 But refuse (to supply) (even)
neighbourly needs.□

Chapter 108

Sūrah Al-Kawthar
(The Abundance)

Translator's Introduction

This very brief early Makkan Sūrah sums up in the single mystic word *Kawthar* (Abundance) the doctrine of spiritual Riches through devotion and sacrifice. The converse also follows: indulgence in hatred means the cutting off of all hopes of this life and the Hereafter.

*** *** ***

In the name of Allah,
Most Gracious, Most Merciful.

1 To you have We granted the Fount (of Abundance). 2 Therefore to your
Lord turn in prayer and sacrifice. 3 For he who hates you, *he* will be cut
off (from Future Hope).□

Chapter 109

Sūrah Al-Kāfirūn
(Those Who Reject Faith)

Translator's Introduction

This is another early Makkan Sūrah. It defines the right attitude to those who reject Faith; in matters of Truth we can make no compromise, but there is no need to persecute or abuse anyone for his faith or belief.

*** *** ***

In the name of Allah,
Most Gracious, Most Merciful.

1 Say: O you that reject Faith! 2 I worship not that which you worship, 3
Nor will you worship that which I worship. 4 And I will not worship that
which you have been wont to worship, 5 Nor will you worship that which
I worship. 6 To you be your Way, and to me mine.□

Chapter 110

Sūrah Al-Naṣr
(The Help)

Translator's Introduction

This beautiful Sūrah was the last of the Sūrahs to be revealed *as a whole,* though the portion of the verse 5:3, "This day have I perfected your religion for you" etc., contains probably the last *words* of the Qur'an to be revealed.

The date of this Sūrah was only a few months before the passing away of the Holy Prophet from this world, Rabī ' al-Awwal, A.H. 11. The place was either the precincts of Makkah at his Farewell Pilgrimage, Dhū al-Ḥijjah, A.H. 10, or Madīnah after his return from the Farewell Pilgrimage.

Victory is the crown of service, not an occasion for exultation. All victory comes from the help of Allah.

*** *** ***

In the name of Allah,
Most Gracious, Most Merciful.

1 When comes the help of Allah, and Victory, 2 And you do see the people enter Allah's Religion in crowds,[1] 3 Celebrate the praises of your Lord, and pray for His Forgiveness: for He is Oft-Returning (in Grace and Mercy).□

---

1. The Prophet migrated from Makkah to Madīnah, a hunted and persecuted man. In Madīnah all the forces of truth and righteousness rallied round him, and the efforts by the Makkans and their confederates to destroy him and his community recoiled on their own heads. Gradually all the outlying parts of Arabia ranged themselves round his standard and the bloodless conquest of Makkah was the crown and prize of his patience and constant endeavour. After that, whole tribes and tracts of country gave their allegiance to him collectively, and before his earthly ministry was finished, the soil was prepared for the conquest of the wide world of Islam. What was the lesson to be learnt from this little epitome of the world's history? Not man's self-glory, but humility; not power, but service; not an appeal to man's selfishness or self-sufficiency, but a realisation of Allah's Grace and Mercy, and the abundant outpouring of Allah's Praises in word and conduct. [6292]

Chapter 111

Sūrah Al-Lahab
(The Flame)

Translator's Introduction

This very early Makkan Sūrah, though it referred in the first instance to a particular incident in a cruel and relentless persecution, carries the general lesson that cruelty ultimately ruins itself. The man who rages against holy things is burnt up in his own rage. His hands, which are the instruments of his action, perish, and he perishes himself. No boasted wealth or position will save him. The women, who are made for nobler emotions, may, if they go wrong, feed unholy rage with fiercer fuel—to their own loss. For they may twist the torturing rope round their own neck. It is a common experience that people perish by the very means by which they seek to destroy others.

*** *** ***

In the name of Allah,
Most Gracious, Most Merciful.

1 Perish the hands of the Father of Flame![1] Perish he! 2 No profit to him
from all his wealth, and all his gains! 3 Burnt soon will he be in a Fire of
blazing Flame! 4 His wife shall carry the (crackling) wood—as fuel!—5
A twisted rope of palm-leaf fibre round her (own) neck!□

1. Abū Lahab: "Father of Flame", was the nickname of an uncle of the Holy Prophet, from his fiery hot temper and his ruddy complexion. He was one of the most inveterate enemies of early Islam. When the Holy Prophet called together the Quraysh and his own kith and kin to come and listen to his preaching and his warning against the sins of his people, the "Father of Flame" flared up and cursed the Holy Prophet, saying, "Perdition to thee!" Abū Lahab's wife was a woman of equally passionate spite and cruelty against the sacred person of the Holy Prophet. She used to tie bundles of thorns with ropes of twisted palm leaf fibre and carry them and strew them about on dark nights in the paths which the Prophet was expected to take. [6294]

Chapter 112

Sūrah Al-Ikhlāṣ (The Purity of Faith)

Translator's Introduction

This early Makkan Sūrah sums up in a few terse words the Unity of the Godhead—often professed, but frequently mixed up in the popular mind with debasing superstitions.

*** *** ***

In the name of Allah,
Most Gracious, Most Merciful.

1 Say: He is Allah,[1] the One and Only;[2] 2 Allah, the Eternal, Absolute;[3]
3 He begets not, nor is He begotten;[4] 4 And there is none like unto
Him.[5]□

---

1. The nature of Allah is here indicated to us in a few words, such as we can understand. The qualities of Allah are described in numerous places elsewhere, *e.g.*, in 59:22-24, 62:1, and 2:255. Here we are specially taught to avoid the pitfalls into which men and nations have fallen at various times in trying to understand Allah. The first thing we have to note is that His nature is so sublime, so far beyond our limited conceptions, that the best way in which we can realise Him is to feel that He is a Personality, "He", and not a mere abstract conception of philosophy. He is near us; He cares for us; we owe our existence to Him. Secondly, He is the One and Only God, the Only One to Whom worship is due; all other things or beings that we can think of are His creatures and in no way comparable to Him. Thirdly, He is Eternal, without beginning or end, Absolute, not limited by time or place or circumstance, the Reality before which all other things or places are mere shadows or reflections. Fourthly, we must not think of Him as having a son or a father, for that would be to import animal qualities into our conception of Him. Fifthly, He is not like any other person or thing that we know or can imagine: His qualities and nature are unique. [6296]

2. This is to negate the idea of Polytheism, a system in which people believe in gods many and lords many. Such a system is opposed to our truest and profoundest conceptions of life. For Unity in Design, Unity in the fundamental facts of existence, proclaim the Unity of the Maker. [6297]

3. *Ṣamad* is difficult to translate by one word. I have used two, “Eternal” and “Absolute”. The latter implies: (1) that absolute existence can only be predicted of Him; all other existence is temporal or conditional; (2) that He is dependent on no person or things, but all persons or things are dependent on Him, thus negating the idea of gods and goddesses who ate and drank. wrangled and plotted, depended on the gifts of worshippers, etc. [6298]

4. This is to negate the Christian idea of the godhead, “the Father”, “the only-begotten Son” etc. [6299]

5. This sums up the whole argument and warns us specially against Anthropomorphism, the tendency to conceive of Allah after our own pattern, an insidious tendency that creeps in at all times and among all peoples. [6300]

Chapter 113

Sūrah Al-Falaq
(The Dawn)

Translator's Introduction

This early Makkan Sūrah provides the antidote to superstition and fear by teaching us to seek refuge in Allah from every kind of ill arising from outer nature and from dark and evil plottings and envy on the part of others.

*** *** ***

In the name of Allah,
Most Gracious, Most Merciful.

1 Say: I seek refuge with the Lord of the Dawn, 2 From the mischief of
created things; 3 From the mischief of Darkness as it overspreads; 4 From
the mischief of those who practise Secret Arts; 5 And from the mischief
of the envious one as he practises envy.□

Chapter 114

Sūrah Al-Nās
(Mankind)

Translator's Introduction

This early Makkan Sūrah is a pendant to the last Sūrah, and concludes the Holy Qur'an, with an appeal to us to trust in Allah, rather than man, as our sure shield and protection. It warns us specially against the secret whispers of evil within our own hearts.

*** *** ***

In the name of Allah,
Most Gracious, Most Merciful.

1 Say: I seek refuge with the Lord and Cherisher of Mankind, 2 The King
(or Ruler) of Mankind, 3 The God (or judge) of Mankind,—4 From the
mischief of the Whisperer (of Evil), who withdraws (after his
whisper),—5 (The same) who whispers into the hearts of Mankind,—6
Among *Jinns* and among Men.□

INDEX